THE
WOMANIST
READER

THE
WOMANIST
READER

EDITED BY LAYLI PHILLIPS

Routledge
Taylor & Francis Group
New York   London

Routledge is an imprint of the
Taylor & Francis Group, an informa business

Routledge
Taylor & Francis Group
270 Madison Avenue
New York, NY 10016

Routledge
Taylor & Francis Group
2 Park Square
Milton Park, Abingdon
Oxon OX14 4RN

Printed in the United States of America on acid-free paper
10 9 8 7 6 5 4 3 2 1

International Standard Book Number-10: 0-415-95411-8 (Softcover) 0-415-95410-X (Hardcover)
International Standard Book Number-13: 978-0-415-95411-2 (Softcover) 978-0-415-95410-5 (Hardcover)

Library of Congress Cataloging-in-Publication Data

The Womanist reader / edited by Layli Phillips.
    p. cm.
    Includes bibliographical references and index.
    ISBN 0-415-95410-X (hardback : alk. paper) -- ISBN 0-415-95411-8 (pbk. : alk.
    paper) 1. Womanism. 2. Women, Black. 3. African American women. 4. Minority
    women. 5. Feminism. I. Phillips, Layli, 1965- II. Title.

HQ1197.W66 2006
305.48'896073--dc22
                                2006007443

Visit the Taylor & Francis Web site at
http://www.taylorandfrancis.com

and the Routledge Web site at
http://www.routledge-ny.com

Permissions

Dedication

For the "Five Grand Mothers" ...
Phyllis,
who was born into slavery and emancipated at age twelve and whom I
know only through a first name and half a torn photograph, seen once.
Laura Glass,
the cigar-smoking supporter of the Universal Negro Improvement
Association and neighborhood root doctor, after whom I am named.
Jannie Glass Worthy Murphy,
who worked three jobs to put two daughters through Spelman College
and turned down her own admission so they could go—a pious church
organist whose only two books were the Bible and Carter G. Woodson's
The Negro in Our History. She was my biggest cheerleader and also
the most stylish and classy woman I ever knew.
Mary N. Worthy and Louise Worthy Geer,
respectively, Mom and Aunt, family philosopher and family historian,
artist and teacher, mothers of five and seven, civil rights activists,
iconoclasts, and free thinkers, through whom I came to know the power
of conversation at the kitchen table.
And for Dad ...
Duane D. Dumbleton
(1939-2006),
who was born a white farm boy in Wisconsin, only to become the kind of
man no one yet imagines possible.
"I don't know about you, but I am universalese."

Contents

Acknowledgments

This project has been my dream for the past ten years, and the roots of its coming into being go back even further. There are many people whom I need to thank for its realization, and I do so with the utmost sincerity. For starters, at Routledge, I want to thank Michael Bickerstaff for having the vision to see the necessity and timeliness of this anthology and David McBride for having the enthusiasm to see its production through to the end. I also want to thank Stephanie Drew for being a fantastic "nuts and bolts" person. I thank Colin Reublinger for giving me a crash course on the publishing business, brainstorming with me, and then going the extra mile on the marketing end. Thank you Nicole Hirshman for your painstaking disk editing and Arlene Belzer for your amazing proofreading—this volume is all the more polished for it. Gratitude to Denise Gupta for the last minute save on the index and Suzanne Lassandro for the tie-breaking votes on all those unanswered questions. Thank you to Brendan O'Neill, Sarah Blackmon, and especially Susan Horwitz for their production magic—we now hold their work in our hands. Thank you to Pearl Chang for the graphic design that transformed my sister's cherished artwork into a book cover. And to all the unsung, behind-the-scenes people at Routledge/Taylor & Francis and affiliated entities without whose labor and attention this text would never have seen the light of day, I express my deepest gratitude now.

My entrée into women's studies came through the door of Black feminism and womanism in the early 1980s, when I was a student at Spelman College. Three people there were profoundly instrumental in my development as a womanist, Black feminist, and postmodern "race woman," namely, Beverly Guy-Sheftall, Barbara Carter, and a dynamic instructor of African art whose name, unfortunately, I can no longer recall. Beverly, who continues to be an esteemed mentor and inspiration to this day, taught with Barbara Carter the first course I took on race, class, and gender. Barbara took a personal interest in my education by encouraging me to apply for a Ford Foundation graduate fellowship at the end of my senior year, when I, toddler in arms and pregnant for the second time, might have given up. This fellowship ultimately funded portions of my graduate education. The instructor of African art modeled radical pedagogy and forever changed my approach to learning and teaching when she spent the first half of our class exposing us to the "forbidden knowledge" of Africology and insisting that we could not understand African art without it. To these three women, I am indebted to your imprint, and I deem you spiritual mothers.

Three more spiritual mothers must also be recognized. To Barbara Smith, *Home Girls: A Black Feminist Anthology* was a watershed in my life and an epiphany of major proportions, and I am honored that I can now call you both friend and elder. Your picture sits on my desk for daily inspiration. To Faye V. Harrison, you are my model for engaged, liberationist, Black feminist, womanist, citizen-of-humanity, spiritualized scholar-activism, and your love, sweetness, and support have sustained me and lit the way for me more times than you know (a shout-out also to William Conwill). To Chela Sandoval, you are my model for taking it from the streets and making the academy pay attention. You are the queen of translation across languages, thought communities, and spiritual dimensions—thank you for giving me the language for things I have always known and for talking back to "them big boyz (and girlz)."

I must also give thanks to the "big three" of womanism: Alice Walker, Chikwenye Okonjo Ogunyemi, and Clenora Hudson-Weems. Thank you for laying the foundation and speaking in three different voices that harmonize and coordinate so well.

Numerous colleagues have provided tangible and intangible assistance to this project over the years, and I want to recognize them by name. From my University of Georgia days, I thank R. Baxter Miller, Barbara McCaskill, Kendra Freeman, Kecia Thomas, and Pat Del Rey. Thanks also to Lynn Szwaja at the Rockefeller Foundation and to everyone associated with the Womanist Studies Consortium (1995–2002), *The Womanist: A Newsletter for Afrocentric Feminist Researchers* (1994–95), and *Womanist Theory and Research* (1995–2002), especially Gerris Farris, Beth McIver, and Emilie Townes. I thank Dionne P. Stephens, Derrick Alridge, and Lee D. Baker (who wins the prize for being on the team longest) for being my crew. I send thanks out to Linda Bell, Susan Talburt, Charlene Ball, Julie Kubala, Charles Jones, Makungu Akinyele, Akinyela Umoja, Carol Marsh-Lockett, Sarah Cook, and Rod Watts at Georgia State University. Thanks to Dean Lauren Adamson, who arranged for my research leave during fall 2004, when the writing for this book began in earnest. Other academic friends in the area include Kim Wallace-Stephens and Vanessa Jackson (a shout-out to our old Black feminist reading circle), M. Bahati Kuumba, Dianne Stewart, Isa Williams, Beth Hackett, and Jude Preissle and Mark Toomey. My national network of people who must be recognized and thanked heartily includes Susan Glisson, Carolyn Fluehr-Lobban, Jean Rahier and Mariama Jaiteh, Pat Washington, Laurie Fuller and Erica Meiners, Yi-Chun Tricia Lin, Mattie Richardson, Marlon Bailey, Jafari Sinclair Allen, Lisa C. Moore, and Jill Nelson. Susan L. Taylor, your columns have been manna. Laura Amazzone, thanks for the connecting work. Thanks also to Pat Hill Collins and Bonnie Thornton Dill for being trailblazers and giving the much-needed nods. Special shout-outs to Asa G. Hilliard III and Robert V. Guthrie (you just departed, but it feels like you're still here), elders who need no introduction; your personal words of wisdom and encouragement, in addition to your world-changing work, have made a difference in my life.

Students have been important to my life and to the development of this project from the beginning. I must thank the students of my womanism classes of summer 2003 and spring 2005 and every section of Black feminist thought and African American lesbian and gay activism that I have ever taught. For particular research assistance, I thank Melinda Mills, Angel Charmain Dupree Paschall, Kerri Reddick-Morgan, BeAnka Nyela/Kym Tate, Max Green, and Stacey Singer. For good conversations in which we all developed our ideas, I thank Charles Stephens, Martha Turner, Shomari Olugbala, Xiumei Pu, Shani Settles, Donna Troka, and Derrick Lanois. For being my connection to Uganda and more, I thank Andrew Ellias State and also Alicia Decker. GSU BlackOUT, your support has been invaluable all along, but special thanks to Samietra Lisenbee for picking up the womanist torch and also to Leah Trotter, Brandy "Calamity" Collier, Marla Stewart, Aza Zuma Sauti/Janelle Allen, Sanjo Kali, Antoine Norwood, and Kyndra Frasier on general principle. Some students go that extra mile, and for that I must thank Taliba Sikudhani Olugbala/Jonelle Shields, Andy Lowry, and Yolo Akili Ifakunle/Micheal Robinson.

Friends and family form the bedrock of our daily lives and emotional survival. For being there, I must thank Lyz Jaeger ("oldest and bestest"), Debra Roberts, Carla Thompson, Susan Gill and Giordana Diaz, Sujata and Kalindi Winfield, and Cara Averhart Reese. My children, Thad and Aliyah, are among my reasons for living. Thank you to the Richman and Phillips clans for being "part of that village." Love to my brothers and sisters—Mary Bahiyyih ("the librarian" and "the artist"—a shout-out on the cover art), Xandra, Rama, and Ben—and also to my father's Wisconsin-rooted people and my mother's Georgia-rooted people. Nancy Cavins, you have earned a special place in my heart. A shout-out goes to my book group, "Book and Circumstance: Responses, Revelations, Resolutions"—Gary Longstreet, LaMiiko Moore, Gerald Phillips, Tyees Douglas, Coy McCall, Julie Jones, Gregory Turner, Alisa Dawson, Miss Culver, and Kendall Clayborne—because it is so nice to talk about books with people outside school! And speaking of books, big thanks to Mutota at Oasis and everybody at Charis for the constant support, both tangible and intangible.

I saved the best for last. I must thank all those who have transitioned and generously provide me with inspiration and help from the "other side"—"we are all interconnected." You know who you are, and I will continue to honor you. Special respect is owed to Ignacio Martin-Baro, Kenneth and Mamie Clark, Audre Lorde, Gloria Anzaldúa, Joseph Antenor-Firmin, Malcolm, Martin, Fela, Jean-Michel, and el Che. I thank the Creator for instilling me with mission, my Higher Self for taking up the charge, and Life itself for providing signposts. Finally, there is not enough I can say or do to thank my visionary counterpart, Baruti KMT, "beloved Abiona," with whom I travel time and space and walk the path.

Introduction

Womanism: On Its Own

LAYLI PHILLIPS

Since 1983, when Alice Walker's *In Search of Our Mothers' Gardens: Womanist Prose* introduced the womanist idea to the general public, feminists of all colors, as well as women of color and others who question or reject feminism, have been debating the uniqueness and viability of womanism as a freestanding concept. Because the definition of *"womanist"* offered by Walker was poetic in nature, it became, on the one hand, immediately attractive to and resonant for many people who were searching for an alternative to "feminist" as an identity or praxis and, on the other hand, theoretically slippery and frustrating to scholars and activists accustomed to working within a decidedly feminist frame. By the end of the 1990s, two things had happened. First, within women's studies per se, these debates had reached a point of exhaustion, prematurely stifling any serious discussion of womanism as a significant discourse within academic feminism or critical theory. Second, outside women's studies, as well as in marginalized corners of the field, the employment of womanism as a theoretical frame had proliferated, by then constituting a venerable and persistent underground movement indicating the ongoing productivity and relevance of the perspective outside the academic mainstream and even beyond the academy itself. Today, in 2006, we can look back on how the twentieth anniversary of the publication of *In Search of Our Mothers' Gardens* was unceremoniously bypassed and observe a major void, namely, the absence of any systematic treatment of the womanist idea and, notably, the absence of any definitive compendium of womanist scholarship documenting what has now been more than a quarter century of womanist scholarly and creative work.

I say "quarter century" because what few people note is that Alice Walker's first use of the term *womanist* occurred in 1979 when her short story "Coming Apart" was published in Laura Lederer's anthology *Take Back the Night*.[1] In this story about a Black husband and wife arguing over the effect of the husband's consumption of pornography on their marriage, there is a line where Walker writes, "The wife has never considered herself a feminist—though she is, of course, a 'womanist.' A 'womanist' is a feminist, only more common." This act of joining the terms *"woman"* and *"common"* at the border of "feminist/not feminist" situated a particular mode of women's resistance activity squarely within the realm of the "everyday," thereby defying both academic and ideological claims on the definition, labeling, and elaboration of women's resistance activity under the exclusive and limited label "*feminist*." In two simple yet pregnant sentences, Walker had opened up a new way of talking about the relationship between women, social change, the struggle against oppression, and the quest for full humanity. In two successively more widely circulated publications, namely, her 1981 book review essay, "Gifts of Power: The Writings of Rebecca Jackson" and her 1983 book *In Search of Our Mothers' Gardens*, she further elaborated the definition of "*womanist*" in ways both explicit and cryptic. From 1983 on, womanism and Alice Walker were inextricably linked in both the popular and the academic imaginations.

Yet there is more to the story. The notion and terminology of womanism must be traced to at least two additional progenitors, namely, Chikwenye Okonjo Ogunyemi, who in 1985 published her article "Womanism: The Dynamics of the Contemporary Black Female Novel in English," and Clenora Hudson-Weems, whose 1993 book *Africana Womanism: Reclaiming Ourselves* resulted from a series of papers presented in the 1980s, including her 1989 article "Cultural and Agenda Conflicts in Academia: Critical Issues for Africana Women's Studies." Each of these authors developed the womanist idea and related terminology independently. Over time, Ogunyemi's perspective came to be known as African womanism, while Hudson-Weems's perspective identified itself as Africana womanism. Each distinct in its own right, Walker's womanism, Ogunyemi's African womanism, and Hudson-Weems's Africana womanism formed the collective basis for an interpolated field of theory and praxis used by a host of people to follow. Significantly, none of these authors created something new; rather, each named something that had been in existence for some time, functioning below the academic and activist radar and outside dominant histories of consciousness. What is significant is that the time had come to name, and ultimately elaborate, this thing.

Womanism: What It Is

That being said, what is womanism? Womanism is a social change perspective rooted in Black women's and other women of color's everyday experiences and everyday methods of problem solving in everyday spaces, extended to the problem of ending all forms of oppression for all people, restoring the balance between people and the environment/nature, and reconciling human life with the spiritual dimension. I take the perspective that womanism is not feminism. Its relationships to feminism (including Black feminism) are important, but its relationships to other critical theories and social-justice movements are equally important, despite being less frequently discussed or acknowledged. Unlike feminism, and despite its name, womanism does not emphasize or privilege gender or sexism; rather, it elevates all sites and forms of oppression, whether they are based on social-address categories like gender, race, or class, to a level of equal concern and action. Womanism's link to gender is the fact that the historically produced race/class/gender matrix that is Black womanhood[2] serves as the origin point for a speaking position that freely and autonomously addresses any topic or problem. Because Black women experience sexism, and womanism is concerned with sexism, feminism is confluent with the expression of womanism, but feminism and womanism cannot be conflated, nor can it be said that womanism is a "version" of feminism.

Since being named, womanism has spawned both passionate affiliation and vigorous debate. Beginning in the mid-1980s, scholars in theology, literature, and history began to employ womanist terminology and explore the implications of womanism in their disciplines. Within a decade, scholars in fields as diverse as film and theater studies, psychology, education, anthropology, communication studies, social work, and nursing, in addition to women's studies and Africana studies, had enlarged this corpus. By the time womanism could claim a quarter century of existence, womanist scholarship could also be found in sexuality studies, public health, and architecture. Womanism has been visible in popular culture since the mid-1980s, appearing in magazines, newspapers, and other media and permeating the worlds of popular music, especially hip-hop, as well as the arts. Neither has womanism been limited to Black American contexts. Explorations of the womanist idea can be found in African, Australian (Aboriginal), Canadian, Caribbean/West Indian, Chinese/Taiwanese, European, Latino/Latina American, Native American Indian, and Southeast Asian/Indian cultural contexts, scholarly and otherwise. Internet searches of the World Wide Web readily locate thousands of womanist-related citations from around the world.

What is interesting is that, since the beginning, the womanist frame has been applied more frequently than it has been written about. That is, more people have employed womanism than have described it. What this reflects is the tendency of womanism to be approached and expressed intuitively rather than analytically. While some might view this as problematic, there are good reasons for it—reasons that only affirm the distinctiveness and incommensurability of womanism vis-à-vis other perspectives with which it might be confused or conflated. On the plus side, this state of affairs has preserved the open-ended, polyvalent, polyvocal, dialogic, noncentralized, and improvisational character of womanism, allowing it to resist canonization, academic appropriation, and ideological subsumption. By maintaining its autonomy outside established intellectual and political structures, womanism has preserved its accessibility to a broad spectrum of people from diverse walks of life and retained its ability to flourish "beneath the radar." On the minus side, however, this state of affairs has allowed the apparent absorption of womanism into various taxonomic schemes within which it is not intelligible and lessened the visibility of womanism in some contexts. The field of women's studies, where womanism has experienced an interesting rise and fall, is a case in point.

The ascent of womanist scholarship and usage of womanist terminology in the popular sphere precipitated ongoing attempts to define womanism in relation to feminism as well as to debate the merits of womanism versus feminism. Several points have been at issue: Is womanism "its own thing" or simply another "version" of feminism? Is womanism the same thing as Black feminism? Who can claim womanism or be womanist? Is womanism activist or simply an identity? Does womanism detract from feminism? Is womanism an alternative to feminism for women who reject feminism? Is womanism soft on sexism and an apology for patriarchy? Is womanism prolesbian or, alternately, soft on homophobia? Is womanism essentially academic or truly vernacular? Interestingly, within the field of women's studies, where these questions have been most vigorously debated and are of greatest concern, initial excitement about womanism yielded to obscurity once the determination was made that womanism was simply a synonym for Black feminism, and a relatively superfluous one at that. This view has been cemented by entries in "official" reference works—encyclopedias and dictionaries—that essentially stripped womanism of its defining features and represented it as a largely unremarkable phenomenon.

For instance, the *American Heritage Dictionary*—which, in 1993, was the first to include such a definition—defines *"womanist"* as "Having or expressing a belief in or respect for women and their talents and abilities beyond the boundaries of race and class."[3] This dictionary definition includes the following quote from Alice Walker: "Womanist … tradition assumes, because of our experiences during slavery, that black women already are capable." To me, this definition seems to be, at best, nonsensical and, at worst, an attempt to neutralize the difference that womanism actually represents. What does "beyond the boundaries of race and class" mean? Clearly, womanism is an ethnically and culturally situated (although not bounded) perspective that does not seek to negate difference through transcending it. Rather, as I explain in greater detail later, womanism seeks to harmonize and coordinate difference so that difference does not become irreconcilable and dissolve into violent destruction. Additionally, womanism does not "begin and end" with women, as the definition suggests. Invocation of Alice Walker's quote affirming the capability of Black women implies that womanism is more or less a recuperation and celebration of women who have been "beat down" by the system. Yet, a careful reading of the extant womanist literature—even Alice Walker's work alone—relays that womanism is a great deal more than this.

The encyclopedia entry on womanism found in *The Reader's Companion to U.S. Women's History* is similarly problematic.[4] It begins, "*Womanist* and *womanism* are culture-specific and poetic synonyms for *Black feminist* and *Black feminism*" (p. 639), and it ends, "See also Feminism, Black" (p. 641). This entry, authored by Gloria Steinem and Diana L. Hayes, briefly acknowledges that some womanist theologians "prefer *womanist* to stand alone" and "do not offer *Black feminist* or *feminist of color* as synonyms" (p. 640), yet it fails to elaborate on this possibility. In addition, this entry, which relies heavily on Alice Walker's womanism, makes no mention of other key progenitors such as Chikwenye Okonjo Ogunyemi or Clenora Hudson-Weems. Even though it was published as late as 1998, the entry makes no mention of womanism's global reach, even in areas like Africa and Europe, where its elaboration was highly significant by that time; rather, it emphasizes a U.S. frame. While a strength of this encyclopedia entry is its nuanced and fairly elaborate treatment of Walker's poetic definition from *In Search of Our Mothers' Gardens,* a reader might walk away from this reference thinking that Walker's womanism is all there is. In addition, such a reader's understanding of womanism might be limited to racialized gender concerns. The entry also suggests that men feel less comfortable with womanism than with feminism or profeminism, while a number of Black male authors, in particular, had by that time clearly expressed that they felt womanism offered a more inclusive context for men's participation than feminism. I point out the shortcomings of Steinem and Hayes's groundbreaking encyclopedia entry not to impugn the intent or expertise of its authors, but rather to make the point that prevailing conceptual schemes make it difficult to understand womanism. The tendency to envelop it within existing conceptual schemes, especially feminism, has been strong, leading to the unfortunate and unintentional tendency to "not see" important aspects of womanism. Thus, womanism has typically been misrepresented or, at least, underarticulated within mainstream histories of consciousness. My goal here is to present womanism in a different light—one that makes womanism visible on its own.

Carol Marsh-Lockett presents a better definition in *The Oxford Companion to African American Literature,* published in 1997.[5] Although this encyclopedia entry, like Steinem and Hayes's, is limited by its singular and almost exclusive focus on Walker's womanist definition, Marsh-Lockett teases out nuances of womanist theory and praxis that extend beyond Walker's 1983 verbiage and begins to allude to the full promise of womanism as a universal perspective authored by Black women. Most notably, Marsh-Lockett links womanism to a "global vision" tied to "attention to the African presence in the Americas" and the "universality of the Black race" (p. 785). A womanist is triply concerned with herself, other Black women, and the entire Black race, female and male—but also all humanity, showing an ever-expanding and ultimately universal arc of political concern, empathy, and activism. As Marsh-Lockett points out, womanists are concerned with not only gender and race, but also "local and international culture in addition to national and global politics and economics" (p. 785). Through a discussion of intersectionality, Marsh-Lockett relates—but does not conflate—womanism and Black feminism, demonstrating that, while there is a relationship between the two, they are not interchangeable. According to Marsh-Lockett, "womanism furnishes a system of analysis and a world view hitherto unavailable to African American women and other women of color" (p. 785). By linking womanism to the writings of authors like Zora Neale Hurston, Lorraine Hansberry, Alice Childress, and others, as well as to the Black women's club movement of the late nineteenth and early twentieth centuries, Marsh-Lockett demonstrates that womanism, while only recently provided nomenclature by Walker and others, nevertheless articulates a long and unique history of Black women's thought and activism. Finally, Marsh-Lockett demonstrates an awareness of the breadth of womanist thought across multiple disciplines and regions in her mention of womanist literary studies and theology as well as her citation of Chikwenye Okonjo Ogunyemi.

In sum, womanism's representation within mainstream histories of consciousness has been problematic. Either womanism has been conflated with feminism or Black feminism, or its full scope has been inadequately captured. Womanism manifests five overarching characteristics: (1) it is antioppressionist, (2) it is vernacular, (3) it is nonideological, (4) it is communitarian, and (5) it is spiritualized. *"Antioppressionist"* supersedes and organizes all labels that reference specific forms of oppression, such as antisexist, antiracist, antiheterosexist, antihomophobic, antixenophobic, and the like,[6] extending the reach of womanism into zones of oppression that may not be related to labelable identities and for which there is not even yet language.[7] A womanist knows oppression when she (or he) sees it, and she (or he) is against it.[8] She lives her life in such a way as to fight and dismantle oppression in whatever ways she can, individually or in organized formations with others. The term *"antioppressionist"* conveys that womanism is identified with liberationist projects of all sorts and that womanism supports the liberation of all humankind from all forms of oppression. Indeed, womanism seeks to enable people to transcend the relations of domination and oppression altogether.

"Vernacular" identifies womanism with "the everyday"—everyday people and everyday life. The soul of womanism is grassroots, identified with the masses of humanity. Use of the term *"masses of humanity"* does not in this case suggest a polarity between "the masses" and "the elites"; rather, it highlights the unifying reality that all people have "everyday" lives and that elite status is something that cloaks this reality more than supplants it. What links people, and thus provides a basis for the harmonization and coordination of difference, are common human concerns—food, shelter, relationships, communication, body and health, love, life, death, and contemplation of the transcendental, to name just a few examples. Like other critical theorists and social-justice activists, womanists view gross differentials in power and resources as highly problematic because they contribute to dehumanization and interfere with individual and collective well-being. Where they differ from many other critical theorists and social-justice activists is in the trust they place in nonelites to envision and accomplish social-justice ends, inside or outside formal structures like organizations or social movements. Womanists

just act in the course of everyday life, and the nature of these actions varies widely from person to person. This diversity is not problematized; rather, it is viewed favorably. The assumption of womanism is that "it all adds up" to positive social change in the end. "Start where you are" might be the womanist credo, and "one step forward" is the standard for progress. As a womanist, there is no need to be "perfect"; personhood is enough to qualify.

"Nonideological" refers to the fact that womanism abhors rigid lines of demarcation and tends to function in a decentralized manner. Statements like "You're either in or you're out" and "You're either with us or against us" do not compute for womanists. Womanism is not about creating lines of demarcation; rather, it is about building structures of inclusiveness and positive interrelationship from anywhere in its network. Ideology is rigid; it relies on internal logical consistency and some degree of central control that seeks the resolution of difference by means of homogenization. Ideological perspectives and, to a lesser extent, movements rely on processes that compel or seduce people to conform and do not deal effectively with difference or paradox. Differences and tension that cannot be elided or erased trouble ideologies, and unresolved paradoxes tend to cause ideologies to crumble and lose efficacy. Womanism is not a rule-based system, and it does not need to resolve internal disagreement to function effectively. It is a nondisciplinary system; there are no "lines in the sand." Womanists rely on dialogue to establish and negotiate relationships; such relationships can accommodate disagreement, conflict, and anger simultaneously with agreement, affinity, and love. From an analytic perspective, womanism appears paradoxical and logically inconsistent, and from an analytic perspective, these are fair assessments—yet womanism's criteria for self-evaluation are not analytic. They are holistic, affective, and spiritual. From a political perspective, legitimation of paradox and logical inconsistency are methods of enabling the harmonization and coordination of difference in ways that are humanizing and respectful of the multitude of ways that people need to express themselves to live in rewarding and authentic ways and to answer to the dictates of their own spiritual evolution.

"Communitarian" refers to the fact that womanism views commonweal as the goal of social change. Commonweal is the state of collective well-being; it is the optimization of well-being for all members of a community. For womanists, community is conceptualized as a series of successively overlapping tiers, beginning with Black women or women of color (the level of the self or identity), followed by the Black community and other communities of color (the level of "tribe" or "kin"), followed by all oppressed people (the level of similarly situated others), and ultimately encompassing all humanity (the universal level). Thus, contrary to the way in which it has been characterized, womanism's main concern is not Black women per se; rather, Black women are the place where this particular form of thinking about commonweal originates. Black women's vision then extends to encompass all humans,

but it does not stop there. Included in this conception of community is what Taliba Sikudhani Olugbala has called "livingkind"[9] (all living things—from humans, to animals, to plants, to microorganisms) as well as the "inanimate" components of Earth, the universe(s) beyond Earth, the spiritual world(s) and transcendental realm(s) encompassing the universe(s), and, ultimately, all of creation. Commonweal is the principle that holds all these dimensions and aspects of creation together in an ideal state of dynamic balance and constant expressive unfoldment. The assumption is that commonweal does not exist at this time, and the purpose of social change activity from a womanist perspective is to bring it about. Thus, womanism seeks to reconcile three relationships: the relationship between people from different groups, the relationship between people and the environment/nature, and the relationship between people and the spiritual/transcendental realms. Womanist methods are those that intervene between or seek to heal wounds and imbalances at any or all of these sites.

"*Spiritualized*" refers to the fact that womanism openly acknowledges a spiritual/transcendental realm with which human life, livingkind, and the material world are all intertwined. For womanists, this realm is actual and palpable, and the relationship between it and humans is neither abstract nor insignificant to politics. AnaLouise Keating has used the term "*spiritualized politics*" to refer to social-justice activism and perspectives that are informed by spiritual beliefs and practices, rooted in the conviction that spiritual intercession and consideration of the transcendental or metaphysical dimension of life enhance and even undergird political action.[10] Perspectives that are more academic or ideological have typically avoided incorporation of spiritual/transcendental considerations. Womanism, on the other hand, is quite adamant about the reality and importance of the spiritual world, with less concern for the diversity of ways that it is conceptualized. Of all the characteristics that distinguish womanism from other critical, theoretical, or ideological perspectives, this one is perhaps the most unique and potentially controversial.

Womanist Methods of Social Transformation

Womanist methods of social transformation cohere around the activities of harmonizing and coordinating, balancing, and healing. These methods work in and through relationship, reject violence and aggression but not assertiveness, and readily incorporate "everyday" activities. These overlapping methods include, but are not limited to, dialogue, arbitration and mediation, spiritual activities, hospitality, mutual aid and self-help, and "mothering." Physical healing and methods of reconciling body, mind, and spirit (including integral medicine and folk healing) are also recognized as methods of social transformation by womanists, based on the notion that physical and psychological well-being provide a necessary foundation for social justice and commonweal.

"Harmonizing and coordinating" involve figuring out how to make disparate elements work together. It requires a type of cognitive mobility that Chela Sandoval refers to as "differential consciousness."[11] Differential consciousness permits movement among and between divergent logics (cultural, religious, ideological, etc.) and conceptual schemes (cosmologies, value systems, ethical codes, etc.), and its hallmark is a higher-order coordinating mechanism ("the differential") that enables them to collectively make sense and work together. It requires the ability to make positive connections between elements that might have seemed unrelatable before; thus, it is associated with creativity, ingenuity, improvisationality, and the proverbial "making a way out of no way."[12] As Sandoval points out, the transcendental-emotive state of love creates a space within and a mechanism by which limiting rational-analytical logics can be dissolved to make different, paradox-superseding logics possible and active. This love, similar to Audre Lorde's "erotics,"[13] has a political expression that Sandoval calls "revolutionary love."[14]

Dialogue is a means by which people express and establish both connection and individuality. Dialogue permits negotiation, reveals standpoint, realizes existential equality, and shapes social reality. Dialogue is the locale where both tension and connection can be present simultaneously; it is the site for both struggle and love. The "kitchen table" is a key metaphor for understanding the womanist perspective on dialogue.[15] The kitchen table is an informal, woman-centered space where all are welcome and all can participate. The table is an invitation to become part of a group amicably comprised of heterogeneous elements and unified by the pleasure and nourishment of food and drink. At the table, people can come and go, agree or disagree, take turns talking or speak all at once, and laugh, shout, complain, or counsel—even be present in silence. It is a space where the language is accessible and the ambience casual. At the kitchen table, people share the truths of their lives on equal footing and learn through face-to-face conversation. When the kitchen table metaphor is applied to political problem-solving situations, the relations of domination and subordination break down in favor of more egalitarian, interpersonal processes.

Arbitration and mediation involve helping warring parties to calm down and return to positive relationship. The arbiter or mediator is the person who serves as a bridge or connector by maintaining simultaneous positive relationships with both parties at once and translating communications in ways that make fresh perspectives possible. In arbitration and mediation, there are no enemies—only parties to a disagreement. The goals of arbitration and mediation are fairness and reconciliation. Ogunyemi refers to womanist arbitration and mediation as *"siddon look"* tactics, literally "sit down and look" or "sit down and cogitate."[16] She characterizes these tactics as "a belligerent form of pacifism," which can easily be related to Walker's womanist, who is "responsible, in charge, *serious*" and who "loves Struggle" and "loves the Folk."[17] When tension, disagreement, or conflict arises, the goal in arbitration and media-tion—unlike war—is not to vanquish, eliminate, or separate one or the other opposing party, but rather to facilitate both parties' return to a state of happy, unhampered, and authentic life pursuit within the context of commonweal. What undergirds the mediation process and gives it moral legitimacy is the appeal to a common humanity, expressed as a family relation, answerable to transcendental, spiritual, or ethical imperatives. Arbitration and mediation, as womanist methods, do not, unlike prevalent conflict resolution models, aspire toward the creation of "unity" through the suppression or neutraliza-tion of difference; rather, they aspire toward an organic and dynamic whole-ness that functions whether the disagreement is resolved or remains. Actions that convey hospitality, care, or nurturance can help this process.

Spiritual activities involve communication between the material and spiritual realms, based on the assumption that these realms are actual, inter-connected, and interpenetrating. Drawing from a diversity of traditions, womanists may use prayer, rituals, meditation, collective visualization, and a host of other means to draw spiritual energy toward social, political, and even physical problem solving and healing. Spiritual methods of social transforma-tion, which may be exercised by individuals or groups, recognize not only the value of power based in the spiritual realm that can be applied toward human problems, but also the importance of maintaining a harmonious relationship between humans, the environment, and the spiritual realm.

Hospitality as method refers to taking good care of guests. Guests are those who, by one or more degrees of difference or separation, are not members of one's house or intimate circle, but are welcomed into one's house and treated in ways that respect their existential worth and integrity. By implication, hos-pitality is a practice that facilitates a positive encounter between people who are strangers or "other" to one another, setting the stage for possible friend-ship or collaboration. Hospitality is fundamental to the management of differ-ence on a global scale. Hospitality is a way of acknowledging dignity, offering nurturance, promoting amity, and providing pleasure to foster positive intra- and intergroup relations. Hospitality preempts the tensions that may arise as a result of difference by providing a means of connection at the beginning of relation. Hospitality can also be used to mediate and reduce conflict through the heartening effects of care, pleasure, and festivity. Hospitality as a method of social transformation emerges out of womanist caretaking sensibilities as they manifest in everyday life activities and reflects traditions of caring for the friend or stranger that have long histories in many of the world's cultures and religions.

Mutual aid and self-help are everyday "do-it-yourself" methods that involve coming together as a group at the grassroots level to solve a common problem. Mutual aid and self-help rely on the principles of strength in numbers, wisdom gained from life experience, self-education, and democratic knowledge sharing. Examples of this womanist social change method can be found in washerwoman Callie House's reparations movement activism during the late 1800s, the Black women's club movement of the late 19th and early 20th centuries (with its motto of "Lifting as We Climb"), the eclectic social work leadership of early to mid-20th century icons Maggie Lena Walker, Elizabeth Ross Haynes, and Mamie Phipps Clark, the civil rights activism style of Ella Baker, the organization and activism of second wave feminist groups like the Third World Women's Alliance (today the Women of Color Resource Center), Salsa Soul Sisters, the Combahee River Collective, and the National Black Women's Health Project—examples are numerous and plentiful.[18] Even the Underground Railroad, spearheaded by Harriet Tubman, could be understood through this lens. Womanist mutual aid and self-help begins with the survival wisdom of women of color, but does not end there—ultimately it welcomes and embraces all who can benefit from this body of knowledge without negating its source or denying the social conditions that created it. Mutual aid and self-help demonstrate two important things: first, that an underestimated genius for problem solving circulates among institutionally dispossessed populations and, second, that such marginalized populations will not be forced to succumb beneath institutional neglect, whether benign or malign. Indeed, at times, mutual aid and self-help are the only means by which intellectually marginalized groups can implement superior methods of problem solving that are either rejected or not acknowledged by the mainstream.

Motherhood as a womanist method of social transformation has its roots in African cultural legacies. Motherhood, here, however, must be dissociated from its purely biological connotation and even from its strictly gendered connotation. In the African context, motherhood is a highly elaborated construct encompassing a number of meanings not generally recognized in the Euroamerican context. As Ogunyemi explains, using examples from West African cultures, most germane here are the notions of spiritual mother (Osun or Chi/Ori), mother as oracle (Odu), childless mother (Mammywata), and community mother (Omunwa/Iyalode).[19] Essentially, motherhood is a set of behaviors based on caretaking, management, nurturance, education, spiritual mediation, and dispute resolution. Anyone—whether female or male, old or young, with or without children, heterosexual or same-gender-loving—can engage in these behaviors and, therefore, mother. In so doing, every individual has the ability to contribute to the ultimate goals of womanism: societal healing, reconciliation of the relationship between people and nature, and the achievement and maintenance of commonweal.

Physical healing is integral to social change for a variety of reasons. Bodily well-being is the foundation for other forms of well-being; the lack of good nutrition, fitness, and health make it hard for people to contribute their energy toward higher-level concerns. In the current social context, many forms of infirmity are the result of oppressive conditions and processes. Arguably, suboptimal bodily health also relates to violence and hatred. Thus, from a womanist perspective, the most basic forms of health and healing are related to rebalancing the world socially, environmentally, and spiritually. Womanist methods of social change—from the simplest acts like cooking food and sharing it, to everyday acts of hospitality and nurturance, to more complex procedures of folk healing and integral medicine, even literacy and education—all seek to enhance the wellness of the body and psyche as a foundation for the wellness of society. Womanists inherently recognize the principle of "as above, so below." As such, bodily health is an indicator of and conduit for societal and environmental health. Due to its association with the everyday and common "Folk," womanism values both traditional, naturalistic, and spiritually based methods of healing as well as a variety of "scientific" methods, as long they recognize the interconnectedness of body, mind, and spirit. In line with liberation psychology, womanists also recognize the role of societal structures in physical and psychological health: peace and justice are health-favoring conditions, while war and injustice are health-compromising conditions.[20] Part of healing/medicine is healing society.

In contrast to established ideological perspectives like feminism, ethnic nationalism, Marxism/socialism, and so on, womanist activism does not focus on the confrontation of institutional structures so much as on the shaping of thought processes and relationships. For womanists, entrenched social and environmental problems originate from a psychological and/or spiritual first cause, only later manifesting in the material or institutional realms. Thus, to attack institutions or physical conditions is to attack the outer layer, rather than the inner layer, of the problem and run the risk of reproducing the same oppression with new actors. War, violence, poverty, environmental degradation, racism, sexism, classism, homophobia, heterosexism, xenophobia, ableism, ageism, inadequate health care, inadequate education, and the like all begin in the realm of beliefs, attitudes, and behaviors. Womanists value everyday activism that involves confronting violence and oppression wherever and whenever they appear across the course of a day. Talking with and organizing those around one, sharing information that can conscientize, but not proselytizing, and being a positive person to interact with are all womanist methods of social change—methods that more ideological perspectives might write off as unimportant, ineffective, or naive. In characteristic fashion, a womanist might respond by adapting the colloquial proverb as follows: "You can catch more flies with honey than vinegar—although a little vinegar does add spice now and then." Methodological purity is not required; indeed, from a womanist perspective, mixed methods, unhampered by ideology, work better.

Womanism and Postmodernity

Given its vernacular loyalties and grassroots sensibilities, it might not be obvious that womanism is uniquely well suited to social and environmental problem solving under conditions of postmodernity.[21] Academic wisdom has it that this honor rests with poststructuralism, a philosophical approach that can claim particularly compelling explanations for how postmodern societies function (and dysfunction). A close reading of both womanist and poststructuralist texts, a full explication of which is beyond the scope of this chapter reveals that the two perspectives are remarkably similar in two respects: first, how they unpack complex oppressive processes and forms of violence, concentrating on the circulation of power; and second, how they promote equality and democracy while respecting difference and freedom.[22] These perspectives differ in three key ways, however: (1) their use of language—womanism is accessible, poststructural theory is not (and this fact has implications for the degree to which each is able to engage and mobilize various segments of humanity for change on a mass scale); (2) their perspectives on identity and community—womanism favors holistic models, while poststructuralism has a particular affinity for perspectives that emphasize fragmentation and dislocation; and (3) spirituality—womanism is explicitly spiritual, poststructuralism is not (which, like accessibility of language, has implications for the degree to which each perspective can engage and mobilize various segments of humanity). In my opinion, womanism and poststructuralism are compatible and mutually enhancing, but poststructuralism would have more impact if its insights were more frequently delivered in plain language. Its failure to use plain language implicates it in processes that reinforce the very relations of domination it theoretically opposes, inside and outside the academy, allowing it to reinscribe white supremacy, patriarchy, class disparity, and a host of other oppressive systems.[23]

The convergence of womanism and poststructuralism at a locale characterized by new forms of community built around lines of affinity rather than identity and a radical respect for responsible freedom would represent the longed-for reconciliation of poor Black women, representing the historical and symbolic bottom of the global social hierarchy, and rich white men, who represent the top, under the current dehumanizing system, thus bringing people of all races, ethnicities, and genders into a new system of relations. Indeed, such a convergence might precipitate the collapse of the very oppressive binary system that drives the relations of domination and oppression altogether. As the Combahee River Collective wrote in 1977, "If Black women were free, it would mean that everyone else would have to be free since our freedom would necessitate the destruction of all the systems of oppression."[24] While such a reconciliation is almost unthinkable at this point in time, it will ultimately be the issue that determines the success or failure of social-justice activism in the twenty-first century. Social forces that will force a resolution of this issue are rapidly gathering momentum. Part of why now is the time to clearly articulate the womanist idea is that womanism can contribute greatly to a successful reconciliation of parties opposed under the current system.

In its theory and praxis, womanism envisions and enacts a world freed from the oppressive and dehumanizing effects of this binary. Without presenting womanism against the backdrop of postmodernity—a task that could scarcely have been accomplished twenty-five years ago—it is nearly impossible to convey womanism's liberatory potential vis-à-vis other perspectives. Womanism is postmodernism at street level.

Womanism's Relationship to Other Perspectives

Having stated that womanism is not feminism and that womanism and poststructuralism are compatible despite some important differences, I now pursue a fuller discussion of the relationship between womanism and other perspectives with which is it often compared or contrasted. To understand womanism's relationship with other perspectives, a general framework for thinking about relationship must be articulated.

The Western academic emphasis on classification and taxonomy obscures the relationship between womanism and other perspectives, especially feminism and Black feminism. These relationships cannot be understood within the frame of taxonomic classification, which relies on lines of demarcation that separate and differentiate. The goal of any taxonomic system is to establish discrete and nonoverlapping categories. Taken a step further, taxonomic systems facilitate prediction and control as well as the formation of oppressive hierarchies. The goal of any familial system of organization is to establish connections and overlaps while demonstrating distinctiveness and individuality through contrast from commonalities. While family models are not necessarily nonhierarchical from a conceptual standpoint, they differ from taxonomic models in three respects. First, their animating impulses of relationship, rather than prediction and control, are, ideally, love and care. Second, they manifest fundamental interconnectedness and interdependence among elements in the system. Third, the hierarchies they embody are, ideally, helpful rather than oppressive.

Taxonomic systems rely on "either/or" logic, while familial organization systems rest on "both/and" logic.[25] Even traditional feminist histories of consciousness are animated by the urge to demonstrate differences between perspectives, and thus isolate and oppose groups of thinkers and actors whose best interests lie in working together—that is, harmonizing and coordinating all while permitting difference and its infinite proliferations. Womanism is a harmonizing and coordinating project, not an isolating and separating project. It seeks to promote relations of interconnectedness and cooperation all while blurring, dissolving, and dismantling ideological lines of demarcation. Thus, womanism has not been and cannot be understood within traditional feminist histories of consciousness insofar as these systems rely on taxonomic systems of classification. To understand womanism and its relation to other perspectives requires a family model.

For purposes of discussion, I separate womanism/feminism as identity and womanism/feminism as politics and discuss the implications of each separately. The relationship between womanist and feminist identities is readily illuminated using a family metaphor. To a lesser extent, the relationship between womanist and feminist politics is also elucidated using this metaphor. But other metaphors, which I elaborate below, further clarify—and add a different slant to—the relationship between womanist and feminist politics. While no metaphor can offer a complete accounting of the thing it analogizes, metaphors can be useful for pointing out new ways of thinking.

In terms of identity and, to a lesser extent, politics, feminism and womanism are cousins. Within a taxonomic system, feminism and womanism are opposed and, potentially, adversarial. Within a familial system, feminism and womanism are related and can be mutually supportive. Under this rubric, they recognize and respect their difference from one another, yet they allow one another to flourish. One problem plaguing the relationship between womanism and feminism heretofore has been the tendency of Euroamerican feminism to assimilate all difference into itself and, in particular, to exhibit both racism and cultural imperialism rather unselfconsciously. While decades of internal work around these issues has fundamentally transformed feminism from the inside—a fact that not all womanist scholars acknowledge—one troubling component of feminism's appropriative tendencies remains, namely, its constant attempts to recenter itself as the only progressive voice or vehicle for women concerned with social-justice issues. This tendency disallows and neutralizes alternative expressions of women's social-justice work or thought, of which feminism is just one—a point well articulated by authors as diverse as Clenora Hudson-Weems, Catherine Obianuju Acholonu, Molara Ogundipe-Leslie, Ada Maria Isasi-Diaz, and Allyson Goce Tintiangco[26]—and is thus disciplinary in the Foucaultian sense. This tendency accounts for much of the tension between some womanists and feminism. To say that one is a womanist is not to say that one is a feminist, even if the two are not mutually exclusive; a person can be either, neither, or both.

For feminists to claim that womanists are being disloyal to feminism or undermining feminism by claiming womanism instead of feminism reflects a lack of understanding about the relationship and difference between the two entities as well as a lack of genuine appreciation for the proliferation of positionalities generated by all ideologies and critical perspectives as they evolve and differentiate. Such an accusation subtly implies that all women should be feminists because feminism is a superior social-justice perspective for women. The womanist perspective holds that, as long as the job of social justice gets done, it scarcely matters what label it falls under; the more perspectives contributing, the better. Self-labeling is a psychologically and politically valuable process, yet all labels and identities are socially negotiated through dialogue. People may or may not agree about how to name a thing, but the process of negotiating the label is healthy and inevitable. For this reason, womanists view womanist identity as an article of avowal (one has to claim it).[27] Yet, womanists exercise the right to describe someone or something else as exhibiting womanist tendencies if it appears that way to them, with the full understanding that someone else might have a different opinion. Thus, use of the term *womanist* retrospectively is not problematic for womanists.

This fact relates back to the fact that womanism is an interpolated perspective rather than an ideology. That is, womanism is not and never has been set in stone; codification and canonization are processes that are antithetical to the spirit of womanism. Womanists function by constantly discerning and synthesizing the various expressions of womanism generated by dialogue (written, verbal, or visual) and inspiration (internal/spiritual creativity) in interaction with the knowledge produced by moving through the world in daily life. Womanism does not function by relating back to a set of rules or principles and evaluating whether one is in conformity. Rather, it functions by constantly moving toward a horizon of healing and commonweal by whatever method seems best in the moment. Thus, the responsibility for "right action" rests with the individual's conscience and the guiding dialogue of the social and spiritual communities within which she embeds herself by affinity.

To continue with the family metaphor, Black feminism and womanism are sisters. Insofar as Black feminism can be distinguished from feminism, with its implied modifier "white," the relationship between Black feminism and womanism is closer than that between womanism and feminism. Black feminism and womanism have common cultural and historical origins. While they "favor" each other, using the old country parlance to denote family resemblance, they are not, as some would argue, one and the same— even if they sometimes seem like twins. Each must be respected for what it contributes uniquely to the struggle for liberation from oppression and to full humanization.[28, 29] Previous confusion about the nature and politics of womanism, not to mention inadequate models for understanding the relation between womanism and other perspectives, has made it appear at times that womanism is opposed or antithetical to Black feminism, but this is not the case. Womanism is opposed to the cultural appropriation and co-optation of Black feminism as well as to feminist deployments of racism and imperialism/ neocolonization, intentional or unintentional, but it is not opposed to the struggle against sexism and violence against women. Some womanists choose to frame Black women's historical antisexist struggle within a Black cultural framework ("race women") rather than a feminist framework in an effort to reclaim the autonomy of Black political action by women, particularly Black women activists of the nineteenth century and early twentieth century;[30] such a move serves antiracist rather than antifeminist ends. Womanism in its interpolated form embraces the creative and politically productive tension between Black women who frame their work in terms of "Black" social movements (e.g., Black nationalism, Pan-Africanism, civil rights, etc.) and those who frame their work in terms of feminism (e.g., Black feminism, African feminism, third world feminism, postcolonial feminism, etc.), as well as those who don't frame their work at all and just do it.

All metaphors have limits, and the limit of the family metaphor is its inability to show that there is a difference of type or kind between womanism and feminism. Thus, comparing feminism and womanism is not like comparing apples and oranges, but rather like comparing apples and pie crust or apples and water. Pie crust (womanism) can work as well with apples (feminism) as it can with blueberries, cherries, or peaches (i.e., other social-justice concerns). Similarly, water (womanism) can just as easily give shape and form to apples (feminism) as it can to fish or glaciers or electricity (i.e., radically different domains of human activity, from politics, to identity, to sexuality). Another metaphor that helps to show this complementary difference of kind between womanism and feminism is musical: we can consider womanism a song and feminism one of many possible instruments on which it can be played. Womanism plays equally well on the violin, the djembe, the gamelan, the koto, or the didjeridu. Ultimately, however, the sound is richest coming from the full orchestra or, put in more global terms, intercultural musical assemblage—and it is just such an assemblage that womanism seeks by working through different instruments, feminism being only one of them. Without each instrument holding its own, the orchestra or assemblage is not possible, yet the song can exist independently of any given instrument. Here's another metaphor: feminism is like a particular kind of magnifying lens that highlights certain womanist political concerns but not others. Other social-justice–oriented critical perspectives could be employed to magnify in the same way. Womanism, then, as politics, is the entire "text" that stands to be so magnified. The point is, prior to now, the relationship between womanism and feminism has been hard to articulate because all speech directed at this topic has been predicated on the notion that womanism and feminism are of the same type. My purpose with these analogies has been to demonstrate that, at least from one angle, they are not.

To summarize, feminism is that critical perspective and social movement that revolves around the eradication of sexism, the dismantling of patriarchy, and the elimination of violence against women. Black feminism is a Black expression of feminism animated by the womanist idea and conveyed through womanist frames. Stated differently, womanism is what's left when feminism is lifted off Black feminism; it is the sound and feel of Black feminism, the politics of Black feminism, and the soul of Black feminism. That being said, however, womanism can infuse any critical perspective or social movement—feminism is not the sole instrument through which it speaks. In the end, womanism is a social-change perspective that focuses on harmonizing and coordinating difference, ending all forms of oppression and dehumanization, and promoting well-being and commonweal for all people, regardless of identity, social address, or origins.

Who Can Be Womanist?

Given womanism's origins with Black women and other women of color, many people wonder who can be womanist. There is a consensus among the main progenitors of womanism, namely, Walker, Ogunyemi, and Hudson-Weems, that people other than Black women or women of color can be womanists; indeed, these authors all suggest that womanism is a perspective open to all humanity. The womanist idea is not owned by Black women and women of color, even if it was developed, launched, articulated, and elaborated primarily by Black women and other women of color. Men of color, particularly Black men, have participated in the womanist enterprise almost from the beginning.[31] White women have questioned whether they, too, might be womanists.[32] To date, I have not seen this question posed by white men, but this fact does not preclude the possibility that White men could be womanists. Again, while such an event is hard to imagine at this time, its possibility must be acknowledged and even envisioned if womanism is to fulfill its full potential as a social-change perspective and praxis.

That being said, womanism is not, at this time, a free-for-all. The working policy is as follows: you're a womanist if you say you're a womanist, but others can contest you or ask you what womanism means for you. Womanism requires that one's ethnic and cultural origins be acknowledged from the outset. Womanism detests race but loves ethnicity and culture, because the concept of race is rooted in the relations of domination and oppression, whereas ethnicity and culture are storehouses of human knowledge that contain such systemic and life-enhancing elements as ancestry, history, memory, geography, cosmology, epistemology, worldview, metaphysics, ethics, aesthetics, logic, psychology, spirituality, traditions, rituals, art, literatures, architecture, food, medicine, science, and language. In other words, culture is rich, while race is impoverished; culture is life affirming, while race is dehumanizing.[33] Far from being a frozen, essentialized entity, culture for the womanist is dynamic and constantly changing. At the same time that traditional cultures are being maintained and reinterpreted in contemporary forms, a hybrid global transculture is also forming. To be a womanist, one must identify one's cultural roots and experience oneself as a cultural or ethnic being rather than a racial being, but one must also be able to see oneself and one's people as part of a larger global body defined by common humanness. Such identification preserves valuable streams of difference for the benefit of all humanity, while simultaneously detaching these streams of difference from particular bodies or identities. From this ground, people can begin the process of struggling for commonweal at the successive levels of community as defined by the womanist—from one's own group, to all humanity, to livingkind, to Earth, to the universe, to all the realms of creation.

Thus, the short answer to the question "Who can be womanist?" is anybody and everybody, assuming they begin with the identification of their individual standpoints and move toward the harmonization and coordination of everyone's standpoints. Ultimately, womanism allows everyone to move toward the same place along different paths: that place is universal community; that path is whatever uniquenesses they have acquired by birth and all their successive travels through different experiences since that time. While this perspective may be unsettlingly nonracial for those who view womanism as merely another name for Black feminism or a Black women-centered perspective, the reality is that one hallmark of womanism is Black women's and other women of color's expression, vision, and articulation of universal sentiments and aspirations.

Beyond Race, Gender, and Class: Womanism and Other Vectors of Difference

With all the focus on race, gender, class, culture, and nation, one question that may arise concerns womanism's position on sexuality issues. Western feminism, gay and lesbian liberation movements, and queer theory have all identified sexual orientation as a critical vector of social difference, and homophobia and heterosexism as oppressive systems of tremendous magnitude. While Walker's womanism clearly endorses same-sex love and relationships, Ogunyemi's African womanism takes a more polyvalent perspective, and Hudson-Weems's Africana womanism rejects homosexuality outright, the process of interpolation that shapes womanist theory and praxis beyond its original progenitors allows room for differences of opinion about sexuality, all while rejecting systematic discrimination and oppression based on sexuality on the basis of its dehumanizing consequences. At this time, womanist perspectives on sexuality are as diverse as sexuality itself, yet womanism still opposes oppression based on sexuality. While questions of sexuality are far from settled among womanists, productive dialogue is taking place.

My personal perspective is that womanism's fundamental affirmation of human diversity and support of spiritually grounded self-expression within the context of commonweal supports the free expression of sexuality and rejects discrimination or oppression based on sexuality as well as the centering or privileging of one sexual group and its practices or norms over another. That is, my womanism is avowedly antihomophobic and antiheterosexist; beyond this, my womanism also rejects discrimination or oppression based on gender expression; transgender status; intersex status; bi-, omni-, pan-, or fluid sexuality; monogamous versus polyamorous or open relationship forms; decisions about whether or not to bear children; and decisions about whether or not to disclose sexuality information about oneself. At the same time as I confidently assert my views, I recognize that others may have different views and I retain my ability to remain in relation with people whose views are different on whatever basis I may decide to do so. Because womanism is nonideological, it does not compel me to separate politically or socially from people whose views are different from mine, although it does place on me the responsibility to pursue dialogue and difficult conversations when my own or others' humanity, safety, or well-being is at stake.

Beyond race, gender, class, ethnicity, culture, and sexuality, there are of course other issues, identities, and vectors of difference to which womanism can and does speak. In focusing primarily on these issues, I hope that I have conveyed enough about the womanist perspective and how it works to allow others to extrapolate how womanism might address any issue not mentioned here. The point is, the universe of issues, identities, and vectors of difference is infinite, inexhaustible, and constantly proliferating. It is impossible to get a handle on and address all issues without taking the position that all oppression is dehumanizing, that all oppression is unified by a common operating principle, namely, the relations of domination and oppression, and that this principle must be transcended, dismantled, and dissolved for any real, substantive change in the direction of justice and healing to take place. The shortcoming of all previous perspectives is that they have defined themselves according to a single issue, identity, or vector of difference, and only after recognizing the reality of intersectionality have they gradually added concern for others.[34] While the recognition of intersectionality improved these various single-issue based ideologies, it did not by itself allow these ideologies to transcend their initial foundations and gain the ability to approach all oppressions with equal concern. Those who came closest to doing so were Black feminists and other feminists of color whose methods and perspectives were born out of generations of survival wisdom gained under conditions of near annihilation and forged in the interstitial spaces between the multiple single-issue movements to which they could lay claim. While it may be controversial, I argue that womanism as I have described it herein is the spirit that animated the perspectives of this "eccentric cohort,"[35] conferring uniqueness on their particular and previously ill-labeled brand of race/class/gender/sexuality/ humanity activism. Furthermore, this same spirit animated the activism of "race women" and other outspoken Black women in the nineteenth and early twentieth centuries, as well as outspoken women of color from other backgrounds during this same period. This connects with my much earlier point that womanism as a way of being in the world goes back much further than 1979 when it was first named. That is, the tradition is longer than the terminology is old.

Why Black Women?

Lest it trouble some that Black women and other women of color are the origin point for a perspective with ramifications for all members of humanity, let me explain this connection further. Why Black women and other women of color? As I have already explained, Black women and other women of color have been at the bottom of every social hierarchy created by man, particularly during the four centuries of the modern era, and multiply so, based on the interaction of race, class, and gender hierarchies and systems of identity. Black women and other women of color have come to understand what it means to live in the margins of multiple communities simultaneously and function, even thrive, in the "in-between," interstitial spaces of other people's structures. They have developed the ability to think and reason using multiple perspectives simultaneously, moving in and out of different cognitive, ideological, cultural, emotional, social, or spiritual frames with relative ease—and the ability to harmonize and coordinate a variety of forms and methods of social movement to respond synthetically and with specificity to an ever-changing variety of social problems and conditions.

Furthermore, Black women and other women of color maintain a relationship with "the masses of the people of humanity," to borrow Angela Davis's phrase,[36] that most other academic and ideological perspectives have lost, abandoned, abdicated, or forgotten, despite their propeople rhetoric. Thus, Black women are connected to—and generally live their daily lives as part of—the primary site of today's most entrenched social problems: the masses. Black women and other women of color rarely "forget who they are" or "forget where they came from," no matter what spaces they circulate in; they can move back and forth with ease between disparate environments, separated by class, race, or other markers of social difference. Black women and other women of color frequently use "everyday methods" of social change that more academic or ideological thinkers refuse to take seriously. Consciousness raising becomes a daily activity, achieved through ongoing streams of microactions.

Black women and other women of color are generally not afraid of or skeptical about spirituality. They recognize the spiritual world, the transcendental dimension of human life, spiritual forces (named or unnamed), and the importance of maintaining a positive and orderly relationship between humans and "the powers that be." In this light, Black women and women of color are emblematic of the majority of humans, for whom a relationship with the spiritual world is actual, palpable, meaningful, and valued. Black women and other women of color also recognize the political implications of this spiritual relationship in ways that few more academically or ideologically inclined perspectives do.

The defining feature of the masses of humanity at this time is the condition of poverty. While academics and politicos euphemistically speak of "class," the real issue is poverty—want, need, and the dehumanizing lack of resources required for survival and quality of life. Black women and other women of color have experienced racialized, gendered forms of economic deprivation at the same time as they have been responsible for the survival, care, and nurturance of others under these conditions. As a result, they have evolved collective wisdom about how to get by on less, which, paradoxically, is what everyone in the world needs to know how to do to overcome environmental degradation and overtaxation as well as to achieve economic parity on a global scale. The real, hands-on knowledge as well as emotional sensibility to live with less will be required of all humans, particularly those who exist at the higher end of the economic spectrum, if the global human community is to get past the precipice of resource depletion based on rampant and unchecked consumerism, as well as all related social conflicts. Thus, Black women and other women of color, based on historical legacies of economic deprivation combined with the previously noted genius of "making a way out of no way," are poised to be leaders for the rest of humanity at a time when humanity is approaching a crisis point in its own survival. Part of this survival wisdom has derived from the maintenance of collectivist values, the teleological end of which is a form of commonweal that could harmonize and coordinate the world's diverse and ever-changing groupings into a workable and peaceable community. Because individual distinctiveness within overall collectivity is valued, there is no tension or paradox between individual and community development.

Black women and other women of color have a history of resisting dehumanization—of "resist[ing] the conditions that thwart life," to cite Katie Cannon[37]—using D.I.Y. or "do it yourself" methods that require neither the validation nor the participation of institutional powers. What differentiates womanism from other social-change perspectives is its indifference toward traditional institutional structures of society. While most modernist social-change camps orient toward one or more institutions of society, defining these institutions as "the problem" or "the enemy," the womanist activist mantra might be, "We can do it with or without you." Historically, Black women and other women of color have not waited for "official" recognition or assistance to move forward when there was a pressing problem to solve.[38] While institutions can be problematic, what is more problematic are the thought processes, emotional structures, attitudes, and social practices that make such institutions, and indeed the relations of oppression and domination wherever they manifest, possible in the first place. Those who nurture human beings recognize, "Change the human being and you change society"; changing social institutions is only a partial or temporary solution because, in the absence of changed minds and changed practices, dismantled social institutions will only re-form in newly oppressive ways. This principle applies both to traditional social institutions as well as to "progressive" social-change organizations, both of which Black women and other women of color have historically felt wary about.

One last point regarding why Black women and other women of color have so ingeniously produced the womanist idea. Contradiction is no problem for Black women and other women of color. People need not be perfect to be good. There is no ideological "party line." To reiterate, *"womanist"* is a term of avowal: once you claim it, it's yours, and you decide what it means and how to enact it. Each person decides whether s/he is in or out, and that decision, while subject to dialogue, debate, and negotiation, is essentially personal. Furthermore, one can participate in "the struggle" and still "have a life." As a result of historical experiences that have whisked them to the brink of psychological annihilation and back, Black women and other women of color recognize that self-nurturance is as important as taking care of others.[39] To require oneself and others to enact one's politics perfectly at all times and under all conditions is an unnecessary burden and may be counterproductive in the long run. Such extremism leads to burnout and alienation, and it defies the reality that change is a process. As I stated earlier, the fundamental social-change process is to "start where you are" and move one step forward. "Forward" is defined by that which moves toward full humanization and commonweal.

Womanism does not assume that only Black women or other women of color hold these perspectives or have had these experiences, yet it recognizes that historical conditions have produced a unique set of circumstances for Black women in particular and women of color in general. This unique set of circumstances, created by the convergence of racism, sexism, and poverty, has yielded certain forms of consciousness and repertoires of skills that any and all occupying such a position ostensibly would have developed. The fact that Black women and other women of color are doing this is controversial only because of the way in which and the degree to which Black women and other women of color have been maligned and dismissed historically, particularly as thinkers. It is hard for people occupying positions of greater social power and privilege to take women of color and their perspectives seriously, to believe that their knowledge and social technologies could actually contain answers to long-standing, deeply entrenched, and increasingly threatening social problems, particularly when Black women and other women of color have so frequently been viewed as the very essence of "the problem." But that is exactly what womanism is doing. Under the radar and beyond surveillance, everyday Black women and other women of color have devised theories and methods for human problem solving that are now taking shape as this thing labeled *womanism*.

The purpose of this anthology is, without undermining the very dynamic and fluid nature of womanism, to highlight and showcase womanism "on its own" and to reveal its very infrastructure through direct exposure of the sites where it has been developed by thinkers who resonate with and endorse it. To read this book is to view a constructive process in process and to engage a ground-level perspective with far-reaching implications for the well-being of planet Earth and all its inhabitants. That no single author has articulated this reality, yet all authors collectively point toward it, is the reason for this compilation. Having said that, I now turn to a discussion of the articles that comprise this volume.

Organization of This Volume

This book is organized into five sections. The first section, "Birthplaces, Birthmothers: Womanist Origins" highlights the work of Alice Walker, Chikwenye Okonjo Ogunyemi, and Clenora Hudson-Weems to drive home the point that womanism is a multiply authored perspective. It is not my intent in this section to suggest that Walker, Ogunyemi, and/or Hudson-Weems "founded" womanism, because I hold firmly to the idea, as do these authors, that the womanist idea is much older that its naming within the last quarter century suggests. Yet these authors played a vital role in the articulation and elaboration of the womanist idea, thus setting the stage for the manifestation of this interpolated perspective that we now refer to as womanism. A further purpose of this section on origins is to highlight the fact that womanism has existed and emerged in diverse locales—in the case of Walker, in the United States and outside the academy, in the creative world; in the case of Ogunyemi, in Africa and, to the extent that traditional African religions and African-derived religions have proliferated outside Africa, in the global African diaspora as well; in the case of Hudson-Weems, in the realms of Africana studies and Black nationalism, evoking the Pan-African arena. While all of these authors are connected to academia on some level, their takes on womanism clearly bridge the academic world with the world outside it, primarily because each brings herself, an everyday woman, into every environment she enters. Each of these womanist authors models this bridging activity and, importantly, each does so with a different voice.

Obtaining an adequate grasp of Walker's womanism requires the simultaneous consideration of her didactic short story "Coming Apart" (1979), in which she introduced and briefly defined "womanist," as well as "Gifts of Power: The Writings of Rebecca Jackson" (1981), in which she reflected on the cultural and sexual autonomy of the womanist, and, finally, her most famous piece, "Womanist" from *In Search of Our Mothers' Gardens: Womanist Prose* (1983). Taken together, these three writings demonstrate the growth of the womanist idea à la Walker and contain many important nuances that, in retrospect, enable us to distinguish womanism from other perspectives. Ogunyemi's essay "Womanism: The Dynamics of the Contemporary Black Female Novel in English" (1985) is included here because it contains her first published use of the term *"womanism,"* although any reading of Ogunyemi's womanism is incomplete without her later book *Africa Wo/Man Palava: The Nigerian Novel by Women* (1996). Similarly, Hudson-Weems's articles "Cultural and Agenda Conflicts in Academia: Critical Issues for Africana Women's Studies" (1989) and "Africana Womanism" (1993) are selected from her large corpus of writings because they reflect her first published works on womanism. A fuller understanding of Africana womanism can only be gained by reading *Africana Womanism: Reclaiming Ourselves* in its entirety (the "Afterword" is particularly interesting) and also examining her book *Africana Womanist Literary Theory* (2004), as well as her many published articles.

The second section of the book, "Womanist Kinfolk: Sisters, Brothers, Daughters, and Sons on Womanism," explores the ways in which others have responded to womanism. Patricia Hill Collins's essay "What's in a Name? Womanism, Black Feminism, and Beyond" and Michael Awkward's "A Black Man's Place in Black Feminist Criticism" reflect Black feminist responses to womanism. Collins's effort revolves around distinguishing womanism from Black feminism, without negating the relationship between the two, while Awkward's article reflects the tendency, particularly on the part of many Black male authors, to view Black feminism and womanism as extremely confluent. My own article with Barbara McCaskill, "Who's Schooling Who? Black Women and the Bringing of the Everyday into Academe, or Why We Started *The Womanist*" and Gary L. Lemons's article "To Be Black, Male, and 'Feminist': Making Womanist Space for Black Men" reflect the birth of a womanist identity, that is, the emergence of "second-generation" womanist scholars who identified with womanism as something distinct from (though not incompatible with) Black feminism. In Lemons's work, in particular, we begin to see recognition of womanism as a perspective with unique possibilities for anti-sexist and antihomophobic Black men (and by association, other men of color) who wish to express and name Black male humanity, in contradistinction to Black masculinity per se.

The third and largest section, "Womanist Theory and Praxis: Womanism in the Disciplines," samples womanist scholarship from diverse fields of study. This is the section in which womanism's development "under the radar"—at a time when womanism was being largely ignored or downplayed by feminists—becomes visible, its history effectively recovered.

One goal of this section is to demonstrate the disciplinary breadth and depth of womanism. Arts and humanities, social sciences, and professions are all represented, as is theology. A second goal is to highlight the cultural and geographical reach of womanism. African American, African, Chinese American, Taiwanese, and Mexican perspectives are all represented in this section. Were space unlimited, I would also have been able to represent womanist perspectives originating in Caribbean, Native American, East Indian, Australian (Aboriginal), and European cultural contexts. A third goal is to illustrate how womanism has been applied in more and less vernacular ways by academic writers, whose very identification with vernacular themes, tropes, methods, or identities has challenged the structure of the academy and its unspoken rules of elitism and exclusivity. Articles published in top-tier journals and books produced by prestigious publishers in the so-called mainstream sit side by side with articles published in more obscure journals and books of limited circulation from the so-called fringes—all of these animated and unified by the womanist idea.

While it would have been desirable to include multiple articles for all of the disciplines in which womanist scholarship has taken expression, page limits precluded such a luxury. Thus, a premium was placed on articles that were either first in their use of womanist terminology or particularly elaborative or demonstrative of the womanist idea. Theology, because it was the first discipline to really latch on to the womanist idea and develop womanism as a unique and freestanding perspective, is presented first. Delores S. Williams's oft-cited short article "Womanist Theology: Black Women's Voices" presents a template for womanist thinking—not just for theology but for other disciplines as well. Cheryl J. Sanders, Katie G. Cannon, Emilie M. Townes, M. Shawn Copeland, bell hooks, and Cheryl Townsend Gilkes's "Roundtable Discussion: Christian Ethics and Theology in Womanist Perspective" models womanist dialogue, incorporating "kitchen table" method and achieving the harmonization and coordination of difference around a variety of issues that are debated within womanism, including differences in spirituality, sexuality issues, and the relation between womanism and feminism.

After theology, womanism proliferated most freely in the humanities, beginning with literary studies, history, and theater and film studies. Sherley Anne Williams's "Some Implications on Womanist Theory" and Elsa Barkley Brown's "Womanist Consciousness: Maggie Lena Walker and the Independent Order of Saint Luke" were landmark publications and are, to this day, widely cited. Mark A. Reid's "Dialogic Modes of Representing Africa(s): Womanist Film" shows both the early appeal of womanism to men and the international, cross-cultural scope of womanist theorizing. Wenying Xu's "A Womanist Production of Truths: The Use of Myths in Amy Tan" illustrates the appeal and applicability of womanism beyond Black and African contexts, in this case speaking to a Chinese cultural context.

In the decade following these developments, womanism took hold in the social sciences (communication and media studies, psychology, and anthropology) and professions (especially education, social work, nursing, and public health, but also architecture). Womanist language permeated quantitative psychology, particularly in the area of identity studies, as early as 1992, although its use was largely devoid of ethnic connotations. Thus, the selection I have chosen for this volume is Kim Marie Vaz's "Womanist Archetypal Psychology: A Model of Counseling for Black Women and Couples Based on Yoruba Mythology." I chose this paper, originally presented as a conference paper in 1995 and published here for the first time, for several reasons. First, it shows how the iconography, philosophy, and spirituality of African cultures provide a more viable, alternative foundation for depth psychology than the usual, Western cultural myths; second, it demonstrates how women of African descent in the West maintain concrete connections to African cultural legacies, applying them in everyday life; and third, it demonstrates how womanism as a discipline was developing as much around the edges of mainstream academia (in this case, the oral medium of conference presentation) as in traditional, "authorized" outlets. Ruth Trinidad Galván's "Portraits of *Mujeres Desjuiciadas*: Womanist Pedagogies of the Everyday, the Mundane and the Ordinary" serves double duty by illustrating womanism in a Latin American context and clearly demonstrating the vernacular genius of womanism. Geneva Smitherman's "A Womanist Looks at the Million Man March" also serves a dual purpose by, first, addressing the controversial topic of womanist support for men-only space and, second, illustrating how a womanist-identified scholar, even after having achieved the highest pinnacle of achievement by traditional academic standards, can continue to affiliate with, speak to, and write about vernacular concerns using vernacular methods without apology. Continuing to explore this theme of vernacularity, Janice D. Hamlet's "Assessing Womanist Thought: The Rhetoric of Susan L. Taylor" takes a look at an icon of Black women's popular spirituality and self-help, the long-time editor of *Essence* magazine and author of two inspirational books, *In the Spirit* and *Lessons in Living,* to demonstrate that her praxis, while unnamed, is highly consistent with the womanist idea.

Given the practical, hands-on, helping-oriented nature of womanism, it is not surprising that scholar-practitioners in applied fields began to explore the ramifications of womanist thought for their respective disciplines. An early example is Vanessa Sheared's "Giving Voice: An Inclusive Model of Instruction—A Womanist Perspective," a particularly important piece because her focus is on adult education—an oft-neglected area in the arena of educational discourse, yet an important site for healing the effects of social inequality and seeking social justice. A later piece, Tamara Beauboeuf-Lafontant's "A Womanist Experience of Caring: Understanding the Pedagogy of Exemplary Black Women Teachers," shows how an expanded concept of mothering, akin to Ogunyemi's community mother, helps define and explain the politically efficacious pedagogical methods of Black women teachers. In Iris Carlton-LaNey's "Elizabeth Ross Haynes: An African American Reformer of Womanist Consciousness, 1908–1940," we can observe methodological parallels between other early twentieth-century womanist activists like Maggie Lena Walker (the subject of Elsa Barkley Brown's contribution) and both Sheared's and Beauboeuf-Lafontant's late twentieth-century teachers. The practices of African American nurses in clinical research settings, as they are documented in JoAnne Banks-Wallace's "Womanist Ways of Knowing: Theoretical Considerations for Research with African American Women," further extend this line of connection.

Sexuality studies is, at this point, ill-defined even as an interdiscipline—yet the importance of this emerging field for bridging women's studies, cultural studies, ethnic studies, and other interdisciplines and representing the reformation of the disciplinary landscape of academia in general cannot be overstated. Sexuality studies is ably represented in this volume by Wenshu Lee's "*Kuaering* Queer Theory: My Autocritography and a Race-Conscious, Womanist, Transnational Turn," in which she laces together "all of the above" and challenges both the Western academy and Western languages of identity through the lens of her own Taiwanese lesbian existence. Perhaps better than any other article in this volume, Lee's piece anticipates and foreshadows new frontiers of womanist emergence on the global horizon.

Finally, as something of an outlier in terms of disciplines, we have architect Epifania Akosua Amoo-Adare's "Critical Spatial Literacy: A Womanist Positionality and the Spatio-temporal Construction of Black Family Life," which takes a critical look at how Western notions of nuclear family and women's connection to private space are applied to urban architecture in Western Africa. The result is that rural West African women (in this case, Ghanaian) who move to urban centers must alter their patterns of social interaction (communal, spiritual, public) in ways that affect their psychology and chip away at life-sustaining cultural practices. The result is the diminishment of women's power, influence, freedom, and, in some cases, happiness. Amoo-Adare's work implies that physical space itself, politically suffused in the form of architecture, serves to mediate the degree to which the values and practices of women of color permeate the larger society, whether local or global, thus contributing to social problem solving.

One thing that becomes apparent upon perusal of the many articles in the third section of this book is that womanists run the gamut in terms of their views on the degree to which womanism is equivalent to Black feminism. My perspective on this question is that, while womanism has been distinct from Black feminism all along, the articulation of this difference has fallen behind the application of it in real-time terms. That is, people doing womanist work knew in their gut that they were doing something different when they called their work "womanist" instead of "(Black) feminist," but the language or context within which to articulate this difference-in-relation had not yet emerged. Part of the purpose of this chapter is to articulate and thus clarify that difference without resorting to an erroneous and destructive polarization of womanism and (Black) feminism—but also without denying the alienating rift that has existed between women's studies and Africana studies in the academy. It is important to allow womanism to be in both places at once and, in certain respects, to begin the process of reconciling and bridging the two disciplines. Here, womanism exhibits its method of arbitration and mediation between "warring" parties and does not shrink from its imperative to call out persistent and often invisibilized racism in women's studies and deeply entrenched sexism and homophobia in Africana studies. Womanism's interpolated perspective makes such a bridging possible without allowing either side to elide responsibility for its real deficits and their consequences.

The fourth section, "Critiquing the Womanist Idea," reflects the reality that womanism has not always been met with open arms. The three most common critiques of womanism are that (1) it allows Black women to reject feminism, minimizing the gains that Black feminists have achieved for all Black women through struggle; (2) it undermines feminist struggle by creating confusing and diversionary new terminology with ambiguous politics and little connection to activism; and (3) like white feminism, it is imperialist insofar as it privileges the views of U.S. Black women and pushes them globally onto womanists of other nations and cultures. Each of these perspectives obtains a hearing in this volume: bell hooks's contribution to the womanist "Round Table" in the third section reflects the first critique; Helen (charles)'s article "The Language of Womanism: Rethinking Difference" voices the second critique; and Inderpal Grewal and Caren Kaplan's "*Warrior Marks*: Global Womanism's Neo-colonial Discourse in a Multicultural Context" elaborates on the third critique.

As womanist theory and praxis become more clearly distinguished from that of feminism, some aspects of these critiques may be answered in a way that they were not during the first quarter century of womanism. For now, let me digress briefly to address each of these critiques. While all three authors make some compelling points, three common weaknesses impact their critiques. First, all three authors refer only to Walker's womanism, without the advantage of an interpolated version of womanism that draws from Ogunyemi's and Hudson-Weems's contributions to the womanist idea as well as insights offered by the many and diverse womanist thinkers and writers who published subsequently. Thus, they rest their premises on an incomplete version of womanism. Second, each fails to distinguish womanism as something of a different type than feminism, succumbing to the problem I identified earlier. That is, each author implies that womanism is a poor and problematic imitation of feminism, not recognizing that womanism is neither an imitation of feminism nor a flight from it—it is something different altogether. Third, each fails to acknowledge the positive (culturally grounded) sources of womanist thought, confining their discussion of womanism to those aspects of womanism that revolve around rejecting racism among feminists and marginalization within feminism. These authors overidentify womanism with "race" and underidentify it with "Africanity" (and/or other culturally situated sources of knowledge and politics). I find myself wondering whether these authors would have advanced similar arguments had they considered a broader, more complete version of womanism.

While it is beyond the scope of this introductory chapter to address the critiques of womanism in detail, it is important to include, acknowledge, and address them earnestly. Grewal and Kaplan's article in particular reminds womanists to be as vigilant as anyone else to avoid reinscribing the very oppressions it rejects. Helen (charles)'s article reminds womanists to exercise the courage of their convictions by clarifying the new and important meanings that ride on their valiantly defended neologism. bell hooks reminds womanists to remember and honor the great strides hard won at great risk by women calling themselves Black feminists and to not use womanism as an excuse to forget—or to reinvent the proverbial wheel. Other critiques of womanism, such as critiques of womanist perspectives on the relationship between women and men or womanist perspectives on sexuality, may be resolved in the process of interpolating womanism as well as the process of dialogue. Womanism, like other perspectives, feminism included, is dynamic and evolving at all times.

Finally, the fifth section, "Womanist Resources," includes an extensive womanist bibliography. With the rapid proliferation of womanism in scholarly and pop culture contexts (particularly on the World Wide Web), as well as the tendency of womanism to appear in marginalized areas, many worthwhile references did not make it onto this list. Nevertheless, it is hoped that this bibliography can serve as a point of departure for those wishing to find out more about womanism on its own as well as for those seeking to deepen their reading within specific disciplines or problem areas. Particular attention has been paid to references that might be helpful in a classroom or research context, especially when the goal is to expand the offerings available in a specific discipline.

For every article that I have included in this volume, I could have included several more. No historically oriented anthology can adequately represent the full field of work that defines a particular era (in this case, the first quarter century of womanism), yet it is the challenge of the anthologist to sample from the universe of available material as fairly and representatively as possible. Because womanism is by definition constituted by the creative tension inherent in diverse perspectives seeking harmonization and coordination, it is difficult to convey the richness of womanism as it exists when having to make decisions about what to include and exclude. In this anthology, I have tried to preserve as much diversity as possible while, at the same time, showing how the womanist idea—as an interpolated phenomenon—has evolved over time. To make up for the fact that I could not republish every worthwhile article, I intend the bibliography as "suggestions for further reading." Admittedly, these suggestions are colored by my own reading, which is not equally extensive across all disciplines. Nevertheless, it is hoped that my suggestions will be of concrete use to teachers and others who are preparing discipline-specific syllabi and the like.

Perhaps a later edition of this volume will be expanded to include some of the material that could not be included here. Yet, a retrospective approach cannot be all there is. Womanism is a vast and growing field of discourse, and this fact will surely lend itself to future anthologies focusing on contemporary womanist scholarship, womanism in the popular arena, womanism in disciplines not represented here, and so on. The prospect of these exciting developments—and, even more, the potential of womanism to inform real-world human problem solving and improve social conditions for the masses of humanity, leading to new solutions to old problems and new models for old situations—is what fuels and inspires womanist productivity. It is to the vision of redemption for a world in crisis affecting all members of humanity that I, a Black woman, dedicate this work.

Notes

1. Another version of this story was published in *Ms.* magazine under the title "A Fable."
2. As I am using it here, the term *"Black womanhood"* references and encompasses a social location that is triply at the bottom of three intersecting social hierarchies, namely, race, gender, and class. Race is defined by the white–Black dichotomy; gender is defined by the male–female dichotomy; and class is defined by the wealth–poverty dichotomy. In each case, the first term names the superior or dominant pole of the dichotomy, and the second term names the inferior or subordinated pole of the dichotomy. By definition, Black women and all women of color (who are not white) occupy the inferior/subordinated pole of the race/gender intersection. Historically, as a result of this double subordination, Black women and other women of color have been more likely than their counterparts to occupy impoverished conditions. Thus, my use of the term *Black womanhood* here encompasses both Black women and other women of color and implies that anyone, regardless of race or gender, who occupies similar subordinated conditions would develop a similar perspective and praxis to the one being described here.
3. This definition is available online at http://www.answers.com/topic/womanism? method=5&linktext=womanist.
4. Gloria Steinem and Diana L. Hayes, "Womanism," in *The Reader's Companion to U.S. Women's History*, ed. Smith et al. (New York: Houghton Mifflin, 1998), 639–41.
5. Carol Marsh-Lockett, "Womanism," in *The Oxford Companion to African American Literature*, ed. William L. Andrews, Frances Smith Foster, and Trudier Harris (New York: Oxford University Press, 1997), 784–86.
6. These "named" forms of oppression have the tendency to proliferate infinitely, making it difficult to be as inclusive as one might wish to be, particularly when one is faced with the task of naming them all.
7. A good example of nonlabelable oppressions or oppressions for which there is not yet language appears in Jeff Schmidt's book, *Disciplined Minds: A Critical Look at Salaried Professionals and the Soul-battering System That Shapes Their Lives* (Lanham, MD: Rowman and Littlefield, 2000). Chela Sandoval also discusses these in terms of the "democratization of vulnerability" in *Methodology of the Oppressed* (Minneapolis: University of Minnesota, 2000).
8. In this chapter, all genders are implied in most statements. To avoid wordy constructions, the pronouns *she* and *her* will be the default, although more inclusive constructions will occasionally be used. It is the perspective of this author that the pronouns *she/her* and *he/him* do not encompass all of the human genders that exist, thus the inadequacy of this system is acknowledged up front, with apology.
9. Personal communication, July 2005.
10. AnaLouise Keating, "Shifting Perspectives: Spiritual Activism, Social Transformation, and the Politics of Spirit," in *Entre Mundos/Among Worlds: New Perspectives on Gloria E. Anzaldúa*, ed. AnaLouise Keating (New York: Palgrave Macmillan, 2005), 241–54. See also "Self-Help, Indian Style? Paula Gunn Allen's *Grandmothers of the Light* and the Politics of Transformation," in *Cultural Sites of Critical Insight: Philosophy, Aesthetics, and Native and African American Women's Writings*, ed. Angela L. Cotten and Christa Davis Acampora (Albany: SUNY Press, forthcoming). I first encountered Keating's use of the term *spiritualized politics* in a public lecture on womanism at the University of Georgia during spring 2000.
11. Sandoval, *Methodology of the Oppressed*, 6.
12. I am indebted to the Black women historians and sociologists who have enlarged on this theme of "making a way out of no way" by documenting and theorizing everyday Black

women's survival genius. These historians and sociologists include but are not limited to Paula Giddings, Darlene Clark Hine, Deborah Gray White, Elsa Barkley Brown, Rosalyn Terborg-Penn, Jacqueline Rouse, Joyce Ladner, Elizabeth Higgenbotham, and Bonnie Thornton Dill. Gerda Lerner's work has also contributed greatly to this effort.

13. Audre Lorde, "Uses of the Erotic: The Erotic as Power," in her own *Sister Outsider: Essays and Speeches* (Freedom, CA: Crossing Press, 1984), 53–59.

14. Sandoval, *Methodology of the Oppressed*, 142.

15. The thread of this metaphor can be followed through sources as diverse as the naming of Kitchen Table: Women of Color Press in the 1970s to Barbara and Beverly Smith's "Across the Kitchen Table: A Sister-to-Sister Dialogue," published in *This Bridge Called My Back: Writings by Radical Women of Color* in 1981, to Olga Idriss Davis's more recent scholarship, "In the Kitchen: Transforming the Academy through Safe Spaces of Resistance," *Western Journal of Communication* 63 (1999): 364–81.

16. Chikwenye Okonjo Ogunyemi, *Africa Wo/Man Palava: The Nigerian Novel by Women* (Chicago: University of Chicago, 1996), 26.

17. Alice Walker, *In Search of Our Mothers' Gardens: Womanist Prose* (San Diego: Harcourt Brace Jovanovich, 1983), xi–xii.

18. In addition to the related chapters in this volume, see Mary Frances Berry, *My Name Is Black Is True: Callie House and the Struggle for Ex-slave Reparations* (New York: Knopf, 2005); Layli Phillips, "Mamie Phipps Clark," in *Notable American Women: A Biographical Dictionary, Completing the Twentieth Century*, ed. Susan Ware and Stacy Braukman, (Cambridge, MA: Harvard University Press, 2005); Susan M. Glisson, *"Neither Bedecked nor Bebosomed": Lucy Randolph Mason, Ella Baker, and Women's Leadership and Organizing in the Struggle for Freedom* (Williamsburg, VA: College of William and Mary, 2000 [dissertation]); Kimberly Springer, *Still Lifting, Still Climbing: African American Women's Contemporary Activism* (New York: NYU Press, 1999) and *Living for the Revolution: Black Feminist Organizations, 1968-1980* (Durham, NC: Duke University Press, 2005).

19. Ogunyemi, *Africa Wo/Man Palava*, 21–61.

20. For more on liberation psychology, see Ignacio Martin-Baro, *Writings for a Liberation Psychology* (Cambridge, MA: Harvard University Press, 1994), and Nicole Hollander, *Love in a Time of Hate: Liberation Psychology in Latin America* (New Brunswick, NJ: Rutgers University Press, 1997).

21. Postmodern conditions include information glut/overload; the proliferation of new technologies, particularly in the telecommunications arena; the evolution of multi-, trans-, and supranational structures of governance and commerce; the mobility of capital and labor across national borders; increasing polarization of wealth and poverty and the global diminishment of the middle classes; increasing surveillance of everyday life; the eclipse of agricultural and manufacturing economies by service, information, and finance economies; cultural and economic globalization; cultural hybridization and mestizaje, combined with global Westernization; moral indeterminism; the increasing impact of simulacra on psychological processes; and the increasing indeterminacy or complexity of identity.

22. For an academic overview of poststructuralist theory as it relates to feminism, see Chris Weedon, *Feminist Practice and Poststructuralist Theory* (Oxford: Blackwell Publishing, 1996). Michel Foucault's works, *Discipline and Punish: The Birth of the Prison* (New York: Vintage, 1995/1978) and *The History of Sexuality: An Introduction* (New York: Vintage, 1990/1978), also provide a reasonable entrée into this philosophical field. For a more accessible introduction to this general area of thought, see Donald D. Palmer, *Structuralism and Poststructuralism for Beginners* (1998), James N. Powell and Joe Lee, *Postmodernism for Beginners* (1997), and Lydia Alix Fillingham and Moshe Susser, *Foucault for Beginners* (1994), all part of the Writers and Readers Documentary Comic Books Series published in New York. Finally, womanism and postmodernism are brought together in Angeletta KM Gourdine, "Postmodern Ethnography and the Womanist Mission: Postcolonial Sensibilities in *Possessing the Secret of Joy*," *African American Review* 30 (1996): 237–44.

23. I have nothing against such ornate language—indeed, I view it, like fancy cake decorating and fine art, among humankind's most exquisite achievements—yet, in a world where educational inequalities are such that the vast majority of people can neither produce nor penetrate such language, its use feeds into systems of oppression, and the energies that

painstakingly craft it could better be employed at this time to eradicate the very educational inequalities that prevent it from being accessible to all.

24. Combahee River Collective, "A Black Feminist Statement," reprinted in Barbara Smith's *Home Girls: A Black Feminist Anthology* (New York: Kitchen Table: Women of Color Press, 1983), 278. The Black Feminist Statement was originally self-published as a pamphlet in 1977.

25. For a good discussion of either/or both/and logics, see Patricia Hill Collins, *Black Feminist Thought: Knowledge, Consciousness, and the Politics of Empowerment*, 2nd ed. (New York: Routledge, 2000).

26. Clenora Hudson-Weems articulates this point in *Africana Womanism: Reclaiming Ourselves* (Troy, MI: Bedford Press, 1993); however, see also Catherine Obianuju Acholonu's *Motherism: The Afrocentric Alternative to Feminism* (Owerri, Nigeria: Afa Publications, 1995), and Molara Ogundipe-Leslie's "Stiwanism: Feminism in an African Context," in her own *Re-Creating Ourselves: African Women and Critical Transformations* (Trenton, NJ: Africa World Press, 1994), 209–41, for perspectives on Black women's critical thought and activism outside feminism. For similar perspectives among Hispanic women, see Ada Maria Isasi-Diaz, Elena Olazagasti-Segovia, Sandra Mangual-Rodriguez, Maria Antonietta Berriozabal, Daisy L. Machado, Lourdes Arguelles, and Raven-Anne Rivero, "Roundtable Discussion: *Mujeristas:* Who We Are and What We Are About," *Journal of Feminist Studies in Religion* 8 (1992): 105–25, and Isasi-Diaz's *En la Lucha/In the Struggle: A Hispanic Women's Liberation Theology* (Minneapolis, MN: Fortress Press, 1993). Allyson Goce Tintiangco addresses a similar theme from a Pilipino perspective in her article "Pinayism," *Maganda Magazine* 10 (1997), http://www.magandamagazine.org/10/pinayism01.html.

27. Emilie M. Townes, "Voices of the Spirit: Womanist Methodologies in the Theological Disciplines," *The Womanist* 1 (1994): 2–3.

28. The list of Black feminist writers, scholars, activists, and artists whose work has altered the course of history in ways both big and small is longer than these pages can contain. In my own personal journey, I am particularly indebted to the following authors, whose work has revolutionized my consciousness and provided me with perpetual inspiration over the years: Barbara Smith, Alice Walker, Audre Lorde, Beverly Guy-Sheftall, Patricia Hill Collins, Patricia Bell Scott, Toni Cade Bambara, M. Jacqui Alexander, Angela Y. Davis, Anna Julia Cooper, Filomena Chioma Steady, Faye V. Harrison, Rose M. Brewer, bell hooks, Pat Parker, Cheryl Clarke, June Jordan, Kimberly Wallace-Sanders, Kimberly Springer, M. Bahati Kuumba, Nah Dove, Cheryl Dunye, Lisa C. Moore, Makeda Silvera, Jill Nelson, Susan L. Taylor, Shirley Chisholm, Essex Hemphill, Marlon Riggs, and, of course, the Combahee River Collective, also Selena Sloan Butler, Mamie Phipps Clark, and Funmilayo Ransome-Kuti, whose lives of activism were their texts. It should be noted that some of these authors, activists, and artists also identify as womanists, and many of them have contributed to the development of my womanist consciousness. In addition, I have also been profoundly influenced and deeply moved by Chicana feminists Gloria Anzaldúa and Chela Sandoval as well as third world/postcolonial feminist Chandra Talpade Mohanty. In addition to all of the above-named individuals, there are numerous other authors, artists, and activists whose works I am on the path to discovering, exploring, and sharing with others.

29. My understanding of the concept of "full humanization" draws heavily from Paulo Freire's in *Pedagogy of the Oppressed* (New York: Continuum, 1999/1970).

30. Clenora Hudson-Weems, *Africana Womanism*.

31. For a few examples of Black men's participation in womanism, see Mark A. Reid's "Dialogic Modes of Representing Africa(s): Womanist Film" (1991), Gary Lemons's "To Be Black, Male, and 'Feminist': Making Womanist Space for Black Men" (1997) and "'When and Where [We] Enter': In Search of a Feminist Forefather—Reclaiming the *Womanist* Legacy of W.E.B. DuBois" (2001), Michael Awkward's "A Black Man's Place in Black Feminist Criticism" (1998), and Rufus Burrow Jr.'s "Enter Womanist Theology and Ethics" (1998) and "Toward Womanist Theology and Ethics" (1999). For a more recent take, see Mark Anthony Neal's online essay, "My Black Male Feminist Heroes," February 26, 2003, http://www.popmatters.com/features/030226-blackfeminists.shtml. Some of these authors claim Frederick Douglass and W.E.B. DuBois as womanist forefathers. Tolagbe Ogunleye claims Martin Robison Delany as an early Africana womanist man in

her article "Dr. Martin Robison Delany, 19th-Century Africana Womanist: Reflections on His Avant-Garde Politics Concerning Gender, Colorism, and Nation Building" (1998).

32. This is a frequent query at conference sessions where womanism is the topic. However, for a published reflection on this topic, see Constance Fulmer, "A Nineteenth-Century 'Womanist' on Gender Issues: Edith J. Simcox in Her *Autobiography of a Shirtmaker*," *Nineteenth Century Prose* 26 (1999): 110–26.

33. I am indebted to Faye V. Harrison's "Introduction: Expanding the Discourse on 'Race,'" *American Anthropologist* 100 (1998): 609–31, Asa Hilliard's *SBA: The Reawakening of the African Mind* (Gainesville, FL: Makare Publishing Company, 1998), and Cheikh Anta Diop's *Civilization or Barbarism: An Authentic Anthropology* (Brooklyn, NY: Lawrence Hill, 1991) for perspectives on this matter.

34. For more detail on intersectionality, see Patricia Hill Collins's *Black Feminist Thought* and Kimberle Crenshaw's "Mapping the Margins: Intersectionality, Identity Politics, and Violence Against Women of Color," in *Applications of Feminist Legal Theory to Women's Lives: Sex, Violence, Work, and Reproduction,* ed. D. Kelly Weisberg (Philadelphia: Temple University Press, 1996).

35. Sandoval, *Methodology of the Oppressed,* 42.

36. Angela Y. Davis, women's history month lecture, Agnes Scott College, March 2004.

37. Katie G. Cannon, "Roundtable: Christian Ethics and Theology in Womanist Perspective," *Journal of Feminist Studies in Religion* 5 (1989): 93.

38. For an interesting case in point, see "The New Amazons," a story about the Womanist Party of India (WPI), published August 15, 2004, in *The Telegraph* newspaper of Calcutta, India, http://www.telegraphindia.com/1040815/asp/look/story_3622999.asp#.

39. Susan L. Taylor's work, especially *In the Spirit* (San Francisco: Amistad, 1993), represents this perspective particularly well.

References

Acholonu, Catherine Obianuju. *Motherism: The Afrocentric Alternative to Feminism.* Owerri, Nigeria: Afa Publications, 1995.

Amoo-Adare, Epifania Akosua. "Critical Spatial Literacy: A Womanist Positionality and the Spatio-temporal Construction of Black Family Life." In *La Familia en Africa y la Diaspora Africana: Estudio Multidisciplinar/Family in Africa and the African Diaspora: A Multidisciplinary Approach,* ed. Olga Barrios and Frances Smith Foster, 63–73. Salamanca, Spain: Ediciones Almar, 2004.

Awkward, Michael. "A Black Man's Place in Black Feminist Criticism." In *Negotiating Difference: Race, Gender, and the Politics of Positionality.* Chicago: University of Chicago Press, 1998.

Banks, JoAnne. "Womanist Ways of Knowing: Theoretical Considerations for Research with African American Women." *Advances in Nursing Science* 22 (2000): 33–45.

Beauboeuf-Lafontant, Tamara. "A Womanist Experience of Caring: Understanding the Pedagogy of Exemplary Black Women Teachers." *The Urban Review* 34 (2002): 71–86.

Berry, Mary Frances. *My Name Is Black Is True: Callie House and the Struggle for Ex-slave Reparations.* New York: Knopf, 2005.

Brown, Elsa Barkley. "Womanist Consciousness: Maggie Lena Walker and the Independent Order of Saint Luke." *Signs: Journal of Women in Culture and Society* 14 (1989): 610–33.

Burrow Jr., Rufus. "Enter Womanist Theology and Ethics." *Western Journal of Black Studies* 22 (1998): 19–29.

———. "Toward Womanist Theology and Ethics." *Journal of Feminist Studies in Religion* 15 (1999): 77–95.

Cannon, Katie G. "Roundtable: Christian Ethics and Theology in Womanist Perspective." *Journal of Feminist Studies in Religion* 5 (1989): 93.

Carlton-LaNey, Iris. "Elizabeth Ross Haynes: An African American Reformer of Womanist Consciousness, 1908–1940." *Social Work* 42 (1997): 573–83.

(charles), Helen. "The Language of Womanism: Re-thinking Difference." In *British Black Feminism: A Reader,* ed. Heidi Safia Mirza, 278–97. London: Routledge, 1997.

Collins, Patricia Hill. *Black Feminist Thought: Knowledge, Consciousness, and the Politics of Empowerment.* 2nd ed. New York: Routledge, 2000.

———. "What's in a Name? Womanism, Black Feminism, and Beyond." *The Black Scholar* 26 (1996): 9–17.

Combahee River Collective. "A Black Feminist Statement." In *Home Girls: A Black Feminist Anthology*, ed. Barbara Smith, 272–82. New York: Kitchen Table: Women of Color Press, 1983.

Crenshaw, Kimberle. "Mapping the Margins: Intersectionality, Identity Politics, and Violence against Women of Color." In *Applications of Feminist Legal Theory to Women's Lives: Sex, Violence, Work, and Reproduction*, ed. D. Kelly Weisberg. Philadelphia: Temple University Press, 1996.

Davis, Olga Idriss. "In the Kitchen: Transforming the Academy through Safe Spaces of Resistance." *Western Journal of Communication* 63 (1999): 364–81.

Diop, Cheikh Anta. *Civilization or Barbarism: An Authentic Anthropology*. Brooklyn, NY: Lawrence Hill, 1991.

Fillingham, Lydia Alix, and Moshe Susser. *Foucault for Beginners*. New York: Writers and Readers, 1994.

Foucault, Michel. *Discipline and Punish: The Birth of the Prison*. New York: Vintage, 1995/1978.

———. *The History of Sexuality: An Introduction*. New York: Vintage, 1990/1978.

Freire, Paulo. *Pedagogy of the Oppressed*. New York: Continuum, 1999/1970.

Fulmer, Constance. "A Nineteenth-Century 'Womanist' on Gender Issues: Edith J. Simcox in Her *Autobiography of a Shirtmaker*." *Nineteenth Century Prose* 26 (1999): 110–26.

Galván, Ruth Trinidad. "Portraits of *Mujeres Desjuiciadas*: Womanist Pedagogies of the Everyday, the Mundane and the Ordinary." *Qualitative Studies in Education* 15 (2001): 603–21.

Glisson, Susan M. *"Neither Bedecked nor Bebosomed": Lucy Randolph Mason, Ella Baker, and Women's Leadership and Organizing in the Struggle for Freedom* [dissertation]. Williamsburg, VA: College of William and Mary, 2000.

Gourdine, Angeletta KM. "Postmodern Ethnography and the Womanist Mission: Postcolonial Sensibilities in *Possessing the Secret of Joy*." *African American Review* 30 (1996): 237–44.

Grewal, Inderpal, and Caren Kaplan. "*Warrior Marks*: Global Womanism's Neo-colonial Discourse in a Multicultural Context." In *Keyframes: Popular Cinema and Cultural Studies*, ed. Matthew Tinkcom and Amy Villarejo. New York: Routledge, 52–71.

Hamlet, Janice D. "Assessing Womanist Thought: The Rhetoric of Susan L. Taylor." *Communication Quarterly* 48 (2000): 420–36.

Harrison, Faye V. "Introduction: Expanding the Discourse on 'Race.' " *American Anthropologist* 100 (1998): 609–31.

Hilliard III, Asa G. *SBA: The Reawakening of the African Mind*. Gainesville, FL: Makare Publishing Company, 1998.

Hollander, Nicole. *Love in a Time of Hate: Liberation Psychology in Latin America*. New Brunswick, NJ: Rutgers University Press, 1997.

Hudson-Weems, Clenora. "Africana Womanism." In *Africana Womanism: Reclaiming Ourselves*, 17–32. Troy, MI: Bedford, 1993.

———. *Africana Womanist Literary Theory*. Trenton, NJ: Africa World Press, 2004.

———. *Africana Womanism: Reclaiming Ourselves*. Troy, MI: Bedford Press, 1993.

———. "Cultural and Agenda Conflicts in Academia: Critical Issues for Africana Women's Studies." *Western Journal of Black Studies* 13 (1989): 185–89.

Isasi-Diaz, Ada Maria. *En la Lucha/In the Struggle: A Hispanic Women's Liberation Theology*. Minneapolis, MN: Fortress Press, 1993.

Isasi-Diaz, Ada Maria, Elena Olazagasti-Segovia, Sandra Mangual-Rodriguez, Maria Antonietta Berriozabal, Daisy L. Machado, Lourdes Arguelles, and Raven-Anne Rivero. "Roundtable Discussion: *Mujeristas*: Who We Are and What We Are About." *Journal of Feminist Studies in Religion* 8 (1992): 105–25.

Keating, AnaLouise. "Self-help, Indian Style? Paula Gunn Allen's *Grandmothers of the Light* and the Politics of Transformation." In *Cultural Sites of Critical Insight: Philosophy, Aesthetics, and Native and African American Women's Writings*, ed. Angela L. Cotten and Christa Davis Acampora. Albany: SUNY Press, forthcoming.

———. "Shifting Perspectives: Spiritual Activism, Social Transformation, and the Politics of Spirit." In *Entre Mundos/Among Worlds: New Perspectives on Gloria E. Anzaldúa*, ed. AnaLouise Keating, 241–54. New York: Palgrave Macmillan, 2005.

Lee, Wenshu. "*Kuaering* Queer Theory: My Autocritography and a Race-Conscious, Womanist, Transnational Turn." *Journal of Homosexuality* 45 (2003): 147–70.

Lemons, Gary L. "To Be Black, Male, and 'Feminist': Making Womanist Space for Black Men." *International Journal of Sociology and Social Policy* 17 (1997): 35–61.

————. "'When and Where [We] Enter': In Search of a Feminist Forefather—Reclaiming the *Womanist* Legacy of W.E.B. DuBois." In *Traps: African American Men on Gender and Sexuality,* ed. Rudolph P. Byrd and Beverly Guy-Sheftall, 71–89. Bloomington: Indiana University Press, 2001.

Lorde, Audre. "Uses of the Erotic: The Erotic as Power." In *Sister Outsider: Essays and Speeches,* 53–59. Freedom, CA: The Crossing Press, 1984.

Marsh-Lockett, Carol. "Womanism." In *The Oxford Companion to African American Literature,* ed. William L. Andrews, Frances Smith Foster, and Trudier Harris, 784–86. New York: Oxford University Press, 1997.

Martin-Baro, Ignacio. *Writings for a Liberation Psychology.* Cambridge, MA: Harvard University Press, 1994.

Nandgaonkar, Satish. "The New Amazons." *The Telegraph,* August 15, 2004,, http://www.telegraphindia.com/1040815/asp/look/story_3622999.asp#.

Neal, Mark Anthony. "My Black Male Feminist Heroes." February 26, 2003, http://www.popmatters.com/features/030226-blackfeminists.shtml.

Ogundipe-Leslie, Molara. "Stiwanism: Feminism in an African Context." In *Re-creating Ourselves: African Women and Critical Transformations,* 209–41. Trenton, NJ: Africa World Press, 1994.

Ogunleye, Tolagbe. "Dr. Martin Robison Delany, 19th-Century Africana Womanist: Reflections on His Avant-Garde Politics Concerning Gender, Colorism, and Nation Building." *Journal of Black Studies* 28 (1998): 628–49.

Ogunyemi, Chikwenye Okonjo. *Africa Wo/Man Palava: The Nigerian Novel by Women.* Chicago: University of Chicago, 1996.

————. "Womanism: The Dynamics of the Contemporary Black Female Novel in English." *Signs: Journal of Women in Culture and Society* 11 (1985): 63–80.

Palmer, Donald D. *Structuralism and Poststructuralism for Beginners.* New York: Writers and Readers, 1998.

Phillips, Layli. "Mamie Phipps Clark." In *Notable American Women: A Biographical Dictionary, Completing the Twentieth Century,* ed. Susan Ware and Stacey Braukman. Cambridge, MA: Harvard University Press, 2005.

Phillips, Layli, and Barbara McCaskill. "Who's Schooling Who? Black Women and the Bringing of the Everyday into Academe, or Why We Started *The Womanist.*" *Signs: Journal of Women in Culture and Society* 20 (1995): 1007–18.

Powell, James N., and Joe Lee. *Postmodernism for Beginners.* New York: Writers and Readers, 1997.

Reid, Mark A. "Dialogic Modes of Representing Africa(s): Womanist Film." *Black American Literature Forum* 25 (1991): 375–88.

Sanders, Cheryl J., Katie G. Cannon, Emilie M. Townes, M. Shawn Copeland, bell hooks, and Cheryl Townsend Gilkes. "Roundtable Discussion: Christian Ethics and Theology in Womanist Perspective." *Journal of Feminist Studies in Religion* 5 (1989): 83–112.

Sandoval, Chela. *Methodology of the Oppressed.* Minneapolis: University of Minnesota, 2000.

Schmidt, Jeff. *Disciplined Minds: A Critical Look at Salaried Professionals and the Soul-battering System That Shapes Their Lives.* Lanham, MD: Rowman and Littlefield, 2000.

Sheared, Vanessa. "Giving Voice: An Inclusive Model of Instruction—A Womanist Model." *New Directions for Adult and Continuing Education* 61 (1994): 27–37.

Smith, Barbara, and Beverly Smith. "Across the Kitchen Table: A Sister-to-Sister Dialogue." In *This Bridge Called My Back: Writings by Radical Women of Color,* ed. Gloria Anzaldúa and Cherrie Moraga. Watertown, MA: Persephone Press, 1981.

Smitherman, Geneva. "A Womanist Looks at the Million Man March." In *Million Man March/ Day of Absence,* ed. Haki R. Madhubuti and Maulana Karenga, 104–107. Chicago: Third World Press, 1996.

Springer, Kimberley. *Living for the Revolution: Black Feminist Organizations, 1968–1980.* Durham, NC: Duke University Press, 2005.

Springer, Kimberley. *Still lifting, Still Climbing: African American Women's Contemporary Activism.* New York: NYU Press, 1999.

Steinem, Gloria, and Diana L. Hayes. "Womanism." In *The Reader's Companion to U.S. Women's History,* ed. Barbara Smith, Gloria Steinem, Gwendolyn Mink, Marysa Navarro, and Wilma Mankiller, 639–41. New York: Houghton Mifflin, 1998.

Taylor, Susan L. *In the Spirit.* San Francisco: Amistad, 1993.

————. *Lessons in Living.* New York: Anchor, 1998.

Tintiangco, Allyson Goce. "Pinayism." *Maganda Magazine* 10 (1997), http://www.magandamagazine.org/10/pinayism01.html.

Townes, Emilie M. "Voices of the Spirit: Womanist Methodologies in the Theological Disciplines." *The Womanist* 1 (1994): 2–3.

Vaz, Kim Marie. "Womanist Archetypal Psychology: A Model of Counseling for Black Women and Couples Based on Yoruba Mythology" (this volume).

Walker, Alice. "Coming Apart." In *Take Back the Night,* ed. Laura Lederer, 84–93. New York: Bantam, 1979.

———. "Gifts of Power: The Writings of Rebecca Jackson." In *In Search of Our Mothers' Gardens: Womanist Prose,* 71–82. San Diego: Harcourt Brace Jovanovich, 1983.

———. *Womanist.* San Diego: Harcourt Brace Jovanovich, 1983.

———. "Womanist." In *Womanist,* xi–xii. San Diego: Harcourt Brace Jovanovich, 1983.

Weedon, Chris. *Feminist Practice and Poststructuralist Theory.* Oxford: Blackwell, 1996.

Williams, Delores S. "Womanist Theology: Black Women's Voices." *Christianity and Crisis,* March 2, 1987, 66–70.

Williams, Sherley Anne. "Some Implications of Womanist Theory." *Callaloo* 9 (1986): 303–308.

Xu, Wenying. "A Womanist Production of Truths: The Use of Myths in Amy Tan." *Paintbrush* 22 (1995): 56–66.

Part 1

Birthplaces, Birthmothers:
Womanist Origins

Alice Walker's Womanism

Coming Apart (1979)

ALICE WALKER

These three paragraphs by Alice Walker tell why she wrote *Coming Apart*: "Many Black men see pornography as progressive because the white woman, formerly taboo, is, via pornography, made available to them. Not simply available, but in a position of vulnerability to all men. This availability and vulnerability diminishes the importance and *power* of color among men and permits a bonding with white men *as men*, which Black men, striving to be equal, not content with being different, apparently desire.

"Many Black women also consider pornography progressive and are simply interested in equal time. But in a racist society, where Black women are on the bottom, there is no such thing as equal time or equal quality of exposure. It is not unheard of to encounter 'erotica' or pornography in which a Black woman and a white woman are both working in 'a house of ill-repute,' but the Black woman also doubles as the white woman's maid.[1] The Black man who finds himself 'enjoying' pornography of this sort faces a split in himself that allows a solidarity of gender but promotes a rejection of race. 'Beulah, peel me a grape' has done untold harm to us all.

"I have, as we all have, shared a part of my life—since the day I was born—with men whose concept of woman is a degraded one. I have also experienced, like the woman in this piece, Forty-second Street; I felt demeaned by the selling of bodies, threatened by the violence, and furious that my daughter must grow up in a society in which the debasement of women is actually *enjoyed*."

* * *

A middle-aged husband comes home after a long day at the office. His wife greets him at the door with the news that dinner is ready. He is grateful. First, however, he must use the bathroom. In the bathroom, sitting on the commode, he opens up the *Jiveboy* magazine he has brought home in his briefcase. There are a couple of Jivemate poses that particularly arouse him. Studies the young women—blonde, perhaps (the national craze); with elastic waists and

3

inviting eyes—and strokes his penis. At the same time, his bowels stir with the desire to defecate. He is in the bathroom a luxurious ten minutes. He emerges spent, relaxed—hungry for dinner.

His wife, using the bathroom later, comes upon the slightly damp magazine. She picks it up with mixed emotions. She is a brownskin woman with black hair and eyes. She looks at the white blondes and brunettes. Will he be thinking of them, she wonders, when he is making love to me?

"Why do you need these?" she asks.

"They mean nothing," he says.

"But they hurt me somehow," she says.

"You are being a) silly, b) a prude, and c) ridiculous," he says. "You know I love you."

She cannot say to him: But they are not me, those women. She cannot say she is jealous of pictures on a page. That she feels invisible. Rejected. Overlooked. She says instead, to herself: He is right. I will grow up. Adjust. Swim with the tide.

He thinks he understands her, what she has been trying to say. It is *Jiveboy*, he thinks, the white women.

Next day he brings home *Jivers,* a Black magazine, filled with bronze and honey-colored women. He is in the bathroom another luxurious ten minutes.

She stands, holding the magazine: on the cover are the legs and shoes of a well-dressed Black man, carrying a briefcase and rolled *Wall Street Journal* in one hand. At his feet—she turns the magazine cover around and around to figure out how exactly the pose is accomplished—there is a woman, a brownskin woman like herself, twisted and contorted in such a way that her head is not even visible. Only her glistening body—her back and derriere—so that she looks like a human turd at the man's feet.

He is on a business trip to New York. He has brought his wife along. He is eagerly sharing Forty-second Street with her, "Look!" he says, "how *free* everything is! A far cry from Bolton!" (The small town they are from.) He is elated to see the blonde, spaced-out hookers, with their Black pimps, trooping down the street. Elated at the shortness of the Black hookers' dresses, their long hair, inevitably false and blonde. She walks somehow behind him, so that he will encounter these wonders first. He does not notice until he turns a corner that she has stopped in front of a window that has caught her eye. While she is standing alone, looking, two separate pimps ask her what stable she is in or if in fact she is in one. Or simply "You workin'?"

He struts back and takes her elbow. Looks hard for the compliment implied in these questions, then shares it with his wife. "*You* know you're foxy?"

She is immovable. Her face suffering and wondering. "But look," she says, pointing. Four large plastic dolls—one a skinny Farrah Fawcett (or so the doll looks to her) posed for anal inspection; one, an oriental, with her eyes, strangely, closed, but her mouth, a pouting red suction cup, open; an enormous eskimo woman—with fur around her neck and ankles, and vagina; and a Black woman dressed entirely in a leopard skin, complete with tail. The dolls are all life-size, and the efficiency of their rubber genitals is explained in detail on a card visible through the plate glass.

For her this is the stuff of nightmares because all the dolls are smiling. She will see them for the rest of her life. For him the sight is also shocking, but arouses a prurient curiosity. He will return, another time, alone. Meanwhile, he must prevent her from seeing such things, he resolves, whisking her briskly off the street.

Later, in their hotel room, she watches TV as two Black women sing their latest hits: the first woman, dressed in a gold dress (because her song is now "solid gold!"), is nonetheless wearing a chain around her ankle—the wife imagines she sees a chain—because the woman is singing: "Free me from my freedom, chain me to a tree!"

"What do you think of that?" she asks her husband.

"She's a fool," says he.

But when the second woman sings: "Ready, aim, fire, my name is desire," with guns and rockets going off all around her, he thinks the line "Shoot me with your love!" explains everything.

She is despondent.

She looks in a mirror at her plump brown and blackskin body, crinkly hair and black eyes and decides, foolishly, that she is not beautiful. And that she is not hip, either. Among her other problems is the fact that she does not like the word "nigger" used by anyone at all, and is afraid of marijuana. These restraints, she feels, make her old, too much like her own mother, who loves sex (she has lately learned) but is highly religious and, for example, thinks cardplaying wicked and alcohol deadly. Her husband would not consider her mother sexy, she thinks. Since she herself is aging, this thought frightens her. But, surprisingly, while watching herself become her mother in the mirror, she discovers that *she* considers her mother—who carefully braids her average length, average grade, graying hair every night before going to bed; the braids her father still manages to fray during the night—*very* sexy.

At once she feels restored.

Resolves to fight.

"You're the only Black woman in the world that worries about any of this stuff," he tells her, unaware of her resolve, and moody at her months of silent studiousness.

She says, "Here, Colored Person, read this essay by Audre Lorde."

He hedges. She insists.

He comes to a line about Lorde "moving into sunlight against the body of a woman I love," and bridles. "Wait a minute," he says. "What kind of a name is 'Audre' for a man? They must have meant 'André.'"

"It *is* the name of a woman," she says. "Read the rest of that page."

"No dyke can tell me anything," he says, flinging down the pages.

She has been calmly waiting for this. She brings in *Jiveboy* and *Jivers*. In both, there are women eating women they don't even know. She takes up the essay and reads:

> This brings me to the last consideration of the erotic. To share the power of each other's feelings is different from using another's feelings as we would use a Kleenex. And when we look the other way from our experience, erotic or otherwise, we use rather than share the feelings of those others who participate in the experience with us. And use without consent of the used is abuse.

He looks at her with resentment, because she is reading this passage over again, silently, absorbedly, to herself, holding the pictures of the phony lesbians (a favorite, though unexamined, turn-on) absentmindedly on her lap. He realizes he can never have her again sexually, the way he has had her since their second year of marriage, as though her body belonged to someone else. He sees, down the road, the dissolution of the marriage, a constant search for more perfect bodies, or dumber wives. He feels oppressed by her incipient struggle, and feels somehow as if her struggle to change the pleasure he has enjoyed is a violation of his rights.

Now she is busy pasting Audre Lorde's words on the cabinet over the kitchen sink.

When they make love she tries to look him in the eye, but he refuses to return her gaze.

For the first time he acknowledges the awareness that the pleasure of coming without her is bitter and lonely. He thinks of eating stolen candy alone, behind the barn. And yet, he thinks greedily, it is better than nothing, which he considers her struggle's benefit to him.

The next day she is reading another essay when he comes home from work. It is called "A Quiet Subversion," and is by Luisah Teish. "Another dyke?" he asks.

"Another one of your sisters," she replies, and begins to read aloud, even before he's had dinner:

> During the Black Power Movement, much cultural education was focused on the Black physique. One of the accomplishments of that period was the popularization of African hairstyles and the Natural. Along with (the Natural) came a new selfimage and way of relating. It suggested that Black people should relate to each other in respectful and supportive ways. Then the movie industry put out *Superfly*, and the Lord Jesus Look and the Konked head, and an accompanying attitude ran rampant in the Black community. ... Films like *Shaft* and *Lady Sings the Blues* portray Black "heroes" as cocaine-snorting, fast-life fools. In these movies a Black woman is always caught in a web of violence. ...

A popular Berkeley, California, theater featured a pornographic movie entitled *Slaves of Love*. Its advertisement portrayed two Black women, naked, in chains, and a white man standing over them with a whip! How such *racist* pornographic material escapes the eye of Black activists presents a problem. ...

Typically, he doesn't even hear the statement about the women. "What does the bitch know about the Black Power Movement?" he fumes. He is angry at his wife for knowing him so long and so well. She knows, for instance, that because of the Black Power Movement (and really because of the Civil Rights Movement before it) and not because he was at all active in it—he holds the bourgeois job he has. She remembers when his own hair was afro-ed. Now it is loosely curled. It occurs to him that, because she knows him as he was, he cannot make love to her as she is. Cannot, in fact, *love* her as she is. There is a way in which, in some firmly repressed corner of his mind, he considers his wife to be *still* Black, whereas he feels himself to have moved to some other plane.

(This insight, a glimmer of which occurs to him, frightens him so much that he will resist it for several years. Should he accept it at once, however unsettling, it would help him understand the illogic of his acceptance of pornography used against Black women: that he has detached himself from his own blackness in attempting to identify Black women only by their sex.)

The wife has never considered herself a feminist—though she is, of course, a "womanist." A "womanist" is a feminist, only more common.[2] So she is surprised when her husband attacks her as a "women's liber," a "white women's lackey," a "pawn" in the hands of Gloria Steinem, an incipient bra-burner! What possible connection could there be, he wants to know, between her and white women— those overprivileged hags, now (he's recently read in *Newsweek*) marching and preaching their puritanical horseshit up and down Times Square!

(He remembers only the freedom he felt there, not her long pause before the window of the plastic doll shop.) And if she is going to make a lot of new connections with dykes and whites, where will that leave him, the Black man, the most brutalized and oppressed human being on the face of the earth? (*Is it because he can now ogle white women in freedom and she has no similar outlet of expression that he thinks of her as still Black and himself as something else? This thought underlines what he is actually saying, and his wife is unaware of it.*) Didn't she know it is over these very same white bodies he has been lynched in the past, and is lynched still, by the police and the U.S. prison system, dozens of times a year *even now*!?

The wife has cunningly saved Tracey A. Gardner's essay for just this moment. Because Tracey A. Gardner has thought about it *all*, not just presently, but historically, and she is clear about all the abuse being done to herself as a Black person and as a woman, and she is bold and she is cold—she is furious. The wife, given more to depression and self-abnegation than to fury, basks in the fire of Gardner's high-spirited anger.

She begins to read:[3]

> Because from my point of view, racism is everywhere, including the Women's Movement, and the only time I really need to say something special about it is when I *don't* see it—and the first time that happens, I'll tell you about it.

The husband, surprised, thinks this very funny, not to say pertinent. He slaps his knee and sits up. He is dying to make some sort of positive dyke comment, but nothing comes to mind.

> American slavery relied on the denial of the humanity of Black folks, on the undermining of our sense of nationhood and family, on the stripping away of the Black man's role as protector and provider, and on the structuring of Black men and women into the American system of *white male domination.*

"In other words," she says, "white men think they have to be on top. Other men have been known to savor life from other positions."

> The end of the Civil War brought the end of a certain "form" of slavery for Black folks. It also brought the end of any "job security" and the loss of the protection of their white enslaver. Blacks were now free game, and the terrorization and humiliation of Black people, especially Black men, began. Now the Black man could have his family and prove his worth, but he had no way to support or protect them, or himself.

As she reads, he feels ashamed and senses his wife's wounded embarrassment, for him and for herself. For their history together. But doggedly, she continues to read:

> After the Civil War, "popular justice" (which meant there usually was no trial and no proof needed) began its reign in the form of the castration, burning at the stake, beheading, and lynching of Black men. As many as 5,000 white people turned out to witness these events, as though going to a celebration. (*She pauses, sighs: beheading?*) Over 2,000 Black men were lynched in the ten-year period from 1889–1899. There were also a number of Black women who were lynched. (*She reads this sentence quickly and forgets it.*) Over 50 percent of the lynched Black males were charged with rape or attempted rape.

He cannot imagine a woman being lynched. He has never even considered the possibility. Perhaps this is why the image of a Black woman chained and bruised excites rather than horrifies him? It is the fact that the lynching of her body has never stopped that forces the wife, for the time being, to blot out the historical record. She is not prepared to connect her own husband with the continuation of that past.

She reads:

If a Black man had sex with a consenting white woman, it was rape. (*Why am I always reading about, thinking about, worrying about, my man having sex with white women? she thinks, despairingly, underneath the reading.*) If he insulted a white woman by looking at her, it was attempted rape.

"Yes," he says softly, as if in support of her dogged reading, "I've read Ida B.—what's her last name?"[4]

By their lynching, the white man was showing that he hated the Black man carnally, biologically; he hated his color, his features, his genitals. Thus he attacked the Black man's body, and like a lover gone mad, maimed his flesh, violated him in the most intimate, pornographic fashion. ...

I believe that this obscene, inhuman treatment of Black men by white men ... has a direct correlation to white men's increasingly obscene and inhuman treatment of women, particularly white women, in pornography and real life. White women, working toward their own strength and identity, their own sexuality and independence, have in a sense become "uppity niggers." As the Black man threatens the white man's masculinity and power, so now do women.

"That girl's onto something," says the husband, but thinks, for the first time in his life, that when he is not thinking of fucking white women—fantasizing over *Jiveboy* or clucking at them on the street—he is very often thinking of ways to degrade them. Then he thinks that, given his history as a Black man in America, it is not surprising that he has himself confused fucking them *with* degrading them. But what does that say about how he sees himself? This thought smothers his inward applause for Gardner, and instead he casts a bewildered, disconcerted look at his wife. He knows that to make love to his wife as she really is, as who she really is—indeed, to make love to any other human being as they really are—will require a soul-rending look into himself, and the thought of this virtually straightens his hair.

His wife continues:

Some Black men, full of the white man's perspective and values, see the white woman or Blond Goddess as part of the American winning image. Sometimes when he is with the Black woman, he is ashamed of how she has been treated, and how he has been powerless, and that they have always had to work together and protect each other. (*Yes, she thinks, we were always all we had, until now.*)

(*He thinks: We are all we have still, only now we can live without permitting ourselves to know this.*)

Frantz Fanon said about white women, "By loving me she proves that I am worthy of white love. I am loved like a white man. I am a white man. I marry the culture, white beauty, white whiteness. When my restless hands caress those white breasts, they grasp white civilization and dignity and make them mine." (*She cannot believe he meant to write "white dignity."*)

She pauses, looks at her husband: "So how does a Black woman feel when her Black man leaves *Playboy* on the coffee table?"

For the first time he understands fully a line his wife read the day before: "The pornography industry's exploitation of the Black woman's body is *qualitatively* different from that of the white woman," because she is holding the cover of *Jivers* out to him and asking, "What does this woman look like?"

When he has refused to see—because to see it would reveal yet another area in which he is unable to protect or defend Black women—is that where white women are depicted in pornography as "objects," Black women are depicted as animals. Where white women are at least depicted as human beings if not beings, Black women are depicted as shit.

He begins to feel sick. For he realizes that he has bought some if not all of the advertisements about women, Black and white. And further, inevitably, he has bought the advertisements about himself. In pornography the Black man is portrayed as being capable of fucking anything ... even a piece of shit. He is defined solely by the size, readiness and unselectivity of his cock.

Still, he does not know how to make love without the fantasies fed to him by movies and magazines. Those movies and magazines (whose characters' pursuits are irrelevant or antithetical to his concerns) that have insinuated themselves between him and his wife, so that the totality of her body, her entire corporeal reality is alien to him. Even to clutch her in lust is to automatically shut his eyes. Shut his eyes, and ... he chuckles bitterly ... dream of England. For years he has been fucking himself.

At first, reading Lorde together, they reject celibacy. Then they discover they need time apart to clear their heads. To search out damage. To heal. In any case, she is unable to fake response—he is unwilling for her to do so. She goes away for a while. Left alone, he soon falls hungrily on the magazines he had thrown out. Strokes himself raw over the beautiful women, spread like so much melon (he begins to see how stereotypes transmute) before him. But he cannot refuse what he knows—or what he knows his wife knows, walking along a beach in some Black country where all the women are bleached and straightened and the men never look at themselves; and are ugly, in any case, in their imitation of white men.

Long before she returns he is reading her books and thinking of her—and of her struggles alone and his fear of sharing them—and when she returns, it is 60% *her* body that he moves against in the sun, her own Black skin affirmed in the brightness of his eyes.

Notes

1. Ed. Note: This is the situation in the movie version of *The Story of O.*
2. "Womanist" encompasses "feminist" as it is defined in Webster's, but also means *instinctively* pro-woman. It is not in the dictionary at all. Nonetheless, it has a strong root in Black women's culture. It comes (to me) from the word "womanish," a word our mothers used to describe, and attempt to inhibit, strong, outrageous or outspoken behavior when we were children: "You're acting *womanish!*" A labeling that failed, for the most part to keep us from acting "womanish" whenever we could, that is to say, like our mothers themselves, and like other women we admired.

   An advantage of using "womanist" is that, because it is from my own culture, I needn't preface it with the word "Black" (an awkward necessity and a problem I have with the word "feminist"), since Blackness is implicit in the term; just as for white women there is apparently no felt need to preface "feminist" with the word "white," since the word "feminist" is accepted as coming out of white women's culture.
3. The excerpts that follow are taken from an earlier, longer version of Tracey A. Gardner's essay, "Racism in Pornography and the Women's Movement."
4. Ida B. Wells, also known as Ida Wells Barnett, Black radical investigative reporter and publisher of the Memphis-based *Free Speech.* She wrote *On Lynchings: A Red Record, Mob Rule in New Orleans: Southern Horrors* (New York: Arno Press, 1969; first published 1892), a brilliant analysis of lynching in America. Wells led the anti-lynching movement in this country.

Gifts of Power: The Writings of Rebecca Jackson (1981)

ALICE WALKER

In the summer of 1830, when Rebecca Cox Jackson was thirty-five years old, she awoke in panic to the loud thunder and flashing lightning of a severe storm. For five years thunderstorms had terrorized her, making her so sick she was forced to wait them out in bed. This time, even the sanctuary of her bed was not enough; she found herself cowering miserably at the top of the garret stairs of her house believing the next blast of thunder would knock her down them. In this condition she called earnestly to "the Lord" to forgive her all her sins, since she was about to die, and to have mercy in the next world on her poor sinner's soul. Instead of dying, however, with the utterance of this prayer her inner storm ceased, the clouded sky inside her cleared, and her heart became "light" with the forgiveness, mercy, and love of God. Her fear of storms left her permanently (she now believed the power of God's spirit would come to her in storms); and she ran from window to window throwing open the blinds to let the lightning stream in upon her. It was, she said, like "glory" to her soul.

This was Rebecca Jackson's first spiritual connection with the divine. She was to have many more.

Rebecca Cox was born in 1795 of free black parents in Philadelphia. Her mother died when she was thirteen, and she spent many years with a beloved grandmother, who also died while she was young. There is no record of her father. Her young adult life, indeed her life until she was nearly forty, was lived in the home of her older brother, Joseph Cox, an elder of the influential Bethel African Methodist Episcopal church, one of the first black churches in America, founded by Richard Allen. Her husband, Samuel Jackson, lived with her in her brother's house and was also deeply involved in the church. They had no children of their own.

After Jackson's spiritual conversion—as she acknowledged it in later years—she found she had been given spiritual "gifts." That she could tell the future through dreams, for example, and nothing was hidden from her "spirit eye." This meant that while speaking to other people or simply observing them (and frequently not even this) she was able to discern their innermost thoughts as well as ways to deal with them. "God" (manifested as an inner voice) spoke to her, she felt, directly, and as long as she did not hesitate to obey Him she could count on His help over any obstacle.

There were many obstacles.

For one thing, Jackson could neither read nor write, in a family and religious community that valued these skills perhaps above all others. As the eldest girl, responsible for the care of younger siblings after her mother died, as well as for her brother's several small children, there was no opportunity to attend school. How she was even to speak intelligently about God, hindered as she was by ignorance of His written word, she could not fathom. She was also a married woman.

It was her brother to whom she turned for help in learning to read, but, tired from his own work and often impatient with Jackson, he succeeded in making her feel even more backward and lost. He also attempted to censor or change what she dictated and wished him to write.

> So I went to get my brother to write my letters and to read them. So he was awriting a letter in answer to one he had just read. I told him what to put in. Then I asked him to read. He did. I said, "Thee has put in more than I told thee. ... I don't want thee to *word* my letter. I only want thee to *write* it." Then he said, "Sister, thee is the hardest one I ever wrote for!" These words, together with the manner that he wrote my letter, pierced my soul like a sword. ... I could not keep from crying. And these words were spoken in my heart, "Be faithful, and the time shall come when you can write." These words were spoken in my heart as though a tender father spoke them. My tears were gone in a moment.

Incredibly, Jackson *was* taught to read and write by the spirit within her.

> One day I was sitting finishing a dress in haste and in prayer. [Jackson earned her living as a dressmaker.] This word was spoken in my mind, "Who learned the first man on earth?" "Why, God." "He is unchangeable, and if He learned the first man to read, He can learn you." I laid down my dress, picked up my Bible, ran upstairs, opened it, and kneeled down with it pressed to my heart, prayed earnestly to Almighty God if it was consisting to His holy will, to learn me to read His holy word. And when I looked on the word, I began to read. And when I found I was reading, I was frightened—then I could not read another word. I closed my eyes again in prayer and then opened my eyes, began to read. So I done, until I read the whole chapter. I came down. "Samuel, I can read the Bible." "Woman, you are agoing crazy!" "Praise the God of heaven and earth, I can read His holy word!" Down I sat and read through. ... When my brother came to dinner I told him, "I can read the Bible! I have read a whole chapter!" "One thee has heard the children read, till thee has got it by heart." What a wound that was to me, to think he would make so light of a gift of God!

From this time on, Rebecca Jackson found she could write her own letters and "read the Bible anywhere." Her scriptural interpretations, however, based solely on personal spiritual instruction, caused strife not only in her own family, but also in the entire religious community of which she was a part. She was a woman, after all, when the church did not permit women as preachers, who, as soon as she received the holy message, moved immediately to spread it. The pastors and elders of the established churches (all male) accused her of "chopping up the churches," since she declined to join any, and of being a heretic, "a woman aleading the men." There were many threats against her and attempts made on her life.

For the most part, Jackson's spiritual insights came from direct, frequently ecstatic, revelation in either a dreaming or a waking state. She was also literally instructed in matters both spiritual and temporal by a spirit who arrived almost daily to give her lessons. One of the most astonishing examples of this instruction (Jackson's "teacher" was a "fatherly" white man dressed in Quaker attire) is the following entry from her journal, "View of the Natural Atmosphere":

> Monday evening, February 18, 1850, I was instructed concerning the atmosphere and its bounds. I saw its form—it is like the sea, which has her bounds. ... It covered land and sea, so far above all moving things, and yet so far beneath the starry heavens. Its face is like the face of the sea, smooth and gentle when undisturbed by the wind. So is the atmosphere, when undisturbed by the power of the sun and moon. When agitated by these, it rages like the sea and sends forth its storms upon the earth. Nothing can live above it. A bird could no more live or fly above its face, than a fish can live or swim out of water. It is always calm and serene between its face and the starry heaven. The sight, to me, was beautiful.

Her dreams are filled with symbols and her own activity. She can fly through the air like a bird (though higher than birds, and, interestingly, white women), walk through walls, visit other realms, and converse with angels. She can touch a hot stove while awake and not be burned, or totter with eyes closed on the very lip of a steep cellar stair and not fall. She preaches the word of God as it is revealed to her and discovers she has the power to pray sick people well and sinful people holy. All glory for these wonders she gives to God alone and repeatedly describes herself as "a little child" or "a worm of the dust."

One of the biggest obstacles to Jackson's new life in Christ (Jesus, she is told, is the second Adam, and essentially a female spirit; the first Adam was essentially male and fell from grace because he permitted lust to replace spirit and therefore obedience to God) was the expectation of her husband that as his wife she must fulfill her sexual obligations toward him. But her inner voice insisted that though she might live with her husband and serve him in every other way, she could not indulge in what she termed "the sin of the fall." To do so would put her in the same category as Adam. Her husband was at first puzzled, then convinced of her holiness, then outraged anyhow. In his wilder moments, Jackson writes, he "sought my life, night and day." But, because her inner voice was always "leading" her, she was able to keep ahead of him, to know what he was "agoing to do" before he knew it himself.

A year after her conversion she left her husband and her brother's house. She became an itinerant minister who found "fellowship" (more accurately "sistership") among other black women who organized "praying bands" that met in small groups in each other's houses to pray, discuss the scripture and sing, and sustain each other in the arduous task of following the "true" voice within them. (Spiritual consciousness-raising groups, one might say.) It was at this time that Jackson formed a relationship with a younger woman, Rebecca Perot. These two women lived together, ate together, traveled together, prayed together, and slept together until the end of Jackson's life, some thirty-odd years after they met.

It was with Rebecca Perot that Jackson became a resident member of the community of Shakers at Watervliet, New York. The Shakers, a religious group that believed in nothing secular—least of all government and man-made laws (they would not fight in America's wars; indeed, they did not recognize the country of America)—were ecstatics who shared the same spiritual views as Rebecca Jackson: they believed God was spirit ("As well ask how Jesus could be a man as how can Jesus be a woman. God is spirit") and should be worshiped as one, preferably in silence unless the spirit itself directs otherwise. They believed in confession and repentance of sin as a prerequisite of inner peace. They believed in physical and moral cleanliness, in plain dress, in meditation and silence, and in living separate from the world. But more important than any of these, from Rebecca Jackson's point of view, they believed in celibacy; the only religious group she ever heard of that did.

During her time with the Shakers, Jackson knew much spiritual richness and love. For the first time in her life she felt understood and warmly treasured as one who revealed obvious gifts from God. As much as she had been despised in the A.M.E. churches for her stand on celibacy (in her view, an absolute necessity if one wanted to lead a spiritual life), she was embraced by the Shakers, who agreed with her that inasmuch as Jesus Christ was unmarried and celibate, this was the example he wished his people to follow.

With the passing of time, however, disagreements surfaced, primarily because Jackson felt compelled *always* to follow her own inner voice or "invisible lead" and could not follow the Shaker leaders unless instructed by her inner lead to do so. Shortly before the Civil War she was commanded by her inner voice to minister to her own people—ravaged by slavery and persecution—whose destitution she felt the Shakers did not adequately address. But when she requested leave to follow the commandment, the Shaker leadership would not give her its blessing to do so. She and Perot left Watervliet anyway, though Jackson was accused of apostasy, of attempting to lead others "in her own gift."

With time, the rift was healed. Rebecca Jackson received instruction from her inner lead that she might accept orders and instruction from the Shaker elders and eldresses. After this submission she was given a Shaker blessing to minister to black people in a black Shaker settlement, which she established in Philadelphia in the 1870s. With this blessing came the authority of being a recognized religious group, as well as a Shaker promise to render aid to the new settlement in time of trouble. There is no record that Jackson either requested or received such aid.

> A core group of sisters lived together in a single large house, supporting themselves by daywork, as seamstresses or laundresses in the city ... [Shaker records tell us]. White Shakers, visiting from Watervliet and New Lebanon in 1872, described the residence of the family in slightly awestruck terms, as "almost palatial" with its modern plumbing, central heating, "a large drawing room, sufficient for twenty souls to sit down," a carpeted meeting room with "marble" mantels ... "very nice, almost extravagantly so." Their description of the services that took place that evening ... is also thoroughly admiring.

In 1878 eight black women, three black children, and three white women (one of them Jewish) lived in the Shaker commune, members of Rebecca Jackson and Rebecca Perot's spiritual family.

The little band of Shaker sisters survived after Rebecca Jackson's death, in 1871, at least until 1908, when the last reports of the group were recorded.

Gifts of Power is an extraordinary document. It tells us much about the spirituality of human beings, especially of the interior spiritual resources of our mothers, and, because of this, makes an invaluable contribution to what we know of ourselves. A simple review could not begin to do it justice, for it is a contribution of many facets, some readily comprehended, some not. What, for instance, are we to make of Rebecca Jackson's obviously gnostic beliefs (that the "resurrection" occurs in life, not after death; that the spirit of "Christ" is manifested through the "mind" in visions and dreams and not through the bureaucracy of the church) a hundred years before the Nag Hammadi "Gnostic Gospels, the Secret Teachings of Christ" was found? What are we to make of her discovery that she had not only a divine Father but also a divine Mother—which is consistent with pre-Western Indian and African religious belief? What are we to make of the reasons that suggest why so many black women (Rebecca Jackson only one of them)[1] abandoned the early black churches to find religious audiences of their own? (The established churches insisted on "civilized" worship, everyone singing at the same time out of the same book; whereas the women wanted the passion and glory of spontaneous *inspired* worship and song, behavior the male leaders of the churches called "heathenish." What the male leaders termed "progress" in the black church, i.e., subdued, calm, rather Presbyterian behavior, the women called "letting the devil into the church.") What are we to make of Jackson's ability to "manufacture" spiritually a "father" she had never had? And what are we to make of the remarkable general power of Rebecca Jackson herself—a woman whose inner spirit directed her to live her own life, creating it from scratch, leaving husband, home, family, and friends, to do so?

Jean McMahon Humez has done a magnificent job in editing *Gifts of Power*. There is only one point at which I stopped, while reading her splendid and thorough introduction, to question her obviously deep knowledge of her material. It is when she discusses the relationship between Rebecca Jackson and Rebecca Perot (known among the Shakers as "the two Rebeccas"). Unlike other black women who were spiritual leaders and were single and traveled alone, Rebecca, Humez writes, "after breaking with her husband and brother ... lived and traveled throughout the rest of her life in close relationship with a single cherished, intimate woman friend who shared her religious ideas. *Perhaps, had she been born in the modern age, she would have been an open lesbian*" (my italics).

Though women ministers who worshiped and lived with other women were perceived by the male leaders of the early churches as "closeted lesbians," because they followed their own inner voices rather than the "fathers" of the church, there is nothing in these writings that seems to make Jackson one. It would be wonderful if she were, of course. But it would be just as wonderful if she were not. One wonders why, since Jackson mentions more than once her "deadness" to sexuality or "lust," Humez implies she was a lesbian? The example she gives of "erotic" activity on Jackson's part is a dream Jackson relates which involves Rebecca Perot's long hair. In the dream another woman combs all her hair out, and Rebecca Jackson is upset because she had worked so hard on Perot's hair and "had got it so long."

Considering that our culture has always treasured long hair nearly as much as reading, and frequently *as* much, I submit that this does not qualify as an erotic dream. A more telling dream, in my opinion, is one related by Rebecca *Perot,* in which she saw herself as queen and Rebecca Jackson as king of Africa.

What I am questioning is a nonblack scholar's attempt to label something lesbian that the black woman in question has not. Even if Rebecca Jackson and Rebecca Perot *were* erotically bound, what was their own word for it? (What would be the name that must have been as black and positive as "bull-dagger"—in more modern times—is black and negative?) Did they see it as a rejection of men? Did it (whatever they did alone together) infringe on their notion of celibacy? Was the "lesbianism" the simple fact that Jackson and Perot lived together? And would this mean that any two women who lived together are lesbians? Is the "lesbianism" the fact that Jackson and Perot lived with other women and founded a religious settlement comprised entirely of women (and their children)? If the "lesbianism" is any of these things, then the charge that the women were "closeted lesbians" was well founded. But the women did not accept this label when it was made, and I think we should at least wonder whether they would accept it now, particularly since the name they *did* accept, *and embrace,* which caused them so much suffering and abuse, was *celibate*. Of course celibates, like lesbians, have a hard time proving they exist. My own guess is that, like Virginia Woolf, whom many claim as a lesbian but who described herself as a "eunuch," the two Rebeccas became spiritual sisters partly *because* they cared little for sex, which Jackson repeatedly states.

The word "lesbian" may not, in any case, be suitable (or comfortable) for black women, who surely would have begun their woman-bonding earlier than Sappho's residency on the Isle of Lesbos. Indeed, I can imagine black women who love women (sexually or not) hardly thinking of what Greeks were doing; but, instead, referring to themselves as "whole" women, from "wholly" or "holy." Or as "round" women—women who love other women, yes, but women who also have concern, in a culture that oppresses all black people (and this would go back very far), for their fathers, brothers, and sons, no matter how they feel about them as males. My own term for such women would be "womanist." At any rate, the word they chose would have to be both spiritual and concrete and it would have to be organic, characteristic, not simply applied. A word that said more than that they choose women over men. More than that they choose to live separate from men. In fact, to be consistent with black cultural values (which, whatever their shortcomings, still have considerable worth) it would have to be a word that affirmed connectedness to the entire community and the world, rather than separation, *regardless* of who worked and slept with whom. All things considered, the main problem with Lesbos as a point of common reference for women who love women is not, as I had once thought, that it was inhabited by Greek women whose servants, like their culture, were probably stolen from Egypt, but that it is an island. The symbolism of this, for a black person, is far from positive.

But this is a small complaint and perhaps an esoteric one. I simply feel that naming our own experience after our own fashion (as well as rejecting whatever does not seem to suit) is the least we can do—and in this society may well be our only tangible sign of personal freedom. It was her grasp of the importance of this that caused Rebecca Jackson to write down her spiritual "travels" that all might witness her individual path. This, that makes her an original. This, that makes us thankful to receive her as a gift of power in herself.

Note

1. Others included Sojourner Truth, Amanda Berry Smith, and Jerena Lee.

Womanist (1983)

ALICE WALKER

Womanist

1. From *womanish*. (Opp. of "girlish," i.e., frivolous, irresponsible, not serious.) A black feminist or feminist of color. From the black folk expression of mothers to female children, "You acting womanish," i.e., like a woman. Usually referring to outrageous, audacious, courageous or *willful* behavior. Wanting to know more and in greater depth than is considered "good" for one. Interested in grown-up doings. Acting grown up. Being grown up. Interchangeable with another black folk expression: "You trying to be grown." Responsible. In charge. *Serious.*

2. Also: A woman who loves other women, sexually and/or nonsexually. Appreciates and prefers women's culture, women's emotional flexibility (values tears as natural counterbalance of laughter), and women's strength. Sometimes loves individual men, sexually and/or nonsexually. Committed to survival and wholeness of entire people, male *and* female. Not a separatist, except periodically, for health. Traditionally universalist, as in: "Mama, why are we brown, pink, and yellow, and our cousins are white, beige, and black?" Ans.: "Well, you know the colored race is just like a flower garden, with every color flower represented." Traditionally capable, as in: "Mama, I'm walking to Canada and I'm taking you and a bunch of other slaves with me." Reply: "It wouldn't be the first time."

3. Loves music. Loves dance. Loves the moon. Loves the Spirit. Loves love and food and roundness. Loves struggle. Loves the Folk. Loves herself. *Regardless.*

4. Womanist is to feminist as purple to lavender.

2

Chikwenye Okonjo Ogunyemi's African Womanism

Womanism: The Dynamics of the Contemporary
Black Female Novel in English (1985)

CHIKWENYE OKONJO OGUNYEMI

> We are not white. We are not Europeans. We are black like the Africans
> themselves. ... We and the Africans will be working for a common goal:
> the uplift of black people everywhere. [Alice Walker, *The Color Purple*]

What does a black woman novelist go through as she comes in contact with
white feminist writing and realizes that Shakespeare's illustrious sisters belong
to the second sex, a situation that has turned them into impotent eunuchs
without rooms of their own in which to read and write their very own literature, so that they have become madwomen, now emerging from the attic,
determined to fight for their rights by engaging in the acrimonious politics of
sex? Does she precipitately enter the lists with them against Euro-American
patriarchy and, in their victory, further jeopardize the chances of her race in
the sharing of political, social, and economic power? Does she imitate their
war effort and throw the gauntlet down to challenge black patriarchy? Does
she light the sexual war some of the time and the racial war at other times?
Does she remain indifferent to the outer sex war and, maintaining a truce in
the black sexual power tussle, fight only the race war?

Many black female novelists writing in English have understandably not
allied themselves with radical white feminists; rather, they have explored the
gamut of other positions and produced an exciting, fluid corpus that defies
rigid categorization. More often than not, where a white woman writer may
be a feminist, a black woman writer is likely to be a "womanist." That is, she
will recognize that, along with her consciousness of sexual issues, she must
incorporate racial, cultural, national, economic, and political considerations
into her philosophy.

It is important to establish why many black women novelists are not feminists in the way that their white counterparts are and what the differences

are between them. African and Afro-American women writers share similar aesthetic attitudes in spite of factors that separate them. As a group, they are distinct from white feminists because of their race, because they have experienced the past and present subjugation of the black population along with present-day subtle (or not so subtle) control exercised over them by the alien, Western culture. These extraliterary determinants have helped to make the black female novel in English what it is today and partly account for the conflict between white and black women over strategies and priorities in sexual politics. To illustrate the black womanist aesthetic, I will cite many novels by black women in both African and Afro-American literatures without going into detailed analysis of them; my intention is to establish that womanism is widespread and to pinpoint the factors that bind black female novelists together under this distinct praxis. On the African side I will refer to Bessie Head's *When Rain Clouds Gather, Maru,* and *A Question of Power* (South Africa); Flora Nwapa's *Idu* and *One Is Enough* (Nigeria); Ama Ata Aidoo's *Our Sister Killjoy* (Ghana); and Mariama Bâ's *So Long a Letter* (Senegal). On the Afro-American side my references turn primarily on Margaret Walker's *Jubilee;* Paule Marshall's *The Chosen Place, the Timeless People* and *Praisesong for the Widow;* Toni Morrison's *The Bluest Eye* and *Song of Solomon;* and Alice Walker's *The Third Life of Grange Copeland* and *The Color Purple.*

* * *

Since the feminist novel is still evolving, the following descriptive statements are tentative and hypothetical but serve as a working base: the feminist novel is a form of protest literature directed to both men and women. Protesting against sexism and the patriarchal power structure, it is unapologetically propagandist or strident or both. It demands that its readers, whether the male oppressors or the female oppressed, be aware of ideological issues in order that it may change their attitudes about patriarchy. For a novel to be identified as feminist, therefore, it must not just deal with women and women's issues but should also posit some aspects of a feminist ideology.[1] A reader can expect to find in it some combination of the following themes: a critical perception of and reaction to patriarchy, often articulated through the struggle of a victim or rebel who must face a patriarchal institution; sensitivity to the inequities of sexism allied with an acceptance of women and understanding of the choices open to them; a metamorphosis leading to female victory in a feminist Utopia, or a stasis, signifying the failure to eliminate sexism; a style spiced with the acrimony of feminist discourse. As with recipes, so with works of art; results are variable. Womanist novels, while they too may possess these characteristics to a greater or lesser degree, lay stress on other distinctive features to leave an impression markedly different from that of feminist works. This divergence, I think, necessitates the separate classification I have given to black female novels.

Consider *Jane Eyre,* a complex and far-reaching novel that Sandra Gilbert and Susan Gubar, in their scintillating analysis, identify as part of the feminist tradition.[2] The feminist character of the novel is apparent in the portrait of Jane as a rebel against patriarchal institutions, represented by such domineering male figures as the Reverend Brocklehurst, Edward Rochester, and St. John Rivers. For the white feminist reader the novel's ending is a positive one: Jane triumphs through achieving acknowledged equality with her husband, Rochester.

For the discerning black reader, however, *Jane Eyre* is not just a feminist novel, but a disarmingly realistic appraisal of white survival ethics. David Cecil in his *Early Victorian Novelists* saw in the Heathcliff–Edgar Linton clash in Emily Brontë's *Wuthering Heights* an economic (and, I might add, a racial) dimension, an interpretation that can be extended to the Bertha-Rochester relationship. The indomitable West Indian mulatto, Bertha Rochester, exploited for her sexual attractiveness and wealth, is locked up because the patriarchal Rochester says she is mad.[3] Rochester, as is typical of exploitative white masters, likes her wealth and her sexual possibilities but dislikes the tint of her skin, the color that, among other factors, made her vulnerable to him in the first place. He casts her aside,[4] has affairs, and attempts to marry a white woman as if the black one has metamorphosed into an invisible woman; for the "mad" Bertha, it is a catch-22 situation. She therefore fights for survival. She wreaks vengeance on the polygynously inclined Rochester and his female accomplice, "virtuous, plain Jane," who should know better than to supplant another female to secure a husband. Bertha burns down Thornfield, the white patriarchal edifice, to the chagrin of the white man and woman. To right the inequities of patriarchy, from the black viewpoint, the white woman must accept a more lowly situation in life, having as mate a man in reduced circumstances, with whom she is equal. So far, so good. However when Brontë allows Bertha, betrayed on all sides by white women—Adele's mother; her guard, Grace Poole; and her rivals for Rochester's love, especially Jane—to die as the patriarchy collapses, she creates a tragic vision of feminism for a black reader. Such an ending makes the novel ambivalent; or is it, perhaps, that the feminist utopia is for white women only? For black women who would be feminists the lesson is simple: in fighting the establishment, the black woman must not be so mad as to destroy herself with the patriarchy. The fact that this lesson has been learned by many black women novelists partly explains their lack of enthusiasm for feminism's implied endorsement of total white control. Hence their womanist stance.

The works of Nigeria's Buchi Emecheta, who has been living in exile in England for almost twenty years and started to write after a marital fiasco, are something of an exception. Emecheta's two autobiographical novels, *In the Ditch* (1972) and *Second-Class Citizen* (1974), are deeply grounded in the British and Irish feminism in which she was nurtured. Adah, Emecheta's alter ego in these novels, is rebellious. Unlike Bertha Mason—a predecessor of Adah's insofar as they are both black women alone in a white society—she success-fully fights patriarchy, experienced as the British welfare slate (*In the Ditch*). She also triumphs over her Nigerian husband, Francis (*Second-Class Citizen*), bestial in his sexuality and economic irresponsibility, even though he is backed by a long Nigerian patriarchal tradition. In England, Adah transcends the female predicament by obtaining a divorce (which would be frowned on in Nigeria), and she also copes with the burden of caring for five children in a hostile environment.

Following the tradition of feminists, Emecheta, in her later nonautobio-graphical works whose titles suggest their feminist slant—*The Bride Price* (1976), *The Slave Girl* (1977), *The Joys of Motherhood* (1979), *Double Yoke* (1982)—tends to feminize the black male, making him weak, flabby, and unsuccessful. This disquieting tendency also calls into question Emecheta's opinion about women. She presents the black male as the "other," a ridiculous "object," to borrow Simone de Beauvoir's apt vocabulary. He is destined to be "killed" by Emecheta but is incongruously resurrected, perhaps in the author's last-minute bid to remain faithful to Nigerian patriarchal reality. Her heroines are mostly strong characters who struggle against patriarchy only to die in childbirth, heroine enslaved in marriage, or die insane, abandoned by the children they nurtured. Emecheta's destruction of her heroines is a femi-nist trait that can be partly attributed to narcissism on the part of the writer.[5] The African feminist writer's position is complicated by the fact that her work sometimes lacks authenticity, since the traditional African woman she uses as protagonist is, in reality, beset by problems of survival and so is hardly aware of her sexist predicament; the feminist desire to present her as rebellious can, in the context of this reality, be merely ludicrous.

If the feminist literary movement desires the illumination of female expe-rience in order to alter the status quo for the benefit of women,[6] the African woman writer's dilemma in a feminist context becomes immediately appar-ent. Black women are disadvantaged in several ways: as blacks they, with their men, are victims of a white patriarchal culture; as women they are victimized by black men; and as black women they are also victimized on racial, sexual, and class grounds by white men. In order to cope, Emecheta largely ignores such complexities and deals mainly with the black woman as victim of black patriarchy. This preoccupation is atypical of black women writers, though Emecheta's indefatigable zeal for black feminism could become catching.

* * *

Interviewed during the feminist book fair in London in June 1984, the white South African journalist Beata Lipman was forthright about the state of women's writing in South Africa. According to her, "Racism is a more urgent matter than sexism,"[7] a statement that can be extended to many Third World areas if we substitute hunger, poverty, or backwardness for "racism." Much as she downplays her power, the white woman has an authority that the black man or woman does not have. Moreover, while the white woman writer protests against sexism, the black woman writer must deal with it as one among many evils; she battles also with the dehumanization resulting from racism and poverty. What, after all, is the value of sexual equality in a ghetto? Black women writers are not limited to issues defined by their femaleness but attempt to tackle questions raised by their humanity. Thus the womanist vision is racially conscious in its underscoring of the positive aspects of black life. The politics of the womanist is unique in its racial-sexual ramifications; it is more complex than white sexual politics, for it addresses more directly the ultimate question relating to power:[8] how do we share equitably the world's wealth and concomitant power among the races and between the sexes?

White feminists consistently compare the situation of white women with that of "slaves," "colonials," the "black minority," "serfs in a feudal system," the "Dark Continent."[9] Since these are demeaning positions to which black people have been assigned and which they still hold in many parts of the world, such comparisons alienate black readers because they underscore yet trivialize black subordination. Indeed, the white feminist stance arouses black suspicion that whites will further suppress blacks to make provision for a female victory in the white, sexual, political game. The black woman writer, therefore, whether in Africa or somewhere in the diaspora, tends to believe that white feminism is yet another ploy, perhaps unintentional, against her and hers. The common black heritage of subjugation by whites, both directly and by the introjection of white values and mores, has determined the nature of modern black life, which S.E. Ogude rightly recognizes as a living tradition of suffering and humiliation.[10] To generate public awareness and understanding of this central fact through the writing of stories that are tellingly appropriate and instructive is the black woman writer's first concern. She is thus not as primarily or exclusively interested in sexism as is the feminist.

The intelligent black woman writer, conscious of black impotence in the context of white patriarchal culture, empowers the black man. She believes in him; hence her books end in integrative images of the male and female worlds. Given this commitment, she can hardly become a strong ally of the white feminist until (perhaps) the political and economic fortunes of the black race improve. With the world power structure as it is, what would the relevance be of a black female character's struggle to be equal to such a black man as, for example, on the Afro-American side, Richard Wright's bestialized Bigger Thomas or Ralph Ellison's eternally hibernating Invisible Man or James Baldwin's sterile Leo Proudhammer; or, on the African side, as Ngugi wa Thiong'o's treacherous male or Wole Soyinka's drifting interpreter or Chinua Achebe's insecure Okonkwo? Just as Baldwin rejects integration into the burning house of the United States, the black woman instinctively recoils from mere equality because, as in Aidoo's *Our Sister Killjoy,* she has to aim much higher than that and knit the world's black family together to achieve black, not just female, transcendence.[11]

Aidoo might have been speaking for most black women writers when she diagnosed the African woman writer's disease: "Life for the African woman writer is definitely 'not crystal stair.' It is a most peculiar predicament. But we also share all, or nearly all the problems of male African writers"—sharing experience that white female writers do not have with their male counterparts.[12] For the African man or woman, there are the basic problems of writing in a borrowed language and form; for most blacks the difficulties in getting published when there are so few black publishing houses remains a critical issue. Then, too, many African novels are slight or lack the profundity found in many black American ones. The tradition of African art with its simplicity and ephemerality—as can be seen in African architecture as well as in oral and performed literatures—has been bequeathed to African women writers. Yet they have to produce novels in a milieu that hankers after the complex and the enduring. At the same time, who will read what they produce when a large proportion of the home audience hates reading or cannot read—a predicament shared by black Americans?

Writing from a position of power, the white female writer does not face such difficulties. Instead she concentrates on patriarchy, analyzing it, attacking it, detecting its tentacles in the most unlikely places. Patriarchy, as it manifests itself in black ghettos of the world, is a domestic affair without the wide reverberations it has in white patriarchy where the issue is real world power. The ultimate difference between the feminist and the womanist is thus what each sees of patriarchy and what each thinks can be changed. Black sexism is a microcosmic replication of Euro-American racism, a concept Alice Walker recognizes. In *The Color Purple*, Nettie writes that the Olinka in not educating girls are "like white people at home who don't want colored people to learn."[13] It follows that for the black woman racism and sexism must be eradicated together.

Since the 1960s, when the idea of independence and nationalism blew through Africa and the diaspora, the white woman has intensified her feminist drive for equality with white men, a position that complicates her response to racial issues and to black feminism. Many white feminist critics have confirmed black suspicion of duplicity by rarely dealing with black women's writing, curtly dismissing it on the pretext of their ignorance of it.[14] This neglect has a positive side in that it has encouraged the emergence of black women critics. The conflict between the white and black positions is concretized in black women's antagonism toward their white counterparts' sexual politics. It shows in the consistently unsympathetic portrayal of white female characters in novels by black women writers—a situation that signals the extent of the conflict between while feminists and black womanists.

A revealing example of this hostility is Aidoo's portrait of the German Marja, wife of Adolf (Hitler?) in *Our Sister Killjoy*. First Marja appears as a tempter when she presents the black girl, Sissie, with numerous offers of fruits in symbolic gestures that lead finally to a sexual advance. Sissie recoils at what she considers abominable, though her horror is mixed with Baldwinian tenderness, and rejects feminism while she moves toward womanism.[15] Similarly, in *A Question of Power* Head demonstrates, through the portrait of Camilla, that the white woman yearns to control black men and women by humiliating them. She is stopped by an open confrontation.

The Afro-Americans have dealt with the white woman even more viciously than have African writers—understandably, since the racist situation is more exacerbating for them than for their average African counterpart. What could be more damaging than Margaret Walker's portrait in *Jubilee* of Big Missy as the hard matriarch or of her daughter, the lily-livered Miss Lillian, in the contrasting stereotype of the fragile, docile woman? Big Missy, for her diabolical treatment of her black slaves, finally receives her just deserts when—with most of her family dead and Yankee guns booming as if at the back of her plantation—she starts emitting flatus and becomes incontinent following a massive stroke. As if that were insufficient, Walker finishes the white female by finally portraying Miss Lillian (who is also adept at emitting flatus at gatherings) as insane and helpless, in sharp contrast to the black Vyry, who thrives under hardships created by Big Missy and other white characters.

Paule Marshall is as devastating as Margaret Walker in her portrait of the white woman in *Brown Girl, Brownstones* and even more trenchant in *The Chosen Place, the Timeless People*. In the latter, she makes an important historical point through her white character Harriet, whose wealth had its origins in the slave trade; like Margaret Walker, Marshall asserts that slavery benefited white women as well as white men. The white woman's dubious role in the racial context is further underscored by the behavior of a white woman, the English lover of the black woman, Merle. The incident has the character of a historical parable. Determined to negate Merle's attempts at connecting with her black African roots through marriage (worldwide unity of blacks), the white woman (Britain), in a symbolic, neocolonialist move, sets the African husband and the West Indian wife against each other, recklessly and treacherously destroying the budding relationship between black people in Africa and the diaspora; she has economic control, and her tactics are to divide and rule.

Neofeminism's "socialist connection" smacks of the black flirtation with communism in the 1940s.[16] A black and white female alliance would have similar characteristics. Like the earlier flirtation, such connections would come to nothing much, since Euro-American economy with its present structure will not readily permit blacks or women to win. So black female writers express in their writing what Sheila Rowbotham has surmised about the world economic situation: "A feminist movement which is confined to the specific oppression of women cannot, in isolation, end exploitation and imperialism."[17] If the ultimate aim of radical feminism is a separatist, idyllic existence away from the hullabaloo of the men's world,[18] the ultimate aim of womanism is the unity of blacks everywhere under the enlightened control of men and women. Each is finally separatist—the one sexually, the other racially—and their different goals create part of the disunity in the women's movement.

Recognition of the impact of racism, neocolonialism, nationalism, economic instability, and psychological disorientation on black lives, when superimposed on the awareness of sexism that characterizes black women's writing, makes concern about sexism merely one aspect of womanism. Black women writers distinguish womanism from feminism, just as their critical perception of black patriarchy and particular concern for black women distinguish the themes in their works from the acceptance of obnoxious male prejudices against women often found in writing by black men.

* * *

I arrived at the term "womanism" independently and was pleasantly surprised to discover that my notion of its meaning overlaps with Alice Walker's. She employs it to denote the metamorphosis that occurs in an adolescent girl, such as Ruth or Celie, when she comes to a sense of herself as a woman; involved is what Morrison, with her Pecola, refers to as "the little-girl-gone-to-woman" and Ntozake Shange represents through the maturing Indigo in *Sassafrass, Cypress & Indigo*. The young girl inherits womanism after a traumatic event such as menarche or after an epiphany or as a result of the experience of racism, rape, death in the family, or sudden responsibility. Through coping with the experience she moves creatively beyond the self to that concern for the needs of others characteristic of adult womanists. While writing on Nwapa, Alison Perry made a comment on Walker's extended usage of the word that tallies with my understanding of it. According to Perry, "If Flora Nwapa would accept a label at all, she would be more at home with Black American author Alice Walker's term 'womanist,' meaning a woman who is 'committed to the survival and wholeness of the entire people, male and female.' "[19]

Black womanism is a philosophy that celebrates black roots, the ideals of black life, while giving a balanced presentation of black womandom. It concerns itself as much with the black sexual power tussle as with the world power structure that subjugates blacks. Its ideal is for black unity where every black person has a modicum of power and so can be a "brother" or a "sister" or a "father" or a "mother" to the other. This philosophy has a mandalic core: its aim is the dynamism of wholeness and self-healing that one sees in the positive, integrative endings of womanist novels.

Black American female writers share with black males the heritage of the blues, whose spiritual dynamics ensure equilibrium in a turbulent world—perhaps because, as Stephen Henderson points out, there is a connection between the blues and the capacity to experience hope. The blues have had a tremendous impact on the Afro-American womanist novel, and, in contrast to feminist novels, most Afro-American womanist novels, culture-oriented as they are, abound in hope.[20] The Afro-American female novelist sometimes even employs the mood and structure of the blues in her novels. As Henderson explains, "The blues ... are a music and poetry of confrontation—with the self, with the family and loved ones, with the oppressive forces of society, with nature, and, on the heaviest level, with fate and the universe itself. And in the confrontation ... a woman discovers her strengths, and if she is a Ma Rainey, *she shares it with the community and in the process becomes immortal*" (emphasis added).[21]

More often than not, in fiction we have many Ma Raineys—women without men: examples include Janie Crawford (Zora Neale Hurston's *Their Eyes Were Watching God*); Vyry (Margaret Walker's *Jubilee*); Merle (Marshall's *The Chosen Place, the Timeless People*); Avey Johnson (Marshall's *Praisesong for the Widow*); Sula and Nel (Morrison's *Sula*); Pilate and Circe (Morrison's *Song of Solomon*); Meridian (Alice Walker's *Meridian*); Ruth (Alice Walker's *The Third Life of Grange Copeland*); Celie and Nettie (Alice Walker's *The Color Purple*). Many such women can be found in the African female novel too: Elizabeth (Head's *A Question of Power*); Sissie (Aidoo's *Our Sister Killjoy*); Ramatoulaye (Bâ's *So Long a Letter*); Idu (Nwapa's *Idu*); and Amaka (Nwapa's *One Is Enough*). In the contemporary literary scene, the Morrisons and Heads and Aidoos and Marshalls are themselves such matriarchs without men.[22] On one level the depiction of such women can be regarded as an antipatriarchal statement on the authors' part. On another these exemplary figures, like Ma Rainey, demonstrate concern for the family—not for the Western nuclear family (as viewed by feminists) but for the black extended family (as viewed by womanists) with its large numbers and geographical spread. From this perspective, Sula is a binding, spiritual force in Medallion; Merle in Bournehills; Sissie amid black people.

Karen Gasten is therefore mistaken in concluding about *The Third Life of Grange Copeland* that "what is needed to bring about a healthy balance in sexual relationships is a generation of Ruths."[23] The book's purpose is not so much the achievement of that feminist goal but the integration of the Ruths into the black world—a womanist objective. The black woman is not as powerless in the black world as the white woman is in the white world; the black woman, less protected than her white counterpart, has to grow independent. These factors generate an affirmative spirit in the womanist novel that is packed full of female achievement.[24] Also, womanists explore past and present connections between black America and black Africa. Like amiable co-wives with invisible husbands, they work together for the good of their people. Charles Chesnutt's Aun' Peggy, the witch-herbalist in *The Conjure Woman*, Hurston's indomitable Janie Crawford, Ayi Kwei Armah's and Ngugi's formidable women—all serve as inspirational sources. Like the younger generation of black aestheticists, black female writers sidetrack the negative spirit of the protest tradition that some feminists still find useful.

In spite of the blues, black women occasionally go mad. Unlike negatively presented white madwomen, the black madwoman in novels written by black women knows in her subconscious that she must survive because she has people without other resources depending on her; in a positive about-face she usually recovers through a superhuman effort, or somehow, aids others. Merle, carrying her national burden of leading Bournehills up a road to progress, recoups her energy after her bouts of insanity and strengthens herself spiritually for the future political struggle by undertaking a pilgrimage to East Africa. In *The Bluest Eye,* the peculiar Pecola goes mad on the surface but acquires an interior spiritual beauty symbolized by the bluest eye (an "I" that is very blue). In this mixed state she acts as the scapegoat so that "all who knew her—felt so wholesome after [they] cleaned [them]selves on her."[25] Merle is comparable to Head's Elizabeth, who—nudged on by self-will, her son, her neighbors, and the medicinal effect of herbal greenery—recovers her sanity to play her part in an agricultural commune. Bâ's Jacqueline recuperates from her nervous breakdown as soon as she understands that her illness is psychosomatic, and she becomes reintegrated into society. After each mental upheaval there is thus a stasis in the womanist novel when the black woman's communion with the rest of the society is established, a consonance that expresses the black way to authenticity and transcendence. Madness becomes a temporary aberration preceding spiritual growth, healing, and integration.

These insights into character portrayal and thematic development have not come easily to the African writer. In an article unfortunately dated in some aspects, Maryse Conde observes that Nwapa and Aidoo "convey the impression that a gifted woman simply has no place in African society." In her analysis this is true "not only because [the gifted woman] cannot find a proper match but because the price she has to pay for her unusual gifts is so high that she would be better born without them," an idea that Juliet Okonkwo reiterates. Conde then concludes, "Here are two gifted women portraying gifted females like themselves, but ultimately destroying them. These murders are the expression of a deeply-rooted conflict."[26] Perhaps. I suggest that this problem partly arises from the fact that early in their careers the African writers tend to model themselves on white feminists, thus putting themselves at variance with polygamy, which is generally accepted in rural Africa and is gaining ground in urban Nigeria.[27]

Conde's 1972 thesis has since been put into question by the appearance of Nwapa's *One Is Enough* (1981) and, most especially, by Aidoo's assertive *Our Sister Killjoy* (1977). In the latter, the strong-headed Sissie wants black men everywhere to undergo a psychological metamorphosis to assert their manhood in world politics, just as she has successfully represented black womanhood in her role as roving ambassador in Europe. A black man with such mastery can then become equal to and united with her. Here, the Ghanaian Aidoo, an Akan by birth, discards her Western consciousness to embrace the Akan matrilineal culture and outlook. Akan women are generally acclaimed for their independence. There, as a proverb goes, the husband cooks and leaves the food to the woman to relish—though, I must hastily add, the woman's brother dishes it out. So, in the denouement of the work, Aidoo envisages black solidarity between men and women in Africa and the diaspora.

The Senegalese novel *So Long a Letter* by Bâ is grounded in a Fulani world where the foreign religion of Islam has, like Christianity, been ruthlessly imposed on Africans. As Bâ demonstrates, both religions bear partial responsibility for the fact that many Africans have suffered psychological and moral disorientation. She generates tension in the novel by exploring the matrilineal perspective of the Fulanis in opposition to the patriarchal tenets of Islam, which advocates polygyny. Her shortish novel takes the form of a long letter written by Ramatoulaye, the determined heroine, to a friend to tell her about the polygynous situation that has ruined her marriage because of her Western expectation of monogyny. Rather than collapsing, she remains undaunted, with little acrimony. Ramatoulaye will not break another woman's heart by marrying that woman's husband as a second wife, and she even sympathizes with the other woman who ruined her (Ramatoulaye's) marriage. Men must be men, it seems, but women do not have to be like them. Having accepted men with their libidinous disposition, she can create a stable life around her numerous children, male and female, along with their spouses. This is womanism in action; the demands of Fulani culture rather than those of sexual politics predominate. Though she recognizes the inequities of patriarchy, she never really fights for her "rights"—a position further expressed by the novel's private, epistolary form. It must be pointed out that these two societies—the Akan and the Fulani—though preferable to the strictly patriarchal societies from a woman's viewpoint, are matrilineal and not truly matriarchal. One can therefore postulate that matrilineal and polygynous societies in Africa are dynamic sources for the womanist novel.

Head's *When Rain Clouds Gather* is a womanist novel achieved on different terms: widowhood involving the care of male and female children. In this idyllic novel, bad men are eliminated so that men and women can live together harmoniously. Similarly, ostracism and ethnicism rather than sexism cause the development of the strong woman in Head's *Maru*. In the end, the untouchable Margaret Cadmore marries the chief and touches other people. The disintegrating forces of apartheid in conjunction with the necessity to care for a black male child cause the toughening up and recovery of the insane heroine in Head's *A Question of Power*. Elizabeth frees herself from racial, ethnic, and male bondage to emerge as an intrepid individual, able to cope with bringing up her son and living harmoniously with others and with nature. It is Head's unique South African experience that makes it possible for her to detribalize the African womanist novel by exploring so many possibilities.

In the United States Alice Walker has been equally inventive. To make her point she uses the woman who is docile (but not helpless as her white counterpart would be), hardworking, and pitted against a terrible fate; her heroines suffer from poverty or racism allied with sexism, and sometimes from all three together. Walker is making the point that the black woman's destiny, in general, radically differs from her white counterpart's. About the latter de Beauvoir observes: "But woman is not called upon to build a better world: her domain is fixed and she has only to keep up the never ending struggle against the evil principles that creep into it; in her war against dust, stains, mud, and dirt she is fighting sin, wrestling with Satan."[28] In couching woman's war in domestic and religious terms, de Beauvoir is playful and somewhat Puritanical; her account does not cover the experience of the black woman for whom Satan is not a metaphysical concept but a reality out there, beyond her home, where she must willy-nilly go to obtain the wherewithal for decent survival as well as for a "better world." Ruth's mother, Mem, does so in *The Third Life of Grange Copeland;* Meridian in *Meridian;* Celie and Nettie in *The Color Purple.*

* * *

Writing in the latter half of the twentieth century, the black womanist has been experimenting with old forms used by her predecessors, male and female. It is significant that the African woman writer emerged with the advent of political independence. Handicapped by writing in a second language, she has sometimes tried to put herself on familiar ground by fusing the familiar oral tradition with the foreign written medium, while also playing the role traditionally reserved for woman: enlightening and entertaining the population left in her care. The classics of the female Afro-American novel came after the heyday of the protest tradition and took for granted the ideological backing of the black power movement. Consequently, female novelists in both continents prefer to tell of life as it is, sometimes of life as it is thought to be, and rarely of life as it ought to be.

With some parallels to Jane Austen's clever exploitation of the gothic in *Northanger Abbey,* Head manipulates the mystique of gothicism in her psychological portrait of the mad Elizabeth in *A Question of Power.* As the private, fantastical "movies," which represent the punishment cells, unreel in Elizabeth's mind and vision, the reader is forced to act the voyeur, transported into an exotic, weird world where the unusual, the eccentric, the traumatic, the frightening, the mysterious become the norm. Elizabeth's interior gothic world is wild, unjust, sexist, as her fight against the two reprehensible men—Dan and Sello—demonstrates. Its power play replicates the outer racist and ethnocentric society whose horrific power mongering leads Elizabeth to a nervous breakdown. Human tenderness and her willpower restore her to a supportable society.

Aidoo's, Bâ's, and Alice Walker's return to the early epistolary form of the novel inherited from eighteenth-century women writers departs from twentieth-century novelistic practice.[29] Their rediscovery of the epistle enables them to exploit its qualities of simplicity, relative intimacy, and candor. As a result, a novel in this form appears more open and more sincere than one written in the autobiographical mode—which tends to be defensively aggressive, narcissistic, self-glorifying, as in the work of some feminists. The letter pretends to be authentic and, like oral narration, gives the impression that the storyteller is not lying. In Aidoo's and Bâ's novels, the correspondents are loving friends. This aura of authenticity has a didactic function, particularly for women readers. Aidoo's use of the form in *Our Sister Killjoy* seems a modification of that employed in Baldwin's *The Fire Next Time*: she retains his clarity of vision and makes an objective assessment of the black global predicament. Her feminine nagging tone resembles Baldwin's sermonizing mode, made acceptable by a tenderness extended to friend and foe alike. In its daring experimentation in form, *Our Sister Killjoy* also resembles Jean Toomer's *Cane*. Like Toomer, Aidoo mixes prose, the sketch, poetry, song, and the like to produce something living, fresh, and lyrical—an oral performance in book form.

Alice Walker's *The Color Purple* is also complex and variable in its structure. The first addressee in its epistles is a power-wielding God. White, patriarchal, he acts the role of the indifferent voyeur. When God metamorphoses into "It," neuter but not quite neutral, in the female imagination, life miraculously improves for womanhood. Also included in the book is the correspondence of two loving and trusting sisters. Like rural, sequestered women, some of their letters remain unopened, hidden in a trunk by an interfering male. Walker then brings the truth of their lives to the world, just as Shug, the enlightened black woman who brings the secluded, "private" Celie into the public world of artistic and economic fulfillment. Celie and the letters resemble Emily Dickinson's poems, sewn up and hidden in a wombed trunk, away from public hostility or public honor, but later delivered for many eyes to see.

Each letter in *The Color Purple* represents a patch in the quilt that puts the whole of southern life with its sexism, racism, and poverty on display. One distinct pattern in the enormous quilt, painstakingly stitched together, shows the black woman's development from slavery to some form of emancipation from both white and black patriarchy. Walker's positivistic stance emerges as the expression of her yearning: a vision of a union of the male and the female, the black American and the African, brought about through women's faith that is in turn sustained by (letter) writing.

The letter with its surface innocuousness is indeed subversive. As a literary form that pretends to be private while it is made public, it ensures an open inquiry into those matters that affect one's material well-being, one's spiritual disposition, one's destiny, and one's relationship both to other people and to the environment. Letters in black female writing finally ensure illumination of the black predicament that precedes black integrity.

It is notable that some black women writers intersperse their novels with songs, verse, reiterated phrases. These seem to have the communal function of the call-and-response usually employed during African storytelling sessions. They relieve the tedium of a long speech or a long stretch of narration and involve the audience in the spinning of the yarn. They are effective during public readings of novels. The writers sometimes use them to emphasize climactic points in the narration where the emotion is so intense that prose can no longer serve as a suitable vehicle; so Aidoo does in *Our Sister Killjoy* and Morrison in *Song of Solomon*. In Margaret Walker's *Jubilee* as well as in Marshall's *Praisesong for the Widow* the numerous songs, wise sayings, and dances link the principals with black tradition, black suffering, black beliefs, and black religion. Ntozake Shange achieves a similar result by including weaving, culinary and medicinal recipes, and herbal lore in *Sassafrass, Cypress & Indigo*; she demonstrates their voodoo-like, "chemical" effects in the black lives involved.

* * *

The force that binds many black female novels in English together is, thus, womanism. As a woman with her own peculiar burden, knowing that she is deprived of her rights by sexist attitudes in the black domestic domain and by Euro-American patriarchy in the public sphere; as a member of a race that feels powerless and under siege, with little esteem in the world—the black female novelist cannot wholeheartedly join forces with white feminists to fight a battle against patriarchy that, given her understanding and experience, is absurd. So she is a womanist because of her racial and her sexual predicament.

The long-standing tradition of black American women writers has helped to define the black American woman's situation. The works of Pauline Hopkins, Mary Etta Spenser, Jean Fauset, Nella Larsen, Dorothy West, Ann Petry, and Zora Neale Hurston, among many others, have all helped to this end.[30] (It will be a useful line of research to find out if these authors' underlying philosophy is womanism too.) This long line of black foremothers—and also of forefathers—gives the Afro-American female writer an advantage over her African counterpart who was forefathered (in the written tradition) with a vengeance. Nevertheless, the black woman writer in Africa and in the United States has finally emerged as a spokeswoman for black women and the black race by moving away from black male chauvinism and the iconoclastic tendencies of feminism to embrace the relative conservatism of womanism.[31] She consequently ensures larger horizons for herself and her people. Indeed, in helping to liberate the black race through her writing she is aiding the black woman who has been and still is concerned with the ethics of surviving rather than with the aesthetics of living. Womanism with its wholesome, its religious grounding in black togetherness, is her gospel of hope. Morrison expresses its nature when she says of black women, "There is something inside us that makes us different from other people. It is not like men and it is not like white women. We talked earlier about the relationship between my women and the men in their lives. When [the women] sing the blues it is one of those 'somebody is gone' kind of thing but there is never any bitterness."[32]

Notes

1. Ama Ata Aidoo dismisses the assumption that all material dealing with women is necessarily feminist: "I am not a feminist because I write about women. Are men writers male chauvinist pigs just because they write about men? Or is a writer an African nationalist just by writing about Africans? ... Obviously not ... no writer, female or male, is a feminist just by writing about women. Unless a particular writer commits his or her energies, actively, to exposing the sexist tragedy of women's history; protesting the ongoing degradation of women; celebrating their physical and intellectual capabilities, and above all, unfolding a revolutionary vision of the role [of women]," he or she cannot be pronounced a feminist. "Unwelcome Pals and Decorative Slaves—or Glimpses of Women as Writers and Characters in Contemporary African Literature," in *Medium and Message: Proceedings of the International Conference on African Literature and the English Language* (Calabar, Nigeria: University of Calabar, 1981), 1:17–37, esp. 33.
2. Sandra M. Gilbert and Susan Gubar, *The Madwoman in the Attic: The Woman Writer and the Nineteenth-Century Imagination* (New Haven, Conn.: Yale University Press, 1979), pp. 338 ff.
3. David Cecil, *Early Victorian Novelists* (London: Constable & Son, 1935), cf. Jean Rhys, *Wide Sargasso Sea* (New York: W.W. Norton & Co., 1967). In this fictional interpretation of *Jane Eyre*, Rhys presents Mrs. Rochester as a Creole. See also Elaine Showalter, *A Literature of Their Own: British Women Novelists from Brontë to Lessing* (London: Virago Ltd., 1978), p. 124.
4. Kate Millett (*Sexual Politics* [London: Sphere Books, 1972], p. 39) asserts that black men are more ready to stand by their white women than white men are prepared to protect their black women.
5. Compare Myra Jehlen, "Archimedes and the Paradox of Feminist Criticism," *Signs: Journal of Women in Culture and Society* 6, no. 4 (Summer 1981): 575–601, esp. 598.
6. Cheri Register, "Literary Criscticism," *Signs: Journal of Women in Culture and Society* 6, no. 2 (Winter 1980): 268–82, esp. 269.
7. "The Feminist Book Fair," *West Africa* (June 18, 1984). p. 1263. The East African writer Grace Ogot considers other dimensions, such as "economic struggle" and the generation gap; see Oladele Taiwo, *Female Novelists of Modern Africa* (London: Macmillan Publishers, 1984), p. 162.
8. Millett, pp. 38–39. She notes that socially the white female has a "higher status" than the black male who is in turn "higher" than the black female.
9. Ibid., p. 33. Millett inherits some of her phraseology from Simone de Beauvoir (*The Second Sex*, trans. H.M. Parshley [Harmondsworth: Penguin Books, 1972], p. 609); see also Barbara Charlesworth Gelpi, "A Common Language: The American Woman Poet," in *Shakespeare's Sisters: Feminist Essays on Women Poets*, ed. Sandra M. Gilbert and Susan Gubar (Bloomington: Indiana University Press, 1979), pp. 269–79, esp. p. 269; Elaine Showalter, "Feminist Criticism in the Wilderness," in *Writing and Sexual Difference*, ed. Elizabeth Abel (Brighton: Harvester Press, 1982), pp. 9–35, esp. p. 31. Recent feminist writing resembles Afro-American male literature from the Harlem Renaissance to the 1960s.
10. S.E. Ogude, "Slavery and the African Imagination: A Critical Perspective," *World Literature Today* 55, no. 1 (Winter 1981): 21–25, esp. 24.
11. Amiri Baraka, "Afro-American Literature & Class Struggle," *Black American Literature Forum* 14, no. 1 (Spring 1980): 5–14, esp. 12. Baraka treats the black female predicament from an economic, racial, and social viewpoint: "Third World women in this country suffer a triple oppression, if they are working women, as workers under capitalism—class oppression, national oppression and oppression because of their sex."
12. Aidoo (n. 1 above), p. 32.

13. Alice Walker, *The Color Purple* (New York: Washington Square Press, 1983), p. 145.
14. Deborah E. McDowell, "New Directions for Black Feminist Criticism," *Black American Literature Forum* 14, no. 4 (Winter 1980): 153–58, esp. 133.
15. Black American writers operate in a more liberal atmosphere than their African counterparts and so tend to portray lesbian relationships more sympathetically: see, e.g., Walker's *The Color Purple*; Ntozake Shange's *Sassafrass, Cypress & Indigo*; Paule Marshall's *The Chosen Place, the Timeless People* and *Praisesong for the Widow*, where lesbianism is depicted tangentially. An exception to the rule in African literature is Rebeka Njau, *Ripples in the Pool* (London: Heinemann Books, 1975).
16. Sheila Rowbotham, *Women's Consciousness, Man's World* (Harmondsworth: Penguin Books, 1973), p. ix.
17. Ibid., pp. 123–24.
18. Rosemary Radford Ruether, *Sexism and God-Talk: Towards a Feminist Theology* (London: SCM Press, 1983), pp. 229 ff.
19. Alison Perry, "Meeting Flora Nwapa," *West Africa* (June 18, 1984), p. 1262.
20. See Annis Pratt, *Archetypal Patterns in Women's Fiction* (Sussex: Harvester Press, 1982), pp. 51 ff.
21. Stephen E. Henderson, "The Heavy Blues of Sterling Brown: A Study of Craft and Tradition," *Black American Literature Forum* 14, no. 1 (Spring 1980): 32–44, esp. 32.
22. Elaine Showalter has noted the strange phenomenon that strong, successful female writers hardly ever portray successful female characters (*A Literature of Their Own* [n. 3 above], pp. 244 ff). This is a feminist rather than a womanist practice, as the strong female characters cited above easily establish.
23. Karen C. Gasten, "Women in the Lives of Grange Copeland," *CLA Journal* 24, no. 3 (March 1981): 276–86, esp. 286.
24. See Barbara Christian, *Black Women Novelists: The Development of a Tradition, 1892–1976* (Westport, Conn.: Greenwood Press, 1980), p. 239.
25. Toni Morrison, *The Bluest Eye* (New York: Holt, Rinehart & Winston, 1970), p. 163.
26. Maryse Conde, "Three Female Writers in Modern Africa: Flora Nwapa, Ama Ata Aidoo and Grace Ogot," *Présence africaine* 82 (1972): 132–43, esp. 139, 143. Juliet Okonkwo, "The Talented Woman in African Literature," *Africa Quarterly* 15, nos. 1, 2 (1975): 36–47, esp. 45.
27. Compare Gilbert and Gubar, *The Madwoman in the Attic* (n. 2 above), p. 78. If one modifies their observation about the relationship between the female writer and her mad or monstrous characters to suit Nwapa's and Aidoo's conceptual dilemma, one sees that the novelists project "their rebellious impulses" into their heroines but lack the courage to make them succeed, thereby demonstrating the authors' "own self-division, then desire both to accept the strictures of patriarchal society and to reject them," evidence of an early feminism mixed with an unconscious gravitation toward womanism.
28. De Beauvoir (n. 9 above), pp. 470–71.
29. According to Showalter (*A Literature of Their Own* [n. 3 above], p. 17), "Most eighteenth-century epistolary novels were written by women."
30. The first Afro-American novel by a woman is Frances Harper's *Iola Leroy; or, The Shadows Uplifted* (1892). The first African novel by a woman is Flora Nwapa's *Efuru* (1966). The Afro-American woman's scribal tradition is, of course, over two hundred years old, dating back to Phillis Wheatley, though the oral tradition in Africa far predates Wheatley.
31. Aidoo (n. 1 above), p. 33.
32. Bettye J. Parker, "Complexity: Toni Morrison's Women—an Interview Essay," in *Sturdy Black Bridges: Visions of Black Women in Literature*, ed. Roseann P. Bell, Bettye J. Parker, and Beverly Guy-Sheftall (Garden City, N.Y.: Anchor Books, 1979), pp. 251–57, esp. p. 255.

3

Clenora Hudson-Weems's
Africana Womanism

*Cultural and Agenda Conflicts in Academia: Critical
Issues for Africana Women's Studies*[1] *(1989)*

CLENORA HUDSON-WEEMS

> Well, chillun, whar dar is so much racket, dar must be something out o'
> kilter. I t'ink dat 'twixt de niggers of de Souf an' de women at de Norf
> all a-talkin' bout rights, de white men will be in a fix pretty soon. ... Dat
> man ober dar say dat women needs to be helped into carriages, and lifted
> ober ditches, and to have de best place everywhere. Nobody eber helped
> me into carriages, or ober mud puddles, or give me any best place. And
> ain't I a Woman? (Truth, 104)

During her lifetime as a staunch upholder of truth and justice, Sojourner
Truth, born a slave in 1797 and freed under the 1827 New York State Emancipation Act, often unexpectedly appeared at antislavery and women's rights
rallies. Her impromptu remarks often refuted antagonistic arguments against
both her race and her sex, and in that order. Her frequently quoted speech
above, which was both unsolicited and initially unwelcomed because of her
color by the White audience at an 1852 Women's Rights Convention in Akron,
Ohio, is used here to demonstrate the critical position of the Africana woman
within the context of the modern feminist movement.

Historically, Africana women have fought against sexual discrimination
as well as race and class discrimination. They have challenged Africana male
chauvinism, but have stopped short of eliminating Africana men as allies in
the struggle for liberation and family-hood. Historically, Africana women
have wanted to be "liberated" to the community, family, and its responsibilities.
The daily evacuation of males and females from the Africana community in
a nine-to-five society has wreaked havoc on the sense of security of Africana
children. The distress of these Africana children and their need for comforting
seems to have been ignored, overlooked and vastly underplayed, suggesting

that these children do not need this kind of support. The result is generations of hurt and rejection. Even Africana women who happen to be on welfare and may be at home are condemned for not having a job and are, thus, often not regarded as positive figures for these children, even though they at least offer an adult presence. With polarized minds, Africanans have bought into this view, embracing all too frequently the stereotype of the Africana woman on welfare and society's disapproval of them. Nevertheless, Africana women are seeking to reclaim security, stability, and nurturing of a family-based community.

According to Africana sociologist Vivian Gordon in *Black Women, Feminism and Black Liberation: Which Way?*:

> To address women's issues, therefore, is not only to address the crucial needs of Black women, it is also to address the historic primacy of the African and African American community; that is, the primacy of its children and their preparation for the responsibilities and privileges of mature personhood. (viii)

Africana women have historically demonstrated that they are diametrically opposed to the concept of many White feminists who want independence and freedom from family responsibility. In the Statement of Purpose, which was issued by the National Organization of Women (NOW) in 1966 and which is still in effect today, "it is no longer either necessary or possible for women to devote the greater part of their lives to child rearing."[2] Some women take this statement a step further and wish to be liberated not only from their families but from their obligation to men in particular. This sentiment may appeal more to radical lesbian feminists or radical feminist separatists. Many White feminists deny traditional familyhood as an integral part of their personal and professional lives.

All too frequently, Sojourner's resounding query, "And ain't I a woman?" is extrapolated from the text in order to force a feminist identification of the speaker without any initial or even later reference to her first obstacle, which is her race. As mentioned earlier, during Sojourner's speech in 1852, Whites had not even deemed her as human, let alone deem her as a woman, which is precisely why she was mocked before they finally allowed her to speak. One may question what this has to do with the modern feminist movement. The fact is that these racist perceptions have not changed significantly as to suggest that Africana women do not yet have to contend with the same problem of insidious racism, with almost equal intensity even though it is somewhat masked today.

In attempting to unearth the historical truths about the feminist movement that divide the White feminist from Africana women, Africana literary theorist Hazel V. Carby asserts that:

> In order to gain a public voice as orators or published writers, black women had to confront the dominant domestic ideologies and literary

conventions of womanhood which excluded them from the definition "women." (Carby, 6)

Moreover, many White feminists ironically have used Sojourner's quotation to justify labeling this freedom fighter as a feminist or a "pre-feminist." Often, they include their interpretation of the Africana experience when it is convenient—Sojourner's experience becomes a dramatization of female oppression. Ironically, Sojourner was not embracing the Women's Rights movement; instead she was attacking that element of the Women's Rights agenda that excluded her. Instead of establishing a feminist alignment, she was engaging in self-actualization, forcing White women in particular to recognize her and all Africana women as women, and as a definite and legitimate part of society in general. During the abolitionist movement White women learned from Africana women techniques on how to organize, hold public meetings, and conduct petition campaigns. As abolitionists, the White women first learned to speak in public and began to develop a philosophy of their place in society and of their basic rights. Africana women, on the other hand, learned and practiced all these same things centuries ago in their ancestral home of Africa.

Procrusteans have mislabeled Africana women activists, like Sojourner Truth, and other prominent Africana women freedom fighters, such as Harriet Tubman and Ida B. Wells, simply because they were women. Indeed, the primary concerns of these women were not of a feminist nature, but rather a commitment to the centrality of the African-American freedom struggle. Their primary concern was the life-threatening plight of all Africana people, both men and women, at the hands of a racist system. To cast them in a feminist mode, which de-emphasizes their major interest, is an abomination and an outright insult to their level of struggle.

Too many Blacks have taken the theoretical framework of "feminism" and have tried to make it fit their particular circumstance. Rather than create their own paradigm and name and define themselves, some Africana women, scholars in particular, have been persuaded by White feminists to adopt or to adapt to the White concept and terminology of feminism. The real benefit of the amalgamation of Black feminism and White feminism goes to White feminists who can increase their power base by expanding their scope with the convenient consensus that sexism is their commonality and primary concern. They make a gender analysis of Africana-American life with the goal of equating racism with sexism. Politically and ideologically for Africana women, such an adoption is misguided and simplistic. Most Africanans do not share the same ideology as traditional White feminists. True, the two groups may share strategies for ending sexual discrimination, but they are divided on how to change the entire political system to end racial discrimination and sexual exploitation. While the White feminist has not sacrificed her major concern, sexism, the Black feminist has, in that she has yielded to her primary concern for racism, and is forced to see classism as secondary and tertiary issues. The modified terminology, "Black Feminism," is some Africana women's futile attempt to fit into the constructs of an established White female paradigm. At best, Black feminism may relate to sexual discrimination outside of the Africana community, but cannot claim to resolve the critical problems within it, which are influenced by racism and classism. White feminist, Bettina Aptheker, accurately analyzes the problem:

> When we place women at the center of our thinking, we are going about the business of creating an historical and cultural matrix from which women may claim autonomy and independence over their own lives. For women of color, such autonomy cannot be achieved in conditions of racial oppression and cultural genocide. ... In short, "feminist," in the modern sense, means the empowerment of women. For women of color, such an equality, such an empowerment, cannot take place unless the communities in which they live can successfully establish their own racial and cultural integrity. (Aptheker, 13)

For many White women, Africana women exist for their purpose—a dramatization of oppression. As for their identity, they consider themselves the definitive woman and thus there is no need, for example, to name their studies "White" Women's Studies. Moreover, while gender-specific discrimination is the key issue for Women's Studies, it unfortunately narrows the goals of Africana liberation and devalues the quality of Africana life. Gender-specific neither identifies nor defines the primary issue for Africana women or other non-White women. It is crucial that Africana women engage in self-naming and self-definition, lest they fall into the trap of refining a critical ideology at the risk of surrendering the sense of identity.

Africana women might begin by naming and defining their unique movement "*Africana Womanism*."[3] The concept of Womanism can be traced back to Sojourner's speech that began to develop and highlight Africana women's unique experience into a paradigm for Africana women. In refining this terminology into a theoretical framework and methodology, "*Africana Womanism*" identifies the participation and the role of Africana women in the struggle, but does not suggest that female subjugation is the most critical issue they face in their struggle for parity. Like Black feminism, *Africana Womanism* acknowledges societal gender problems as critical issues to be resolved; however, it views feminism, the suggested alternative to these problems, as a sort of inverted White patriarchy, with the White feminist now in command and on top. Mainstream feminism is women's co-opting themselves into mainstream patriarchal values. According to Gordon, "The Movement fails to state clearly that the system is wrong; what it does communicate is that White women want to be a part of the system. They seek power, not change" (47).

The Africana womanist, on the other hand, perceives herself as the companion to the Africana man, and works diligently toward continuing their established union in the struggle against racial oppression. Within the Africana culture, there is an intrinsic, organic equality that has always been necessary for the survival of the Africana culture, in spite of the individual personal problems of female subjugation that penetrated the Africana family structure as a result of the White male cultural system. This issue must be addressed. However, the White male's privilege is not the Africana men's or women's personal problem but rather a political problem of unchallenged gender chauvinism in the world. Critiquing Women's Studies, Aptheker concludes that:

> ... women's studies programs operate within a racist structure. Every department in every predominantly white institution is centered on the experience, history, politics, and culture of white men, usually of the elite. What is significant, however, is that women's studies, by its very reason for existence, implies a reordering of politics, a commitment to community, and an educational purpose, which is inherently subversive of its institutional setting. ... Insofar as women's studies replicates a racial pattern in which white rule predominates, however, it violates its own principles of origin and purpose. More to the point: it makes impossible the creation of a feminist vision and politics. (13)

Africanans have critical and complex problems in their community, most of which stem from racial oppression. The Africana woman acknowledges the problem of classism, a reproachable element in America's capitalistic system. However, even there the plight of the middle-class Africana woman becomes intertwined with racism. Given that both the Africana womanist and the Black feminist address these critical issues and more, there must be something that makes the issues of the Africana womanist different, and that something is prioritizing on the part of the Africana woman. She realizes the critical need to prioritize the antagonistic forces as racism, classism and sexism, respectively. In the final analysis, *Africana Womanism* is connected to the tradition of self-reliance and autonomy, working toward participation in Africana liberation.

Observe the importance of Africana identity in the case of Sojourner Truth, for example. Before one can properly address her much-quoted query, one must, as she did, first consider her color, for it was because of color that Sojourner was initially hissed and jeered at for having the gall to address the conflict between men and women and the rights of the latter. Before Sojourner could hope to address gender problems, she had to first overcome discrimination from her White audience. Clearly, gender was not her primary concern. By reiterating "And ain't I a Woman," Sojourner insisted that she, too, possessed all the traits of a woman, notwithstanding her race and class, that the dominant culture used to exclude her from that community. The key issue for the Africana woman, as well as for the Africana man, is racism, with classism intertwined therein.

While women of all ethnic orientations share the unfortunate commonality of female subjugation, it is naive, to say the least, to suggest that this kind of oppression should be the primary concern of all women, particularly women of color. When the Black feminist buys the White terminology, she also buys its agenda. Because Africana women share other forms of oppression that are not necessarily a part of the overall White women's experiences, their varied kinds of victimization need to be prioritized. Instead of alienating the Africana male sector from the struggle today, Africanans must call for a renegotiation of Africanan male–female roles in society. In so doing, there must be a call to halt once and for all female subjugation, while continuing the critical struggle for the liberation of Africana people worldwide.

As previously stated, the notion of Africana women moving "from margin to center"[4] of the feminist movement, as proposed by bell hooks is ludicrous. For how can any woman hope to move from the peripheral to the center of a movement that, historically, has not included her on the agenda? Even during the resurgence of the Women's Liberation Movement of the mid-1960s the critical concerns of the Africana woman were not part of the agenda. Be that as it may, hooks complains that contemporary Africana women do not join together for women's rights because they do not see womanhood as an important aspect of their identity. Further, she states that racist and sexist socialization have conditioned Africana women to devalue their femaleness and to regard race as their only relevant label of identity. In short, she surmises that Africana women have been asked to deny a part of themselves and they have. Clearly this position evokes some controversy, as it does not take into account the reasons for the Africana woman's reluctance to embrace feminism.

Consider the experience of a woman who said that from so many feet away, her race was noticed; as she got into closer proximity, her class was detected; but that it was not until she got in the door that her sex was known. Does not that suggest the need for prioritizing? The prioritizing of the kinds of relegation to which the Africana woman is subjected should be explored in a serious effort to recognize and to understand the existence of her total sense of oppression. What one really wants to do is appreciate the triple plight of Africana women. Society needs to deal with all aspects of the oppression of the Africana woman in order to better combat them. Race and class biases are the key issues for non-Whites and must be resolved even before gender issues if there is any hope for human survival. It is impossible to conceive of any human being succumbing to absolute regression without an outright struggle against it.

Sojourner Truth demonstrated early on in the Women's Rights Movement that a commonality exists between the Africana men and women of the South and the women of the North in their struggle for freedom. Clearly, the Africana woman had, neither then nor now, no exclusive claim on the struggle for equal rights apart from her male counterpart. Africana men and Africana women are and should be allies, struggling as they have since the days of slavery for equal social, economic, and political rights as fellow human beings in the world. There is an inherent contradiction in the ideology of "Black Feminism" that should be reevaluated. A more compatible concept is "*Africana Womanism*." Indeed, this issue must be properly addressed if Women's Studies is to be truly respected and if a positive agenda for Africana Women's Studies is to be truly realized.

Notes

1. This chapter is reprinted with permission from *The Western Journal of Black Studies*, which first appeared in the Winter 1989 issue.
2. NOW Statement of Purpose (Adopted at the organizing conference in Washington, DC, October 29, 1966).
3. The author introduced the "*Africana Womanism*" concept at the National Council for Black Studies Conference, March 1988.
4. See bell hooks' *Feminist Theory: From Margin to Center*.

Africana Womanism (1993)

CLENORA HUDSON-WEEMS

Black Feminism, African Feminism, Womanism ...

> Feminism. You know how we feel about that embarrassing Western philosophy? The destroyer of homes. Imported mainly from America to ruin nice African women. (Ama Ata Aidoo, 1986)

Central to the spirit of Africanans (Continental Africans and Africans in the diaspora) regarding feminism in the Africana community is the above quotation by internationally acclaimed African novelist and critic, Ama Ata Aidoo. One of today's most controversial issues in both the academy and the broader community is the role of the Africana woman within the context of the modern feminist movement. Both men and women are debating this issue, particularly as it relates to Africana women in their efforts to remain authentic in their existence, such as prioritizing their needs even if the needs are not of primary concern for the dominant culture. The ever-present question remains the same: what is the relationship between an Africana woman and her family, her community, and her career in today's society that emphasizes, in the midst of oppression, human suffering, and death, the empowerment of women and individualism over human dignity and rights?

While many academics uncritically adopt feminism, the established theoretical concept based on the notion that gender is primary in women's struggle in the patriarchal system, most Africana women in general do not identify with the concept in its entirety and thus cannot see themselves as feminists.[1] Granted, the prioritizing of female empowerment and gender issues may be justifiable for those women who have not been plagued by powerlessness based on ethnic differences; however, that is certainly not the case for those who have—Africana women. For those Africana women who do adopt some form of feminism, they do so because of feminism's theoretical and methodological legitimacy in the academy and their desire to be a legitimate part of the academic community. Moreover, they adopt feminism because of the absence of a suitable framework for their individual needs as Africana women. But while some have accepted the label, more and more Africana women today in the academy and in the community are reassessing the historical realities and the agenda for the modern feminist movement. These women are concluding that feminist terminology does not accurately reflect their reality or their struggle.[1] Hence, feminism, and more specifically, Black feminism, which relates to African-American women in particular, is extremely problematic as labels for the true Africana woman and invites much debate and controversy among today's scholars and women in general.

It should be noted here that there is another form of feminism that is closely identified with Africana women around the world. While African feminism is a bit less problematic for Africana women than is feminism in general, it is more closely akin to *Africana womanism*. According to African literary critic Rose Acholonu in a paper she presented in July 1992 at the International Conference on Africana women in Nigeria:

> The negative hues of the American and European radical feminism have succeeded in alienating even the fair-minded Africans from the concept. The sad result is that today [the] majority of Africans (including successful female writers), tend to disassociate themselves from it.[2]

Hence, in spite of the accuracy of Filomina Chioma Steady in *The Black Woman Cross-Culturally* in her astute assessment of the struggle and reality of Africana women, the name itself, African feminism, is problematic, as it naturally suggests an alignment with feminism, a concept that has been alien to the plight of Africana women from its inception. This is particularly the case in reference to racism and classism, which are prevailing obstacles in the lives of Africana people, a reality that the theorist herself recognizes. According to Steady:

> Regardless of one's position, the implications of the feminist movement for the black woman are complex. ... Several factors set the black woman apart as having a different order of priorities. She is oppressed not simply because of her sex but ostensibly because of her race and, for the majority, essentially because of their class. Women belong to different socio-economic groups and do not represent a universal category. Because the majority of black women are poor, there is likely to be some alienation from the middle-class aspect of the women's movement which perceives feminism as an attack on men rather than on a system which thrives on inequality. (23–24)

In "African Feminism: A Worldwide Perspective," from *Women in Africa and the African Diaspora*, Steady asserts that

> For the majority of black women poverty is a way of life. For the majority of black women also racism has been the most important obstacle in the acquisition of the basic needs for survival. Through the manipulation of racism the world economic institutions have produced a situation which negatively affects black people, particularly black women. ... What we have, then, is not a simple issue of sex or class differences but a situation which, because of the racial factor, is castelike in character on both a national and global scale. (18–19)

It becomes apparent, then, that neither the terms Black feminism nor African feminism are sufficient to label women of such complex realities as Africana women, particularly as both terms, through their very names, align themselves with feminism.

Why not feminism for Africana women? To begin with, the true history of feminism, its origins and its participants, reveals its blatant racist background, thereby establishing its incompatibility with Africana women. Feminism, earlier called the Woman's Suffrage Movement, started when a group of liberal White women, whose concerns then were for the abolition of slavery and equal rights for all people regardless of race, class and sex, dominated the scene among women on the national level during the early to mid-nineteenth century. At the time of the Civil War, such leaders as Susan B. Anthony and Elizabeth Cady Stanton held the universalist philosophy on the natural rights of women to full citizenship, which included the right to vote. However, in 1870 the Fifteenth Amendment to the Constitution of the United States ratified the voting rights of Africana men, leaving women, White women in particular, and their desire for the same rights, unaddressed. Middle-class White women were naturally disappointed, for they had assumed that their efforts toward securing full citizenship for Africana people would ultimately benefit them, too, in their desire for full citizenship as voting citizens. The result was a racist reaction to the Amendment and Africanans in particular. Thus, from the 1880s on, an organized movement among White women shifted the pendulum to a radically conservative posture on the part of White women in general.

In 1890 the National American Woman Suffrage Association (NAWSA) was founded by northern White women, but "southern women were also vigorously courted by that group" (Giddings, 81), epitomizing the growing race chauvinism of the late nineteenth century. The organization, which brought together the National Woman Suffrage Association and the American Woman Suffrage Association, departed from Susan B. Anthony's original women's suffrage posture. They asserted that the vote for women should be utilized chiefly by middle-class White women, who could aid their husbands in preserving the virtues of the Republic from the threat of unqualified and biological inferiors (Africana men) who, with the power of the vote, could gain a political foothold in the American system. For example, staunch conservative suffragist leader Carrie Chapman Catt and other women of her persuasion insisted upon strong Anglo Saxon values and White supremacy. They were interested in banding with White men to secure the vote for pure Whites, excluding not only Africanans but White immigrants as well. Historians Peter Carrol and David Noble quoted Catt in *The Free and the Unfree* as saying that "there is but one way to avert the danger. Cut off the vote of the slums and give it to [White] women." She continued that the middle class White men must recognize "the usefulness of woman suffrage as a counterbalance to the foreign vote, and as a means of legally preserving White supremacy in the South" (296). These suffragists felt that because Africana people, Africana men in particular with their new status as voters, were members of an inferior race, they should not be granted the right to vote before them, which did not come until much later with the August 1920 Nineteenth Amendment. Thus, while the disappointment of being left out in the area of gaining full citizenship, i.e., voting rights, for White women was well founded, their hostility and racist antagonistic feelings toward Africanans in general cannot be dismissed lightly.

Feminism, a term conceptualized and adopted by White women, involves an agenda that was designed to meet the needs and demands of that particular group. For this reason, it is quite plausible for White women to identify with feminism and the feminist movement. Having said that, the fact remains that placing all women's history under White women's history, thereby giving the latter the definitive position, is problematic. In fact, it demonstrates the ultimate of racist arrogance and domination, suggesting that authentic activity of women resides with White women. Hence, in this respect for White women, Africana women activists in America in particular, such as Sojourner Truth (militant abolition spokesperson and universal suffragist), Harriet Tubman (Underground Railroad conductor who spent her lifetime aiding Africana slaves, both males and females, in their escape to the North for freedom), and Ida B. Wells (anti-lynching crusader during the early twentieth century), were prefeminists, in spite of the fact that the activities of these Africana women did not focus necessarily on women's issues. Considering activities of early Africana women such as those mentioned above and countless other unsung Africana heroines, what White feminists have done in reality was to take the lifestyle and techniques of Africana women activists and used them as models or blueprints for the framework of their theory, and then name, define, and legitimize it as the only real substantive movement for women. Hence, when they define a feminist and feminist activity, they are, in fact, identifying with independent Africana women, women they both emulated and envied. Such women they have come in contact with from the beginning of American slavery, all the way up to the modern Civil Rights Movement with such Africana women activists as Mamie Till Mobley, the mother of Emmett Louis Till,[3] and Rosa Parks, the mother of the Modern Civil Rights Movement—and the aftermath. Therefore, when Africana women come along and embrace feminism, appending it to their identity as Black feminists or African feminists, they are in reality duplicating the duplicate.

Africana Womanism is a term I coined and defined in 1987 after nearly two years of publicly debating the importance of self-naming for Africana women. Why the term "*Africana Womanism*"? Upon concluding that the term "Black Womanism" was not quite the terminology to include the total meaning desired for this concept, I decided that "*Africana Womanism*," a natural evolution in naming, was the ideal terminology for two basic reasons. The first part of the coinage, *Africana*, identifies the ethnicity of the woman being considered, and this reference to her ethnicity, establishing her cultural identity, relates directly to her ancestry and land base—Africa. The second part of the term, *Womanism,* recalls Sojourner Truth's powerful impromptu speech "And Ain't I [a] Woman," one in which she battles with the dominant alienating forces in her life as a struggling Africana woman, questioning the accepted idea of womanhood. Without question, she is the flip side of the coin, the co-partner in the struggle for her people, one who, unlike the White woman, has received no special privileges in American society. But there is another crucial issue that accounts for the use of the term woman(ism). The term "woman," and by extension "womanism," is far more appropriate than "female" ("feminism") because of one major distinction—only a female of the human race can be a woman. "Female," on the other hand, can refer to a member of the animal or plant kingdom as well as to a member of the human race. Furthermore, in electronic and mechanical terminology, there is a female counterbalance to the male correlative. Hence, terminology derived from the word "woman" is more suitable and more specific when naming a group of the human race.

The Africana womanist is not to be confused with Alice Walker's "womanist" as presented in her collection of essays entitled *In Search of Our Mothers' Gardens.* According to Walker, a womanist is:

> A black feminist or feminist of color ... who loves other women, sexually and/or nonsexually. Appreciates and prefers women's culture ... [and who] sometimes loves individual men, sexually and/or nonsexually. Committed to survival and wholeness of entire people, male and female. ... Womanist is to feminist as purple to lavender. (xi, xii)

Clearly the interest here is almost exclusively in the woman, her sexuality and her culture. The culminating definition, "womanist is to feminist as purple to lavender," firmly establishes the author's concept of the affinity between the womanist and the feminist. There is hardly any differentiation, only a slight shade of difference in color. The Africana womanist, on the other hand, is significantly different from the mainstream feminist, particularly in her perspective on and approach to issues in society. This is to be expected, for obviously their historical realities and present stance in society are not the same. Africana women and White women come from different segments of society and, thus, feminism as an ideology is not equally applicable to both.

Neither an outgrowth nor an addendum to feminism, *Africana Womanism* is not Black feminism, African feminism, or Walker's womanism that some Africana women have come to embrace. *Africana Womanism* is an ideology created and designed for all women of African descent. It is grounded in African culture, and therefore, it necessarily focuses on the unique experiences, struggles, needs, and desires of Africana women. It critically addresses the dynamics of the conflict between the mainstream feminist, the Black feminist, the African feminist, and the Africana womanist. The conclusion is that *Africana Womanism* and its agenda are unique and separate from both White feminism and Black feminism, and moreover, to the extent of naming in particular, *Africana Womanism* differs from African feminism.

Clearly there is a need for a separate and distinct identity for the Africana woman and her movement. Some White women acknowledge that the feminist movement was not designed with the Africana woman in mind. For example, White feminist Catherine Clinton asserts that "feminism primarily appealed to educated and middle-class White women, rather than Black and White working-class women" ("Women Break New Ground," 63). Steady, in her article entitled "African Feminism: A Worldwide Perspective," which appears in *Women in Africa and the African Diaspora,* admits that:

> Various schools of thought, perspectives, and ideological proclivities have influenced the study of feminism. Few studies have dealt with the issue of racism, since the dominant voice of the feminist movement has been that of the white female. The issue of racism can become threatening, for it identifies white feminists as possible participants in the oppression of blacks. (3)

Africana men and women do not accept the idea of Africana women as feminists. There is a general consensus in the Africana community that the feminist movement, by and large, is the White woman's movement for two reasons. First, the Africana woman does not see the man as her primary enemy as does the White feminist, who is carrying out an age-old battle with her White male counterpart for subjugating her as his property. Africana men have never had the same institutionalized power to oppress Africana women as White men have had to oppress White women. According to Africana sociologist Clyde Franklin II:

> Black men are relatively powerless in this country, and their attempts at domination, aggression, and the like, while sacrificing humanity, are ludicrous. (112)

Joyce Ladner, another Africana sociologist, succinctly articulates the dynamics of the relationship between Africana men and women and does not view the former as the enemy of the latter in *Tomorrow's Tomorrow:*

> Black women do not perceive their enemy to be black men, but rather the enemy is considered to be oppressive forces in the larger society which subjugate black men, women and children. (277–78)

Since Africana women never have been considered the property of their male counterpart, Africana women and men dismiss the primacy of gender issues in their reality, and thus dismiss the feminist movement as a viable framework for their chief concerns. Instead, they hold to the opinion that those Africana women who embrace the feminist movement are mere assimilationists or sellouts who, in the final analysis, have no true commitment to their culture or their people, particularly as it relates to the historical and current collective struggle of Africana men and women.

Second, Africana women reject the feminist movement because of their apprehension and distrust of White organizations. In fact, White organized groups in general, such as the Communist Party and the National Organization for Women (N.O.W.), have never been able to galvanize the majority of Africana people. On the whole, Africanans are grassroots people who depend on the support and confidence of their communities and who, based on historical instances of betrayal, are necessarily suspicious of organizations founded, operated, and controlled by Whites. In general, unlike members of the dominant culture, Africanans are not issue-oriented. Instead they focus on tangible things that can offer an amelioration of or exit from oppression, which are of utmost importance for survival in the Africana community. Those Africana intellectuals who insist on identifying with organizations that offer them neither leadership nor high visibility generally subordinate their Blackness to being accepted by White intellectuals. Unfortunately for those Africana intellectuals, philosophy and scholarship surpass even self-identity, and they seem to be sufficiently appeased by merely belonging to a White group.

Having established that the major problem with the African feminist is that of naming, what is the major problem with the Black feminist? Briefly stated, the Black feminist is an Africana woman who has adopted the agenda of the feminist movement to some degree in that she, like the White feminist, perceives gender issues to be most critical in her quest for empowerment and selfhood. On the outskirts of feminist activity, Black feminists possess neither power nor leadership in the movement. Black feminist bell hooks obviously realizes this, as she makes a call for Africana women to move "from margin to center" of the feminist movement in her book entitled *Feminist Theory: From Margin to Center*. Receiving recognition as heralds of feminism by way of legitimating the movement through their identification with it, Black feminists are frequently delegated by White feminists as the voice of Africana women. However, this peripheral promotion of Black feminists is only transient, as they could never reach the same level of importance as that of White feminists. It is quite obvious, for example, that bell hooks will never be elevated to the same status as either Betty Friedan or Gloria Steinem. At best, she and other Black feminists like her are given only temporary recognition as representatives and spokespersons for Africana people in general and Africana women in particular. Black feminists advance an agenda that is in direct contravention to that in the Africana community, thereby demonstrating a certain lack of African-centered historical and contemporary perspective. Although White feminists contend that the movement is a panacea for the problems of Africana women, they have been unsuccessful in galvanizing the majority of Africana women as feminists. In fact, there is no existing group of White women controlling the majority of Africana women to the extent of directing and dictating the latter's thought and action.

While Africana women do, in fact, have some legitimate concerns regarding Africana men, these concerns must be addressed within the context of African culture. Problems must not be resolved using an alien framework, i.e., feminism, but must be resolved from within an endemic theoretical construct—*Africana Womanism*. It appears that many Africana women who become Black feminists (or who are inclined more in that direction) base their decisions upon either naiveté about the history and ramifications of feminism or on negative experiences with Africana men. For example, because there are some Africana women who pride themselves on being economically independent—which was the way of life for Africana women long before the advent of feminism—and because one of the chief tenets of feminism in the larger society is that a woman is economically independent, many Africana women unthinkingly respond positively to the notion of being a feminist. To be sure, Africana women have always been, by necessity, independent and responsible co-workers and decision-makers. But while this naiveté can be easily corrected, negative personal experiences cannot be rectified so readily.

True, one's personal experiences are valid ways of determining one's world view; however, the resulting generalization that many Black feminists share—that all or most Africana men are less worthy than women—is based upon intellectual laziness, which requires effortless rationalization. By the same analysis, it is easy for some people to believe that all White people or all people of any race or sex are a certain way, and it is difficult for them to treat people as individuals. This is important because in reality, relationships are based upon individual particularities rather than upon an overriding group characteristic. For example, an Africana brother having a bad experience with an Africana woman might conclude that all Africana women are undesirable, thus castigating this entire group of people. A classic example of gross exaggeration based not on facts but on polemics or limited personal experiences, is Michele Wallace's book entitled *Black Macho and the Myth of the Superwoman* (1980). In this book, the author makes a serious attack on Africana men by categorizing them as super macho men who physically and mentally abuse Africana women. It is apparent that the author's personal negative experiences with Africana men, which she relates throughout the book, influenced her ideology. The tragedy is that her book, which was encouraged in different ways by the many feminists listed in the Acknowledgments, received such wide exposure that it consequently influenced the thoughts of an entire generation, thereby representing a watershed in the development of modern Black feminist thought.

If one considers the collective plight of Africana people globally, it becomes clear that we cannot afford the luxury, if you will, of being consumed by gender issues. A supreme paradigm of the need for Africana women to prioritize the struggle for human dignity and parity is presented by South African woman activist Ruth Mompati. In her heart-rending stories of unimaginable racial atrocities heaped upon innocent children, as well as upon men and women, Mompati asserts the following:

> The South African woman, faced with the above situation, finds the order of her priorities in her struggle for human dignity and her rights as a woman dictated by the general political struggle of her people as a whole. The national liberation of the black South African is a prerequisite to her own liberation and emancipation as a woman and a worker. The process of struggle for national liberation has been accompanied by the politicizing of both men and women. This has kept the women's struggle from degenerating into a sexist struggle that would divorce women's position in society from the political, social, and economic development of the society as a whole.
>
> From the South African women who together with their men seek to liberate their country, come an appeal to friends and supporters to raise their voices on their behalf. (In Daphne Williams Ntiri's *One [I]s Not a Woman, One Becomes,* 112–13)

Overall, "human discrimination transcends sex discrimination … the costs of human suffering are high when compared to a component, sex obstacle" (Ntiri, 6). Furthermore, according to Steady in *The Black Woman Cross-Culturally:*

> for the black woman in a racist society, racial factors, rather than sexual ones, operate more consistently in making her a target for discrimination and marginalization. This becomes apparent when the "family" is viewed as a unit of analysis. Regardless of differential access to resources by both men and women, white males and females, as members of family groups, share a proportionately higher quantity of the earth's resources than do black males and females. There is a great difference between discrimination by privilege and protection, and discrimination by deprivation and exclusion. (27–28)

Steady's assessment here speaks directly to the source of discrimination that Africana women suffer at the hands of a racist system. There is the oppression of the South African woman who must serve as maid and nurse to the White household with minimum wage earnings, the Caribbean woman in London who is the ignored secretary, and the Senegalese or African worker in France who is despised and unwanted. There is the Nigerian subsistence farmer, such as the Ibo woman in Enugu and Nsukka, who farms every day for minimum wages, and the female Brazilian factory worker who is the lowest on the totem pole. Clearly, the problems of these women are not inflicted upon them solely because they are women. They are victimized first and foremost because they are Black; they are further victimized because they are women living in a male-dominated society.

The problems of Africana women, including physical brutality, sexual harassment, and female subjugation in general perpetrated both within and outside the race, ultimately have to be solved on a collective basis within Africana communities. Africana people must eliminate racist influences in their lives first, with the realization that they can neither afford nor tolerate any form of female subjugation. Along those same lines, Ntiri summarizes Mompati's position that sexism "is basically a secondary problem which arises out of race, class and economic prejudices" (5).

Because one of the main tensions between Africana men and women in the United States involves employment and economic opportunity, Africanans frequently fall into a short sighted-perception of things. For example, it is not a question of more jobs for Africana women versus more jobs for Africana men, a situation that too frequently promotes gender competition. Rather, it is a question of more jobs for Africanans in general. These jobs are generated primarily by White people, and most Africanans depend on sources other than those supplied by Africana people. The real challenge for Africana men and women is how to create more economic opportunities within Africana communities. Many people talk about the need for enhanced Africana economic empowerment. If our real goal in life is to be achieved—that is, the survival of our entire race as a primary concern for Africana women—it will have to come from Africana men and women working together. If Africana men and women are fighting within the community, they are ultimately defeating themselves on all fronts.

Perhaps because of all the indisputable problems and turmoil heaped upon the Africana community, much of which is racially grounded, Africanans frequently fail to look closely at available options to determine if those options are, in fact, sufficiently workable. Rather than create other options for themselves, Africanans become confluent with White privileged-class phenomenon, as in the case of feminism. On the other hand, when a group takes control over its struggle, tailoring it to meet its collective needs and demands, the group is almost always successful. When success in one's goals is realized, it makes for a more peaceful reality for all concerned, and one is more inclined to a wholesome and amicable relationship with others, knowing that the concerns of the people are respected and met. As *Africana Womanism*—rather than feminism, Black feminism, African feminism, or womanism—is a conceivable alternative for the Africana woman in her collective struggle with the entire community, it enhances future possibilities for the dignity of Africana people and the humanity of all. In short, the reclamation of Africana women via identifying our own collective struggle and acting upon it is a key step toward human harmony and survival.

Notes

1. For many reasons, many White women as well as African women have become disenchanted with feminism.
2. Rose Acholonu presented a paper entitled "Love and the Feminist Utopia in the African Novel" at the International Conference on Women in Africa and the African Diaspora: Bridges Across Activism and the Academy at the University of Nigeria-Nsukka, July 1992.
3. Emmett Louis "Bobo" Till was the 14-year-old Africana Chicago youth who was lynched in 1955 in Money, Mississippi for whistling at a 21-year-old White woman. For a detailed explanation of Till's importance to the Modern Civil Rights Movement, read Clenora Hudson's (Hudson-Weems') 1988 doctoral dissertation entitled *Emmett Till: The Impetus for the Modern Civil Rights Movement* and *Emmett Till: The Sacrificial Lamb of the Civil Rights Movement*.

Part 2
Womanist Kinfolk: Sisters, Brothers, Daughters, and Sons on Womanism

4

Sisters and Brothers: Black Feminists on Womanism

What's in a Name? Womanism, Black Feminism, and Beyond (1996)

PATRICIA HILL COLLINS

Black women are at a decision point that in many ways mirrors that faced by African Americans as a collectivity. Building on the path breaking works by Toni Cade Bambara, Ntozake Shange, Angela Davis, Toni Morrison, June Jordan, Alice Walker, Audre Lorde and other black women who "broke silence" in the 1970s, African American women in the 1980s and 1990s developed a "voice," a self-defined, collective black women's standpoint about black womanhood (Collins 1990). Moreover, black women used this standpoint to "talk back" concerning black women's representation in dominant discourses (hooks 1989). As a result of this struggle, African American women's ideas and experiences have achieved a visibility unthinkable in the past.

But African American women now stand at a different historical moment. Black women appear to have a voice, and with this new-found voice comes a new series of concerns. For example, we must be attentive to the seductive absorption of black women's voices in classrooms of higher education where black women's texts are still much more welcomed than black women ourselves. Giving the illusion of change, this strategy of symbolic inclusion masks how the everyday institutional policies and arrangements that suppress and exclude African Americans as a collectivity remain virtually untouched (Carby 1992; DuCille 1994). Similarly, capitalist market relations that transformed black women's writing into a hot commodity threaten to strip their works of their critical edge. Initially, entering public space via books, movies, and print media proved invigorating. But in increasingly competitive global markets where anything that sells will be sold regardless of the consequences, black women's "voices" now flood the market. Like other commodities exchanged in capitalist markets, surplus cheapens value, and the fad of today becomes the nostalgic memory of tomorrow.

While a public voice initially proved dangerous, black women's coming to voice ironically fostered the emergence of a new challenge. The new public safe space provided by black women's success allowed longstanding differences among black women structured along axes of sexuality, social class, nationality, religion, and region to emerge. At this point, whether African American women can fashion a singular "voice" about the black *woman's* position remains less an issue than how black women's voices collectively construct, affirm, and maintain a dynamic black *women's* self-defined standpoint. Given the increasingly troublesome political context affecting black women as a group (Massey and Denton 1993; Squires 1994), such solidarity is essential. Thus, ensuring group unity while recognizing the tremendous heterogeneity that operates within the boundaries of the term "black women" comprises one fundamental challenge now confronting African American women.

Current debates about whether black women's standpoint should be named "womanism" or "black feminism" reflect this basic challenge of accommodating diversity among black women. In her acclaimed volume of essays, *In Search of Our Mothers' Gardens*, Alice Walker (1983) introduced four meanings of the term "womanist." According to Walker's first definition, a "womanist" was "a black feminist or feminist of color" (xi). Thus, on some basic level, Walker herself uses the two terms as being virtually interchangeable. Like Walker, many African American women see little difference between the two since both support a common agenda of black women's self-definition and self-determination. As Barbara Omolade points out, "black feminism is sometimes referred to as womanism because both are concerned with struggles against sexism and racism by black women who are themselves part of the black community's efforts to achieve equity and liberty" (Omolade 1994, xx).

But despite similar beliefs expressed by African American women who define themselves as black feminists, as womanists, as both, or, in some cases, as neither, increasing attention seems devoted to delineating the differences, if any between groups naming themselves as "womanists" or "black feminists." The *name* given to black women's collective standpoint seems to matter, but why?

In this paper, I explore some of the theoretical implications of using the terms "womanism" and "black feminism" to name a black women's standpoint. My purpose is not to classify either the works of black women or African American women themselves into one category or the other. Rather, I aim to examine how the effort to categorize obscures more basic challenges that confront African American women as a group.

Womanism

Alice Walker's multiple definitions of the term "womanism" in *In Search of Our Mothers' Gardens*, shed light on the issue of why many African American women prefer the term womanism to black feminism. Walker offers two contradictory meanings of "womanism." On the one hand, Walker clearly sees womanism as rooted in black women's concrete history in racial and gender oppression. Taking the term from the Southern black folk expression of mothers to female children "you acting womanish," Walker suggests that black women's concrete history fosters a womanist worldview accessible primarily and perhaps exclusively to black women. "Womanish" girls acted in outrageous, courageous, and willful ways, attributes that freed them from the conventions long limiting white women. Womanish girls wanted to know more and in greater depth than what was considered good for them. They were responsible, in charge, and serious.

Despite her disclaimer that womanists are "traditionally universalist," a philosophy invoked by her metaphor of the garden where room exists for all flowers to bloom equally and differently, Walker simultaneously implies that black women are somehow superior to white women because of this black folk tradition. Defining womanish as the opposite of the "frivolous, irresponsible, not serious" girlish, Walker constructs black women's experiences in opposition to those of white women. This meaning of womanism sees it as being different from and superior to feminism, a difference allegedly stemming from black and white women's different histories with American racism. Walker's much cited phrase, "Womanist is to feminist as purple to lavender" (1983, xii) clearly seems designed to set up this type of comparison—black women are "womanist" while white women remain merely "feminist."

This usage sits squarely in black nationalist traditions premised on the belief that blacks and whites cannot function as equals while inhabiting the same territory or participating in the same social institutions (Pinkney 1976; Van Deburg 1992). Since black nationalist philosophy posits that white people as a group have a vested interest in continuing a system of white supremacy, it typically sees little use for black integration or assimilation into a system predicated on black subjugation. Black nationalist approaches also support a black moral superiority over whites because of black suffering.

Walker's use of the term womanism promises black women who both operate within these black nationalist assumptions and who simultaneously see the need to address "feminist" issues within African American communities partial reconciliation of these two seemingly incompatible philosophies. Womanism offers a distance from the "enemy," in this case, whites generally and white women in particular, yet still raises the issue of gender. Due to its endorsement of racial separatism, this interpretation of womanism offers a vocabulary for addressing gender issues within African American communities without challenging the racially segregated terrain that characterizes American social institutions.

This use of womanism sidesteps an issue central to many white feminists, namely, finding ways to foster interracial cooperation among women. African American women embracing black nationalist philosophies typically express little interest in working with white women—in fact, white women are defined as part of the problem. Moreover, womanism appears to provide an avenue to foster stronger relationships between black women and black men, another very important issue for African American women regardless of political perspective. Again, Walker's definition provides guidance where she notes that womanists are "committed to survival and wholeness of entire people, male *and* female" (xi). Many black women view feminism as a movement that at best, is exclusively for women and, at worst, dedicated to attacking or eliminating men. Sherley Williams takes this view when she notes that in contrast to feminism, "womanist inquiry ... assumes that it can talk both effectively and productively about men" (1990, 70). Womanism seemingly supplies a way for black women to address gender oppression without attacking black men.

Walker also presents a visionary meaning for womanism. As part of her second definition, Walker has a black girl pose the question "Mama, why are we brown, pink, and yellow, and our cousins are white, beige, and black?" (xi). The response of "the colored race is just like a flower garden, with every color flower represented," both criticizes colorism within African American communities and broadens the notion of humanity to make all people people of color. Reading this passage as a metaphor, womanism thus furnishes a vision where the women and men of different colors coexist like flowers in a garden yet retain their cultural distinctiveness and integrity.

This meaning of womanism seems rooted in another major political tradition within African American politics, namely, a pluralist version of black empowerment (Van Deburg 1992). Pluralism views society as being composed of various ethnic and interest groups, all of whom compete for goods and services. Equity lies in providing equal opportunities, rights, and respect to all groups. By retaining black cultural distinctiveness and integrity, pluralism offers a modified version of racial integration premised not on individual assimilation but on *group* integration. Clearly rejecting what they perceive as being the limited vision of feminism projected by North American white women, many black women theorists have been attracted to this joining of pluralism and racial integration in this interpretation of Walker's "womanism." For example, black feminist theologian Katie Geneva Cannon's (1988) work *Black Womanist Ethics* invokes this sense of the visionary content of womanism. As an ethical system, womanism is always in the making—it is not a closed fixed system of ideas but one that continually evolves through its rejection of all forms of oppression and commitment to social justice.

Walker's definition thus manages to invoke three important yet contradictory philosophies that frame black social and political thought, namely, black nationalism via her claims of black women's moral and epistemological superiority via suffering under racial and gender oppression, pluralism via the cultural integrity provided by the metaphor of the garden, and integration/assimilation via her claims that black women are "traditionally universalist" (Van Deburg 1992). Just as black nationalism and racial integration coexist in uneasy partnership, with pluralism occupying the contested terrain between the two, Walker's definitions of womanism demonstrate comparable contradictions. By both grounding womanism in the concrete experiences of African American women and generalizing about the potential for realizing a humanist vision of community via the experiences of African American women, Walker depicts the potential for oppressed people to possess a moral vision and standpoint on society that grows from their situation of oppression. This standpoint also emerges as an incipient foundation for a more humanistic, just society. Overall, these uses of Walker's term "womanism" creates conceptual space that reflects bona fide philosophical differences that exist among African American women.[1]

One particularly significant feature of black women's use of womanism concerns the part of Walker's definition that remains neglected. A more troublesome line for those self-defining as womanist precedes the often cited passage, "committed to survival and wholeness of entire people, male *and* female" (xi). Just before Walker offers the admonition that womanists, by definition, are committed to wholeness, she states that a womanist is also "a woman who loves other women, sexually and/or nonsexually" (xi). The relative silence of womanists on this dimension of womanism speaks to black women's continued ambivalence in dealing with the links between race, gender and sexuality, in this case, the "taboo" sexuality of lesbianism. In her essay "The Truth That Never Hurts: Black Lesbians in Fiction in the 1980s," black feminist critic Barbara Smith (1990) points out that African American women have yet to come to terms with homophobia in African American communities. Smith applauds the growth of black women's fiction in the 1980s, but also observes that within black feminist intellectual production, black lesbians continue to be ignored. Despite the fact that some of the most prominent and powerful black women thinkers claimed by both womanists and black feminists were and are lesbians, this precept often remains unacknowledged in the work of African American writers. In the same way that many people read the Bible, carefully selecting the parts that agree with their worldview and rejecting the rest, selective readings of Walker's womanism produce comparable results.

Another significant feature of black women's multiple uses of womanism concerns the potential for a slippage between the real and the ideal. To me, there is a distinction between describing black women's historical responses to racial and gender oppression as being womanist, and using womanism as a visionary term delineating an ethical or ideal vision of humanity for all people. Identifying the liberatory *potential* within black women's communities that emerges from concrete, historical experiences remains quite different from claiming that black women have already *arrived* at this ideal, "womanist" endpoint. Refusing to distinguish carefully between these two meanings of womanism thus collapses the historically real and the future ideal into one privileged position for African American women in the present. Taking this position is reminiscent of the response of some black women to the admittedly narrow feminist agenda forwarded by white women in the early 1970s. Those black women proclaimed that they were already "liberated" while in actuality, this was far from the truth.

Black Feminism

African American women who use the term black feminism also attach varying interpretations to this term. As black feminist theorist and activist Pearl Cleage defines it, feminism is "the belief that women are full human beings capable of participation and leadership in the full range of human activities— intellectual, political, social, sexual, spiritual and economic" (1993, 28). In its broadest sense, feminism constitutes both an ideology and a global political movement that confronts sexism, a social relationship in which males as a group have authority over females as a group.

Globally, a feminist agenda encompasses several major areas. First and foremost, the economic status of women and issues associated with women's global poverty, such as educational opportunities, industrial development, environmental racism, employment policies, prostitution, and inheritance laws concerning property, constitute a fundamental global women's issue. Political rights for women, such as gaining the vote, rights of assembly, traveling in public, officeholding, the rights of political prisoners, and basic human rights violations against women such as rape and torture constitute a second area of concern. A third area of global concern consists of marital and family issues such as marriage and divorce laws, child custody policies, and domestic labor. Women's health and survival issues, such as reproductive rights, pregnancy, sexuality, and AIDS constitute another area of global feminist concern. This broad global feminist agenda finds varying expressions in different regions of the world and among diverse populations.

Using the term "black feminism" positions African American women to examine how the particular constellation of issues affecting black women in the United States are part of issues of women's emancipation struggles globally (Davis 1989; James and Busia 1994). In the context of feminism as a global political movement for women's rights and emancipation, the patterns of feminist knowledge and politics that African American women encounter in the United States represent but a narrow segment refracted through the dichotomous racial politics of white supremacy in the United States. Because the media in the United States portrays feminism as a for-whites-only movement, and because many white women have accepted this view of American apartheid that leads to segregated institutions of all types, including feminist organizations, feminism is often viewed by both black[s] and whites as the cultural property of white women (Caraway 1991).

* * *

Despite their media erasure, many African American women have long struggled against this exclusionary feminism and have long participated in what appear to be for-whites-only feminist activity. In some cases, some black women have long directly challenged the racism within feminist organizations controlled by white women. Sojourner Truth's often cited phrase "ain't I a woman" typifies this longstanding tradition (Joseph 1990). At other times, even though black women's participation in feminist organizations remains largely invisible, for example, Pauli Murray's lack of recognition as a founding member of NOW, black women participated in feminist organizations in positions of leadership. In still other cases, black women combine allegedly divergent political agendas. For example, Pearl Cleage observes that black feminist politics and black nationalist politics need not be contradictory. She notes, "I don't think you can be a true Black Nationalist, dedicated to the freedom of black people *without* being a feminist, black *people* being made up of both men and *women,* after all, and feminism being nothing more or less than a belief in the political, social and legal equality of women" (1994, 180).

Using the term "black feminism" disrupts the racism inherent in presenting feminism as a for-whites-only ideology and political movement. Inserting the adjective "black" challenges the assumed whiteness of feminism and disrupts the false universal of this term for both white and black women. Since many white women think that black women lack feminist consciousness, the term "black feminist" both highlights the contradictions underlying the assumed whiteness of feminism and serves to remind white women that they comprise neither the only nor the normative "feminists." The term "black feminism" also makes many African American women uncomfortable because it challenges black women to confront their own views on sexism and women's oppression. Because the majority of African American women encounter their own experiences repackaged in racist school curricula and media, even though they may support the very ideas on which feminism rests, large numbers of African American women reject the term "feminism" because of what they perceive as its association with whiteness. Many see feminism as operating exclusively within the terms white and American and perceive its opposite as being black and American. When given these two narrow and false choices, black women routinely choose "race" and let the lesser question of "gender" go. In this situation, those black women who identify with feminism must be recoded as being either non-black or less authentically black. The term "black feminist" also disrupts a longstanding and largely unquestioned reliance on black racial solidarity as a deep tap root in black political philosophies, especially black nationalist and cultural pluralist frameworks (Dyson 1993). Using family rhetoric that views black family, community, race and nation as a series of nested boxes, each gaining meaning from the other, certain rules apply to all levels of this "family" organization. Just as families have internal naturalized hierarchies that give, for example, older siblings authority over younger ones or males over females, groups defining themselves as racial-families invoke similar rules (Collins forthcoming). Within African American communities, one such rule is that black women will support black men, no matter what, an unwritten family rule that was manipulated quite successfully during the Clarence Thomas confirmation hearings. Even if Anita Hill was harassed by Clarence Thomas, many proclaimed in barber shops and beauty parlors, she should have kept her mouth shut and not "aired dirty laundry." Even though Thomas recast the life of his own sister through the framework of an unworthy welfare queen, in deference to rules of racial solidarity, black women should have kept our collective mouths shut. By counseling black women not to remain silent in the face of abuse, whoever does it, black feminism comes into conflict with codes of silence such as these.

Several difficulties accompany the use of the term "black feminism." One involves the problem of balancing the genuine concerns of black women against continual pressures to absorb and recast such interests within white feminist frameworks. For example, ensuring political rights and economic development via collective action to change social institutions remains a strong focal point in the feminism of African American women and women of color. Yet the emphasis on themes such as personal identity, understanding "difference," deconstructing women's multiple selves, and the simplistic model of the political expressed through the slogan the "personal is political," that currently permeate North American white women's feminism in the academy can work to sap black feminism of its critical edge. Efforts of contemporary black women thinkers to explicate a long-standing black women's intellectual tradition bearing the label "black feminism" can attract the attention of white women armed with a different feminist agenda. Issues raised by black women not seen as explicitly "feminist" ones, primarily issues that affect only women, receive much less sanction. In a sense, the constant drumbeat of having to support white women in their efforts to foster an anti-racist feminism that allows black women access to the global network of women's activism diverts black women's energy away from addressing social issues facing African American communities. Because black feminism appears to be so well-received by white women, in the context of dichotomous racial politics of the United States, some black women quite rightfully suspect its motives.

Another challenge facing black feminism concerns the direct conflict between black feminism and selected elements of black religious traditions. For example, the visibility of white lesbians within North American feminism overall comes into direct conflict with many black women's articles of faith that homosexuality is a sin. While individual African American women may be accepting of gays, lesbians and bisexuals as individuals, especially if such individuals are African American, black women as a collectivity have simultaneously distanced themselves from social movements perceived as requiring acceptance of homosexuality. As one young black woman queried, "why do I have to accept lesbianism in order to support black feminism?" The association of feminism with lesbianism remains a problematic one for black women.

Reducing black lesbians to their sexuality, one that chooses women over men, reconfigures black lesbians as enemies of black men. This reduction not only constitutes a serious misreading of black lesbianism—black lesbians have fathers, brothers, and sons of their own and are embedded in a series of relationships as complex as their heterosexual brothers and sisters—it simultaneously diverts attention away from more important issues (Lorde 1984). Who ultimately benefits when the presence of black lesbians in any black social movement leads to its rejection by African Americans?

The theme of lesbianism and its association with feminism in the minds of many African Americans also overlaps with another concern of many African American women, namely their commitment to African American men. Another challenge confronting black feminism concerns its perceived separatism—many African Americans define black feminism as being exclusively for black women only and rejecting black men. In explaining her preference for "womanism," Sherley Anne Williams notes, "one of the most disturbing aspects of current black feminist criticism (is) its separatism—its tendency to see not only a *distinct* black female culture but to see that culture as a separate cultural form having more in common with white female experience than with the facticity of Afro-American life" (1990, 70). This is a valid criticism of black feminism, one that, in my mind, must be addressed if the major ideas of black feminism expect to avoid the danger of becoming increasingly separated from African American women's experiences and interests. But it also speaks to the larger issue of the continuing difficulty of positioning black feminism between black nationalism and North American white feminism. In effect, black feminism must come to terms with a white feminist agenda incapable of seeing its own racism as well as a black nationalist one resistant to grappling with its own sexism (White 1990). Finding a place that accommodates these seemingly contradictory agendas remains elusive (Christian 1989).

Beyond Naming

African American women's efforts to distinguish between womanism and black feminism illustrates how black women's placement in hierarchical power relations fosters different yet related allegiances to a black women's self-defined standpoint. While the surface differences distinguishing African American women who embrace womanism and black feminism appear to be minimal, black women's varying locations in neighborhoods, schools, and labor markets generate comparably diverse views on the strategies black women feel will ultimately lead to black women's self-determination. In a sense, while womanism's affiliation with black nationalism both taps an historic philosophy and a set of social institutions organized around the centrality of racial solidarity for black survival, this position can work to isolate womanism from global women's issues. At the same time, while black feminism's connections to existing women's struggles both domestically and globally fosters a clearer political agenda regarding gender, its putative affiliation with whiteness fosters its rejection by the very constituency it aims to serve.

No term currently exists that adequately represents the substance of what diverse groups of black women alternately call "womanism" and "black feminism." Perhaps the time has come to go beyond naming by applying main ideas contributed by both womanists and black feminists to the over-arching issue of analyzing the centrality of gender in shaping a range of relationships within African American communities. Such an examination might encompass several dimensions.

First, it is important to keep in mind that the womanist/black feminist debate occurs primarily among relatively privileged black women. Womanism and black feminism would both benefit by examining the increasing mismatch between what privileged black women, especially those in the academy, identify as important themes and what the large numbers of African American women who stand outside of higher education might deem worthy of attention. While these African American women physically resemble one another and may even occupy the same space, their worlds remain decidedly different. One might ask how closely the thematic content of newly emerging black women's voices in the academy speak for and speak to the masses of African American women still denied literacy. Black women academics explore intriguing issues of centers and margins and work to deconstruct black female identity while large numbers of black women remain trapped in neighborhoods organized around old centers of racial apartheid. Talk of centers and margins, even the process of coining to voice itself, that does not simultaneously address issues of power leaves masses of black women doing the dry cleaning, cooking the fast food, and dusting the computer of the sister who has just written the newest theoretical treatise on black women.

Second, shifting the emphasis from black women's oppression to how institutionalized racism operates in gender-specific ways should provide a clearer perspective on how gender oppression works in tandem with racial oppression for both black women and men. This shift potentially opens up new political choices for African Americans as a group. Just as feminism does not automatically reside in female bodies, sexism does not reside in male ones. It may be time to separate political philosophies such as black nationalism, Afrocentrism, and feminism, from the socially constructed categories of individuals created by historical relations of racism and sexism. Black men cannot have black women's experiences but they can support African American women by advocating anti-racist and anti-sexist philosophies in their intellectual and political work (see, e.g., Marable 1983; hooks and West 1991; and Awkward 1995). Focusing on gender as a structure of power that works with race should provide the much needed space for dialogues among black women, among black men, and between black women and men.

This approach promises to benefit the black community as a collectivity because it models sensitivity to the heterogeneity concerning not only gender, but class, nationality, sexuality, and age currently operating within the term "black community." Thus, the womanism/black feminism debate also provides an excellent opportunity to model a process of building community via heterogeneity and not sameness. For African American women, breathing life into Alice Walker's seemingly contradictory meanings of "womanist" and "black feminist" means engaging in the difficult task of working through the diverse ways that black women have been affected by interlocking systems of oppression. Some black women will have to grapple with how internalized oppression has affected them because they are poor while others must come to terms with the internalized privilege accompanying their middle- and upper-class status. Other black women must grapple with the internalized privileges that accrue to them because they engage in heterosexual behaviors or how American citizenship provides them rights denied to women elsewhere in the Diaspora. Working through the interconnected nature of multiple systems of oppression and potential ways that such intersectionality might foster resistance becomes significant in moving quite diverse African American women forward toward Walker's visionary term "womanism." A commitment to social justice and participatory democracy provide some fundamental ground rules for black women and men concerning how to relate across differences.

Finally, despite the promise of this approach, it is important to consider the limitations of womanism, black feminism, and all other putatively progressive philosophies. Whether labeled "womanism," "black feminism," or something else, African American women could not possibly possess a superior vision of what community would look like, how justice might feel, and the like. This presupposes that such a perspective is arrived at without conflict, intellectual rigor, and political struggle. While black women's particular location provides a distinctive angle of vision on oppression, this perspective comprises neither a privileged nor a complete standpoint. In this sense, grappling with the ideas of heterogeneity within black women's communities and hammering out a self-defined, black women's standpoint leads the way for other groups wishing to follow a similar path. As for black women, we can lead the way or we can follow behind. Things will continue to move on regardless of our choice.

Note

1. For a detailed treatment of Alice Walker's and other black feminist writers' connection to black nationalist politics, see Dubey (1994).

References

Awkward, Michael. 1995. *Negotiating Difference: Race, Gender, and the Politics of Positionality.* Chicago: University of Chicago Press.
Cannon, Katie G. 1988. *Black Womanist Ethics.* Atlanta: Scholars Press.
Caraway, Nancie. 1991. *Segregated Sisterhood: Racism and the Politics of American Feminism.* Knoxville: University of Tennessee Press.

Carby, Hazel. 1992. "The Multicultural Wars." pp. 187–99 in *Black Popular Culture*, edited by Michele Wallace and Gina Dent. Seattle: Bay Press.

Christian, Barbara. 1989. "But Who Do You Really Belong To—Black Studies or Women's Studies?" *Women's Studies* 17, 1–2: 17–23.

Cleage, Pearl. 1993. *Deals with the Devil and Other Reasons to Riot*. New York: Ballantine Books.

Collins, Patricia Hill. 1990. *Black Feminist Thought: Knowledge, Consciousness, and the Politics of Empowerment*. New York: Routledge, Chapman and Hall.

———. forthcoming. "Intersections of Race, Class, Gender, and Nation: Some Implications for Black Family Studies." *Journal of Comparative Family Studies*.

Davis, Angela. 1989. *Women, Culture, and Politics*. New York: Random House.

Dubey, Madhu. 1994. *Black Women Novelists and the Nationalist Aesthetic*. Bloomington: Indiana University Press.

DuCille, Ann. 1994. "The Occult of True Black Womanhood: Critical Demeanor and Black Feminist Studies." *Signs* 19(3): 591–629.

Dyson, Michael. 1993. *Reflecting Black: African-American Cultural Criticism*. Minneapolis: University of Minnesota Press.

hooks, bell. 1989. *Talking Back: Thinking Feminist, Thinking Black*. Boston: South End Press.

———, and Cornel West. 1991. *Breaking Bread: Insurgent Black Intellectual Life*. Boston: South End Press.

James, Stanlie, and Abena Busia, eds. 1994. *Theorizing Black Feminisms*. New York: Routledge.

Jordan, June. 1992. *Technical Difficulties: African-American Notes on the State of the Union*. New York: Pantheon Books.

Joseph, Gloria I. 1990. "Sojourner Truth: Archetypal Black Feminist." pp. 35–47 in *Wild Women in the Whirlwind*, edited by Joanne Braxton and Andree Nicola McLaughlin. New Brunswick: Rutgers University Press.

Lorde, Audre. 1984. *Sister Outsider*. Trumansburg, NY: The Crossing Press.

Marable, Manning. 1983. "Grounding with My Sisters: Patriarchy and the Exploitation of Black Women." pp. 69–104 in *How Capitalism Underdeveloped Black America*. Boston: South End Press.

Massey, Douglas S., and Nancy A. Denton. 1993. *American Apartheid: Segregation and the Making of the Underclass*. Cambridge: Harvard University Press.

Omolade, Barbara. 1994. *The Rising Song of African American Women*. New York: Routledge.

Pinkney, Alphonso. 1976. *Red, Black, and Green: Black Nationalism in the United States*. London: Cambridge University Press.

Smith, Barbara. 1990. "The Truth That Never Hurts: Black Lesbians in Fiction in the 1980s." pp. 213–245 in *Wild Women in the Whirlwind*, edited by Joanne Braxton and Andree Nicola McLaughlin. New Brunswick: Rutgers University Press.

Squires, Gregory D. 1994. *Capital and Communities in Black and White: The Intersections of Race, Class, and Uneven Development*. Albany: SUNY Press.

Van Deburg, William L. 1992. *New Day in Babylon: The Black Power Movement and American Culture, 1965–1975*. Chicago: University of Chicago Press.

Walker, Alice. 1983. *In Search of Our Mothers' Gardens*. New York: Harcourt Brace Jovanovich.

White, E. Frances. 1990. "Africa on My Mind: Gender, Counter Discourse and African-American Nationalism." *Journal of Women's History* 2, 1 (Spring): 73–97.

Williams, Sherley Anne. 1990. "Some Implications of Womanist Theory." pp. 68–75 in *Reading Black, Reading Feminist: A Critical Anthology*, edited by Henry Louis Gates. New York: Meridian.

A Black Man's Place in Black Feminist Criticism (1998)

MICHAEL AWKWARD

Many essays by male and female scholars devoted to exploring the subject of male critics' place in feminism generally agree about the uses and usefulness of the autobiographical male "I." Such essays suggest that citing the male critical self reflects a response to (apparent) self-difference, an exploration of the disparities between the masculine's antagonistic position in feminist discourse on the one hand and, on the other, the desire of the individual male critic to represent his difference with and from the traditional androcentric perspectives of his gender and culture. Put another way, in male feminist acts, to identify the writing self as biologically male is to emphasize the desire not to be ideologically male; it is to explore the process of rejecting the phallocentric perspectives by which men traditionally have justified the subjugation of women.[1]

In what strikes me as a particularly suggestive theoretical formulation, Joseph Boone articulates his sense of the goals of such male feminist autobiographical acts:

> In exposing the latent multiplicity and difference in the word "me(n)," we can perhaps open up a space within the discourse of feminism where a male feminist voice *can* have something to say beyond impossibilities and apologies and unresolved ire. Indeed, if the male feminist can discover a position *from which* to speak that neither elides the importance of feminism to his work nor ignores the specificity of his gender, his voice may also find that it no longer exists as an abstraction ... but that it in fact inhabits a body: its own sexual/ textual body.[2]

Because of an awareness that androcentric perspectives are learned, are transmitted by means of specific sociocultural practices in such effective ways that they come to appear natural, male feminists such as Boone believe that, through an informed investigation of androcentric and feminist ideologies, individual men can work to resist the lure of the normatively masculine. That resistance for the aspiring male feminist requires, he says, exposing "the latent multiplicity and difference in the word 'men,' " in other words, disrupting both ideologies' unproblematized perceptions of monolithic and/or normative maleness (as villainous, antagonistic "other" for feminism, and, for androcentricism, powerful, domineering patriarch). At this early stage of male feminism's development, to speak self-consciously—autobiographically—is to explore, implicity or explicitly, why and how the individual male experience (the "me" in men) has diverged from, has created possibilities for a rejection of, the androcentric norm.

And while there is not yet agreement as to what constitutes an identifiably male feminist act of criticism or about the usefulness of such acts for the general advancement of the feminist project, at least one possible explanation for a male critic's self-referential discourse is that it is a response to palpable mistrust—emanating from some female participants in feminism and perhaps from the writing male subject himself—about his motives. A skeptical strand of opinion with regard to male feminism is represented by Alice Jardine's "Men in Feminism: Odor di Uomo or Compagnons de Route?" Having determined that the most useful measure of an adequately feminist text is its "*inscription of struggle*—even of *pain*"—an inscription of a struggle against patriarchy which Jardine finds absent from most male feminist acts, perhaps because "the historical fact that is the oppression of women [is] … one of their favorite blind spots"—she admits to some confusion as to the motivations for males' willing participation: "Why … would men want to be in feminism if it's about struggle? What do men want to be in—in pain?"[3]

In addition to seeking to cure its blindness where the history of female oppression is concerned, a male feminism must explore the motivations for its participation in what we might call, in keeping with Jardine's formulations, a discourse of (en)gendered pain. If one of the goals of male feminist self-referentiality is to demonstrate to females that individual males can indeed serve as allies in efforts to undermine androcentric power—and it seems that this is invariably the case—the necessary trust cannot be gained by insisting that motivation as such does not represent a crucial area that must be carefully negotiated. For example, I accept as accurate and, indeed, reflective of my own situation Andrew Ross's assertion that "there are those [men] for whom the *facticity* of feminism, for the most part, goes without saying … who are young enough for feminism to have been a primary component of their intellectual formation."[4] However, in discussions whose apparent function is a foregrounding of both obstacles to and possibilities of a male feminism, men's relation(s) to the discourse can never go "without saying"; for the foreseeable future at least, this relation needs necessarily to be rigorously and judiciously theorized, and grounded explicitly in the experiential realm of the writing male subject.

But no matter how illuminating and exemplary one finds self-referential inscriptions of a male feminist critical self, if current views of the impossibility of a consistently truthful autobiographical act are correct, there are difficulties implicit in any such attempt to situate or inscribe that male self. Because, as recent theorizing on the subject of autobiography has demonstrated, acts of discursive self-rendering unavoidably involve the creation of an idealized version of a unified or unifiable self, we can be certain only of the fact that the autobiographical impulse yields but some of the truths of the male feminist critic's experiences.[5] As is also the case for female participants, a male can never possess or be able to tell the whole truth and nothing but the truth about his relationship to feminist discourse and praxis.

But while autobiographical criticism, like the genre of autobiography itself, is poised tenuously between the poles of closure and disclosure, between representation and re-presentation, between a lived life and an invented one, I believe that even in the recoverable half-truths of my life are some of the materials that have shaped my perceptions, my beliefs, the self or selves that I bring to the interpretive act. In these half-truths is the source of my desire both to inscribe a black male feminism and to inscribe myself as a self-consciously racialized version of what Jardine considers a potentially oxymoronic entity— "male feminist"—whose literal, it not ideological or performative "blackness" is indisputable, and whose adequacy vis-à-vis feminism others must determine. By examining discussions of the phenomenon of the male feminist—that is to say, by reading male and female explorations of men's places in feminist criticism—and exploring responses of others to my own professional and personal relationships to feminism, I will identify autobiographically and textually grounded sources for my belief that while gendered difference might be said to complicate the prospect of a non-phallocentric black male feminism, it does not render such a project impossible.

At the outset, I acknowledge that mine is a necessary participation with regard to black feminist criticism in the half-invention, half-perception which, in Houston Baker's compelling formulation, represents every scholar's relationship to cultural criticism.[6] Such an acknowledgment is not intended to indicate that my male relationship to feminism is that of an illegitimate child, as it were. Rather, it is meant to suggest, like Elizabeth Weed's insistence on "the impossibility" of both men's and women's "relationship to feminism," my belief that while feminism represents a complex, sometimes self-contradictory "utopian vision" which no one can fully possess, a biological male can "develop political, theoretical [and, more generally, interpretive] strategies" which, though at most perhaps half-true to all that feminist ideologies are, nevertheless can assist in a movement toward actualizing the goals of feminism.[7]

I have been forced to think in especially serious ways about my own relationship to feminist criticism since I completed the first drafts of *Inspiring Influences,* my study of Afro-American women novelists.[8] I have questioned neither the explanatory power of feminism nor the essential importance of developing models adequate to the analysis of black female-authored texts, as my book—in harmony, I believe, with the black feminist project concerned with recovering and uncovering an Afro-American female literary tradition—attempts to provide on a limited scale. Instead, I have been confronted with suspicion about my gendered suitability for the task of explicating Afro-American women's texts, suspicion which has been manifested in the form of both specific responses to my project and general inquiries within literary studies into the phenomenon of the male feminist.

For example, a white female reader of the manuscript asserted—with undisguised surprise—that my work was "so feminist" and asked how I'd managed to offer such ideologically informed readings. Another scholar, a black feminist literary critic, recorded with no discernible hesitation her unease with my "male readings" of the texts of Zora Neale Hurston, Toni Morrison, Gloria Naylor, and Alice Walker. I wondered about the possibility of my being simultaneously "so feminist" and not so feminist (i.e., so "male"), about the meanings of these terms both for these scholars and for the larger interpretive communities in which they participate. Consequently, in what was perhaps initially an act of psychic self-protection, I began to formulate questions for which I still have found no consistently satisfactory answers. Were the differences in the readers' perceptions of the ideological adequacy of my study a function of their own views of feminist criticism, a product, in other words, of the differences not simply *within me* but *within feminism itself*? And if the differences within feminism are so significant, could I possibly satisfy everybody with "legitimate" interests in the texts of Hurston et al. by means of my own appropriated versions of black feminist discourse, my unavoidably half-true myth of what that discourse is, means, and does? Should my myth of feminism and its mobilization in critical texts be considered naturally less analytically compelling than that of a female scholar simply as a function of my biological maleness? And how could what I took to be a useful self-reflexivity avoid becoming a debilitating inquiry into a process that has come to seem for me, if not "natural," as Cary Nelson views his relationship to feminism, at least *necessary*?[9]

Compelled, and, to be frank, disturbed by such questions, I searched for answers in others' words, others' work. I purchased a copy of *Men in Feminism*, a collection which examines the possibility of men's participation as "comrades" (to use Toni Morrison's term) in feminist criticism and theory. Gratified by the appearance of such a volume, I became dismayed upon reading the editors' introductory remarks, which noted their difficulty in "locating intellectuals, who, having shown interest in the question, would offer, for instance, a gay or a black perspective on the problem."[10] While a self-consciously "gay ... perspective" does find its way into the collection, the insights of nonwhite males and females are conspicuously absent.[11]

Even more troubling for me than the absence of black voices or, for that matter, of general inquiries into the effects of racial, cultural, and class differences on males' relationship to feminism, was the sense shared by many contributors of insurmountable obstacles to male feminism. In fact, the first essay, Stephen Heath's "Male Feminism," begins by insisting that "men's relation to feminism is an impossible one."[12] For me, Heath's formulations are insightful and provocative, if not always persuasive, as when he claims: "This is, I believe, the most any man can do today: to learn and so to try to write and talk or act in response to feminism, and so to try not in any way to be anti-feminist, supportive of the old oppressive structures. Any more, any notion of writing a feminist book or being a feminist, is a myth, a male imaginary with the reality of appropriation and domination right behind."[13] Is male participation in feminism restricted to being either appropriative and domineering or not antifeminist? Must we necessarily agree with Heath and others who claim that men cannot be feminists? To put the matter differently, is gender really an adequate determinant of "class" position?

Despite the poststructuralist tenor of Heath's work generally and of many of his perspectives here, his is an easily problematized essentialist claim—that, in effect, biology determines destiny and, therefore, one's relationship to feminist ideology, that womanhood allows one to become feminist at the same time that manhood necessarily denies that status to men. And while Heath embraces its notions of history as a narrative of male "appropriation and domination" of gendered others, he appears resistant at this point in his discourse to evidence of a powerful feminist institutional *present* and *presence*. I believe that we must acknowledge that feminism represents, at least in areas of the American academy, an incomparably productive, influential, and resilient ideology and institution that men, no matter how cunning, duplicitous, or culturally powerful, will neither control nor overthrow in the foreseeable future, one whose perspectives have proved and might continue to prove convincing even to biological males. In surveying the potential implications or the participation of biological men in feminism, we must therefore be honest about feminism's current persuasiveness and indomitability, about its clarifying, transformative potential, and about the fact that the corruptive possibility of both the purposefully treacherous and the only half-convinced male is, for today at least, slight indeed. Surely it is neither naive, presumptuous, nor premature to suggest that feminism as ideology and reading strategy has assumed a position of exegetical and institutional strength capable of withstanding even the most energetically masculinist acts of subversion.

Below I want to focus specifically on the question of a black male feminism. Rather than seeing it as an impossibility or as a subtle new manifestation of and attempt at androcentric domination, I want to show that certain instances of afrocentric feminism provide Afro-American men with an invaluable means of rewriting—of *re-vis(ion)ing*—our selves, our history and literary tradition, and our future.

Few would deny that black feminist literary criticism is an oppositional discourse constituted in large part as a response against black male participation in the subjugation of Afro-American women. From Barbara Smith's castigation of black male critics for their "virulently sexist ... treatment" of black women writers and her insistence that they are "hampered by an inability to comprehend Black women's experience in sexual as well as racial terms" to Michele Wallace's characterization of the "black male Afro-Americanists who make pivotal use of Hurston's work" as "a gang," Afro-American men are generally perceived as non-allied others of black feminist discourse.[14] And, as is evident in Wallace's figuration of male Hurston scholars as intraracial street warriors, they are viewed at times as always already damned and unredeemable, even when they appear to take black women's writing seriously. We—I—must accept the fact that black male investigations informed by feminist principles, including this one, may never be good enough or ideologically correct enough for some black women who are feminists.

This sense of an unredeemable black male critic/reader is in stark contrast to perspectives offered in such texts as Sherley Anne Williams's "Some Implications of Womanist Theory." In her essay, she embraces Alice Walker's term "womanist"—which, according to Williams, connotes a commitment "to the survival and wholeness of an entire people, female and male, as well as a valorization of women's works in all their varieties and multitudes"—because she considers the black feminist project to be separatist in "its tendency to see not only a distinct black female culture but to see that culture as a separate cultural form" from "the facticity of Afro-American life."[15]

I believe that a black male feminism, whatever its connections to critical theory or its specific areas of concern, can profit immensely from what female feminists have to say about male participation. For example, Valerie Smith's suggestion in "Gender and Afro-Americanist Literary Theory and Criticism" that "Black male critics and theorists might explore the nature of the contradictions that arise when they undertake black feminist projects"[16] seems to me quite useful, as does Alice Jardine's advice to male feminists. Speaking for white female feminists, Jardine addresses white males who consider themselves to be feminists: "We do not want you to *mimic* us, to become the same as us; we don't want your pathos or your guilt: and we don't even want your admiration (even if it's nice to get it once in a while). What we want, I would even say what we need, is your *work*. We need you to get down to serious work. And like all serious work, that involves struggle and pain."[17] The womanist theoretical project that has been adopted by Williams, Smith, and others provides aspiring Afro-American male feminists with a useful model for the type of self-exploration that Smith and Jardine advocate. What Williams terms "womanist theory" is especially suggestive for Afro-American men because, while it calls for feminist discussions of black women's texts and for critiques of black androcentricism, womanism foregrounds a general black psychic health as a primary objective. Williams argues that "what is needed is a thoroughgoing examination of male images in the works of black male writers"; her womanism, then, aims at "ending the separatist tendency in Afro-American criticism," at leading black feminism away from "the same hole The Brother has dug for himself—narcissism, isolation, inarticulation, obscurity," at the creation and/or continuation of black "community and dialogue."[18]

If a black man is to become a useful contributor to black feminism, he must, as Boone argues, "discover a position *from which* to speak that neither elides the importance of feminism to his work nor ignores the specificity of his gender." However multiply split we perceive the subject to be, however deeply felt our sense of "maleness" and "femaleness" as social constructions, however heightened our sense of the historical consequences and current dangers of black androcentricism, a black male feminism cannot contribute to the continuation and expansion of the black feminist project by being so identified against or out of touch with itself as to fail to be both self-reflective and at least minimally self-interested. A black male feminist self-reflectivity of the type I have in mind necessarily would include examination of both the benefits and the dangers of a situatedness in feminist discourse. The self-interestedness of a black male feminist would be manifested in part by his concern with exploring a man's place. Clearly if convincing mimicry of female-authored concerns and interpretive strategies—speaking *like* a female feminist—is not in and of itself an appropriate goal for aspiring male participants, then a male feminism necessarily must explore males' various situations in the contexts and texts of history and the present.

Perhaps the most difficult task for a black male feminist is striking a workable balance between male self-inquiry/interest and an adequately feminist critique of patriarchy. To this point, especially in response to the commercial and critical success of contemporary Afro-American women's literature, scores of black men have proved unsuccessful in this regard. As black feminist critics such as Valerie Smith and Deborah McDowell have argued, the contemporary moment of black feminist literature has been greeted by many Afro-American males with hostility, self-interested misrepresentation, and a lack of honest intellectual introspection. In "Reading; Family Matters," a useful discussion for black male feminism primarily as an exploration of what such a discourse ought not do and be, McDowell speaks of widely circulated androcentric male analyses of Afro-American feminist texts by writers such as Toni Morrison and Alice Walker:

> Critics leading the debate [about the representation of black men in black women's texts] have lumped all black women writers together and have focused on one tiny aspect of their immensely complex and diverse project—the image of black men—despite the fact that, if we can claim a center for these texts, it is located in the complexities of black female subjectivity and experience. In other words, though black women writers have made black women the subjects of their own family stories, these male readers/critics are attempting to usurp that place for themselves and place it at the center of critical inquiry.[19]

Although I do not believe that "the image of black men" is as microscopic an element in Afro-American women's texts as McDowell claims, I agree with her about the reprehensible nature of unabashed androcentricism found in formulations she cites by such writers as Robert Staples, Mel Watkins, and

Darryl Pinckney. Nevertheless, in relation to the potential development of a black male feminism, I am troubled by what appears to be a surprisingly explicit determination to protect turf. In their unwillingness to grant that exploration of how Afro-American males are delineated by contemporary black female novelists is a legitimate concern that might produce illuminating analyses, McDowell's formulations echo in unfortunate ways those of antifeminist male critics, white and black, who consider feminism to be an unredeemably myopic and unyielding interpretive strategy incapable of offering subtle readings of canonical, largely male-authored texts. Despite the circulation of reprehensibly masculinist responses to Afro-American women's literature, black feminist literary critics do not best serve the discourses that concern them by setting into motion homeostatic maneuvers intended to devalue all forms of inquiry except for those they hold to be most valuable (in this particular case, a female-authored scholarship that emphasizes Afro-American women's writings of black female subjectivity). If the Afro-American women's literary project is indeed "immensely complex and diverse," as McDowell claims, bringing to bear other angles of vision, including antipatriarchal male ones, can assist in analyzing aspects of that complexity.

While the views of Staples and others are clearly problematic, those problems do not arise specifically from their efforts to place males "at the center of critical inquiry" any more than feminism is implicitly flawed because it insists, in some of its manifestations, on a gynocritical foregrounding of representations of women. Rather, these problems appear to result from the fact that the particular readers who produce these perspectives do not seem sufficiently to be, in Toril Moi's titular phrase, "men against patriarchy."[20] Certainly, in an age when both gender studies and Afro-American women's literature have achieved a degree of legitimacy within the academy and outside of it, it is unreasonable for black women either to demand that black men not be concerned with the ways in which they are depicted by Afro-American women writers, or to see that concern as intrinsically troubling in feminist terms. If female feminist calls for a non-mimicking male feminism are indeed persuasive, then black men will have very little of substance to say about contemporary Afro-American women's literature, especially if we are also to consider as transgressive any attention to figurations of black manhood. It seems to me that the most black females in feminism can insist upon in this regard is that examinations which focus on male characters treat the complexity of contemporary Afro-American women novelists' delineations of black manhood with an antipatriarchal seriousness which the essays McDowell cites clearly lack.

From my perspective, what is potentially most valuable about the development of black male feminism is not its capacity to reproduce black feminism as practiced by black females who focus primarily on "the complexities of black female subjectivity and experience."[21] Rather, its potential value lies in the possibility that, in being antipatriarchal and as self-inquiring about their relationship(s) to feminism as Afro-American women have been, black men can expand the range and utilization of feminist inquiry and explore other fruitful applications for feminist perspectives, including such topics as obstacles to a black male feminist project itself and new figurations of "family matters" and black male sexuality.

For the purpose of theorizing about a black male feminism, perhaps the most provocative, enlightening, and inviting moment in feminist or in "womanist" scholarship occurs in Hortense Spillers's "Mama's Baby, Papa's Maybe: An American Grammar Book." Indeed, Spillers's essay represents a fruitful starting point for new, potentially nonpatriarchal figurations of family and of black males' relationship to the female. Toward the end of this illuminating theoretical text, which concerns itself with slavery's debilitating effects on the Afro-American family's constitution, Spillers envisions black male identity formation as a process whose movement toward successful resolution seems to require a serious engagement of black feminist principles and perspectives. Spillers asserts that as a result of those specific familial patterns which functioned during American slavery and beyond and "removed the African-American male not so much from sight as from *mimetic* view as a partner in the prevailing social fiction of the Father's name, the Father's law," the African-American male "has been touched ... by the *mother, handed* by her in ways that he cannot escape." Because of separation from traditional American paternal name and law, "the black American male embodies the *only* American community of males which has had the specific occasion to learn *who* the female is within itself. ... It is the heritage of the *mother* that the African-American male must regain as an aspect of his own personhood—the power of 'yes' to the 'female' within."[22]

Rather than seeing the "female" strictly as other for the Afro-American male, Spillers's afrocentric revisioning of psychoanalytic theory insists that we consider it an important aspect of the repressed in the black male self.[23] Employing Spillers's analyses as a starting point, we might regard Afro-American males' potential "in-ness" vis-à-vis feminism not, as Paul Smith insists in *Men in Feminism,* as a representation of male heterosexual desires to penetrate and violate female spaces[24] but rather as an acknowledgment of what Spillers considers the distinctive nature of the Afro-American male's connection to the "female." If Afro-American males are ever to have anything to say about or to black feminism beyond the types of reflex-action devaluations and diatribes about divisiveness that critics such as McDowell and Valerie Smith rightly decry, the investigative process of which womanist acts by Spillers and Williams speak is indispensable. Such a process, if pursued in an intellectually rigorous manner, offers a means by which black men can participate usefully in and contribute productively to the black feminist project.

Black womanism demands neither the erasure of the black gendered other's subjectivity, as have male movements to regain a putatively lost Afro-American manhood, nor the relegation of males to prone, domestic, or other limiting positions. What it does require, if it is indeed to become an ideology with widespread cultural impact, is a recognition on the part of both black females and males of the nature of the gendered inequities that have marked our past and present, and a resolute commitment to work for change. In that sense, black feminist criticism has not only created a space for an informed Afro-American male participation, but it heartily welcomes—in fact, insists upon—the joint participation of black males and females as *comrades*, to invoke, with a difference, this paper's epigraphic reference to *Sula*.

Reading "Mama's Baby, Papa's Maybe" was of special importance to me in part because it helped me to clarify and articulate my belief that my relationship to feminism need not mark me necessarily as a debilitatingly split subject. The source of that relationship can only be traced autobiographically, if at all. Having been raised by a mother who, like too many women of too many generations, was the victim of male physical and psychological brutality—a brutality which, according to my mother, resulted in large part from my father's frustrations about his inability to partake in what Spillers calls masculinity's "prevailing social fiction"—my earliest stories, my familial narratives, as it were, figured "maleness" in quite troubling terms. My mother told me horrific stories, one of which I was, in a sense, immediately involved in: my father—who left us before I was one year old and whom I never knew—kicked her in the stomach when my fetal presence swelled her body, because he believed she'd been unfaithful to him and that I was only "may be" his baby.

As a youth, I pondered this and other such stories often and deeply, in part because of the pain I knew these incidents caused my mother, in part because, as someone without a consistent male familial role model, I actively sought a way to achieve a gendered self-definition. As one for whom maleness as manifested in the surrounding inner city culture seemed to be represented only by violence, familial abandonment, and the certainty of imprisonment, I found that I was able to define myself with regard to my gender primarily in oppositional ways. I had internalized the cautionary intent of my mother's narratives, which also served as her dearest wish for me: that I not grow up to be like my father, that I not adopt the definitions of "maleness" represented by his example and in the culture generally. Because the scars of male brutality were visibly etched—literally marked, as it were—on my mother's flesh and on her psyche, "maleness," as figured both in her stories and in my environment, seemed to me not to be a viable mimetic option. I grew up, then, not always sure of what or who I was with respect to prevailing social definitions of gender but generally quite painfully aware of what I could not become.

In order to begin to understand who my mother was, perhaps also who my father was, what "maleness" was and what extra-biological relationship I could hope to have to it, I needed answers that my mother was unable [to] provide. I found little of value in the black masculinist discourse of the time, which spoke endlessly of the dehumanization and castration of the Afro-American male by white men and black women—our central social narrative for too long—for this rhetoric seemed simplistic and unself-consciously concerned with justifying domestic violence and other forms of black male brutality.

Afro-American women's literature, to which I was introduced along with black feminism in 1977 as a sophomore at Brandeis University, helped me move toward a comprehension of the world, of aspects of my mother's life, and of what a man against patriarchy could be and do. These discourses provided me with answers, nowhere else available, to what had been largely unresolvable mysteries. I work within the paradigm of black feminist literary criticism because it explains elements of the world about which I care most deeply. I write and read what and as I do because I am incapable of escaping the meanings of my mother's narratives for my own life, because the pain and, in the fact of their enunciation to the next generation, the sense of hope for better days that characterizes these familial texts are illuminatingly explored in many narratives by black women. Afro-American women's literature has given me parts of myself that—incapable of a (biological) "Fatherly reprieve"—I would not otherwise have had.

I have decided that it is ultimately irrelevant whether these autobiographical facts, which, of course, are not, and can never be, the whole story, are deemed by others sufficient to permit me to call myself "feminist." Like Toril Moi, I have come to believe that "the important thing for men is not to spend their time worrying about definitions and essences ('am I *really* a feminist?'), but to take up a recognizable anti-patriarchal position."[25] What is most important to me is that my work contribute, in however small a way, to the project whose goal is the dismantling of the phallocentric rule by which black females and, I am sure, countless other Afro-American sons have been injuriously "touched."

My indebtedness to Spillers's and other womanist perspectives is, then, great indeed, as is my sense of their potential as illuminating moments for a newborn—or not-yet-born—black male feminist discourse. But to utilize these perspectives requires that we be more inquiring than Spillers is in her formulations, not in envisioning liberating possibilities of an acknowledgment of the "female" within the black community and the male subject, but in noting potential dangers inherent in such an attempted adoption by historically brutalized Afro-American men whose relationship to a repressed "female" is not painstakingly (re)defined.

Clearly, more thinking is necessary not only about what the female within is but about what it can be said to represent for black males, as well as serious analysis of useful means and methods of interacting with a repressed female interiority and subject. Spillers's theorizing does not perform this task, in part because it has other, more compelling interests and emphases—among which is the righting/(re)writing of definitions of "woman" so that they will reflect Afro-American women's particular, historically conditioned "female social subject" status—but a black male feminism must be especially focused on exploring such issues if it is to mobilize Spillers's suggestive remarks as a means of developing a fuller understanding of the complex formulations of black manhood found in many texts and contexts, including Afro-American women's narratives.

I want to build briefly on Spillers's provocative theorizing about the Afro-American male's maturational process and situation on American shores. To this end, I will look at an illuminating moment in Toni Morrison's *Sula*, a text that is, to my mind, not only an unparalleled Afro-American woman's writing of the complexities of black female subjectivity and experience but also of black males' relationship to the female within as a consequence of their limited access to "the prevailing social fiction" of masculinity. In this novel, the difficulty of negotiating the spaces between black male lack and black female presence is plainly manifested in such figures as the undifferentiatable deweys; BoyBoy, whose name, in contrast to most of the authorial designations in *Sula*, speaks unambiguously for him; and Jude, whose difficulty in assuming the mantle of male provider leads him to view his union with Nel as that which "would make one jude."[26]

The response of Plum, the most tragic of *Sula*'s unsuccessful negotiators of the so-called white man's world, vividly represents for me some of the contemporary dangers of black male "in-ness" vis-à-vis the "female." Despite a childhood which included "float[ing] in a constant swaddle of love and affection" and his mother's intention to follow the Father's law by bequeathing "everything" to him (38), Plum appears incapable of embracing hegemonic notions of masculinity. Instead, he returns from World War I spiritually fractured but, unlike a similarly devastated Shadrack, lacking the imaginative wherewithal to begin to theorize or ritualize a new relationship to his world. He turns to drugs as a method of anesthetizing himself from the horrors of his devastation and, in his mother's view, seeks to compel her resumption of familiar/familial patterns of caretaking. In the following passage, Eva explains to Hannah her perception of Plum's desires, as well as the motivation for her participation in what amounts to an act of infanticide:

> When he came back from that war he wanted to git back in. After all that carrying' on, just gettin' him out and keepin' him alive, he wanted to crawl back in my womb and well ... I ain't got the room no more even if he could do it. There wasn't space for him in my womb. And he was crawlin' back. Being helpless and thinking baby thoughts and dreaming baby dreams and messing up his pants again and smiling all the time. I had room enough in my heart, but not in my womb, got no more. I birthed him once. I couldn't do it again. He was growed, a big old thing God-havemercy, I couldn't birth him twice. ... A big man can't be a baby all wrapped up inside his mamma no more; he suffocate. I done everything

I could to make him leave me and go on and live and be a man but he wouldn't and I had to keep him out so I just thought of a way he could die like a man not all scrunched up inside my womb, but like a man. (62)[27]

What is significant about this passage for an analysis of the possibilities of a non-oppressive black male relationship to feminism—to female experience characterized by a refusal to be subjugated to androcentric desires—is its suggestiveness for our understanding of the obstacles to a revised male view of the repressed "female," obstacles which result in large part from black males' relative social powerlessness. If black feminism is persuasive in its analysis of the limitations of Afro-American masculinist ideology, emphasizing as it does achievement of black manhood at the expense of black female subjectivity, and if we can best describe an overwhelming number of Africa's American male descendants as males-in-crisis, the question a black male feminism must ask itself is, On what basis, according to what ideological perspective, can an Afro-American heterosexual male ground his notions of the female? Beyond its heterosexual dimension, can the "female" truly come to represent for a traditional black male-in-crisis more than a protective maternal womb from which he seeks to be "birthed" again? Can it serve as more than a site on which to find relief from or locate frustrations caused by an inability to achieve putatively normative American male socioeconomic status? If embracing normative masculinity requires an escape from the protection and life-sustaining aspects symbolized by maternal umbilical cords and apron strings and an achievement of an economic situation wherein the male provides domestic space and material sustenance for his dependents (including "his woman"), black manhood generally is, like Plum, in desperate trouble. And if, as has often been the case, a black female can be seen by an Afro-American male-in-crisis only if she has been emptied of subjectivity and selfhood, if she becomes visible for the male only when she is subsumed by male desire(s), then the types of refiguration and redefinition of black male subjectivity and engagement with the "female" central to Spillers's formulations are highly unlikely.

This question of seeing and not seeing, of the male gaze's erasure and re-creation of the female, is crucial to *Sula*'s general thematics. It seems to me that in all of her novels Morrison's figuration of black female subjectivity is largely incomprehensible without some serious attention both to her representation of black manhood and to her exploration of the relationships between socially constructed gendered (and racial) positions. To return explicitly to the case of Eva: What Eva fears, what appears to be a self-interested motivation for her killing of her intended male heir, is that Plum's pitiful, infantile state has the potential to reduce *her* to a static female function of self-sacrificing mother, which, according to Bottom legend, had already provoked her decision to lose a leg in order to collect insurance money with which to provide for her children. Having personally lost so much already, Eva chooses, instead of sacrificing other essential parts of her self, to take the life of her self-described male heir. And if Plum dies "like a man" in Eva's estimation, his achievement of manhood has nothing to do with an assumption of traditional masculine traits, nothing to do with strength, courage, and a refusal to cry in the face of death. Instead, that achievement results from Eva's creation of conditions that have become essential components of her definition of manhood: death forces him to "leave" her and to "keep ... out" of her womb. It would appear that manhood is defined here not as presence as typically represented in Western thought, but—by and for Eva at least—as liberating (domestic and uterine) absence.

One of the intentions of this chapter is to suggest that feminism represents a fruitful and potentially not oppressive means of reconceptualizing, of figuratively birthing twice, the black male subject. But, as a close reading of the aforementioned passage from *Sula* suggests, interactions between men and women motivated by male self-interest such as necessarily characterizes an aspect of male participation in feminism are fraught with possible dangers for the biological/ideological female body of an enactment of or a capitulation to hegemonic male power. Indeed, if it is the case that, as Spillers has argued in another context, "the woman who stays in man's company keeps alive the possibility of having, one day, an unwanted guest, or the guest, deciding to 'hump the hostess,' whose intentions turn homicidal, then male proximity to feminism generally creates the threat of a specifically masculinist violation."[28] If, as I noted earlier, the dangers of a hegemonic, heterosexual Euro-American male's "inness" vis-à-vis feminism include (sexualized) penetration and domination, then those associated with a heterosexual black male's interactions with the ideological female body are at least doubled, and potentially involve an envisioning of the black female body as self-sacrificingly maternal or self-sacrificingly sexual. Because of a general lack of access to the full force of hegemonic male power, Afro-American men could see in increasingly influential black female texts not only serious challenges to black male fictions of the self but also an appropriate location for masculine desires for control of the types of valuable resources that the discourses of black womanhood currently represent.

But a rigorous, conscientious black male feminism need not give in to traditional patriarchal desires for control and erasure of the female. To be of any sustained value to the feminist project, a discourse must provide illuminating and persuasive readings of gender as it is constituted for blacks in America and sophisticated, informed, contentious critiques of phallocentric practices in an effort to redefine our notions of black male and female textuality and subjectivity. And in its differences from black feminist texts that are produced by individual Afro-American women, a black male feminism must be both rigorous in engaging these texts and self-reflective enough to avoid, at all costs, the types of patronizing, marginalizing gestures that have traditionally characterized Afro-American male intellectuals' response to black womanhood. What a black male feminism must strive for, above all else, is to envision and enact the possibilities signaled by the differences feminism has exposed and created. In black feminist criticism, being an Afro-American male does not mean attempting to invade an/other political body like a lascivious soul snatcher or striving to erase its essence in order to replace it with one's own myth of what the discourse should be. Such a position for black men means, above all else, an acknowledgment and celebration of the incontrovertible fact that "the Father's law" is no longer the only law of the land.

Notes

1. Joseph Boone's and Gerald MacLean's essays in *Gender and Theory* assume that the foregrounding of gendered subjectivity is essential to the production of a male feminist critical practice. Consequently, in an effort to articulate his perspectives on the possibilities of a male feminist discourse, Boone shares with us professional secrets—he writes of his disagreement with the male-authored essays in Alice Jardine and Paul Smith's *Men and Feminism,* and of being excluded, because of his gender, from a Harvard feminist group discussion of Elaine Showalter's "Critical Cross-Dressing." And MacLean's essay discloses painfully personal information about his difficult relationship with his mother, his unsatisfying experience with psychoanalysis, and an incident of marital violence.

2. Joseph Boone, "Of Me(n) and Feminism: Who(se) Is the Sex That Writes?" in *Gender and Theory,* 158–80. Here and below, I quote from p. 159. For my purposes, Boone's remarks are suggestive despite their use of language that might seem to mark them as a heterosexualization of men's participation in feminism ("open up a space," "discover a position"). I believe that Boone's passage implies less about any desire for domination on his part than it does about the pervasiveness in our language of terms which have acquired sexual connotations and, consequently, demonstrates the virtual unavoidability of using a discourse of penetration to describe interactions between males and females. But it also appears to reflect a sense of frustration motivated by Boone's knowledge that while feminism has had a tremendous impact on his thinking about the world he inhabits, many feminists do not see a place in their discourse for him or other like-minded males. In order to make such a place for himself, violation and transgression seem to Boone to be unavoidable.

3. Alice Jardine, "Men in Feminism: Odor di Uomo or Compagnons de Route?" in *Men in Feminism,* 58.

4. Andrew Ross, "No Question of Silence," in *Men in Feminism,* 86.

5. See Georges Poulet, "Criticism and the Experience of Interiority," in *Reader-Response Criticism: From Formalism to Post-Structuralism,* ed. Jane P. Tompkins (Baltimore: Johns Hopkins University Press, 1980), 41–44.

6. Houston A. Baker, Jr., *Afro-American Poetics,* 8.

7. Elizabelh Weed, "A Man's Place," in *Men in Feminism,* 75.

8. Michael Awkward, *Inspiriting Influences: Tradition, Revision, and Afro-American Women's Novels* (New York: Columbia University Press, 1989).

9. About his relationship to feminism, Nelson writes: "Feminism is part of my social and intellectual life, has been so for many years, and so, to the extent that writing is ever 'natural,' it is natural that I write about feminism" (153). Nelson's "Men, Feminism: The Materiality of Discourse" (*Men in Feminism,* 153–72) is, in my estimation, a model for self-referential male feminist inquiries that assume—or, at the very least, seek to demonstrate—a useful place for males in the discourse of feminism.

10. Jardine and Smith, *Men in Feminism,* vii–viii.

11. See Craig Owens, "Outlaws: Gay Men in Feminism," in *Men in Feminism,* 219–32. It is hard to believe that Jardine and Smith's difficulty reflected a lack of interest among Afro-Americans in exploring the relationship of men to black feminism. A number of texts give evidence of interest in "the problem": the 1979 *Black Scholar* special issue devoted to investigating black feminism as manifested primarily in Ntozake Shange's *for colored girls* and Michele Wallace's *Black Macho and the Myth of the Superwoman.* Mel Watkins, "Sexism, Racism, and Black Women Writers," *New York Times Book Review,* June 15, 1986, p. l; Darryl Pinckney, "Black Victims, Black Villains," *New York Review of Books 34* (January 29, 1987: 17–20); and essays by Valerie Smith and Deborah McDowell from which I draw below.

Jardine and Smith's difficulties might have stemmed from the facts that most of the men who had spoken publicly on the subject were open about their hostility to black feminism, and most of them did not speak the language of contemporary theory, a high academic idiom which demonstrates that the contributors to *Men in Feminism* are, despite significant differences among them, members of the same speech community.

12. Stephen Heath, "Male Feminism," *Men in Feminism*, 1.
13. Ibid., 9.
14. Barbara Smith, "Toward a Black Feminist Criticism," 173, 172; Michele Wallace, "Who Dat Say Dat When I Say Dat? Zora Neale Hurston Then and Now," *Village Voice Literary Supplement*, April 1988, p. 18.
15. Sherley Anne Williams, "Some Implications of Womanist Theory," *Callaloo* 9 (1986): 304.
16. Valerie Smith, "Gender and Afro-Americanist Literary Theory and Criticism," in *Speaking of Gender*, 68.
17. Jardine, "Men in Feminism," *Men in Feminism*, 60.
18. Williams, "Some Implications," 307.
19. Deborah McDowell, "Reading Family Matters," in *Changing Our Own Words: Essays on Criticism, Theory, and Writing by Black Women*, ed. Cheryl Wall (New Brunswick: Rutgers University Press, 1989), 84.
20. Toril Moi, "Men against Patriarchy," in *Gender and Theory*, 181–88.
21. McDowell's views notwithstanding, constructions of black male and black female subjectivity are too obviously interrelated in black women's narratives for feminist criticism to profit in the long run from ignoring—or urging that others ignore—the important function that delineations of black male subjectivity play in these narratives' thematics. Certainly the threat of antifeminist male critical bias is not cause to erase or minimize the significance of black male characters in these writers' work.
22. Spillers, "Mamas Baby, Papa's Maybe: An American Grammar Book," 80.
23. In this sense, Spillers's perspectives complement those of Sherley Anne Williams, for the latter demands, in effect, that we consider the extent to which black male repression of the "female" results from an attempt to follow the letter of the white Father's law.
24. Paul Smith, "Men in Feminism: Men and Feminist Theory," *Men in Feminism*, 3.
25. Moi, "Men against Patriarchy," 184.
26. Toni Morrison, *Sula* (New York: Plume, 1973), 71. Subsequent references to this novel appear in the text in parentheses.
27. At least one other reading of Eva's murder of her son is possible: as protection against the threat of incest. In a section of her explanation to Hannah—very little of which is contained in my textual citation of Sula—Eva discusses a dream she has had concerning Plum:

    > I'd be laying here at night and he be downstairs in this room, but when I closed my eyes I'd see him ... six feet tall smilin' and crawlin' up the stairs quietlike so I wouldn't hear and opening the door soft so I wouldn't hear and he'd be creepin' to the bed trying to spread my legs trying to get back up in my womb. He was a man, girl, a big old growed-up man. I didn't have that much room, I kept on dreaming it. Dreaming it and I knowed it was true. One night it wouldn't be no dream. It'd be true and I would have done it, would have let him if I'd've had the room but a big man can't be a baby all wrapped up inside his mamma no more; he suffocate. (72–73)

    Morrison reverses to some extent the traditional dynamics of the most prevalent form of intergenerational incest. Instead of the male parent creeping to the bed and spreading the legs of his defenseless female child, in Eva's dream her man-child Plum is the active agent of violation. Eva's emphasis on Plum's immensity and her own uterus's size makes connections to incestuous creeping and spreading possible. It is not difficult to imagine given Plum's constantly drugged state, that frustrations caused by an inability to re-insert his whole body into his mother's womb during what Eva views as an inevitable encounter might lead to a forced insertion of a part that "naturally" fits, his penis. At any rate, a reading of this scene that notes its use of language consistent with parent–child incest serves to ground what appear to be otherwise senseless fears on Eva's part concerning both the possible effects of Plum's desire for reentry into her uterine space and her own inability to deny her son access to that space ("I would have done it, would have let him").
28. Spillers, "Black, White, and in Color, or Learning How to Paint: Toward an Intramural Protocol of Reading."

5

Daughters and Sons: The Birth of Womanist Identity

Who's Schooling Who? Black Women and the
Bringing of the Everyday into Academe, or
Why We Started *The Womanist* (1995)

LAYLI PHILLIPS AND BARBARA McCASKILL

A Story: Layli

I became a womanist the moment I read Michele Russell's "Black-Eyed Blues Connections: Teaching Black Women" in Gloria T. Hull, Patricia Bell Scott, and Barbara Smith's *All the Women Are White, All the Blacks Are Men, but Some of Us Are Brave: Black Women's Studies* (Russell 1982). At the time, I was a single-parenting, food stamp-getting, 'hood-living graduate student in supposed preparation for a high-powered, mainstream, solidly middle-class career in teaching and research. Before I read Michele Russell's essay, my life was the story of polarities: going back and forth between the food stamp line and the graduate seminar, between the WIC appointment and the halls of academe. I tried as hard as possible to keep the two worlds separate, to act as though my less than optimal grades (despite my "stellar" intellect) had nothing to do with the fact that I could not afford the textbooks and had no food in the refrigerator, and as though my "strange" way of raising my kids had nothing to do with the fact that I was being trained as a developmental psychologist and was, by virtue of the nature of graduate school, spending most of my time around considerably older, better-heeled, and "differently cultured" colleagues/models of parenthood than with other young sister-mothers with young children like myself. It was a schizophrenic existence, and "Black-Eyed Blues Connections" came to the rescue.

In her essay, Michele Russell writes:

> In Detroit, I am at the Downtown YWCA. Rooms on the upper floors are used by Wayne County Community College as learning centers. It is 10 A.M. and I am convening an introductory Black studies class

for women on Community and Identity. The twenty-two women who appear are all on their way from somewhere to something. This is a breather in their day. They range in age from nineteen to fifty-five. They all have been pregnant more than once and have made various decisions about abortion, adoption, monogamy, custody, and sterilization. Some are great-grandmothers. A few have their children along. They are a cross-section of hundreds of Black women I have known and learned from in the past fifteen years. … We have an hour together. The course is a survey. The first topic of conversation—among themselves and with me—is what they went through just to make it in the door, on time. That, in itself, becomes a lesson. (1982, 196–97)

She continues, describing the beginnings of a working methodology:

We start where they are. We exchange stories of children's clothes ripped or lost, of having to go to school with sons and explain why Che is always late and how he got that funny name, anyway, to teachers who shouldn't have to ask and don't really care. They tell of waiting for men to come home from the night shift so they can get the money or car necessary to get downtown, or power failures in the neighborhood, or administrative red tape at the college, or compulsory overtime on their own jobs, or the length of food stamp lines, or just being tired and needing sleep. Some of the stories are funny, some sad; some elicit outrage and praise from the group. It's a familiar and comfortable ritual in Black culture. It's called testifying. (197)

Finally she concludes: "The role of the teacher? Making the process conscious, the content significant. … Learn what daily survival wisdom these women have. Care. Don't let it stop at commiseration. Try to help them generalize from the specifics" (197). Encapsulated, her view is that "political education of Black women in America … becomes radical when, as teachers, we develop a methodology that places daily life at the center of history and enables Black women to struggle for survival with the knowledge that they are making history" (196).

White men have had the luxury of knowing that they are making history. All the history books—the histories of every discipline—attest to this. Black women, on the other hand, have had to construct this knowledge outside the traditional locale of knowledge validation, that is, outside the academy. Over many generations of constructing this knowledge and gradually chipping away at the impermeability of the academy, Black women intellectuals, whether inside or outside the academy, have created systems of translation between these two milieus—the academic and the everyday. They have created tools with which to work on the problems of exclusion and marginalization.

Michele Russell's essay, as emblematized by her subtitle, spoke to and reconciled both sides of my dilemma: the teacher (i.e., the academic) and the Black woman. It translated and connected the two worlds for me. As a result of her essay, I was able to reformulate these disparate yet fundamental elements of my existence in terms of complementarity rather than tension and to realize that both could be harmonized without the sacrifice of either. Her essay had been a tool, the ultimate function of which was my liberation.

It has been traditional to conceptualize education as emanating out from the academy to "the community" and to conceptualize helping as emanating out from those with more socially sanctioned power and wealth to those who are considered disenfranchised or marginal. This schematic has perpetually placed Black women—who have since their arrival in this country borne the brunt of the triple oppression of race, class, and gender—on the receiving end of every handout or supposed charitable act, as if to proclaim, "You are only needy; you have nothing to offer." Such posturing has been a long-standing insult to Black women as human beings and as participants in society, not to mention to Black women as card-carrying members of the sweat equity club and possessors of a unique wisdom born of a particular social and cultural history. Such posturing has permitted the interpretation that the academy has nothing to gain from everyday Black women and their experiences and that everyday Black women have everything to gain from the academy. In addition, this unspoken assumption has permitted—even tacitly encouraged—a dismissal of everyday Black women's experiences as material worthy of scholarly investigation and of everyday Black women themselves as capable generators, interpreters, or validators of knowledge, even when that knowledge pertains to their own experiences. My argument, however, is that this exquisite and ironic marginalization has not only hurt Black women, it has hurt the academy.

In her essay, Russell focuses on the education of everyday Black women and the validation of Black women's everyday experiences by Black women themselves within academic settings. The concealed premise is that entry into academic settings for everyday Black women has been facilitated by a "teacher"—a Black woman who has, in all historical probability, "played the game" well enough and long enough to persuade the academy that she is nonthreatening and will not subvert its traditional objectives. Yet, this Black woman, this teacher, has, like the Trojan horse or trickster, managed to maintain, cultivate, or shield her Black womanness beyond the academy's line of vision. It—her Black womanness—has become her secret weapon for both the liberation of more sisters and the revolutionizing of the academy itself.

When Black women enter the academy, they bring with them different kinds of lives—lives shaped by the ubiquitous and historically inescapable fact of triple oppression. All Black women, regardless of their social background, have had to formulate themselves in response to this fact. It becomes inevitable, then, that when Black women enter academe, they bring with them all of the knowledge and expertise that has accrued around this particular fact of their existence. Black women's lives are not, however, defined by the fact of triple oppression; Black women also bring with them intergenerationally transmitted experiential and metatheoretical frameworks based on their ancient African origins and what it meant to be a woman in Black Africa. Together, these two facts—triple oppression and African origins—generate unique thematic concerns and interpretive frameworks that, when brought in by Black women, enrich the academy, further humanize it, and make it more accessible to a wider segment of humanity, including, but not limited to, Black women.

Examples of these themes, which can be gleaned from the writings of numerous womanist and Black feminist scholars, include spirituality, struggle and activism, work, and the politics of interlocking oppressions. Black women draw interpretive frameworks from their unique social, cultural, and historical experiences. For example, from their integral knowledge of extended family, Black women have drawn valuable models of harmonizing complex and diverse social systems. From their notion of sisterhood, Black women have drawn models of research in which research "subjects" are not "subjected" to objectification, anonymity, and power imbalances but, rather, are elevated to esteemed research collaborators, named historical personages, and empowered citizens. From their history of dance, Black women have constructed polyrhythmic understandings of complex natural and human phenomena. The metaphors Black women bring to the table of scholarly activity have the potential to benefit both the humanities and the sciences, whether social, biological, or physical, by increasing the number and variety of models and frames available for the explanation of phenomena and the construction of knowledge.

Perhaps the central organizing principle of womanism (if it can be said that there is one) is the absolute necessity of speaking from and about one's own experiential location and not to or about someone else's. Black women's scholarship has placed Black women and their experiences at the center of analysis just like traditional White men's scholarship has placed White men and their experiences at the center of analysis; the crucial difference is that Black women's scholarship has articulated and owned the centering, whereas traditional White men's scholarship has not. Black women's scholarship does not parade as universal, but rather it emanates from a point of acute authenticity and invites others to participate in a similar, equally authentic, process. While traditional White men's scholarship presumes to have a monopoly on content as well as method, Black women's scholarship underscores the fallacy and pomposity of such a presumption. Ironically, universality emerges not from the imposition of sameness and the enforced proclamation that "we're all just human underneath it all," but from the careful and respectful acknowledgment that both individuals and groups have experiences that generate differences in both vision and concern and the recognition that these differences can contribute to the robustness and optimal functioning of the human race as a whole.

Because Black women are intimately familiar with the experience of having one's experience appropriated, exploited, misconstrued, and ultimately dismissed, Black feminists and womanists have developed an epistemological stance that demands the acknowledgment of one's particular location prior to the pronouncement of knowledge. Furthermore, because Black women carry with them an Afrocentric cultural ethos that purports that reality is both spiritual and material, that self-knowledge is the basis of all knowledge, that knowledge can be obtained through the use of symbolic imagery (metaphor/parable) and rhythm (pattern), and that positive relationships among humans are the highest value (Myers 1991), Black feminists and womanists offer a methodological stance that is dialogic or conversational in approach, that views the relationship between researcher and research subject as collaborative and equal, that incorporates activism into the scientific method, and that does not discount the importance of spiritual as well as material (including concrete, everyday) scientific concerns (Collins 1990). Black feminist/womanist science speaks unapologetically and authoritatively in the first person and resists the excessive canonization that would suggest that science and scholarship are essentially exclusive or objective pursuits. In fact, Black feminist/womanist science and scholarship utilize dialogue and story as metaphors for knowledge construction and validation.

Another Story: Barbara

I am an endangered species, but I sing no victim's song.
I am a woman. I am an artist. And I know where my voice belongs.
(Diana Reeves 1994)

This is my location. It is not at all easy to revolutionize the question and to ask, What is it that nonacademic, everyday women bring to womanist scholarship in the academy? I am troubled by this question. Perhaps I am troubled because, as a predominately white university-trained scholar of literature and literary history, I am disciplined to think all too often from the center—my center, my area of specialization, my research orientation, or what have you—and then to spiral out. More than this, I am troubled by what I perceive to be this question's concealed ahistorical, elitist assumption, in spite of Layli's appropriate recentering of everyday women, that the center of an aspiring womanist academic originates in academe. This question and its reverse seem, first, to propose that a kind of Demilitarized Zone distinguishes universities from the communities that surround them; then, that this Zone, once transgressed by Someone Like Me, morphs to an Ivory Curtain crashing down between the esoteric womanist scholars that Someone Like Me aspires to and the nonscholars, relevant and accountable, that Someone Like Me once resembled. I would like to see womanist scholarship progress so that neither this question nor an inversion of it necessitates a proposal in the first place. To me, both sides of the question constitute the tip of a glacier to which many of us black women scholars cling.[1] Meanwhile, our base is evaporating at warp speed in a terminal moment of meltdown. And our hands are slipping.

So I am going to practice what I preach in my approach to this issue of the intersection of womanist scholarship and black women *out there*, by referring in my section of this viewpoint to both nonacademic and academic, womanist and nonwomanist black women as *we*. I will extend Layli's first-person statement to the first-person plural. Because I am *out there*, too—and more frequently, at times with staccato, fortissimo frequency, than I am *in here*. I am *out there* when white students complain that I read race in every text, and when students and faculty, both black and white, insinuate that I owe my appointment solely to such benefactors as "generous standards," "admissions adjustments," "administrative pressures"/"administrative rewards," and "minority initiatives." I am *in here* when I read article after article on the endangered black male species, and when my analyst's mind engages such facts as my mother is fighting breast cancer and so little research dispatches specific protocols for black women, that black women are soaring in the AIDS statistics, that black women are most likely to suffer depression and least likely to have this depression diagnosed, that black women are the most underpaid of all Americans. I am a virtual simulcast of *out there* and *in here*.

So where do I hang the curtain rods?
Where do you?

And what exactly do we everyday, academic black women bring to womanist scholarship, to womanist research and practice? Foremost, I think we bring an assumption that what we accomplish becomes relevant and accountable especially when and since our lives do not dovetail materially, culturally, socially, or historically. Layli's observation bears repeating here: "Black women's scholarship does *not* parade as universal." In "The Responsibility of Intellectuals in the Age of Crack," a November 1993 forum at the Massachusetts Institute of Technology, Regina Austin commented, "The issue is not whether intellectuals are doing well; it's whether other folks are doing well. And other folks are not doing well" (1994, 6). By virtue of its interdisciplinary and multilateral focus, womanist scholarship proposes that as long as "other folks" are not doing well, academics—be they womanists, feminists, Marxist feminists, postmodernists, anarchists, or what have you—are not doing well either. I guess that I am offering womanist scholarship as a critique of the assumption that an electrified ideological barricade a priori stands between us based on academic pedigree, class affiliation, sexual preference, make and plate of car, degree of literacy attained, pre- or postmarital status, and other factors. This is not to say that we do not disagree or divide among ourselves. Rather, at the center of womanist scholarship stands a for-gone conclusion that we do demonstrate the capabilities of collaborating and withstanding the walls that divide us. And we do this more frequently and harmoniously than is reported.

In womanist scholarship operates a mystique that many of us surely rec-ognize. Michele Russell's classes at the downtown YWCA speak to this mys-tique. With no romanticization or exoticism intended, I think of this as the mystique of the Tribe. In my high school, circa 1975, a microscopic nucleus of African American students diverged in many directions on just about every issue. Yet we thought of ourselves as the Tribe. We came from different classes. We were tracked at different levels. Some of us had traveled; some had families that never had moved from the same hometown. We had naturals and perms, platforms and loafers, A-line skirts and attitudes, the latest issues of *X-Men* and the library's only copy of *War and Peace*. Yet we thought of ourselves as the Tribe.

The Tribe did not contravene these distinctions; rather, it proliferated them and exploited their potential. We were the Family Stone and the P-Funk Moth-ership Connection, and sometimes our attire came pretty close to rivaling Sly, George, Bootsie, Maceo, and the rest! When one of us became pregnant and school policy dictated her expulsion, the Tribe, all nine of us then as I recall, left our tasks and trooped before the entranceway's heavy double doors so that she saw us when the principal rifled the contents of her locker and ushered her away. Thus, we were a community that theorized: we critiqued the stigmas and stereotypes that estranged our lives from academic protocol, and in opportune moments we mobilized and blew the suckers up! Every Tribal member carved her or his niche; where none was apparent, one was nurtured: sports, chemistry, debate, even clowning. The Tribe was delicate and solid, consensual, a self-gen-erated configuration that easily slipped into the dictatorial or patriarchal, but most of the time meant a dynamic construction that accomplished results.

This is the sort of impulse that we bring to womanist scholarship. By dint of our differences, womanist scholarship is composed of transformative har-mony, proactive tension, and regenerative collaboration. Womanist scholar-ship resists dogma, and it offers a vision of intellectual leadership in which reliance and responsibility are not approached as handicaps but as liberatory strategies. Joy James's theory of black women autobiographers/activists as "liv-ing thinkers" concretizes this philosophy and resists "the worldview that cor-porate academia sells: self-reliant isolation and competition" (1993, 43). James presents such revolutionary black women as Assata Shakur, Bernice Johnson Reagon, Anne Moody, and Angela Davis as such living thinkers whose theoriz-ing "requires understanding or at least recognizing the conditions and sources of oppression, both specific to one people and universal," as thinkers whose theorizing "bound to the community, forces a response not only to |their| struggles as a revolutionary but to those of the community as well" (1993, 41).

So the hardest part for many of us is not bringing womanist pedagogy/womanist practices *into* anything. The difficulty is generating *out* of self-reliant, self-serving academic societies, like the proverbial round peg in the square hole, the responsibility for collective well-being, women's and men's, and the reliance upon each other that are second nature to most contemporary womanist enterprises. As we practice a community-bound scholarship, we black women often find ourselves divided between official commitments to our disciplinary homes and commitments to cultivating black women's studies in sociopolitical realms that we often consider more satisfying, and our peers regard as less enriching, than the former. Just how many of us, for example, are cultivating curricula vitae in two departments for tenure? And of this population, how many of us hold appointments in only one institute, department, or program? As we strive to create a community-bound intellectual record, we black women are too often asked to make an all-or-nothing choice: either generate our own scholarship or retrieve and evaluate the talents of other generations of black women and risk dire consequences. Just how many of us have risked the breach, editing as many projects as we have authored individually? How many of us are guilty of sneaking in just one more lecture to a student or civic group during Kwanzaa or black or women's history month, even though we know our colleagues mightily disapprove?

The academy bifurcates our pursuits into two paths—focused (or tenurable) and scattered (or irrelevant). It pits us in an adversarial relationship that opposes home, family, neighborhood, church, and culture versus Quality Time on the PC for our focused, relevant, academic projects. This dichotomy stands as another exquisite marginalization that harms both black women and the academy. It implies that well-roundedness is a pathology, the equivalent of academic arrested development, and it condemns our real black women's lives as at best inconsequential precisely because we find this well-roundedness unavoidable and vital.

Black women, Latina women, Asian women, Native women, white women—*women*—all, to greater and lesser degrees, experience the restrictions of this Hobson's choice between scholarship and community. Yet there are palpable cultural perspectives that influence how black women experience and negotiate these restrictions differently from other women. Black culture converges the meanings of the terms *intellectual, teacher,* and *activist.* Black culture views academic institutions as vehicles for knowledge production, preservation, and dissemination that are irreducible to four walls, one canon, and scores of competing theoretical and discursive fiefdoms. Black culture, finally, defines a community as inclusive of both individual, blood-related, family members and broader social networks. These legacies, among others, make pursuing an academic profession more than any single black woman's choice of family time over career advancement. It is a choice that places the body of black female intellectual endeavor on a course that collides head-on with academic culture.

Womanist philosophy jettisons these tensions and helps us black women to understand that our well-roundedness fulfills our highest expectations as scholars and can function as its own reward. Womanist philosophy appreciates and cultivates the well-rounded, dialectical teachers/researchers, the Michele Russells of knowledge construction. Womanism resists the dichotomy between focused and scattered pursuits by its emphasis on the community work that is foundational in the collective histories of black women. "Community work," as Cheryl Townsend Gilkes explains, "is a constant struggle, and it consists of everything that people do to address oppression in their own lives, suffering in the lives of others, and their sense of solidarity or group kinship" (1994, 231). When we integrate this womanist interpretation of community work into our colleges and universities, we arrest focus and elevate struggle. We write, produce, grade papers, edit *The Womanist* in the ghettoes of midnight work sessions and the gulped-down, solitary lunch hours at our desks—between classes, committees, advising sessions, seminars, and consultations. We struggle on, determined to accomplish our efforts without sacrificing our commitments for focus, because those workers that we know—workers, incidentally, who we are—know that the efforts must be made.

Finally, we bring to womanist enterprises the insight that culture thrives on a creole diet. Womanists sample. Another way to articulate this is to say, as one of my Afrocentric students loved to proclaim, that we clothe ourselves in our culture. "Go to the source," advice we have often heard as students and scholars, is a moot point to us. We *are* the sources, the everyday black women, as much as we are the gatherers/interpreters of the data, the "capable generators," as Layli describes us. We are like rappers who engage each other's rhythms and rhymes: borrowing from records, infiltrating them with our own lyrics and sounds, and then becoming the new source that is borrowed. In other words, we do not have a problem with our own subjectivity. To speak from our own locations, as Layli has put it, is not an issue. As Patricia Hill Collins writes, "For ordinary African-American women, those individuals who have lived through the experiences about which they claim to be experts are more believable and credible than those who have merely read or thought about such experiences" (1990, 209). Wherever we are as womanists, "lived through" or "read about," out there or in here, we bring a confidence in evaluating our own experiences, dictating our own discourses, and defining our own terms. Maybe this is what we bring the most. Maybe this is where we belong.

Why We Started *The Womanist*: Layli and Barbara

The idea for *The Womanist: A Newsletter for Afrocentric Feminist Researchers* was born out of a desire to empower others as Michele Russell and other Black feminists/womanists had empowered us as well as a desire to "create more space" for Black feminism and womanism in the academy. Knowing that the project entailed some professional risk, we initially vacillated, but our decision to publish it, one way or another, was cemented when we attended the first national conference of Black women academics, "Black Women in the Academy: Defending Our Name, 1894–1994," held at the Massachusetts Institute of Technology, January 13–15, 1994. Good fortune followed in the form of a grant from the Institute for African-American Studies at the University of Georgia, under the direction of R. Baxter Miller, who agreed to underwrite the production.

The Womanist: A Newsletter for Afrocentric Feminist Researchers was conceived as a forum for the exposition of theory and research. Quoting from the statement of purpose that appeared on the initial announcement for *The Womanist*, "*The Womanist* is meant to be a gathering place for Afrocentric feminist researchers who are struggling to devise, develop, and disseminate womanist methodologies within traditional (or non-traditional) academic disciplines ... a place where we can share ideas, ask questions, and engage in supportive criticism, in order to strengthen our mission, de-marginalize our activities, and provide wider access to our perspectives" (*The Womanist* 1994). The essential purpose of the publication was to help Black women who are trying to bring the everyday into the academy as well as to help the academy by presenting the everyday in a format that academicians could understand. The idea was to disrupt the traditional notion that Black women are merely the beneficiaries of academia in favor of the notion that the academy, particularly in this era of anxiety about "changing demographics," is the beneficiary of Black women's presence. In addition, the idea was to provide validation for Black women that, having entered the doors of academia, we nevertheless have not left our beloved everyday lives behind. The choice of a one-word moniker—womanist—reflected our position that Afrocentric feminism is more than just the sum of Afrocentrism and feminism.

We view *The Womanist* as a tool—a testament to the fact that, with all respect to Audre Lorde (1984), you *can* dismantle the master's house with the master's tools (after all, that's what he built it with) at the same time as you are forging new tools and building new structures. In addition, we view *The Womanist* as part of a larger project on the part of Black women everywhere: to make the institutional realm more accurately reflect our presence and our experiences. In such an endeavor, however, Black women also open the door for other marginalized or excluded groups and for the inclusion and institutional validation of their experiences and concerns. For this reason, Black feminism/womanism is a crucial aspect of the reformulation of the academy as a whole.

In sum, to interrogate "Who's Schooling Who?" is to look at what the academy has to gain (and has gained) from Black women, Black feminists, womanists, and their kin. It is to recognize how Black women have educated and can educate the academy about knowledge—its collection, its generation, its validation, and its dissemination. It is our hope that *The Womanist* can in some way assist in this undertaking.

Note

1. The difference in the capitalization of the term *black* in the two parts of this essay is intentional, marking a difference of opinion between the authors. One of the main tenets of womanism is such accommodation of diversity.

References

Austin, Regina. 1994. "The Responsibility of Intellectuals in the Age of Crack." *Boston Review* 19 (11): 3–9.

Collins, Patricia Hill. 1990. *Black Feminist Thought: Knowledge, Consciousness, and the Politics of Empowerment.* New York: Routledge.

Gilkes, Cheryl Townsend. 1994. " 'If It Wasn't for the Women ... : African American Women, Community Work, and Social Change." In *Women of Color in U.S. Society,* ed. Maxine Baca Zinn and Bonnie Thornton Dill, 229–46. Philadelphia: Temple University Press.

James, Joy. 1993. "African Philosophy, Theory, and 'Living Thinkers.' " In *Spirit, Space and Survival: African American Women in (White) Academe,* ed. Joy James and Ruth Farmer, 31–46. New York: Routledge.

Lorde, Audre. 1984. *Sister Outsider.* Trumansburg, N.Y.: Crossing.

Myers, Linda James. 1991. "Expanding the Psychology of Knowledge Optimally: The Importance of Worldview Revisited." In *Black Psychology,* ed. Reginald Jones, 15–28. Berkeley: Cobb & Henry.

Reeves, Diana. 1994. "Endangered Species." Song 6 on her compact disc *Art and Survival.* EMI Records.

Russell, Michele. 1982. "Black-Eyed Blues Connections: Teaching Black Women." In *All the Women Are White, All the Blacks Are Men, but Some of Us Are Brave: Black Women's Studies,* ed. Gloria T. Hull, Patricia Bell Scott, and Barbara Smith, 196–207. New York: Feminist Press.

The Womanist. 1994. *The Womanist: A Newsletter for Afrocentric Feminist Researchers,* promotional flyer. Presented at "Black Women in the Academy: Defending Our Name, 1894–1994," Massachusetts Institute of Technology, Boston, January 13–15.

To Be Black, Male, and "Feminist": Making Womanist Space for Black Men (1997)

GARY L. LEMONS

If black men and women take seriously Malcolm [X]'s charge that we must work for our liberation "by any means necessary," then we must be willing to explore the way feminism as a critique of sexism, as a movement to end sexism and sexist oppression, could aid our struggle to be self-determining.[1]

—**bell hooks**

Womanist. ... A black feminist or feminist of color ... [c]ommitted to survival and wholeness of entire people, male *and* female. ... Womanist is to feminist as purple to lavender.[2]

—**Alice Walker**

bell hooks says in "Reconstructing Black Masculinity" that "[c]ollectively we can break the life threatening choke-hold patriarchal masculinity imposes on black men and create life sustaining visions of a reconstructed black masculinity that can provide black men ways to save their lives and the lives of their brothers and sisters in struggle" (113). Toward the work of political (re)unification of the genders in black communities today, black men must acknowledge and begin to confront the existence of sexism in black liberation struggle as one of the chief obstacles impeding its advancement. Making womanist space for black men to participate in allied relation to feminist movement to oppose the oppression of women means black men going against the grain of the racist and sexist mythology of black manhood and masculinity in the U.S. Its underlying premise rooted in white supremacist patriarchal ideology continues to foster the idea that we pose a racial and sexual threat to American society such that our bodies exist to be feared, brutalized, imprisoned, annihilated—made invisible.

It has been the fear of emasculinization originating in the history of black male lynching where the power of white (male) supremacy performed itself in the ritual act of castration (the violent sexual *dis*membering of our bodies) as a tool "to put/keep us in our place"—expressly because we were *black* and *male*—to "feminize" us. Thus, it is the fear of feminization in the minds of many black men that has led us to over-determine our sexuality, believing the idea that our identity as men resides only in the power of our penises. Against the inhumanity of our past—we must create a place/space to make ourselves over again in our own image. It must not be one reconstructed in the very mythology which sexually demonized our bodies as the scourge of white womanhood, but rather one which frees us *to be black* in the most radically revolutionary manner, *to be male* in the most non-oppressive, anti-sexist way, *to be feminist* in the most supportive, non-patriarchal way to bring about an end to the domination, subordination, and mistreatment of women exactly because they are women.

I believe *womanism*, as Alice Walker conceived it, to be a liberatory location for remaking black manhood toward a male identity that transgresses the boundaries of patriarchy—freeing us from the oppressive racist/sexist, sexually "othered" space we occupied in the past. Theorizing a womanist space for black men means focusing on the historical impact castration and lynching have had on the black male psyche and on ways we construct our identity as men. It may begin to tell us why many black men have internalized the racist sexual myths of black manhood and masculinity such that images of "black macho" and the super sexual "buck/stud" have prevailed in black communities as legitimate representations of black male power. hooks maintains that "[B]lack men who are most worried about castration and emasculation are those who have completely absorbed white supremacist patriarchal definitions of masculinity" ("Reconstructing Black Masculinity," 93). The black buck stereotype, conceived in the white racist imagination during the period of slavery, signified that every black male (who did not fit the "Uncle Tom," older non-sexualized type) stood as the symbol of the sexually brutalizing phallus operating always already as a sexual threat to the purity of white womanhood—thus the need for castration.

As a controlling image in the contemporary period, phallic representations of black masculinity in the Black Power Movement of the 1960s manifested themselves in popular culture via the performance of hyper-masculinity as witnessed in the popularity of blaxploitation films in the 1970s (a genre made famous by the movie *Shaft* and a host of others featuring the "superfly" or the hyper-cool black male stereotype). Yet the mythology of black machismo remains grounded in the black man as super-sexual savage created to control black men during slavery.[3] The (re)production and perpetuation of a hyper-sexualized, hard black manhood/masculinity in white supremacist capitalist media is fed by stereotypical portrayals of black males. The very sexually over-determined images that have "essentially" typed us through history are played out repeatedly on the contemporary scene in the arena of popular culture, where the "dick-clutching" posture of many black male rappers has obtained as a status symbol of male power in Hip-hop.

I defy the notion that black manhood and masculinity is about a "dick thing." Progressive black men renouncing sexist, misogynist, and patriarchal

practice against women—that is the taproot of the "dick thing" mentality—
begin to mediate the painful historical memory of our own dehumanization.
Challenging the white supremacist stereotype of the "super dick" (that so
many black men have internalized as the symbol of black male power) means
resisting the racist/sexist sexual mythology created to control us. It would
have us believe that we are no more than one big collective "walking, brutalizing phallus." When we begin to interrogate its oppressive power over
us, we start to perceive the interrelated ways racism and male supremacist
privilege work together to dehumanize all black men. Understanding the
link between white privilege and male privilege—realizing that empowered
images of black manhood do not rest in the reclamation of lost phallic power
(the pre-eminent fallacy of manhood thinking in general)—black men come
to experience transformative, liberatory power as men. When we begin to
claim our bodies as our own—beyond the bounds of white supremacist capitalist patriarchal control—we no longer have to fear that our penises will be
cut off for being black and male. When we fully realize this, we confront the
psychic/sexual wound/violation that castration/lynching represents, discovering that our quest for power in the myth of the "big black dick" is a self-
dehumanizing act—physically, psychologically, and spiritually. Black men
coming to feminist consciousness signifies a radical departure from the rac-
ist/sexist ideology of black manhood/masculinity that has consumed many
of us. Black men moving to reclaim our womanist/feminist past contest the
power of the phallus in our lives and the lives of women, toward truly liberatory
meanings of manhood.

Theorizing Black Men as Pro-feminist Comrades

In this essay, I address the problematics of being a black male feminist focusing
on African-American men's historic relation to feminism and their relationship to black liberation struggle and issues of sexism, patriarchy, misogyny.
Examining the interrelation of these modes of female oppression to racism
in the light of black feminist critique of the multiplicity of oppression in the
history of black women's lives in the United States, I call for the creation of
a political space for black men "in" feminism grounded in the history of the
fight African-Americans waged for race and gender rights.

In the process, I address a set of questions which strike at the core of contemporary black resistance to feminism, while critically asserting the need
for contemporary black men (and women) to come together in "womanist"
solidarity to reclaim black male commitment to a liberatory movement rooted
in struggle against racism and sexism. Can black people in the U.S. reconceive
a freedom movement beyond the imperatives of male identity toward a progressive platform which opposes not only racism, sexism, and classism—but
homophobia as well? Can feminist and anti-racist strategies share the same
political agenda in the spirit of coalition movement?

In a period when white supremacist groups are re-emerging in the form of a militia movement, when a new black manhood movement predicated on the black patriarchal capitalist ideas of Louis Farrakhan—can a progressive coalition movement against domination be forged that transgresses the borders of identity politics to affect a truly liberatory ideology that embraces a multiplicity of struggle? Can the academy be a site of oppositional struggle where progressive educators employ the classroom as a strategic location for liberatory education practice? And finally, what difference can a black male feminist make toward a vision of "wholeness" in black communities, where every individual woman, man, and child is valued and cared for? Addressing these questions, as a black male feminist, I envision a space in feminism where black men can work to empower themselves in feminist solidarity—working in the tradition and spirit of their womanist legacy.

Today black men must begin remembering their feminist past, one in which the fight against racist oppression was integrally linked to women's liberation struggle. Comprehending the power of this crucial fact, we will have to rethink the meaning of contemporary black liberation struggle. Beyond the exclusionary politic of anti-racist strategizing based solely on a masculinist recuperation of manhood, black men must begin resisting sexist propaganda that tells us wrongfully that to be fully empowered as black men we should strive to "atone" for its loss. Progressive black people in the U.S., calling out sexist and misogynist practice perpetrated by black men, create counter-hegemonic black male and female space where locations of race, gender, and sexual healing are created. At this particular historical moment, considering the fact that there is an emerging movement around the repatriarchalization of black masculinity, black men in particular need to recognize the vital link between the histories of feminist movement and black liberation movement connected to womanist concerns—acting to reconnect politically the integral line that connects both struggles. Only then will black men achieve a status of dignity and self-worth that is not always already tied to patriarchy—constructing an integrative, holistic movement against the dehumanizing power of patriarchal thinking.

In 1925, Amy Jacques Garvey, editor of the "Women's Page" of the *Negro World* and wife of Marcus Garvey, declared—

> We are tired of hearing Negro men say, "There is a better day coming" while they do nothing to usher in the day. We are becoming so impatient that we are getting in the front ranks and serve notice that we will brush aside the halting, cowardly Negro leaders. ... Mr. Black Man watch your step! ... Strengthen your shaking knees and move forward, or we will displace you and lead on to victory and glory. (quoted in Giddings, 195)

Exhorting black men to act more aggressively toward racial progress or be "displace[d]" by more radically mobilized black women, Amy Garvey wrote without regard to the disposition of the black male ego. From the rise of black

feminism in the second half of the 19th century and the fervor of its movement in the 1920s, through its re-emergence in the writings of contemporary
black women novelists, critics, poets, theorists, and academics—black women
feminists have determined for themselves a course of action often set against
the grain of black racial and gender party lines. Always having to weigh their
actions with regard to notions of race solidarity and the defense of themselves
as women, black feminists share a history of liberation struggle cultivated in a
political (inter)relation of racism and sexism.

In the text above Amy Jacques Garvey (author)itatively calls into question
black male power (without compromising the movement for racial liberation).
(Re)writing the destiny of black women in liberation struggle, she proclaims
the power of black female agency. Yet when black women have written or spoken out in critique of black male status, privilege, and/or sexism—black men
have accused them of perpetuating white supremacist emasculation of the black
male. In the contemporary period, feminist black women writers continue to
be "object" of anti-feminist rhetoric. Thinking about the *Black Scholar* essay
Robert Staples' wrote in 1979 which initiated "The Debate on Black Sexism," I
maintain that the critique he wrote opposing black feminist writings by Michele
Wallace and Ntozake Shange foreshadowed subsequent attacks on Alice Walker,
Gayle Jones, Gloria Naylor, Toni Morrison, and Paule Marshall, among others,
through the 1980s and '90s marked by the onslaught of black male criticism
against the film version of Terry McMillan's recent novel *Waiting to Exhale*.

The anti-womanist response many black men voiced against the film echoed
the negative reaction expressed toward the cinematic representation of *The
Color Purple*, Alice Walker's epistolary novel of black female search for self-
empowerment. Scoring big at the box office during the first weeks it played,
Waiting to Exhale generated significant dialogue among black women and men
on the current state of gender relations in black communities. Yet many black
men contested male representation in the film asserting that once again a black
woman had misrepresented them, focusing on negative images. Viewing it as
nothing more than black male bashing, they saw no redeeming value to "airing
the dirty laundry of black people." Listening to a radio program in which call-
ers discussed their views of the film, I found myself wondering why every male
who phoned in severely lambasted McMillan for having "(mis)treated black
men in such stereotypical ways." A couple of weeks earlier, one black man I
encountered one afternoon while sitting on a bus came on equipped with a
copy of *Waiting to Exhale* in his hand ranting to black female passengers that
he *had* to read "another male-bashing-book by a sister." Rather than challenge
my black "brother" to rethink his misguided notion of black women writers, I
sat in silence remembering the outspoken manner in which I had defended the
book and film version of *The Color Purple* more than a decade ago.

As a black feminist man (having declared my political affiliation to feminism some years ago as the only [black] male student in a graduate women's

feminist organization) the manner in which I have articulated a pro-feminist positionality has taken many turns—some representing a radical "out" posture, others affecting a more subversive stance. In part, this essay works to oppose black male anti-feminist contempt and mistrust of contemporary black women writers as my work is an attempt to recover and reaffirm the history of black men in pro-feminist alliance with black and white women begun in the Woman Suffrage Movement. It also functions to assert the idea that black feminist critique of sexism and misogyny in black communities is not about "black male bashing"—but about black women confronting the reality of patriarchy acted out by black men. The "black male bashing" attitude only perpetuates popular media sensationalization of black life grounded in the myth of a black gender war. Creating space for progressive dialogues on the prevalence of black sexism need not be governed by male supremacist thinking as if the black male ego remains too fragile for the rigor of critique, even as black women labor under the myth of the matriarch, a castrating "superwoman." Recovering black men's pro-feminist past acts to engender a politic of intervention whereby black men (and women) come to understand the necessity of feminist critique in liberation struggle as a critical means to empower all black people.

Black Women Writing to Liberate Themselves: Breaking a Tradition of Silence

If the first wave of American feminism in the 19th century represented the struggle of black women to be recognized as "women"—the second movement for women's liberation set the stage for a renaissance of black women writers who employed literature as a vehicle for self-empowerment. Misguidely, the liberatory writings of black women have become the targets of black male anti-feminists precisely because many believe that the sole aim of black female writers is to bash them. Critical dialogue during and since "The Debate on Black Sexism" has continued around what black male detractors of feminism consider the emasculation of black men by "angry black feminists," Robert Staples calls Wallace and Shange. Black men opposed to feminism, such as Ishmael Reed, have accused black women writers of complicity with white women feminists toward the racist castration of all black men.

Black women writers have been accused of breaking faith with a standing agreement with their male counterparts and black female representation of black men said to be counter-productive to African-American struggle against racist oppression. Yet few of the black male critics of black women writers are willing to acknowledge the reality of sexism in black communities. In "Family Plots: Black Women Writers Reclaim Their Past," Thulani Davis articulates the perceived attack on black men this way—

Contemporary [women] writers are being accused of pillorying black men, promoting homosexuality, ignoring sociological overviews of black oppression—and they're often pegged as the first black writers to commit such sins. (14)

To the extent that black women have embraced feminism, many black anti-feminists believe it has led them into acts of betrayal through a "(Ms.)representation" of black men. The price black women writers pay is expulsion from the Tradition of ("racial uplift") writing hereto dominated by African-American male writers. According to Mel Watkins in "Sexism, Racism and Black Women Writers,"

> Those black women writers who have chosen black men as a target have set themselves outside a tradition that is nearly as old as black American literature itself. They have, in effect, put themselves at odds with what seems to be an unspoken but almost universally accepted covenant among black writers. (36)

The "unspoken covenant" to which Watkins refers resides in myth. Black writers have never had such an unstated agreement. In African-American literary history, prescriptive notions of representation have traditionally met opposition (example: the Harlem renaissance). To suggest (as Watkins does later in his article) that the Harlem renaissance was a period during which "the earliest fiction by American blacks, produced by the Talented Tenth school of writers ... [was] characterized by [its] emphasis on establishing humane, positive images of blacks" (36) reveals a limited knowledge of the period's literary crisis regarding the representation of blacks in fiction. Watkins completely ignores the many black female *and male* writers who contested the provincialism, sexism, and homophobia of the black middle class. Watkins' claim that contemporary African-American women writers initiated a trend toward negative images of black men ignores those less than positive portrayals created by a number of black male writers. Like Watkins, Robert Staples would have us believe Shange and Wallace were the first (rightly) "angry black feminists." How would black men like Mel Watkins and Robert Staples read the feminist writings of Frederick Douglass and W.E.B. Du Bois? Would they be called "angry black feminists"? Apparently, contemporary black men who oppose feminism have no knowledge of Shange and Wallace's historical black male womanist counterparts.

(Re)constructing a Black Male Feminist Past, toward a Black Womanist Future

Considering the difference race makes in relation to black men and feminism, my analysis of black male feminism is situated in the historical light of African-American male participation in the Woman Suffrage Movement. It forms the basis for theorizing black male feminism as a site of resistance to anti-womanist thinking and a location for gender solidarity, where transformative ideas of black manhood and masculinity in support of women's rights work against the ideology of male supremacy. Contesting black male attacks on black feminists—from Michele Wallace and Ntozake Shange in the late 1970s to Alice Walker and Terry McMillan in the following decades—black men understanding the longstanding relationship between black women and men in coalition struggle for woman suffrage in the 1920s disrupts the contemporary myth that all black men are anti-feminists. (Re)establishing a black men's womanist history represents an important step toward ending the myth of feminism as an (alien)ating force in black lives.

On the one hand, racial imperatives articulated in the framework of race and cultural nationalism since the 1960s—during the rise of the Black Power Movement and most recently in the call for black male repatriarchalization by Louis Farrakhan with the Million Man March—"blackness" has again become synonymous with "maleness," reinscribing a male-centered view of race that always already ignores issues of sexism. On the other, in the '60s issues of gender equality and women's rights led the agenda of the Women's Liberation Movement, principally dominated by middle class white women. And for many white women feminists still, the relation of men to feminism continues to be articulated in terms of gender alone, excluding the impact race has had and continues to have on gender relations in the U.S. By the end of the Black Power Movement, just as racial injustice had come to be identified mostly with the plight of the black male, so at the height of the Women's Liberation Movement the oppression of women had come to be associated with women who were white and middle class.

Reflecting on the race and gender politics of the 1960s, I have come to view the Black Power Movement and the second wave of feminism as important clarifying moments in my evolution as a black male feminist teacher in the 1990s. But like black women feminists advocating the struggle against racism, black men supporting women against sexism find ourselves on the margins of both black liberation and women's movements. Often having to confront the question: Are you "black" first or "feminist"? we find ourselves walking a race/gender tight-rope always having to negotiate a position of split allegiance. For black women feminists, emphasis on their status as women in many black communities has been equated with a betrayal of race solidarity and lesbianism (as if heterosexual affiliation alone should determine one's affinity to blackness).

The absence of a large-scale political pronouncement of black men in support of anti-sexist activism suggests that in the contemporary period something called "black male pro-feminism" is invisible. And in many ways, being black and male in feminist alliance means being an "invisible (wo)man"—not a woman but neither a man in traditional phallocentric terms. Without oversimplifying this condition, perhaps, there is a kind of gender/race ambiguity that informs the idea of black male feminist positionality. But, as I have stated before, it is the idea of feminism connected to a perverse notion of the feminine that in the historical memory of black men conjures up images of feminization, castration, and ultimately death which may partly account for contemporary black male antifeminism. Thus, in white supremacist capitalist patriarchal culture, to many black men feminism represents a threat to their vision of black masculinity and manhood—of familial and cultural authority, responsibility, nationhood, and "manliness." Many view feminism in synonymous relation to white supremacist attempt to reinact the sexual "un-maning" of black men as the prime spectacle in the contemporary period of a "high tech" lynching.

Yet we can no longer use the myth of feminism as a racist ploy to emasculate black men while we assert our power as men to oppress women. Progressive black men, whether or not we advocate feminism, ought to begin divesting ourselves of male privilege in support of black women. Opposing sexism and misogyny, we embrace our history of pro-feminist alliance in women's rights struggle. Confronting the fear of the feminine that feminism represents to many men, black men begin to formulate effective, liberatory strategies of gender empowerment in black communities which affirm the rights of all women. Moreover, as we insist upon our right to be treated with dignity and respect in this society, we do so not because we are men but because we are human beings. Black men need to know that feminism—as a belief rooted in the right of women to lead non-oppressive, non-objectified lives—is not racist, sexist, or classist. We must vigorously denounce black male anti-feminist rhetoric that reduces the feminism of black women to a diatribe against black men.

If black women feminists are "angry" with black men (to recite Robert Staples' choice of words), then we need to ask why—without the cloak of self-pity that so many of us wear as we hide behind the wall of sexist denial to defend our oppressive behavior and misogynist ways. We can no longer construct ourselves as innocent victims of racism—castrated by "our" women who have no sympathy for the battle we wage against the (white) "Man" who refuses us a bigger slice of patriarchal pie. Black men in the Woman Suffrage Movement speaking and writing in feminist alliance rejected the "black-man-as-victim" status as they fought to obtain social, economic, and political rights for black men and women—while working to secure certain rights for women particularly based on the condition of gender oppression across the boundaries of race. Why can't we?

Black Men Speaking and Writing in Feminist Alliance

Fundamentally, it must be stated that from Frederick Douglass to W.E.B. Du Bois, feminist movement in black communities has had a significant impact on the representation of African-Americans in black discourse. The emergence of a black female intelligentsia in the last decade of the 19th century was preceded by the rise of Douglass as one of the century's most recognized black intellectuals, and followed by Du Bois as the major arbiter of the intellectual and artistic movement known as the Harlem renaissance. In the African-American literary tradition these men stand as acknowledged leaders of the "race," but each in his own right commanded more than one discursive field in which he spoke and wrote on the subject of women's rights. To view Douglass and Du Bois only as race leaders obscures and diminishes their distinguished careers as advocates of women's rights. To overlook their active participation in the developing stage of black women's intellectual and political enterprise (from which African-American feminist movement emerged) represents a grave oversight. Frances Ellen Harper, Pauline Hopkins, Anna Julia Cooper, and Ida B. Wells, among others, constituted a feminist intellectual body of which Frederick Douglass and W.E.B. Du Bois were an integral part.

As pro-woman speakers and writers, these men fit within the black feminist tradition at the incisive juncture of black women's political and social activism, characterized in the writings of the "Woman's Era." I assert the importance of the pro-woman position Douglass and Du Bois held partly to counter the phallocentric identification of blackness, though at times both men represented themselves in rather traditionally patriarchal ways. In recovering the women's rights discourse of Douglass and Du Bois as models of black male pro-feminism, I employ it to counterpose contemporary black male anti-feminist sentiment. I argue that the vision of liberation struggle these men constructed around a race/gender coalition politic holds transformative possibilities for black liberation movement today. The liberatory nature of feminist writings by Douglass and Du Bois rest precisely on the conjoinment of gender and race issues. This way of thinking is representative of the ideals early coalition strategists conceived in linking abolitionism to feminism. Douglass, Elizabeth Cady Stanton, and Susan B. Anthony among others viewed gender and race oppression in coterminous relation (notwithstanding the racist ideology of the Woman Suffrage Movement). Therefore, a movement to oppose gender and race oppression could constitute a much more politically viable and powerful location from which to strategize black enfranchisement and the political freedom of women.

Relying on black feminists theorizing race, gender, and class as interlocking systems of oppression, I look to the work of Paula Giddings, Angela Davis, and hooks on the history of black women and men in feminist movement to clarify the dual positions Douglass and Du Bois occupied as race spokesmen and advocates of women's rights. As standpoints determining their views of black liberation, race/gender duality inform the complex ideological structure of the men's feminist writings. Grasping the strategy Douglass and Du Bois conceived to advance the struggle of black people enables contemporary black men to reconceptualize a movement in resistance to white supremacy which encompasses strategies that oppose the oppression of women.

While the history of joint movement involving black and white people against racism and sexism in the U.S. presents less than a glowing model of success, as a feminist I believe progressive feminism (founded on the liberation of all people, female and male) remains a crucial site in which to foster a coalition politic—linking political resistance to gender, race, class, and sexual oppression (across the boundaries of identity politics). I believe the infusion of coalition politics, informed by feminist thinking, in black people's movement for liberation would transform the dynamics of gender relations in black communities such that no one—regardless of sex, sexual preference, and/or class—is excluded from the battle for black people to live as whole beings. In the process, black men interrogating meanings of manhood (beyond white supremacist patriarchal denial of black male humanity) come to view feminism as a life-sustaining way of thinking that enhances rather than threatens our lives. As woman suffragists and advocates of women's rights, Frederick Douglass and W.E.B. Du Bois have much to offer us as black male feminists.

"(Black) Men in Feminism?" The "Ins" and "Outs" of (White) Male Feminism

In the 1980s male feminism was debated in *Men in Feminism* (1987), edited by Alice Jardine and Paul Smith. Centering on the theoretical problematics of male feminism, essays in the anthology focused on issue of men's relation (or nonrelation) to feminist theory. Given the ever-increasing presence of male critical and theoretical discourse on women, a volume such as *Men in Feminism* possessed the potential to be crucially important to a continuing dialogue on where men stand in relation to feminism. But it woefully failed. The essays, for the most part, exclude a discussion of race and sexuality. The volume includes not one essay by a woman or man of color. What references there are to black men and women are only incidental. The relation of men of color to feminism is never addressed. We remain invisible at nearly every level of discussion. Only one essay written by a white gay man overtly engages "men in feminism" and male sexuality. Jardine and Smith blame the virtual absence of gay and nonwhite perspectives on their "trouble locating intellectuals, who, having shown interest in the question, would offer ... a gay or black perspective on the problem." Rather than simply confess to the failure of their search, they point to academia's lack of institutional commitment to diversity in its hiring practices (vii–viii).

I seriously question how extensively the editors' looked for the "Other" perspective when by 1987 bell hooks had already written on the relationship of men of color to feminism in *Feminist Theory: From Margin to Center*, 1984. In spite of its glaring silence on the subject of black men and feminism, conceptually *Men in Feminism* raises a fundamental question as to whether male feminists can work to empower women in non-patriarchal ways. In "Male Feminism," Stephen Heath addresses this question asserting that "[m]en's relation to feminism is an impossible one ... politically. Men have a necessary relation to feminism ... and that relation is also necessarily one of a certain exclusion ... no matter how 'sincere,' 'sympathetic' or whatever, we are always in a male position which brings with it all the implications of domination and appropriation ..." (1). The idea that men cannot in feminist alliance with women politically subvert the power of male supremacy is like saying white people in anti-racist solidarity with black people cannot divest themselves of white supremacist thinking.

Considering the institutionalization of women's studies in the academy and the proliferation of feminist scholarship by men (mostly white), I too am suspicious of male presence into this arena—particularly when so much of it appears appropriative, motivated by professional advancement. Yet male feminism situated in activist relation to feminist movement demonstrates a necessary engagement in theory and practice. Otherwise, the "in" space of "feminist" men construct can only be patriarchal—one of control, penetration, and violation. Discovering and writing about the lives of Douglass and Du Bois as woman suffragists has helped me to free myself from the kind of paralyzing male feminist theorizing trap that Stephen Heath sets up. If all feminist men concluded as he does that our relation to feminism is indeed an impossible one, we would never get on with the task at hand—to end sexism and the oppression of women. The history of black male pro-feminist relation to women's movement against sexism shows that despite the patriarchal baggage all men carry, we can be men without being oppressors of women.

(Black) male feminism as a politic of intervention (opposing sexism in black communities) represents a crucial step toward educating men on the ill-effects of male domination. According to bell hooks, the struggle against sexist oppression will be most successfully fought when men undergo feminist transformation—only when we are challenged by women to understand that the oppression of women is a form of self-oppression. Women can no longer afford to theorize men on the margin of feminism when sexist practice impacts the lives of women daily as its victims and men as its perpetrators. Women accepting progressive men as feminist allies end the stigma of feminist movement as a separatist enterprise. While separatist thinking may free women from the presence of men, it does not eradicate sexism in the society at large. Instead, it mirrors the very sexist behavior feminist women seek to end.

"Re-membering" in Feminist Solidarity, Renewing Progressive Partnerships between Black Women and Men

As the 1960s brought forth with it a renaissance of black women writers, so it gave birth to a new generation of black female scholar/critics who would become the architects of a black feminist theory and criticism. From the re-emergence of feminism in black communities in the 1960s, came some of today's most outspoken black feminists. Of them, bell hooks, more than any other has addressed the necessity of black men in feminist movement. "Men:

Comrades in Struggle" (in *Feminist Theory: From Margin to Center*) critically addressed the need for men's political engagement in feminism. In one of her most radical essays on the subject, "Feminist Focus on Men" (from *Talking Back: Thinking Feminist, Thinking Black*, 1989)—she calls for women scholars to begin writing on men:

> Now we [women] can acknowledge that the reconstruction and trans-formation of male behavior, of masculinity, is a necessary and essen-tial part of feminist revolution. ... While it is critical that male scholars committed to feminist struggle do scholarship that focuses on men, it is equally important that women scholars focus on men. (127, 132)

Putting into practice that which she advocates, hooks works in the tradi-tion of 19th and early 20th-century black feminist coalition struggle. *Yearn-ing: Race, Gender, and Cultural Politics* (1990) includes "Black Women and Men: Partnership in the 1990s," a dialogue between herself and Cornel West. *Breaking Bread: Insurgent Black Intellectual Life* (1991), co-authored with West, opens with the essay above as the basis for what represents a book-length continuation of the conversation the two began earlier. As intellectual "part-ners" discussing the challenge of integrating radical intellectualism into the struggle against racism, sexism, and the economic and cultural exploitation of African-Americans, they become comrades of the mind negotiating—

> [T]he point of connection between black women and men [that is the] space of recognition and understanding, where we know one another so well, our histories, that we can take the bits and pieces, the fragments of who we are, and put them back together, re-member them. (19)

In "re-member[ing]" black women and men's histories, hooks and West remember the legacy of those gone before them, who fought for the liberation of black people. That hooks and West would frame their coming together in the tradition of African-American intellectualism brings a new, even more lucid understanding of a historic exchange between black women and men. Well known dialogues have been recorded between Frederick Douglass and black women intellectuals including Sojourner Truth, Frances Harper, and Ida B. Wells-Barnett, among others. Dialogues have been documented which took place between W.E.B. Du Bois and Mary Church Terrell, Anna Julia Cooper, and Jessie Fauset—as well as those he had with a number of other black female thinkers of his day. *Breaking Bread* is about maintaining and preserving the historical continuity of black intellectual life. In the company of Douglass and Du Bois, bell hooks and Cornel West find their dialogue solidly grounded in a long history of black female/male "partnership" in feminist movement.

Claiming the feminist positionality of Douglass and Du Bois as a critical standpoint from which to call contemporary black men into renewed dialogue with black women on the status of gender relations in black communities, as a feminist black male college professor teaching African-American literature, I have constructed a cluster of courses in which the focus is the examination of the gender, race, class, and sexual politics of black people in the U.S. Teaching as a feminist, I aim my courses (while focusing on the experiences of black Americans) to engender the anti-racist/anti-sexist agenda Douglass and Du Bois conceived. The remainder of this essay works to explain the performance of anti-racist-feminism in my education practice—where the classroom is employed as a space not only for teaching progressive race and gender politics but for creating a liberatory location in which students learn about the transformative power of human rights activism.

From Theory to Practice: Teaching Feminism to Re-member

Committed to progressive feminist movement as articulated by hooks, I envision teaching as a process of "re-membering" in which African-American literary narratives become agents of social healing, across the boundaries of race, gender, class, and sexuality. Many students interested in ways these categories intersect come to my classes seeking an approach to understand the complex relation between them. I set up the political struggle of black Americans recounted in fiction, poetry, and/or essay form as a model for liberation politics.

Over the past five years, I have developed a course repertory grounded in feminism.[4] Working from my background in African-American literature, the courses I teach apply a sociological perspective to the representation of black female/male gender relations rather than a strictly traditional "literary" interpretation. This approach illustrates the juncture where the personal, political, and pedagogical meet to establish the classroom as a space of feminist activism, where teaching black literature serves a liberatory purpose.

But it is the standpoint from which I perform an anti-racist/feminist pedagogy in the classroom that distinguishes my teaching as a male feminist. Thinking about ways to contest male privilege, sexism, and patriarchal hegemony and the power of the maternal in my life as a man, a husband, a father, and a teacher—I have come to draw upon the style, attitudes, and critical thinking about life experience my mother passed on to me. For me, performing a black male feminist positionality in the classroom means tapping into the maternal as a transformative space in which to nurture the development of critical consciousness in my students. I work to achieve a relationship with them associated with a maternal posture rather than paternal, patriarchal, or traditionally masculine-identified interaction. Following Sara Ruddick's progressive line of thought that "a man who engages in mothering to some extent takes on the female condition and risks identification with the feminine" (45), I claim the act of "mothering" as a liberatory location to employ the maternal as a strategy of nurturance in my pedagogical practice in opposition to ways of the Father.

Growing up in a patriarchal household where my father's experience as a military officer informed the masculine rigidity of its day-to-day operation—as an often withdrawn timid little boy, I came to fear, despise, and later resist his notions of manhood, manliness, and masculinity. But in reflection, I was never drawn to the idea of male supremacy. More than anything, I identified with my mother's condition as black woman who, as a house-keeper/cook for a period in her life working tirelessly at the whims of elite white women, always had to enter the back door of their elegantly appointed homes to perform her duties as a servant. But it is my mother's sharp tongue, her resolute will to struggle, her critical understanding of the way race shaped her experience as a black female working class mother and wife that have informed how and what I teach. Teaching students (male students in particular) to resist anti-feminist ideas that men embracing feminism necessarily means a loss of a masculinity, I hold to Ruddick's idea that: "The fear of becoming 'feminine'...is a motivating force behind the drive to master women and whatever is 'womanly.' ... [G]rown men should confront the political meaning of 'femininity' and their own fear of the feminine. A man does not, by becoming a mother, give up his male body or any part of it. To be sure, by becoming a mother he will, in many social groups, challenge the ideology of masculinity" (45).

It stands to reason that men who embrace feminist thinking risk having their masculinity called into question; this is the point exactly. A man advocating and teaching feminism means taking risks—breaking through barriers of manhood and masculinity inscribed in patriarchy, where qualities of nurturance and mothering are devalued. The maternal, as Ruddick insists, possesses *transgendered* capabilities.

Since my first course in feminism nearly ten years ago in graduate school when I read *Feminist Theory: From Margin to Center* for the first time, hooks' progressive vision of feminist movement against all forms of domination has shaped and guided my vision of the classroom as a space for liberatory education practice. But feminism itself remains a contested ideology in and outside the classroom not only because it subverts patriarchal power but also because it is bound up in complicated issues of race, class, and sexuality. For any teacher—whether female or male, black or not, gay or straight—employing progressive feminist politics to teach against white supremacy and male domination represents a transgressive act. Anti-racist feminist practice in the classroom requires risk-taking by the teacher and student. Often it means speaking from the personal, a space loaded with ideological baggage in need of exposure and examination.

When declaring to students that I am a feminist, they always react in complex ways, depending upon their race, gender, and sexual affiliations. But a feminist black man in (or outside) the classroom is an oddity. First of all, I am at odds with many white students' fear of black men and racist attitudes about black people in general. Secondly, I am at odds with many black students whose rage against and contempt for all white people blind them to the possibilities of progressive coalition movement across racial boundaries in resistance to racism, when we begin to de-essentialize "blackness." I am also at odds with male students especially (of color and not) who buy into male supremacist ideas of manhood and masculinity. They view me as a traitor to *man*kind, a misanthrope of the worst kind!

As a black man teaching feminism as a strategy to combat racism, I take risks in the classroom posing a particular challenge to essentialized meanings of black liberation and racial solidarity linked to narrow ideas of black manhood and masculinity. Like black women feminists, my commitment to black struggle against racism is called into question by students of color who (always few in number at my institution) argue that "feminism is a white woman's thing." As a black man teaching in a predominately white, private institution who advocates an end to male privilege, sexism, and misogyny from a particularly "black" feminist perspective, my color and gender pose problems for white students in my classes. While white male presence in them is rare, those white men they do attract are often in the process of coming to grips with their fear of "blackness"—especially that personified in negative stereotypes of black men. Similarly, white women in my classes, whether feminist or not, respond to me in ways that suggest they too are working to figure out their own relationship to a "feminist black man." Feminist students who are female (of color and not), suspicious of men's motives for teaching and claiming feminist alliance, often display attitudes of distrust toward the notion of a male feminist. Generally, in the minds of both white students and students of color, I represent an image of black manhood and masculinity out of synch with the racist and sexual mythologies inscripted on the black male body over the course of time. I am not a Sambo, an Uncle Tom, a buck, a rapist, or a dope-dealer. But I am a black man who must downplay the fact of my tallness (6'4") and my "loud" voice (which I have been told by white females in my classes that these aspects of my identity frighten them)—because I am specifically "black" and "male."

By the same token, disclaiming a patriarchal nationalist black masculinity (as represented by the ideas of Farrakhan dramatically played out in the Million Man March), I am viewed by many black male students as not only having sold out my blackness but my manhood as well because I critically opposed the March and most of its "Mission Statement." I maintain that a major contributing factor to the failure of black liberation movement in the 1960s had to do with its over-emphasis on issues relating to the needs of black men that excluded those of black women. The inability of the movement to sustain a successful oppositional stance and resistance to white supremacy and white supremacist capitalist patriarchal exploitation of black culture resided in the fact that many black men who participated in the movement viewed the struggle against racism solely in male-identified terms as I have already argued.

Black students in my classes (often because they feel threatened by implicit and explicit acts of racism perpetrated by white administrators, faculty members, and staff persons in a predominately white university setting) resist my claim that anti-racist ideology must be affected through a number of radical strategies—beyond the limited perspective of black male identity politics. Toward bell hooks' liberatory vision of "education as the practice of freedom," I claim a pedagogical strategy rooted in the politics of progressive feminist movement against all forms of domination, where teachers committed to coalition building cross race, gender, class, and sexual borders teach students ways to oppose the dehumanization of all people.

Contemporary black men actively calling into question male supremacy represents a potentially powerful voice for rethinking black masculinity. Transformative strategies of black liberation linked to a liberatory vision of black manhood and masculinity reflect a critically oppositional view of black men's racial oppression and the power we possess to oppress women precisely because we are men. When black men begin to construct a large-scale movement against racism *and sexism,* we embark upon a new path of struggle— one of feminist reclamation, not patriarchal atonement. Accepting our past as black men fighting racism as we waged with women the battle for gender rights, we claim a destiny beyond the bounds of patriarchy.

Notes

1. Excerpted from Alice Walker's definition of "womanist" in *In Search of Our Mothers' Gardens* (San Diego: Harcourt Brace Jovanovich, Publishers), 1983.
2. From "Reconstructing Black Masculinity" in *Black Looks: Race and Representation* (Boston: South End Press), 1992.
3. In *Soul on Ice* and *Sex and Racism in America,* respectively, both Eldridge Cleaver and Calvin Hernton offer provocative versions of U.S. race, gender sexual hierarchy in which the racist sexualization of the black male operates.
4. For example, students in a course I teach called "Black Female Representation in the Harlem Renaissance" focus on the politics of gender and race in the U.S. during the 1920s. They study fictional accounts of "mixed-race" women in the African-American literary genre known as the "novel of passing." Examining the impact of miscegenation on the female body, students call into question "race" as an inherently natural category while analyzing the interrelated ways white supremacy, male privilege, classism, and homophobia function to shape the destiny of "biracial" women. Female and male students reading, discussing, and writing about the dilemma of "the tragic mulatta" come to understand the value of progressive feminist critique to engage the multiple oppression she experiences. Interrogating the fallibility of racial categorizing and the fallacy of whiteness, they comprehend the oppression of women as bound up in complex matrix of competing power relations. Moreover, they come to understand that all forms of domination are interconnected. I suggest to them that for individuals concerned with issues of social justice, coalition politics rooted in feminist movement can be a powerful force toward mobilizing people across borders. For me, the classroom serves as a viable site for the development of critical consciousness that values coalition building that resists the dehumanization of all people. Teaching in the spirit of feminist black men like Frederick Douglass and W.E.B. Du Bois advocating feminism who have come before me, I put into practice the anti-racist-feminist legacy they created.

Bibliography

Cleaver, Eldridge. *Soul on Ice.* New York: Dell Publishing Co., Inc., 1968.

Davis, Thulani. "Family Plots: Black Women Writers Reclaim the Past." *Voice Literary Supplement* Mar. 1987: 14–17.

Giddings, Paula. *When and Where I Enter: The Impact of Black Women on Race and Sex in America.* New York: Bantam Books, 1984.

Hernton, Calvin. *Sex and Racism in America.* New York: Grove Press, 1965.

hooks, bell. *Feminist Theory: From Margin to Center.* Boston: South End Press, 1984.

——. *Talking Back: Thinking Feminist, Thinking Black.* Boston: South End Press, 1989.

——. *Yearning: Race, Gender, and Cultural Politics.* Boston: South End Press, 1990.

——. *Black Looks: Race and Representation.* Boston: South End Press, 1992.

hooks, bell, and West, Cornel. *Breaking Bread: Insurgent Black Intellectual Life.* Boston: South End Press, 1991.

Jardine, Alice and Paul Smith, eds. *Men in Feminism.* New York: Routledge, 1987.

Ruddick, Sara. *Maternal Thinking: Toward a Politics of Peace.* New York: Ballantine Books, 1989.

Staples, Robert. "The Myth of Black Macho: A Response to Angry Black Feminists." *The Black Scholar.* Mar.–Apr. 1979: 24–32.

Walker, Alice. *In Search of Our Mothers' Gardens.* San Diego: Harcourt Brace Jovanovich, Publishers, 1983.

Watkins, Mel. "Sexism, Racism and Black Women Writers." *The New York Times Book Review.* June 1986: 36.

Part 3
Womanist Theory and Praxis: Womanism in the Disciplines

6

Theology

Womanist Theology: Black Women's Voices (1986)

DELORES S. WILLIAMS

Daughter:	Mama, why are we brown, pink, and yellow, and our cousins are white, beige, and black?
Mother:	Well, you know the colored race is just like a flower garden, with every color flower represented.
Daughter:	Mama, I'm walking to Canada and I'm taking you and a bunch of slaves with me.
Mother:	It wouldn't be the first time.

In these two conversational exchanges, Pulitzer Prize–winning novelist Alice Walker begins to show us what she means by the concept "womanist." The concept is presented in Walker's *In Search of Our Mothers' Gardens,* and many women in church and society have appropriated it as a way of affirming themselves as *black* while simultaneously owning their connection with feminism and with the Afro-American community, male and female. The concept of womanist allows women to claim their roots in black history, religion, and culture.

What then is a womanist? Her origins are in the black folk expression "You acting womanish," meaning, according to Walker, "wanting to know more and in greater depth than is good for one … outrageous, audacious, courageous and *willful* behavior." A womanist is also "responsible, in charge, serious." She can walk to Canada and take others with her. She loves, she is committed, she is a universalist by temperament.

Her universality includes loving men and women, sexually or nonsexually. She loves music, dance, the spirit, food and roundness, struggle, and she loves herself "Regardless."

Walker insists that a womanist is also to "committed survival and wholeness of entire people, male and female." She is no separatist, "except for health." A womanist is a black feminist or feminist of color. Or Walker says, "Womanist is to feminist as purple to lavender."

Womanist theology, a vision in its infancy, is emerging among Afro-American Christian women. ... Ultimately many sources—biblical,[1] theological, ecclesiastical, social, anthropological, economic, and material from other religious traditions—will inform the development of this theology. As a contribution to this process, I will demonstrate how Walker's concept of womanist provides some significant clues for the work of womanist theologians. I will then focus on method and God-content in womanist theology. This contribution belongs to the work of prolegomena—prefatory remarks, introductory observations intended to be suggestive and not conclusive.

Codes and Contents

In her definition, Walker provides significant clues for the development of womanist theology. Her concept contains what black feminist scholar bell hooks in *From Margin to Center* identifies as cultural codes. These are words, beliefs, and behavioral patterns of a people that must be deciphered before meaningful communication can happen cross-culturally. Walker's codes are female-centered and they point beyond themselves to conditions, events, meanings, and values that have crystalized in the Afro-American community *around women's activity* and formed traditions.

A paramount example is mother-daughter advice. Black mothers have passed on wisdom for survival—in the white world, in the black community, and with men—for as long as anyone can remember. Female slave narratives, folk tales, and some contemporary black poetry and prose reflect this tradition. Some of it is collected in "Old Sister's Advice to Her Daughters," in *The Book of Negro Folklore* edited by Langston Hughes and Arna Bontemps (Dodd Mead, 1958).

Walker's allusion to skin color points to an historic tradition of tension between black women over the matter of some black men's preference for light-skinned women. Her reference to black women's love of food and roundness points to customs of female care in the black community (including the church) associated with hospitality and nurture.

These cultural codes and their corresponding traditions are valuable resources for indicating and validating the kind of data upon which womanist theologians can reflect as they bring black women's social, religious, and cultural experience into the discourse of theology, ethics, biblical and religious studies. Female slave narratives, imaginative literature by black women, autobiographies, the work by black women in academic disciplines, and the testimonies of black church women will be authoritative sources for womanist theologians.

Walker situates her understanding of a womanist in the context of non-bourgeois black folk culture. The literature of this culture has traditionally reflected more egalitarian relations between men and women, much less rigidity in male-female roles, and more respect for female intelligence and ingenuity than is found in bourgeois culture.

The black folk are poor. Less individualistic than those who are better off, they have, for generations, practiced various forms of economic sharing. For example, immediately after Emancipation mutual aid societies pooled the resources of black folk to help pay for funerals and other daily expenses. *The Book of Negro Folklore* describes the practice of rent parties which flourished during the Depression. The black folk stressed togetherness and a closer connection with nature. They respect knowledge gained through lived experience monitored by elders who differ profoundly in social class and world view from the teachers and education encountered in American academic institutions. Walker's choice of context suggests that womanist theology can establish its lines of continuity in the black community with non-bourgeois traditions less sexist than the black power and black nationalist traditions.

In this folk context, some of the black female-centered cultural codes in Walker's definition (e.g., "Mama, I'm walking to Canada and I'm taking you and a bunch of slaves with me") point to folk heroines like Harriet Tubman, whose liberation activity earned her the name "Moses" of her people. This allusion to Tubman directs womanist memory to a liberation tradition in black history in which women took the lead, acting as catalysts for the community's revolutionary action and for social change. Retrieving this often hidden or diminished female tradition of catalytic action is an important task for womanist theologians and ethicists. Their research may well reveal that female models of authority have been absolutely essential for every struggle in the black community and for building and maintaining the community's institutions.

Freedom Fighters

The womanist theologian must search for the voices, actions, opinions, experience, and faith of women whose names sometimes slip into the male-centered rendering of black history, but whose actual stories remain remote. This search can lead to such little-known freedom fighters as Milla Granson and her courageous work on a Mississippi plantation. Her liberation method broadens our knowledge of the variety of strategies black people have used to obtain freedom. According to scholar Sylvia Dannett, in *Profiles in Negro Womanhood,*

> Milla Granson, a slave, conducted a midnight school, for several years. She had been taught to read and write by her former master in Kentucky ... and in her little school hundreds of slaves benefited from her learning. ... After laboring all day for their master, the slaves would creep stealthily to Milla's "schoolroom" (a little cabin in a back alley). ... The doors and windows ... had to be kept tightly sealed to avoid discovery. Each class was composed of twelve pupils and when Milla had brought them up to the extent of her ability, she "graduated" them and took in a dozen more. Through this means she graduated hundreds of slaves. Many of whom she taught to write a legible hand [forged] their own passes and set out for Canada.

Women like Tubman and Granson used subtle and silent strategies to liberate themselves and large numbers of black people. By uncovering as much as possible about such female liberation, the womanist begins to understand the relation of black history to the contemporary folk expression: "If Rosa Parks had not sat down, Martin King would not have stood up."

While she celebrates and *emphasizes* black women's culture and way of being in the world, Walker simultaneously affirms black women's historic connection with men through love and through a shared struggle for survival and for productive quality of life (e.g., "wholeness"). This suggests that two of the principal concerns of womanist theology should be survival and community building and maintenance. The goal of this community building is, of course, to establish a positive quality of life—economic, spiritual, educational—for black women, men, and children. Walker's understanding of a womanist as "not a separatist" ("except for health"), however, reminds the Christian womanist theologian that her concern for community building and maintenance must *ultimately* extend to the entire Christian community and beyond that to the larger human community.

Yet womanist consciousness is also informed by women's determination to love themselves. "Regardless." This translates into an admonition to black women to avoid the self-destruction of bearing a disproportionately large burden in the work of community building and maintenance. Walker suggests that women can avoid this trap by connecting with women's communities concerned about women's rights and well-being. Her identification of a womanist as also a feminist joins black women with their feminist heritage extending back into the nineteenth century in the work of black feminists like Sojourner Truth, Frances W. Harper, and Mary Church Terrell.

In making the feminist-womanist connection, however, Walker proceeds with great caution. While affirming an organic relationship between womanists and feminists, she also declares a deep shade of difference between them. ("Womanist is to feminist as purple to lavender.") This gives womanist scholars the freedom to explore the particularities of black women's history and culture without being guided by what white feminists have already identified as women's issues.

But womanist consciousness directs black women away from the negative divisions prohibiting community building among women. The womanist loves other women sexually and nonsexually. Therefore, respect for sexual preferences is one of the marks of womanist community. According to Walker, homophobia has no place. Nor does "Colorism" (i.e., "yella" and half-white black people valued more in the black world than black-skinned people), which often separates black women from each other. Rather, Walker's womanist claim is that color variety is the substance of universality. Color, like birth and death, is common to all people. Like the navel, it is a badge of humanity connecting people with people. Two other distinctions are prohibited in Walker's womanist thinking. Class hierarchy does not dwell among women who "... love struggle, love the Folks ... are committed to the survival and wholeness of an entire people." Nor do women compete for male attention when they "... appreciate and prefer female culture ... value ... women's emotional flexibility ... and women's strength."

The intimations about community provided by Walker's definition suggest no genuine community building is possible when men are excluded (except when women's health is at stake). Neither can it occur when black women's self-love, culture, and love for each other are not affirmed and are not considered vital for the community's self-understanding. And it is thwarted if black women are expected to bear "the lion's share" of the work and to sacrifice their well-being for the good of the group.

Yet, for the womanist, mothering and nurturing are vitally important. Walker's womanist reality begins with mothers relating to their children and is characterized by black women (not necessarily bearers of children) nurturing great numbers of black people in the liberation struggle (e.g., Harriet Tubman). Womanist emphasis upon the value of mothering and nurturing is consistent with the testimony of many black women. The poet Carolyn Rogers speaks of her mother as the great black bridge that brought her over. Walker dedicates her novel *The Third Life of Grange Copeland* to her mother "... who made a way out of no way." As a child in the black church, I heard women (and men) give thanks to God for their mothers "... who stayed behind and pulled the wagon over the long haul."

It seems, then, that the clues about community from Walker's definition of a womanist suggest that the mothering and nurturing dimension of Afro-American history can provide resources for shaping criteria to measure the quality of justice in the community. These criteria could be used to assure female-male equity in the presentation of the community's models of authority. They could also gauge the community's division of labor with regard to the survival tasks necessary for building and maintaining community.

Womanist Theology and Method

Womanist theology is already beginning to define the categories and methods needed to develop along lines consistent with the sources of that theology. Christian womanist theological methodology needs to be informed by at least four elements: (1) a multidialogical intent, (2) a liturgical intent, (3) a didactic intent, and (4) a commitment both to reason *and* to the validity of female imagery and metaphorical language in the construction of theological statements.

A multidialogical intent will allow Christian womanist theologians to advocate and participate in dialogue and action with *many* diverse social, political, and religious communities concerned about human survival and productive quality of life for the oppressed. The genocide of cultures and peoples (which has often been instigated and accomplished by Western white Christian groups or governments) and the nuclear threat of omnicide mandates womanist participation in such dialogue/action. But in this dialogue/action the womanist also should keep her speech and action focused upon the slow genocide of poor black women, children, and men by exploitative systems denying them productive jobs, education, health care, and living space. Multidialogical activity may, like a jazz symphony, communicate some of its most important messages in what the harmony-driven conventional ear hears as discord, as disruption of the harmony in both the black American and white American social, political, and religious status quo.

If womanist theological method is informed by a liturgical intent, then womanist theology will be relevant to (and will reflect) the thought, worship, and action of the black church. But a liturgical intent will also allow womanist theology to challenge the thought/worship/action of the black church with the discordant and prophetic messages emerging from womanist participation in multidialogics. This means that womanist theology will consciously impact *critically* upon the foundations of liturgy, challenging the church to use justice principles to select the sources that will shape the content of liturgy. The question must be asked: "How does this source portray blackness/darkness, women and economic justice for nonruling-class people?" A negative portrayal will demand omission of the source or its radical reformation by the black church. The Bible, a major source in black church liturgy, must also be subjected to the scrutiny of justice principles.

A didactic intent in womanist theological method assigns a teaching function to theology. Womanist theology should teach Christians new insights about moral life based on ethics supporting justice for women, survival, and a productive quality of life for poor women, children, and men. This means that the womanist theologian must give authoritative status to black folk wisdom (e.g., Brer Rabbit literature) and to black women's moral wisdom (expressed in their literature) when she responds to the question, "How ought the Christian to live in the world?" Certainly tensions may exist between the moral teachings derived from these sources and the moral teachings about obedience, love, and humility that have usually buttressed presuppositions about living the Christian life. Nevertheless, womanist theology, in its didactic intent, must teach the church the different ways God reveals prophetic word and action for Christian living.

These intents, informing theological method, can yield a theological language whose foundation depends as much upon its imagistic content as upon reason. The language can be rich in female imagery, metaphor, and story. For the black church, this kind of theological language may be quite useful, since the language of the black religious experience abounds in images and metaphors. Clifton Johnson's collection of black conversion experiences, *God Struck Me Dead,* illustrates this point.

The appropriateness of womanist theological language will ultimately reside in its ability to bring black women's history, culture, and religious experience into the interpretive circle of Christian theology and into the liturgical life of the church. Womanist theological language must, in this sense, be an instrument for social and theological change in church and society.

Who Do You Say God Is?

Regardless of one's hopes about intentionality and womanist theological method, questions must be raised about the God-content of the theology. Walker's mention of the black womanist's love of the spirit is a true reflection of the great respect Afro-American women have always shown for the presence and work of the spirit. In the black church, women (and men) often judge the effectiveness of the worship service not on the scholarly content of the sermon nor on the ritual nor on orderly process. Rather, worship has been effective if "the spirit was high," i.e., if the spirit was actively and obviously present in a balanced blend of prayer, of cadenced word (the sermon), and of syncopated music ministering to the pain of the people.

The importance of this emphasis upon the spirit is that it allows Christian womanist theologians, in their use of the Bible, to identify and reflect upon those biblical stories in which poor oppressed women had a special encounter with divine emissaries of God, like the spirit. In the Hebrew Testament, Hagar's story is most illustrative and relevant to Afro-American women's experience of bondage, of African heritage, of encounter with God/emissary in the midst of fierce survival struggles. Kate Cannon among a number of black female preachers and ethicists urges black Christian women to regard themselves as Hagar's sisters.

In relation to the Christian or New Testament, the Christian womanist theologian can refocus the salvation story so that it emphasizes the beginning of revelation with the spirit mounting Mary, a woman of the poor: ("... the Holy Spirit shall come upon thee, and the power of the Highest shall overshadow thee ..." Luke 1:35). Such an interpretation of revelation has roots in 19th-century black abolitionist and feminist Sojourner Truth. Posing an important question and response, she refuted a white preacher's claim that women could not have rights equal to men's because Christ was not a woman. Truth asked, "Whar did your Christ come from? ... From God and a woman! Man had nothin' to do wid Him!" This suggests that womanist theology could eventually speak of God in a well-developed theology of the spirit. The sources for this theology are many. Harriet Tubman often "went into the spirit" before her liberation missions and claimed her strength for liberation activity came from this way of meeting God. Womanist theology has grounds for shaping a theology of the spirit informed by black women's political action.

Christian womanist responses to the question "who do you say God is?" will be influenced by these many sources. Walker's way of connecting womanists with the spirit is only one clue. The integrity of black church women's faith, their love of Jesus, their commitment to life, love, family, and politics will also yield vital clues. And other theological voices (black liberation, feminist, Islamic, Asian, Hispanic, African, Jewish, and Western white male traditional) will provide insights relevant for the construction of the God-content of womanist theology.

Each womanist theologian will add her own special accent to the understandings of God emerging from womanist theology. But if one needs a final image to describe women coming together to shape the enterprise, Bess B. Johnson in *God's Fierce Whimsy* offers an appropriate one. Describing the difference between the play of male and female children in the black community where she developed, Johnson says:

> the boys in the neighborhood had this game with rope ... tug-o'-war ... till finally some side would jerk the rope away from the others, who'd fall down. ... Girls ... weren't allowed to play with them in this tug-o'-war; so we figured out how to make our own rope—out of ... little dandelions. You just keep adding them, one to another, and you can go on and on. ... Anybody, even the boys, could join us. ... The whole purpose of our game was to create this dandelion chain—that was it. And we'd keep going, creating till our mamas called us home.

Like Johnson's dandelion chain, womanist theological vision will grow as black women come together and connect piece with piece. Between the process of creating and the sense of calling, womanist theology will one day present itself in full array, reflecting the divine spirit that connects us all.

Note

1. [The following was a box in the original article]

Womanist Theology: Some Beginnings

Black female theologians, ethicists, sociologists, and scholars in religious studies are exploring the meaning of womanist. Ethicist Katie G. Cannon speaks of a black womanist tradition in her contribution, "The Emergence of Black Feminist Consciousness," in *Feminist Interpretation of the Bible* (Westminster Press, 1985). This tradition "identifies those [biblical] texts which help black womanists to celebrate and rename ... innumerable incidents of unpredictability in empowering ways. The black womanist identifies with those biblical characters who hold on to life in the face of formidable oppression."

At the Womanspirit Rising Conference sponsored by the United Campus Ministries of Ohio University October 1986, Sandra Overby of Wilberforce University and Payne Theological Seminary convened a workshop entitled Womanist Theology: A Theology with Black Women at the Center.

Sociologist Cheryl Townsend Gilkes claims that much of Walker's definition of a womanist converges with the idea of "holy boldness" possessed by certain women in our society. They are the women who occasionally remind us, quite assertively, that "if it wasn't for the women you wouldn't have a church." These ideas are presented in "The Role of Women in the Sanctified Church," in the Spring-Summer 1986 issue of the *Journal of Religious Thought*.

Theologian Jacqueline Grant, at Inter-denominational Theological Center, is also pioneering in womanist theology. In her major lecture at the last meeting of the Women's Inter-Seminary Conference, Grant used a womanist framework to structure her message. My own paper, "Poke Sallit, Mullein, Sassafras, and God: Survival Resources in Black Women's Literature," given in the women's section at the 1985 meeting of the American Academy of Religion, considers the possible task of a womanist theology in light of the survival concerns expressed in black women's literature.

Roundtable Discussion: Christian Ethics and Theology in Womanist Perspective (1989)

CHERYL J. SANDERS, KATIE G. CANNON, EMILIE M. TOWNES, M. SHAWN COPELAND, bell hooks, AND CHERYL TOWNSEND GILKES

Cheryl J. Sanders

One of the most exciting developments in the theological scholarship of the 1980s has been the emergence of womanist ethics and theology. *Womanist* refers to a particular dimension of the culture of black women that is being brought to bear upon theological, ethical, biblical and other religious studies. These new interpretations of black women's religious experience and ideas have been sparked by the creative genius of Alice Walker. She defines the term womanist in her 1983 collection of prose writings *In Search of Our Mothers' Gardens.*[1] In essence, womanist means black feminist.

As early as 1985, black women scholars in religion began publishing works that used the womanist perspective as a point of reference. The major sources for this work are the narratives, novels, prayers and other materials that convey black women's traditions, values and struggles, especially during the slavery period. Methodologically, womanist scholars tend to process and interpret these sources in three ways: (1) the celebration of black women's historical struggles and strengths; (2) the critique of various manifestations of black women's oppression; and (3) the construction of black women's theological and ethical claims. The content of womanist ethics and theology bears the distinctive mark of black women's assertiveness and resourcefulness in the face of oppression. The womanist ideal impels the scholars who embrace it to be outrageous, audacious and courageous enough to move beyond celebration and critique to undertake the difficult task of practical constructive work, toward the end of black women's liberation and wholeness.

Does the term womanist provide an appropriate frame of reference for the ethical and theological statements now being generated by black women? To answer this question, it is necessary first to examine critically Walker's own understanding and use of the term, and then to construct some basis for assessing its adequacy as a rubric for Christian ethical and theological discourse.

In 1981 Alice Walker wrote a review of *Gifts of Power: The Writings of Rebecca Jackson* for *The Black Scholar.*[2] The review lifts up the spiritual legacy

126

of the nineteenth-century black Shaker, Rebecca Jackson, who had an unusual conversion experience, left her husband for a life of celibacy, and lived thereafter in close relationship with a Shaker sister, Rebecca Perot. Walker gives high praise to editor Jean McMahon Humez, but takes exception to Humez's suggestion that Jackson was a lesbian. Walker identifies at least three errors in judgment by Humez with respect to Jackson's sexual orientation: (1) her disregard of Jackson's avowed celibacy; (2) her questionable interpretation of Jackson's dreams about Perot as erotic; and (3) her attempt to "label something lesbian that the black woman in question has not." Walker's own position regarding Jackson's sexual orientation is that it would be "wonderful" either way. Having thus disclaimed the moral significance of Jackson's alleged lesbianism, she then goes on to suggest that lesbian would be an inappropriate word in any case, not only for Jackson, but for all black women who choose to love other women sexually. Walker offers her own word *womanist* as a preferred alternative to *lesbian* in the context of black culture. Her concern is to find a word that affirms connectedness rather than separation, in view of the fact that Lesbos was an island whose symbolism for blacks "is far from positive." Furthermore, Walker concludes that "the least we can do," and what may well be for black women in this society our only tangible sign of personal freedom, is to name our own experience after our own fashion, selecting our own words and rejecting those words that do not seem to suit.

Walker gives a more complete definition of womanist as a preface to *In Search of Our Mothers' Gardens,* her 1983 collection of womanist prose that includes the *Gifts of Power* review. This definition has four parts, the first showing the word's derivation from *womanish* (opposite of *girlish*) and its primary meaning "black feminist" or "feminist of color." The second part conveys the sense of the word as explained in the book review; as a woman who loves other women but is committed to the survival and wholeness of entire people; who is not separatist, but is "traditionally" universalist and capable (these traits being illustrated with excerpts of dialogue between mother and daughter). The third part celebrates what the womanist loves—music, dance, the moon, the Spirit, love, food, roundness, struggle, the Folk, herself—ending with the word "regardless," presumably an allusion to Walker's earlier call in the review for a word that affirms connectedness to the community and the world "*regardless* of who worked and slept with whom." The fourth and final part of the definition compares womanist to feminist as purple to lavender, expressing in vivid terms the conclusion that womanist has a deeper and fuller meaning than feminist.

Walker's definition of womanist represents a shift in emphasis from her earlier discussion of womanist in the book review. In the first instance womanist carries the connotation of black *lesbian,* and in the second it denotes black *feminist,* a designation that includes women who love women and those who love men. In both cases, however, her point is to name the experience of audacious black women with a word that acknowledges their sensibilities and traditions in ways that the words *lesbian* and *feminist* do not. Walker's womanist definition and writings send a clear and consistent signal to celebrate the black woman's freedom to choose her own labels and lovers. It is apparent that a few black women have responded to this call for celebration by writing womanist theology and womanist ethics and by calling themselves womanist scholars.[3] Those who have made use of the term womanist in their writing have cited the definition that Walker gives in her preface to *In Search of Our Mothers' Gardens* generally without giving attention to Walker's explanation of womanist in her review of *Gifts of Power*. Walker's definition has been subjected each time to the writer's own editing and interpretation, partly because each writer seems compelled to construe its meaning in light of her own thought. This process of appropriation and adaptation merits close scrutiny. In our efforts to tailor Walker's definition to suit our own purposes, have we misconstrued the womanist concept and its meaning? Is the word womanist being co-opted because of its popular appeal and used as a mere title or postscript for whatever black women scholars want to celebrate, criticize or construct? Are we committing a gross conceptual error when we use Walker's descriptive cultural nomenclature as a foundation for the normative discourse of theology and ethics? On what grounds, if any, can womanist authority and authenticity be established in our work? In other words, what is the necessary and sufficient condition for doing womanist scholarship? To be a black woman? A black feminist? A black lesbian?

One approach to resolving these concerns would be to devise some reasonable categories for evaluating the extent to which womanist theological and ethical thought conforms to (or deviates from) Walker's basic concern for black women's freedom to name their own experience and to exercise prerogatives of sexual preference. If we assume, rather boldly, that Walker never intended to reserve exclusive authority to use the word as her own private vehicle of expression, it can be argued that the authority to label one's work as a womanist derives directly from one's ability to set forth an authentic representation of Walker's concept in that work. Three categories are suggested here as grounds for comparison and evaluation: context, criteria, and claims.

The context of the womanist perspective is set forth quite clearly in Walker's long definition of the word. While its general context is the folk culture of black women, its specific context is the intergenerational dialogue between black mothers and their daughters in an oppressive society. The origin of the word *womanist* is a traditional warning given by black mothers to their daughters, "You acting womanish," in response to their precocious behavior (i.e., "You trying to be grown"). The behavior in question is further described as outrageous, audacious, courageous, and willful, words suggesting rebellion against the mother's authority, as well as resistance to oppressive structures that would limit knowledge and self-realization. However, it is evident that Walker's concern is to include the mother in the womanist context by ascribing to her the role of teacher and interpreter, and by portraying her as resigned to the daughter's assertion of her womanhood. This can be seen in the mother-daughter dialogues cited to illustrate the meaning of "traditionally universalist," with reference to the diversity of skin tones among blacks, and "traditionally capable," i.e., the determination of slaves to persist in their pursuit of freedom.

The criteria of the womanist perspective are very clearly spelled out in Walker's definition. To summarize, the womanist is a black feminist who is audacious, willful and serious; loves and prefers women, but also may love men; is committed to the survival and wholeness of entire people; and is universalist, capable, all loving, and deep. Perhaps it is unrealistic to expect complete compliance with all of these criteria as a prerequisite for employing womanist nomenclature. But it is intellectually dishonest to label a person, movement or idea as womanist on the basis of only one or two of these criteria to the exclusion of all the others. Two of these criteria tend to have the broadest appeal in theological-ethical statements: commitment to the survival and wholeness of entire people and love of the Spirit. The reason for this should be obvious; these two criteria point directly to the self-understanding of the black church. However, they would seem not to merit the prominence theologians and ethicists ascribe to them, especially in view of the fact that they are not given any particular priority within the definition itself. In other words, it may be a distortion of Walker's concept to lift up these two criteria because they resonate with black church norms, while quietly dismissing others that do not. The fact is that womanist is essentially a secular cultural category whose theological and ecclesial significations are rather tenuous. Theological content too easily gets "read into" the womanist concept, whose central emphasis remains the self-assertion and struggle of black women for freedom, with or without the aid of God or Jesus or anybody else. The womanist concept does lend itself more readily to ethical reflection, given that ethics is often done independently of theology, as philosophical discourse with greater appeal to reason than to religious dogma. Walker's definition comprises an implicit ethics of moral autonomy, liberation, sexuality and love that is not contingent upon the idea of God or revelation. In any case, to be authentically "womanist," a theological or ethical statement should embrace the full complement of womanist criteria without omissions or additions intended to sanctify, de-feminize or otherwise alter the perspective Walker intended the word *womanist* to convey.

Despite the proliferation of theological claims that have been issued under the authority of the womanist rubric, Walker's womanist nomenclature makes only one claim—that black women have the right to name their own experience. This claim is inclusive of the prerogative of sexual preference; to choose one's own labels and lovers is a sign of having fully come into one's own. It may be understood theologically as the right to name one's own deity and sources of revelation, but to do so is to move beyond interpretation to the more dubious task of interpolation. Moreover, neither Walker's definition nor her discussion of womanist addresses the nature and purpose of God in relation to the plight of the oppressed, as blacks and/or as women. So it appears that womanist theology, with its liberatory theological claims, has been built upon a cultural foundation that not only was not intended to sustain theological arguments, but actually was fashioned to supplant ideas and images, theological or otherwise, that might challenge the supremacy of self-definition. This is not to deny the possibility of a genuine congruence between womanist theological-ethical discourse and the claim of personal and collective self-definition. The real problem here is the appropriation of the womanist concept as the prime ground and source for theological claims that have been extracted from the testimony of black women whose theology and ethics rested upon other foundations, and who, given the opportunity to choose labels, might have rejected womanist even as a name for their own experience.

It would seem that to do ethics in womanist perspective presents less of a problem, insofar as the construction of ethical claims can be pursued independently of theological considerations. Even so, one must take care not to force the ethical statements of one era into the ethical categories of another, nor to ascribe to our black foremothers womanist sensibilities shaped by a modernist impulse that they might not have endorsed or understood.

The necessary and sufficient condition for doing womanist scholarship has to be adherence to the context, criteria, and claims inherent in Walker's definition; it would be a mistake to recognize anything that any black woman writes with a womanist title or reference as womanist discourse simply because the author is black and female. Ultimately, the authority to determine what qualifies as womanist discourse rests with Alice Walker, who has defined and demonstrated the meaning of the word in her writing with great skill and consistency. However, given the fact that so many black female scholars have already taken the liberty of using her word in our work, we need to come to terms with the responsible exercise of the authority we have claimed.

I am fully convinced of the wisdom of Walker's advice to black women to name our own experience after our own fashion and to reject whatever does not suit. It is upon the authority of this advice that I want to explore further the suitability of the term womanist for theological-ethical discourse. The context, criteria, and claims of the womanist perspective provide an appropriate basis for raising critical questions concerning the suitability of this label for the work black women scholars are currently doing in theology and ethics.

First, there are contextual problems, beginning with tensions inherent in the dialogues presented in Walker's definition. There is an intergenerational exchange where the traditional piety of the acquiescent mother is in conflict with the brash precociousness of the womanish daughter. The definition conveys a spirit of celebration, evoking approval of the daughter's rebellion and the mother's resignation to it. This push to be "womanish" or "grown" also bears a hint of self-assertion in a sexual sense, where sexual freedom is a sign of moral autonomy. Thus, the context of womanist self-assertion includes two apparently inseparable dimensions: the personal struggle for sexual freedom and the collective struggle for freedom in the political-social sense. Yet, in the theological-ethical statements womanist is used to affirm the faith of our mothers principally in the collective sense of struggle, that is, for freedom from racist and sexist oppression. Further, it should be noted that although the question of Rebecca Jackson's sexual orientation is Walker's point of departure for discussing the meanings of womanist, she refrains from applying the term to Jackson. Walker chides Humez for not taking seriously Jackson's description of herself as celibate, but Jackson's choice of celibacy (i.e., not to love either women or men sexually, not even her own husband) as an act of submission to a spiritual commitment to follow Jesus Christ evidently is not regarded by Walker as a womanist assertion of sexual freedom. Thus it would seem inappropriate to label as womanist those saintly rebels (e.g., Sojourner Truth) whose aim was not to assert their sexual freedom but rather to work sacrificially toward the liberation of their people as followers of Jesus Christ. To designate a historic figure as womanist solely on the basis of political-social engagement without addressing the personal-sexual dimension is a contextual error typical of womanist theological-ethical discourse. To be authentically grounded in the womanist context, these statements cannot be simply celebrations of black women's assertiveness, but must also give attention to the inherent dialogical and intergenerational tensions within the black woman's struggle for freedom, and to both dimensions of that struggle, the personal-sexual and the political-social.

A further contextual problem stems from the fact that Walker's definition gives scant attention to the sacred. Womanist is defined in secular terms, centered on a worldly premise of self-assertion and self-sufficiency. The womanist's concern for the sacred is demonstrated in the definition by italicizing the verb in the statement that she "*loves* the Spirit," but otherwise finds no distinctiveness among her loves for other aspects of nature and culture (she also "*loves* the folk"). The term *womanist theology* is in my view a forced hybridization of two disparate concepts and may come to resemble another familiar hybrid, the mule, in being incapable of producing offspring. Novelist Zora Neale Hurston once declared in the voice of one of her characters that the black woman is "the mule of the world," but unlike the mule the black woman has often sought to cast upon the Lord those burdens too hard for her to bear, and has reproduced herself, body and spirit, through many generations. Not only does this scant attention to the sacred render the womanist perspective of dubious value as a context for theological discourse, but it ultimately subverts any effort to mine the spiritual traditions and resources of black women.

The use of black women's experience as a basis for theology is futile if that experience is interpreted apart from a fully theistic context. One might argue here that it is inappropriate to make such an issue of the distinctiveness of the sacred in black theological discourse in view of our African heritage that allegedly draws no such distinctions, at least not the way they are drawn in the West. In the African tradition, however, the basis for denial of the distinction between sacred and secular is the notion that the sacred pervades everything. By contrast, Western modernity exalts the secular to the point of disregarding or circumscribing the sacred in unhealthy ways. African American Christians, poised historically in a peculiar position between two incompatible world views, have tended to resolve this dilemma by fashioning for ourselves a world view that derives its power, character, and spirit from the sacred realm, from which we have drawn wisdom and hope to survive within the profane world of those who have oppressed us in the name of God and mammon. Thus it would appear incongruous to try to do black women's theology, or ever, just to articulate it in words, within a context that marginalizes the sacred within black women's existence. The search for our mothers' gardens, and our own, seems pointless if we remain oblivious to our mothers' gods.

The womanist concept sets forth a variety of criteria that convey specific moral values, character traits and behavior, especially with regard to sexuality. One important question to raise is whether or not the sexual ethics implied by the womanist concept can serve the best interests of the black family, church, and community. Part of Walker's original intent was to devise a spiritual, concrete, organic, characteristic word, consistent with black cultural values, that would describe black women who prefer women sexually, but are connected to the entire community. *Womanist* is a preferred alternative to *lesbian* because it connotes connectedness and not isolation, and womanist is one who loves other women, sexually and/or nonsexually, and who appreciates and prefers women's culture. Clearly, in Walker's view, sexual preference is not a morally or ethically significant factor in determining whether or not one is "committed to the survival and wholeness of entire people, male *and* female." But the affirmation of the connectedness of all persons within the black community regardless of sexual preference is not the only issue at stake with respect to the well-being of black people. In my view there is a fundamental discrepancy between the womanist criteria that would affirm and/or advocate homosexual practice, and the ethical norms the black church might employ to promote the survival and wholeness of black families. It is problematic for those of us who claim connectedness to and concern for the black family and church to engage these criteria authoritatively and/or uncritically in the formulation of theological-ethical discourse for those two institutions. If black women's ethics is to be pertinent to the needs of our community, then at least some of us must be in a position to offer intellectual guidance to the church as the principal (and perhaps only remaining) advocate for marriage and family in the black community. There is a great need for the black churches to promote a positive sexual ethics within the black community as one means of responding to the growing normalization of the single-parent family, and the attendant increases in poverty, welfare dependency, and a host of other problems. Moreover, it is indisputably in the best interest of black children for the church not only to strengthen and support existing families, but also to educate them ethically for marriage and parenthood. The womanist nomenclature, however, conveys a sexual ethics that is ambivalent at best with respect to the value of heterosexual monogamy within the black community.

Thirdly, it is problematic for black women who are doing womanist scholarship from the vantage point of Christian faith to weigh the claims of the womanist perspective over against the claims of Christianity. The womanist perspective ascribes ultimate importance to the right of black women to name our own experience; in the Christian perspective, Christ is the incarnation of claims God makes upon us as well as the claims we make upon God. While there may be no inherent disharmony between these two assertions, the fact remains that there are no references to God or Christ in the definition of womanist. For whatever reason, christology seems not to be directly relevant to the womanist concept. And if we insist upon incorporating within the womanist rubric the christological confessions of black women of faith, or discerning therein some hidden or implicit christology, then we risk entrapment in the dilemma of reconciling Christian virtues such as patience, humility and faith, with the willful, audacious abandon of the womanist. Walker only obscures the issue by making vague references to the spirit instead of naming Christian faith and practice. For example, she uses terms like general power and inner spirit to describe Rebecca Jackson's motive for leaving husband, home, family, friends and church to "live her own life." Yet it seems obvious that Jackson would name her own experience simply as a call to follow Christ. I suspect that it is Christianity, and not womanism, that forms the primary ground of theological and ethical identity with our audacious, serious foremothers.

In conclusion, the womanist perspective has great power, potential and limitations; it may be useful as a window to the past, but a truly womanist tradition has yet to be fully created and understood. I have raised some questions concerning the suitability of womanist as a rubric for black women's ethics and theology, yet I have no better word to offer, nor do I feel especially compelled to come up with one. I am aware that many of my colleagues in theological scholarship are wholly committed to the womanist perspective, and my principal aim has been to prod us all further in the direction of critique and construction. If we are going to be serious about the constructive task, then we must be celebrative and critical at the same time, neither letting ourselves become so enraptured in celebrating our heroines and ideals that we sweep aside the critical questions, nor allowing the critical process to dampen our zeal for the content of our work. I have great faith that black female theologians and ethicists are on target to give significant direction to both church and society by further exposing the roots of oppression in all its forms and manifestations, and by discovering more keys to our personal and collective survival, regardless of which labels we embrace.

Note

1. Alice Walker, *In Search of Our Mothers' Gardens* (San Diego and New York: Harcourt Brace Jovanovich, 1983).
2. Jean McMahon, ed., *Gifts of Power: The Writings of Rebecca Jackson (1795–1871), Black Visionary, Shaker Eldress* (Amherst: Univ. of Massachusetts Press, 1981); Alice Walker, review of *Gifts of Power: The Writings of Rebecca Jackson (1795–1871), Black Visionary, Shaker Eldress,* edited with an introduction by Jean McMahon Humez, in *Black Scholar* (November–December 1981): 64–67. Reprinted in Alice Walker, *In Search of Our Mothers' Gardens,* 71–82.
3. See, for example, Katie Geneva Cannon, *Black Womanist Ethics* (Atlanta: Scholars Press, 1988); Toinette M. Eugene, "Moral Values and Black Womanists," *Journal of Religious Thought* 44 (Winter–Spring 1988): 23–34; Jacquelyn Grant, "Womanist Theology: Black Women's Experience as a Source for Doing Theology, with Special Reference to Christology," *Journal of the Interdenominational Theological Center* 13 (Spring 1986): 195–212; Renita J. Weems, *Just a Sister Away* (San Diego: LuraMedia, 1988); and Delores S. Williams, "Womanist Theology: Black Women's Voices," *Christianity and Crisis* (July 14, 1986): 230–232.

Katie G. Cannon

In preparing to write this response, I found myself repeatedly stopped by waves of anger at Dr. Cheryl Sanders' treatment of womanist as a secular terminological issue. It was not clear to me what I, a self-avowed, practicing, Black-Womanist-Liberationist-Christian Ethicist, was doing responding to Professor Sanders' paper. Was I trying to persuade practitioners of Afro-Christian culture to hold on to this organic concept until we debunk, unmask, and disentangle the political parameters of gender, class and patriarchal authority in the Black Church community? Was I trying to convince white establishment scholars that there is genuine merit in womanist discourse? Was I trying to rethink my own previous work about Alice Walker's definition of womanist[4]— a definition that has given new meaning to the Afro-Christian ambience in which I live, move and have my being? Was I angry with Cheryl Sanders, the white academy, or the African-American theological guild?

Well, all of the above. What finally struck me was the fact that I needed to transform the power of my anger into the radical work of love:[5] I needed to be pro-active rather than reactive in my analysis of Sanders' paper. I needed to place myself simultaneously at the center of the controversy and at the edge of constructive envisioning. It was as though I were asking Sanders to answer some of her own questions. Thus, I will focus my response on what I perceive to be her major concern: "Does the term *womanist* provide an appropriate frame of reference for the ethical and theological statements now being generated by black women?"

Yes, I think it does. A womanist liberation theo-ethical framework is an endeavor to identify African-American women's moral agency, eliminating, as far as possible, contradictory directives for character and behavior. We must identify the principles we act upon as agents of faith and determine how these are related to the principles to which we give intellectual assent (lip-service and down-to-earth expediency), in order to assess the codified ethical standards and justice aims of women actively involved in the Black Church community.

In this definition I am attempting a critical reappropriation of Afro-Christian culture. By looking beyond and through historical "facts" for Black women's consciousness,[6] womanist scholars undertake the systematic questioning and critical examination of the moral reasoning that enables Black women to refuse dehumanization and to resist the conditions that thwart life.[7] A womanist liberation theo-ethical critique is a theoretical frame of reference that is at once a comparative and an ideal construct, asking new questions of the Black Church community, in order to examine and confront openly the ideological nature and function of patriarchy in the Black Church.

For example, as womanist ethicists, we need to ask ourselves the following questions: Why are particular images of Black church women included and promoted in sermons and others excluded?[8] What effect does the objectification, degradation, and subjection of the female in Black preaching have on women's social relations? How disruptive are androcentric sermons for the Black family? Are the images of Afro-Christian feminists congruent with social reality? What are the ideological and theological forces, the "specific determinations" that equate Black feminism and lesbianism? Whom does this equation serve? A womanist liberation theological ethic rejects heuristic concepts such as "heteropatriarchal familialist ideology"[9] and "compulsory heterosexism"[10] but seeks instead heuristic models that explore sacred power and benevolent cohumanity.

The concrete locus of womanist Christian praxis is the particularity of Black women's efforts to comprehend and transform alienating experiences and oppressive social structures. For instance, particular attention is given to analyzing the social power relations and organization of the Black Church—curricula, music, leadership expectations, pastor–member interactions—as well as outright sex discrimination. Far too often the organization of the church mirrors male domination in the society and normalizes it in the eyes of both female and male parishioners.

In essence, a womanist liberation theological ethic places Black women at the center of human social relations and ecclesiastical institutions. It critiques the images and paradigms that the Black Church uses to promote or exclude women. A womanist theo-ethical critique serves as a model for understanding the silences, limitations and possibilities of Black women's moral agency, by identifying Afro-Christian cultural patterns and forms, perspectives, doctrines, and values that are unique and peculiar to the Black Church community, in order to assess the dialectical tensions in Black women's past social relations as well as our current participation in the Black Church. A Black womanist liberation Christian ethic is a critique of all human domination in light of Black women's experience, a faith praxis that unmasks whatever threatens the well-being of the poorest woman of color.[11]

Note

4. Katie G. Cannon, "Hitting a Straight Lick with a Crooked Stick: The Womanist Dilemma in the Development of a Black Liberation Ethic," *The Annual: The Society of Christian Ethics* (1987): 165–177; Alice Walker, *In Search of Our Mothers' Gardens: Womanist Prose* (San Diego and New York: Harcourt Brace Jovanovich, 1983), xi–xii.
5. Beverly Wildung Harrison, "The Power of Anger in the Work of Love: Christian Ethics for Women and Other Strangers," in *Making the Connections: Essays in Feminist Social Ethics* (Boston: Beacon Press, 1985), 3–21.
6. Elisabeth Schüssler Fiorenza, *In Memory of Her: A Feminist Theological Reconstruction of Christian Origins* (New York: Crossroads, 1986).
7. Beverly Wildung Harrison, "Toward a Christian Feminist Liberation Hermeneutic for Demystifying Class Reality in Local Congregations," in *Beyond Clericalism*, ed. Joseph C. Hough, Jr. and Barbara G. Wheeler (Atlanta: Scholars Press, 1988), 137–51.
8. W. Lawrence Hogue, *Discourse and the Other* (Durham: Duke University Press, 1986).

9. Cheryl Clarke, "Lesbianism: An Act of Resistance," in *This Bridge Called My Back: Writings by Radical Women of Color,* ed. Cherrie Moraga and Gloria Anzaldua (Watertown, MA: Persephone Press, 1981): 128–37.
10. Adrienne Rich, "Compulsory Heterosexuality and Lesbian Existence," *Signs* 5, no. 4 (Summer 1980): 631 ff.
11. Harrison, "Toward a Christian Feminist Liberation Hermeneutic," 142.

Emilie M. Townes

Cheryl Sanders's essay is an ambitious attempt to raise critical and constructive questions regarding the use of the term *womanist* as a point of reference for recent Afro-American women's scholarship in theological and ethical inquiry. She raises both foundational and methodological questions to encourage critical precision and substantive depth. I join in her enthusiasm and advocacy for a thorough, rigorous, self-critical stance for Afro-American women's scholarship.

Sanders's essay, however, is problematic for me. Although I applaud the attempt, I find that she begins with an integral conceptual error that leads her down an unproductive path. Her understanding of Walker's discomfort with Humez's imposition of the term "lesbian" to describe Rebecca Jackson's life, and Walker's subsequent choice of "womanist" as possibly more descriptive of Jackson, leans too heavily on the lesbian lifestyle. As I read Walker's essay, I believe she attempts to define a style of living:

> I can imagine black women who love women (sexually or not) hardly thinking of what Greeks were doing; but, instead, referring to themselves as "whole" women, from "wholly" or "holy." Or as "round" women— women who love other women, yes, but women who also have concern, in a culture that oppresses all black people … for their fathers, brothers, and sons, no matter how they feel about them as males.[12]

This style of living is not necessarily lesbian for Walker as she stresses "sexually or not." Walker is unwilling to condemn or question lesbianism as a lesser order of creation within the Afro-American community. The focus I find in Walker is a concern for the survival and flourishing of the Afro-American community in its diversity: age, gender, sexuality, radical activity, accommodationist stance, creative promise. In short, her definition models what Peter Paris calls the fundamental principle of the black Christian tradition: Human equality under God is categorical, absolute, unconditional, and universally applicable.[13] Walker challenges the Afro-American community's heterosexism, which places conditions on the universality of God's grace and acceptance. Many womanist Christian ethicists and theologians extend Walker's challenge to serious questioning of what and who constitutes family structures and healthy models of love and growth for Afro-Americans living in these pre–twenty-first century times.

The four parts of Walker's definition of womanist must be considered as a whole, yet distinct in their focus. One part of her definition features the intergenerational dialogue between mother and daughter. The daughter is willful, courageous, audacious, and outrageous. She is about the business of defining self. Framed within an ethical context, she is asking a fundamental moral question in her actions: What should I be as a person? This person is a sexual being but she does not hold her sexuality as a sign of moral autonomy, as Sanders suggests. Walker's womanist is an integrated woman and would not hold parts of herself as distinct from the wholly, holy, round, whole woman she is. Moral autonomy for Walker's womanist is a woman's ability to define and celebrate herself and her people as agents of a human community.

Rather than fall victim to solipsism, she is in dialogue with her ancestors. Having been a participant in such dialogue in my youth, I can attest that the mother involved is far from resigned to such independent behavior. As a true mentor, she endeavors to encourage, restrain, and guide assertions of moral autonomy, liberation, and sexuality in a hostile society. She is an active participant in the liberative process, but also a circumspect guide. Both women are in tension, yoking dynamically the quest for personal growth and liberation with collective struggle.

The most terse, yet salient part of Walker's use of womanist is in the latter two sections of the definition in which she understands the womanist as enriching, strengthening, descriptive understanding of feminist as well as a woman who celebrates life and the Spirit. To suggest Walker lacks a concentration on the sacred is, I believe, to miss the crux of her spirituality. Walker clearly spells out her conception of the divine, the Spirit, in the dialogue between Celie and Shug in *The Color Purple.* This view is implicit in her definition of womanist. Shug tells Celie:

> God is inside of you and inside of everybody else. You come into the world with God. But only them that search for it inside find it. And sometimes it just manifest itself even when you not looking, or don't know what you looking for.[14]

This radically immanent concept of the divine is not readily found within the Afro-American religious experience. There is however a strong tradition of a personal Jesus who walks with us and shares our burdens and knows our sorrows. Walker's understanding of the Spirit challenges the Afro-American religious community to do what Delores Williams suggests—to create a well-developed theology of the Spirit.[15]

Rather than finding Walker's understanding of the sacred marginal, I perceive her understanding of the Spirit as woven intricately into the very fabric of existence itself. To embrace fully and to articulate such an understanding of the sacred can only enhance the black religious tradition of the parenthood of God and the kinship of all people. It challenges Afro-Americans to explore the profundity of the parenthood of God with its promise-invoking images of birthing and nurturing whole peoples into freedom and wholeness.

Walker's understanding of the sacred in her definition of womanist and the current and future appropriations of this term have a rich historical context for Afro-feminists in this country. Ida B. Wells-Barnett spoke of the God of freedom when she urged the twelve Afro-American men jailed for allegedly inciting the Elaine, Arkansas riot of 1919:

> I have been listening to you for nearly two hours. You have talked and sung and prayed about dying, and forgiving your enemies, and of feeling sure you are going to be received in the New Jerusalem. ... But why don't you pray to live and ask to be freed? ... Let all of your songs and prayers hereafter be songs of faith and hope that God will set you free; ... Quit talking about dying; if you believe your God is all powerful, believe he is powerful enough to open these prison doors, and say so. ... Pray to live and believe you are going to get out.[16]

With such a fertile inheritance from our Afro-American foremothers, a seasoned theology of the Spirit is vital for Afro-American women and men committed to putting their faith in action as we enter the twenty-first century. The articulation of the black Christian tradition demands from the womanist and her people strategies for the survival of the Afro-American community and the transformation of the socio-political structures of the United States.

The womanist perspective provides abundant promise for ethical and theological reflection within the Afro-American community. The Afro-American women who base their scholarship on an unapologetic womanist perspective hold in tension the roots of the Afro-American religious tradition as they challenge that tradition at its points of exclusivity and limited vision. The liberating promise of an exploration of a theology of the Spirit as Afro-American women (whether they term themselves womanist, black feminist, Afro-feminist, or black/Afro-American women) can further strengthen and ripen the Afro-American community's conception of not only God, but Jesus Christ.

Such an exploration challenges us to take a hard look at our understanding and interpretation of the trinity. Sanders is helpful in raising the question of how womanist Christian ethicists and theologians integrate christology with a radically immanent concept of the divine—the Spirit, and traditional understandings of God within the Afro-American religious context. And perhaps more to the point, how can womanist Christian ethicists and theologians do so with integrity and in true dialogue with history, with the contemporary Afro-American religious community, and with the larger Afro-American community?

The agenda of womanist Christian ethics and theology must articulate an understanding of liberation concerned with human equality and the ever-present, ever-sustaining, judging, and redeeming nature of God. Our additional task is to promote the full partnership of women and men in creation with God—to model and embody inclusivity enveloped by justice. Womanist Christian ethics and theology searches for the possibilities and is so bold as to have the will to grasp them.

Note

12. Alice Walker, "Gifts of Power: The Writings of Rebecca Jackson," in *In Search of Our Mothers' Gardens* (San Diego and New York: Harcourt Brace Jovanovich, 1984), 81.

13. Peter J. Paris, *The Social Teachings of the Black Churches* (Philadelphia: Fortress Press, 1985), 14.

14. Alice Walker, *The Color Purple* (New York: Washington Square Press, 1982), 177.

15. Delores Williams, "Womanist Theology: Black Women's Voices," *Christianity and Crisis* (2 March 1987): 70.

16. Ida B. Wells, *Crusade for Justice,* ed. Alfreda Duster (Chicago: University of Chicago Press, 1970), 403.

M. Shawn Copeland

In "Christian Ethics and Theology in Womanist Perspective," Professor Cheryl J. Sanders probes the appropriation and adaptation of Alice Walker's term *womanist* by other African American women scholars in ethics and in theology. Her essay intends a foundational concern with the status, function, and implications of method in theology: What is it that African American women ethicists and theologians are doing when they appropriate and adapt "the secular term" womanist in doing Christian ethics and theology? What are the implications of such usage for resulting ethical and theological proposals and claims? What implications are posed by the use of this multivalent term for the moral, ethical, and theological teaching and practice of the black church?

Sanders charges that Walker's secular term has been pried loose from the contexts in which it was developed.[17] Since each African American woman scholar has construed the meaning of womanist in light of her own thought, Sanders questions whether the term is being adopted and applied uncritically. Quite properly she asks, "Are we committing a gross conceptual error when we use Walker's descriptive cultural nomenclature as a foundation for the normative discourse of theology and ethics?" (This question reminds us precisely that fiction is Alice Walker's primary method for recording, apprehending, understanding, evaluating, judging, criticizing, transforming African American culture and life.) "What," then inquires Sanders "is the necessary and sufficient condition for doing womanist scholarship? To be a black woman? A black feminist? A black lesbian?" Professor Sanders proposes to answer this question by evaluating the extent to which womanist ethical and theological proposals conform to or deviate from Walker's coinage.

Professor Sanders takes seriously the appropriation and adaptation of the term womanist by our colleagues. This, in itself, makes the essay important. Yet, notably absent from her analysis are quotations from works by those scholars who use womanist to describe their work. Their voices are silenced. Without their words, it is not possible to determine the accuracy of Sanders' understanding, interpretation, and judgment of their work. It is not possible to judge her evaluation of their claims and proposals in any specific way. My response (1) comments on some of the issues that emerge in the ways Sanders understands, interprets, and judges the meanings of the term womanist and (2) suggests other possible interpretations of the term for theology.

By positing consistency and conformity to Walker's definition of womanist as normative for authentic use, and by insisting on its secularity in relation to Christian themes, the essay overlooks the creativity of Christian thinkers who historically have bent and shaped secular feasts, festivals, and fables to Christian ends. Feminist theologians, likewise, have appropriated and adopted a secular term, reworking it to include meanings and concerns which neither Betty Friedan nor Gloria Steinem would have imagined. If it is possible to speak of secular feminists and Christian feminists, surely it is possible to speak of secular womanists and Christian womanists.

More importantly, such an appeal for conformity yields the authoritative ground of the ethical and theological enterprise. That ground is the attentive, intelligent, rational, responsible mind of the scholar, the ethicist, the theologian *herself*. To that ground the essay, in my judgment, mistakenly opposes the Christian tradition. Theologians and ethicists have minds and *must* use them: Not to use one's mind is to fail the tradition which is not a chain, but a living root; not to use one's mind is to fail the discipline which is not rote catechesis, but speculative exploration only begun; not to use one's mind is to fail the mind.

Sanders suggests that use of the term womanist has been more celebratory than critically reflective. I agree. Yet, perhaps, the adaptation of the term signals the acute and seething dissatisfaction of African American women scholars at the "stepsister" treatment we, and indeed all women of color, have received from white feminists inside and outside the church. The embrace of the term womanist by African American women scholars signifies our demand for serious, sustained, and substantive dialogue with white feminists. Such dialectic is crucial given Walker's *first* definition of womanist: "A black feminist or feminist of color." The very term, then, implies black women's reworking of the notion and term *feminist*. What do black women mean by feminist, by feminism? I believe that Walker would approve the definition furnished by black feminist literary critic, Barbara Smith.

> Feminism is the political theory and practice that struggles to free all women: women of color, working-class women, poor women, disabled women, lesbians, old women—as well as white, economically privileged, heterosexual women. Anything less than this vision of total freedom is not feminism, but merely female self-aggrandizement.[18]

Given Walker's and Smith's definitions, it seems to me that black feminists and/or womanists seek a new and common ground from which all women and men may vigorously oppose racism, sexism, homophobia, ageism, class exploitation, intentional limitation of the disabled, and—I add, as Christians must—anti-Semitism. Black feminists and/or womanists apprehend these oppressions as interlocking and mutually conditioning; their interaction structures the conditions of our lives.[19]

At issue in the appropriation of the term womanist is the power of definition, of self-definition, of self-naming. In *Beloved,* Toni Morrison captures the importance of this audacious act. After having killed, cooked, and eaten a shoat Sixo argues with schoolteacher that he did not *steal* the shoat rather he was "improving [his master's valuable] property." Schoolteacher questions Sixo's veracity and the meaning of his statement.

Sixo plant rye to give the high piece a better chance. Sixo take and feed the
soil, give you more crop. Sixo take and feed Sixo give you more work.

Clever, but schoolteacher beat him anyway to show that definitions
belonged to the definers—not the defined.[20]

African American women scholars are struggling to define themselves and
their experiences—to be definers. For an African American woman scholar
to define herself to name herself womanist is to embrace, to love her culture
and religio-cultural traditions, her people, her people's struggle, her own
embodiment (Walker's third definition). For an African American scholar to
define herself, to name herself womanist is to tap the roots of the historical
traditional liberation capability of black women (Walker's second definition).

With the term womanist, African American women scholars of religion
also signal our African American male colleagues. Womanist intimates a critical posture towards sexism, towards misogyny, towards the objectification
and abuse of black women within the academy, within the African American
community, within the dominant patriarchal culture.

Black women are among the last admitted to full participation in the theological academy. In the formative years of black theology, which coincided
in large measure with the civil rights movement, little note was taken of the
black woman's peculiar position as an oppressed person within an oppressed
group. The enduring and mythical sociological label of that period which
black women continue to bear is "matriarch." Nor did black theology in those
formative years take note of black men's sexism and their admittance—albeit,
grudgingly—through patriarchy's male-bonding into limited privileges and
places. Use of the term womanist communicates to black men scholars, that
black women scholars are aware of the complexity of our differing positions as
African American scholars within the academy and within the larger socio-
cultural matrix; that black women scholars consciously name and reject the
intimidations, manipulations, and seductions of patriarchal power, privilege,
and place; and that black women scholars self-consciously link the historical
and explicit struggle of the race with the struggles of *all* oppressed, marginalized, brutalized, ostracized women and men.

It seems to me that a womanist perspective can contribute to the reshaping
and expansion of black theology. Indeed, the continued rethinking of black
theology is the requisite task of each African American man and woman
who calls himself or herself a theologian, an ethicist. In the past decade, a
renewed, prophetic black theology took up social analysis, recital, and denunciation to challenge the commitment and ethical and moral responsibility of
a growing black middle class to the demands and imperatives of the Gospel
and to our African American people. Materials that convey black women's
traditions—narratives, novels, and prayers—only recently have become an
explicit resource for black theology. The term womanist makes visible and

gives voice to African American women scholars in religion who are in the midst of the struggle to shape a distinctive perspective that takes seriously the experiences and traditions of black women as a source for theologizing on the black experience.

Sanders seems to identify the term womanist almost exclusively with Walker's second and complex definition which treats sexual orientations and sexual practices. Sanders worries that the "womanist nomenclature conveys a sexual ethics that is ambivalent" with respect to the "value of heterosexual monogamy within the black community." I agree with Sanders that young (and some not so young) African Americans need thorough education and preparation for responsible, i.e., ethical and moral, life-partnership or marriage and parenthood. I agree as well that poverty, welfare dependency, unemployment, crime, drugs, and AIDS have infiltrated the African American community in most pervasive and virulent strains. Yet, I believe the pathology that has metastasized in our community results from our angular social-cultural-economic-political location in the United States under late-twentieth-century supremacist capitalism, rather than from womanist nomenclature, its range of meanings, and appropriation by a handful of scholars of religion.

I conclude by repeating what I noted earlier. The term womanist makes visible and gives voice to African American women scholars in religion who are in the process of crafting a distinctive perspective that takes the experiences and traditions of black women as a source for theologizing on the black experience. Indeed, Walker's definitions admit a womanist continuum. By taking the meanings and implications of the term seriously, Professor Sanders reminds us of the need for on-going study and conversation about the sources and methods to be employed in the continued reshaping of black theology. Perhaps, in a few years time, we shall see a substantial corpus of womanist works; perhaps, conversations like this one shall have contributed to its development or, perhaps, to its demise. Time's gift of wisdom will have afforded us a longer and more comprehensive viewpoint. Seven years ago Michele Wallace mused that black feminists seemed, of necessity, to exist as individuals—monadic, isolated, separated—some well-known, others unknown. Wallace wrote:

> We exist as women who are Black who are feminists, each stranded for the moment, working independently because there is not yet an environment in this society remotely congenial to our struggle—because, being on the bottom, we would have to do what no one else has done: we would have to fight the world.[21]

In appropriating and adapting Alice Walker's multivalent term womanist, sifting old notions and themes through its sieve, lacing obstacles thrown up against them from within and without the African American community and the academy, some of our colleagues are struggling to create an environment more congenial for the struggle of African American women theologians and ethicists, indeed, for all men and women committed to the sacred work of human liberation with and before the Great God of our forebears.

Note

17. Walker's first use of the term *womanist* may have been in the "introduction," "fable," "story," entitled "Coming Apart: By Way of Introduction to Lorde, Teish and Gardner," which she wrote for an anthology on pornography, *Take Back the Night*. The material was subsequently published in *Ms.* and reprinted in Walker's collection of short stories, *You Can't Keep a Good Woman Down* (New York: Harcourt Brace Jovanovich, 1981), 41–53, especially 48. In this article, Walker writes, "A womanist is a feminist, only more common" (48). The context Walker creates for this use is a discussion about pornography between a black woman and man, who are wife and husband. The wife objects to her husband's use of pornography; she feels demeaned by his reliance on it and is angry. He "attacks" her as a "women's libber," a "white women's lackey," a "pawn" (48). Given this context, I take the womanist to be an ordinary (common) black woman who does not want to be objectified or displaced under the pornographic gaze of the black man she loves.

    See Alice Walker, *In Search of Our Mothers' Gardens* (San Diego and New York: Harcourt Brace Jovanovich, 1983), xi–xii, 71–82. Here Walker grounds the derivation of womanist in the black folk expression womanish. In this longer treatment of the term, Walker notes that the expression would have been used by adult black women (mothers or grandmothers or great-grandmothers or aunts) to comment on the assumption of adult (precocious and audacious) behavior by female children. She extends the definition to include liberatory action à la Harriet Tubman; universalism; celebration of what the womanist loves—music, dance, the moon, the Spirit, love, food, roundness, struggle, the Folk, herself; and to propose the analogue: womanist is to feminist as purple is to lavender. It is in the review of *Gifts of Power* that Walker treats the sexual connotation of womanist.

    Sanders insightfully notes the general and specific contexts for Walker's usage and development—black folk culture and the intergenerational dialogue between black mothers and their daughters. Given the title of the text in which the term is located, I suggest that there may be an even further context for consideration—*the gardens, our mothers' gardens*. In Jewish and Christian symbolism, the garden is the site of creation, light, and life, as well as of destruction, gloom, and death. The garden is the home of the first parents—the first father, (the first) Adam, the first mother, Eve; the garden is the place of their trial, temptation, and sin. For Christians, the garden is also the site of the struggle and revelation of the Second Adam. The garden is the place in which knowledge and ignorance, good and evil, sorrow and joy, blood, sweat and resurrection are revealed.

18. Barbara Smith, "Racism and Women's Studies," in Gloria T. Hull, Patricia Bell Scott, and Barbara Smith, eds., *All the Women Are White, All the Blacks Are Men: But Some of Us Are Brave* (Old Westbury, N.Y.: Feminist Press, 1982), 49.

19. See the Combahee River Collective, "A Black Feminist Statement," in *All the Women Are White*, 13–22; also, Patricia Bell Scott, "Selected Bibliography on Black Feminism," *All the Women Are White*, 23–33.

20. Toni Morrison, *Beloved* (New York: Alfred A. Knopf, 1987), 190.

21. Michele Wallace, "A Black Feminist's Search for Sisterhood," in *All the Women Are White*, 12.

bell hooks

As one who is politically engaged with the construction of theoretical paradigms that call attention to the ways sexism and sexist oppression affect the lives of black women and all black people, I believe feminist thinking and the feminist movement are a crucial part of the black liberation struggle. Were all African-Americans practicing feminist thinking there would be greater political solidarity between black women and men. In my *Feminist Theory: From Margin to Center*, feminism is defined as a movement to end sexism and sexist oppression.[22] This definition does not privilege any race, class, or gendered group. It does not suggest that men are the problem or that feminism is a white feminist movement. It places the emphasis on eradicating a particular politic of domination based on gender.

As black women and men who are victimized and suffer within white supremacist capitalist patriarchy, we have much to gain from using feminism as a critical standpoint to critique sexism and as a basis for collective struggle. Alice Walker's re-visioning of the term womanist is another way of naming feminism, particularly black feminism, by many black women. Use of this term is problematic. Often it is used to deflect attention from feminism as a political struggle to end sexism and sexist domination and to focus attention instead on black female cultural practice and lifestyle.

Cheryl Sanders's essay begins with this shift in focus. It does not cite the emergence of the contemporary feminist movement, its impact on gender-based scholarship, its insistence on the relevance of constructing theory from a feminist standpoint in all scholarly areas, especially theology, as the dynamic force motivating black female exploration of these issues. Sanders suggests that "new interpretations of black women's religious experience and ideas have been sparked by the creative genius of Alice Walker." Black women writers have been a courageous vanguard fictively exploring various politics of domination in black life—racism, sexism, and capitalism—and questioning institutions religious and secular that reinforce and uphold these structures. Their writing necessarily inspires black women scholars attempting to create new critical direction. Within theology, black women scholars have been among the most willing to acknowledge this supportive influence, identifying it as one of many traditions shaping their theoretical perspectives.

Significantly, Katie Cannon, in her introduction to *Black Womanist Ethics*, situates her concern with Christian ethics within a historical framework that encompasses various movements: black religious experience, the struggle for black liberation, the development of black literary traditions (especially the writing of black women), and the feminist movement.[23] Appropriating the term womanist has allowed black women scholars to do feminist thinking using a term that does not imply absence of concern for race or the survival of black people. Sanders acknowledges this effort, emphasizing that "in essence, womanist means black feminist." Yet it is this key aspect of its definition Sanders ignores (for Walker separates her descriptions of the term suggesting not a singular meaning but multiple definitions—one need not encompass the other). Without reflecting on feminism, or black feminism, Sanders focuses on the aspects of the definition that connect womanist with audacity, rebellion against authority and/or affirmation of black women as desiring subjects asserting autonomous choice to engage in varied sexual practices, especially lesbianism.

This focus produces a blindspot. Extensive critical exploration of womanism as an aspect of feminism would have indicated the powerful transformative impact of feminist theorizing within traditional theological discourse and the field of Christian ethics. By collapsing all of Walker's definitions of womanist into a single category, Sanders constructs a paradigm that makes it appear that a womanist perspective is in many ways inimical to Christian belief and practice. She can then conclude that "womanist is essentially a secular cultural category whose theological and ecclesial significations are rather tenuous." The aspect of Walker's definition that has the most intense resonance for many black female theologians has been the affirmation of a feminist standpoint that privileges the historical experiences of black women and our perspectives.

Walker's term is enabling for women who are fearful that explicitly identifying themselves as feminists would alienate them from black communities. Evoking the term womanist, they are able to affirm their ties to black traditions while simultaneously rethinking and re-visioning black experience from a feminist standpoint. Sanders implies that these scholars are using a womanist perspective to "supplant" theological concerns "that might challenge the supremacy of self-definition." Affirming the necessity of black female self-definition is not to make that act a supreme gesture. In actuality black women scholars are searching for new intellectual paradigms that will expand our understanding of theological ethical discourse and its contemporary relevance for our lives. Sanders opposes the two, declaring, "it would seem inappropriate to label as womanist those saintly rebels (e.g., Sojourner Truth) whose aim was not to assert their sexual freedom but rather to work sacrificially toward the liberation of their people as followers of Jesus Christ." Acknowledging that religious black women like Jarena Lee, Rebecca Jackson, and a host of others have had to critique and re-vision gender roles in order to participate fully in Christian practice, to step out on faith, is not heretical. There is a profound connection between this commitment to spiritual practice and feminist struggle. Again, by focusing exclusively on sexuality, Sanders ignores this vital connection. Failure to affirm the importance of a black feminist standpoint as it has emerged historically, politically devalues both the tremendous radical work of black women in the church and their devout spiritual commitment. If the black church experience is to survive and sustain its revolutionary theological mission, feminist re-visioning is essential. It would enable the black church to acknowledge that families vary, that they are not all heterosexually based or centered on couples. Single-parent households are as in need of support and affirmation as dual-parent families. Sanders makes family synonymous with heterosexual coupling. Feminist thinking enables us to imagine new church traditions that can affirm heterosexual marriage and, as Sanders suggests, "promote a positive sexual ethics" without promoting homophobia or reinscribing heterosexism as the only spiritually acceptable relational choice.

Concurrently, black religious traditions are informed by varied spiritual practices and teachings as well as Christianity. Any black church person concerned with the survival of black families and black people must encourage respect for varied religious experience. A Christian scholar concerned with the mystical dimensions of religious experience may focus more attention on the construction of our sense of divine spirit than on Christology; this does not make her less devoted to Christian practice. Sanders concludes her essay with the insightful recognition that "a truly womanist tradition has yet to be fully created and understood." To reach that goal, religious black women and men, and theological scholars in particular, must courageously explore the transformative potential of feminist struggle, the ways it can enable us to survive as a people, and enhance our understanding of the importance of spirituality in modern life.

Note

22. bell hooks, *Feminist Theory: From Margin to Center* (Boston: South End Press, 1984).
23. Katie Geneva Cannon, *Black Womanist Ethics* (Atlanta: Scholars Press. 1988).

Cheryl Townsend Gilkes

When I first read Alice Walker's definition of "womanist," it engendered the same joy and sense of good feeling within me that I felt that day, now twenty years ago, when I acquired my "Afro" (a hairstyle I still wear). It just felt good. It fit. It provided a way of stating who I was and how I felt about a lot of things. I would like to think that Alice Walker used the format of a dictionary definition to invite a liberating and wide-ranging appropriation that reflects the diversity of women of color. Womanist also brought to mind a day several years earlier when, uncomfortable with the term feminist because of the abuse I had experienced at the hands of insensitive and racist white women and because of the silliness I perceived in many of the issues discussed by white women calling themselves feminist, I had declared myself "pro-woman" in my attitudes and feelings, "period!" I said in my heart, "Thank you, Lord, for Alice Walker."

As a more critical and publicly accessible exercise, I also examined my own work on community workers and on church women in light of Walker's definition. I was particularly fascinated by its resonance with the women I met in the Sanctified Church.[24] Indeed, I was attached to Walker's term and her definition of it because I perceived that it was the most accurate distillation of the distinctiveness of the African-American female experience as I had both observed and partaken of it. It fit.[25] It felt good. And, it provided a bridge between forces faced by women my age and younger, and the more traditional African-American women's institutions within church and community. Walker's definition became a vehicle upon which Harriet Tubman (our foremother who walked north to freedom taking her family and community with her), Mary Church Terrell (our foremother who felt "the Race" should be called "colored" because it was so visually diverse), Mrs. Rippy (the very round, big-voiced, gospel soloist in my church who loved to laugh, cook, and bug us all and who testified openly at the church dinner table of the importance of caring for oneself through facial massage and through choosing life, by mastectomy if need be, as she did, all the while depending on the Holy Ghost, a.k.a. "the Spirit," to bring her "from a mighty long way"), Margaret (my friend who organized the very first Third World Women's Conference I ever attended), many many "homegirls,"[26] community and church mothers, and myself could all ride together as women wishing to penetrate the complexities of life as African-American women in the United States and its colonial antecedent.

Now Alice Walker is not the only person ever to think comprehensively about being black and female but she provided an "ahah!" experience that brought together my own thinking and research on women in the community and in diverse churches with black women's literary and creative traditions. Her idea seemed consistent with her other writings which are full of allusions and appropriations from the core of the African-American religious experience,[27] and which draw deeply from the well of African-American women's history as inseparable from the history of a total community—"... entire people, male *and* female." While not primarily religious, Walker's definition manages to draw upon the central indigenous theme of African-American spirituality, church formation, and construction of the pillars of religious experience: the importance of the Spirit as the operative manifestation of God in everyday life. For the vast majority of black people that emphasis has been contextualized in Christian settings, and Walker's use of the term "the Spirit," for us, automatically means "the Holy Ghost"—an actualization of Jesus's assertion to "the woman at the well" in John 4:24 that "God is a Spirit." While Walker herself may not claim an explicitly Christian spirituality and allegiance (and a recent quotation in *Jet* affirms that she does not), my reading of her assertion that a womanist *"Loves the Spirit"* resonates with my every encounter with "shouts" and "saints." It points to the Christian mysticism that undergirds the most radical actions of our foremothers and continues to spill over into the lives of the most secular of black women activists.

When considering the importance of Walker's definition as a *concept* or frame of reference for ethical and theological discourse, one has to be clear about what the term conveys for thinking about people as agents of history, not for thinking about God. Her focus is on human action, an appropriate focus for concepts and ideas used in ethics. Race, ethnicity, class, and gender are similar issues and terms now considered appropriate foci for ethical and theological thinking. "Womanist" is a term like "afrocentric" (or more properly "africentric"). Both terms make dramatic epistemological demands on the users while at the same time providing clear channels for creative thinking that do not have to answer to the theoretical and ideological assumptions surrounding terms such as "feminist" and "non-western." I find that Walker's definition demands that we take seriously the whole of African-American women's experience. I read in the definition more than "folk culture." I read in that definition the importance of the political and cultural traditions of clearly identifiable foremothers who insisted in their practice and in their thinking that black people must embrace one another wholeheartedly in a constructive life-affirming way,[28] an action that fits important understandings of *love. And Walker clearly emphasizes love.* The term love appears eleven times in the definition.

When one refers back to her discussion concerning Rebecca Jackson, a discussion whose real emphasis is distorted by an exaggerated focus on sexual preference, one finds Walker insisting that the issue of "woman-bonding" has to be carried back farther than the island of Lesbos in classical Greek tradition. Walker points to the probability that these were "Greek women whose servants, like their culture, were probably stolen from Egypt. ..."[29] What is critical here is that she seems to agree with George G.M. James and others that Greek civilization had its origins in Egypt, an African civilization.[30] Walker's insistence that "black women ... surely would have begun their woman-bonding earlier than Sappho's residency on the Isle of Lesbos"[31] points to older African traditions of institutionalized acceptance of women's organization and sisterhood as an essential part of the economic and family system.[32] The central issue for Walker around Lesbos is not really sexuality, but rather the isolation and aloofness implied in the notion of an island. She concludes, "The symbolism of [an island], for a black person, is far from positive."[33]

If we are to evaluate the thought of Alice Walker, thought which is highlighted and summarized in her definition but not presented as a fully elaborated system, then we must take seriously her emphasis on the importance of Martin Luther King in the shaping of our generation. I consider her statement, "... that if it had not been for ... Dr. King, I would have come of age believing in nothing and no one," a valid directional in ethical evaluation of her thinking.[34] For Walker and for King, the emphasis is on love, *agape* love—the kind of love that embraces everyone for the purposes of healing, change, and liberation, and on the connectedness of the black struggle to the emancipation of humanity and, ultimately, creation. For Walker particularly there is an emphasis on the centrality of black women in that struggle.

Finally, I read the last reference to love, "... herself. *Regardless*," to be a critical admonition for those seeking to emancipate and empower women, especially and most critically black women. The "self" component of the command to "love thy neighbor as thy*self*" matches social scientists' understandings of self-esteem. The failure to love self makes it impossible to love others, and our hateful acts toward others are often a measure of our feelings about self. Some of the greatest threats to human development among the poor and the non-poor, among the black and the non-black, are rooted in the lack of self-esteem. Teenage pregnancy, learning problems, toleration of abusive behavior, addictive and self-destructive behaviors, and hyper/unprincipled sexuality all seem to be related to problems of low self-esteem. I also think that many of the problems related to political apathy are functions of both individual and group self-esteem. I, personally, found that the emphasis on "black is beautiful" taught many of us to stop speaking in terms that reflected low self-esteem, for instance "bad hair," and to recognize that chemically assaulted skin and "oppressed hair" cannot inherit the kingdom.[35] If we are to explore the work of Alice Walker for ethical content or for direction in constructing ethics and in thinking theologically, I think that the most fruitful course is her artful advocacy of unconditional love that starts with our acceptance of ourselves as divinely and humanly lovable.

In her most recent book, Walker resurrects one of our favorite characters, Shug, making her the founder of a church in the tradition of many African-American "sisters of the Spirit." Walker also authors a pamphlet called "The Gospel According to Shug." Consistent with Walker's most subtle appropriations and reworking of the biblical imagery, ethics, and rhetoric implicit in the faith of our mothers, Walker presents us with a reworking of the beatitudes in which "Blessed" is replaced with the term "HELPED." The theme of love for all who are living is interwoven with twenty-seven explicit admonitions to embrace the cosmos, to pray for peace and justice, to help the existence of others, and to forgive. A close reading of Shug's gospel suggests that Walker affirms a connection between the *agape* love of Christian ethics and a variety of ethical systems concerned with the relations among human beings, their world, and their Creator. For Walker, and admittedly this is my reading, there is a consistent challenge to relate to all human beings with an all-encompassing non-violent, indeed *anti*-violent, love that challenges, changes, and liberates. "HELPED are those who love and actively support the diversity of life. ..."[36] In my reading of Walker, and this would make an excellent ethical study encompassing all of her work, this love is the greatest issue in human existence and the critical point of convergence between her creative thinking and the task of Christian ethics. Like many of us who were raised cuddling against our many mothers and aunts under the African-American preaching tradition, the greatest issue gleaned from those sermons was love. For Walker and many others, still "the greatest of these is love" and all else is commentary.

Note

24. Cheryl Townsend Gilkes, "The Role of Women in the Sanctified Church," *Journal of Religious Thought* 43 (Spring/Summer 1986): 24–41.
25. See Delores S. Williams, "The Color of Feminism: Or Speaking the Black Woman's Tongue," *Journal of Religious Thought* 43 (Spring/Summer 1986): 42, where she notes the problem posed for black Christian women by the word "feminist," using the metaphor of a dress shop. She writes, "The black woman in group 'A' said: This all reminds me of the day I went into a fancy dress shop downtown and saw a real pretty dress. ... There just wasn't enough material in that dress to make it fit me. ... And what I'm wondering is: if you black feminists try to make feminism fit me, will you have the same thing?"
26. Barbara Smith, ed., *Home Girls: A Black Feminist Anthology* (New York: Kitchen Table: Women of Color Press, 1983). See pp. xix–lvi for a discussion of the term "home girls," an earlier version of Walker's definition that uses the term "herstorically" rather than historically, some penetrating ethical issues around the misplaced black panic over homosexuality, and the need to critique the nature of heterosexuality in the black community.
27. See especially Walker's short story "The Welcome Table," in *In Love and In Trouble: Stories of Black Women* (New York: Harcourt Brace Jovanovich, 1973), 81–87.
28. I disagree with Gloria Watkins's assertion that "the term womanist is not sufficiently linked to a tradition of radical political commitment to struggle and change." Her complaint misses Walker's very cogent reading of black women's political history. bell hooks, *Talking Back: Thinking Feminist, Thinking Black* (Boston: South End Press, 1989), 182.
29. Alice Walker, "Gifts of Power: The Writings of Rebecca Jackson," in *In Search of Our Mothers' Gardens* (San Diego and New York: Harcourt Brace Jovanovich, 1983), 81–82.
30. George G.M. James, *Stolen Legacy* (London: The African Publication Society, 1954). Walker's discussion alludes to James's argument that the Greeks were not the authors of philosophy and civilization but appropriated the ideas and systems of the Egyptians, a North African people. Walker further elaborates her agreement with critiques of white supremacist hegemony in the study of ancient civilizations in her most recent novel, *The Temple of My Familiar* (Orlando, Florida: Harcourt Brace Jovanovich, 1989).
31. Walker, "Gifts of Power," 81.
32. For a more extended discussion of African women's traditions and their importance for understanding the roles of powerful women in black churches and communities, see Cheryl Townsend Gilkes, "The Roles of Church and Community Mothers: Ambivalent

American Sexism or Fragmented African Familyhood?" *Journal of Feminist Studies in Religion* 2 (Spring 1986): 41–59.

33. Walker, "Gifts of Power," 82.
34. Alice Walker, "Coretta King, Revisited," in *In Search of Our Mothers' Gardens*, 147.
35. See Alice Walker's essay, "Oppressed Hair Puts a Ceiling on the Brain," in *Living By the Word: Selected Writings 1973–1987* (New York: Harcourt Brace Jovanovich, 1988), 69–74.
36. Walker, *Temple of My Familiar*, 287–289.

A Final Rejoinder, by Cheryl J. Sanders

I want to begin by expressing my profound appreciation for these fresh and vigorous defenses of the womanist concept and nomenclature as an appropriate point of departure for doing ethics and theology as black women. If nothing else has been accomplished by this discussion, we have succeeded, I believe, in giving clear definition and direction to the terms of womanist discourse. Katie Cannon offers a helpful and significant formulation of a womanist liberation theological ethic to be used as a critical tool for constructing a faith praxis for black women. Emilie Townes's view of the womanist idea as a model of the fundamental principle of the black Christian tradition invites intense theological reflection upon the question of how christology can be integrated with a radically immanent concept of the divine. M. Shawn Copeland's concern for theological method, for the reshaping of black theology, and for Walker's derivation and development of the term enlightens our understanding of the womanist concept as "normative for adoption, adaptation, and authentic use." bell hooks envisions womanism as an aspect of feminism that invites black women to construct theoretical paradigms which call attention to the workings of sexist oppression, and to become engaged in the transformative potential of feminist struggle. And Cheryl Gilkes helps us to ground our understanding of womanist as a frame of reference for ethical and theological discourse by giving attention to the vital historical-cultural content and social ethical focus conveyed by the definition. I am satisfied that some of my most fundamental critical questions have been thoughtfully addressed by these several statements of how the womanist concept shapes and directs our ethical and theological work as black women scholars.

Each of my colleagues has taken issue on some level with two specific areas of concern lifted up in my essay—the use of womanist as a descriptive cultural nomenclature for normative ethical and theological discourse, and the relevance of sexual preference in assessing the use and applicability of the term. In fact, I perceive that my respondents are disturbed as much by my raising these questions as by whatever underlying assumptions and biases are revealed in them. After giving careful consideration to their concerns and objections, with particular sensitivity to Katie Cannon's expressions of anger, I became aware of an important factor that I did not explicitly raise in my statement but that does influence my thought and convictions on these issues. As a member of the Church of God, having been brought up in this church from my childhood as the third generation in Church of God from both sides of my family, and having served this church in positions of ministerial and educational leadership for much of my adult life, I identify very closely with the holiness tradition. My education in the liberal arts (Swarthmore College) and liberal theological (Harvard Divinity School) tradition notwithstanding, I suspect that my identification with the holiness tradition, perhaps more than any other factor, accounts for my position on these two issues, i.e., my insistence upon making hard and fast distinctions between the sacred and the secular in theory, and my deep concern for the moral significance of sexual norms in praxis.

Moreover, I think it is precisely at this juncture that I feel compelled to take issue with the fact that Rebecca Jackson, Sojourner Truth and other foremothers are named in womanist discourse without giving attention to the theological conservatism and evangelical fervor that undergirds much of their thought and action. In other words, I sense that these two major points of contention in the roundtable discussion are energized by the conflict between liberal and conservative theological perspectives more than by a lack of consensus regarding the appropriate terms, procedures and content of womanist ethics and theology. To further complicate matters, in the Church of God tradition, in theory if not also in practice, our commitment to Christian unity causes us to look with suspicion upon any effort to define church in terms of race, gender, class or denomination.[37] Our regard for the Bible as the supreme source of our understanding of the nature of divinity and the situation of humanity makes it difficult to ascribe independent revelatory authority to any other sources or concepts in doing theology apart from the light of Scripture. Thus, it is problematic for me to incorporate terms, concepts, practices and approaches into my own theological and ethical reflection that contradict my limited but growing understanding of the Word of God. I might add that I am helped in my dilemma by M. Shawn Copeland's suggestion that we can speak of secular womanists and Christian womanists. In any case, I applaud the diversity of perspectives represented in this roundtable discussion, and sincerely hope that my own deviance from the liberal norm does not compromise my continued participation in this dialogue.

I hope that our debate on the specificities of theological method and the relevance of sexual preference will not deter us from forthright consideration of the concrete concern that is at the root of these womanist ethical and theological statements, which is justice. The experience of sexism and racism focuses the black woman's attention on the question of justice in a unique way. But our participation as black women in the upper echelons of graduate theological education can be as "the blind leading the blind" if we do not bring to our work a passionate commitment to the transformative liberatory praxis which bell hooks and others have persistently brought to our attention. I believe that the womanist concept, in addition to giving us an opportunity to name our own experience after our own fashion, compels us to celebrate, critique and construct resources provided through the lives of black women to confront the structures of injustice and oppression and other forms of evil that would destroy us individually and collectively. One of the strengths of the womanist perspective in this regard is the ease with which it lends itself to analysis of both the personal and political dimensions of the pursuit of justice, because of its implicit focus on the individual rights and collective responsibilities of black women.

To summarize, I discern within this roundtable discussion the emergence of several encouraging signs of the potential impact of womanist theological scholarship upon the life of the academy, the church and the community. It did my soul good to observe the extent to which my colleagues drew upon black women's sources in formulating their responses. The fact that almost all of their footnotes are derived from the writings of black women sends the important signal that we are appreciating, analyzing and appropriating our own sources, and also those of black men, without appealing, for the most part, to white sources for sanction or approval of what we ourselves have said. This observation is especially significant in view of the fact that in a racist society, self-hatred manifests itself as unmistakably in the academy as in the ghetto when we are pressured to employ our oppressors' criteria to evaluate our own work and worth. To see black women embracing and engaging our own material is a celebration in itself. It may be that the best contribution womanist scholars can make to the church (and to the academy as well) by means of discussions such as these is to force the issue of acceptance of the diversity of perspectives, experiences and approaches to human wholeness. These responses represent for me some exciting combinations of content and method; indeed, the womanist concept invites and encourages dialogue across the disciplines. Moreover, the fact that we are far from uniform even in some of our basic assumptions and ideas enlightens and enlarges the discussion in my view. Given the implicit and explicit pastoral concerns expressed in each of the responses, it is my hope that womanist ethics and theology can generate the practical enablement of oppressed persons in the society through the instrumentality of the church and the academy. This is not to suggest that the value of womanist thought is strictly reduced to its immediate applicability to pastoral ministry, but rather to recognize that a practical concern for enablement is the expected outcome of theological reflection and action rooted in the real experience and struggle and power represented by the womanist concept. The intergenerational emphasis of the womanist definition can form the basis for developing more effective strategies and resources for parents in the black community and beyond, who are faced with the responsibility of finding ways to equip our children to name and to overcome the many scourges and plagues which obscure our past, complicate our present and threaten our future. Thus it is with deep gratitude and hope that I exhort my sister scholars to continue the work of crafting tools and breaking ground and planting seeds for a new day.

Note

37. I have addressed the conflict between the doctrine of holiness and unity and the practice of racism and sexism in the Church of God in a chapter entitled "Ethics of Holiness and Unity in the Church of God," in *Called to Minister, Empowered to Serve*, ed. Juanita Leonard (Anderson, Indiana: Warner Press, 1989).

7

Literature and Literary Criticism

Some Implications of Womanist Theory* (1986)

SHERLEY ANNE WILLIAMS

I am an Afro-Americanist and enough of an Africanist to know something of the enormous differences between African literatures and Afro-American literature, and something, too, of the remarkable parallels and similarities between them. We do in English, after all, trace our literary roots back to the same fore-parents, the Senegalese American, Phillis Wheatley and the Nigerian American Gustavas Vassa or Olaudah Equino, the African. So you must make your own analogies with what follows here; I am assuming that feminist criticism receives much the same reception it has met with among Afro-American critics, male and female. Often, feminist concerns are seen as a divisive, white importation that further fragments an already divided and embattled race, as trivial mind-games unworthy of response while black people everywhere confront massive economic and social problems. I don't deny feminism's potential for divisiveness, but the concerns of women are neither trivial nor petty. The relation between male and female is the very foundation of human society. If black men refuse to engage the unease at the race's heart, they cannot speak or even see truthfully anywhere else.

Feminist readings can lead to mis-apprehensions of particular texts or even of a whole tradition, but certain of its formulation offer us a vocabulary that can be made meaningful in terms of our own experience. Feminist theory, like black aesthetics, offers us not only the possibility of changing one's *reading* of the world, but of changing the world itself. And like black aesthetics, it is far more egalitarian than the prevailing mode. What follows, then, is both a critique of feminist theory and an application of that branch of it Alice Walker has called "womanist."[1] It is as much *bolekaja* criticism as "feminist" theory for black women writers had been urging black men, not so much to "come down [and] fight," as to come down and talk, even before Chinweizu, Jemie and Madubuike coined a critical term to describe our challenge.[2]

---

* Presented at the African Literature Conference, April 17, 1986.

Feminist criticism, to paraphrase Elaine Showalter's words in the "Introduction" to *The New Feminist Criticism*,[3] challenges the fundamental theoretical assumptions of literary history and criticism by demanding a radical rethinking and revisioning of the conceptual grounds of literary study that have been based almost entirely on male literary experiences. Some of the implications of this radical revisioning have already been realized in Afro-American literature. The works of forgotten black women writers are being resurrected and critics are at work revising the slighting, often misinformed, critical opinions of these works. We have a fuller understanding of these writers because feminist criticism has begun to eliminate much of the phallocentrism from our readings of their work and to recover the female aesthetics said to distinguish female creativity from male. We can see the results of this inquiry in the numerous monographs and articles that have appeared in the nine years since the publication of Barbara Smith's groundbreaking essay, "Towards a Black Feminist Criticism,"[4] and in that some black male critics are now numbered among the ranks of feminist critics.

Much of the present interest in black feminist criticism is rooted in the fact that black women writers are among the most exciting writers on the contemporary American literary scene, but it began in the confrontation of black women readers in the early '70s with black female portraiture (or its lack) in fiction by black male writers. Debra McDowell, in "New Directions for Black Feminist Theory,"[5] values these pioneering studies of negative and derogatory female portraiture as an impetus to early black feminist inquiry and acknowledges that a black feminist criticism must do more than "merely focus on how black men have treated black women in literature." McDowell's major concern is with encouraging the development of theories that will help us to see properly and understand the themes, motifs and idioms used by black women writers, but she raises other important issues as well. She touches upon one of the more disturbing aspects of current black feminist criticism: its separatism; its tendency to see not only a *distinct* black female culture but to see that culture as a separate cultural form having more in common with white female experience than it has with the facticity of Afro-American life. This proposition is problematic, even as a theoretical conjecture, especially since even its adherents have conceded that, until quite recently, black women's literary experiences were excluded from consideration in the literature of white feminists. For this reason, I prefer Alice Walker's term, *womanist,* as the referent for what I attempt here. Womanist theory is, by definition, "committed to the survival and wholeness of entire people," female *and* male, as well as a valorization of women's works in all their varieties and multitudes. That commitment places it squarely within the challenge of engagement implicit in *bolekaja* criticism.

McDowell also calls for black feminist critics to turn their attention to the "challenging and necessary task" of a thoroughgoing examination of the works of black male writers, and suggests a line of inquiry that implicitly affirms kinship among Afro-American writers, "the countless thematic, stylistic, and imagistic parallels between black male and black female writing." Her call, however, does not go far enough. By limiting the studies of writings by black males to efforts "to determine the ways in which these commonalities are manifested differently in black women's writings and the ways in which they coincide with writings by black men," she seems to imply that feminist inquiry can only illuminate works by women and works that include female portraiture, that our re-readings of female images will not also change our readings of men. Womanist inquiry, on the other hand, assumes that it can talk both effectively and productively about men. This is a necessary assumption because the negative, stereotyped images of black women are only a part of the problem of phallocentric writings by black males. In order to understand that problem more fully, we must turn to what black men have written about themselves.

Much literature, classic and popular, by white American males valorizes the white patriarchal ideals of physical aggression, heroic conquest, and intellectual domination. Recognizing that a difference in actual circumstances forced distinguishing and different characteristics on would-be black patriarchs, a conventional feminist reading of literature by black males would see these ideals only partially "encoded" in their writings. Even so, such ideals would be the desired ones, and deviation from them taken as signs of diminished masculine self-esteem. That is, explicit social protest about racial prohibitions that restrict black men from exercising patriarchial authority is part of their "heroic quest" because they don't possess all the privileges of white men. Such a reading, of course, tends to reduce the black struggle for justice and equal opportunity to the right to beat one's wife and daughter. Many black men refused to exercise such "rights," and many black women resisted those who tried.[6] Nor was physical aggression really a value in the literature of black males before 1940. Physical force, even when used by non-heroic black men, was almost always defensive, especially against white people, and, when used against other blacks, generally symbolized the corruption wrought by slavery. The initial *formulation,* however, does serve to illuminate some instances of black male self-portraiture, particularly in nineteenth century non-fiction prose narrative and fiction.

Nineteenth century black men, confronted with the impossibility of being the (white) patriarch, began to subvert certain of patriarchy's ideals and values to conform to their own images. Thus, the degree to which, and the basis on which, the hero avoids physical aggression was one means of establishing the hero's noble stature and contributed to the hero's intellectual equality—not dominance—with the collective white man. Frederick Douglass' 1845 autobiography, *Narrative of the Life of Frederick Douglass, An American Slave,*[7] offers several instances of this subversion and redefinition of white patriarchal ideals. I focus on what he will later call "The Fight."[8] Douglass, an "uppity" slave, is hired out to Covey, a "nigger-breaker," to have his spirit curbed. Douglass' "fight" with Covey marks the turning point in his development from slave to free man. In the instant he refuses to be whipped, Douglass ceases "to be a slave in fact." Yet Douglass is not the aggressor. Douglass seizes Covey by the throat when the later tries to tie him up and holds him "uneasy"; though Douglass does draw Covey's blood, he actually touches him only with the ends of his fingers. Douglass brings the white man to the ground but never lays violent hands on him; rather, he "seizes him by the collar." Douglass is thus able to dominate Covey by his own self-restraint and self-control rather than *force major*. Douglass took a great delight in having bested Covey while conforming to a semblance of the master–slave relationship. In the later re-telling of the episode he returns "a polite, 'Yes, sir,' " to Covey's outraged, " 'Are you going to continue to resist?' " and concludes, I was "victorious because my aim had not been to injure him but to prevent his injuring me." Robert B. Stepto, in *From Behind the Veil*[9] (itself a brilliant example of the use to which genre studies can be put), details the brilliant strokes by which "Douglass reinforces his posture as an articulate hero"—i.e., the intellectual equal of the white men who introduce and thus vouch for the authenticity of Douglass and his narrative before the white world. Suffice it here to say that in "supplant[ing the white men] as the definitive historian[s] of his past" Douglass self-consciously reverses the usual patterns of authentication in black texts and that this manifestation of his intellectual independence is characterized by the same restraint and subtlety as his description of his successful psychological rite of passage.

The pattern of self-restraint, of physical self-control as an avenue to moral superiority and intellectual equality vis-à-vis white society, dominates male self-portraiture in the nineteenth century, where achieving heroic stature is most often the means by which the black male hero also assumes the mantel of the "patriarch." But the black patriarch in the nineteenth century has more to do with providing for and protecting his "dependents" than with wielding authority or exploiting their dependency so as to achieve his own privilege. Once free, Douglass marries, takes a job, becomes a leader in the struggle for the abolition of slavery; Josiah Henson, the model for Harriet Beecher Stowe's Uncle Tom,[10] escapes from slavery with his wife beside him and two children on his back, works on the Underground Railroad, and founds a black township in Canada. Dr. Miller, the hero of Charles Chestnutt's turn-of-the-century novel, *The Marrow of Tradition*,[11] is a husband, father, son, and founder of a hospital and school for blacks. In other words, black male heroic stature was most often achieved within the context of marriage, family, and black community—all of which depend on a relationship with, if not black women, at least other black people.

The nature of the black male character's heroic quest and the means by which the hero achieves intellectual parity begin to change in the twentieth century. The heroic quest through the early thirties was a largely introspective one whose goal was the reintegration of the educated hero with the unlettered black masses who symbolized his negro-ness.[12] But the valuation of black community and black family (often an extended family) continues until 1940. Richard Wright's *Native Son* began a period in which the black heroic quest was increasingly externalized. A perceptive, though not necessarily articulate or educated, protagonist seeks recognition from the white power structure and in the process comes to recognize—and realize—himself. By the mid 1960s white society was typically characterized in the literature by physically frail and cowardly, morally weak, sexually impotent, effeminate white men and super-feminine white women who personified the official standard of feminine beauty—delicate, dainty, sexually inhibited until liberated by a hyper-potent black man.[13] The goal of the black hero's quest was to dominate the one and marry the other. Black community, once the object of heroic quest, was, in these works, an impediment to its success; black female portraiture, when present, was often no more than demeaning stereotypes used to justify what even the hero sometimes recognized as a pathological obsession with the white woman. This kind of heroic quest is a dominant feature in some important contemporary texts; however, black male self-portraiture, by the late 1970s, was presented within a broader spectrum of themes—patriarchal responsibility, sibling relations, and male bonding—that were self-questioning rather than self-satisfied or self-righteous.[14] These few texts can be construed as a positive response to the black feminist criticism of the early 1970s. Yet they are largely neglected by the Afro-American critical establishment which, by and large, leaves to the *New York Times* the task of canonizing our literature. The present interest in black women's writing arose outside that hegemony as had the interest in black poetry in the late 1960s. And, like the black aesthetics that arose as a response to black arts poetry, black feminist criticism runs the risk of being narrowly proscriptive rather than broadly analytic.

* * *

Using a combination of fiction and non-fiction prose by Richard Wright, Ralph Ellison, James Baldwin, Norman Mailer, and Eldridge Cleaver, Michele Wallace suggested, in *Black Macho and the Myth of the Superwoman*,[15] a black feminist reading of the development of modern black male self-image that is similar to what I have said here. Wallace was roundly damned and told by sister feminists "to read it again" as though we ourselves had not suspected, even suggested, these things before. And no one has quite dared since then to hold up the record black men have written of themselves. Rather, since black men gave little evidence of talking to us, we talked to each other.

Having confronted what black men have said about us, it is now time for black feminist critics to confront—and to confront black male writers—with what they have said about themselves. What is needed is a thoroughgoing examination of male images in the works of black male writers. This is a necessary step in ending the separatist tendency in Afro-American criticism and in achieving, in Afro-American literature, feminist theory's avowed aim of "challenging the fundamental theoretical assumptions of traditional literary history and criticism." Black women as readers and writers have been kept out of literary endeavor, so we had, and have, a lot to say. But to focus solely on ourselves is to fall into the same hole The Brother has dug for himself—narcissism, isolation, inarticulation, obscurity. Of course we must keep talking to and about ourselves but literature, as Chinweizu and Walker remind us, is about community and dialogue; theories or ways of reading ought actively to promote the enlargement of both.

Notes

1. Alice Walker, *In Search of Our Mothers' Gardens* (New York, 1984).
2. Chinweizu, Onwuchekwa Jemi, and Ihechukwu Madubuike, *Toward the Decolonization of African Literature* (Washington, D.C., 1983).
3. Elaine Showalter, ed., *The New Feminist Criticism* (New York, 1985).
4. Barbara Smith in Showalter, *op. cit.*
5. In Showalter, *op. cit.*, 186–99.
6. Further research in both traditional and contemporary Afro-American orature just might document that the community valued going "upside" anyone's head as a *last,* rather than the first, resort at least as much as they admired the ability or will to do so.
7. Benjamin Quarles, ed. (Cambridge, 1960).
8. *My Bondage and My Freedom* (1855; rep. New York, 1969).
9. Urbana, 1979.
10. *Father Henson's Own Story* (1849; rep. Upper Saddle River, N.J., 1970).
11. 1901; rep. Ann Arbor, Michigan, 1969.
12. The key texts include James Weldon Johnson's *The Autobiography of an Ex-Colored Man* (1912), Jean Toomer's *Cane* (1923), and Langston Hughes's *Not without Laughter* (1930).
13. The terminology is drawn from Eldridge Cleaver's *Soul on Ice* (New York, 1968) but the portrayal can be found in the works of black male writers from Richard Wright and Ralph Ellison to Ishmael Reed.
14. Ernest J. Gaines's *In My Father's House* (1978), Wesley Brown's *Tragic Magic* (1978) come most readily to mind; however, the works of William Melvin Kelley, John McCluskey, and John A. Williams present a range of black male characters that still await close discussion.
15. New York, 1978.

A Womanist Production of Truths: The Use of Myths in Amy Tan (1995)

WENYING XU

Women as sexed subjects[1] are produced by centuries of ideological indoctrination inscribing social and sexual mores in girls and women. Mythologies are one of the most appetizing, saturating, and thus most vicious components of gender ideologies, for mythologies are capable of shaping female subjects who take as their own vital survival the perpetuation of existent social and sexual order. As we have often seen and read, sometimes women have a more desperate sense of peril than men when there is any transgression of sexual morals, particularly if the transgression is done by another woman. Humanist and individualist traditions have further captivated women under their oppression with the philosophy of the Intended Subject. If one fails to recognize the subject as ideologically molded and thus fractured and incoherent, one cannot understand women as gendered subjects who are not identical to their intentions. If there were a self before language and culture that was identical to its intentions, it has been irretrievably lost.

It is not my desire, however, to speculate on the nature of the primordial; rather I would like to discuss through the reading of Amy Tan's novels how women can take possession of myths and make them produce truths that enable women to revise their self-understanding and thus gain a renewed sense of self. Their production of truths is an act of transgression against established norms and ideals, facilitating the loosening of the foundations of female subject constitution.

How Asian American writers use myths and legends has been at the center of a debate concerning the truthfulness of the representation of Chinese culture. In *The Big Aiiieeeee!* Frank Chin tries to distinguish the real Chinese myths and legends from the fake ones as he finds them in Maxine Hong Kingston, Amy Tan, and David Henry Hwang.[2] Chin accuses these Asian American writers of having "faked" Chinese legends and myths to confirm "the white racist" belief that Chinese are cruel and misogynous. These writers' revision of Chinese myths and legends is condemned as "a device for destroying history and literature" (Chin 2–3).

It seems that what Frank Chin demands of Chinese American writers is their loyalty to their ancestral culture and history to such an extent that it precludes any concern about gender issues which challenge the patriarchal order, for his charge against Kingston, Tan, and Hwang is that these writers have rewritten Chinese myths and legends in order to highlight either the victimization of women or women's self-empowerment. As a man well versed in Chinese culture and history, Chin has to work very hard to forget the misogynous portrayals of women in Chinese literature and the gendered Chinese language. In his "This Is Not an Autobiography," Chin's repeated use of "Chinaman" functions to demarcate "the yellow agents of yellow extinction" or "ornamental orientals" (among whom he locates Maxine Hong Kingston, Betty Bao Lord, and David Henry Hwang) from the "real Chinaman" (Chin 110). This male universal as the incorruptible genuine embodiment of Chinese culture and history further blinds Chin to the blatant male domination inherent in the Chinese language. He writes: "Whatever language a Chinaman speaks, it is always Chinaman, and the first person pronoun I, in any language, means 'I am the law' " (Chin III). In order to make this Kwan Kung bold statement (Chin 121–22), Chin must forget the humble Chinese female pronoun "I" (nu) which is synonymous with slave.

Chin's desire to separate the real from the fake is thus gender driven. In opposing the feminization of Chinese myths or legends, he is not simply (and naively) guarding the purity of his ancestral culture; he is glorifying and continuing the male militant heroism in that culture.[3] What Frank Chin does not seem to understand is the fact that myths and legends are neither immutable nor unmediated in the sense of being sacred and gender free. The story of Fa Mu Lan, for example, has several versions in the Tang, Ming, and Qing dynasties as well as in the modern period.[4] Myths and legends also are the very stuff that renders ideologies invisible.[5]

For me it was a rare pleasure to find in Amy Tan's novels revisions of mythologies that subvert gender ideologies and gain women a measure of freedom from patriarchal domination. The two main myths Amy Tan uses are the myth of the Moon Lady in *The Joy Luck Club* (1989) and that of the Kitchen God in *The Kitchen God's Wife* (1991).[6] For my purpose I will give a fuller account of both myths than that given by Amy Tan.

The Moon Lady myth tells the story of the master archer, Yi, and his wife, Chang Eh, who became the Moon Lady.[7] Both were originally lesser gods but as a punishment they had been turned into mere mortals by the supreme father god and his wife, the sun goddess. Normally only one solar son at a time was permitted to appear in the sky and meet the needs of the mortals on earth. Once, however, choosing to be playful rather than dutiful, all ten sons appeared at the same time, scorching the earth. Yi, the master archer, had been sent to earth merely to discipline the sons of the sun goddess so as to restore the order normal to the relation between the heaven and the earth. Yi, in overzealous compassion for mortals, angrily shot down nine of the sons and thus, with his wife, was forced to become mere mortals. Yi and Chang Eh never gave up hope of recapturing immortality. Yi eventually found a creature who possessed a tree on which grew a ten-thousand-year rare fruit which either could provide human immortality for two people or could send one to heaven as a god. Because of Yi's earlier compassion for mortals, the creature gave him the fruit, and in similar compassion he chose to share it with his wife so both could become immortal. His wife, Chang Eh, however, who had killed no one but still had been punished along with her husband, was not content to share the fate of being merely an immortal human with her husband; she ate the fruit by herself in order to again become a goddess. Instantly, she felt as light as a feather and floated out of an open window up to the moon. In one ending of the myth, as soon as she got to the moon she became a toad in punishment for her disloyalty. In the other ending, she was compelled to live for eternity on the moon as a beautiful but utterly lonely young woman. In *The Joy Luck Club* Ying-Ying recalls a celebration of the Moon Festival in her childhood. The opera of the Moon Lady is customarily staged on the night of August 15 when the moon is the fullest. After the Moon Lady takes the "peach" of immortality, the drama turns didactic.

> As soon as she tasted it, she began to rise, then fly—not like the Queen Mother—but like a dragonfly with broken wings. "Flung from this earth by my own wantonness!" she cried just as her husband dashed back home, shouting, "Thief! Life-stealing wife!" ... there stood the poor lady against a moon as bright as the sun. Her hair was now so long it swept the floor, wiping up her tears. An eternity had passed since she last saw her husband, for this was her fate: to stay lost on the moon, forever seeking her own selfish wishes.
>
> "For woman is yin," she cried sadly, "the darkness within, where untempered passions lie. And man is yang, bright truth lighting our minds." (*Club* 81)

The moral lesson of the Moon Lady aims at curbing women's desire for agency by describing it as "wanton" and "selfish." Myths mapping such explicit limitations on women's desires and actions are analogous to what Spivak calls "symbolic clitoridectomies" (10). They mark, expose, and slice off the place of women's desire. The agents of perpetrating such removal of desire are often women themselves. Myths and traditional wisdom engender and legitimate the removal of agency in women. As a child Waverly Jong learns from her mother "Bite back your tongue. ... Strongest wind cannot be seen" (*Club* 89). Only silent wishes get fulfilled. Ying-Ying as a child cannot understand why a secret wish is "what you want but cannot ask." She demands an answer from Amah, "Why can't I ask?" "It's because ... if you ask it ... it is no longer a wish but a selfish desire," says Amah. "Haven't I taught you that it is wrong to think of your own needs? A girl can never ask, only listen" (*Club* 70).

The real beginning of the narrative of *The Joy Luck Club* is the mother's killing secret. When Jing-mei is summoned by her father to take her mother's "corner" at the mah jong table, he tells her his suspicions: "My Father thinks she was killed by her own thoughts."

" 'She had a new idea inside her head,' said my father. 'But before it could come out of her mouth, the thought grew too big and burst. It must have been a very bad idea' " (*Club* 19). It is a desire too great to be good for a woman. A mortal woman dies because of a great desire and an immortal woman becomes exiled for it. Tales or myths of this sort are gendering and regulating biographies for the constitution of the sexed subject. Through them Chinese women learn not to desire, not to demand, not to act out of their wishes. Winnie remembers that all the stories she knows

> had to do with lessons learned too late—not to eat too much, not to talk too loudly, not to wander out at night by yourself—in any case, always about people who fell off the earth and into the sky because of their willful ways. (*Wife* 230)

Amy Tan gives the Moon Lady an alternative ending that counteracts the gendering "truth" of the myth. After the opera is over, Ying-Ying follows the Moon Lady hoping to get her wish granted.

> "I have a wish," I said in a whisper, and still she did not hear me. So I walked closer yet, until I could see the face of the Moon Lady: shrunken cheeks, a broad oily nose, large glaring teeth, and red-stained eyes. ... And as the secret wish fell from my lips, the Moon Lady looked at me and became a man. (*Club* 82)

This ending removes the glamour of the Moon Lady as a beautiful yet pitiful sinner, thus disclosing the ugliness of women's victimization and crystallizing the insidious "secret" behind the making of the myth. Now if we recall the truth uttered by the Moon Lady at the end of the opera, "Women are yin, the darkness within. ... And man is yang, bright truth lighting our minds," we see the comical twist in Tan's telling of the Moon Lady. The "truth," declared by a declining man disguised as a beautiful young woman, now appears to be a bad joke that strips the grandeur of the universal claim about the sexes. With this comical twist of the story of the Moon Lady, Amy Tan reminds her reader that mythologies are not authorless and therefore free from intentions to manipulate. Rather myths have been authored by the intentions of gender ideologies to subjugate women and turn them into sexed subjects.

In *The Kitchen God's Wife* Winnie Louie chooses to tell the unknown story of a god's wife who was the hand behind his glory and wealth.

> Fish jumped in his river, pigs grazed his hand, ducks flew around his yard as thick as clouds. And that was because he was blessed with a hardworking wife named Guo. She caught his fish and herded his pigs. She fattened his ducks, doubled all his riches, year after year ... (*Wife* 54)

But the husband "was not satisfied" and began philandering around (54). His wife, refusing to wait on his lovers, left him for good. Years later, having squandered all his wealth, Zhang as a beggar met his wife again, who now was a lady of a rich house. Out of shame he jumped into the fireplace and his ashes flew up to heaven. "For having the courage to admit you were wrong," the Jade Emperor (ruler of heaven) declared to Zhang, "I make you Kitchen God, watching over everyone's behavior. Every year you let me know who deserves good luck, who deserves bad" (*Wife* 55).

In one of the common versions of the Kitchen God myth, the god began as a good, hard working, and honest man, fated, however, to be poor all his life.[8] The extreme poverty forced him to sell his wife to a wealthy man as a concubine. She never forgot him and once when he came to work for her new husband, even though he never even recognized her, she gave him some cakes into which she had hidden money. Not knowing they contained money, this man on his way home shared one of them with a hungry stranger at a tea house. Discovering the money in the cake, the stranger swindled him into selling them for almost nothing. Later, learning that his ever loving former wife had filled the cakes with money, he decided that his fate was too heavy and ended his own life. With his efforts in this life receiving no reward, he nevertheless was rewarded by being appointed the God of the Kitchen.

Winnie's rendition of the myth focuses on the injustice that the wife suffered. Winnie also denaturalizes the husband's poverty, explaining it as the result of his bad character rather than his fate. In her story the husband and his lover "slaughtered ducks just to eat a plate of their tongues. And in two years' time, all of Zhang's land was empty, and so was his heart" (*Wife* 54). Such revision enables Winnie to indignantly disavow this myth. "Why should I want that kind of person to judge me, a man who cheated his wife? His wife was the good one, not him" (*Wife* 55).

For someone from the old China, Winnie is not only courageous but also enlightened to denounce the god and demand justice for the forgotten wife. After all, as she very well knows,

> "All year long you have to show him [the kitchen god] respect—give him tea and oranges. When Chinese New Year's time comes, you must give him even better things—maybe whiskey to drink, cigarettes to smoke, candy to eat, that kind of thing. You are hoping all the time his tongue will be sweet, his head a little drunk, so when he has his meeting with the big boss, maybe he reports good things about you. This family has been good, you hope he says. Please give them good luck next year." (*Wife* 55)

Following further Winnie's account of her life in China, one finds out that the story of the Kitchen God is also her own story. She is the kind-hearted hard-working wife, who is constantly humiliated and abused by her ruthless and black hearted husband, Wen Fu. It seems that her life in China is an unbreakable chain of bad luck—female child of a concubine, abandoned by both parents, married to a murderous man, two dead children, several abortions, China's war with Japan, and her one and half years in jail. ... Perhaps it is her incessant bad luck that has made her defiant of the Kitchen God, for she certainly deserves good luck because of her unbending observation of the traditional codes for women. But in contradiction with the tradition she also learns that being born a female (in the old China) certifies all kinds of rotten luck to appear on her path of life.[9]

In her narrative of her past life, Winnie casts herself in the role of the Kitchen God's wife whose good behavior secured her nothing. She has followed closely the prescription of a virtuous woman and a good wife, but she has always been made to feel inadequate by her husband's dissatisfaction expressed in torrents of abuse. Winnie becomes furious but helpless as she watches her husband being rewarded with good luck for simply being his horrible self. Winnie's revision of the myth of the Kitchen God produces the truth of the masculine use of women as instruments of self-assertion. She makes it clear that it is through the use of women that Zhang became a kitchen god, and it is by abusing women that Wen Fu perceives himself as a "real man."

When Winnie finally understands that if she does not fight back, she will be like many other women who become sacrifices on the altar of the patriarchal tradition, she casts off the respectable robe of tragedy and compares herself to "a chicken in a cage, mindless, never dreaming of freedom, but never worrying when your neck might be chopped off" (*Wife* 313). It is this recognition of the inhumanity of her life that finally motivates her to seek a change in life. In retrospect she tells her daughter, "If I had had to change the whole world to change my own life, I would have done that" (*Wife* 355–56).

To save herself Winnie chooses to do what only "bad" women do—running away from her husband and moving in with the man she loves. Only when she refuses to be a virtuous woman and good wife does good luck begin to flow into her life. Even the good luck, however, does not come without the company of patriarchal bullying. When Winnie is sued by her husband, Wen Fu, the court sentences her to two years in prison for "deserting her husband" (*Wife* 373). Already disentangled from the grip of her traditional female consciousness, Winnie feels no shame but anger over the injustice of China's legal system. After one and half years in prison, after being raped by Wen Fu once again, and after she has pointed his gun at his head, Winnie finally gains her freedom from Wen Fu and begins her new life with Jimmie Louie in America. In the new country she refuses to continue the tradition that demands in women silent desires and self-effacement. She teaches her daughter with her own life stories the courage to be "selfish."[10]

At the end of *The Kitchen God's Wife*, Winnie shops for a goddess for the red altar which her daughter Pearl has inherited from Auntie Du. Dissatisfied with all the existent goddesses, who are helplessly entrenched in the tradition of female servility, she tells the shop owner: "I am looking for a goddess that nobody knows. Maybe she does not yet exist" (*Wife* 413). The shop owner is delighted to part with the statue of a goddess on which the factory forgot to inscribe her name.

> So I bought that mistake. I fixed it. I used my gold paint and wrote her name on the bottom. ... I could see this lady statue in her new house, the red temple altar with two candlesticks lighting up her face from both sides. She would live there, but no one would call her Mrs. Kitchen God. Why would she want to be called that, now that she and her husband are divorced. (*Wife* 414)

This "mistake," the object that has made the husband of the shop owner "so mad," takes on the life that has been traditionally impossible for women—she is named "Lady Sorrowfree" (*Wife* 414–15). Now divorced and deified, she finally becomes a goddess by her own merit. "She will listen. She will wash away everything sad with her tears. She will use her stick to chase away everything bad" (*Wife* 414–15).

This gesture of celebration and self-affirmation is also present in Tan's use of the myth of the Moon Lady. At the end of her children's book, *The Moon Lady* (1992),[11] Nai-nai (Grandma Ying-Ying) tells her three granddaughters that her secret wish to the Moon Lady has already been answered—"I had found myself. I found out what kind of tiger I really was. ... And I knew what the best wishes were: those I could make come true by myself" (*Lady* 27). The story ends with Nai-nai and her granddaughters dancing "by the light of the full moon," casting Nai-nai as the *new* Moon Lady who has outlived the punishment, the misery, and the loneliness (*Lady* 27).

Notes

1. See Gayatri Spivak, *The Post-Colonial Critic: Interviews, Strategies, Dialogues* (New York: Routledge, 1990) Chapter 1.
2. See Frank Chin's "Come All Ye Asian American Writers of the Real and the Fake," *The Big Aiiieeeee!*, 1–92.
3. For an excellent study of Frank Chin's charge against Kingston's feminist revision of Chinese myths, see King-Kok Cheung, "The Woman Warrior versus the Chinaman Pacific: Must a Chinese American Critic Choose between Feminism and Heroism?" *Conflicts in Feminism*, eds. Marianne Hirsch et al.
4. See Sau-ling Cynthia Wong, "Kingston's Handling of Traditional Chinese Sources," in *Approaches to Teaching Kingston's* Woman Warrior, 26–36. (New York: The Modern language Association of America, 1991).
5. My critique focusing on the issue of gender should not be interpreted as a total rejection of Chin's criticism of Asian Americans for buying into the hegemonic Christian culture.
6. Amy Tan, *The Joy Luck Club* (New York: G.P. Putnam's Sons, 1989). *The Kitchen God's Wife* (New York: G.P. Putnam's Sons, 1991). All further references to these editions will be cited parenthetically in the text, as *Club* and *Wife*.
7. My narration of the myth is based on the untranslated *Chinese Mythology* by Yuan Ke.
8. This version of the Kitchen God is based on "The Kitchen Deity" in *Folk Tales of China*, ed. Wolfram Eberhard.
9. Marina Heung succinctly describes the life of women in the old China. She writes: "Because of their historical devaluation, women in the Chinese family are regarded as disposable property or detachable appendages despite their crucial role in maintaining the family

line through childbearing. Regarded as expendable 'objects to be invested in or bartered,' the marginal status of Chinese women shows itself in their forced transfer from natal families to other families through the practice of arranged marriage, concubinage, adoption, and pawning. The position of women—as daughters, wives, and mothers—in Chinese society is therefore markedly provisional, with their status and expendability fluctuating according to their families' economic circumstances, their ability to bear male heirs, and the proclivities of authority figures in their lives" (601).

10. This, of course, does not guarantee that the daughter would be less vulnerable than her mother to gender ideologies. In Amy Tan America does not dissolve women's oppression. She has An-mei, Rose's mother, complain: "I was raised the Chinese way; I was taught to desire nothing, to swallow other people's misery, to eat my own bitterness. And even though I taught my daughter the opposite, still she came out the same way ... she was born a girl" (*Club* 215). Through the stories of the daughters in *The Joy Luck Club*, Tan successfully portrays the asymmetrical power relations between men and women in this country. However, Tan is also naive in seeing sexism in the U.S. mainly as unmediated male domination in families and heterosexual relationships. This critique will be the subject of another essay.

11. Amy Tan, *The Moon Lady* (New York: Macmillan, 1992). All further references will be to this edition and will be cited parenthetically in the text, abbreviated *Lady*.

References

Chan, Jeffery Paul et al. eds. *The Big Aiiieeeee!* New York: A Meridian Book, 1991.

Cheung, King-Kok, "The Woman Warrior versus The Chinaman Pacific: Must a Chinese American Critic Choose between Feminism and Heroism?" *Conflicts in Feminism*, eds. Marianne Hirsch et al. New York: Routledge, 1990. 234–51.

Chin, Frank, "This Is Not an Autobiography," *Genre* 18 (Summer 1985): 109–30.

Eberhard, Wolfram, ed. *Folk Tales of China*. Chicago: The University of Chicago Press, 1965.

Heung, Marina. "Daughter-Text/Mother-Text: Matrilineage in Amy Tan's *Joy Luck Club*," *Feminist Studies* Fall 1993: 597–616.

Lim, Shirley Geok-lin. *Approaches to Teaching Kingston's* The Woman Warrior. New York: The Modern Language Association of America, 1991.

Spivak, Gayatri. *The Post-Colonial Critic: Interviews, Strategies, Dialogues*. New York: Routledge, 1990.

Tan, Amy. *The Joy Luck Club*. New York: G.P. Putnam's Sons, 1989.

———. *The Kitchen God's Wife*. New York: G.P. Putnam's Sons, 1991.

———. *The Moon Lady*. New York: Macmillan, 1992.

Yuan, Ke. *Chinese Mythology*. Beijing: Chinese Book Bureau Press, 1960.

8

History

Womanist Consciousness: Maggie Lena Walker and
the Independent Order of Saint Luke (1989)

ELSA BARKLEY BROWN

In the first decades of the twentieth century Maggie Lena Walker repeatedly challenged her contemporaries to "make history as Negro women." Yet she and her colleagues in the Independent Order of Saint Luke, like most black and other women of color, have been virtually invisible in women's history and women's studies. Although recent books and articles have begun to redress this,[1] the years of exclusion have had an impact more significant than just the invisibility of black women, for the exclusion of black women has meant that the concepts, perspectives, methods, and pedagogies of women's history and women's studies have been developed without consideration of the experiences of black women. As a result many of the recent explorations in black women's history have attempted to place black women inside feminist perspectives which, by design, have omitted their experiences. Nowhere is this exclusion more apparent than in the process of defining women's issues and women's struggle. Because they have been created outside the experiences of black women, the definitions used in women's history and women's studies assume the separability of women's struggle and race struggle. Such arguments recognize the possibility that black women may have both women's concerns and race concerns, but they insist upon delimiting each. They allow, belatedly, black women to make history as women or as Negroes but not as "Negro women." What they fail to consider is that: women's issues may be race issues, and race issues may be women's issues.[2]

Rosalyn Terborg-Penn, in "Discontented Black Feminists: Prelude and Post-script to the Passage of the Nineteenth Amendment," an essay on the 1920s black women's movement, of which Walker was a part, persuasively discusses the continuing discrimination in the U.S. women's movement and the focus of black women on "uplifting the downtrodden of the race or ... representing people of color throughout the world." Subsequently she argues for the "unique nature of feminism among Afro-American women." The editors of *Decades of Discontent: The Women's Movement, 1920–1940,* the 1983 collection on post–Nineteenth Amendment feminism, however, introduce Terborg-Penn's article by mistakenly concluding that these black women, disillusioned and frustrated by racism in the women's movement, turned from women's issues to race issues. Using a framework that does not conceive of "racial uplift, fighting segregation and mob violence" and "contending with poverty" as women's issues, Lois Scharf and Joan Jensen succumb to the tendency to assume that black women's lives can be neatly subdivided, that while we are both black and female, we occupy those roles sequentially, as if one cannot have the two simultaneously in one's consciousness of being.[3] Such a framework assumes a fragmentation of black women's existence that defies reality.

Scharf and Jensen's conclusion is certainly one that the white feminists of the 1920s and 1930s, who occupy most of the book, would have endorsed. When southern black women, denied the right to register to vote, sought help from the National Woman's Party, these white feminists rejected their petitions, arguing that this was a race concern and not a women's concern. Were they not, after all, being denied the vote not because of their sex but because of their race?[4]

Black women like Walker who devoted their energies to securing universal suffrage, including that of black men, are not widely recognized as female suffragists because they did not separate their struggle for the women's vote from their struggle for the black vote. This tendency to establish false dichotomies, precluding the possibility that for many racism and sexism are experienced simultaneously, leads to discussions of liberation movements and women's movements as separate entities.

Quite clearly, what many women of color at the United Nations Decade for Women conference held in Nairobi, Kenya, in 1985, along with many other activists and scholars, have argued in recent years is the impossibility of separating the two and the necessity of understanding the convergence of women's issues, race/nationalist issues, and class issues in women's consciousnesses.[5] That understanding is in part hampered by the prevailing terminology: feminism places a priority on women; nationalism or race consciousness, a priority on race. It is the need to overcome the limitations of terminology that has led many black women to adopt the term "womanist." Both Alice Walker and Chikwenye Okonjo Ogunyemi have defined womanism as a consciousness that incorporates racial, cultural, sexual, national, economic, and political considerations.[6] As Ogunyemi explains, "black womanism is a philosophy" that concerns itself both with sexual equality in the black community and "with the world power structure that subjugates" both blacks and women. "Its ideal is for black unity where every black person has a modicum of power and so can be a 'brother' or a 'sister' or a 'father' or a 'mother' to the other. ... [I]ts aim is the dynamism of wholeness and self-healing."[7]

Walker's and Ogunyemi's terminology may be new, but their ideas are not. In fact, many black women at various points in history had a clear understanding that race issues and women's issues were inextricably linked, that one could not separate women's struggle from race struggle. It was because of this understanding that they refused to disconnect themselves from either movement. They instead insisted on inclusion in both movements in a manner that recognized the interconnection between race and sex, and they did so even if they had to battle their white sisters and their black brothers to achieve it. Certainly the lives and work of women such as Anna Julia Cooper, Mary Church Terrell, and Fannie Barrier Williams inform us of this. Cooper, an early Africanamerican womanist, addressed the holistic nature of the struggle in her address to the World's Congress of Representative Women:

> Let woman's claim be as broad in the concrete as in the abstract. *We take our stand on the solidarity of humanity,* the oneness of life, and the unnaturalness and injustice of all special favoritisms, whether of sex, race, country, or condition. If one link of the chain be broken, the chain is broken. ... We want, then, as toilers for the universal triumph of justice and human rights, to go to our homes from this Congress, demanding an entrance not through a gateway for ourselves, our race, our sex, or our sect, but a grand highway for humanity. The colored woman feels that woman's cause is one and universal; and that not till ... race, color, sex, and condition are seen as the accidents, and not the substance of life; ... not till then is woman's lesson taught and woman's cause won— not the white woman's, nor the black woman's, nor the red woman's, but the cause of every man and of every woman who has writhed silently under a mighty wrong. *Woman's wrongs are thus indissolubly linked with all undefended woe, and the acquirement of her "rights" will mean the final triumph of all right over might,* the supremacy of the moral forces of reason, and justice, and love in the government of the nations of earth.[8]

One of those who most clearly articulated womanist consciousness was Maggie Lena Walker. Walker (1867–1934) was born and educated in Richmond, Virginia, graduating from Colored Normal School in 1883. During her school years she assisted her widowed mother in her work as a washerwoman and cared for her younger brother. Following graduation she taught in the city's public schools and took courses in accounting and sales. Required to stop teaching when she married Armstead Walker, a contractor, her coursework had well prepared her to join several other black women in founding an insurance company, the Woman's Union. Meanwhile, Walker, who had joined the Independent Order of Saint Luke at the age of fourteen, rose through the ranks to hold several important positions in the order and, in 1895, to organize the juvenile branch of the order. In addition to her Saint Luke activities, Walker was a founder or leading supporter of the Richmond Council of Colored Women, the Virginia State Federation of Colored Women, the National Association of Wage Earners, the International Council of Women of the Darker Races, the National Training School for Girls, and the Virginia Industrial School for Colored Girls. She also helped direct the National Association for the Advancement of Colored People, the Richmond Urban League, and the Negro Organization Society of Virginia.[9]

Walker is probably best known today as the first woman bank president in the United States. She founded the Saint Luke Penny Savings Bank in Richmond, Virginia, in 1903. Before her death in 1934 she oversaw the reorganization of this financial institution as the present-day Consolidated Bank and Trust Company, the oldest continuously existing black-owned and black-run bank in the country. The bank, like most of Walker's activities, was the outgrowth of the Independent Order of Saint Luke, which she served as Right Worthy Grand Secretary for thirty-five years.

The Independent Order of Saint Luke was one of the larger and more successful of the many thousands of mutual benefit societies that have developed throughout Africanamerican communities since the eighteenth century. These societies combined insurance functions with economic development and social and political activities. As such they were important loci of community self-help and racial solidarity. Unlike the Knights of Pythias and its female auxiliary, the Courts of Calanthe, societies like the Independent Order of Saint Luke had a nonexclusionary membership policy; any man, woman, or child could join. Thus men and women from all occupational segments, professional/managerial, entrepreneurial, and working-class, came together in the order. The Independent Order of Saint Luke was a mass-based organization that played a key role in the political, economic, and social development of its members and of the community as a whole.[10]

Founded in Maryland in 1867 by Mary Prout, the Independent Order of Saint Luke began as a women's sickness and death mutual benefit association. By the 1880s it had admitted men and had expanded to New York and Virginia. At the 1899 annual meeting William M.T. Forrester, who had served as Grand Secretary since 1869, refused to accept reappointment, stating that the order was in decline, having only 1,080 members in fifty-seven councils, $31.61 in the treasury, and $400.00 in outstanding debts. Maggie Lena Walker took over the duties of Grand Worthy Secretary at one-third of the position's previous salary.[11]

According to Walker, her "first work was to draw around me *women*."[12] In fact, after the executive board elections in 1901, six of the nine members were women: Walker, Patsie K. Anderson, Frances Cox, Abigail Dawley, Lillian H. Payne, and Ella O. Waller.[13] Under their leadership the order and its affiliates flourished. The order's ventures included a juvenile department, an educational loan fund for young people, a department store, and a weekly newspaper. Growing to include over 100,000 members in 2,010 councils and circles in twenty-eight states, the order demonstrated a special commitment to expanding the economic opportunities within the black community, especially those for women.

It is important to take into account Walker's acknowledgment of her female colleagues. Most of what we know about the Order of Saint Luke highlights Walker because she was the leader and spokeswoman and therefore the most visible figure. She was able, however, to function in that role and to accomplish all that she did not merely because of her own strengths and skills, considerable though they were, but also because she operated from the strength of the Saint Luke collective as a whole and from the special strengths and talents of the inner core of the Saint Luke women in particular. Deborah Gray White, in her work on women during slavery, underscores the importance of black women's networks in an earlier time period: "Strength had to be cultivated. It came no more naturally to them than to anyone. … If they seemed exceptionally strong it was partly because they often functioned in groups and derived strength from numbers. … [T]hey inevitably developed some appreciation of one another's skills and talents. This intimacy enabled them to establish the criteria with which to rank and order themselves." It was this same kind of sisterhood that was Walker's base, her support, her strength, and her source of wisdom and direction.[14]

The women of Saint Luke expanded the role of women in the community to the political sphere through their leadership in the 1904 streetcar boycott and through the *St. Luke Herald*'s pronouncements against segregation, lynching, and lack of equal educational opportunities for black children. Walker spearheaded the local struggle for women's suffrage and the voter registration campaigns after the passage of the Nineteenth Amendment. In the 1920 elections in Richmond, fully 80 percent of the eligible black voters were women. The increased black political strength represented by the female voters gave incentive to the growing movement for independent black political action and led to the formation of the Virginia Lily-Black Republican Party. Walker ran on this ticket for state superintendent of public instruction in 1921.[15] Thus Walker and many other of the Saint Luke women were role models for other black women in their community activities as well as their occupations.

Undergirding all of their work was a belief in the possibilities inherent in the collective struggle of black women in particular and of the black community in general. Walker argued that the only way in which black women would be able "to avoid the traps and snares of life" would be to "band themselves together, organize, … put their mites together, put their hands and their brains together and make work and business for themselves."[16]

The idea of collective economic development was not a new idea for these women, many of whom were instrumental in establishing the Woman's Union, a female insurance company founded in 1898. Its motto was The Hand That Rocks the Cradle Rules the World.[17] But unlike nineteenth-century white women's rendering of that expression to signify the limitation of woman's influence to that which she had by virtue of rearing her sons, the idea as these women conceived it transcended the separation of private and public spheres and spoke to the idea that women, while not abandoning their roles as wives and mothers, could also move into economic and political activities in ways that would support rather than conflict with family and community. Women did not have to choose between the two spheres; in fact, they necessarily had to occupy both. Indeed, these women's use of this phrase speaks to their understanding of the totality of the task that lay ahead of them as black women. It negates, for black women at least, the public/private dichotomy.

Saint Luke women built on tradition. A well-organized set of institutions maintained community in Richmond: mutual benefit societies, interwoven with extended families and churches, built a network of supportive relations.[18] The families, churches, and societies were all based on similar ideas of collective consciousness and collective responsibility. Thus, they served to extend and reaffirm notions of family throughout the black community. Not only in their houses but also in their meeting halls and places of worship, they were brothers and sisters caring for each other. The institutionalization of this notion of family cemented the community. Community/family members recognized that this had to be maintained from generation to generation; this was in part the function of the juvenile branches of the mutual benefit associations. The statement of purpose of the Children's Rosebud Fountains, Grand Fountain United Order of True Reformers, clearly articulated this:

> Teaching them ... to assist each other in sickness, sorrow and afflictions and in the struggles of life; teaching them that one's happiness greatly depends upon the others. ... Teach them to live united. ... The children of different families will know how to ... talk, plot and plan for one another's peace and happiness in the journey of life.
>
> Teach them to ... bear each other's burdens ... to so bind and tie their love and affections together that one's sorrow may be the other's sorrow, one's distress be the other's distress, one's penny the other's penny.[19]

Through the Penny Savings Bank the Saint Luke women were able to affirm and cement the existing mutual assistance network among black women and within the black community by providing an institutionalized structure for these activities. The bank recognized the meager resources of the black community, particularly black women. In fact, its establishment as a *penny* savings bank is an indication of that. Many of its earliest and strongest supporters were washerwomen, one of whom was Maggie Walker's mother. And the bank continued throughout Walker's leadership to exercise a special commitment to "the small depositor."[20]

In her efforts Walker, like the other Saint Luke women, was guided by a clearly understood and shared perspective concerning the relationship of black women to black men, to the black community, and to the larger society. This was a perspective that acknowledged individual powerlessness in the face of racism and sexism and that argued that black women, because of their condition and status, had a right—indeed, according to Walker, a special duty and incentive—to organize. She argued, "Who is so helpless as the Negro woman? Who is so circumscribed and hemmed in, in the race of life, in the struggle for bread, meat and clothing as the Negro woman?"[21]

In addition, her perspective contended that organizational activity and the resultant expanded opportunities for black women were not detrimental to the home, the community, black men, or the race. Furthermore, she insisted that organization and expansion of women's roles economically and politically were essential ingredients without which the community, the race, and even black men could not achieve their full potential. The way in which Walker described black women's relationship to society, combined with the collective activities in which she engaged, give us some insight into her understanding of the relationship between women's struggle and race struggle.

Walker was determined to expand opportunities for black women. In fulfilling this aim she challenged not only the larger society's notions of the proper place of blacks but also those in her community who held a limited notion of women's proper role. Particularly in light of the increasing necessity to defend the integrity and morality of the race, a "great number of men" and women in Virginia and elsewhere believed that women's clubs, movements "looking to the final exercise of suffrage by women," and organizations of black professional and business women would lead to "the decadence of home life."[22] Women involved in these activities were often regarded as "pullbacks, rather than home builders."[23] Maggie Walker countered these arguments, stressing the need for women's organizations, saying, "Men should not be so pessimistic and down on women's clubs. They don't seek to destroy the home or disgrace the race."[24] In fact, the Richmond Council of Colored Women, of which she was founder and president, and many other women's organizations worked to elevate the entire black community, and this, she believed, was the proper province of women.

In 1908 two Richmond men, Daniel Webster Davis and Giles Jackson, published *The Industrial History of the Negro Race of the United States,* which became a textbook for black children throughout the state. The chapter on women acknowledged the economic and social achievements of black women but concluded that "the Negro Race Needs Housekeepers ... wives who stay at home, being supported by their husbands, and then they can spend time in the training of their children."[25] Maggie Walker responded practically to those who held such ideas: "The bold fact remains that there are more women in the world than men; ... if each and every woman in the land was allotted a man to marry her, work for her, support her, and keep her at home, there would still be an army of women left uncared for, unprovided for, and who would be compelled to fight life's battles alone, and without the companionship of man."[26] Even regarding those women who did marry, she contended, "The old doctrine that a man marries a woman to support her is pretty nearly thread-bare to-day." Only a few black men were able to fully support their families on their earnings alone. Thus many married women worked, "not for name, not for glory and honor—but for bread, and for [their] babies."[27]

The reality was that black women who did go to work outside the home found themselves in a helpless position. "How many occupations have Negro Women?" asked Walker. "Let us count them: Negro women are domestic menials, teachers and church builders." And even the first two of these, she feared, were in danger. As Walker perceived it, the expansion of opportunities for white women did not mean a corresponding expansion for black women; instead, this trend might actually lead to an even greater limitation on the economic possibilities for black women. She pointed to the fact that white women's entry into the tobacco factories of the city had "driven the Negro woman out," and she, like many of her sisters throughout the country, feared that a similar trend was beginning even in domestic work.[28]

In fact, these economic realities led members of the Order of Saint Luke to discuss the development of manufacturing operations as a means of giving employment and therefore "a chance in the race of life" to "the young Negro woman."[29] In 1902 Walker described herself as "consumed with the desire to hear the whistle on our factory and see our women by the hundreds coming to work."[30] It was this same concern for the economic status of black women that led Walker and other Saint Luke women to affiliate with the National Association of Wage Earners (NAWE), a women's organization that sought to pool the energies and resources of housewives, professionals, and managerial, domestic, and industrial workers to protect and expand the economic position of black women. The NAWE argued that it was vital that all black women be able to support themselves.[31] Drawing on traditional stereotypes in the same breath with which she defied them, Walker contended that it was in the self-interest of black men to unite themselves with these efforts to secure decent employment for black women: "Every dollar a woman makes, some man gets the direct benefit of same. Every woman was by Divine Providence created for some man; not for some man to marry, take home and support, but for the purpose of using her powers, ability, health and strength, to forward the financial ... success of the partnership into which she may go, if she will. ... [W]hat stronger combination could ever God make—than the partnership of a business man and a business woman."[32]

By implication, whatever black women as a whole were able to achieve would directly benefit black men. In Walker's analysis family is a reciprocal metaphor for community: family is community and community is family.

But this is more than rhetorical style. Her discussions of relationship net-works suggest that the entire community was one's family. Thus Walker's references to husbands and wives reflected equally her understandings of male/female relationships in the community as a whole and of those rela-tionships within the household. Just as all family members' resources were needed for the family to be well and strong, so they were needed for a healthy community/family.

In the process of developing means of expanding economic opportunities in the community, however, Walker and the Saint Luke women also confronted white Richmond's notions of the proper place of blacks. While whites found a bank headed by a "Negress" an interesting curiosity,[33] they were less receptive to other business enterprises. In 1905 twenty-two black women from the Inde-pendent Order of Saint Luke collectively formed a department store aimed at providing quality goods at more affordable prices than those available in stores outside the black community, as well as a place where black women could earn a living and get a business education. The Saint Luke Emporium employed fifteen women as salesclerks. While this may seem an insignificant number in comparison to the thousands of black women working outside the home, in the context of the occupational structure of Richmond these women constituted a significant percentage of the white-collar and skilled working-class women in the community. In 1900 less than 1 percent of the employed black women in the city were either clerical or skilled workers. That num-ber had quadrupled by 1910, when 222 of the more than 13,000 employed black women listed their occupations as typists, stenographers, bookkeepers, sales-clerks, and the like. However, by 1930 there had been a reduction in the numbers of black women employed in clerical and sales positions. This under-scores the fact that black secretaries and clerks were entirely dependent on the financial stability of black businesses and in this regard the Independent Order of Saint Luke was especially important. With its fifty-five clerks in the home office, over one-third of the black female clerical workers in Richmond in the 1920s worked for this order. The quality of the work experience was significantly better for these women as compared to those employed as labor-ers in the tobacco factories or as servants in private homes. They worked in healthier, less stressful environments and, being employed by blacks, they also escaped the racism prevalent in most black women's workplaces. Additionally, the salaries of these clerical workers were often better than those paid even to black professional women, that is, teachers. While one teacher, Ethel Thompson Overby, was receiving eighteen dollars a month as a teacher and working her way up to the top of the scale at forty dollars, a number of black women were finding good working conditions and a fifty-dollar-per-month paycheck as clerks in the office of the Independent Order of Saint Luke. Nev-ertheless, black women in Richmond, as elsewhere, overwhelmingly remained employed in domestic service in the years 1890–1930.[34]

Located on East Broad Street, Richmond's main business thoroughfare, the Saint Luke Emporium met stiff opposition from white merchants. When the intention to establish the department store was first announced, attempts were made to buy the property at a price several thousand dollars higher than that which the Order of Saint Luke had originally paid. When that did not succeed, an offer of ten thousand dollars cash was made to the order if it would not start the emporium. Once it opened, efforts were made to hinder the store's operations. A white Retail Dealers' Association was formed for the purpose of crushing this business as well as other "Negro merchants who are objectionable ... because they compete with and get a few dollars which would otherwise go to the white merchant." Notices were sent to wholesale merchants in the city warning them not to sell to the emporium at the risk of losing all business from any of the white merchants. Letters were also sent to wholesale houses in New York City with the same warning. These letters charged that the emporium was underselling the white merchants of Richmond. Clearly, then, the white businessmen of Richmond found the emporium and these black women a threat; if it was successful, the store could lead to a surge of black merchants competing with white merchants and thus decrease the black patronage at white stores. The white merchants' efforts were ultimately successful: the obstacles they put in the way of the emporium, in addition to the lack of full support from the black community itself, resulted in the department store's going out of business seven years after its founding.[35] Though its existence was short-lived and its demise mirrors many of the problems that black businesses faced from both within and without their community, the effort demonstrated the commitment of the Order of Saint Luke to provide needed services for the community and needed opportunities for black women.

Maggie Walker's appeals for support of the emporium show quite clearly the way in which her notions of race, of womanhood, and of community fused. Approximately one year after the opening of the emporium, Walker called for a mass gathering of men in the community to talk, in part, about support for the business. Her speech, "Beniah's Valour: An Address for Men Only," opened with an assessment of white businessmen's and officials' continuing oppression of the black community. In her fine rhetorical style she queried her audience. "Hasn't it crept into your minds that we are being more and more oppressed each day that we live? Hasn't it yet come to you, that we are being oppressed by the passage of laws which not only have for their object the degradation of Negro manhood and Negro womanhood, but also the destruction of all kinds of Negro enterprises?" Then, drawing upon the biblical allegory of Beniah and the lion, she warned, "There is a lion terrorizing us, preying upon us, and upon every business effort which we put forth. The name of this insatiable lion is prejudice. ... The white press, the white pulpit, the white business associations, the legislature—all ... the lion with whom we contend daily ...

in Broad Street, Main Street and in every business street of Richmond. Even now … that lion is seeking some new plan of attack."[36]

Thus, she contended, the vital question facing their community was how to kill the lion. And in her analysis, "the only way to kill the Lion is to stop feeding it." The irony was that the black community drained itself of resources, money, influence, and patronage to feed its predator.[37] As she had many times previously, Walker questioned the fact that while the white community oppressed the black, "the Negro … carries to their bank every dollar he can get his hands upon and then goes back the next day, borrows and then pays the white man to lend him his own money."[38] So, too, black people patronized stores and other businesses in which white women were, in increasing numbers, being hired as salesclerks and secretaries while black women were increasingly without employment and the black community as a whole was losing resources, skills, and finances.[39] Walker considered such behavior racially destructive and believed it necessary to break those ties that kept "the Negro … so wedded to those who oppress him."[40] The drain on the resources of the black community could be halted by a concentration on the development of a self-sufficient black community. But to achieve this would require the talents of the entire community/family. It was therefore essential that black women's work in the community be "something more tangible than elegant papers, beautifully framed resolutions and pretty speeches." Rather, "the exercising of every talent that God had given them" was required in the effort to "raise … the race to higher planes of living."[41]

The Saint Luke women were part of the Negro Independence Movement that captured a large segment of Richmond society at the turn of the century. Disillusioned by the increasing prejudice and discrimination in this period, which one historian has described as the nadir in U.S. race relations, black residents of Richmond nevertheless held on to their belief in a community that they could collectively sustain.[42] As they witnessed a steady erosion of their civil and political rights, however, they were aware that there was much operating against them. In Richmond, as elsewhere, a system of race and class oppression including segregation, disfranchisement, relegation to the lowest rungs of the occupational strata, and enforcement of racial subordination through intimidation was fully in place by the early twentieth century. In Richmond between 1885 and 1915 all blacks were removed from the city council; the only predominantly black political district, Jackson Ward, was gerrymandered out of existence; the state constitutional convention disfranchised the majority of black Virginians; first the railroads and streetcars, and later the jails, juries, and neighborhoods were segregated; black principals were removed from the public schools and the right of blacks to teach was questioned; the state legislature decided to substitute white for black control of Virginia Normal and College and to strike "and College" from both name and function; and numerous other restrictions were imposed. As attorney

J. Thomas Hewin noted, he and his fellow black Richmonders occupied "a peculiar position in the body politics":

> He [the Negro] is not wanted in politics, because his presence in official
> positions renders him obnoxious to his former masters and their descen-
> dants. He is not wanted in the industrial world as a trained handicrafts-
> man, because he would be brought into competition with his white brother.
> He is not wanted in city positions, because positions of that kind are
> always saved for the wardheeling politicians. He is not wanted in State
> and Federal offices, because there is an unwritten law that a Negro shall
> not hold an office. He is not wanted on the Bench as a judge, because
> he would have to pass upon the white man's case also. Nor is he wanted
> on public conveyances, because here his presence is obnoxious to white
> people.[43]

Assessing the climate of the surrounding society in 1904, John Mitchell, Jr., editor of the *Richmond Planet*, concluded, "This is the beginning of the age of conservatism."[44] The growing movement within the community for racial self-determination urged blacks to depend upon themselves and their community rather than upon whites: to depend upon their own inner strengths, to build their own institutions, and thereby to mitigate the ways in which their lives were determined by the white forces arrayed against them. Race pride, self-help, racial cooperation, and economic development were central to their thinking about their community and to the ways in which they went about building their own internal support system in order to be better able to struggle within the majority system.

The Saint Luke women argued that the development of the community could not be achieved by men alone, or by men on behalf of women. Only a strong and unified community made up of both women and men could wield the power necessary to allow black people to shape their own lives. Therefore, only when women were able to exercise their full strength would the community be at its full strength, they argued. Only when the community was at its full strength would they be able to create their own conditions, conditions that would allow men as well as women to move out of their structural isolation at the bottom of the labor market and to overcome their political impotence in the larger society. The Saint Luke women argued that it was therefore in the self-interest of black men and of the community as a whole to support expanded opportunities for women.

Their arguments redefined not only the roles of women but also the roles and notions of manhood. A strong "race man" traditionally meant one who stood up fearlessly in defense of the race. In her "Address for Men" Walker argued that one could not defend the race unless one defended black women. Appealing to black men's notions of themselves as the protectors of black womanhood, she asked on behalf of all her sisters for their "FRIENDSHIP, ...

LOVE, ... SYMPATHY, ... PROTECTION, and ... ADVICE": "I am asking you, men of Richmond, ... to record [yourselves] as ... the strong race men of our city. ... I am asking each man in this audience to go forth from this building, determined to do valiant deeds for the Negro Women of Richmond."[45] And how might they offer their friendship, love, and protection; how might they do valiant deeds for Negro womanhood? By supporting the efforts of black women to exercise every talent;[46] by "let[ting] woman choose her own vocation, just as man does his";[47] by supporting the efforts then underway to provide increased opportunities—economic, political, and social—for black women.[48] Once again she drew upon traditional notions of the relationship between men and women at the same time that she countered those very notions. Black men could play the role of protector and defender of womanhood by protecting and defending and aiding women's assault on the barriers generally imposed on women.[49] Only in this way could they really defend the race. Strong race consciousness and strong support of equality for black women were inseparable. Maggie Walker and the other Saint Luke women therefore came to argue that an expanded role for black women within the black community itself was an essential step in the community's fight to overcome the limitations imposed upon the community by the larger society. Race men were therefore defined not just by their actions on behalf of black rights but by their actions on behalf of women's rights. The two were inseparable.

This was a collective effort in which Walker believed black men and black women should be equally engaged. Therefore, even in creating a woman's organization, she and her Saint Luke associates found it essential to create space within the structure for men as well. Unlike many of the fraternal orders that were male or female only, the Order of Saint Luke welcomed both genders as members and as employees. Although the office force was all female, men were employed in the printing department, in field work, and in the bank. Principal offices within the order were open to men and women. Ten of the thirty directors of the emporium were male; eight of the nineteen trustees of the order were male. The Saint Luke women thus strove to create an equalitarian organization, with men neither dominant nor auxiliary. Their vision of the order was a reflection of their vision for their community. In the 1913 Saint Luke Thanksgiving Day celebration of the order, Maggie Walker "thank[ed] God that this is a *woman's* organization, broad enough, liberal enough, and unselfish enough to accord equal rights and equal opportunity to men."[50]

Only such a community could become self-sustaining, self-sufficient, and independent, could enable its members to live lives unhampered by the machinations of the larger society, and could raise children who could envision a different world in which to live and then could go about creating it. The women in the Order of Saint Luke sought to carve a sphere for themselves where they could practically apply their belief in their community and in the potential that black men and women working together could achieve, and they sought to infuse that belief into all of black Richmond and to transmit it to the next generation.

The Saint Luke women challenged notions in the black community about the proper role of women; they challenged notions in the white community about the proper place of blacks. They expanded their roles in ways that enabled them to maintain traditional values of family/community and at the same time move into new spheres and relationships with each other and with the men in their lives. To the larger white society they demonstrated what black men and women in community could achieve. This testified to the idea that women's struggle and race struggle were not two separate phenomena but one indivisible whole. "First by practice and then by precept."[51] Maggie Lena Walker and the Saint Luke women demonstrated in their own day the power of black women discovering their own strengths and sharing them with the whole community.[52] They provide for us today a model of womanist praxis.

Womanism challenges the distinction between theory and action. Too often we have assumed that theory is to be found only in carefully articulated position statements. Courses on feminist theory are woefully lacking on anything other than white, Western, middle-class perspectives; feminist scholars would argue that this is due to the difficulty in locating any but contemporary black feminist thought. Though I have discussed Maggie Lena Walker's public statements, the clearest articulation of her theoretical perspective lies in the organization she helped to create and in her own activities. Her theory and her action are not distinct and separable parts of some whole; they are often synonymous, and it is only through her actions that we clearly hear her theory. The same is true for the lives of many other black women who had limited time and resources and maintained a holistic view of life and struggle.

More important, Maggie Lena Walker's womanism challenges the dichotomous thinking that underlies much feminist theory and writing. Most feminist theory poses opposites in exclusionary and hostile ways: one is black and female, and these are contradictory/problematical statuses. This either/or approach classifies phenomena in such a way that "everything falls into one category or another, but cannot belong to more than one category at the same time."[53] It is precisely this kind of thinking that makes it difficult to see race, sex, and class as forming one consciousness and the resistance of race, sex, and class oppression as forming one struggle. Womanism flows from a both/and worldview, a consciousness that allows for the resolution of seeming contradictions "not through an either/or negation but through the interaction" and wholeness. Thus, while black and female may, at one level, be radically different orientations, they are at the same time united, with each "confirming the existence of the other." Rather than standing as "contradictory opposites," they become "complementary, unsynthesized, unified wholes."[54] This is what Ogunyemi refers to as "the dynamism of wholeness." This holistic consciousness undergirds the thinking and action of Maggie Lena Walker and the other

Saint Luke women. There are no necessary contradictions between the public and domestic spheres; the community and the family; male and female; race and sex struggle—there is intersection and interdependence.

Dichotomous thinking does not just inhibit our abilities to see the lives of black women and other women of color in their wholeness, but, I would argue, it also limits our ability to see the wholeness of the lives and consciousnesses of even white middle-class women. The thinking and actions of white women, too, are shaped by their race and their class, and their consciousnesses are also formed by the totality of these factors. The failure, however, to explore the total consciousness of white women has made class, and especially race, nonexistent categories in much of white feminist theory. And this has allowed the development of frameworks which render black women's lives invisible. Explorations into the consciousnesses of black women and other women of color should, therefore, be a model for all women, including those who are not often confronted with the necessity of understanding themselves in these total terms. As we begin to confront the holistic nature of all women's lives, we will begin to create a truly womanist studies. In our efforts Maggie Lena Walker and black women like her will be our guide.

Notes

1. The recent proliferation of works in black women's history and black women's studies makes a complete bibliographical reference prohibitive. For a sample of some of the growing literature on black women's consciousness, see Evelyn Brooks, "The Feminist Theology of the Black Baptist Church, 1880–1900," in *Class, Race, and Sex: The Dynamics of Control,* ed. Amy Swerdlow and Hanna Lessinger (Boston: G.K. Hall, 1983), 31–59; Hazel V. Carby, *Reconstructing Womanhood: The Emergence of the Afro-American Woman Novelist* (New York: Oxford University Press, 1987); Elizabeth Clark-Lewis, " 'This Work Had a' End': The Transition from Live In to Day Work," Southern Women: The Intersection of Race, Class, and Gender Working Paper no. 2 (Memphis, Tenn.: Memphis State University, Center for Research on Women, 1985); Patricia Hill Collins, "The Social Construction of Black Feminist Thought," *Signs: Journal of Women in Culture and Society* 14, no. 4 (Summer 1989), forthcoming; Cheryl Townsend Gilkes, " 'Together and in Harness': Women's Traditions in the Sanctified Church," *Signs* 10, no. 4 (Summer 1985): 678–99; Deborah Gray White, *Ar'n't I a Woman? Female Slaves in the Plantation South* (New York: Norton, 1985). Also note: *Sage: A Scholarly Journal on Black Women,* now in its fifth year, has published issues that focus on education, health, work, mother–daughter relationships, and creative artists.

2. On a contemporary political level, this disassociation of gender concerns from race concerns was dramatically expressed in the 1985 United Nations Decade for Women conference held in Nairobi, Kenya, where the official U.S. delegation, including representatives of major white women's organizations but not one representative of a black women's organization, insisted upon not having the proceedings become bogged down with race and national issues such as apartheid so that it could concentrate on birth control and other "women's" issues. Delegates operating from such a perspective were unable to see African, Asian, and Latin American women who argued for discussion of national political issues as anything other than the tools of men, unfortunate victims unable to discern true women's and feminist struggles. For a discussion of the ways in which these issues were reflected in the Kenya conference, see Ros Young, "Report from Nairobi: The UN Decade for Women Forum," *Race and Class* 27, no. 2 (Autumn 1985): 67–71; and the entire issue of *African Women Rising,* vol. 2, no. 1 (Winter–Spring 1986).

3. See Rosalyn Terborg-Penn, "Discontented Black Feminists: Prelude and Postscript to the Passage of the Nineteenth Amendment," 261–78; Lois Scharf and Joan M. Jensen, "Introduction," 9–10, both in *Decades of Discontent: The Women's Movement, 1920–1940*, ed. Lois Scharf and Joan M. Jensen (Westport, Conn.: Greenwood, 1983).

4. Terborg-Penn, 267. A contemporary example of this type of dichotomous analysis is seen in much of the discussion of the feminization of poverty. Drawing commonalities between the experiences of black and white women, such discussions generally leave the impression that poverty was not a "feminine" problem before white women in increasing numbers were recognized as impoverished. Presumably, before that black women's poverty was considered a result of race, now it is more often considered a result of gender. Linda Burnham has effectively addressed the incompleteness of such analyses, suggesting that they ignore "class, race, and sex as *simultaneously* operative social factors" in black women's lives ("Has Poverty Been Feminized in Black America?" *Black Scholar* 16, no 2 [March/April 1985]: 14–24 [emphasis mine]).

5. See, e.g., Parita Trivedi, "A Study of 'Sheroes,' " *Third World Book Review* 1, no 2 (1984): 71–72; Angela Davis, *Women, Race, and Class* (New York: Random House, 1981); Nawal el Saadawi, *The Hidden Face of Eve: Women in the Arab World*, trans. Sherif Hetata (Boston: Beacon, 1982); Jenny Bourne, "Towards an Anti-Racist Feminism," *Race and Class* 25, no. 1 (Summer 1983): 1–22; Bonnie Thornton Dill, "Race, Class, and Gender: Prospects for an All-inclusive Sisterhood," *Feminist Studies* 9, no. 1 (Spring 1983): 131–50; Evelyn Nakano Glenn, *Issei, Nisei, War Bride: Three Generations of Japanese American Women in Domestic Service* (Philadelphia: Temple University Press, 1986); Audre Lorde, *Sister Outsider: Essays and Speeches* (Trumansburg, N.Y.: Crossing Press, 1984); Barbara Smith, "Some Home Truths on the Contemporary Black Feminist Movement," *Black Scholar* 16, no. 2 (March/April 1985): 4–13; Asoka Bandarage, *Toward International Feminism: The Dialectics of Sex, Race and Class* (London: Zed Press, forthcoming). For a typology of black women's multiple consciousness, see Deborah K. King, "Race, Class, and Gender Salience in Black Women's Feminist Consciousness" (paper presented at American Sociological Association annual meeting, Section on Racial and Ethnic Minorities, New York, August 1986).

6. Alice Walker's oft-quoted definition is in *In Search of Our Mothers' Gardens: Womanist Prose* (New York: Harcourt, Brace, Jovanovich, 1983), xi–xii: "Womanist. 1. ... Responsible. In Charge. *Serious.* 2. ... Appreciates ... women's strength. ... Committed to survival and wholeness of entire people, male *and* female. Not a separatist, except periodically, for health. Traditionally universalist. ... Traditionally capable. ... 3. ... Loves struggle. *Loves* the Folk. Loves herself. *Regardless* 4. Womanist is to feminist as purple is to lavender." Cheryl Townsend Gilkes's annotation of Alice Walker's definition ("Women, Religion, and Tradition: A Womanist Perspective" [paper presented in workshop at Summer Research Institute on Race and Gender, Center for Research on Women, Memphis State University, June 1986]) has been particularly important to my understanding of this term.

7. Chikwenye Okonjo Ogunyemi, "Womanism: The Dynamics of the Contemporary Black Female Novel in English," *Signs* 11, no. 1 (Autumn 1985): 63–80.

8. May Wright Sewall, ed., *World's Congress of Representative Women* (Chicago, 1893), 715, quoted in Bert James Loewenberg and Ruth Bogin, eds., *Black Women in Nineteenth-Century American Life: Their Words, Their Thoughts, Their Feelings* (University Park: Pennsylvania State University Press, 1976), 330–31 (emphasis mine). See also Anna Julia Cooper, *A Voice from the South: By a Black Woman of the South* (Xenia, Ohio: Aldine. 1892), esp. "Part First."

9. Although there exists no scholarly biography of Walker, information is available in several sources. See Wendell P. Dabney, *Maggie L. Walker and The I.O. of Saint Luke: The Woman and Her Work* (Cincinnati: Dabney, 1927); Sadie Iola Daniel, *Women Builders* (Washington, D.C.: Associated Publishers, 1931), 28–52; Sadie Daniel St. Clair, "Maggie Lena Walker," in *Notable American Women, 1607–1960* (Cambridge, Mass.: Harvard University Press, Belknap, 1971), 530–31; Elsa Barkley Brown, "Maggie Lena Walker and the Saint Luke Women" (paper presented at the Association for the Study of Afro-American Life and History 69th annual conference, Washington, D.C., October 1984), and " 'Not Alone to Build This Pile of Brick': The Role of Women in the Richmond, Virginia, Black Community, 1890–1930" (paper presented at the Midcontinental and North Central

American Studies Association joint conference, University of Iowa, April 1983); Lily Hammond, *In the Vanguard of a Race* (New York: Council of Women for Home Missions and Missionary Education Movement of the United States and Canada, 1922), 108–18; A.B. Caldwell, ed., *Virginia Edition,* vol. 5 of *History of the American Negro* (Atlanta: A.B. Caldwell, 1921), 9–11; Rayford Logan, "Maggie Lena Walker," in *Dictionary of American Negro Biography,* ed Rayford W. Logan and Michael R. Winston (New York: Norton, 1982), 626–27; Gertrude W. Marlowe, "Maggie Lena Walker: African-American Women, Business, and Community Development" (paper presented at Berkshire Conference on the History of Women, Wellesley, Mass., June 21, 1987); Kim Q. Boyd, " 'An Actress Born, a Diplomat Bred'; Maggie L. Walker, Race Woman" (M.A. thesis, Howard University, 1987); Sallie Chandler, "Maggie Lena Walker (1867–1934): An Abstract of Her Life and Activities," 1975 Oral History Files, Virginia Union University Library, Richmond, Va., 1975; Maggie Lena Walker Papers, Maggie L. Walker National Historic Site, Richmond, Va. (hereafter cited as MLW Papers). Fortunately, much of Walker's history will soon be available; the Maggie L. Walker Biography Project, funded by the National Park Service under the direction of Gertrude W. Marlowe, anthropology department, Howard University, is completing a full-scale biography of Walker.

10. Noting the mass base of mutual benefit societies such as the Independent Order of Saint Luke, August Meier has suggested that the activities of these organizations "reflect the thinking of the inarticulate majority better than any other organizations or the statement of editors and other publicists" (*Negro Thought in America, 1880–1915: Racial Ideologies in the Age of Booker T. Washington* [Ann Arbor: University of Michigan Press, 1963], 130).

11. *50th Anniversary—Golden Jubilee Historical Report of the R.W.G. Council I.O. St. Luke, 1867–1917* (Richmond, Va.: Everett Waddey, 1917), 5–6, 20 (hereafter cited as *50th Anniversary*).

12. Maggie L. Walker, "Diary," March 6, 1928, MLW Papers. My thanks to Sylvester Putman, superintendent, Richmond National Battlefield Park, and Celia Jackson Suggs, site historian, Maggie L. Walker National Historic Site, for facilitating my access to these unprocessed papers.

13. *50th Anniversary,* 26.

14. White (n. 1 above), 119–41. Although I use the term "sisterhood" here to refer to this female network, sisterhood for black women, including M.L. Walker, meant (and means) not only this special bond among black women but also the ties amongst all kin/community.

15. Of 260,000 black Virginians over the age of twenty-one in 1920, less than 20,000 were eligible to vote in that year's elections. Poll taxes and literacy tests disfranchised many; white Democratic election officials turned many others away from the polls; still others had given up their efforts to vote, realizing that even if they successfully cast their ballots, they were playing in "a political game which they stood no chance of winning" (Andrew Buni, *The Negro in Virginia Politics, 1902–1965* [Charlottesville: University of Virginia Press, 1967], 77–88). The high proportion of female voters resulted from whites' successful efforts to disfranchise the majority of black male voters, as well as the enthusiasm of women to exercise this new right: see, e.g., *Richmond News-Leader* (August–October 1920); *Richmond Times-Dispatch* (September–October, 1920). Rosalyn Terborg-Penn (n. 3 above, 275) reports a similarly high percentage of black female voters in 1920s Baltimore. In Richmond, however, black women soon found themselves faced with the same obstacles to political rights as confronted black men. Independent black political parties developed in several southern states where the lily-white Republican faction had successfully purged blacks from leadership positions in that party; see, e.g., George C. Wright, "Black Political Insurgency in Louisville, Kentucky: The Lincoln Independent Party of 1921," *Journal of Negro History* 68 (Winter 1983): 8–23.

16. M.L. Walker, "Addresses," 1909, MLW Papers, cited in Celia Jackson Suggs. "Maggie Lena Walker." TRUTH: *Newsletter of the Association of Black Women Historians* 7 (Fall 1985): 6.

17. Four of the women elected to the 1901 Saint Luke executive board were board members of the Woman's Union, which had offices in Saint Luke's Hall; see advertisements in *Richmond Planet* (August 1898–January 3, 1903).

18. Some of the societies had only women members, including some that were exclusively for the mutual assistance of single mothers. For an excellent discussion of the ties among the

societies, families, and churches in Richmond, see Peter J. Rachleff, *Black Labor in the South: Richmond, Virginia, 1865–1890* (Philadelphia: Temple University Press, 1984).

19. W.P. Burrell and D.E. Johnson, Sr., *Twenty-Five Years' History of the Grand Fountain of the United Order of True Reformers, 1881–1905* (Richmond, Va.: Grand Fountain, United Order of True Reformers, 1909), 76–77.

20. Saint Luke Penny Savings Bank records: Receipts and Disbursements, 1903–1909; Minutes, Executive Committee, 1913; Cashier's Correspondence Book, 1913; Minutes, Board of Trustees, 1913–1915, Consolidated Bank and Trust Company, Richmond. Va.; *Cleveland Plain Dealer* (June 28, 1914), in Peabody Clipping File, Collis P. Huntington Library, Hampton Institute, Hampton, Va. (hereafter cited as Peabody Clipping File), no. 88, vol. 1. See also Works Progress Administration, *The Negro in Virginia* (New York: Hastings House, 1940), 299.

21. This analysis owes much to Cheryl Townsend Gilkes's work on black women, particularly her "Black Women's Work as Deviance: Social Sources of Racial Antagonism within Contemporary Feminism," working paper no. 66 (Wellesley, Mass.: Wellesley College Center for Research on Women, 1979), and " 'Holding Back the Ocean with a Broom': Black Women and Community Work," in *The Black Woman*, ed. LaFrances Rodgers-Rose (Beverly Hills, Calif.: Sage, 1980). Excerpt from speech given by M.L. Walker at 1901 annual Saint Luke convention, *50th Anniversary* (n. 11 above), 23.

22. The prevailing turn-of-the-century stereotype of black women emphasized promiscuity and immorality; these ideas were given prominence in a number of publications, including newspapers, periodicals, philanthropic foundation reports, and popular literature. The attacks by various segments of the white community on the morality of black women and the race at the turn of the century are discussed in Beverly Guy-Sheftall, " 'Daughters of Sorrow': Attitudes toward Black Women. 1830–1920" (Ph.D. diss., Emory University, 1984), 62–86; Darlene Clark Hine, "Lifting the Veil, Shattering the Silence: Black Women's History in Slavery and Freedom," in *The State of Afro-American History: Past, Present, and Future*, ed. Darlene Clark Hine (Baton Rouge: Louisiana State University Press, 1986), 223–49, esp. 234–38; Willi Coleman, "Black Women and Segregated Public Transportation: Ninety Years of Resistance," TRUTH: *Newsletter of the Association of Black Women Historians* 8, no. 2 (1986): 3–10, esp. 7–8; and Paula Giddings, *When and Where I Enter: The Impact of Black Women on Race and Sex in America* (New York: William Morrow, 1984), 82–86. Maggie Walker called attention to these verbal attacks on Negro womanhood in her speech, "Beniah's Valour: An Address for Men Only," Saint Luke Hall, March 1, 1906, MLW Papers (n. 9 above). It was in part the desire to defend black women and uplift the race that initiated the formation of the National Federation of Black Women's Clubs.

23. Charles F. McLaurin, "State Federation of Colored Women" (n.p., November 10, 1908). Peabody Clipping File, no. 231, vol. 1.

24. Chandler (n. 9 above), 10–11.

25. Daniel Webster Davis and Giles Jackson, *The Industrial History of the Negro Race, of the United States* (Richmond Virginia Press, 1908), 133. Similar attitudes expressed in the *Virginia Baptist* in 1894 had aroused the ire of the leading figures in the national women's club movement. The *Baptist* had been particularly concerned that women, in exceeding their proper place in the church, were losing their "womanliness" and that "the exercise of the right to suffrage would be a deplorable climax to these transgressions"; see discussion of the *Baptist* in *Women's Era* 1, no. 6 (September 1894): 8.

26. M.L. Walker, "Speech to Federation of Colored Women's Clubs," Hampton, Va., July 14, 1912, MLW Papers (n. 9 above).

27. M.L. Walker, "Speech to the Negro Young People's Christian and Educational Congress," Convention Hall, Washington, D.C., August 5, 1906, MLW Papers.

28. Quotations are from M.L. Walker, "Speech to the Federation of Colored Women's Clubs." These ideas, however, were a central theme in Walker's speeches and were repeated throughout the years. See, e.g., "Speech to the Negro Young People's Christian and Educational Congress" and "Beniah's Valour: An Address for Men Only" (n. 22 above). See also the *St. Luke Herald*'s first editorial, "Our Mission" (March 29, 1902), reprinted in *50th Anniversary* (n. 11 above), 26.

29. Excerpt from speech given by M.L. Walker at 1901 annual Saint Luke convention *50th Anniversary*, 23.

30. See "Our Mission" (n. 28 above).
31. The NAWE, having as its motto "Support Thyself—Work," armed at making "the colored woman a factor in the labor world." Much of its work was premised upon the belief that white women were developing an interest in domestic science and other "Negro occupations" to such an extent that the prospects for work for young black women were becoming seriously endangered. They believed also that when white women entered the fields of housework, cooking, and the like, these jobs would be classified as professions. It therefore was necessary for black women to become professionally trained in even domestic work in order to compete. Container 308, Nannie Helen Burroughs Papers, Manuscript Division, Library of Congress.
32. M.L. Walker, "Speech to Federation of Colored Women's Clubs" (n. 26 above).
33. See, e.g., "Negress Banker Says If Men Can, Women Can," *Columbus Journal* (September 16, 1909), Peabody Clipping File (n. 20 above), no. 231, vol. 7, see also Chandler (n. 9 above), 32.
34. In 1900, 83.8 percent of employed black women worked in domestic and personal service; in 1930, 76.5 percent. U.S. Bureau of the Census, *Twelfth Census of the United States Taken in the Year 1900, Population Part 1* (Washington, D.C.: Census Office, 1901), *Thirteenth Census of the United States Taken in the Year 1910*, vol. 4: *Population 1910—Occupation Statistics* (Washington, D.C.: Government Printing Office, 1914), 595, and *Fifteenth Census of the United States: Population*, vol. 4: *Occupations, by States* (Washington, D.C.: Government Printing Office, 1933); Benjamin Brawley, *Negro Builders and Heroes* (Chapel Hill: University of North Carolina Press, 1937), 267–72; U.S. Bureau of the Census, *Fourteenth Census of the United States Taken in the Year 1920*, vol. 4: *Population 1920—Occupations* (Washington, D.C.: Government Printing Office, 1923); Ethel Thompson Overby, *"It's Better to Light a Candle Than to Curse the Darkness": The Autobiographical Notes of Ethel Thompson Overby* (1975), copy in Virginia Historical Society, Richmond.
35. The business, which opened the Monday before Easter 1905, officially closed in January 1912. Information on the emporium is found in *50th Anniversary* (n. 11 above), 55, 70, 77. *New York Age*, March 16, 1905, Peabody Clipping File, no. 88, vol. 1, "Maggie Lena Walker Scrapbook," MLW Papers (n. 9 above); Daniels (n. 9 above), 41. The most detailed description of the opposition to the emporium is in M.L. Walker, "Beniah's Valour: An Address for Men Only" (n. 22 above), quote is from this speech.
36. M.L. Walker, "Beniah's Valour: An Address for Men Only."
37. Ibid.
38. Chandler (n. 9 above), 30.
39. M.L. Walker, "Beniah's Valour: An Address for Men Only."
40. Chandler, 30.
41. *New York Age* (June 22, 1909), Peabody Clipping File, no. 231, vol. 1.
42. Rayford W. Logan, *The Betrayal of the Negro from Rutherford B. Hayes to Woodrow Wilson* (New York: Collier, 1965; originally published in 1954 as *The Negro in American Life and Thought: The Nadir*).
43. J. Thomas Hewin, "Is the Criminal Negro Justly Dealt with in the Courts of the South?" in *Twentieth Century Negro Literature, or a Cyclopedia of Thought on the Vital Topics Relating to the American Negro*, ed. D.W. Culp (Toronto: J.L. Nichols, 1902), 110–11.
44. *Richmond Planet* (April 30, 1904).
45. M.L. Walker, "Beniah's Valour: An Address for Men Only" (n. 22 above).
46. *New York Age* (June 22, 1909), Peabody Clipping File, no. 231, vol. 1.
47. M.L. Walker, "Speech to the Federation of Colored Women's Clubs" (n. 26 above).
48. M.L. Walker, "Beniah's Valour: An Address for Men Only." This appeal for support of increased opportunities for black women permeated all of Walker's speeches. In her last speeches in 1934 she continued her appeal for support of race enterprises (newspaper clipping [n.p., n.d.], "Maggie Laura Walker Scrapbook," MLW Papers [n. 9 above]). Maggie Laura Walker is Walker's granddaughter.
49. W.E.B. DuBois, who explored extensively the connection between race struggle and women's struggle in "The Damnation of Women," also challenged men's traditional roles: "The present mincing horror of a free womanhood must pass if we are even to be rid of the bestiality of a free manhood; *not by guarding the weak in weakness do we gain strength, but by making weakness free and strong*" (emphasis mine, *Darkwater, Voices from within the Veil* [New York: Harcourt, Brace, & Howe, 1920], 165).

50. M.L. Walker, "Saint Luke Thanksgiving Day Speech," City Auditorium, March 23, 1913, MLW Papers (n. 9 above).
51. M.L. Walker, "Address—Virginia Day Third Street Bethel AME Church," January 29, 1933, MLW Papers.
52. Ogunyemi (n. 7 above, 72–73) takes this idea from Stephen Henderson's analysis of the role of the blues and blues women in the Africanamerican community.
53. The essays in Vernon J. Dixon and Badi G. Foster, eds., *Beyond Black or White: An Alternate America* (Boston: Little, Brown, 1971) explore the either/or and the both/and worldview in relation to Africanamerican systems of analysis; the quote can be found in Dixon, "Two Approaches to Black–White Relations," 23–66, esp. 25–26.
54. Johnella E. Butler explores the theoretical, methodological, and pedagogical implications of these systems of analysis in *Black Studies: Pedagogy and Revolution: A Study of Afro-American Studies and the Liberal Arts Tradition through the Discipline of Afro-American Literature* (Washington, D.C.: University Press of America, 1981), esp. 96–102.

9

Theater and Film Studies

Dialogic Modes of Representing Africa(s):
Womanist Film (1991)

MARK A. REID

One has only to peruse the shelves of a university bookstore or page through "academic" journals to discover that members of the academy have indirectly reified feminism as a discourse by, for, and about white, heterosexual, Western women. Corrective energy is best directed toward the development of theories of representation which describe the voices that mainstream feminism ignores, for the employment of critical approaches which consider race, class, and sexual affiliation would cure academic feminism of its narcissistic gaze upon the white, middle-class female subject.

In an effort to assist in the building of a black feminist theory of film production and reception, this paper presents a "womanist" interpretation of three aspects of black independent film. First, I explore the term *black womanist film* in the context of the production and reception of any womanist film. Second, I discuss the politics of black womanist discourse as a form of resistance to a raceless feminism and a phallocentric pan-Africanism. Third, I analyze three spectatorial relationships that black womanist films elicit from two "interested" spectatorial groups—feminists and pan-Africans. Finally, informed by my description of black womanist film, its politics of blackness and womanness, and its three receptive modes, I interpret how certain narrative films present African and African diasporic women's subjectivity as a polyvalent idea.

I do not intend to prescribe conditions for black womanist filmmaking or its spectatorial readings. Nonetheless, I do consider how certain processes of representation and reception permit different readings of black womanist films. Finally, when I speak of African or black women, I am making reference to the many black African women who exist, survive, and struggle in Africas throughout the world. Therefore, I am explicating an international black womanist theory—a theory which rejects the closures of nation, race, gender, and class exclusivity. However, I must limit this present study to an analysis of black-directed independent films.

Black Womanist Film: A Working Definition

Throughout this paper, I will employ the term *black womanist film* to refer to narrative constructions as well as viewing positions which permit "womanish," as opposed to "girlish," processes of black female subjectivity. Films belonging to this category dramatize the shared experiences of black women. I have borrowed the term *womanist* from Alice Walker, who provides, as one of its principal definitions:

> A woman who loves other women, sexually and/or nonsexually. Appreciates and prefers women's culture, women's emotional flexibility ... and women's strength. Sometimes loves individual men, sexually/or nonsexually. Committed to survival and wholeness of entire people, male *and* female. Not a separatist, except periodically, for health. Traditionally universalist, as in: "Mama, why are we brown, pink, and yellow, and our cousins are white, beige, and black?" (xi)

In relation to black film, the term *womanism* refers to certain black-oriented films (not their authors) and reading strategies whose narrative and receptive processes permit polyvalent female subjectivity.

The term *black womanist film* describes two levels of filmic production: (1) the narrative content which constructs black womanist subjectivity and (2) the various processes by which an audience might receive the narrative's construction of this subjectivity. The two levels conjoin and articulate an ideology of black womanism as a twofold process of construction and reception. *Black womanist film* does not describe *all* films made by African and African diasporic women. However, black womanist film results from imaginatively representing the socio-psychic and socio-economic experiences of African and African diasporic women. This film calls forth "black womanist spectators" and creates a spectatorial space for such an audience.

The concept *black womanist spectatorship* should *not* be taken "to refer directly to the [black] woman who buys her ticket and enters the movie theater as the member of an audience, sharing a social identity but retaining a unique psychical history. Frequently, [it] do[es] not even refer to the spectator as a social subject but, rather, as a psychical subject, as the effect of signifying structures."[1] Black womanist spectatorship, then, is a socio-psychical process, not a biological trait. It cannot totally exclude or include its audience based on race or gender.

Womanism and Post-Negritude: Theorizing Black Experience

Black womanism is a form of resistance to a raceless feminism and a phallocentric pan-Africanism. As a theoretical tool, it requires that one scrutinize how its closest supporter decodes black womanist film. This is especially true for feminism and pan-Africanism, because each of these movements has ignored the triple oppression of black women. Black female subjectivity, as woman and African, is historically positioned at the boundaries of gender, sexuality, and race. This subjectivity conjoins the two limit-texts of feminism and pan-Africanism, but has been heretofore on the margins of these discourses. As an effect of a womanist ideology, black womanist films resist dramatizing one-dimensional struggles which ignore the black woman's three-pronged oppression. Therefore, Safi Faye's *La passante* (*The Passerby*, Senegal, 1972) criticizes the sexist expectations of a white French man as well as a black African man; Sara Gomez's *De cierta manera* (*One Way or Another*, Cuba, 1974/1977) presents sexism in post-revolutionary Cuba; and Michelle Parkerson's *Storme: The Lady of the Jewel Box* (USA, 1987) constructs black gay history while documenting the life of Storme, a male impersonator. These black womanist films question patriarchal and heterosexist notions of black female subjectivity. Additionally, each film creates a spectatorial position which speaks to micro- as well as macro-struggles against *phallic* forms of knowledge and power within and without the black community.[2]

A theory and practice of black film, if based on a womanist ideology of the polyphony of blackness, initiates *possible* receptive processes. A womanist reception occurs only after an "interested" spectator actively participates in a systematic critique of the singularity of canonical (con)texts. Stressing the importance of an "interested" reader in the production of a plural text, Catherine Belsey writes,

> In the writable ... wholly plural text all statements are of indeterminate origin, no single discourse is privileged, and no consistent and coherent plot constrains the free play of the discourses. The totally writable, plural text does not exist. At the opposite extreme, the readable text is barely plural. The readable text is merchandise to be consumed, while the plural text requires the production of meanings through the identification of its polyphony. (105)

Thus, black womanism, as a theory of reception and production, requires an "interested" spectator to decode the plurality of (con)texts, which include intra- as well as interracial forces that dehumanize the community. Equally, black womanist critical strategies deconstruct narrative systems and viewing positions which reduce racial, sexual, and class differences to one of gender. Black womanism, as Alice Walker suggests, represents universalist notions of blackness which conjoin African and African diasporic cultures. Consequently, the black womanist film project constructs a post-*Negritude* theory of reception and production.

Before defining post-*Negritude*, I would like to suggest the polyphonic quality of the movement and concept that preceded it and shares in its global concerns. Nigerian philosopher Abiola Irele writes that Negritude

> has acquired, in the way it has been used by different writers, a multiplicity of meanings covering so wide a range that it is often difficult to

form a precise idea of its particular reference at any one time or in any one usage. The difficulty stems from the fact that, as a movement and as a concept, Negritude found its origin and received a development in a historical and sociological context whose implications for those whom it affected were indeed wide-ranging, and which ultimately provoked in them a multitude of responses [readings] that were often contradictory, though always significant. ... The term has thus been used in a broad and general sense to denote the black world in its historical being, in opposition to the West, and in this way resumes the total consciousness of belonging to the black race, as well as an awareness of the objective historical and sociological implications of that fact. (67)

Similarly, *post-Negritude* refers to any moment when members of the black community, through their literature, art, and politics, recognize that black culture "is, concretely, an open-ended, creative dialogue of subcultures, of insiders and outsiders, of diverse factions." Correspondingly, these members share a language of black subjectivity that celebrates "the interplay and struggle of regional dialects, professional jargons, generic commonplaces, the speech of different age groups, individuals, and so forth" (Clifford 46). Contrary to Negritude, the recognition and shared productivity of the post-Negritude project result from the active participation of an *interested* audience that decodes the black subject using discourses which surround and construct representations of gender, race, class, sexuality, and nation. An "interested" audience scrutinizes the incorporation of these images as an internal regulatory agency of the representation as well as themselves. Through this shared post-Negritude recognition, respective black audiences will question their own (and, by implication, others') interpretations (Hutcheon 180).

Reception: Resistance, Accommodation, Assimilation

In the analysis of black womanist films, I propose three general modes of reception—resistance, accommodation, and assimilation. These three receptive modes represent the dialogic quality of any particular black womanist film. In the *resistance* mode, the source of the rejection of a particular black womanist film lies in its inability to mirror a given audience's partial vision of themselves. The desired image that a group holds of itself may be derivative of an authorized hegemonic image, a resistant radical image, or a combination of the two which produces a constant tension for both the viewer and artist in question. This tension combines race, sexuality, and gender subjectivity. The blurring of racial, sexual, and gender hierarchies permits free zones of discourse and makes the black womanist project a most dynamic movement. Theorizing this post-Negritude moment permits one to understand the reception of any black womanist film.

Since spectatorship is a psychical investiture, certain black womanist texts permit spectatorial positions that criticize sexism but maintain black communal solidarity. Contrarily, black womanist films which depict non-sexist men may threaten the psychical desires of certain feminists—for example, separatists who deplore any feminism which includes men. In addition, non-black feminist spectators who maintain a hierarchic allegiance to a raceless, classless, and nondescript sexuality may deplore this form of black feminism, because it criticizes racial, class, and sexual discrimination within the women's movement. Nonetheless, such feminists may still enjoy black womanist films. Enjoyment demands that black womanist films represent, and their viewers/listeners identify with, some *nexus of* desire which results in *accommodative* readings of these films. The same criterion is equally true for raceless feminists and for phallocentric pan-African spectators.

Certain pan-Africans might regard black womanist narratives as too hostile toward black patriarchal figures or might view black feminism as a threat to black communal solidarity because, according to them, the natural place for black women is within a nuclear family as the provider of moral support to her husband. Generally speaking, this point of view naturalizes the subordination of women; it reflects a phallic hierarchical system which processes false notions of black masculinity and femininity. Consequently, this phallic type of pan-African thought denies both male and female pan-Africans the ability to appreciate black womanist ideology as represented in film. Black psychologist Vickie M. Mays writes,

> The Afro-American woman has been denied power and privilege. She has been raised expecting to work, as she will need to assist in supporting her family. She will also be asked to do all she possibly can to advance the Black man and the Black race—at the cost of ignoring the oppression of sexism. Indeed, the Black woman has been taught from early childhood that one way to survive in this society is through marriage or in a male-female relationship. (75)

Pan-Africans who deny or devalue the oppression of black women are as demeaning as white feminists who disregard racial and class factors. Yet, on viewing black womanist films, these same pan-Africans might identify with the cinematic use of African and African diasporic elements, while resisting the elements that evoke identification among non-black feminists. Thus, like some non-black feminists, pan-Africans may assume an accommodative viewing relationship to a black womanist film.

Contrary to the two discussed accommodative positions, an *assimilative* reception tends to accept a film as a "realistic" vision, rather than an imaginative representation open to *revision* of black womanhood. Assimilative spectatorial positions, as organizing concepts, promote authoritarian conformity among creator, discursive apparatus, and consumer. Authoritarian discourses eliminate the tension between the desire to resist and the desire to accommodate. In the assimilative mode, audience members' consumptive habits are eased when their identity (their imagined subjectivity) is not threatened by what they feel are contradictory images of themselves. Singularity is also part of the spectatorial mode which produces resistance among certain feminists and pan-Africans when they view the more radical aspects of black womanist ideology as constructed in films.

The authoritarian discourse process is present in rigid systems as well as those contesting on the margins of discourse. Like any discursive apparatus, the black womanist film has an assimilative mode of construction and reception capable of denying "unauthorized" readings. If effective, this mode protects against uncritical acceptance and duplication of black womanist discursive strategies. Once black womanist theory moves from the periphery to the center, assimilative readings of black womanist discourses might retain their protective strategies and oppose their initial, heteroglossic conception of black womanism. The move from liberation to repression occurs because modernist projects require a closure of their *imagined* boundaries—a reflection of hegemony's need to contain polyvalent subjectivity by maintaining segregated sites of "resistance," such as women's liberation, gay liberation, and black liberation. Black womanist subjectivity, however, blurs these imagined boundaries of black selfhood. This post-Negritude blurring reflects the dialogic possibilities of blackness in womanist film.

Black Womanist Praxis

Some of the earliest work of black women filmmakers appeared in the 1970s and was filmed by women from the Americas and Africa. Madeline Anderson, Sarah Maldoror, Safi Faye, and Sara Gomez are representative of the first wave of black womanist filmmakers. The beginning of an international black feminist film practice is reflected in Anderson's *I Am Somebody* (USA, 1970), Maldoror's *Des Fusils pour Banta* (*Guns for Banta*, Guinea-Bissau, 1971), and Gomez's *De cierta manera* (*One Way or Another*, Cuba, 1974/1977). Admitting the historical importance of these filmmakers and their works, I confine my analysis to Alile Sharon Larkin's *A Different Image* (USA, 1981), Safi Faye's *La passante* (*The Passerby*, Senegal, 1972), and Kathleen Collins's *Losing Ground* (USA, 1982). I will conclude with some general statements on black womanist films and post-Negritude.

In 1981, Alile Sharon Larkin focused on sexism and African heritage in *A Different Image*. Interestingly, the film previewed at the Second International Women Filmmakers Symposium, which underlines the film's importance to this audience. In addition to being a woman-centered film, *A Different Image* is equally resilient in its celebration of a pan-African consciousness which is at odds with the sexism and racism of the West. Larkin says, "The film deals with assimilation ... of Western sexism and how racism is inherently a part of that, ... can't be separated from it. When I say that the racism and the sexism are inseparable, this also applies to definitions of manhood as well as womanhood" (*"Your Children"*). Larkin underscores the black womanist belief that racism is an inherent part of sexism, and to ignore this fact is counterproductive to the black womanist struggle for equality.

The film focuses on Alana, a young black woman, and her friend Vincent, an equally young black man. After a male acquaintance has ridiculed Vincent's platonic relationship with Alana, Vincent tries to assert his manhood by forcing himself on Alana, who has fallen asleep on his bedroom floor. After Alana accuses him of attempted rape and severs their friendship, Vincent, missing her companionship, reexamines the question of the appropriate kind of relationship between a man and a woman. Finally, he initiates a reconciliation by giving her earrings shaped like the Egyptian goddess Isis.

In the film, Larkin focuses on a touchy gender-related problem within the black community: Black women are expected to submit to the sexual desires of their black male friends. Larkin does not limit this problem to America. By introducing the film with a collage of photographs of black women, and by using an African goddess as the symbol of Vincent's effort of reconciliation, Larkin underscores the correspondence between the experiences of black women in America and Africa. She writes,

> If you look at Africa today, you see that people there face the same problem with sexism[; therefore,] I am saying that there were other cultures and other ways that men and women related to each other ... before the African slave trade, before Islam, before the patriarchal religions came in. So, we have to study those ways before we [black people] took on these [patriarchal] values. (*"Your Children"*)

Larkin understands the need for solidarity among black filmmakers around a commonly shared ideology that reflects a post-Negritude openness to feminism, classism, and sexuality. She writes, "An ideology or belief which attempts to compartmentalize the nature and form of the oppression of African people solely into gender and/or class is ultimately destructive to our achieving genuine equality and liberation" ("Black Women" 158). Larkin refuses to permit authoritarian ideologies of opposition to determine or speak for a black womanist film practice. She recognizes the ease with which some groups have co-opted the civil rights struggle to benefit their very white agendas:

> As a Black woman I experience all areas of oppression—economic, racial, and sexual. I cannot "pick and choose" a single area of struggle. I believe it is in this way that feminists and other progressive whites pursue their own interests at the expense of those of us subjected to racism. They do not have to deal with the *totality of oppression*, and instead may conform to, or accept the policies of, institutional racism. ...
>
> Feminism succumbs to racism when it segregates Black women from Black men and dismisses our history. ("Black Women" 158)

To understand *A Different Image* as an articulation of feminist ideas, as opposed to black womanist ideology, would be aberrant reading and would instance the authoritarian mode of feminism. Larkin argues,

> The assumption that Black women and white women share ... similar histories and experiences presents an important problem. ... Both historically and currently, white women participate in and reap the benefits of white supremacy. Feminism must address these issues[;] otherwise its ahistorical approach towards Black women can and does maintain institutional racism. ("Black Women" 158–59)

A pan-African reading which recognizes the abuses black women experience will produce a different set of articulations and assumptions about the similar histories of women and men in the black community. For example, if the viewer focuses on the visual allusions to African women and Alana's colorful dress, and if this viewer listens to the musical score, which connotes an African rhythm, then this viewer/listener might perceive Alana as the female representative of pan-African subjectivity, which, for the woman of color, is more dynamic than a generalized female subjectivity. I am not proposing that the black womanist and the feminist readings are binary opposites. I merely want to show that the same text can activate certain *accommodative* readings for these two audiences.

A black womanist reading would combine the latter two spectatorial positions—feminist and pan-African—and articulate the importance of the *refigured* African-American male, Vincent. This dialogic reading of *A Different Image* would resist the processes of gender and racial closure. In discussing the problematics of feminist thinking, Hortense J. Spillers writes, "Sexuality as a term of power belongs to the empowered. Feminist thinking often appropriates the term in its own will to discursive power in a sweeping, patriarchal, symbolic gesture that reduces the human universe of women to its own image" (78). Equally, certain forms of black nationalism belong to the empowered, and such nationalist thinking often appropriates the term *pan-African culture* in its own will to discursive power in a sweeping, patriarchal, symbolic gesture that reduces black humanity to its own image. Both of these reductive forms of empowerment deny the micro-politics of struggle within their specific groups. They attempt to force the assimilation of radical members by creating a politics of binary opposition which discounts individual differences. Alile Sharon Larkin's film dramatizes the micro-politics of difference within the black community and portrays the shared phallic notions that some men and women act upon. The film denies a hypothetical sweeping, patriarchal gaze as biologically determined, since the patriarchal gaze is an "ideological construct" which is figured in men as well as women. The film privileges a text constructed on pan-African historical subjects who are embedded in the *maternal* voice of Alana's mother and the embodied portraits of African women.

The black womanist reading/viewing position avoids the inherent sexual dualism which engenders both the "dominant, male-centered position" and its appropriation by a "female-phallic position." It acknowledges that the goals of black feminist theory are a revision of gender relations and an open-ended sexuality. Womanist goals do not attempt a simple appropriation of hierarchic systems to continue oppressive processes of subjectivity. Consequently, the black womanist film project proposes the collective refiguration of the pan-African community. Such a purpose requires an artist/critic/audience to re-vision "possible" black others in a post-Negritude world.

Alile Sharon Larkin's *A Different Image* pursues the refiguration of gender through deconstructing the illusion that all black men are phallocrats and all black women are oppressed by such men. The film presents sexism as an ideological construct rather than a biological trait of the male. Larkin's film portrays how phallic ideas call forth (hail) men, women, boys, and girls. According to the film, phallocentric thought is not limited to men; it is present in the baiting that Vincent receives from his male friend as well as the teasing that Alana receives from her female friend. Larkin's womanist film demystifies the totalizing effects of phallic ordering. The reconciliation of the Alana–Vincent friendship resists patriarchal closure. The idea that men are contentedly contained within a sexist system is revised, and the unquestioned fate of women as sex objects or reproductive apparati-in-waiting is denied.

Black filmmakers in Africa have represented black Africa through womanist discourse strategies in which the experiences of women are central to the film narrative. This is true of the first black-directed African feature film, Ousmane Sembene's *La Noire de* (Senegal, 1968), as well as other African films directed by black men (Vieyra 162).

Concurrent with the development of black African cinema in the late '60s, Safi Faye, an African-born Senegalese, directed African films. Faye's first film, *La passante* (*The Passerby*, Senegal, 1972), depicts the Parisian experiences of an African woman who is preyed upon by African and French men. Interestingly, Faye was both filmmaker and the filmed subject, since she performed the role of the female who is the object of the gaze of both men. Faye does not agree with the closed status of the male gaze[3] but views the male gaze as a matter of who is behind, who is in front of, and who belongs to the audience that participates in this relationship. In *The Passerby*, a 10-minute narrative film, she disrupts the male gaze upon female body parts by giving the female object a transitive quality and, thereby, both reversing the source of the gaze and providing an "other" meaning. A series of shot-reverse shots and point-of-view shots decenters the authority of the male point of view, as well as its discourse, and exposes the polyvalent quality of the male gaze.

Thus, as early as 1972, Faye was constructing a black womanist gaze to resist dominant viewing relationships. This permitted spectatorial positions of resistance, accommodation, and assimilation. While I have not attempted an in-depth study of the possible receptions of this film, I find Faye's *The Passerby* equal in receptive possibilities to Larkin's *A Different Image*. Each film criticizes a sexism that crosses racial boundaries. Yet Safi Faye rejects identification as a woman filmmaker:

> I never say that I am a woman filmmaker. I think I am a human being like the others. I never put someone under me but I never accept to be placed in a submissive position. The only difference between me and a man is my familial responsibilities. When I think about my daughter Zeiba, I say OK, I am a woman. But when I think of my job or a film project, I am like … African men. (Reid)

Faye's response raises two important issues. First, the product should not be confused with its author any more than authorial intent should describe the final product. Second, Faye refuses the label *woman filmmaker* because, according to her, her films are not solely about women. She views the struggle in a larger frame—a sort of womanist struggle to counter dehumanizing relationships which oppress men and women.

The representation of black African women should not be limited by a choice between motherhood and a career. Faye, for instance, acknowledges that African Serrer customs form her concept of womanhood—womanism. She feels a deep commitment to motherhood, but is equally committed to filmmaking:

> Since I am an African woman, I was educated in this way. I have remained close to the traditional role of mother, and this responsibility is not a burden to me. I try to keep my job near my eight-year-old daughter. Men do not have the responsibilities of caring for children, because they have wives to care after them. When I think about this, I realize that I am a woman. But I cannot be a filmmaker without being a mother. As an African woman filmmaker, the two are very much a part of me. (Reid)

Like Safi Faye, there are other black women filmmakers who see motherhood and filmmaking as inseparable. Kathleen Collins was, until her death in 1988, a mother, a writer, a university professor, and the first African-American woman to direct a feature-length film, *Losing Ground*.

Womanist Film and the Black Professional

In 1982, Kathleen Collins directed *Losing Ground*, in which she dramatized a critique of sexism. Here, however, she did not employ the pan-African sensibility of Larkin's film. Sara, her protagonist, is a black professor of philosophy who is married to an insensitive black artist. Perceiving her husband's interest in an attractive, extroverted Puerto Rican woman, the introverted

Sara reevaluates her career, marriage, and life. Altering her inhibited beliefs about actions appropriate to women professors, Sara takes a role as Johnnie in a dramatization of the story in which Johnnie shoots and kills her boyfriend Frankie because he has proved unfaithful. At the end of the film, Sara, turning the blank pistol away from the man playing Frankie, symbolically points it at her own philandering husband. *Losing Ground* marks the first appearance of a black professional woman as protagonist in black independent film, and it is one of very few portrayals of developing consciousness in a black professional woman in any feature-length film.

It is beneficial neither to feminism nor to black womanist creativity to collapse the socio-economic differences of race and gender into a generalized feminist or women's film aesthetic of purity. Collins speaks of an "imperfect synthesis" of the African-American condition. She is "willing to recognize that being Black is without purity. That one cannot achieve [racial] purity in ... [American] culture. That one can only achieve some kind of emotional truth. ... That's what characterizes my work. ... I am much more concerned with how people resolve their inner dilemma in the face of external reality" (Nicholson 12). But Collins is quick to affirm the cultural differences between black women filmmakers and their white colleagues, and acknowledges that such differences inform the aesthetic choices of these filmmakers:

> I would think that there is a Black aesthetic among Black women filmmakers. Black women are not white women by any means; we have different histories, different approaches to life, and different attitudes. Historically, we come out of different traditions; sociologically, our preoccupations are different. However, I have a lot of trouble with this question because I do not feel that there has been a long enough tradition. (Campbell 62)

Granted, the history of black filmmaking presents a discontinuous pattern of false starts and long production gaps. Yet there are films to document these attempts. The archaeology of the black woman's participation is no more than a twenty-year effort. Nevertheless, black womanist films have pioneered creative processes for the reception and production of racialized, sexualized, and engendered black subjectivities. Cultural studies and visual research must freely consult the sacred (legitimized) discourses on blackness as well as those deemed profane in order to make visible the histories of the ignored members of the black community, and to permit a dialogue within this community and across its *imagined* boundaries of race, gender, sexuality, class, and nation.

If the dialogic aspects of blackness(es) remain invisible and ignored, then we further the fragmentation of black communities. It is time to affirm and celebrate the sonorous polyphony of black voices. Let us not welcome them only to deny their voices and our attention. Why imitate the history that humbled and shamed us?

204 • The Womanist Reader

Notes

1. Mary Ann Doane writes, "It is important to specify precisely what is meant by the 'female spectator' or 'female spectatorship.' Clearly these terms are not meant to refer directly to the woman who buys her ticket and enters the movie theater as the member of an audience, sharing a social identity but retaining a unique psychical history. Frequently, they do not even refer to the spectator as a social subject but, rather, as a psychical subject, as the effect of signifying structures. … Women spectators oscillate or alternate between masculine and feminine positions, … and men are capable of this alternation as well" (8).
2. When referring to phallic forms of knowledge and power within the black community, I make reference to discourses which reflect a "tendency in every form to harden its generic skeleton and elevate the existing norms to a model that resists change. … Canonization is that process that blurs heteroglossia; that is, that facilitates a naive, single-voiced reading" (Bakhtin 425). Phallic gender or race reasoning reflects any socio-psychical attempt to disavow the fact that the male (and white) subject, like the female (and black) subject, is surrounded by and constructed through discourses which he also incorporates as an internal regulatory agency (see Silverman 99).
3. Taking a different approach, Laura Mulvey argues that the "male gaze" is an inherent and uncontestable property of narrative cinema.

References

Bakhtin, M.M. *The Dialogic Imagination: Four Essays by M.M. Bakhtin.* Ed. Michael Holquist. Trans. Caryl Emerson and Michael Holquist. Austin: U of Texas P, 1981.
Belsey, Catherine. *Critical Practice.* New York: Methuen, 1980.
Campbell, Loretta. "Reinventing Our Image: Eleven Black Women Filmmakers." *Heresies* 4.4 (1983): 58–62.
Clifford, James. *The Predicament of Culture: Twentieth-Century Ethnography, Literature, and Art.* Cambridge: Harvard UP, 1988.
Doane, Mary Ann. *The Desire to Desire: The Woman's Film of the 1940s.* Bloomington: Indiana UP. 1987.
Faye, Safi. Personal interview. 26 May 1986.
Hutcheon, Linda. *A Poetics of Postmodernism: History, Theory, Fiction.* New York: Routledge, 1988.
Irele, Abiola. *The African Experience in Literature and Ideology.* London: Heinemann, 1981.
Larkin, Alile Sharon. "Black Women Filmmakers Defining Ourselves: Feminism in Our Own Voice." Ed. E. Deidre Pribram. *Female Spectators: Looking at Film and Television.* London: Verso, 1988. 157–73.
———. *"Your Children Come Back to You and a Different Image."* Debate "Lutte actuelle des noirs américains" (Debate on "The Afro-American Contemporary Struggle"), 8eme Festival du Cinéma des Minorités Nationales (Eighth Festival of National Minority Cinema). Douarnenez, France. 28 Aug. 1985.
Mays, Vickie M. "I Hear Voices but See No Faces." *Heresies* 3.4 (1981): 74–76.
Mulvey, Laura. "Visual Pleasure and Narrative Cinema." 1975. *Visual and Other Pleasures.* Bloomington: Indiana UP, 1989. 14–26.
Nicholson, David. "A Commitment to Writing: A Conversation with Kathleen Collins Prettyman." *Black Film Review* 5.1 (1988–89): 6–15.
Pfaff, Francoise. *Twenty-Five Black African Filmmakers.* New York: Greenwood, 1988.
Silverman, Kaja. *The Acoustic Mirror: The Female Voice in Psychoanalysis and Cinema.* Bloomington: Indiana UP, 1988.
Spillers, Hortense J. "Interstices: A Small Drama of Words." *Pleasure and Danger: Exploring Female Sexuality.* Ed. Carole S. Vance. Boston: Routledge, 1984. 73–100.
Vieyra, Paulin Soumanou. *Le Cinéma africain: Des origines à 1973.* Paris: Éditions Présence Africaine, 1975.
Walker, Alice. *In Search of Our Mothers' Gardens.* New York: Harcourt, 1983.

Filmography

Anderson, Madeline. *I Am Somebody.* USA, 1970. 30 min., 16mm. Documentary on the 1969 hospital workers' strike in Charleston, SC.

Collins, Kathleen. *Losing Ground*. USA, 1982. 86 min., 16mm.

Faye, Safi. *La passante* (*The Passerby*). Senegal, 1972. 10 min., 16mm.

Gomez, Sara. *De cierta manera* (*One Way or Another*). Cuba, 1974/1977. 97 min., 16mm. Semi-documentary depicting post-revolutionary sexism in an individual's relationship that affects his lover as well as the men with whom he works; ends with a political analysis of the protagonist's actions.

Larkin, Alile Sharon. *A Different Image*. USA, 1981. 51 min., 16mm.

Maldoror, Sarah. *Des Fusils pour Banta* (*Guns for Banta*). Guinea-Bissau, 1971. 105 min., 35mm. Portrays a Guinea-Bissau woman who develops a program of armed resistance against the Portuguese but dies before the actual struggle begins. According to Francoise Pfaff, this film "never went beyond the editing stages" due to a verbal confrontation Maldoror had with a high-ranking Algerian officer (207).

Parkerson, Michelle. *Storme: The Lady of the Jewel Box*. USA, 1987. 21 min., 16mm. Archival materials used to document the story of Storme DeLarverie, a male impersonator and former master of ceremonies at the Jewel Box Revue, considered to be America's first integrated female impersonation show.

10

Communication and Media Studies

A Womanist Looks at the Million Man March (1996)

GENEVA SMITHERMAN

Womanist: referring to an African American woman who is rooted in the Black community and committed to the development of herself and the entire community.

I saw all that crowd, and I thought, uh-oh, But I never heard so many "Scuse me's" and "Sorry, Brothaman's" in my life. —Kofi, my 15-year-old nephew from Detroit, who attended the March with his father.

The Million Man March—and make no mistake about it, at least a million Black men were there—on October 16, 1995, in the nation's capitol, marked the culmination of Minister Louis Farrakhan's "Stop the Killing" lecture campaign, which he embarked on several years ago. Controversy surrounding Farrakhan notwithstanding, everyone agrees that the condition of Black males is at an unprecedented low. The indices are undeniable. One in three Black males in the age group 20–29 is under the criminal justice system. There are 72 Black male homicide victims per 100,000, compared to 9.3 homicides per 100,000 for white males. In terms of work, 11.1% of Black males are unemployed, compared to 4.9% of white males. For at least the past seven years, in the age group 16–19, the Black male unemployment rate has been over 50%; it hit 59.3% in 1993. For those fortunate enough to be holding down a job, there is still an inequity in wages: the median salary for Black men is $23,020, compared to $31,090 for white men. And in a nation rapidly deindustrializing, 30.7% of Black males' jobs are in the category of industrial labor.

For me as the mother of a son, a Womanist, and an educator, the Million Man March brought back memories of the King ("Black English") Federal court case: of the eleven children remaining in the case—several had moved away—by the time it finally came to trial in July of 1979, nine were boys. The King case involved a group of African American women, all single parents living in a housing project, who had sued the Ann Arbor, Michigan School District for failing to provide equal educational opportunities for their children. I served as an expert witness and advocate for these Sisters who had been frustrated for years as their children, of normal and above average intelligence, were labelled "learning disabled," tracked, and trapped in remedial classes. They were not taught and were not expected to learn. The ruling in our favor essentially mandated the School District to educate the children and teach them to read, rather than throwing them upon the ash heap of special education merely because of their language (and cultural) differences. As a much-too-young parent during my son's elementary schooling, I had almost let this same thing happen to him because his school had deemed him "hyperactive" and in need of medication and special classes. Only the intervention of an older Sister that I used to baby-sit for saved him. I remember her words well: "Well, I ain't got no whole lotta education, but ain't nothing wrong with that boy—it just don't sound right to me." Compared to Black females, and white males and females, Black males are disproportionately placed in special education and other kinds of slow track classes in the educational systems of this nation. Still today. Yeah, we needed that March—and anything else that will highlight what is happening to our boys and our men.

There were two marches, the one in D.C. and the "march" at home. Black folk on the homefront used the day to gather in churches, community centers, and around television sets and discuss the Black condition, critique the speakers, and debate African American issues. All over African America, block clubs, community organizations, and individuals who don't belong to any organization came out to participate in local marches and to hear speeches about the crises facing African Americans and ways of addressing these problems. Any forward thinking Black person had to love it. For that one day we were all focused on the same thing. What if we did that all year long, over the long haul, on other issues? That's movement.

Yet some Blacks, such as 1960's activist and writer, Amiri Baraka, took issue with the March because it did not include women. Baraka remarked that if he were going to war, he wouldn't leave half the army at home. In fact, only half the army has been fighting the war over the past two decades! With so many Black men dead or injured from street violence, in jail, on drugs, or unemployed, it is Black women who have been raising the children, battling school boards for adequate education for Black youth, providing financial support for the Black elderly, sustaining the churches, and doing most of the work in the NAACP, the Urban League, PUSH, and other Black institutions. Props to Brother Farrakhan for sounding the clarion call to wake up the other half of the Black army.

A group of Black women intellectuals, notable among them 1960's activist, Angela Davis, called a press conference to denounce the March on the grounds of sexism. To be sure, the request for women to remain home may have seemed to resonate with patriarchal prescriptions of old. However, women were not urged to stay at home for the sake of staying at home. Rather, the charge to women was to use this time to revisit Black issues and Black historical traditions. Further, women, and men who would not be journeying to D.C., were urged to implement a work stoppage and an economic boycott of places of business on the day of the March.

Black women must be wary of the seductive feminist trap. White males hold the power in this society, not Black males. (Does it need saying? It seems so obvious.) Black males—as well as all members of the UNworking class—are victims of the machinations of a capitalist monopoly and a technology-gone-wild system which has been set up and continues to be run by white males. To launch an attack against the first mass-based, sorely needed, long overdue, positive effort by Black men on the grounds of sexism is to engage in a misguided, retrogressive brand of feminism. With the ratio of Black men to women being 33 to 100, I would think my Sisters are weary of bearing the burden of the Black family and the Black struggle alone. The fact of the matter is we *can't* do it alone. Sisters have been climbing up the rough side of the mountain, and, yes, we have produced some successes here and there. But the crisis of Black youth sharply demonstrates what happens when only half the army is doing battle. And unless we do something quick, this will be the plight of the next generation of African Americans in the 21st century.

This is not to argue that Black men don't display sexist attitudes. Of course. Such attitudes are in the very fiber of American society; they have infected us all—including women. However, the practice of patriarchy, the subordination of women, and men, requires power, on a grand scale, and control over the nation's institutions. Sorry, but the Brothers ain't there.

Sadly, many Black intellectual women, like those at the anti-March press conference, seem out of touch with mainstream Black women in our communities. Lacking the privileged station of the "D" women (i.e., Ph.D., M.D., J.D., etc.), our less fortunate Sisters do not have the luxury of debating the possible sexism of the Million Man March. They know that their/our men need healing, inspiration, uplift, and a Farrakhanesque talk about responsibility, respecting women, caring for children, standing up, and stopping the killing. I'm sure these feelings were on the minds of Black Women Behind the March, a Los Angeles group organized to raise money to send Brothers to the March. According to a report in *Newsweek*, one Sister said, "I think the March will last us a while. I really think the Brothers got the message this time." Another talked about the telephone call from her husband the night of the March: "He ... began telling me how much he loved me and how much he wanted to make what we had work. He hadn't said that to me in years ... I haven't heard him this happy in a long time ... I don't know how long this will last, but I'm going to ride it as long as I can."

About the numbers. 400,000? One million? 670,000? Two million? Minister Farrakhan attacked the National Park Service's count of 400,000 as a racist effort to write the hundreds of thousands of Black men at the March out of history. He threatened to sue. A reanalysis of the Park Service's photographs by Boston University's Center for Remote Sensing produced an estimate of between 670,000 and 1.04 million men. A *Detroit Free Press* headline four days after the March stated: "New estimate: 870,000." All of the men I've talked to who attended the March estimated the attendance figure as "easily a million."

Contrary to Black journalist Carl Rowan's dismissive comment that this is a "stupid debate," the numbers are crucial because they provide political leadership with a gauge of the people's will. The expression of public opinion, via support of a march in the nation's capital, provides the potential for shaping public policy. In the case of African American men, marginalized in so many ways, their political will is unknown since many do not vote and few write letters to their Congresspersons. But over a million showed up for the March. Farrakhan had his hand on something.

I have said little about Minister Louis Farrakhan, the "messenger" as the media hyped his role. That is because in the final analysis, the Million Man March was not his. Yes, he called it. And yes, given the current leadership vacuum, he is the only one a million men would have journeyed to Washington for.

Quiet as it's kept, Farrakhan is respected by millions of African Americans, on all socio-economic levels, for his courage in standing up to an oppressive system and his penchant for calling white folk out. Truly "unbought and unbossed," he often says the things that many Blacks feel but don't have the freedom to express. According to a poll reported in *Time*, 59% of Blacks believe Farrakhan is a good role model for Black youth and that he speaks the truth. (Since the March, some Black folk have started saying things like: "Now, I tell you what the problem is with her son, even though it's gon hurt, cause I'm like Farrakhan, uhma tell the truth.")

When Farrakhan sent out the call to the Black universe, the March took on a life of its own. Men—and yes, women—battlescarred, weary, and hungry for creative answers and new thought vibed with the call. And gradually "Farrakhan's March" became Black people's March—a defining moment in our history calling all Black men to task. In an article in *The New York Times,* a Brother from Maryland, speaking from the Update Barber Salon, summed it up this way: "The March is a line. This is where we cut the madness off."

Now, a little more than two weeks after the March, one looks for signs of the March's impact. To be sure, in the long run, we have to come to grips with the profound economic and structural problems plaguing African Americans. Jobs are few and decreasing rapidly, even for those with a four-year college degree. Wealth continues to be concentrated in a small white male segment of the population. And the Republicans' "Contract with America" only increases America's economic injustices. The systemic problems of inequality, which hurt African Americans more than any other group, will have to be dealt with.

In the short run, though, the focus has to be on those areas in African America that we ourselves can do something about—right now. In his talk at the March, Farrakhan outlined an eight-point agenda for Black men which included some things that could be put into place as soon as they returned home, such as setting aside their individualism and joining organizations working for Black uplift.

Signs of renewed social commitment are emerging. *Newsweek* described Thomas J. Miller of Atlanta who came home, turned over management of his company to his wife, and volunteered to work full-time at the Southern Christian Leadership Conference to help in that organization's community work. In Los Angeles, former members of the Crips and Bloods, Charles Rachal and Leon Gulette, renewed their pledge to work with gangbangers to get them to lay down their weapons. (My nephew Kofi couldn't believe his eyes when he saw rival gang members hugging each other at the March.)

In the city I know best, the "Big D," as we Detroiters call it, the after-effects of the March are being displayed everywhere. The new Big Brothers–Big Sisters mentoring center is now getting daily phone calls from Black men. Associate Pastor Mangedwa Nyathi, of Detroit's Hartford Memorial Baptist Church, said that for the first time, 150 men attended their recent men's group, which focuses on problems of the elderly and economic development. The "East Side Chapter-Million Man March" has been established to work on problems of blight, crime, and other ills plaguing Detroit's east side neighborhoods. A Detroit Public Schools-based organization has been formed to recruit Black male mentors for every Detroit Public School. One hundred fifty men, including a State Representative and members of the New Marcus Garvey Movement, marched on Detroit's west side to protest a crack house that has been operating there for the past two years.

The big pay-off for my city was the reduced arson rate for the Halloween period, a long-standing problem for Detroiters. This year, with over 30,000 volunteers (compared to about 3,000 in 1994), the number of fires for the three-day period was 158, compared to 354 last year. While the Mayor (who attended and spoke at the March) did significantly more to mobilize the community this year, credit and praise must be given to the people themselves, especially Black men inspired by the March, who turned out in such large numbers. One of the first-time volunteers, Brother J.J. Webster, a 42-year-old cook who attended the March, put it this way: "... there's a new spirit of determination by Black men in the city."

As a Womanist, I am encouraged by these signs of the Brothers' involvement in our struggle to be free. In the absence of a movement that would provide a space to focus our pain, to analyze it, and devise ways to stop it, our men (and a few of my Sisters too) seemed to have resigned themselves to powerlessness, given up on the ability to make our communities work, and retreated from responsibility to and for Black youth. The Million Man March was a symbolic reminder to Brothers of middle class persuasion not to forget the ones they have left behind. It was an admonition to Brothers of "thug life" persuasion to abandon the streets and reclaim their legacy of strength, pride and brotherhood. And it was rejuvenation for all of the faithful who have stayed on the battlefield of the Struggle: the posse is on the way, yall just keep on keepin' on.

Assessing Womanist Thought: The Rhetoric of Susan L. Taylor (2000)

JANICE D. HAMLET

Rhetoric has always been an instrument for liberation in African American thought. The power of rhetoric to transform racial consciousness has given sustenance and inspiration to African Americans in their darkest hours. However, within the parameters of African American rhetoric, there has always existed a rich and diverse women's rhetoric that has traditionally been devalued if not ignored. Through the sharing of common lived experiences and modes of expression, African American women have created ways that specifically address their realities and ways of knowing while also offering an antidote of motherwit (common sense) to the nation's ills.

These modes of expression were not created out of a desire to be creative, but out of a deep necessity to survive, due to the fact that both historically and contemporaneously, African American women are perceived negatively in this country. Stereotypes depicting them as inherently evil, loud, emasculating (toward African American males), unattractive, sexually promiscuous, unintelligent, and fiercely strong and independent dominate the American psyche. Consequently, these stereotypes have served to dehumanize and objectify African American women regardless of their individual professional and social status. So successful are these stereotypes that many African American women contribute to their own victimization by internalizing the stereotypes, which has led to a high rate of depression and suicide among them.

Equally significant, as noted by Deborah K. King in her ground-breaking essay, "Multiple Jeopardy, Multiple Consciousness: The Context of a Black Feminist Ideology" (1988), the experiences of African American women are assumed though never explicitly articulated to be synonymous with either African American males or white females. Because the experiences of both are equivalent, a discussion of African American women in particular is considered to be unnecessary. This position erroneously takes for granted that either there is no difference in being African American and female from being generically African American or generically female (p. 45). The emergence and development of a womanist epistemology and methodology presents African American women and the scholarship about them as distinct subjects of the human family worthy of acknowledgment and study.

Womanist thought is an area of study that combines race, gender, and class in critically assessing the historical, cultural, intellectual, socio-political, and spiritual consciousness of African American women. Its focus suggests a more holistic understanding of African American women, their history, culture, and lived experiences thereby instilling and/or enhancing a rhetoric of self-affirmation and self-healing. In doing so, womanist thought has provided the missing components that have alienated African American women from traditional feminist perspectives and respectful inclusion in academia as well as society.

The term, womanist, first coined by novelist and poet, Alice Walker, refers to a black feminist or feminist of color (Walker, 1983). Womanist scholarship positions African American women at the center of their own experiences and, in doing so, connects the everyday lives of African American women with the intellectual positions held by African American academicians and others in the academy. An elaboration of this cultural perspective can be found in Patricia Hill Collins' seminal text, *Black Feminist Thought: Knowledge, Consciousness, and the Politics of Empowerment* (1990). In this body of work, Hill Collins defines how the black feminist operates.

The black feminist:

- Refuses to reinforce the social relations of domination. Her work is accessible to women from many walks of life while still being rigorous and well researched.
- Does not privilege elites but rather recognizes that everyone has a privileged view from their own vantage point.
- Encourages people to examine their location, share their location, and pay attention to other peoples' locations.
- Places Black women's experiences and ideas at the center of analysis.
- Does not try to accommodate the dominant or traditional discourse by using its language to fit in.
- Incorporates the everyday unapologetically.
- Rejects dualism and objectivity in favor of both/and perspectives.
- Is actively challenging the existing notions of intellect as well as traditions of knowledge production and validation.

Thus, the black feminist or womanist challenges the public discourse about African American women by presenting themselves as they know themselves to be and not as others choose to see them. This area of thought and study was originated from the premise that despite age, marital status, social status, sexual orientation, regionality, or profession, all African American women share a common culture and common experiences. This commonality of experiences suggests that certain core themes shape African American women's rhetoric and rhetorical behavior. These core themes are: (a) a legacy of struggle against racism, sexism, classism and other "isms"; (b) the search for voice as African American women battle their invisibility and fight to erase the controlling images that continue to denigrate them; (c) the interdependence of thought and action whereby intellectualism and political activism are conjoined; and (d) empowerment in the context of everyday life (pp. 19–38).

From these core themes emanating from the history of African American women, black feminism/womanism has emerged as the intellectual and social voice and vision of an African American women's consciousness. This consciousness grew out of African American women's need to define their own realities, shape their own identities, hear their own voices, and find inner peace.

The Rhetoric of Susan L. Taylor

One rhetor whose work has contributed to womanist thought is Susan L. Taylor, communications director and former editor of *Essence,* the nation's largest lifestyle monthly magazine for African American women. Her most notable contribution to womanism is strongly reflected in her monthly column entitled "In the Spirit."

The purpose of this essay is to illuminate a cultural conceptual framework in which to evaluate the rhetoric of African American women by presenting Susan L. Taylor as a rhetor who uses the tenets of womanist epistemology and methodology as a means of transforming African American women's race, gender and class consciousness. Taylor's columns are not only informative, but also overtly rhetorical, designed to change attitudes and establish a healthier agenda among her readers. Taylor's methodology consists of linking African American women's "ways of knowing" with their quest for empowerment by teaching them how to tap into and use their spirituality.

Taylor is an ideal subject for scholarly analysis for several reasons. First, by using her work as the data for rhetorical and cultural analysis, I am attempting to influence and connect two communities simultaneously: the field of communication by introducing to this scholarly community an important figure to African American women—both academic and non-academic; the community of African American women who read and admire Susan L. Taylor by putting a different angle, the academic angle, on her work. In doing so, I am attempting to bridge the gap between the academic and the everyday, the very foundation on which womanist epistemology originated, thereby forging a connection between the two which has ranged from underacknowledged to non-existent.

Taylor is also an ideal subject for scholarly analysis because she represents the multiple oppressions indicative of womanist thought or what sociologist Rose Brewer refers to as "the polyvocality of multiple social locations" (1994, p. 13). Taylor can speak as a poor, single mother, or as a middle-class professional simultaneously, and therefore to both groups equally well because in her own life she has known both experiences and has forgotten neither. Polyvocality of voice is an essential feature of most African American women's standpoints and from which they speak simultaneously (i.e., race, gender, class, and sometimes sexuality) in their daily experiences.

Finally, a study of Taylor's commentaries challenges the existing focus of the male-centered Afrocentric perspective. Her writing offers empirical evidence of how a female Afrocentric standpoint might be different from a male Afrocentric standpoint because Afrocentric theories have marginalized African American women's history and experiences just as traditional feminist theories have done.

In the following discussion, Taylor is presented as a rhetorical figure and her writings as rhetoric developed within a womanist framework. A brief discussion of *Essence* magazine is provided followed by an analysis of a sample of her columns. Finally, I will explain Taylor's worldview and purpose as well as her contribution to African American women's rhetorical and womanist scholarship.[1]

Essence *Magazine*

Essence was born out of the Civil Rights Movement. As African Americans were fighting for their civil rights, African American women were at the center of this monumental upheaval, although their participation was marginalized and their voices were silenced. Ironically, *Essence* was the brainchild of four African American men. Although they had no experience in magazine publishing, they were interested in creating a magazine that would showcase African American women's intellect, beauty, and talent. When *Essence* debuted in 1970, many predicted a magazine catering to African American women would fail because African American women were positioned at the bottom of the socio-political and economic ladder. Moreover, many took for granted that African American women did not have an existence and/or agenda apart from white women or African American men (Oder, 1995, p. 26).

Most women's magazines (e.g., *Ms., McCall's,* and *Cosmopolitan*) have space devoted to the voice of the extant editor. These editorial comments usually address current events, recent issues relevant to women, or a comment celebrating the specific month and/or season. Taylor's "In the Spirit" column, however, serves a more significant purpose than merely to offer an editorial comment. Unlike most columns from editors, which are found in the front of the magazine, Taylor's columns have always been prominently positioned in the middle of *Essence.* This position is significant because the spirituality component that the column offers to the magazine aligns itself with other columns, articles, essays and sometimes short stories focusing on such diverse topics as relationships, workplace politics, health and beauty care, economics, and education. In doing so, the magazine communicates that our lives exist on several planes: the physical, the emotional, the intellectual and the spiritual and all of these planes need to be nurtured. As we begin to improve ourselves, we must be aware of these planes and keep them in balance. This spiritual component is so significant that even though a new editor now heads the magazine with her own column called "Within," Taylor's "In the Spirit" column continues to be featured in *Essence* and remains within the body of the magazine.

With the first issue, however, *Essence* became a lifeline for African American women showcasing their existence. The founders had originally planned to call the magazine *Sapphire*. Although the word means "a precious jewel," it was rejected by African American women because it was also the name of a stereotypical bossy and emasculating African American female character on the early sitcom, "Amos 'n Andy." The name *Essence* was suggested by Ruth Ross, the magazine's first editor and was enthusiastically received (Lewis, 1990, p. 20). Although the magazine started out as a conventional fashion magazine, different editors gradually shifted the focus of the magazine from fashion to social conscience issues such as single parenting, sexual harassment, health issues, employment skills and issues, racism, sexism and classism (Wolseley, 1990). Later years would include issues related to lesbianism and biraciality.

Susan L. Taylor, a former fashion and beauty editor with the magazine, assumed the position of editor in 1981, giving a spiritual dimension to the magazine. When she took over the magazine, she informed readers:

> I want *Essence* to give readers a clear vision of themselves and their world. I want to help my sisters realize all their opportunities for self-actualization. Now more than ever *Essence* must be a source for black women, a handbook that inspires and informs us. (Taylor, 1990, p. 263)

Taylor's "In the Spirit" column made its debut in May 1981. This monthly column focused on self-actualization and personal growth and urged readers to take control of their lives.

In the succeeding two decades, Taylor's columns provided inspiration for many of *Essence*'s 7.2 million readers of which over fifty percent are African American women. Although twenty-seven percent of *Essence*'s subscribers are African American males and an additional twenty percent are white women, *Essence* focuses unapologetically on African American women (Essence Communications, 2000). So popular are the "In the Spirit" columns, that collections of them have been published in two volumes, *In the Spirit* (1993) and *Lessons in Living* (1995), both selling over 350,000 copies each (Janis, 1995). These columns and books have been instrumental in making Taylor a national motivational speaker on college campuses and African American women's conferences across the nation.

Methodology

Taylor published 228 columns from July 1981 to July 2000 (although the columns debuted in May of 1981, I chose to begin with July, thereby selecting the last six columns of that first year). In addition to these six columns, I selected six columns from the succeeding years. My method of selection was as follows: beginning with the six columns in 1981 (July–December), I selected the January through June columns for 1982; the July through December columns for 1983 and so on in this rotating pattern of either the first six columns or the second six columns of each year from 1981 to 2000. This selection process resulted in 120 columns for critical analysis.

These columns advocated African American women's race, gender, and social consciousness and revolved around seven interrelated themes. The themes were identified by using a methodological approach known as cluster analysis (Burke, 1961; Berthold, 1976). Cluster analysis is a tool that helps the critic discover a rhetor's worldview. The meanings that key terms have for the rhetor are discovered by charting the symbols that cluster around those key terms in the rhetorical artifact. Significance of terms is determined on the basis of frequency and intensity.[2]

Often the terms selected as key terms are considered "god" and "devil" terms. "God" terms represent the rhetor's view of what is best or perfect. "Devil" terms represent what the rhetor perceives as negative or evil (Burke, 1945).

To discover the meanings a rhetor has for key terms and what those meanings suggest about the worldview of the rhetor, the critic using cluster analysis goes through four steps: (1) identification of key terms or symbols in the rhetorical artifact; (2) charting of terms that cluster around the key terms; (3) discovery of patterns in the clusters around the key term to determine the meaning of the key terms; and (4) meaning of the rhetor's worldview on the basis of the meanings of the terms (Foss, 1989, p. 368).

Although cluster analysis was used to identify the themes in the columns, an analysis of the messages categorized under each theme was done using the components of womanist epistemology. Epistemology refers to the study of the philosophical problems in concepts of knowledge and truth. However, a womanist epistemology violates traditional epistemological thought and assumptions in the social sciences by incorporating specialized knowledge and experiences of African American women that are used as criteria for meaning, thereby challenging the knowledge validation system. Womanist epistemology combines Afrocentric and feminist consciousness with the uniqueness of African American female history, culture, and experiences. This epistemology consists of (a) the use of concrete experience as a criterion for meaning, rendering knowledge as subjective and relying on the wisdom of African American women; (b) the use of humanizing dialogue that is rooted in the oral tradition of the African American culture and recognizes the connectedness as a primary characteristic of women's ways of knowing; (c) an ethic of caring that emphasizes individual uniqueness, personal expressiveness, emotion and empathy; (d) an ethic of personal accountability, whereby African American women assume full responsibility for the positions they take (Hill Collins, 1990).

Significantly inclusive in this Afrocentric/feminist worldview is the notion of an "optimal conceptual system" (Myers, 1988). An optimal conceptual system assumes that the way a person views the world is so important because it ultimately determines our experience and history. All people view the world based upon their own particular belief systems. The conceptual system to which a person subscribes, determines the way that individual perceives, thinks, feels, and experiences the world. A deeper appreciation of one's own culture and respect for other cultures is a result of optimal psychology. Racism and anger are the result of sub-optimal systems (p. 12).

This Afrocentric ideal, based on feminist principles, is described as "optimal" because it is structured toward the achievement of everlasting peace and happiness. The role of consciousness is primary. Consciousness is identifying that permeating essence or pervasive energy known as spirit. The role and importance of consciousness in African thought is evident in concepts such as Mdw Ntr (divine speech) and Nommo (power of the spoken word) (p. 12).

The role of power is also significant in the optimal conceptual system. Power is the ability to define reality. All of us have the same amount of power. What differentiates us, notes Myers, is that some of us give up our power more readily to the definition of others and our own fear arising from sub-optimal reasoning. In the process of people of African descent rediscovering their heritage, this way of viewing life in total is recaptured, and is consequently termed Afrocentric (pp. 12–13).

Within this cultural framework, Taylor's "In the Spirit" columns about life—how to survive it, embrace it, and rejoice in it—offer African American women an agenda on how to achieve the power to define themselves and to transform their realities, thus reducing some of the complexities in their lives. And, in the process, they may begin see an old world in a new way. Taylor is effective in articulating these messages to her audience because she speaks as one of them. What then does Susan L. Taylor have to say to African American women about combating the negative stereotypes and other complexities they confront in their daily lives?

The Themes

Following is a womanist analysis of the seven interrelated themes identified in Taylor's columns: (1) spirit power; (2) harmony and balance; (3) self-affirmation; (4) cultural history and ancestral reverence; (5) love; (6) collective power; and (7) self-destruction.

Spirit Power

Being in tune with the Creator and maintaining a spiritual connection dominate Taylor's writings having been identified in 50 of her columns. Spirit is the life force of every living element in the universe; the life essence that is covered and protected by the skeletal frame and flesh we call the body. Spirit is the energy of the Creator manifesting itself in many forms. According to Afrocentric thought, there exists the notion that there is an all-pervasive energy that is the source, the sustainer, and the essence of all phenomena. In this regard, everything becomes one thing, spirit manifesting. When an individual adheres to the spiritual/material ontology, that person loses the sense of individualized ego/mind and experiences the harmony of the collective identity of being one with the source of all good. Consubstantiation, the whole being in each of its parts, is assumed (Frye, 1979). Based on this African belief of being one with the spirit, Taylor advises African American women to tap into and feed their spiritual selves on a daily basis. This, she argues, is the key to survival and achievement. Here are a few typical statements from her columns:

> There is something within us, God power, that has the answer to every human crisis, that is stronger and more potent than any external force or worry we could ever experience. Each of us is gifted with that creative spirit. It's always waiting to serve us and help us make the most of our lives. We need only to recognize it and reach for it. (*Essence*, March 1983)

> If I have a gripe it's that I wasn't taught about inner power in my youth. After eight years of religious school training and going to church seven times a week I came to adulthood with a limited view of myself, ignorant of my inner power. But one of the most wonderful things about living this life is that no matter how off track we may seem at times, we can get on course whenever we decide to use our superintelligence. (*Essence*, April 1984)

> Each of us has the inner power to make what we will of our lives. We can make our own miracles. Our challenge is to not let other people's negative ideas and the unreal standards that are inculcated in us through media confuse us about ourselves and one another. (*Essence*, April 1984)

According to Taylor, the thing that unites African American women is sharing the same spiritual base, homes that relate to the power of God. However, while the grandmother might believe in God in the traditional sense, younger women might see God as a force or energy. Therefore, in addition to using the words, "God" and "Spirit," words and phrases like "energy," "consciousness," "mind," "the creative force," "divine assurance," "presence," "divine order," and "spiritual communion" cluster around the identification of spirit power. These substitutions do not change the meaning of spirituality in Afrocentric thought; they enhance it. Also, an Afrocentric feminist perspective deems it important to note how spirit manifests. Human behavior is spirit made evident and readily perceived by the senses. Through their behavior, people are revealing to you what is in their consciousness, what thoughts and emotions are in it, and how they interact within their conceptual framework. All speech and actions become telling from this perspective. Therefore, it is important that African American women exercise control over their thoughts because words have power. They label experience and therefore give thoughts form (Myers, 1988, p. 41).

Through the use of self-affirming language, which communicates a "can-do spirit," Taylor teaches African American women how to rely on their own power, the power of their deep-seated and cosmic spirituality and the power that comes from the ultimate unshakable inner knowledge of their own value and talent.

> Awakening to our spirituality requires that we regularly create quiet spaces in our lives to listen to our own sacred voice—our intuition—and that we trust and practice acting from our inner wisdom in our daily lives. (*Essence,* August 1994)

Harmony and Balance

Staying centered or seeking a balanced life is a major component of Afro-centric thought. The terms "focused," "in tune," "stability," "equilibrium," and "centered" used in her columns also relate to this key theme. The theme appeared in 30 of the columns.

In Afrocentric thought, everything is functionally connected. We are one with nature. To destroy one category of our existence would cause the destruction of our total existence. As in the traditional African cultural reality, there is no formal distinction between the sacred and the secular, religious and nonreligious, spiritual and material areas of life. Therefore, Afrocentric thought constitutes looking at the whole rather than specifics within the whole (Asante, 1980). Balance comes in the realization that one's self-analysis is guided by an infinite wisdom accessed by letting go of one's sense of separateness, and subsequent individual ego and personality needed to control and compete with nature and the infinite (Myers, p. 33).

Taylor builds on this Afrocentric thinking when she encourages African American women to make a commitment to take care of themselves spiritually, physically, psychologically, intellectually, and morally. Thus, when we feed the spirit, the mind and body respond in kind. This notion is related to the Judeo-Christian teachings that proclaims "all things work together for those who love the Lord" (*Rom.* 8:28).

In one column Taylor advises:

> We are a part of nature, governed by its laws. To feel in tune, to function in divine order, we must have balance. … For lasting success we must understand and develop every aspect of our multifaceted selves. We must be in touch with and nurture our wholeness. (*Essence,* April 1986)

> A positive mind-set doesn't change things; it changes you. It changes the energy field surrounding you. It brightens your aura, makes you stronger, clearer, healthier. Yes, it's simple. And it's true. I'm a witness. When you're focused on that which is good in your life, you think good thoughts, speak high, loving words. And this fills your heart and mind with love and hope, which opens the way. (*Essence,* September 1990)

Taylor suggests that self-empowerment begins with being healthy and feeling strong. Achieving harmony and a balanced life is the most politically important work African American women can do for themselves.

> Everything in nature is in harmonious balance. God has wisely given us mountains for our valleys, summers for our winters, days and nights, work and rest, and music in which silences are as vital to the song as the notes that are sung. Life breathes, and in quietly breathing in and out we find the rhythms by which life itself creates and maintains balance. Create a new way of living that has your total well-being at its center. Eliminate anything that is not nourishing, nurturing or life-sustaining. Don't wait until mental and physical exhaustion force you to make changes. Take steps to begin and see how quickly the universe sends forth encouragement for your efforts. (*Essence*, January 1999)

Consequently, Taylor argues, if we would take time to explore our interior world and listen to our inner voice, we would master ourselves and our lives. Then we would not feel overwhelmed or out of harmony. By heeding our inner voice we affirm our self-worth.

Self-Affirmation

From a spiritual perspective, we can create our reality through speech. Africans refer to it as "Afose," the power to bring about occurrence through the power of speech. The process is called "affirmation" and it requires that we use our thoughts and emotions to create what we want and then speak the words which will then manifest as reality. Everything we say—positive or negative—is an affirmation. The universe does not censor what we say, it simply creates it (Vanzant, 1992, p. 62). By one's statement of affirmation, the person is planting a powerful suggestion in her mind. Affirmation is the foundation from which mutual respect with others can be established and maintained.

In response to the assigned status of African American women given by mainstream society, Taylor advises African American women to affirm their individual intelligence, beauty, and inner strength by defying the stereotypes and myths that have been attached to them.

> We all need affirmation. We need to feel valued and appreciated in order to keep on with gusto. We may be too busy to give one another regular encouragement, but it's crucial to our feelings of self-worth that we encourage and reflect on the wonder of our lives. Affirm that you have the power to control your life and to live in harmony with yourself and those around you. Affirm that any discordant thoughts and feelings keeping you from realizing your best self are dissolved. Affirm that each day you will take time to get still, to step out of the world and into yourself, to stay in touch with who you are, what you're

feeling and to celebrate yourself for coming this far. (*Essence*, May 1987)

We must make the words "I love you, I celebrate you" our Mantra, a daily affirmation. If we Black women don't celebrate our own successes, if we don't give ourselves and one another our due, who will? (*Essence*, March 1989)

Afrocentric psychology (Myers, p. 14) informs us that it is the sub-optimal worldview that is faulty because it socializes its adherents to follow a system that, by its nature, can never work. Self-worth, that basic sense of security, peace, and value that all human beings seek, can never be achieved through the external, which by its very nature is temporary. The only thing that can happen is that you get some, you want more, you get more, you want more and more, and so on. Consequently, the sense of inadequacy, anxiety, depression, guilt, resentment, and hostility that builds up within can only be turned outward. When you feel good about yourself, you feel good about others, the reverse is true as well. Nothing can come out of you that is not first in you. Related terms she often uses to advocate self-affirmation are "acknowledge," "declare," "vow," "praise," "commemoration," "glorify," "honor," and "rejoice." The theme was identified in 30 of the columns.

Cultural History and Ancestral Reverence

In Afrocentric thought, each person is a product of her (or his) individual history, but they are all standing on the shoulders of their ancestors. Ancestry is the sum of the accumulated wisdom of the race, it manifesting itself in the living. In the Afrocentric worldview, the center of the African's morality was the life process and the sacredness of those who brought them into existence. Africans' relationship to the future was determined by their relationship to the young. Their relationship to the past was determined by their relationship to their parents. The maintenance of this continuity from generation to generation was justification for their being and the basis on which they determined proper behavior (Stuckey, 1987, p. 41).

Taylor's columns reinforce this belief through her discussion of African American history and ancestral reverence and an allegiance to the African/ African American past.

Think about our ancestors who were cargoed to this alien land. It was faith that sustained them. Have we become too sophisticated to believe? Faith played a big part in all our grandmothers' lives—that should tell us something. They were strong women, sensitive and sensible. They took us higher. Truth gave them the inner security to know they could overcome all the forces arrayed against them even when they couldn't see the light. (*Essence*, July 1981)

Assessing that African Americans have been taught European history for so long that they've forgotten their own, Taylor continually reminds readers that if a people are unaware of their history, then their personal and collective experiences and challenges will overwhelm them. African American history gives African Americans perspective and strength. If African Americans tap into their history they will discover that the survival of African American people in the Western Hemisphere is a great story of the triumph of the spirit and the will to survive. This success can serve as a motivator to African Americans in facing daily challenges. Taylor professes:

> We also have a historical power we can draw from for inspiration and direction. Ours is a potent legacy that has gathered strength from generations of black women who've overcome greater obstacles than we'll ever face. We see our lives in clearer perspective, too, when we acknowledge the struggles and triumphs of our mothers and grandmothers. We are the most blessed generation of black women ever, and we must affirm that our lives are precious and worth preserving. When we're tired and burned out, we lose sight of who we are, of our magnificence and the incredible contributions we make to this world. (*Essence,* May 1987)

Through the use of this key theme, Taylor teaches that even though most people use political, economic and social status as motives to help manage the conflicts in their lives, African American women should also use their cultural history as instruments of inspiration and empowerment.

> Our foreparents' endurance must awaken in us renewed courage and determination. It must make us surrender any untruths we hold about ourselves, about weaknesses or incompleteness. It must dash those fears and doubts that limit our thinking and performance and ensure that we never underbid or devalue ourselves. We must hold fast to our history, feel empowered by it. (*Essence,* February 1992)

Other words like "culture," "past," "history," "the elders," "motherland," "foreparents" are related terms Taylor uses to communicate this theme which was discovered in 34 of the columns.

Love

Love in its various forms is stressed throughout the history of Taylor's columns, beginning with self-love. Before one can genuinely love others, one must first learn to love oneself. Once self-love is established, then and only then, writes Taylor, can we begin to love others.

> When you allow love to express itself through all facets of your being, your life isn't so much of a struggle. You are living on higher ground. Love is like a magnet; it attracts the best of everything. Looking to a

relationship for love is like looking outside yourself for a lifeline. It's also putting the cart before the horse. The simple truth is that until you discover love within yourself you can't recognize it or appreciate it in anyone else. Without loving feelings swelling up inside, we confuse love with good sex, good looks and money in the bank. Trying to find love is a fruitless quest. First we must let love flow from our inexhaustible supply within. (*Essence,* February 1984)

We don't have to settle for the confusion, anxiety and turmoil that have become the collective consciousness of humanity. Because love is our source and the substance of who we are, and because loving is the very purpose of our existence, our capacity to love is never lost. We can return to love at any moment. We only need to recognize the Holy Presence everywhere we are—as the night sky, each blade of grass, our own heartbeat, love enfolds you simply because you live and breathe. You can enter the kingdom of love and begin healing your life just by choosing to turn the key that is your mind. (*Essence,* August 1993)

In celebrating love for others, Taylor advocates:

Together, we also have the ability and the responsibility to develop a collective consciousness to take care of one another and this good earth too. (*Essence,* July 1984)

Each of us is at a different point in self-awareness and understanding of life. We must try to love one another as God loves us, with a Divine love. God's love is unchanging, not arbitrary, or conditional. It supports us whether we are right or wrong, whether we behave lovingly or badly. (*Essence,* February 1992)

Taylor's messages about love inform us that with or without a relationship, love exists in us. Relationships merely provide opportunities to express it. Words such as "affection," "passion," "emotion," "charity," "joy," "adoration," and "friendship" are also related terms Taylor regularly uses. The theme of love was noted in 30 of the columns.

Collective Power

Another principle of Afrocentric thought is the survival of the group. The individual cannot and does not exist alone, but owes her/his very existence to other members of the group or community, including ancestors and those yet unborn. The essence of this principle is best summarized by the African adage: "I am because we are, and because we are therefore I am" (Mbiti, 1970). "I" is the individual and the infinite whole. "We" represents the individual and collective manifestation of all that is "Self" and includes all ancestors, the unborn, the entire community, and all of nature (Myers, 1988, p. 13).

Taylor communicates this principle by first focusing on the individual, the notion of African American women identifying themselves for themselves, taking care of themselves—physically, mentally and spiritually, and taking care of one another. A strong healthy individual contributes to the making and continuity of a strong healthy community. Individually, African American women have long displayed varying types of consciousness regarding their shared angle of vision. But by aggregating and articulating these individual expressions of consciousness, a focused collective consciousness becomes possible.

African American women's ability to forge these individual unarticulated, yet potentially powerful expressions of everyday consciousness into an articulated self-defined, collective standpoint is the key to African American women's survival (Hill Collins, 1990, p. 26). Knowledge is gained not by solitary individuals but by African American women as socially constituted members of a group (Narayan, 1989). Taylor advocates collective power and support among African American women.

> Our combined power is greater than our individual power. We draw strength from the triumphs of other women. (*Essence*, May 1987)

> Africans on both sides of the Atlantic need to embrace the truth and be made whole by it. It's an ancient political strategy to divide those you wish to conquer; to fight among ourselves is to give up our power. Instead we must be one another's eyes and ears and voices. We must lift one another up, protect one another, show love and compassion for one another. Otherwise we probably won't survive. (*Essence*, May 1989)

> Today, a thirst for spiritual communion is pushing Black women to meet at the well. We may call it our book club, sister circle, study group or just hanging with the girls, but these sisterhood gatherings are the spaces we claim to speak the truth about our lives and drink the life-giving water. However we regularly gather—in small intimate groups or large councils, in coalitions or sororities—we are called to have on our agenda a project that benefits our people. (*Essence*, May 1999)

Acknowledging that in many instances African Americans are their own worst enemies, Taylor teaches that they must celebrate each other's victories as well as encourage one another. Most importantly, they must not allow jealously or envy to interfere with individual and collective progress. The message is simple: for African American women, unity is not only a strength but a necessity.

The theme of collective power is not only reflected in what Taylor communicates but also in how she communicates. The collective pronoun "we" dominates her writing. It is important to note that when the rhetor, regardless of her educational or socio-economic status, is a member of the same gender or racial group that she is addressing, the voice is a familiar one symbolized through the use of the collective pronouns "we," "our," "us," "unity, " and "my sisters." Advocating collective power was identified in 25 of the columns.

Self-Destruction

Finally, self-destruction is an important "devil" term significant in Taylor's writing, appearing in 20 of her columns. Taylor reminds African American women of the things that they have allowed to get in the way of obtaining success, happiness, and inner peace: anger, bitterness, self-doubt, self-pity, holding on to the past, fear, and so on. However, Taylor reinforces how one can proceed to eliminate these feelings. She argues that when a person is centered in her wholeness and oneness with her spiritual center, these feelings don't knock you out. There are no physical, mental or financial difficulties that can overtake you. One can possess the spiritual armor to be empowered or to be destroyed.

> Stress is cumulative. If we don't take time to examine our feelings and to regenerate, we're bound to end up with the warning signs of illness— insomnia and anxiety, migraines, depression and more. Stress weakens the defense making the body vulnerable to illness. Ultimately, stress destroys. (*Essence,* April 1985)

> It's rare that we go from feeling great to feeling out of sorts overnight. Depression usually works its way into our lives gradually, as we accept self-limiting thoughts of doubt and fear. But we do have a defense against the gravity of negative ideas that threaten to drag us into a downward spiral. (*Essence,* October 1986)

> In this society we find it easy to use self-destructive methods to anesthetize ourselves. We turn to drugs, alcohol, food—anything that seems to soothe the tempest within. But we can't slay our fears by avoiding them or denying them or sedating ourselves. To overcome fears we must admit to them. Being truthful with ourselves is the first step toward personal freedom. (*Essence,* April 1988)

Words such as "chaos," "confusion," "disempowering," "war," "hurt," "failure," "disappoint," "defeat," "depression," "fearful," "untrusting," "destroy," "self-doubt," "self-pity," "anger," "greed," "racism," "sexism," "sin," "evil," "homophobia," "violence," and "rejecting one's culture" are related devil terms that Taylor uses.

Taylor's Worldview

Worldview refers to how we make sense of the nature of the universe, and the effects of the operation of the universe on our social environment (Dodd, 1982). The Afrocentric worldview is rooted in the historical, cultural, and philosophical tradition of African people. This worldview interprets African American behaviors and psychological functioning from the perspectives of a value system, which prioritizes the affirmation of African American life. It is defined by two guiding principles: "a oneness with nature" and "survival of the group" (Baldwin, 1980; Mbiti, 1970; Nobles, 1980).

The principle of "oneness with nature" asserts that all elements in the universe are interconnected. The principle of "survival of the group" as noted earlier, prioritizes the survival of the community, which includes self, ancestors, all people of African descent. This Afrocentric perspective encourages the interaction between the individual and the group. Africans believed that the community made, created, or produced the individual. Thus, unless the individual was corporate or communal, she or he did not exist (Nobles, 1972, p. 29). Cultural values consistent with these basic principles of the Afrocentric worldview are interdependence, cooperation, unity, mutual responsibility, and reconciliation (Dixon, 1976; Nobles, 1972). All worldviews are accessible through an individual's consciousness.

Taylor's worldview embraces this Afrocentric consciousness, but she also embraces the often overlooked feminist consciousness in Afrocentric thought. Taylor's worldview can be described as an optimal womanist epistemology, rooted in an Afrocentric worldview and a feminist consciousness. It is optimal because it is structured to yield maximally positive experiences in a holistic way.

Implicit in Taylor's worldview is the interdependence of the individual and the community. The individual is empowered through spirituality, self-affirmation, love, achieving harmony, and balance, and by not allowing jealousy, stress, and anger to lead to self-destruction. An empowered individual has the potential to contribute to an empowered community strengthened by its cultural history, ancestral reverence and collective power.

Even a cursory examination of African American life and culture informs us that African American women are the center of the African American community; the keepers of the culture, the healers of the community. Taylor, however, teaches that African American women cannot be effective centers of the community if they are not centered themselves. When a community loses its center, things fall apart. Therefore, African American women have to become serious about establishing their own agendas, affirming and celebrating themselves and each other. They must also build bridges with African American males, establishing and maintaining healthy supportive relationships while maintaining their own identity and voice.

Dominant in Taylor's worldview is the distinction of spirituality as being separate but interdependent from religion. African Americans have long been regarded as a religious people. But Taylor focuses on spirituality as a separate entity, an experience that has more to do with receiving inner power than an outward display of emotion and ritual. A major argument consistent in all of her columns is the belief that "divinity is within." We are socialized to think that spiritual power is outside of us in churches, synagogues and mosques, etc. But Taylor teaches, through her columns, that understanding our power begins with understanding the spirit within us. When we allow our spirituality to take charge, we affirm ourselves and others. Thus, Taylor advocates internal power leading to outward manifestations of the divinity within us.

The columns take a "hey girl" approach with readers, offering a sister-to-sister dialogue about African American women taking responsibility for everything that happens in their space and being wise enough to learn from their pain. "We journey for a purpose: to discover our divinity and to use its power. This is the simple truth we were born to discover," notes Taylor (Manning, 1995). This affirmation is the dominant thread that connects all of the themes discovered in Taylor's columns.

Taylor began calling her monthly columns "In the Spirit" because they were a reflection of her own spiritual journey. They also express other African American women's realities as well as their spiritual, physical, intellectual, and artistic potential within the dominant culture with race and gendered-centered analysis.

Taylor's columns are designed to communicate to African American women a sense of consciousness and culture. The columns are also a metaphor of the struggle of African American women to attain a dignified and self-conscious womanhood. As a result, Taylor articulates a set of values African American women need to adopt in order to become healthier functioning members of American society rather than to be destroyed by it.

Conclusion

Susan L. Taylor's "In the Spirit" columns articulate a rhetoric of womanist thought. Grounded in Afrocentric philosophy and feminism, the columns conjoin spirituality and intellect, appreciate subjectivity, reject duality, and advocate multiplicity of voice and social locations. But most importantly, the columns place African American women's experiences at the center of these discussions. With the style of a wise and loving girlfriend, Taylor weaves her own struggles into each subject as if to assure readers that she knows what they are experiencing because she has also had challenging experiences.

Black feminist thought demonstrates African American women's emerging power as agents of knowledge. By portraying African American women as self-defined, self-reliant individuals confronting race, gender, and class oppressions, Afrocentric feminist thought speaks to the importance that knowledge plays in empowering oppressed people (Hill Collins, 1990, p. 221). Equally significant, when African American women define themselves, they clearly reject the assumption that those in positions granting them the authority to interpret their reality are entitled to do so. Regardless of the actual content of African American women's self-definitions, the act of insisting on African American female self-definition validates African American women's power as human subjects (Hill Collins, 1990, pp. 106–07).

The power of such texts as Taylor's "In the Spirit" columns to educate, inspire, and empower African American women readers lies in its inclusivity and its epistemology.

Theoretically, if this gendered Afrocentric epistemology were followed African Americans as well as all Americans would not experience the dualities so conflictual and commonplace in this society, i.e., mind/body, theory/practice, art/science, and so on, nor racism/sexism to the degree that they do in this society. Equally significant, Taylor's columns are reflective of this growth of a more explicit feminist message in African American women's rhetoric. This is her contribution to rhetorical and womanist scholarship. Only a womanist/black feminist perspective that acknowledges the polyvocality of multiple social locations in the lives of African American women will acknowledge African American women's rhetoric as the transformer of consciousness that it is.

Notes

1. Although there exists public debate among African American female scholars as to which label, *Black feminist* or *womanist,* is more appropriate, I choose to use the terms interchangeably. Call it *Black feminism* or *womanism.* This perspective is about the recognition of a distinct African American women's standpoint, both intellectually and socially.

2. It is important to note that a complete interpretation of the cluster of terms would also include an analysis of the rhetor's motive as well as an agon analysis. An agon analysis involves the critic identifying oppositions among key terms in an attempt to better understand any conflicts in the rhetor's discourse. However, in this essay, cluster analysis was used only as a means of identifying important themes for Afrocentric feminist analysis.

References

Asante, M.K. (1980). *Afrocentricity: The theory of social change.* Buffalo, New York: Amulefi Publishing Co.

Baldwin, J. (1980). The psychology of oppression. In M.K. Asante and A. Vandi (Eds.), *Contemporary Black thought: Alternative analyses in social and behavioral science.* Beverly Hills, CA: Sage.

Berthold, C.A. (1976). Kenneth Burke's cluster-agon method. *Central States Speech Journal, 27* (pp. 302–309).

Brewer, R. (1994). "Theorizing race, class, gender: The new scholarship of black feminist intellectuals and black women's labor": In S.M. James and A.P.A. Busia (Eds.), *Theorizing black feminism* (p. 13). New York: Routledge.

Burke, K. (1945). *A grammar of motives.* Berkeley: University of California Press.

Burke, K. (1961). *Attitudes toward history.* Boston: Beacon Press.

Dixon, V. (1976). World views and research methodology. In L. King, V. Dixon and W. Nobles (Eds.), *African philosophy: Assumptions and paradigms for research on Black persons.* Los Angeles: Fanon Center.

Dodd, C.H. (1982). *Dynamics of intercultural communication.* Dubuque, Iowa: William C. Brown Publishers.

Essence Communications, Inc. Essence *celebrates 30 years.* Retrieved April 13, 2000, from World Wide Web: http://www.essence.com/

Foss, S.K. (1989). *Rhetorical criticism: Explorations and practice.* Prospect Heights, IL: Waveland Press.

Frye, C. (1979). *Einstein and African religion and philosophy: The hermatic lattice.* Hempstead, New York: Albert Einstein Centennial Conference, Hofstra University.

Hill Collins, P. (1990). *Black feminist thought: Knowledge, consciousness and the politics of empowerment.* New York: Routledge.

Janis, P. (1995). The essence of Susan Taylor. *The Detroit News* (November 28).

King, D.K. (1988). Multiple jeopardy, multiple consciousness: The context of a black feminist ideology. *Signs: The Journal of women in culture and society* 14(1) (August): 42–72.

Lewis, E. (1990). In celebrating of our twentieth anniversary. *Essence* (May), 20.

Manning, K. (1995). Profile of Susan L. Taylor. *St. Louis Post-Dispatch* (December 23).

Mbiti, J. (1970). *African religions and philosophy.* New York: Doubleday Press.

Myers, L.J. (1988). *Understanding an Afrocentric world view: Introduction to an optimal psychology.* Dubuque, Iowa: Kendall-Hunt.

Narayan, U. (1989). The project of feminist epistemology: Perspectives from a nonwestern feminist. In A.M. Jaggar and S.R. Bordo (Eds.), *Gender/body/knowledge: Feminist reconstructions of being and knowing* (pp. 256–69). New Brunswick, NJ: Rutgers University Press.

Nobles, W. (1972). African philosophy: Foundations for black psychology. In R. Jones (Ed.), *Black psychology* (p. 29). New York: Harper and Row.

Oder, N. (1995). Essence. *Publishers Weekly,* Vol. 242, 37, p. 26.

Stuckey, S. (1987). *Slave culture.* New York: Oxford University Press.

Taylor, S.L. (1981, July). Coming to faith, *Essence,* 63.

Taylor, S.L. (1983, March). Reach for it, *Essence,* 65.

Taylor, S.L. (1984, February). You are love, *Essence,* 69.

Taylor, S.L. (1984, April). Inner power, *Essence,* 73.

Taylor, S.L. (1984, July). Our time! *Essence,* 69.

Taylor, S.L. (1985, April). Take time, *Essence,* 57.

Taylor, S.L. (1986, April). Sweet success, *Essence,* 81.

Taylor, S.L. (1986, October). Say yes to life, *Essence,* 49.

Taylor, S.L. (1987, May). Affirmation, *Essence,* 55.

Taylor, S.L. (1988, April). Slaying our fears, *Essence,* 55.

Taylor, S.L. (1989, March). Celebrating success, *Essence,* 47.

Taylor, S.L. (1989, May). A call for unity, *Essence,* 59.

Taylor, S.L. (1990). In R. Wolseley, *The black press, U.S.A.* Iowa: Iowa State University Press, p. 263.

Taylor, S.L. (1990, September). Give thanks, *Essence,* 57.

Taylor, S.L. (1992, February). Word from the motherland, *Essence,* 49.

Taylor, S.L. (1993, August). The power of love, *Essence,* 55.

Taylor, S.L. (1994, August). The flow of life, *Essence,* 59.

Taylor, S.L. (1993). *In the spirit.* New York: Amistad Press.

Taylor, S.L. (1995). *Lessons in living.* New York: Amistad Press.

Taylor, S.L. (1999, January). A new way of living, *Essence,* 85.

Taylor, S.L. (1999, May). Claiming a space, *Essence,* 117.

Vanzant, I. (1992). *Tapping the power within: A path to self-empowerment for black women.* New York: Harlem River Press, p. 62.

Walker, A. (1983). *In search of our mothers' gardens: Womanist prose.* New York: Harcourt, Brace, Jovanovich, pp. xi–xii.

Wolseley, R. (1990). *The black press, U.S.A.* Iowa: Iowa State University Press, p. 263.

11

Psychology

Womanist Archetypal Psychology: A Model of Counseling
for Black Women and Couples Based on
Yoruba Mythology (2006/1995)

KIM MARIE VAZ

Yemoja, the Great Mother, was once married to Ogun, the Great God of the Hunters, and together they had two children. In contracting their marriage, both revealed their respective taboos to one another. Ogun knew not to insult Yemoja's breasts and Yemoja knew not to touch Ogun's medicines. Once Ogun was out hunting and he left his medicines outside to dry in the sun. It began to rain and Yemoja wanted to put Ogun's medicine inside to avoid its being damaged. She covered her eyes and used a stick and a broken pot to remove the medicine and threw it in his room. Ogun knew instantly that his medicine had been touched. He returned home demanding to know who had touched his medicine. Realizing that it had been Yemoja, he insulted her breasts. Yemoja withdrew from him and became cold. She took his pot of medicinal herbs, placed it on her head, put her suckling infant on her back and swallowed her other child. She began to walk quickly away from him. Ogun did not want her to leave and he reached out to grab her but she quickly eluded him and kept walking. She began to sing a jingle about informing people of one's taboos. Ogun leapt over hills trying to cut off her progress. She fell down as he pursued her and medicinal water started oozing out of the pot. The spot at which she fell is known as Yemoja's river, called the River Oggun, the river of medicine. Ogun used his own magical medicines to try and increase his power to prevent the river from flowing past the hills. Yemoja called on her son Sango to split the hills for her and she rolled on past Ogun, forming nine estuaries and ending in a lagoon. Because he could not control the force of the river, Ogun abandoned his pursuit.

Among the Yoruba, symbolically, female power is contained in vessels and women's breasts are vessel-like structures. Yemoja forbids anyone from touching

233

her breasts or speaking ill of them. The violation of her taboo can be read as an aggression against women's power. Yemoja's breasts encapsulate an enormous amount of power, since she is the mother of all *orisa* (i.e., the pantheon of Yoruba divinities). She is known as "the woman whose breast is so long, she must wrap it in white cloth." In myth, Ogun, Yemoja's husband, either touches her breast or insults it. By either slipping through his fingers or outpacing him as the river, her transformation makes her elusive to male control. In another version of this myth, Ogun wants to please Yemoja. He goes into the kitchen to prepare a meal for her, but he winds up breaking her pots. Because they agreed to keep each other's taboos, which, for Ogun, meant not touching her pots and, for Yemoja, meant not insulting his bloodshot eyes, Ogun's action is read as a violation of their marital agreement. Not waiting for an explanation from Ogun, Yemoja immediately proceeds to ridicule his eyes. He strikes her, and she falls out. As he tries to revive her by stroking her breasts, she transforms into a river.

In this paper, I describe a syncretic counseling approach for treating narcissistically injured adults. The syncretism involves the self-psychology of Heinz Kohut and the mystical practices of priests and priestesses of the Yoruba religion known as the Ifa system, to form a therapy approach grounded in "womanism." As a theoretical system, womanism entails an "empowering assertion of black women's voice," "a critical reflection of black women's place in the world," and an examination of the social construction of black womanhood in the context of gender, race, class, and sexuality. It seriously considers the contributions of the African ancestral heritage and Africans' life today and pursues the sanctity of the family broadly defined (Thomas 1998). Womanism validates the past lives of enslaved African women by remembering, affirming, and glorifying their contributions. After excavating analytically and reflecting critically on the life stories of our foremothers, the methodology entails a construction and creation of a novel paradigm. We who are womanists concoct something new that makes sense for how we are living in complex gender, racial, and class social configurations. We use our foremothers' rituals and survival tools to live in hostile environments.

As a relational psychoanalytic theory, self-psychology privileges the view of the individual as embedded within a social environment as opposed to viewing the individual as a lone soul pursuing a reduction of those phenomena that cause stress, tension, and unpleasure. Kohut outlines the individual's psychic structure as deriving in infancy from the interactions with empathetic, affirming caretakers whose ministrations enable the child to develop the psychic structure he calls the "self." The self is seen as having two dimensions: an exhibitionist side that needs to feel great and powerful (*mirroring*) and an idealizing side that holds others in high esteem and derives a sense of self-worth from the identification with highly valued individuals (*idealizing mode*). The healthy dimensions of these two poles are the transformation of mirror-hunger into assertiveness, empathy, and respect, on one hand, and idealizing modes that must be transformed into realistically seeing oneself and the valued object and the development of an independent center of initiative (i.e., one has an independent set of ideas rather than merely mimicking the idealized other). The sturdy adult personality is built largely around one of these two poles. When there is not sufficient development in at least one pole, narcissistic psychopathology develops. The narcissistically injured person sees the self as defective, and self-esteem regulation as a chore. Obsessions break through the repression barrier. Destructive aggression predominates, others need to be controlled to ensure a steady stream of feeling personally validated, and much energy is invested in shoring up a faltering sense of self.

Narcissistically wounded individuals are said to arise because these are individuals who in their early childhood interactions encountered chronic empathic failures from their caretakers. Also, early caretaker psychopathology gives rise to children who become "mirror-hungry individuals." The developmental arrest in the pole of mirroring leads to the narcissistically vulnerable person experiencing even the slightest turn of attention away from him or her as an attack on the integrity of the self. Mirror-hungry people are those who need to see themselves as perfect and have others admire them ("I am perfect and you admire me") (Greenberg and Mitchell 1983, p. 354). Individuals who operate within the idealizing mode seek to merge with powerful others to regulate their self-esteem. They harbor the conviction that "You are perfect and I am part of you" (Greenberg and Mitchell 1983, p. 354).

Womanism, with its attention to social forces that subject African American people to race, class, and gender discrimination, offers to the Kohutian explanation further environmental factors that strain the intrapsychic processes of people of African descent. The dominant society, which continues to marginalize black women, only reinforces deficits in the self-structure, complicating the intrapsychic processes in black women, making them strain for the mirror either by undermining aspects of their self-confidence through invalidating images and microaggressions[i] or by forcing them to merge with idealized objects that subvert their well-being (e.g., the cultural press to engage in crass materialism, unhealthy intimate relationships, drug addictions, and the like). Only a psychology that is grounded in the tenets of womanism can develop pragmatic social changes and therapeutic responsiveness for women of color.

Narcissistic Rage

Narcissistic rage, according to Kohut (1972), is an insatiable search for revenge after an individual has incurred a narcissistic injury. Such injuries in vulnerable individuals stem from a range of behaviors on the part of others, from not being acknowledged in return for one's show of concern or another's "failure" to laugh at the individual's joke. Responses to these actual and perceived wounds are either shamefaced withdrawal (manifested by a desire to flee from the situation or the wish to disappear, or indicated by downcast eyes) or narcissistic rage (i.e., the thirst for revenge). Narcissistic rage is a specific type of aggression and differs from mature aggression. Narcissistic rage is characterized by a desire for retribution—the unrelenting need to right a wrong or undo a hurt by any means. It is marked by a "boundless wish to redress an injury and obtain revenge." Mature aggression, on the other hand, is marked by those activities that flow from mature causes. Mature aggression is not limitless; its goal is definite (such as victory over those who would block one's progress toward an important goal); is under the control of the ego; and the individual can recognize that the opponent is separate from herself or himself and that is that the other is "a center of independent initiative" (Kohut 1972, p. 362).

Narcissistic rage occurs in those possessing a grandiose self—a belief that the self is more unique, perfect, clever, attractive, or strong than anyone else—and is distinguished by the narcissistically fixated adult insisting on being admired by archaic self-objects (transferences of the early objects of infancy and childhood into present-day situations) and a compulsion to control them so that they deliver the desired mirroring and affirmation. It is a self characterized by the compulsive need to exercise control over other people who are seen not as they are, not as autonomous beings but rather as extensions of the self. It is a desperate attempt to maintain needed narcissistic supplies to prevent the self from fragmenting. It is a Herculean attempt to modulate the regulatory system of self-esteem maintenance. The self is felt to be under threat of annihilation. Such a self wants control and wants it completely, expecting to dominate those it sees as part of itself. Aggression in the grandiose self is mobilized in the service of maintaining the conception of the self as knowing all and outshining all. Rage develops when either the individual or the other person (who is designated as part of the self and who is expected to function in a particular capacity) "fails" to live up to its assigned role. This is particularly irritating to the vulnerable self because it serves as a reminder that s/he is not in full control. The "offender" is not seen as having her or his own needs and desires but is thought of as "a recalcitrant part of an expanded self over which he expects to exercise full control and whose mere independence or otherness is an offense" (Kohut 1972, p. 385).

To correct this outrage, the wounded person cannot settle down until s/he has blotted out the one who "dared to oppose her," dared to disagree with her, or "outshone" her (or him). Those in the throes of a narcissistic rage show an absolute lack of empathy toward the "offender." In the story at the beginning of this chapter, Ogun's omniscience immediately allows him to know that his medicine has been handled, and this is against his strict prohibitions. That there may have been reasonable cause for the handling of his medicines never gives him pause. His word has been issued, and he expects it to be followed absolutely. Kohut suggests that the tendency toward narcissistic rage may never be cured totally, and one may have to become aware of the need to monitor this reaction. For Kohut, signs of incomplete analytic work in the narcissistic sector include a person's inability to "mobilize even a modicum of empathy for the person who is the target of that anger"—"there exists a total and abiding lack of compassion for the offender" and "an arrogant and rigid refusal even to consider the other's person's position or motivation" (Kohut 1972, p. 393). Clearly Ogun's unforgiving fury, his utter determination to stop Yemoja from fleeing, and his attempt to cut her off at every turn are an archetypal drama that replays itself in couples across centuries and across cultures.

Human Nature and the Change Process

Self-psychology and human change. Kohut's self-object psychology holds that all human beings have a self-structure that begins developing through experiences with significant others during childhood. The formation of a strong self is dependent on the following: childhood experiences of being affirmed, admired, respected, and protected; opportunities to observe role models; opportunities to oppose or disagree with others while remaining connected with those same others; and opportunities to demonstrate one's capabilities while still a child, despite the presence of more powerful, competent adults. The adult with a strong self (who on occasion may still feel somewhat drained, diminished, or less than cohesive) organizes her or his environment in a way that fulfills these needs. These self-objects do not necessarily have to be human; they can be anything that affirms or soothes the self; for example, music. The individual with a strong self can engage in "the rough and tumble of everyday life, not without fear, but undeterred" (Wolf 1989, p. 102). The environmental responses to the child mold and shape the self and, if too many inimical human exchanges take place, the child's self ends up fragile. Faulty self-object experiences lead to individuals' feeling fragmented and empty. They feel diminished or less than they were before the experience took place and may engage in a number of destructive activities to restore feelings of cohesion. Change in the self is forthcoming only when the individual reexperiences the archaic trauma in the here and now with an empathic therapist whom the client experiences as affirming.

Yoruba cosmology and human change. Yoruba cosmology includes predestination through its concept of *ori* or "inner head." The *ori* is selected by the individual before she or he is born. Life becomes a process of discovering what that destiny is and what must be done to fulfill it, if it is a good destiny, and what to do to avert its dangers and secure one's desires if the destiny is undesirable. People rely on "readings" from various divinatory systems to discover their destinies. The findings of divinatory systems are generally relayed in poetic verses, such as the *Odu Ifa*, where stories of mythic characters who have faced similar dilemmas as the client are recounted. How the mythical figure resolved the problem is key to understanding what must be done in the current instance. The more such readings an individual obtains over the course of a lifetime, the better s/he or he understands the self and the more prepared s/he is to face life's challenges and emerge victorious (Drewal 1992).

Womanist Psychology and the Orisas as Archetypes

As an African American woman, I am keenly aware of the damaging images and unique stressors that African Americans face. Living in this society, our primary self-object needs are constantly under attack by a disaffirming society. Thus, whatever damage is done in the early developmental period affecting our object relations is exacerbated by living in a racist, sexist, classist, homophobic, ageist, lookist society, and whatever strengths one has issuing forth from positive early object relations development can be compromised by these stressors. Since Western psychology does not construct models of effective personal functioning from the mythology of African cultural sources, wherein strong Black womanhood is routinely represented, it cannot and does not adequately account for the nature of Black women's psychosocial challenges or fully guide the development of sturdy egos that must effectively cope with the demeaning images of womanhood and Blackness that originate in the West.

In developing a theory of womanist psychology, I draw on the mythology of the powerful Yoruba female divinities (e.g., Odu, Osun, and Yemoja) as archetypes for creative personal functioning (Abiodun 1989). These female divinities are described in the oral literature of West Africa, as well as African-derived religions around the globe, as self-possessed, wealthy, and intelligent leaders who dispense gifts that afford humans status and prestige, as well as well-being. Literary critic Chikwenye Ogunyemi (1996) notes the myths of Yoruba female deities resemble those of Isis and Demeter, among others in that "themes of beauty, love, sexuality, rape, immaculate conception, fertility, grief, separation, mediation, and reconciliation are interconnected motifs in Yoruba, Egyptian, Greek, Roman, and Christian myths. The protagonists are all variations on the theme of the great ancestral mother in a hostile universe. Her greatness lies in her policy of containment of her anguish for the good of all" (p. 23).

Oya, Odu, and Osun, for example, represent primal emotional states that are routinely seen in the therapy office. In *Oya, In Praise of an African Goddess,* Judith Gleason (1992) writes of the Yoruba deity Oya—virginal river, tornado witch, and buffalo woman. Oya is the wind that comes before the thunderstorm (i.e., her husband Sango). The author applies the idea of Oya as tornado—contrasting streams of dry air (energy) accumulated and then released violently to roam earth and sky—to the individual psyche. The storm hits anything in its way. "Then suddenly, somebody's house, enveloped in low-pressure casing, explodes from within and the roof whirls off, joints, struts, and all to be deposited in somebody else's yard" (p. 20). Using the tornado Oya as a metaphor, Gleason proposes that Western patriarchal society has turned away from the storm at the door and thus courts danger. Western patriarchy discounts powerful emotions, and compliant Western mothers coach their daughters to stifle rather than outride their inner storms, to dam and conceal their own floods. Tornados prefer warm and unstable air-mass parcels as opposed to cool and stable ones; hotheadedness and instability give rise to insanity and domestic violence. The solution is to claim one's tornadoes (Oya), that is, to own "one's violence thereby transforming its capricious destructive aspects into creative libidinal energy" (p. 40).

Margaret Drewal (1992) in her study of *Yoruba Ritual: Performers, Play, Agency* discusses the Yoruba idea of "rituals as journeys." Parades, masking displays, and possession trances are all aspects of symbolic journeys signaling the transformative experiences of ritual. She describes several such ceremonies, but one of the most exciting for the purposes of this chapter is the *Itefa* ritual. In this event, Odu, wife of the chief diviner Orunmila, teaches him how to bring about the rebirthing of an individual with a scattered, shattered life and how to help individuals from infancy to avoid the pitfalls that keep them from being "together." Yoruba scholar and *Awise Awo Ni Agbaye*[2] Wande Abimbola (1975) discusses the odus (i.e., the verses of the Ifa system), as codes of conduct that counsel the reorganization of one's social relationships that would make possible the attainment of their destinies. Odu is a female orisa that contains all wisdom and embodies the system of knowledge that male Ifa priests study through long periods of apprenticeship and ironically try to keep out of the hands of women.

Literary critic Diedre Badejo (1989) suggests that the images of Osun conveyed in her oral literature feature the coexistence of power and femininity. In this literature, Osun is characterized as having played a pivotal role in the creation of human civilization, seeking to learn the art of divination, and having protected the town of Osogbo against invasions in the nineteenth century, as well as being a wife, mother, and orisa. She is depicted as strong in character, self-defining, and life sustaining.

The intimate relationships of the river deities Oya, Odu, Osun, and Yemoja with a variety of other divinities, mostly male, provide a mythic source of information that can inform relationship counseling. Power struggles are endemic to the nature of the relationships between male and female orisa. Chikwenye Ogunyemi (1996) observes that masculinist Ifa tradition strives to make Odu Ifa's "insignificant" other. Odu offers psychological stability to supplicants because she contains secret knowledge of their destiny. Collecting readings from the odus offers solutions and interpretations for life predicaments. Yet the masculinist Ifa tradition tries to "displace Odu through the continual appropriation of her power" (p. 28). In her iconography, Osun was the lone female, along with seventeen male deities, sent to help establish the earth. In the building of the community, they excluded her, and in turn she made reproduction and fertility of land impossible for them. Forced by Olodumare, a higher power, to reconcile, the men came to learn of Osun's power.[3] She was pregnant, and they were in awe of the womb, "stunned by the silence of the womb which they could not hear, the darkness they could not read, the mystery of the womb they could not decipher" (p. 22). In her exile from the male community, she established her life on the bank of a river and continued her profession of her hair braiding. They needed her and the water she had come to reside next to.

The clash in the myth about the relationships between two widely worshiped deities,[4] Ogun and Yemoja, who were once husband and wife, symbolizes the essence of a narcissistically injured spouse's interpretation of her or his partner's "failure" to respond in a way that affirms. These times of not being responded to as one would wish/expect/demand to be remind the "injured" spouse of her or his painfully alone position in the world and engender feelings of disappointment that s/he has not achieved the desired merger or oneness with a protecting, approving, constantly supporting, nurturing other. Instead s/he is reminded of her or his powerlessness or separateness. The response is then to rage or withdraw to escape the excruciating feelings and make the other respond as desired. These instances of "failure to respond as needed" often lead to the most virulent fights between couples, causing not only hard feelings and demoralization but, as in the instance of Ogun and Yemoja, domestic violence.

The Psychodynamic Therapy Approach

The goal of self-object therapy is to strengthen the self. The goal from the Yoruba side is to obtain *asé* (pronounced ah-SHAY)—the ability to be calm, composed, and self-possessed. Techniques and procedures required to attain this goal in self-object psychology include the therapeutic ambience and the disruption-restoration process of the therapeutic transference. During therapy, as the narcissistic rage emerges as part of the transference, Kohut suggests that this act is a sign that the rigid personality structure is loosening. The therapist should accept this rage, but not confuse it with mature aggression. For Kohut, transformation of narcissistic rage is not achieved directly, that is, through appeals to the ego to increase its control over the furious impulses. Instead, focus is on the web of narcissism from which the rage arises. Archaic exhibitionism and grandiosity have to be transformed into aim-inhibited self-esteem (widening the range of experiences that bring self-respect) and realistic ambitions. The wounded, psychologically immature individual gets into trouble because of her or his desire to win approval by doing something (exhibiting herself or himself in some way), as well as the desire to be totally and completely one with another person. The aspiration to merge with an archaic omnipotent self-object has to be substituted with attitudes that are within the conscious control of the ego. In this way the rage reaction subsides. The client must know to monitor her/his propensity for rage. It is hoped that through the empathic therapeutic relationship, the client will grow more tolerant and accepting of the demands of the grandiose self and its tendency for rage in the same way that the therapist is understandingly tolerating.

The techniques in the Yoruba problem-solving system, whether physical, spiritual, or emotional, always begin with a reading from one of the divinatory systems. The Yoruba recognize Ifa as containing their collective history, mythology, and philosophy. Through their preliterate academic system, Yoruba priests were rigorously trained in religion and philosophy and also in psychiatry, midwifery, and medicine—taking one of the three areas as their specialty. The Ifa system involves literature, art, and ritual. Ifa is thought to have the answers to all human problems. Ifa is consulted for any important decisions and to find out the true path of one's destiny. Some of the most important instruments of Ifa are the sixteen palm nuts used with a wooden Ifa tray and the divining chain. It is through the manipulation of the nuts or the chain and the resulting *odu,* which is one of the 256 configurations that may result from their manipulation, that the priests advise clients on the nature of the problem and the sacrifices necessary to alleviate it. In the Ifa system, the world is conceived as a continuous battle with the malevolent powers of death, illness, and loss. These are the eternal enemies of human life, and the forces associated with them must be placated through sacrifice. The food offered for sacrifice is actually eaten by the family, pets, neighbors, or wild animals. Although there are 256 *odu,* or poems, with numerous versus, only 16 are considered "major," and each priest will know more of some verses than others. Many of the *odus* are associated with various minor divinities and deified ancestors. Within the verses of the *odus* are contained the life histories of these divinities or ancestors, the problems they encountered, and the sacrifices they made to alleviate them. In addition to sacrifices made, the verses outline the codes of conduct and reorganizations of social relationships that these figures engaged in to make possible the attainment of their destinies.

The counselor, if versed in these systems, can do a reading for the client or use one that has been done by a practitioner. The results of these readings can be analyzed for their immediate relevance to the situation. There are a host of other relevant techniques that might include the mixing and application of certain oils, the wearing of certain beads, the performance of certain rituals, and so forth. In both self-object therapy and Yoruba religion, the empathic intuitiveness of the counselor and priest provide a crucial affirming self-object experience for the client. The mystic provides a deeper experience because so many more modalities are incorporated, deeper regressions are facilitated, and so on.

Applicable Situations

Numerous African Americans are turning toward African religions not only to provide the affirmation and expansion of the self, but also to form new communities that ensure a sense of belonging to its members, literally as privileged children. The priest is the spiritual mother or father of the *omo-orisa* (i.e., the child of the goddesses and gods). Thus, those following the various Yoruba traditions and those individuals wanting an African-based healing system will find this approach useful.

Therapeutic issues where competition for power is the central psychodynamic force. Power struggles characterize the narcissistically injured adults' relationship patterns. In one version of the myth, Yemoja wants to protect Ogun's medicine and therefore prepares to handle them for the stated purposes of shielding them from harm. In another version of the myth, Ogun wants to please Yemoja by making her a meal and thus touches her pots and subsequently destroys them. We can interpret the myth at face value in line with their stated aims as an intention to be kind to the spouse. The manifestly stated love for the spouse is seen by the other person as malicious behavior, and the misadventure goes terribly wrong to the point of the destruction of the marriage. I do not want to interpret the myth so literally, and I chose to read it as a wish to possess and destroy what the other has; it is a problem of spousal envy and territoriality. Yemoja would like either to have access to Ogun's powerful medicines (that allow him to fashion metal into objects than enable the domestication of the forest, e.g., knives and guns) or to at least not be subjected to a relationship in which he has certain secret and privately controlled powers. Ogun would like to be able to use Yemoja's pots, a euphemism perhaps for her powerful womb, an attribute completely unavailable to him, so he tries to appropriate or destroy her source of power. Destructive rage can be mobilized because of an "indomitable self-interest" (Raphling 1998, p. 103) and can rationalize itself as "indignant sense of being wronged" to justify the use of violence and destruction to achieve one's aims (p. 101). The couple's prohibitions regarding the breaking of their taboos stand as cover for the lack of communication around sharing resources and abilities. In satisfying their need for revenge, each becomes a social isolate and a tad paranoid (Ornstein 1998). They become harpy and hypervigilant. "Who is daring to touch my pots [medicine]?" they both bellow. Yemoja, operating within the "strong black woman matrix,"[5] withdraws into defensive autonomy.[6] In leaving, she takes something that is shared to possess fully for herself—their children. She swallows one and fuses the other to her. She uses her relationship with her son Sango, commanding him to split the mountain, to humiliate and defeat her husband. The problem for the developing psyches of each is how to become related and autonomous at the same time, avoiding "sacrificing relationship to a disturbed autonomy and sacrificing autonomy to a disturbed relationship" (Layton 1990, p. 427).

A womanist perspective is necessary in the field of psychology because women of African descent live within a historic context that promotes their need to be autonomous, that is, to be income earning, to be the pillar of the church and community, and to try for sexual relationships only to be frustrated often with a life of celibacy in the long and later years. Her defensive autonomy has been enforced by the social workings of racism involving the African American community as a whole, sexism applied in a racist way, and economic exploitation of her group. The paradigm of white women's psychoanalysis that engages her in a cultural split between the autonomous man and the communal woman (Layton 1990) is outside the purview of the woman of African descent. Most women of African descent have always been forced to be both. Because her potential pool of mates also encounters the slews and arrows of race and class stratification, her moving from reactive and defensive autonomy to healthy relatedness is a liberatory and intrapsychic struggle.

Therapeutic issues where feeling of the inferiority of the body is the central psychodynamic force. Ogun, Yoruba god of iron/technology, and war, is fierce and tough and very sensitive about his bloodshot eyes. If one states the obvious fact of the life and terror blazing through his eyes, it is to risk life and limb. Ogun's bloodshot eyeballs hint at his concerns about his virility and masculinity in a displacement of the genitals upwards. All people owe their existence to Yemoja, primeval mother, yet her exquisite sensitivity to the unevenness in the length of her breasts cannot be mentioned without incurring her destructiveness. These two powerhouses can coexist only if their femininity and masculinity are not commented on, and they cannot talk to each other about their vulnerabilities. Mere discussion about their bodies risks their experiencing psychic pain. Gutwinski (1997) describes a phenomenon where a person would regress to "early bodily experiences of unpleasure and pain whenever the psychic insights" provided in therapy became intolerable (p. 54). In Gutwinski's view, pain is the opposite of language, signaling a terrible feeling of being completely alone. Painful bodily states can be used as a defense against hearing perspectives that seem too difficult to consider. The painful aloneness is preferred over the genuine connectedness to another, and the energy used to form relationships with others is withdrawn and injected into an organ of the body. Even though is it preferred to object relatedness, the organ also becomes hated, because it too inflicts pain.

Kohut (1972) suggests that the shame felt by an adult when a defective body part is looked at by another and the accompanying belief that others are staring at it stems from a cathexis of the defective body part with the childhood wish to exhibit one's body and have it admired. Kohut believed that narcissistic vulnerability came not from the defect but from the failures in responsiveness and rejection of the child's body by early caretakers. The therapeutic endeavor can reduce the outbreaks of narcissistic rage, then, by helping to make the self more cohesive. Rage "arises from the matrix of a fragmented self or a self that is threatened with fragmentation. In the course of treatment, what appears as a 'transformation' of the rage into a signal affect is, in reality, indicative of the changes that had occurred in the structure of the self: the increased consolidation of the self reduces the threat of fragmentation and narcissistic rage may then be experienced in the form of fleeting annoyance" (Ornstein 1998, p. 57).

Given the archaic origins of narcissistic vulnerability, Almansi's (1960) observation is useful here in that when regressed, adults can experience a fusion of two images, the breast (with the nipples as the eyes of the breasts) and the face, and equate them. From the very origins of life, the infant gazes at the mother's face and her breasts, and the mother's face and breasts gaze back as sometimes "loving and inviting" and sometimes "angry and forbidding" (p. 43). Considering the breast–eye conflict for Yemoja and Ogun, I posit the following: seeing the breast and not getting it on demand, Ogun judges Yemoja as withholding, attacking, and sadistic and insists on enacting his omnipotence by attempting to gain absolute control over her to force her to accommodate his need for affirmation.

Growing themselves to psychic maturity and softening the association of their bodily defects with their infantile desires to be admired will lead to "an increase in self-cohesion" and "an increase in self-reflection and insight" (Ornstein 1998, p. 65). Here is where Odu can assist. Through continued readings with diviners of the Yoruba religion, the dilemmas and solutions about ordinary human problems that are contained within the sacred literature can help to further the development of reflective capacities, to review codes of conduct, and to evaluate social engagements with the aim of helping people work well and love well.

Skills Required of the Therapist

The therapist must be well versed in self-psychology literature and techniques and, most important, must have a concrete and firsthand knowledge of Yoruba religious practices as well as some positive connection with practitioners. When consultations are needed, both Western-trained therapists and priests of particular orisa/deities (known as *iyaolorishas* when female and *babalorishas* when male) and priests of Ifa (*iyan 'ifas* when female and *babalawos* when male) are potential professionals with whom one might want to discuss a case.

Limitations

Because so much knowledge about Yoruba religion is required, the therapist must be willing to go deeply into the tradition, ideally being initiated into one of the groups. This is so because ritual knowledge is shared only with the initiated and those with solid and long-standing ties to practitioners. Currently, the availability of such dually trained counselors is limited; however, given the growth of participation in African-derived religions by people outside Africa, this number probably will increase over time. Another limitation is that while there is much research on Yoruba religion, there is less research—in fact, no published book-length studies currently exist—outlining Yoruba religion's significant psychotherapeutic efficacy in combination with Western-oriented insight and behavioral-change techniques. Thus, this field is brand new. Unfortunately, the need for it issues forth from a past that has provided only the most stereotyped and caricatured information on African religion—a deliberate attempt to demoralize and cause fragmentation to the selves of Africans, African Americans, and other people of African descent worldwide. Bridging Western and African approaches to counseling and therapy will go far in healing the fragmentation caused by these conditions as well as open the door to the consideration of psychological insights gleaned from numerous cultures and spiritual systems currently ignored by or underrepresented within the field of psychology.

This chapter addressed the narcissistic vulnerability that leads to intense rage reactions that defeat the ambitions of people of African descent to have healthy interpersonal relationships. According to Cannon, Johnson, and Sims (2005), "We oppressed people tend to fashion ourselves as the imagined others by generating a contrasting identity from that of an imposed negative self, with the hope of locating ourselves closer to those in power." By sanctioning the use of the African wisdom tradition, womanism does not consign the African theological traditions to academic mutism and insignificance. Instead womanism champions the inclusion of biotexts of ordinary women of African descent and the epic tales of African people as material for scholarly deliberation in the central conversations of academic disciplines. When traditional scholarly paradigms fail to account for the complex sources of intrapsychic fragmentations of people of African descent, we can, by working within the womanist theoretical tradition that attributes the perpetuation of negative self-images and problems in self-esteem regulation to a system to internalized oppressions, widen the scope of learning about ourselves through a critical use of psychodynamic observations.

Notes

1. Microaggressions are subtle and cumulative forms of racism and prejudice (Delgado and Stefancic 2001).
2. Spokesperson and ambassador for the Yoruba religion and culture in the world. This is a position he was chosen to fill in 1987 by the assembled elder *babaláwos* of Nigeria. Cited from http://www.louisville.edu/a-s/lbst/calendar.html.
3. Recently, a non–African American colleague narrating her experience as the lone woman in an all-white male committee said she threatened to leave the committee because the men, though very nice and well intentioned, were not interested in pursuing the issues that were important to her. To their credit, they rallied and became more inclusive in their collective work. Woman's exclusion from male centers of power can be accounted for by a womanist psychology that is grounded in African epic literary and psychodynamic thought.
4. This pair is revered and appears in the mythologies of African-derived religions in Trinidad, Cuba, Brazil, Haiti, and Puerto Rico.

5. The concept of the "strong black woman" is the idea passed down in African American families from mother to daughter that Black women can survive anything (Beauboeuf-Lafontant 2003).
6. Defensive autonomy contains the elements of stereotypical self-sufficiency and is generally defined as a "powerful resistance to intimacy" (Alperin 2001, p. 146).

References

Abimbola, W. 1975. *Sixteen great poems of Ifa*. Zaria, Nigeria: UNESCO.

Abiodun, R. 1989. Woman in Yoruba religious images. *African Languages and Cultures* 2:1–18.

Almansi, R.J. 1960. The face–breast equation. *Journal of the American Psychoanalytic Association* 8:43–70.

Alperin, R.M. 2001. Barriers to intimacy. *Psychoanalytic Psychology* 18:137–56.

Badejo, D. 1989. The goddess Osun as a paradigm for African feminist criticism. *Sage* 6:27–32.

Beauboeuf-Lafontant, T. 2003. Strong and large black women? Exploring relationships between deviant womanhood and weight. *Gender and Society* 17:111–21.

Cannon, K.G., A. Johnson, and A.D. Sims. 2005. Living it out: Womanist works in word. *Journal of Feminist Studies in Religion* 21:135–46.

Delgado, R., and J. Stefancic. 2001. *Critical race theory*. New York: New York University Press.

Drewal, M. 1992. *Yoruba ritual: Performers, play, agency*. Bloomington: Indiana University Press.

Gleason, J. 1992. *Oya: In praise of an African goddess*. San Francisco: Harper.

Greenberg, J., and S. Mitchell. 1983. *Object relations in psychoanalytic theory*. Cambridge, MA: Harvard University Press.

Gutwinski, J. 1997. Hypochondria versus the relation to the object. *International Journal of Psychoanalysis* 78:53–68.

Kohut, H. 1972. Thoughts on narcissism and narcissistic rage. *The Psychoanalytic Study of the Child* 27:360–400.

Layton, L. 1990. A deconstruction of Kohut's concept of the self. *Contemporary Psychoanalysis* 26:420–29.

Ogunyemi, C.O. 1996. *Africa wo/man palava: The Nigerian novel by women*. Chicago: University of Chicago Press.

Ornstein, A. 1998. The fate of narcissistic rage in psychotherapy. *Psychoanalytic Inquiry* 18:55–70.

Raphling, D.L. 1998. The narcissistic basis of aggression. *Psychoanalytic Inquiry* 18:100–106.

Thomas, L. 1998. Womanist theology, epistemology, and a new anthropological paradigm. *Cross Currents* 48 (4), http://womenshistory.about.com/gi/dynamic/offsite.htm?site=http%3A%2F%2Fwww.aril.org%2Fthomas.htm (accessed December 22, 2005).

Wolf, E. 1989. *Treatment of the self*. New York: Guilford.

12

Anthropology

Portraits of Mujeres Desjuiciadas: *Womanist Pedagogies of the Everyday, the Mundane and the Ordinary¹ (2001)*

RUTH TRINIDAD GALVÁN

On the way to a *pequeño group de ahorro* (small savings group), I gaze over the land. It is an arid place, where the lack of rainfall has made the growing of crops nearly impossible. Upon entering Jovita's² rural community, ten women sit directly in front of their small church. In spite of the low production of crops, the women have gathered to save money. Jovita, *la animadora* (motivator/educator), begins her reunion with new information. She stands nervously in front of the women of her community. At times her voice breaks, but she continues to read slowly through the information in her notebook. After the meeting she mentions secretively: *"No sé, no sé de donde saco las fuerzas"* ("I don't know, I don't know where I get the strength from"). This humble woman finds the courage and proceeds to read. The women listen attentively. Immediately after finishing the text, Jovita asks: *"¿Qué podemos aprender de ésta lectura?"* ("What can we learn from this story?"). The question sparks a discussion that reminds the women of the need to *rescatar* (recover) the history, stories and legends of their ancestors. Immediately after the discussion, the women gather briskly to pick up their *morrales* (small bags). As a closing ritual Jovita, Doña Berta, Doña Pilar, Rocio, Mariana, Doña Cristina, a group of young *catequists* and myself proceed to enter the church. The meeting ends with a short station of the rosary and songs, all dedicated to their patron— El Señor San José.

This reunion unfolds in the midst of a five year dry spell affecting Jovita's and other neighboring communities. Furthermore, the overall development of these communities and their inhabitants are affected by various economic and socio-cultural factors. These factors influence the manner *campesinas* (rural women) come together and the teachings and learning, or pedagogies, they enact. The small savings groups (SSG), like the one led by Jovita, represent a space where some of the women of these communities cultivate *compañerismo* (companionship) and build strength to tackle the numerous personal and communal problems they confront every day.

The small savings group constitutes an organizing method utilized in various states of the Mexican Republic. In poverty-stricken countries where families struggle to make ends meet one might ask the purpose of these small savings groups. The long held tradition of grassroots organizing and popular education in Latin America (Cagan, 1999; Fink, 1992; McKelvey, 1999; Puig-grós, 1983; Valdes, 1992), and parts of the United States (Delgado Bernal, 1997; Torruellas et al., 1991; Young & Padilla, 1990) has mainly focused on diverse methods of organizing marginalized groups of people to make changes in their communities. Similarly, the small savings groups function as organizing mechanisms because as groups of people come together to save, they engage in critical reflections and discussions. The SSGs operate with the help of three leading coordinators and its members. The *animadora*,[3] for instance, fosters the engagement of members in various activities, such as, a habit for saving, an increase in reading and writing, and the direction of group reflections and conversations. Each member of the group has a *morral* (small bag) in the communal box where they place their money. The *tesorera* (treasurer) responsible for the savings box, is in charge of distributing and collecting the *morrales* from every member, while the *vigilanta* (guard) is in charge of securing the money by handling the key. Individual groups choose a day in the week, time and meeting place. During the group's weekly meetings the members save and engage in various activities, such as, the reflection and solution of personal and communal problems. Furthermore, because it is mainly women who attend and direct the groups, they also find in the SSGs a space for fostering *compañerismo*.

Campesinas, like other underprivileged women, find possibilities for creating solidarity, resiliency and support in intimate community spaces. These spaces, like the SSGs, for example, symbolize safe locations among close compañeras with similar experiences (Scott, 1990). Collins finds these same safe spaces among Black women who intimately relate to one another in Black churches (Collins, 1991). Similarly, *campesinas* find comfort in each other's company, in church spaces and in projects stimulating the development of their communities. These spaces foster feelings of easiness in which women may exercise their right to remain silent, to *conversar* or be confrontational. The PLAMAC project leader, for example, states:

> *No tengan miedo opinar, no siempre vas a convencer a las demás, pero por lo menos diste tu punto de vista.* (Group discussion, May 2000)

> (Don't be afraid to give your opinion, you're not always going to convince others, but at least you gave your point of view.)

Mae Henderson refers to women's ability to "voice" their differences and similarities by describing it as both a "dialogic of difference and a dialectic of identity." "Thus, the contours of women's 'voice' are simultaneously confrontational (in response to different interests) and collaborative (in response to shared interests)" (as cited in Collins, 1998, p. 238). While some of the women of the SSGs may share similar experiences or differ in their personal interests, all of these contours influence their *campesina* pedagogies.

I consider the pedagogies emanating from the SSGs as encompassing a womanist perspective because they are altered by and representative of women's diverse experiences and the arenas in which they take place. Thus, *campesina* pedagogies of the everyday highlight the mundane and the ordinary as powerful sites for learning and teaching. Consequently, an understanding of *campesina* pedagogies requires a context-embedded understanding of women's realities and that of their communities, as well as an exploration of *campesinas'* socio-cultural and economic daily conditions. In this manner, the idea of "pedagogy" is extended to include everyday teachings and learning within a multitude of spaces (Hernández, 1997).

In this article, I address the multiple enactments of *campesina* teachings and learning as "pedagogical forms." Consequently, I seek to excavate new understandings of pedagogy by eliciting the pedagogical forms *en la vida cotidiana de mujeres campesinas* (in the everyday lives of *campesinas*). I aim to demonstrate its womanist qualities with portraits of women's intimate relations with family and community, as well as the many socio-cultural and economic factors affecting these relations. Certainly, these portraits of new and multiple pedagogical forms cue us into the teachings and learning, knowledge creation, and identity production in often "forgotten" communities. These portraits also challenge critical educators to transform our notions of "pedagogy" in centering the lives and sensibilities of women *en la vida cotidiana*.

Womanist Pedagogies de Mujeres Desjuiciadas

The scene is a fairly new neighborhood on the outskirts of town. The main street is newly paved, however, Carolina's house still sits on a dirt road. Her home is a place for another small savings group. As the women enter continually, "*las Buenas Tardes*" ("Good Afternoon") are heard for at least half an hour. Carolina, then, opens her notebook and begins to call out the members' names. Julieta approaches and hands Carolina her money and places a coin in a communal bag. Later in the week, Carolina will take a bus downtown and secure the women's money in a popular savings bank to earn interest. On this occasion, the small savings group's discussion focuses on the literacy training of three group members. During the session, Carolina, Fabiola, and Julieta discuss their unexpected position as future educators. They are amused at the irony that as formally uneducated women they are handed the responsibilities of educators. They laugh loudly and tears of joy roll down their cheeks when Fabiola first refers to themselves as *"Mujeres Desjuiciadas, mujeres sin juicio"* (women lacking judgement or care). *"Estamos bien locas"* ("we're crazy") is Carolina's response. We all laugh for the next half hour. Their amusement and fancy confirmed to me their great self-assurance and oath to their endeavor.

Mujeres desjuiciadas, Carolina, Julieta and Fabiola describe themselves as women "lacking sense, reason or sanity." This description is very similar to one of Alice Walker's definitions of womanist, derived from womanish, "usually referring to outrageous, audacious, courageous or willful behavior" (Walker, 1983, p. xi). Women actively involved in the small savings groups are labeled by men and women in their communities as uncontrollable women who "govern" their husbands and want "to know more and in greater depth than is considered 'good' for them" (Walker, 1983, p. xi). Carolina, Julieta and Fabiola, however, consider their behavior and interests as expressing *"una inquietud"* (a restlessness for more), both in their choice to be on the "street" working with people and in their fury to learn more about their community's social conditions. This fusion of dedication and impulse, *una inquietud,* is what inspires women of these rural communities to act upon their community's problems.

That same *inquietud* inspired me to leave my comfort zone to trial the fields of the intelligencia and rummage through the archives of my ancestry and culture. While my initial encounter with Carolina, Julieta and Fabiola came as a result of my affiliation with PLAMAC (*Proyectos Laubach de Alfabetización Popular en México, Asociación Civil*—Laubach Popular Literacy Projects in Mexico, Civil Association), a grassroots organization, our friendship flourished as I associated my own "willful behavior," untamed soul and spiritual nature to their self-definition of *mujeres desjuiciadas*. Initially, I was interested in the impact the ideology and methodology of the organization had on the rancherias. Interestingly enough, it was the women's own appropriation of the SSGs that eventually became the focus of my study. Seven rancherias and one *colonia* (neighborhood), all centred in a historical city in the state of Guanajuato, are involved in PLAMAC's popular literacy programs. I participated in and observed their intimate spaces of home, church, business and alternative medical treatments. However, my insider/outsider position (Villenas, 1996) as a Mexic Amerindian/Xicana[4] ethnographer in Central Mexico was also an issue I contended with. My Mexicanidad, as the daughter of a Mexican couple once forced to immigrate to the United States, facilitated my entrance and our future relationship. Conversely, my affiliation to a country set on keeping families apart raised some questions and distrust, but helped me understand the many barriers separating and disrupting entire communities. The barriers women of these communities encounter led me to examine the SSGs as more than mere savings groups. A reconceptualization of pedagogy evolved centering *campesinas'* diverse teachings and learning as they were enacted in the small savings groups. Consequently, after participating and bearing witness to the women's various pedagogical forms, existing notions of pedagogy seemed far less liberating.

Thus, to expand the idea of pedagogy it is necessary to untangle how inclusive or exclusive the discourse on pedagogy has been, and how and where barriers are placed in terms of what may be considered pedagogical. Certainly, great strides have been made to conceptualize a more encompassing notion of pedadogy (Freire, 1998), by emphasizing the co-construction of knowledge and furthering the unidirectional view of teaching traditionally enacted in the school system by an instructor towards his/her students. However, reference to pedagogy in this manner fails to account for the everyday teachings and learning of ordinary women. Because *campesinas'* multiple subject positions represent an interlocking of multiple oppressions, where one is not more important than the other; neither a solely classed (Freire, 1998; Shor, 1993) or gendered (Ellsworth, 1992; Gore, 1992; Luke, 1992) analysis captures and explains their pedagogical form. Furthermore, everyday ways of learning and teaching that arise around kitchen tables, on church steps, in local stores, and in family courtyards remain untheorized as distinct pedagogical forms (Guerra, 1998). Traditionally, reference to the kitchen table, for example, is still considered too personal and not rigorous enough (Collins, 1991). Consequently, some scholars underestimate the importance of the "where" of teaching and learning. For instance, a well-known critical pedagogue in response to my critique of male and public dominant pedagogical spaces, stated, "no, the classroom is not the kitchen table, and thus it can not be run like one." Indeed, the classroom is not the kitchen table, but the kitchen table and church steps must also be analyzed as real pedagogical spaces for many underprivileged groups. Instead, consideration of the multiplicity of factors affecting *campesinas'* personal and communal development requires an expanded conception of pedagogy that accounts for the severe discrimination their *campesina* status represents (as poor women in a highly migratory sector of the country). For instance, Fink states, "with Paulo Freire, popular education has tried to create a pedagogy for the oppressed, but it has not delved deeply enough into how to address the problem of women. A popular education that does not recognize women's subordination is not removed from the reproduction of the sex-gender system of domination" (1992, p. 278). Womanist pedagogies advance traditional notions of "pedagogy" by situating it among groups of people traditionally unheard and spaces continually unexplored. Moreover, womanist pedagogies of the everyday, enacted by everyday people serve to reclaim *campesina* intellectual traditions, like those found among ourselves in our churches, our reunions, and in our everyday learning and teachings with our family and community members (Collins, 1991). Furthermore, analyses of these spaces open a different window to our notion of pedadogy and the knowledge created. To sit under the family tree is to hear the spoken, but untold stories, those not entering the classroom of white privileged male scholars. In addition, the pedagogies, knowledge and experiences that arise further expand our understanding of Mexicana/o, Latina/o knowledge (Behar, 1993; Carger, 1996; Delgado-Gaitan & Trueba, 1991; Guerra, 1998; Valdés, 1996; Vasquez et al., 1994; Vélez Ibáñez & Greenberg, 1992) and the theories emerging.

While some Feminists of Color speak directly to the issue of pedagogy (Hernández, 1997; Villenas & Moreno, 2001) and others indirectly (Anzaldúa, 1987, 1990; Behar, 1993; Collins, 1991; Davis, 1981; hooks, 1989; Walker, 1983), their analyses of Third World women's knowledge and experience provide great insight and understanding to womanist pedagogies encompassing women's ways of expressing and sharing their lived realities. Our perceptiveness emanates from our personal and communal experience as Women of Color with inseparable ties to our people's socio-economic and historical conditions. We often share the experiences of operating "in a pluralistic mode" (Anzaldúa, 1987, p. 79), as well as an understanding that ultimately all these experiences shape the diverse ways we engage, teach and learn from one another. Women's perceptiveness and vision draw attention to "other forms of life" and "worldviews" traditionally ignored (Hernández, 1997, p. 24), so as women conceive of communal change it is acutely informed by their personal vision. Hernández writes, "the conception of the subject as 'compound identities' points to a pedagogy that recognizes not only a multiplicity of subject positions, but also the tension among them" (1997, p. 19). I would add that the "multiplicity of subject positions" and "tensions among them" construct a diversity of pedagogical forms (spirituality, well-being and *convivencia*, for instance) enacted in women's reunions. Moreover, equally important to the knowledge being constructed among *campesinas* is the spatial choice fostering fruitful sharing.

The pedagogies Julieta, Carolina and Fabiola live everyday reflect restlessness for learning and teaching. The small savings groups represent a space where the women find personal growth and community in a manner flexible to their positions as heads of households and working women. The creation of community in the SSGs establishes coalitions of women ready to provide each other moral, spiritual, curative, and economic support. Hence, the portraits are a glimpse into the lived realities of *Mexicanas* participating in the small savings groups. They describe a "collective response to … class [gender and other] problems, where to fight for the whole community is to fight for oneself" (Collins, 1998, p. 27). The SSGs, therefore, provide women a space from which to theorize about the larger context and build the strength to deal with communal problems. The barriers, discussed next, offer an examination of the larger context in which *campesinas* find themselves every day.

High Wire Fences: Ruptures in Family and Community Composure

A womanist focus encompasses the reasons why groups of people come together as they do. It is clear that people's socio-historical and economic conditions determine how they come together and for what ends, thus, it is equally important and inevitable to discuss whole groups of peoples and the factors affecting their livelihood. Poor and discriminated women do not count on the privilege of ignoring the social and economic conditions that keep their families from living with dignity and subsisting economically. Womanist pedagogies, therefore, emerge to include whole communities of people—elders, women, men and children of entire communities kept on the margins of Mexico's socio-political and economic development. Womanist pedagogies respond to the necessities of entire groups of peoples by confronting and engaging with those factors or barriers most affecting their personal and communal development.

Environmental and Socioeconomic Conditions

The most prominent high wire fence affecting this region of the country and its inhabitants is the lack of precipitation, and the semi-desert, and ruggedness of the land. Established agricultural areas struggle to produce just enough for the personal consumption of their population. In town, men and women can only expect to make minimum wages in the production of crafts, pottery, textiles, and footwear. In the state of Guanajuato, the two most important occupations are those dedicated to the agriculture and livestock industry (21.7%) and craftsmanship (18.5%) (Guanajuato Demográfico, 1995). In both occupations women play an important role. In the *rancherias,* for example, women work both out in the field and in their homes. Similarly, in town, women work both in their home *talleres* (shops) and attend to numerous household chores. Because most of the women perform their work at home or nearby the percentage of economically inactive women in the state is said to be high (80%) (Consejo Estatal de Poblacion, 1995). These numbers, however, clearly ignore in-house *talleres* and women's work in the home space.

Another factor limiting local development is the lack of roads and poor transportation in town, which is easily disrupted by what little rainfall there is. These factors make low-paying jobs in town unattractive and higher education impossible. Student and teacher attendance is sporadic, since both must walk long distances and in potentially fatal conditions. For instance, young women must literally carry their younger siblings through the river to get to school.

One determining factor explaining the high concentration of all women SSGs is the absence of men in the communities. Womanist pedagogies are non-exclusionary and the men of these communities can equally benefit from the educational, spiritual, and collective support of these reunions. However, as a result of the high wire fences mentioned earlier, these communities witness the emigration of about 80% of their men. Some men migrate to larger cities in the Mexican republic, but most are known to enter Mexico's neighboring country to the north. Rural communities suffer from higher numbers of emigration, but the state, in general, ranks third in the country with the highest expulsion of migrants (Consejo Estatal de Poblacion, 1997). These numbers leave almost every family with one or no men. Consequently, what remain are whole communities of women with few men over the age of 14. Women are left to assume the production of the land, the care and education of the children, and the overall management of the community.

Socially Constructed Gender-Specific Beliefs

Many of the high wire fences affecting Mexico's rural communities directly implicate women. Barriers affecting women are of domestic, social, and economic nature. For instance, many women still find themselves restricted to their household chores without the freedom to come and go, even to church activities. Both family obligations and male domination hinder women's personal and social development outside the home. Housework and attending to the needs of the family keep women fully occupied. Women find this work exhausting, monotonous, and spiritually dead. In relation to getting out of the house, Julieta, for instance, states:

> *Yo quiero salir de la rutina de la casa, y quiero relacionarme am los demás. No nomás estar ahí [en la casa], como muerta—] si yo vivo! Y cuando sal go me distraigo más, ya no ando de malas, y hasta regreso a la casa con más ganas de hacer el quehacer y atender a los niños.* (Interview, March 28, 2000)

> (I want to get out of the routine and connect with others. Not just be there [at home], like I am dead—I am alive! And when I get out, I amuse myself, and am not in a bad mood. I even get back home with more energy to do my chores and attend to the children.)

Like the women in Villenas's study (2001), the women of these communities have great respect and admiration for the home and the work they do in it. However, they also find that it is unrecognized and unappreciated work and it is from these attitudes that the monotony and feeling of complete seclusion from the rest of the community arise.

Many of the women's chores and family obligations restrict their time outside the home. This is apparent in their absenteeism and "fate" to save but not participate in the conversation or *convivencia* (gathering) of the small savings groups. Moreover, they have been socialized to believe that spending time with other women denotes extraneous unproductive gossiping. Further restricting the engagement of women is the lack of time women are "allowed" to spend outside the home. Marisol, a SSG participant, comments that she can only get out once a day because the work she does in the field, in her home, and her husband's attitude towards her "extraneous" activities do not allow for more. She states:

> Es que es difícil para la mayoría de las mujeres salir. No podemos salir a la hora que queremos. Después que me regreso a la casa ya no me dejan salir. Mi esposo se pone muy sospechoso de lo que hago en éstas reuniones (pequeños grupos de ahorro). (Informal interview, September 20, 1999)

> (It's difficult for the majority of the women to get out. We can't just get out at whatever time we please. After I get back home I don't have permission to get out anymore. My husband gets real suspicious of what I do at these reunions [small savings groups].)

Campesínas organizing is limited both by their workload and by the overall attitudes of the men and community at large. Socially constructed beliefs of women's place in the home remain a huge barrier for campesinas. Even though a large portion of the men of the communities are not physically present their beliefs with regard to women's place in society holds strong. Women are collectively forsaken for not conforming to community gender-specific expectations. The overall dynamic of the group, then, changes when androcentric attitudes infiltrate SSG spaces. For example, Angelica explains the influence one man had on the overall ambience of her small savings group:

> Yo si he tenido problemas ahora que ha llegado mi cuñado de los Estados Unidos. No deja a su esposa participar, y como que el grupo ha cambiado. El no deja a nadie participar (agusto). Como él no hace nada (Group discussion, October 21, 1999)

> (I have had problems now that my brother-in-law has arrived from the United States. He doesn't let his wife participate, and like the group has changed. He doesn't let anyone participate [comfortably]. Since he doesn't do anything.)

Apparent in Angelica's comment is the degree of influence absent men (through their constant communication with family and male returnees) and socially constructed ideals of gender roles have on the overall group. Thus, women constantly struggle not only with the men in their immediate family (present or absent) but against gender-specific attitudes deeply embedded in the culture of the community. This is also apparent in a popular saying used both by the men and women of these communities: Las mujeres juntas, sólo difuntas (Women together, only dead). Or when Jovita's husband says to her Primero la obligatión y lue go la devoción (First to your obligation and then to your devotion). Sayings like these are founded on the idea that women must first attend to their chores and obligations and then to "extraneous" activities. Moreover, if the activities involve only women they are considered dangerous and undeserving. *Campesinas* who dare to organize and *convivir* in very womanist ways expose themselves to ridicule and criticism not only of themselves but also of their husband and family. They are many times referred to as women *que no tienen gobierno; viejas huevonas que no tienen quehacer; traen el viejo entre las patas y él no las puede controlar* (they don't have anyone to govern them; they are lazy women that don't have anything better to do; they've got their husband between their feet and he can't control them). These attitudes demoralize even the few husbands who do support their wives, by questioning their manliness and ability to "govern" in their home.

The small savings groups, therefore, serve as organizing mechanisms intended to solve some of the above economic and social dilemmas. For instance, the SSGs offer credit possibilities to men and women, resulting in viable alternatives to generate self- or communal employment, suitable to the region. For example, one objective of the small savings groups is to decrease the level of consumerism and instead emphasize the production of goods. Women are encouraged to invest in farm animals, the production of fruit trees, and reforestation. The small savings groups also serve as educational settings by creating a space of *convivencia* (coming together), recovery of history, identity and self-esteem of the community, as well as the promotion of literacies (Street, 1984). The lessons learned and experienced contribute to the overall organization and leadership of women and men, ultimately contributing to the overall development of their communities. Consequently, what pedagogical form does women's teachings and learning take in the small savings groups? As mentioned previously, womanist pedagogies are formed through and from the conditions of women and their communities. Women of the SSG, dedicated to the wholeness of their entire community, express their teachings and learning in what I found to be three pedagogical forms: spirituality, well-being and *convivencia*.

Campesina Pedagogical Forms

Spirituality: A Pervasive Force in Women's Lives (Austin, 1999)

Campesinas' spiritual inclination is intimately tied to their everyday teachings and learning. In Latin America and Mexico the church represents one of the few human development options for women in rural communities. In this part of the country church activities are/were one of the only means of personal, spiritual, and intellectual growth for women. Similarly today, church activities continue to be spaces where women can participate in a "dignified" manner outside the home (Consejo Estatal de Poblacion, 1994). At the same time that the church is partially responsible for the repressive patriarchal ideologies among Latinas/os, Popular Catholicism[5] remains a presence of spiritual and moral support against injustices. For example, prominent figures of the church played important roles in Mexico's independence from Spain, the Chicano/a movement of the 1960s (Hurtado, 1996), and recently in the uprising of indigenous peoples in Chiapas. On a more personal and everyday level, however, the spiritual connection men and women have to Popular Catholicism serves as a means to deal with daily problems. Women's spirituality serves as a catalyst with which to struggle and combat the daily turmoil of their home, work or community. As Collins states, "spirituality comprises articles of faith that provide a conceptual framework for living everyday life" (Collins, 1998, p. 245). Pedagogies, henceforth, manifest in the manner *campesinas* learn, teach and express themselves in their spirituality. This is apparent in the manner in which spirituality permeates women's everyday activities and language, such as women's frequent reference to the Virgin Mary, Jesus, and God in their speech. When they state *"Dios se lo pague"* or *"Dios mediante nos vemos mañana"* ("God will repay you" or "God willing we will see each other tomorrow"), their statements represent not only their recognition of some spiritual form in their lives, but Its power to help them and others through the day. Their spiritual inclination is also apparent in their direct and indirect participation in the church. Directly, many of the women are involved as *honorarias,* participate actively in the *pastoral social,*[6] and in their reverence of the Sacred Heart of Jesus. Indirectly, many attend *pastoral social* workshops on such themes as alternative medicine and nourishment.

Women's involvement in the *pastoral social* is an influential motivator to their participation in other communal activities. For instance, most of the women involved in the SSGs, especially in Carolina's group, are members of the *pastoral social.* Carolina describes the work of the *pastoral social* as follows:

> *Vieron (la iglesia) que Jesus cuando vino aquí no trabajo sólo lo espiritual, trabajo también lo social, y lo político. El anduvo afuera, allá viendo como trabajaban, que hacian. Siempre se intereso en los demás. Y por los demás es que ... nace la pastoral social.* (Interview, January 18, 2000)

> (They [the church] understood that when Jesus was here, he didn't just work the spiritual, rather also the social and the political. He was out, seeing how people worked and what they did. He was always interested in others, in helping others. And for others is that ... the *pastoral social* is born.)

The *pastoral social* serves as a medium for the Catholic Church to have the laity reflect on their condition, spirituality, rights as humans, health, and nutrition. Through the *pastoral social* the women attend various workshops on such themes as human rights, alternative medicine, and nutrition. These workshops are an attempt to provide poor communities alternative ways of being in the world. Thus, women's direct or indirect participation in the church gives them access to personal or communal development programs. Foremost, women's involvement in the church demonstrates women's mode of learning and sharing knowledge is intimately tied to their spiritual expression.

Apparent in the portraits is the presence of women's spirituality as the driving force igniting their personal growth and ability to act on their commitment to community. Further theorizing the concept of pedagogy needs to include the manner in which women live their spirituality everyday, since it is through their spirituality that they find the strength to defy their fears and embark on new ground. Women, like Carolina, find in their spirituality and commitment the strength to lead groups of women in prayer, organization, and *convivencia* (gathering). She describes her experience in the *honorarias* as follows:

> *Me costó mucho [hablar y organizar a la gente]. Te juro que lagrimas me costaron porque yo no sabia hablar … yo empezaba a leer el ritual delante del grupo, hijole sentia que me ponia bien colorada, sentia fellisimo. Y lue go tenia que llevarles la semilla eucaristica, y muchas cosas no las sabia hacer. Y llevar la lista de cada una, y los aportes, pagar las misas y todo, todo. Llegaba a mi casa y hijole hasta queria dejarme caer ahí y revolcarme. "Soy una imítil no se hacer nada," así me decia, por que no estaba acostumbrada hablar, bien encerrada. No pues ahora hablo más que una perica.* (Interview, January 19, 2000)

> (It cost me a lot [to speak and organize people]. I swear it cost me tears, because I didn't know how to speak. I would start to read the ritual in front of the group, and boy I would feel myself getting all red, and I just felt awful. And then I had to take them the Eucharist, and there were many things I didn't know. Like take roll and all their contributions, pay masses, everything. I would come home and boy I even wanted to throw myself there and roll on the ground, "I am useless, I can't do anything." That's what I use to say to myself. All of that because I wasn't use to speaking in front of people, always confined. But now I talk more than a parrot.)

Carolina mentions that from her spiritual inclination to help others she felt compelled to get out of her home and become more involved. It was her involvement in the *honoraria* group mentioned above that prepared her to later act as director and *animadora* of the *pastoral social* and small savings group, respectively. Her experience is grounded in a web of interpersonal relations with her spiritual self, her commitment to others and her involvement in the church (Rodriguez, 1994). Indeed, women's spirituality permeates their daily living by manifesting itself subtly or boldly in their speech and actions. Even though it usually "manifests in the form of Catholicism because it is the religion she has been taught" it is the spirituality "which has been with women since pre-Conquest times and which precedes Christianity in Europe, [which] is the unspoken key to her strength and endurance as a female throughout all the ages" (Castillo, 1994, p. 95).

Jovita's small savings group in the second portrait is also an example of women's spiritual nature. Their spirituality manifests itself in their speech and actions, as well as their meeting choice. Their small chapel represents a sacred intimate safe space inviting women to converse, learn, and *convivir*. A finalizing prayer and song also accompany their reunions, a giving of thanks for a day's accomplishment and living another day. The small savings groups are also given a name, a way of remembering community elders now deceased but not forgotten. Some groups choose to name their group after a saint. One group mimed their group in homage to *Nuestra Virgen de Guadalupe,* Virgin of the Americas. In order to foster the practice of reading and writing the groups are also encouraged to write songs about the initiation of their savings groups. These women's songs talk about the joyful spirit of what has been learned, of the accomplishments and of their *convivencia.* Many songs give thanks to those involved, while others rejoice women's existence and their devotion to Our Lady of Guadalupe. One group in particular sang reverence to Our Lady of Guadalupe in the form of a *corrido* (Mexican ballad/song), to the music of *La Carta Abierta,* with the following words:

Voy a formar un grupo de unas doce personas para animarlos ha ahorrar y también, y también a estudiar, y así poder lograr muchas cosas más. El nombre de muestro grupo es la Guadalupana, es la que siempre guía, a toditas nuestras almas para hacer todo bien y querernos también ... (Personal communication, June 14, 2000)

(I am going to form a group of about 12 people, so that I can encourage them to save and also to learn, and then accomplish lots more things. The name of our group is the *Guadalupana*. She is the one that always guides our souls to do things right and also to love each other.)

The women have also written communal prayers. In them they ask for the strength to defend their rights as women and help their communities move forward. In the reading and writing aspect of their small savings groups the women have also learned humility to teach others. The reading and writing method used emphasizes the need to meet the spiritual needs of the groups, their self-esteem, security, independence, self-improvement, participation, and affection (Documento de Educación de Adultos). Their actions are informed by the Laubach method of literacy, which intends to cultivate these characteristics in people in order to prepare them to change their community and society.

Jovita and Carolina's groups, as well as other small savings groups, manifest a spirituality reflexive of their Mexicanidad, as women of rural communities with ties to Otomi and Chichimeca peoples,[7] as well as an undeniably strong Catholic influence. Women's spirituality prevails as the most significant energy in women's lives. It continues to be the driving force for women's commitment to family and community, their dedication in search of alternative answers, and the source from which women find the strength to overcome and deal with the daily turmoil of life. How pedagogies manifest themselves through women's spirituality is of an essence to expanding our notion of pedagogy. However, the connections between spirituality and women's well-being and folk traditions are inseparable. Ideally, to speak of pedagogies is to converse simultaneously with women's spirituality, use of folk medicine, and *convivencia*.

Folk Medicine and Campesina Well-Being

On this day Carolina is not her usual self, she is serene and walks cautiously throughout the room. As the women enter, she quietly opens her notebook and begins to call end mimes. Upon finishing, several women ask about her health. "*¿Esta bien Doña Carolina?*" ("Are you alright?") Carolina, then, spiritually compelled to share what to her was a calling from God, proceeds to share her recent miscarriage. "*Sentí morirme, y lo único que pude pensar es que me voy a morir y nadie ésta aquí. Como es posible que teniendo siempre reuniones con mujeres me vaya morir sola.*" ("I felt like dying, and the only thing I could think of is that I will die and no one is here. How can it be possible that if I always have reunions with women I will die alone.") Carolina shares her anguish, need for assistance and distrust of doctors and mainstream medicine. Doña Celina, then, reminds the group to remain close, to continue building *compañerismo* so that no woman feels alone in a time of need. Several suggestions and alternative medical treatments come out of the discussion. Alone with me, Carolina ends the reunion pondering how much she still feels she needs to do: "*Señor no me lleves porque todavía no me realizo, falta mucho que corregir*" ("Lord, don't take me, I am not yet fulfilled, there is still so much to correct").

For hundreds of years as *Mexicanas* we have both celebrated and problematized our *mestizaje* (the union of two worlds) (Anzaldúa, 1987, 1990; Castillo, 1994; Moraga & Anzaldúa, 1983; Paz, 1996). This union, more like a collision, has in actuality forced us to reject our Indianness, its knowledge and belief system, and privileged what was once considered a more civilized and advanced culture. As Castillo writes, "as Christianized mestizas we have been conditioned for generations to reject our indigena blood, as well as invalidate folk medicine for Western medical practices" (Castillo, 1994, p. 87). Traditions and beliefs lost and in many cases destroyed include ancient and natural ways of healing the body and soul. Some of these natural methods endured colonization, imperialism, and genocide, while others forever lost or just now resurrecting symbolize attempts at revitalizing strong pieces of ourselves. "In other words, we are reclaiming all that which was taken away from us by the particular direction civilization took. We will determine for ourselves what makes us feel whole, what brings us tranquility, strength, courage to face the countless—not for one moment imagined—obstacles in the path on our journey toward being fulfilled human beings" (Castillo, 1994, p. 147). As Castillo states, poor women of color face tremendous daily turmoil that positions us to search for the means to proceed as "fulfilled human beings." *Campesina* well-being, consequently, relies on the nature of her spirituality to find solutions to ailments, a spirituality that takes many forms, such as: an affinity to her *Cristianismo,* devotion to a particular saint, seeking the help of folk practitioners (who themselves use various spiritual mediums), *curanderos* (folk healers), *espiritistas* (spiritual guides or psychics), *hueseros* (folk chiropractors), and a reliance on her dreams and intuition (Castillo, 1994). Many *Mexicanas* utilize their indigenous and Spanish curative and spiritual ties to withstand life's lesions and live a joyful existence. Julieta, for instance, during many of our visits together commented on her health and state of mind. The absence of her husband coupled with her added responsibilities as sole parent, provider, and educator to her four children resulted in various health problems. Occasionally she relied on her dreams and intuition to determine the source of her health problems and from them detect possible solutions. Such remedies included a *limpia* (spiritual cleansing) she herself conducts, preparation of particular herbs she is familiar with, or a visit to her local *dispensario* (dispensary), *curandera* or traditional doctor. Most commonly, if personal treatment of her ailments did not function, attendance at the town's *dispensario* or local *curandera* was the next choice of preference.

The *dispensario,* located in a room adjacent to the town's Catholic Cathedral, represents what seems to be the church's attempt to *trabajar lo social* (work the trenches of its congregation) and recover what it once lived to annihilate. The *dispensario* provides herbal, therapeutic, and chiropractic healing at extremely low cost by utilizing various methods being revived and implemented by professionals in Mexico and Cuba. One method in particular is the *Microdosis* (literally meaning minute dosage). *La microdosis* is a therapeutic method used in small quantities on the tongue, skin or ear, utilizing plants, patent medication, and fetal or adult tissue. The origin, development, and future of the *Microdosis* are based on the herb tradition. Indigenous medicine people, women and *campesino* elders bestow their knowledge with regards to identifying plants, their habitat, method, and time of collection. Andrea, Carolina, and Julieta, aside from frequenting the *dispensario* for their own health purposes, refer other women and families to the *dispensario,* attend workshops on the implementation of the *Microdosis,* and engage in the personal processing and consumption of plants in their communities.

El *Curanderismo* (folk medicine), another frequent curative method utilized by some of the women in the small savings groups, embodies "Judeo-Christian religious beliefs, symbols, and rituals; early Arabic medicine and health practices (combined with Greek humoral medicine, revived during the Renaissance); medieval and later European witchcraft; Native American herbal lore and health practices; modern beliefs about spiritualism and psychic phenomena; and scientific medicine" (Trotter II & Chavira, 1997, p. 25). This tradition continues to exist in Mexico and Mexican and Mexican-American communities in the United States (Rose, 1978; Sherman, 1975; Trotter II & Chavira, 1997). *Curanderismo* continues to be popular among Mexicanas/os in Mexico and the United States for various reasons. First, Mexicanas/os' "cultural framework acknowledges the existence of two sources of illness, one natural and one supernatural" (Trotter II & Chavira, 1997, p. 42). Each treated by its respective healer; Mexicanos/as treat the "natural" source through modern medicine and the "supernatural" by *curanderos* (Trotter II & Chavira, 1997) or other folk healers (i.e., *espritistas*). Second, the high cost of traditional health care, bureaucracy, and discrimination within the system represent another obstacle. Andrea, for instance, refused to visit a medical doctor during the extent of her pregnancy and only delivered in a medical clinic after her mother refused to serve as her *partera* (midwife). Her experience in the delivery room made her vow to never again deliver in a medical office (she delivered her first two children in her home with the help of her mother and sisters). Inappropriate questions with regard to the number of children she already had and her rural demarcation as a *mujer de rancho* (rural woman) hinted at the obvious discrimination. Third, "*curanderismo*, as an alternative system of health care, places a strong emphasis on the social, psychological, and spiritual factors contributing to illness and poor health" (Trotter II & Chavira, 1997, p. 45). For women raised with the belief that our well-being is linked to our body, soul, and state of mind and that all are affected by elements transpiring around our daily existence, it is not difficult to conceive of our well-being as not necessarily bound to a medical disposition internal to our bodies, but rather to an affected psychic, soul, or aura. Lastly, *curanderismo* represents a traditionally cultural choice for many *Latino Americanos*. As mentioned earlier, Mexicanos/as utilize one curative method over another depending on the source of their illness. Women who frequent *curanderas* make a conscientious choice to heal intuitive lesions in their spirit, body, and mind. It is their inner self informing them.

Women's experience, intuitive sense, and participation in the processing and use of alternative medical treatments and the frequenting of *curanderas* emerge in the small savings groups. Pedagogies, in this sense, encompass an articulation of health issues, such as the discovery of remedies, and the sharing and alleviation of illnesses. This is apparent in Carolina's portrait regarding her recent miscarriage. Not only was she able to ease the feeling of anguish and near-death experience, but she also received healing suggestions and *compañera* support.

The everyday pedagogies of poor women include conversations surrounding health issues far removed from a doctor's office. Women also find that even if a cure is not recommended, *el desaho go* (alleviation) exists. Doña Imelda, for instance, does not attend the SSGs to save, as much as she does to *desahogarse,* relieve herself of ailments she can share with the group. The SSGs are places where women can share health problems amongst *compañeras* that will not judge their situation as medically untreatable. Poor women tire or lose faith in the misdiagnosis of traditional medicine's surmise of their ailments as psychological and untreatable, explaining the frequency of their resort to *curanderas.* Instead, women's ailments are recognized in the SSGs as real symptoms of real health problems many times caused by life's lesions (Finkler, 1994). Julieta, Andrea, and Fabiola's life lesions, for example, are intensified by the absence of their husbands or sons, the anguish of their illegality in the US and sometimes their disappearance or death. Many women grieve day and night as they pray for the safe arrival of their men in the United States.[8] Fabiola's prayers, however, were to no avail; her son disappeared in the Rio Grande 18 months ago. Many of these "health problems" go undetected or ignored by traditional medical staff who treat only the body. Womanist pedagogies embody conversations surrounding women's ailments, which serve as relief systems, as well as moral, spiritual, and medical support. Hence, as Castillo states, once a woman's knowledge and experiences are shared and reaffirmed (as they often are in the SSGs), she uses the affirmation "to strengthen herself and to share her knowledge with others. Ultimately we seek to propel ourselves into a collective state of being, which is so ancient we will consider it new" (1994, p. 160). Clearly, to expand our understanding of pedagogies they must be understood as a collective form of teaching and learning responding to the everyday, ordinary, and mundane lesions and joys of all peoples. Pedagogies, in this sense, can be understood as taking various forms depending on those groups of peoples engaging in them. The intuitive and experiential knowledge women hold, however, should be shared, and so the beauty of *convivencia* (coming together) lies in the teachings and learning materializing every day.

Convivencia: We Gather to LIVE among One Another

The word *convivir* literally means to live life among others, to learn and share. The women of the small savings groups frequently use the word *convivir* when describing their reunions. For the women *la convivencia* is a way of gathering to live, to coexist. The most frequent answer to the questions "What have you learned in the small savings groups?" and "How have you benefited from the small savings groups?" is *convivir can los demás* (to gather and live among others). *La convivencia,* which the SSGs foster, brings people together to share their everyday problems, ideas, knowledge, and experiences. The women of the small savings groups learn they share similar experiences, such as the migration of the men in their family. They are not alone in their feelings that they act as father and mother of the family, lack the support of another adult, and their children respond aggressively to the absence of male figures in the family. However, women not only share mutual experiences but also encounter and try to make sense of their diverse experiences. This is apparent in a *Community experience recovery workshop*,[9] in which the women discussed the migration problem in their communities. Part of the conversation is as follows:

> Marlen: *Pues yo veo que están mejor económicamente (las que tienen esposos en los Estados Unidos). La manera de vivir es diferente, cambian su cuartito su cuartito viejo por uno nuevo, visten mejor.*
> Angelica: *Pent no es tanto, pierden (los niños) el amor del padre. Los hijos se rebelan.*
> Julieta: *Mi opinión es como que si les afecta mucho (a los hijos), se enferman mucho, se ponen agresivos. Y yo estoy igual que las demás (económicamente), pero ellas lo disfrutan más. No nos podemos resignar. Es horrible, sabe horrible.* (Workshop discussion, January 18, 2000)
> (Marlen: Well, I see that they are better off economically [women who have husbands in the United States]. Their living style is different, they change their old room for a new one, they dress better.
> Angelica: But it is not that much, they [the children] lose the love of their father. Our children become rebellious.
> Julieta: My opinion is it does affect them [the children], they are sick more often, they become aggressive. I am the same [economically] as the rest, but they enjoy what they have more. We can't resign ourselves to this situation. It's horrible, it tastes horrible.)

The conversation brought women with similar and different experiences together to learn and negotiate pre-existing ideas of a common theme. Even though Marlen later sympathizes with the other women, her closing remarks, "poor but together" (with regard to her own situation) further demonstrate that a constant exchange of ideas and experiences is needed to make sense of even familiar problems. The connections made with women who we sometimes think have quite similar experiences turn out to be moments of reflection and problem solving. The *convivencia* women live in the SSGs nurtures the (re)discovery of experiences as well as a defiance of old held beliefs.

Work and traditional perceptions of women's place in the home persist as high wire fences disabling women's organization. Thus, recognition and not criticism is urgently needed for the overall development of *campesinas* and their communities. Patriarchal perceptions of what women's roles are in society materialize into negative attitudes towards women deviating from traditional roles. As women come together they attempt to shatter a discourse socially enmeshed with the idea of governance, where to be singled out as a woman without "government" (*mujeres sin gobierno*) requires great strength, self-assurance, and resiliency. An integral part of the SSGs, therefore, is the continual support of women's personal development. For example, the SSG program leaders attempt to deal with community antagonism of women's work outside the home by encouraging the *animadoras* to have group reflections about women's roles and the sharing of dilemmas or barriers encountered (such as Angelica's example of her disruptive brother-in-law). Guillermina, PLAMAC leader, highlights women's changing views as starting points for the whole community, when she states to the women:

> *Piensen en la educación que estamos obteniendo, el cambió de Mujer, nuestro cambió de actitud, ahí esta el cambió.* (Group discussion, May 2000)

> (Think of the education we are gaining, the change in what is Woman, the change in our attitude, *there* is the change.)

Women in the SSGs are responding to changes by taking great pride in the work they do in their home and community. For instance, Rebeca is quick to mention she has never neglected her family obligations for those of her community. She demonstrates great pride in her ability to compliment both, since both are essential for her well-being and development. This change, nevertheless, requires strength to endure the hostility of those opposed to change. For this and the reasons mentioned earlier, *campesinas* need to build alliances with other women who support these changes. The small savings groups, hence, represent spaces where women learn to help each other with simple tasks, such as their knitting work, and with hard times, such as during economic troubles. These alliances also serve as networking mechanisms for the implementation of new community development programs, attendance at workshops, and employment possibilities. *Campesinas* connect with other women, create friendships and alliances, and break from the monotony of housework. Hence, pedagogies need to be re-examined as a coming together to live, pedagogies of everyday living.

Conclusion

Clearly, womanist pedagogies help explore the multiple ways women and men live, learn, and teach each other every day. Mexico's proximity to the US simplifies the border-crossing of *campesina* portraits that shed light on many Mexican and Latin American immigrant communities in the US. The high wire fences mentioned here refer to conditions affecting groups of Mexicanas/os both in Mexico and in the United States. Most specifically, my reference to Guanajuato's migration dilemma provides further insight to groups of people residing in or entering the United States. Studies (Behar, 1993; Carger, 1996; Castillo, 1994; Delgado-Gaitan & Trueba, 1991; Diaz Soto, 1997; Finkler, 1994; Guerra, 1998; Paz, 1996; Rodriguez, 1994; Valdés, 1996; Vasquez et al., 1994; Vélez Ibáñez & Greenberg, 1992; Villenas, 2001) stressing the wealth of knowledge immigrant communities "demonstrate that members of the immigrant groups currently transforming the complexion of this country bring rich caches of social, cultural, linguistic, and discursive values and practices that have the potential to enrich rather than impoverish the nation as a whole" (Guerra, 1998, p. 158). Furthermore, *campesina* pedagogies expand US knowledge of immigrant peoples' values and experiences, as well as the way they live, learn, and teach each other every day. Their vision and method of organization also provide a design for diverse racial and ethnic groups who may benefit from their organizational insight. These pedagogies, "committed to the survival and wholeness" of entire peoples, key us into ways groups of peoples may maintain/recover their history and traditions (Walker, 1983, p. xi). Ultimately, the everyday, mundane and ordinary portraits of *campesinas* inspire us to reflect on the connections groups make as they gather, and "propel [us] into a collective state of being everyday" (Castillo, 1994, p. 160). Evidently, people's history and traditions, intimately tied to their spiritual expression and material conditions, and the many obstacles *campesinas* and other groups, confront, transform our understanding of what shapes the concept of pedagogies. By utilizing womanist pedagogies the overall understanding of pedagogies becomes more encompassing of the everyday, the mundane, and the ordinary, and the spaces fostering them.

Notes

1. *Can todo mi respeto y cariño le doy las gracias a las mujeres de la cuenca que me confiaron sus experincias, prestaron sus palabras, y instruyeron con sus conocimientos. Gracias par las tortillas.*
2. Pseudonyms are used throughout to protect the anonymity of the women's identity.
3. The *animadora* takes on many functions and no translation entirely conveys her responsibilities. Generally, she is the motivator/educator of the group, since she has been trained in the Laubach literary method by the organization and receives frequent workshops and in-services on ways to motivate or direct the group in various discussions. She also serves as liaison for the organization and her community.
4. Ana Castillo's (1994) reference to Mexic Amerindian strives to "assert both our indigenous blood and the source, at least in part, of our spirituality" by turning to our ethnic and racial makeup (p. 10). Xicanisima also makes reference to our unique positionality as hybrid peoples with multiple ties and struggles to contend with. Xicanisima situates Chicana Feminism ideologically and theoretically outside the confines of White Feminism and the White Women's movement who have ignored the discrimination and struggles of Women of Color. Keen on focusing on gender specific discrimination, White feminists incessantly ignore/refuse to discuss their class and race privileges, thus making little room in their movement for the multiple discriminatory struggles of Women of Color. A Xicanisima take, consequently, places *campesina's*, for instance, multiple issues at the forefront. For further discussion on these themes see Moraga, C. & Anzaldúa, G. (1983). *This bridge called my back: Writings by radical women of color*. Lanthan, New York: Kitchen Table: Women of Color Press.
5. Popular Catholicism encompasses the spiritual beliefs and traditions handed down through generations, not institutionalized by the Catholic church, because of its historical and spiritual ties to indigenous cultures. See Rodriguez, J. (1994). *Our Lady of Guadalupe: Faith and empowerment among Mexican-American women*. Austin: University of Texas Press.
6. Considered part of the Catholic church's pastoral mission, women participating in the *pastoral social* partake in church related activities to benefit the people in their community. For instance, some women assist the ill by serving as company and taking them meals. Many of the women in the *pastoral social* are also *honorarias*. *Honorarias* are a special women's prayer group that meets once a month and pays homage to *el santisimo* (Christ in the form of the Eucharist) as it is exposed in the *custodia* (monstrance). As it is exposed, Christ is considered *en presencia, potencia y divinidad* (in presence, power

and divinity). Women, through constant prayer and songs, stand guard throughout the day, while men pay homage during the night. Once a year every participating community takes a special trip to the church located on a remarkable hill of the state capital (*serro del cubilete*). All through the night men and woman pay this special homage to *el santisimo*. I had the great fortune of participating, with the women of the communities I worked with, in this special observance during the year I lived there.

7. The women's ancestry goes back to Otomi and Chichimeca peoples. The Otomi peoples, in particular, continue to maintain their language and culture in this and surrounding states.

8. Consider, for example, Arizona's recent anti-immigration uproar, where Arizonan ranchers have shot at undocumented men and women attempting to cross the U.S./Mexico border. Furthermore, such is the antagonism of many US citizens against Latino/a immigrants that recently the death of two immigrants was video taped as they attempted to cross the Rio Bravo without a rescue attempt. The Mexican community I was in at the time was deeply affected and disgusted by the apathetic attitudes of the overseeing authorities. As was expected, this triggers immense fear to the many families in these *rancherias* (and Mexicans in general) whose husbands, brothers, sons or friends consider entering the United States in the same manner.

9. PLAMAC, as well as other grassroots organizations, are also dedicated to the recovery and documentation of community history and culture. One of the ways PLAMAC promotes literacy in rural communities is through the investigation and recording of the community's history and culture. On this occasion, the women of the SSGs were being trained by project leaders in the recovery of their history and culture.

References

Alfabetización Laubach Mexicana, A. C. *Documento de Educatión de Adultos*. México. D.F.

Anzaldúa, G. (1987). *Borderlands/La frontera: The new Mestiza*. San Francisco: Aunt Lute Books.

Anzaldúa, G. (1990). *Making faces, making soul: Creative and critical perspectives by feminists of color*. San Francisco: Aunt Lute Books.

Austin, R. (1999). Popular history and popular education: El consejo de educación de adultos de América Latin. *Latin American Perspectives*, 26(4), 39–68.

Behar, R. (1993). *Translated woman: Crossing the border with Esperanza's story*. Boston: Beacon Press.

Cagan, E. (1999). Women and grassroots democracy in El Salvador. In J. Bystydzienski & J. Sekhon (Eds.), *Democratization and women's grassroots movements* (pp. 173–195). Indianapolis: Indiana University Press.

Carger, C. (1996). *Of borders and dreams: A Mexican-American experience of urban education*. New York: Teachers College Press.

Castillo, A. (1994). *Massacre of the dreamers: Essays on Xicanisima*. London: Plume Book.

Collins, P. (1991) *Black feminist thought: Knowledge, consciousness, and the politics of empowerment*. New York: Routledge.

Collins, P. (1998). *Fighting words: Black women and the search for justice*. Minneapolis: University of Minnesota Press.

Consejo Estatal de Población. (1994). *Informe sobre la situación de la mujer en el estado de Guanajuato—Un reconocimiento*. Guanajuato.

Consejo Estatal de Población. (1995). *Guanajuato demografico*. Guanajuato.

Consejo Estatal de Población. (1997). *GENTE. Guanajuato.*

Davis, Angela. *Woman, Race and Class*. New York, Random House, 1981.

Delgado Bernal, D. (1997). Grassroots leadership reconceptualized: Chicana oral histories and the 1968 East Los Angeles school blowouts. *Frontiers: A Journal of Women's Studies*, 19(2), 113–142.

Delgado-Gaitan, C., & Trueba, H. (1991). *Crossing cultural borders: Education for immigrant families in America*. London: Falmer Press.

Diaz Soto, L. (1997). *Language, culture, and power: Bilingual families and the struggle for quality education*. Albany: State University of New York Press.

Ellsworth, E. (1992). Why doesn't this feel empowering? Working through the repressive myths of critical pedagogy. In C. Luke & J. Gore (Eds.), *Feminisms and critical pedagogy* (pp. 60–119). New York: Routledge.

Fink, M. (1992). Women and popular education in Latina America. In N. Stromquist (Ed.), *Women and education in Latin America: Knowledge, power, and change* (pp. 171–193). Boulder: Lynne Rienner.

Finkler, K. (1994). *Women in pain: Gender and morbidity in Mexico.* Philadelphia: University of Pennsylvania Press.

Freire, P. (1998). *Pedagogy of the oppressed.* Albany: State University of New York Press.

Gore, J. (1992). What we can do for you! What can "We" do for "You"? In C. Luke & J. Gore (Eds.), *Feminisms and critical pedagogy* (pp. 54–73). New York: Routledge.

Guerra, J. (1998). *Close to home: Oral and literate practices in a transnational Mexicano community.* New York: Teachers College Press.

Hernández, A. (1997). *Pedagogy, democracy, and feminism: Rethinking the public sphere.* New York: State University of New York Press.

hooks, b. (1989). *Talking back: Thinking feminist, thinking black.* Boston: South End Press.

Hurtado, A. (1996). *The color of privilege: Three blasphemies on race and feminism.* Ann Arbor: University of Michigan Press.

Luke, C. (1992). Feminist politics and radical pedagogy. In C. Luke & J. Gore (Eds.), *Feminisms and critical pedagogy* (pp. 25–53). New York: Routledge.

McKelvey, C. (1999). Feminist organizations and grassroots democracy in Honduras. In J. Bystydzienski & J. Sekhon (Eds.), *Democratization and women's grassroots movements* (pp. 196–213). Indianapolis: Indiana University Press.

Moraga, C., & Anzaldúa, G. (1983). *This bridge called my back: Writings by radical women of color.* Kitchen Table: Women of Color Press.

Paz, O. (1996). *El laberinto de la soledad.* Mexico: Fondo de Cultura Económica.

Puiggrós, A. (1983). Discusiones y tendencies en la educación popular latinoamericana. *Nueva antropolugía-Revista de Ciencias Sociales,* VI(21), 15–40.

Rodriguez, J. (1994). *Our lady of Guadalupe: Faith and empowerment among Mexican-American women.* Austin: University of Texas Press.

Rose, L. (1978). *Disease beliefs in Mexican-American communities.* San Francisco: R & E Research Associates.

Scott, J. (1990). *Domination and the arts of resistance: Hidden transcripts.* New Haven: Yale University Press.

Sherman, J. (1975). *Spiritualistic Curanderismo.* Doctoral dissertation, United States International University [Dissertation Information Service].

Shor, I. (1993). *Empowering education: Critical teaching for social change.* Chicago: University of Chicago Press.

Street, B. (1984). *Literacy in theory and practice.* Cambridge: Cambridge University Press.

Torruellas, R., Benmayor, R., Goris, A., & Juarbe, A. (1991). Affirming cultural citizenship in the Puerto Rican community: Critical literacy and the El Barrio Popular Education Program. In C. E. Walsh (Ed), *Literacy as praxis: Culture, language, and pedagogy* (pp. 183–219). Norwood, New Jersey: Ablex.

Trotter II, R., & Chavira, J. (1997). *Curanderismo: Mexican American folk healing.* Athens: University of Georgia Press.

Valdés, G. (1996). *Con respeto: Bridging the distances between culturally diverse families and schools.* New York: Teachers College Press.

Valdes, X. (1992). The women's rural school: An empowering educational experience. In N. Stomquist (Ed.), *Women and education in Latin America: Knowledge, power, and change* (pp. 277–302). Boulder: Lynne Rienner.

Vasquez, O., Pease-Alvarez, L., & Shannon, S. (1994). *Pushing boundaries: Language and culture in a Mexicano community.* New York: Cambridge University Press.

Vélez Ibáñez, C., & Greenberg, J. (1992). Formation and transformation of funds of knowledge among U.S.-Mexican households. *Anthropology and Education Quarterly,* 23(4), 313–335.

Villenas, S. (1996). Colonizer/colonized Chicana ethnographer: Identity marginalization, and co-optation in the field. *Harvard Educational Review,* 66(4), 711–731.

Villenas, S. (2001). Latina mothers and small town racism: Constructing narratives of dignity and moral education in North Carolina. *Anthropology and Education Quarterly.*

Villenas, S., & Moreno, M. (this issue). To valerse por si misma: Between race, capitalism, and patriarchy—Latina mother/daughter pedagogies in North Carolina. *International Qualitative Studies in Education,* 16(5).

Walker, A. (1983). *In search of our mothers' gardens: Womanist prose.* New York: Harcourt Brace.

Young, E., & Padilla, M. (1990). Mujeres unidas en acción: A popular education process. *Harvard Educational Review,* 60(1), 1–17.

13

Education

Giving Voice: An Inclusive Model of Instruction—
A Womanist Perspective (1994)

VANESSA SHEARED

> Be the best! If you are a thief, be the best one that you can be. If you are
> a doctor, be the best.
>
> **—Ms. Jones, seventh-grade teacher**

These words are ingrained in my memory. To the ordinary reader, they might
not mean very much, but to that seventh grader who heard these words, the
meaning was quite clear. For me growing up in one of the many varied communities on the south side of Chicago, these words reflected the reality of the
many faces and voices in that classroom. This teacher knew that some children would go on to become teachers, lawyers, doctors, and entrepreneurs.
And she knew that others would live their lives in constant retreat from the
law. She understood their differing worlds and realities, and she interpreted
and reflected these realities in the words that she spoke.

As adult educators, we do not always get an opportunity to encourage our
students to become the best that they can be. Their worlds, ideas, perceptions,
and values have already been molded, perhaps by someone like the teacher
whom I encountered at the impressionable age of twelve. So what is the role
of the adult educator? Is it to continue to mold the worlds of students? Or are
we to become instruments through which our students begin to reflect on the
multiple and varied realities that they, like we, bring to the classroom? And if
the latter is the case, then through what means must we instruct them?

Educators in general and adult educators in particular are becoming increasingly concerned by the question, How are we to deliver course content in such
a way that classroom discourse acknowledges all voices—the multiple ways
in which people interpret and reflect their understandings of the world? Multiculturalism, Africentrism,[1] bilingualism, feminism, womanism, perspective
transformation, critical consciousness, cooperative learning are just some of
the methods and theoretical constructs that adult educators have explored or

269

are currently exploring and implementing (Colin and Preciphs, 1991; Freire, 1970; Hayes, 1989; Mezirow, 1978; Ross-Gordon, 1991). Each of these methods and constructs reflects an attempt to give voice to political, economic, and social life stories, experiences, cultures, and histories that have been excluded from the educational mainstream.

This chapter has three goals: to introduce the womanist critique into the discourse on gender and race in adult education, to challenge adult educators to incorporate polyrhythmic realities into their instructional practices, and to define the role and purpose of education by offering a womanist instructional methodology intended to give voice to those whom traditional and unidimensional methods of instruction have silenced.

The womanist methodology acknowledges the ways in which the polyrhythmic realities (Barkley-Brown, 1990) of the instructor and students help to shape the learning environment. These polyrhythmic realities either limit or increase the individual's ability to engage in critical reflective learning at a given moment in time. The concept of polyrhythmic reality reflects the belief that individuals do not just have multiple realities and distinct understandings of them. Instead, individuals experience intersecting realities simultaneously—their realities are polyrhythmic. This concept represents a radical departure from Western, linear notions of the world and reality. Polyrhythms are characteristic of the aesthetic sense as reflected in African American art, music, and dance, as well as language. Barkley-Brown (1988, pp. 11–12) describes this aesthetic in African American quilts as "creating the impression of several patterns moving in different directions or multiple rhythms within the context of a controlled design. ... The symmetry in African-American quilts does not come from uniformity as it does in Euro-American quilts; rather, the symmetry comes through the diversity." Applying the concept to individuals, she suggests the importance of recognizing that "people and actions do move in multiple directions at once. If we analyze these people and actions by linear models, we will create dichotomies, ambiguities, cognitive dissonance, disorientation, and confusion in places where none exist" (Barkley-Brown, 1988, pp. 17–18).

This concept is analogous to the womanist perspective proposed by Walker (1983). The womanist perspective seeks to expose the differences and similarities that human beings experience in the classroom as a result of skin color, language, economic status, and personal experiences. These experiences are relevant to individuals' social, cultural, political, and historical understanding of themselves in relation to others. According to Williams (1990, p. 70), use of the term *womanist* represents a "commitment to the survival and wholeness of entire people—men and women." I believe that the womanist perspective is more inclusive and that it challenges us to think critically about such issues as racism, sexism, language, religious orientation, and sexual orientation. More important, its aim is to reinterpret the word—the ways in which we read, hear, and ultimately speak and listen to one another. This perspective, along with its corresponding relationship to giving voice, will be discussed more fully in this chapter. The discussion that follows is intended to be in relevant for all practitioners in adult education programs, whether they work in adult literacy classes, adult graduate programs, or training programs. The terms *Africentric feminist* and *womanist* are used interchangeably throughout this discussion.

Silencing of Others

Since the 1960s, historians, educators, political activists, and others have raised concerns that the contributions of women, African Americans, and other groups to the historical, economical, and political development of the United States are invisible. Studies on gender and race have shown that the exclusion of these groups from written texts has silenced their voices. While the primary locus has been on the silencing by the dominant culture of others' voices in written texts, concerns also have been raised about the silencing of voices in public speaking.

The Africentric feminist perspective is not just about the voices that have been silenced on the grounds of race or gender but instead considers the simultaneous effects of race and gender (Collins, 1990). While both Africentric and feminist scholars discuss the silencing of voices and marginalization, Africentric feminist scholars suggest that Africentric scholars and feminist scholars fail to address both gender and race as a unifying whole (Collins, 1991; hooks, 1984). As a result, the black woman's voice, as well as other marginalized voices, has been silenced. Wallace (1990, p. 70) asserts that "there is no question ... that the unrelenting logic of dualism or polar opposition, such as black and white, good and evil, male and female, is basic to the discourse of the dominant culture and tends to automatically erase black female subjectivity." Thus, black women's issues become secondary to the dominant discourse on race, gender, and class.

The Womanist Perspective

The womanist perspective acknowledges the intertwining realities that human beings experience within society. Race, gender, and class are interwoven. The relationship between race, gender, class, and the womanist perspective can best be illustrated with a triangle. Race, gender, and class are intersecting lines of reality, and the womanist perspective views these realities from within the triangle. The womanist perspective is grounded in the African American woman's marginalized status in relation to race, gender, and class.

Although her experiences are grounded in this experience, her reality is shaped by others. The womanist perspective is born of a direct response to the exclusion of the African American woman's voice from the discourse on race, gender, and class. Many European American feminist scholars as well as scholars engaged in the discourse on race would say that, when they speak on issues related to women or race, they include the voice of the African American woman. However, African American feminist scholars do not believe this to be true (Collins, 1990; Dill, 1990; King, 1990).

Some African American women scholars use the term *feminist,* while others use the term *womanist.* Many have used the term *womanist* to reflect an understanding of race, gender, and class that is grounded in "a commitment to the survival and wholeness of entire people—men and women—as well as to a valorization of women's works in all their varieties and multitudes" (Williams, 1990, p. 70). People's race, gender, ethnicity, sexual preference, and religious orientation must be acknowledged and examined for individuals to be recognized in their fullness as interconnected human beings.

"Black women," as opposed to "blacks and women," is used by Africentric feminist scholars to indicate that African American women are not "both/or" but rather "both/and." King (cited by Collins, 1990, p. 309) has described the both/and orientation as "the act of being simultaneously a member of a group and yet standing apart from it." The experience of African American women has been further described as the other of the other (Wallace, 1990). According to this perspective, African American women's voices have been silenced because the discourse on race and gender has negated their significance. It excludes their unique experiences in favor of the larger good (Sheared, 1992).

A both/and nondichotomous relationship represents the wholeness and the connectedness of entire people. It does not tear them apart. It is grounded in an understanding of what King (1990) describes as a double or multiple consciousness that develops as a result of the multiple jeopardies that women and blacks have experienced historically, socially, and economically. The womanist perspective shapes the both/and reality into a connected polyrhythmic whole. We no longer see ourselves as separate beings but as communal spirits. We are more than black and woman. We are black women connected to all brothers and sisters engaged in the struggle against oppression based on race, gender, and class.

A Womanist Perspective on Adult Education

Many marginalized or underrepresented adult students enrolled in adult education classes confront the experience that King (1990) describes as both/or and Wallace (1990) as the other of the other—that is, the individual's voice is negated as the result of being grouped with others on the basis of similarities in race and gender. Each student brings a set of experiences to the learning environment that reflects his or her status at work and at home and within his or her family, his or her relative positions in time (history), and his or her understandings of these factors. Polyrhythmic reality reflects the wholeness, the uniqueness, and—most important—the connectedness of individuals to others in society, their both/and realities.

Barkley-Brown (1990) has described quilting by African American women as analogous to what occurs between teachers and students in the classroom. It is useful in helping us to understand the relationship of instruction to both/ and reality. First, the designs used in these quilts are not necessarily symmetrically organized. Instead, the quilting reflects an aesthetic understanding by the makers of what the quilt represents for them in their everyday experience. For instance, pieces of cloth from old family clothes and heirlooms are used to represent an interconnectedness that goes beyond the confines of geometrically correct forms. The shape of the quilt results from the meanings that individual quilters give to the pieces that compose it. Barkley-Brown (1990) uses the Creole term *gumbo ya ya*—everybody talking at once—to describe this art form.

African American women's quilting and gumbo ya ya can be used to describe what Barkley-Brown (1990) calls the polyrhythmic way of understanding. In other words, rather than espousing one uniform center or reality, the student and the teacher embrace multiple or dualistic realities. The teacher must decenter or disempower himself or herself in order to empower the students. The teacher allows students to seek and interpret their world and their words in a political, social, historical, and economic context. The self is understood in relation to its connectedness with others and their perceptions of reality. The process is a communal experience.

Our goal as adult educators is to find ways in which we can uncover and acknowledge the voice of each student; to recognize that we, like our students, bring polyrhythmic realities to the learning environment; to find ways of disempowering ourselves in the learning environment so that students begin to take responsibility for their learning; and to understand that the information we proffer is grounded in a political, social, historical, sexual, racial, and economical context that is unique to us (in other words, we recognize that our subjective understandings of the world are different yet interconnected).

How is this learning environment created? The next section describes a process that adult educators can use to create a learning environment that meets the goals just outlined.

Giving Voice

As noted earlier, giving voice has become an aim of those who seek to provide students and educators with an opportunity to become engaged in a critically reflective dialogue regardless of the subject matter. This aim is based on the proposition that all knowledge is grounded in a social, political, economic, and historical context. To give voice requires us to acknowledge different realities and understand that there are different ways of interpreting reality. "Voice is related to the means whereby teachers and students attempt to make themselves present in history and to define themselves as active authors of their own worlds" (Weiler, 1989, p. xiii). According to this author, it "represents those multiple subjectivities, discourses, and biographies that constitute teachers and students alike within relations of power, history, and experience" (Weiler, 1989, p. xiii). Giroux and McLaren (1986, p. 235) state that the "concept of voice constitutes the focal point for a theory of teaching and learning ... as well as new and challenging ways of confronting and engaging in everyday life." Voice is the active engagement of students and teachers in dialogue with one another. Both are heard and "define themselves as active authors of their worlds ... it is the unique instance of self-expression through which students affirm their own class, cultural, racial, and gender identities" (Giroux and McLaren, 1986, p. 235).

Quite simply, giving voice allows students and teachers to engage and disengage in polyrhythmic realities. Giroux and McLaren (1986, p. 235) concluded that voice is not static but rather used "to make ourselves understood and listened to and to define ourselves as active participants in the world." An Africentric feminist analysis acknowledges voice in the contextual framework of social class, historical and political hegemony, and its relationship with gender and racial oppression. It recognizes but does not negate the realities of both the oppressed and the oppressor, the learned and the learner.

My research (Sheared, 1992) incorporates the Africentric feminist epistemology (Collins, 1990, 1991) because it clearly communicates the oppositional worldview that was essential to understanding the educational, political, and social realities of African American women receiving public assistance. The Africentric feminist epistemology diminishes the negative effects of what King (1990) describes as multiple consciousness and the both/or orientation. It supports Dill's (1990) dialectics of black womanhood and Wallace's (1990) other of the other. The Africentric episteme allows the stories of African American women to be told in ways that do not tear apart or objectify their lives. It also does not obfuscate or mystify the words that they use to interpret and understand the word and the world.

Collins (1990, 1991) depicts the Africentric epistemology as a method that Africentric scholars can use to uncover and describe knowledge produced within the African diaspora. I believe that adult educators can use the following process to reach the goal of giving voice to the many realities that students bring to the learning environment. The process is grounded in two epistemological and two axiological assumptions.

Concrete experience is used as a criterion of meaning. This assumption acknowledges that there is more than one way of knowing. Both knowledge and wisdom are important. Knowledge is grounded in the individual's race, gender and class. Knowledge consists of one's everyday lived experiences and understandings of that reality in terms of dominance and authority. In contrast, wisdom is what one uses to read, interpret, and speak in order to survive, given the information that one receives.

Collins (1990) concludes that the narrative method is one way of uncovering the criterion of meaning. An individual's words tell her or his story and are narrated either in print or by voice. The story is "not torn apart in analysis, and trusted as core belief, not admired as science" (Collins, 1990, p. 312). Students are given an opportunity to read and listen to the words that they use to describe a particular event or a skill that they use to accomplish a particular task. Ultimately, the way in which students read and interpret the symbols used to communicate information must change. They must act on that information in the class, on the job, or in their personal life.

For example, math learning for literacy students can be enhanced if students talk about the mathematical skills that they use in their everyday lives. These skills can include measuring ingredients for cooking and determining the distance between point A and point B or the time that it takes to prepare and cook a certain dish. These skills can be incorporated into a lesson on counting, addition, or subtraction skills. Discussion of these concepts in relationship to everyday examples enables the teacher and others in the class to introduce ways in which numbers and simple mathematical processes affect us in a political, social, economical, and historical context. For example, questions can be asked about the ways in which escalating costs have affected people's ability to prepare certain meals. How do they affect the learner and his or her ability to purchase ingredients? What can the learner do or what has the learner done to change his or her ability to purchase the products needed? This is just one example of the way in which individuals' concrete frame of reference can be used either to teach new skills or to show learners that they already have the power or information necessary to create change within their own environment.

Dialogue is the basis for assessing knowledge claims. A primary epistemological assumption is that connectedness rather than separation is essential to the knowledge validation process. Collins (1990, p. 317) concludes that the use of dialogue for African American women might be a way of "invoking a particular female way of knowing." Belenky, Clinchy, Goldberger, and Tarule (1986) list several ways in which women construct their realities about truth, knowledge, and authority. They conclude that women proceed through several stages as they move from silence to an ability to construct knowledge. They contend that these stages illustrate that women move from a position of total subordination to one in which they share equal voice, or connectedness, in the decisions and choices that they make. Dialoguing gives students an opportunity to challenge the knowledge constructed by others. In so doing, they apply their own understanding to determine what needs to be done.

As students dialogue with one another, they begin to explore alternative ways of viewing the world. More important, they begin to voice their understanding of the ways in which they have learned to operate within the world. If we return to the example just used, math students begin to see how the mathematical skills that they have used affect their lives while at the same time learning new ways of using skills to create changes in their lives.

An ethic of caring emphasizes the uniqueness of individuals, elicits appropriate emotion from the dialogue, and recognizes empathetic understanding. The three elements of an ethic of caring permeate African American culture. One example is the call-and-response discourse that many African American preachers have used in churches. The minister is responsible for pointing out principles from the Bible in a way that evokes a response of understanding from the congregation. Both the affective and the cognitive domains are involved. The process goes beyond simple questions and answers to questions that invoke complex responses. Moreover, the preacher shares a part of himself with the congregation. He must be willing to listen to its responses, react, and then follow up with responses that suggest he understands them as well as they understand him. In other words, the minister and the congregation talk back and forth to each other. It represents an interconnectedness based on an understanding of the meanings that they each have of what they hear and observe in that moment.

For educators, an ethic of caring creates an environment in which participants come to an interconnected state of being through call and response. The question and the answer determine the level of trust and caring that is necessary if learning is to occur.

An ethic of personal accountability guides both teaching and learning. Not only must individuals develop their knowledge claims through dialogue, but they must present these claims in a style proving their concern for their ideas. People are held accountable for what they want to learn. The teacher is accountable for structuring the learning experience and enabling the students. In other words, the responsibility for learning is not just the domain of the teacher but of the learner as well.

I used this method in a course titled "Educating Disadvantaged Adults." In one activity, students were asked to rethink the title of the course in relationship to the materials that they read (the narration) and the discourse that had occurred in class (the dialogue). Each student was responsible for rethinking and renaming the course. Students worked individually and in groups to uncover their own biases and the impact that these had on the ways they thought and taught those whom they considered to be disadvantaged. At the end of the course, each student presented his or her title to the entire group. Students were given an opportunity to question and respond to the ideas presented.

At the end of the course, students acknowledged that they had changed their opinions about who the disadvantaged were. They also stated that they had begun to change the way in which they taught them—because they no longer saw them as beings outside and unconnected to who they were. No longer did my students dichotomize *us* and *them*. It became *we* as the term *disadvantaged* became relative. It helped them to gain an understanding of their political, economical, social, and historical being and its connectedness to their race, gender, and class status. Change had occurred not only in students' thought but in their proposed behavior.

Conclusion

Although the womanist method helps us to understand and grapple with our polyrhythmic realities, it is in no way meant to be the only method that educators use to help their students activate their voices in the confines of formal and informal educational settings. To limit ourselves to one methodological paradigm risks silencing those to whom we hope to give voice. As long as we couch issues in the terms of a black cause or white woman's cause, we maintain the risk of negating black women as well as others. In other words, the womanist perspective must be placed in a context that allows voices to be heard and specific content information to be learned. Alternative instructional methods need to note this caveat: "Feminist readings can lead to misapprehensions of particular or even of a whole tradition, but certain of its formulations offer us a vocabulary that can be meaningful in terms of our own experience, Feminist theory ... offers us not only the possibility of changing one's reading of the world but of changing the world itself" (Wallace, 1990, p. 68).

The womanist perspective is aimed at aiding the instructional process, not at becoming the content. Giving voice acknowledges that there are multiple ways of presenting and interpreting information and knowledge. This then means that one accepts and celebrates the polyrhythmic realities of both the student and the teacher in the learning environment.

As a final recommendation, before any adult educator initiates a particular method or model, she or he should engage in the following call and response activity. I have provided some suggested responses, but your own may vary.

CALL: What is my role and goal as an adult educator?

RESPONSE: I believe that my role and my goal as an adult educator is to help students reflect on the multiple realities of gender, race, and class and their relationship to history, socioeconomics, and politics. More important, I should seek not only to uncover discrepancies and injustices within our educational process, but I must seek to help create environments for change.

CALL: Should my role be primarily to shape and mold the worlds of students, or should I become an instrument through which students begin to reflect on the polyrhythmic realities that they and I bring to the classroom environment?

RESPONSE: I am not here to shape or mold my students' thinking, but I am here to be used as a vessel to help students uncover the polyrhythmic realities that they and I possess in the learning environment.

CALL: Through what means must I instruct them?

RESPONSE: I must learn to give voice to my students. Giving voice occurs as a result of me decentering and centering self along with my students. Together we develop new meanings, understandings, and ways of thinking about the world and the word. In other words "we must pivot" the center in order to center in another's experience (Aptheker, 1989; Barkley-Brown, 1990). The dignity and rights of all—men and women—must be valued through the way we teach, speak, and interact with one another.

If your responses are similar to the ones shown here, then you should review readings and materials aimed at giving voice to your students. Some of the references used in this chapter can help you to begin this process.

Note

1. The use of *Africentrism* rather than the more common *Afrocentrism* is explained [in the original source, ed.].

References

Aptheker, B. *Tapestries of Life.* Amherst: University of Massachusetts Press, 1989.

Barkley-Brown, E. "African American Women's Quilting: A Framework for Conceptualizing and Teaching African American Women's History." In M. Malson, E. Mudimbe-Boyi, J. O'Barr, and M. Wyer (eds.), *Black Women in America: Social Science Perspectives.* Chicago: University of Chicago Press, 1990.

Belenky, M., Clinchy, B., Goldberger, N.R., and Tarule, J.M. *Women's Ways of Knowing: The Development of Self, Voice, and Mind.* New York: Basic Books, 1986.

Colin, S.A.J., III, and Preciphs, T.K. "Perceptual Patterns and the Learning Environment: Confronting White Racism." In R. Hiemstra (ed.), *Creating Environments for Effective Adult Learning.* New Directions for Adult and Continuing Education, no. 50. San Francisco: Jossey-Bass, 1991.

Collins, P.H. "The Social Construction of Black Feminist Thought." In M. Malson, E. Mudimbe-Boyi, J. O'Barr, and M. Wyer (eds.), *Black Women in America: Social Science Perspectives.* Chicago: University of Chicago Press, 1990.

Collins, P.H. *Black Feminist Thought.* New York: Routledge, 1991.

Dill, B.T. "The Dialectics of Black Womanhood." In M. Malson, E. Mudimbe-Boyi, J. O'Barr, and M. Wyer (eds.), *Black Women in America: Social Science Perspectives.* Chicago: University of Chicago Press, 1990.

Freire, P. *Pedagogy of the Oppressed.* New York: Herder and Herder, 1970.

Giroux, H.A., and McLaren, P. "Teacher Education and the Politics of Engagement: The Case for Democratic Schooling." *Harvard Educational Review,* 1986, 56(3), 213–238.

Hayes, E. "Insights from Women's Experiences for Teaching and Learning." In E. Hayes (ed.), *Effective Teaching Styles.* New Directions for Continuing Education, no. 43. San Francisco: Jossey-Bass, 1989.

hooks, b. *From Margin to Center.* Boston: South End Press, 1984.

King, D.K. "Multiple Jeopardy, Multiple Consciousness. The Context of Black Feminist Ideology." In M. Malson, E. Mudimbe Boyi, J. O'Barr, and M. Wyer (eds.), *Black Women in America: Social Science Perspectives.* Chicago: University of Chicago Press, 1990.

Mezirow, J. "Perspective Transformation," *Adult Education,* 1978, 18(2), 100–110.

Ross-Gordon, J.M. "Needed: A Multicultural Perspective for Adult Education Research." *Adult Education Quarterly*, 1991, 42(1), 1–16.

Sheared, V. "From Workfare to Edfare: African American Women and the Elusive Quest for Self-Determination." Unpublished doctoral dissertation, Department of Leadership and Educational Policy Studies, Northern Illinois University, 1992.

Walker, A. *In Search of Our Mothers' Gardens*. San Diego, Calif.: Harcourt Brace Jovanovich, 1983.

Wallace, M. "Variations on Negation and the Heresy of Black Feminist Creativity." In H. Gates (ed.), *Reading Black, Reading Feminist: A Critical Anthology*. New York: Meridian Books, 1990.

Weiler, K. *Women Teaching for Change (Gender, Class, and Power)*. Boston: Bergin and Garvey, 1989.

Williams, S.A. "Some Implications of Womanist Theory." In H. Gates (ed.), *Reading Black, Reading Feminist: A Critical Anthology*. New York: Meridian Books, 1990.

A Womanist Experience of Caring: Understanding the Pedagogy of Exemplary Black Women Teachers (2002)

TAMARA BEAUBOEUF-LAFONTANT

Over the last 15 years, educational researchers and theorists have decried the lack of caring in our schools (Grumet, 1988; Noddings, 1984; Valenzuela, 1999). As researchers have sought to address this problem, they have called for teachers to transform themselves into adults who can relate to and thus more effectively teach all children in our schools (e.g., Bartolome, 1994; Cochran-Smith, 1995; Delpit, 1995; Nieto, 1999). Amidst these calls for teacher transformation have been examples of the types of teachers who are effective. Striking about such portrayals is that a number of these exemplars are black women, which I believe is more than coincidence. I believe that researchers have come across a womanist tradition of caring that extends throughout the history of African-American women.

Womanism

Womanism is a standpoint epistemology (Collins, 1991). It is derived from Alice Walker's (1983) term *womanist* and is used generally to represent the cultural, historical, and political positionality of African-American women, a group that has experienced slavery, segregation, sexism, and classism for most of its history in the United States. Used interchangeably with *black feminism,* it is a theoretical perspective that sees the experiences of black women as normative, not as a derivation or variation of black male or white female behavior (Collins, 1991). Womanists recognize that because so many black women have experienced the convergence of racism, sexism, and classism, they often have a particular vantage point on what constitutes evidence (Collins, 1991), valid action (Welch, 1990), and morality (Cannon, 1995). Three central points support womanism. First, womanists understand that oppression is an interlocking system, providing all people with varying degrees of penalty and privilege. Second, they believe that individual empowerment combined with collective action is key to lasting social transformation. Last, they embody a humanism, which seeks the liberation of all, not simply themselves (Collins, and Tamarkin 1990/1982). Given that womanism seeks to elucidate the experiences, thoughts, and behaviors of black women, in order to understand the caring demonstrated by African-American women teachers, it is critical that we contextualize their thoughts and actions within their particular cultural and historical legacies. In doing so, three characteristics are noteworthy: the embrace of the maternal, political clarity, and an ethic of risk.

Embrace of the Maternal

In both lay and academic analyses of exemplary teachers committed to social justice, the maternal image is particularly visible in the pedagogy of African-American women teachers. A public example of such teaching is that of Marva Collins, the founder of the renowned Westside Preparatory School in Chicago. Over the last 25 years, Collins has drawn out "extraordinary" capabilities from her students, who are "at risk" for school and social failure because they are poor African-American children living in the neighboring housing projects. While her successes are clearly significant and have garnered the attention of many Americans wanting to see improvements in our public schools, notable about her work is the maternal sensibility she brings to her pedagogy. As the jacket of her book, *"Ordinary" Children, Extraordinary Teachers* (1992), reads:

> Marva Collins embodies all that is meant by that hallowed word … teacher. She gives of herself tirelessly so that those whose minds are supple may grasp knowledge and power through her love. Indeed love, like that of a mother for her children, is the essence of the Marva Collins Way … love of learning, love of leaching, and love of sharing.

Such a connection with a maternal form of caring is also evident in Collins's own descriptions of her work. Reflecting on her frustration with the public school she left to begin her own academy, Collins explicitly connects her teaching visions to her sensibilities as a mother:

> The search for a school for my own three children opened my eyes: the public schools had no monopoly on poor education. … What was once the poor man's burden had become everyone's.
>
> With this came another realization, that I couldn't escape the problem, as a teacher or as a mother. These parts of my life were inextricably interwoven; at Delano I was fighting for the kind of education I wanted for my own children. As a parent I tended to be protective, and I always felt that same driving concern as a teacher. I could never walk out of Delano at 3:15 and leave the school and the students entirely behind me. Were my students going home or would they wander the streets? Were their clothes warm enough? Would their stomachs be full tonight and would they have sheets on their beds? (Collins and Tamarkin, 1990/ 1982, p. 73)

Collins views her inability not to mother her students as a matter of fact, and as an emotional strength rather than as a weakness. If anything, her parenting experiences as a mother seem to have informed her teaching so that she has brought the same standards of care and accountability to her students as she would to her own children. "If the school was going to be good enough for other children, it had to be good enough for my own," she reasoned (Collins and Tamarkin, 1990/1982, p. 80). As a public school teacher, caring like a mother focused her decision to take maternal steps, that is, to create a structure in which she could educate and shelter her students/children from adversity. Indeed, in the Ten Teaching Commandments that she has developed for her own faculty, the first reads, "Thou shalt love thy students as you would love your own children" (Collins, 1992, p. 178).

Such a maternal caring for students is also a central theme of a *People* magazine article entitled "Momma Knows Best." Affectionately called "Momma Hawk" by her middle-school students, Corla Hawkins is another Chicago teacher. Like Collins, Hawk began her own school, Recovering the Gifted Child Academy, after seeing too many poor children systematically failed by the public schools. For Hawkins, her teaching very clearly emanates from a vocation to extend herself to those children who needed her most:

> I felt I could take the dysfunctional family structure these children were used to and replace it with a new family structure that stresses success, personal achievement and self-esteem. ... God gave me a dream—to take care of children of rejection. I literally saw myself going around the world hugging and loving children nobody else wanted. (Valente, 1996, pp. 45, 47)

Describing Momma Hawk, a board member of the school says, "Corla is so successful because she is so human. ... She's not on a pedestal. She feels things deeply. She hurts" (Valente, 1996, p. 46). At the same time, however, such emotional connection with her students does not preclude Hawkins from "run[ning] my school based on a corporate model" (p. 46), complete with a time clock and strict discipline.

As educator Lisa Delpit (1995) and others have described, schools too often replay the racial and economic biases of the larger society. Distinctions, both overt and subtle, abound between majority member students ("our children") and children from minority groups ("other people's children"). Drawing attention to this split, Delpit identifies educational reform as centrally concerning our identities and relationships as educators:

> The teachers, the psychologists, the school administrators ... look at "other people's children" and see damaged and dangerous caricatures of the vulnerable and impressionable beings before them. ... What are we really doing to better educate poor children and children of color? ... What should we be doing? The answers, I believe, lie not in a proliferation of new reform programs but in some basic understandings of who we are and how we are connected to and disconnected from one another. (Delpit, 1995, pp. xiii, xiv, xv)

If school failure is a result of a "relational breakdown" (Ward, 1995) between teachers and students, where both groups see little in common or shared in purpose, then the academic success of poor, immigrant, and minority children lies very much in the quality of the relationships that their teachers establish with them.

Exemplary African-American women teachers use the familiar and familial mother–child relationship as a guide for their interactions with students. As Kathe Jervis (1996) concludes in her article about an innovative public school:

> For such a promise of personalized schools to be fulfilled, faculties have to adopt Carrie's [an African-American teacher's] attitude about children. She often says, "When I am in a quandary about how to handle a child, I think, 'What would I do if that child were my child?' and 'How would I want that child handled were my son or daughter in that situation?' " Parents have an urgency about their own children. We need to feel the same urgency when we teach other people's children. (p. 570)

However, to have such an urgency about children is to recognize that teachers may be failing precisely those students considered to be failures. As Momma Hawk notes, when a student is disruptive, "the teacher's first reaction is to get him out of the class instead of saying maybe this child doesn't have anybody" (Valente, 1996, p. 44). Too often, in her opinion, teachers lacking a parental urgency take the easy, nonfamilial/nonmaternal way out of difficult situations.

As insightful and active as the maternal connection to students appears among womanist teachers, not all women adopt it in their pedagogy. Kathleen Casey's (1990, 1993) phenomenological study of teaching and women-identified values perhaps best illuminates the differences in caring among women. Investigating the role of such values in the work of socially progressive Jewish, Catholic, and African-American teachers, Casey (1990) found that many of these women had a desire to "deconstruct the maternal." Both the secular Jewish women and the Catholic nuns interviewed saw schools as sites of the patriarchal domination closely resembling traditional middle-class families. In these families, maintains Casey, there is a pattern of "maternal nurture and paternal authority" (p. 307). Significantly, neither group of teachers had experienced this stereotypical family pattern in their own upbringing. However, both the Jewish and Catholic teachers felt that the only concept of mother that they could manifest in the classroom was that prescribed by the school culture: "mother" as an agent of the patriarchal domination of women and children. As a result, they sought to assert an identity in the classroom that challenged such a conception of teacher as mother.

In a very real manner, these educators were trapped in a mainstream, patriarchal notion of teaching. Significantly, they did not call on the ennobling models of women as mothers from their personal lives and use these to resist the patriarchal expectations of women. Rather, as they decried hierarchical gender distinctions, the Jewish teachers resented the gender stereotyping within schools and thought of teaching "in terms of intellectual challenge and political efficacy" (p. 305), not in terms of making school family-like. Similarly, in their criticism of school patriarchy, the Catholic nuns portrayed themselves as the sisterly allies of students. In other words, for both groups of these women educators, commitments to social justice hinged on their reworking of their professional relationships, as women, to both children/students and men/administrators. Casey's (1990) interviews with older white teachers who taught before and after raising their own children led her to conclude that "since the maternal relationship can leave a woman in our society so materially and psychologically vulnerable, it is no wonder that so many look for another metaphor to describe their connections with children" (p. 313).

The black women teachers in Casey's study, however, did not evidence a domesticated view of womanhood or mothering in their reflections on their educational philosophies and practice. Within their cultural construction of womanhood, they profoundly embraced a maternal image. Based on their lives and experiences outside the classroom, the maternal served as a relational compass for their teaching. Like the Jewish teachers and Catholic nuns, these educators did not accept the definition of "mother" found in the schools and in society. However, unlike their colleagues, the African-American women did not rely on the school's appropriation of the maternal to circumscribe their own desire to relate to students in a familiar, maternal way. In fact, these teachers saw their maternal qualities and the mother–child relationship as *central* to their resistance to domination, both patriarchal and racial. As Casey (1990) clarifies the black teachers' maternal orientation to students:

> The relationship between mother and child is not exclusive and private, but is part of the wider family which is one's "people." … Because of the social context out of which this understanding has been constructed, the maternal is not seen as an individual burden, but as reciprocity among members of the group. Whatever nurture these teachers provide, it comes back to them; as one teacher says about her students, "they love your very soul." (p. 316)

Rather than envision mothering primarily in terms of women's individual relationships with men and children (as Casey reports the Jewish and Catholic teachers doing), the African-American teachers regarded mothering broadly as a communal responsibility. Casey (1990) explains, "The definition of nurture which is presented in the narratives of these Black women teachers is inclusive in several senses: it is not limited to women, it is expressive of relationship within community and it is not separate from the exercise of authority. An exceedingly powerful version of nurture emerges from this particular social context" (p. 317).

Racism and the collective struggle against injustice comprise the particular social context of which Casey speaks. The black women teachers were raised in households in which their identity as African-Americans, as people treated as second-class citizens in a democracy, was discussed. Furthermore, in conceptualizing their own agency, these black women did not believe that their view of maternal responsibility implicated them in a patriarchal family structure. Drawing on the cultural norms of West Africa and the oppressive realities that people of African descent have faced in this country, these women viewed the maternal as a profound commitment to the well-being and survival of black children and black people. The maternal lens they brought to their practice powerfully connected their personal relationships with students to an active engagement with social reality.

Several recent studies have suggested a similar cultural connection between the pedagogy of culturally relevant black teachers and a concept of the maternal in their practice (Case, 1997; Delpit, 1995; Foster, 1993). For example, Michele Foster (1993) maintains that the use of kin terms among black women teachers as "mothers, aunts, and grandmothers" toward their students is a long-standing practice within black communities. In this tradition, teachers often see themselves as "othermothers" or women who, through feelings of shared responsibility, commit themselves to the social and emotional development of all children in a community (Collins, 1991). "Othermothering" has also been described as a "universalized ethic of care" or a "collective social conscience" (Case, 1997, pp. 26, 36) in which the caring that othermothers engage in is not simply interpersonal but profoundly political in intent and practice. Explains Patricia Hill Collins (1991):

> By seeing the larger community as responsible for children and by giving other-mothers and other nonparents "rights" in child rearing, African-Americans challenge prevailing property relations. It is in this sense that traditional bloodmother/other-mother relationships in women-centered networks are "revolutionary." (p. 123)

This concept of othermothering is germane to education because teaching in the African-American community, as in other ethnic groups, has been dominated by women since the turn of the 20th century. However, the profound relational capacities of womanist teachers are vitally connected to another dimension—their identity as political beings who make constant parallels between schooling and society, school practices and social reality. Thus, as the traditions of caring in which black women have been involved have had an explicit focus on helping other women and their children survive the degradations of physical, economic, and political enslavement (Collins, 1991), so has womanism provided an interpersonal base for social action in education.

Political Clarity

Political clarity is the recognition by teachers that there are relationships between schools and society that differentially structure the successes and failures of groups of children (Bartolome, 1994). Womanist teachers see racism and other systemic injustices as simultaneously social *and* educational problems. Consequently, they demonstrate a keen awareness of their power and responsibility as adults to contest the societal stereotypes imposed on children.

The presence of political clarity among womanist teachers is a recurring theme in historical and autobiographical analyses of black segregated schools that were valued by their communities (Beauboeuf-Lafontant, 1999). In taking on the role of surrogate parents toward their students (Cecelski, 1994; Siddle-Walker, 1996), the teachers believed that they were both ethically and "ethnically responsible for preparing these youth for future leadership and for making contributions to this unique mission, namely the liberation and enhancement of the quality of life for Black people" (Adair, 1984; cited in Siddle-Walker, 1996, p. 206). Educators were exhorted to use their sense of collective responsibility to help the masses of their fellow African-Americans understand and act on their rights as citizens in a democracy (Higginbotham, 1992; Perkins, 1983).

As a result, their concern was for the "whole child," not simply their students' academic well-being. As Mamie Garvin Fields (1983) recalls from her lifetime of teaching in the segregated state of South Carolina:

> I taught the schoolchildren the same way I taught my sons, but not everybody approved. …
>
> My point always was that the "good manners" of some black people didn't help their black child to "come up in the world." Those manners kept us "in our place." They conditioned us in the Old South ways. So the next thing you know, that black child is grown up and calling white people "sir" and "ma'am." … For example, many teachers would say, "Don't bother the white people to get necessities for your school." Afraid, you see. My attitude was, "He's a man and speaks English. I will ask him." So the other teachers would send me to see Mr. Welch in his office. I became the spokesman. (p. 221)

Most black teachers during segregation had few illusions about their freedom and knew that, even as adults, they were considered inferior to all whites. Thus, for Mamie Fields to refuse to model subservience for all her children— those of her family as well as of her classroom—was to "teach against the grain" (Cochran-Smith, 1993) in a profoundly political manner. As she also says, "White people had so many ways to degrade the Negro. I always tried to oppose that" (Fields, 1983, p. 214). Thus, her caring and pedagogy were very much contextualized by and responsive to the needs of her students for someone who would value them and expect greatness of them, even if the larger society (and some of their other black teachers) did not. In the words of one former student of a segregated school, "Our teachers could see our potential even when we couldn't, and they were able to draw out our potential. They helped us imagine possibilities of life beyond what we knew" (Foster, 1997, p. 99).

In a similar way, Marva Collins emphasizes the promise of her students, finding something admirable about each child every day (Collins and Tamarkin, 1990/1982, p. 61). This habit is tied to her fundamental belief that

> a good teacher can always make a poor student good and a good student superior. The word *teacher* has its roots in the Latin word meaning *to lead* or *to draw out*. Good teachers draw out the best in every student; they are willing to polish and shine until the true luster of each student comes through. (p. 6; emphasis in original)

In "shining" her students, Collins also confronts them with social reality. In other words, she does not uncritically glorify children. Nor does she simply strive to make students feel good about themselves. The purpose of her teaching is much more political: to help them question reality along with her and to discuss its implications for them.

Because Collins's students are poor children from housing projects located in an urban ghetto, the social assumption (and perhaps desire) is that they will fail, both in school and in life. Rather than ignoring or minimizing the presence of derogatory stereotypes, Collins makes the political ramifications of their failures to learn clear to them:

> If you throw away your life, you're just letting society have its way. ... You know, boys and girls, there are some people who look at places like this, neighborhoods like Garfield Park, and they say, "Oh, children from there are not very smart. They aren't going to grow up to be anyone or do anything special." If you decide to waste your lives, you are letting all those people be right. No one can tell you what you will be. Only you have the power to decide for yourselves. (Collins and Tamarkin, 1990/ 1982, p. 85)

While Collins speaks of her children needing to make choices that have life-long implications, she also recognizes that they need guidance and sponsors, in their families as well as in their school:

> In this messed up world, the only children who are going to make something of themselves are those who come from strong parents or those who have had a strong teacher. One or the other. Or both. (Collins and Tamarkin, 1990/1982, p. 54)

As a result, Collins repeats to her students, "I am not going to give up on you. I am not going to let you give up on yourself" (Collins and Tamarkin, 1990/ 1982, p. 87).

Very significantly, Collins lays bare the political realities that her students, all elementary-aged, are experiencing. Such honesty about the stakes of getting an education, particularly when one is marginalized and oppressed by society, is not common practice in our schools, even at the secondary level (Fine, 1991). Teachers apparently fear that being truthful with minority children will demoralize them even further and seal their fate. Yet, from the perspective of these African-American teacher-mothers, to withhold knowledge *is* to disempower those children.

Politically clear womanist educators understand the necessity of seeing through stereotypes as false representations of children's realities and possibilities. As one communications teacher remarks:

> I teach you the way I perceive you to be. … [One of the problems I had with Teach for America] is that, you know, "White savior" type thing. Susie Bonnie Joe … is going into 125th, you know, and Adam Clayton Powell Boulevard, and teaching people who *look* nothing like her, people who are of a *totally* different economic class, and she's "taming the savages." But she sees them as savages. She's perpetuating [bitter chuckle] the very self-hatred and degradation that, I think, is characteristic of so many people who have been othered by our society. … So you've got to start with a base level of understanding these kids as *human beings.* We're all subject to the stereotypes of our society, and we can't assume that because we're well-intended [chuckle], we don't carry with us all of that. You know, that sheltering, "Don't teach them that history." Or, "Don't tell them that." Or, "I feel so sorry for you. I *expect* you to be poor. I know you only have one parent. Your mother probably doesn't know how to be a mother" [all said in a gentle, yet condescending voice]. Hey, you've got to help them see within their own situation the strength and the richness. (Beauboeuf, 1997, pp. 122–123)

Thus, womanist teachers readily demonstrate their political clarity: With their students, both in deed and in word, they share their understanding of society, an understanding that does not shy away from the reality of domination nor from the existence of resistance struggles against oppression. In essence, loving students means discussing such insights with them, not withholding knowledge from them. Audrey Thompson (1998) describes the cultural significance of such openness: "Caring in the Black family has had to be, in part, *about* the surrounding society, because it has had to provide children with the understanding and the strategies they need to survive racism. … [Thus] love and caring [in the womanist tradition] do not step back from the world in order to return to innocence, but step out into the world in order to change it" (p. 532; emphasis in original). Being a womanist educator entails more than simply having a professed love for children: A womanist educator loves children, especially those considered "other" in society, out of a clear-sighted understanding of how and why society marginalizes some children while embracing others.

While political clarity and a maternal sensibility are central to the everyday practice of womanist teachers, their overall investment in the teaching profession emerges from an ethical perspective of risk taking. It is this ethic of risk that provides such educators with the moral fortitude and vision to persevere in their fundamentally political and maternal form of caring.

An Ethic of Risk

A womanist engagement with oppressive realities occurs in spite of an educator's recognition that social injustice is deep-seated and not easily dismantled. Sharon Welch (1990), a white feminist theologian, has remarked on the "ethic of risk" she observed in the literature of noted black women authors, all of whom describe intergenerational struggles against injustice:

> Within an ethic of risk, actions begin with the recognition that far too much has been lost and there are no clear means of restitution. The fundamental risk constitutive of this ethic is the decision to care and to act although there are no guarantees of success. ... It is an ethos in sharp contrast to the ethos of cynicism that often accompanies a recognition of the depth and persistence of evil. (p. 68)

Thus, when Momma Hawk (Valente, 1996) speaks of her dream of "tak[ing] care of children of rejection" or of her belief that "every child is a gift from God and our job as teachers is to find the gift in each" (p. 44), she frames her teaching as a mission and sees herself as a child of God and as having the spiritual resources to undertake that mission. A similar belief in students and in oneself emanates from a high school English teacher's conviction that students "can be *great* achievers. It's so *much* in them, you know, but it takes a *skillful* teacher, it takes a skillful *woman* to draw it out" (Beauboeuf, 1997, p. 83). Or in the words of a junior high school communications educator, teaching becomes a process of "manifest[ing] the divinity within you":

> And that means for me ... I want to develop a *kindness* and a *love* and a *patience* ... [a] level of *understanding*, of *humility*, of *groundedness*, of *goodness*. ... I think that there's something really *spiritual* about being an educator, because I think the only reason to learn is to teach. (Beauboeuf, 1997, p. 126)

Because their ethic of risk is rooted in their sense of an existential interdependence, womanist educators recognize and accept "not that life is unfair, but that the creation of fairness is the task of generations, that work for justice is not incidental to one's life but is an essential aspect of affirming the delight and wonder of being alive" (Welch, 1990, p. 70).

While individuals have an ethic of risk, their commitments to working for social justice rest on a concept of self that is part of rather than apart from other people. From their embrace of an ethic of risk, womanist educators understand morality not in abstract principles but in personal, and specifically maternal, terms (Colby and Damon, 1992; Koonz, 1987). In other words, their capacity to act morally is based on "the ability to perceive people in their own terms and to respond to need" (Gilligan, 1986, p. 292). It is an intimacy with and not an aloofness from other people that motivates womanist educators to see personal fulfillment in working toward the common good.

From this sense of interdependence, womanist educators establish classroom routines that model such mutual responsibility. Such routines are well described by educational researcher George Noblit (1993) in his ethnography of the classroom dynamics of one African-American teacher, Pam. Noblit maintains that Pam created rituals with her second-grade students so that as they performed daily tasks—such as cleaning the board, sharpening pencils, and reading the calendar—they were "serv[ing] the collective good" (p. 29). Moreover, academically weak children were not left to themselves, and no one was ever singled out for praise at the cost of others. In her interactions with students who were unable to answer questions, Pam still held them responsible for acquiring academic skills; however, she allowed them to do so in a supportive environment filled with "a lot of coaching to get it right and a lot of room to figure it out for yourself" (p. 29). Even when asking a question and choosing one student to answer, Pam would try to include the whole class: She would "let the hands wave for a while—long enough to allow the maximum number of hands to raise … smile and make eye contact with all she could" (p. 33). And regardless of whether the answer given was correct, "she would connect for a brief moment with her eyes, words, humor, and attention" (p. 33). Instructive about Pam's teaching is how she acknowledged, but did not resign herself to, the "difficult" students and parents: "She could laugh at a lot of the tribulations of classroom life because neither the events nor her enjoyment of her students threatened her authority. In many ways, they constituted her moral authority" (Noblit, 1993, pp. 27, 28).

In emic discussions of African-American culture, such an assertion of the individual existing within a web of community and history is very common (Collins, 1991; Hord and Lee, 1995). Not only is the tie between the individual and the community a guiding cultural belief, but the conditions of slavery and continued oppression have heightened this interdependence as not simply a preferred existential state but a critical component of survival: "Black service providers and community activists alike have long recognized that their own destiny was inextricably linked to the destiny of other Blacks, and that in forging ties of mutual support, collective survival and racial progress would be achieved" (Ward, 1995, pp. 176–177). Significant about this concept of interdependence is its charge that "you *must* have some practical *purpose* and *benefit* to others and to self. You *must*" (Beauboeuf, 1997, p. 83). As a junior-high-school history teacher explains, the interdependence of woman-ist caring requires that teachers see both teaching and change as interpersonal processes:

> I mean, it's not that you have all the answers. ... I think you have to have the right attitude, the right outlook that, "I'm about change; I'm not per-fect." ... And I think we've got to sort of remove it from being sort of a personal attack to like trying to help us understand who we are so that we can help our students understand better who they are. (Beauboeuf, 1997, p. 95)

Because they include self-change in the project of social change, womanist educators are guided by a humility in their teaching:

> To suggest "I'm going to change you," is to suggest, "I know everything, and I have the right answer." ... *People aren't victories.* It's about, "So, what have you got to tell me? So let's talk for awhile, let's keep the conver-sation going, and maybe we'll both be changed by the end of this." ... [Change] is increments. It's little steps. And I value the process. ... It's the process through which we go that's often the time during which you learn the most. (Beauboeuf, 1997, p. 127; emphasis added)

Thus, informed by an ethic of risk, womanist caring encourages educators to see their action as a humble, yet essential, contribution to an extensive, collaborative, and enduring project of social change.

Conclusion and Implications

If black women exemplars are truly models of the types of teachers that our students need, then recognizing a womanist orientation to teaching compels us to reconsider several assumptions we may make about women, caring, and education. First, it suggests that caring need not be regarded simply as an inter-personal, dyadic, and apolitical interaction; to see caring in such terms is to disregard its potential for communal engagement and political activism. Fur-thermore, to see children as innocent and incapable of wondering about the problems of our society is in fact to condemn them to the same despair we have about our social ills. Once we begin to see caring and mothering in larger, sociohistorical realms, we can recognize how in sharing knowledge we can also share power. As Alice Walker (1983) notes, womanists pride themselves on "wanting to know more and in greater depth than is considered 'good' for one" because they like being "responsible. In charge. Serious" (p. xi). Thus, for those women (and men) uncomfortable with the political nature of teaching, we might ask, "Whose limitations are they embracing as their own? And to what end?" Noblit's (1993) admission of his own uneasiness with the authority and caring of Pam's womanist pedagogy is instructive here:

> I understood caring as relational and reciprocal. ... I, who saw power linked to oppression in everything, did not want caring to be about power, and thereby about oppression. ... I wanted the "ethic of caring" to be pristine, to be somehow beyond issues of power that I considered to be essentially hegemonic and masculine. (p. 26)

By associating power with masculininty and oppression and caring with femininity and liberation, Noblit acknowledges that he erroneously left no room to explain the pedagogy of Pam, a woman whose pedagogy combined both power and caring. However, as a result of being instructed in her methods as a participant-observer in her class, he realized that power in and of itself is not hurtful and that power is not the same as the exploitation or oppression of another person. As a result, he concludes that the real task of teaching is to find ways of holding truth to power, of using power to promote rather than thwart human development. A key way of manifesting this "good" power, notes Noblit, is heeding Pam's "emphasis on collectivity ... as a corrective for the seemingly rampant individualism of Americans in general" (p. 37).

Lacking such interdependence and an ethic of risk, one can easily succumb to despair given the many problems of urban education. However, to subscribe to a form of mothering in which the nature and purpose of one's caring are not interrogated, out of the belief that good intentions necessarily result in good actions, is also deeply problematic. Alice McIntyre (1997) describes the politically unclear caring of several white female students in a preservice teaching program:

> The observations that are made by the participants reveal several stereotypes about students of color (e.g., unkempt, violent, unprepared). Confounding that is the fact that the participants' perceptions of themselves as caring and benevolent teachers make it difficult for them to even recognize those stereotypes. ... Rather than expressing anger and rage at children coming to school with no coats and "not having" what "they have," the participants' discourse lacked a sense of urgency about the need to restructure educational institutions. The participants conceptualize the problem as being internal to their students. The solution then is to "save" them. (pp. 667, 668)

In resorting to such a paternalistic pedagogy or what Sara Ruddick (1992) terms "maternal militarism" (p. 147), women fail to see or care about "others," those beyond their immediate families and communities. As teachers, they also run the risk of succumbing to self-righteous despair about the enormity of the social problems of poverty, racism, and general injustice, by seeing these problems as insurmountable because they are rooted in the ways of "other people."

Womanism, however, in positing our fundamental interdependence, regardless of the social divisions of class, race, and gender, offers heartening, yet sobering, information about the nature of social activism. It suggests that caring may not result in immediate, self-congratulatory successes. In fact, because the struggle is long and social in nature, one cannot egocentrically base one's commitment on seeing instantaneous change: One must have the faith, as Noblit (1993) writes of Pam, that "You'll love me more after you leave me." As a womanist educator, one must reconcile oneself to the paradox that "peace is the struggle"—that is, "life is [lived] on the edge, and that's when the best self emerges" (Beauboeuf, 1997, p. 150). Thus, womanist teachers see themselves as dynamic agents for social justice precisely because they define themselves as having a sense of connection with and responsibility to the human struggle for freedom and justice. In other words, the hopefulness of the ethic of risk keeps people from falling into the numbness and self-absorption of despair. From a womanist standpoint, we understand that oppression, as a misuse of power, occurs when there is a disconnection between people—when people refuse or fail to care for each other. As a result, womanist teaching offers ways to repair such relational breakdowns by emphasizing the following: the agency that each of us has to treat others as our own; the obligation we have to understand as fully as we can the world around us; and the responsibility we have to make sure that our actions contribute to the larger human goal of freedom for all.

I have intended the foregoing examples of black womanist teachers to help teachers reflect on their own pedagogy. Not all black teachers are womanists, and not all womanists are African-American women. Because womanism is a politicized appropriation of some of the cultural values of black women, people choose whether or not to become womanists. It is my hope that teachers will use the womanist tradition to inform their own pedagogy and professional identities and will begin to see themselves as part of a long-standing *American* tradition in which women and men have seen teaching as their contribution to the making of a socially just society. We exist at a time when our access to multicultural histories is a powerful tool at our disposal for "rewriting autobiography" (Cochran-Smith, 1995) to create empowering images of our possibilities, culled from various cultural and political legacies.

References

Bartolome, L. (1994). Beyond the methods fetish: Toward a humanizing pedagogy. *Harvard Educational Review* 64(2): 173–194.

Beauboeuf, T. (1997). *Politicized Mothering among African American Women Teachers: A Qualitative Inquiry.* Unpublished doctoral dissertation, Cambridge, Harvard Graduate School of Education.

Beauboeuf-Lafontant, T. (1999). A movement against and beyond boundaries: "Politically relevant teaching" among African American teachers. *Teachers College Record* 100(4): 702–723.

Cannon, K. (1995). *Katie's Canon: Womanism and the Soul of the Black Community.* New York: Continuum.

Case, K. (1997). African American othermothering in the urban elementary school. *The Urban Review* 29(1): 25–39.

Casey, K. (1990). Teacher as mother: Curriculum theorizing in the life histories of contemporary women teachers. *Cambridge Journal of Education* 20(3): 301–320.

Casey, K. (1993). *I Answer with My Life: Life Histories of Women Teachers Working for Social Change.* New York: Routledge.

Cecelski, D. (1994). *Along Freedom Road: Hyde County, North Carolina and the Fate of Black Schools in the South.* Chapel Hill: University of North Carolina.

Cochran-Smith, M. (1993). Learning to teach against the grain. In K. Geismar and G. Nicoleau (Eds.), *Teaching for Change: Addressing Issues of Difference in the College Classroom,* pp. 191–223. Cambridge, MA: Harvard College.

Cochran-Smith, M. (1995). Uncertain allies: Understanding the boundaries of race and teaching. *Harvard Educational Review* 65(4): 541–570.

Colby, A., and Damon, W. (1992). *Some Do Care: Contemporary Lives of Moral Commitment.* New York: Free Press.

Collins, M. (1992). *"Ordinary" Children, Extraordinary Teachers.* Charlottesville, VA: Hampton Roads.

Collins, M., and Tamarkin, C. (1990/1982). *Marva Collins' Way: Returning to Excellence in Education.* New York: Putnam.

Collins, P. (1991). *Black Feminist Thought: Knowledge, Consciousness, and the Politics of Empowerment.* New York: Routledge.

Delpit, L. (1995). *Other People's Children: Cultural Conflict in the Classroom.* New York: The New Press.

Fields, M. (1983). *Lemon Swamp and Other Places: A Carolina Memoir.* New York: Free Press.

Fine, M. (1991). *Framing Dropouts: Notes on the Politics of an Urban Public High School.* Albany: State University of New York Press.

Foster, M. (1991). Constancy, connectedness, and constraints in the lives of African American teachers. *NWSA Journal* 3(2): 233–261.

Foster, M. (1993). Othermothers: Exploring the educational philosophy of black American women teachers. In M. Arnot and K. Weiler (Eds.), *Feminism and Social Justice in Education: International Perspectives,* pp. 101–123. Washington, DC: Falmer Press.

Foster, M. (1997). *Black Teachers on Teaching.* New York: New Press.

Gilligan, C. (1986). Exit-voice dilemmas in adolescent development. In A. Foxley, M. McPherson, and G. O'Donnell (Eds.), *Development, Democracy and the Art of Trespassing: Essays in Honor of Albert O. Hirschman,* pp. 283–300. South Bend, IN: University of Notre Dame.

Grumet, M. (1988). *Bitter Milk: Women and Teaching.* Amherst: University of Massachusetts.

Higginbotham, E. (1992). *Righteous Discontent: The Women's Movement in the Black Baptist Church, 1880–1920.* Cambridge, MA: Harvard University.

Hord, F., and Lee, J. (1995). *I Am Because We Are: Readings in Black Philosophy.* Amherst: University of Massachusetts.

Jervis, K. (1996). "How come there are no brothers on that list?" Hearing the hard questions all children ask. *Harvard Educational Review* 66(3): 546–576.

Koonz, C. (1987). *Mothers in the Fatherland: Women, the Family, and Nazi Politics.* New York: St. Martin's Press.

Ladson-Billings, G. (1994). *The Dreamkeepers: Successful Teachers of African American Children.* San Francisco: Jossey-Bass.

McIntyre, A. (1997). Constructing an image of a white teacher. *Teachers College Record* 98(4): 653–681.

Nieto, S. (1999). *The Light in Their Eyes: Creating Multicultural Learning Communities.* New York: Teachers College Press.

Noblit, G. (1993). Power and caring. *American Educational Research Journal* 30(1): 23–38.

Noddings, N. (1994). *Caring: A Feminine Approach to Ethics and Moral Education.* Berkeley: University of California.

Perkins, L. (1983). The impact of the "Cult of True Womanhood" on the education of black women. *Journal of Social Issues* 39(3): 17–28.

Ruddick, S. (1992). From maternal thinking to peace politics. In E. Cole and S. Coultrap-McQuin (Eds.), *Explorations in Feminist Ethics: Theory and Practice,* pp. 141–155. Bloomington: Indiana University.

Siddle-Walker, V. (1996). *Their Highest Potential: An African American School Community in the Segregated South*. Chapel Hill: University of North Carolina.

Thompson, A. (1998). Not the color purple: Black feminist lessons for educational caring. *Harvard Educational Review* 68(4): 522–554.

Valente, J. (1996). Momma knows best: Chicago's Corla Hawkins simply won't let kids fail. *People* (November 18).

Valenzuela, A. (1999). *Subtractive Schooling: US-Mexican Youth and the Politics of Caring*. Albany: SUNY Press.

Walker, A. (1983). *In Search of Our Mothers' Gardens: Womanist Prose by Alice Walker*. New York: Harcourt Brace Jovanovich.

Ward, J. (1995). Cultivating a morality of care in African American adolescents: A culture-based model of violence prevention. *Harvard Educational Review* 65(2): 175–188.

Welch, S. (1990). *A Feminist Ethic of Risk*. Minneapolis: Fortress Press.

14

Social Work

Elizabeth Ross Haynes: An African American Reformer
of Womanist Consciousness, 1908–1940 (1997)

IRIS CARLTON-LaNEY

As a pioneer social worker, author, politician, "race woman," and community activist, Elizabeth Ross Haynes constantly advocated and agitated for the rights of African Americans and for the rights of women. In 1937 she challenged her contemporaries with the following question:

> If Frances Perkins (the Honorable Frances Perkins), secretary of labor, can fill one of the most difficult posts in the Cabinet of the President of these United States—and this she had done superbly despite any criticisms—is not the time ripe for women, black and white, to extend and enlarge the opportunity fought for by Susan B. Anthony and Sojourner Truth, especially since the latter could neither read nor write? (Haynes, n.d.)

Haynes offered herself as a role model. She involved herself in researching, writing, and speaking about women's labor issues, women's spiritual and Christian growth, women's roles in the political arena, and women's use of all their talents and skills and did these to such an extent that she can be described as a pioneer in the women's movement of the Progressive Era and beyond.

Like most African American women of her time, however, Haynes has been virtually ignored in the study of women's contributions to social welfare history and to the development of social welfare institutions for African Americans and for the larger community. This invisibility of African American women in history leaves gaps in social workers' cognition, distorting the knowledge base. As Brown (1989) noted, an even greater problem is that because of the exclusion of African American women like Haynes, the "concepts, perspectives, methods, and pedagogues of women's history and women's studies have been developed without consideration of the experiences of black women" (p. 610). Furthermore, recent efforts to uncover African American women's history occurred parallel to the development of feminist theory. The consequence of this timing is that African American women's history is often couched inside the feminist perspective, which, according to Brown, was designed to omit the experiences of women of color. African American women generally have held marginal positions in the feminist movement. The misperception is that African American women deal either with women's issues or with race issues, and then sequentially, not simultaneously. White women have complained that they did not want to dissipate their energies dealing with issues of race, because their time could be better spent addressing issues of importance to all women (Giddings, 1984; Smith, 1985). For them, the primacy of female oppression denies the structured inequalities of race. On the other hand, McDougald (1925) stated that the African American woman's "feminist efforts are directed chiefly toward the realization of the equality of the races, the sex struggle assuming a subordinate place" (p. 691).

Some writers (Palmer, 1983; Terborg-Penn, 1983) have argued that the term "feminism" is partly responsible for the exclusion that African American women feel, because "feminism" puts a priority on gender, not race. To deal with the problem of terminology, author Alice Walker (1983) and others (Hine, 1996; Ogunyemi, 1985) have used the words "womanist" and "womanism" to describe the African American female experience. Walker defined *womanist* as a consciousness that incorporates racial, cultural, sexual, national, economic, and political considerations for all people. Hine believed that *womanism* speaks to a double legacy of oppression and a resistance movement among African American women. The term may be uncomfortable for some, but its ideals are descriptive of the life careers of many African American pioneer social welfare leaders of the Progressive Era. Leaders such as Ida B. Wells-Barnett, Janie Porter Barrett, and Birdye Henrietta Haynes knew that their oppressed positions in society resulted from both gender and race and that their struggle must include both, because they were not fragmented individuals but whole and holistic in consciousness and purpose.

This article focuses on Haynes's work in the interest of African American social welfare. With race and gender consciousness as the foundation of her social welfare activism, Haynes worked with African American women through the Young Women's Christian Association (YWCA) and the U.S. Department of Labor's Women in Industry Service (WIS). Her role as an elected leader in Harlem's 21st Assembly District is also discussed as one of several mechanisms for planned change on the community level.

"Womanist Race Worker"

Throughout her life, Haynes, affectionately known as "Rossie," articulated a womanist consciousness. It is unlikely that Haynes would have considered herself a feminist. She may well have been affronted by such a label, because her life's work incorporated the numerous issues of race, gender, culture, economics, and politics. Born in Mount Willing, Lowndes County, Alabama, in 1883, Haynes was the only child of Henry and Mary Ross. Lowndes County was one of the poorest areas in Alabama, where African Americans far outnumbered white people. The Ross family amassed some wealth through the purchase of land, which eventually grew to become a 1,500-acre plantation, giving them the luxury of educating their daughter at a level well beyond that of most African Americans of their time (Bogin, 1980; Lasch-Quinn, 1993). Haynes attended the State Normal School in Montgomery and later won a scholarship to Fisk University, where she was awarded an AB degree in 1903. She taught school in Alabama and Texas for several years after graduation, and during the summers of 1905 and 1907 she attended summer school at the University of Chicago.

In 1908 Haynes was invited to work with "colored students" for the Student Department of the National Board of the YWCA. She traveled to college campuses and cities where branches of the YWCA were established for African Americans. Although Haynes resigned from paid employment with the YWCA in 1910 when she married George Edmund Haynes, cofounder and first executive director of the National Urban League, her work with this organization continued for many years thereafter (Bogin, 1980). Her concern for women's equity and economic well-being was just beginning.

Labeling Haynes is a challenge, because the scope of her work is so broad and varied. McDougald (1925) described the following four groups into which African American women were divided during the 1920s, based on their work and activities:

> First, comes a very small leisure group—the wives and daughters of men who are in business, in the professions, and in a few well-paid personal service occupations. Second, a most active and progressive group, the women in business and the professions. Third, the many women in the trades and industry. Fourth, a group weighty in numbers struggling on in domestic service, with an even less fortunate fringe of casual workers, fluctuating with the economic temper of the times. (p. 689)

Haynes defies McDougald's categorization. Although she had a fairly privileged childhood and later gave up paid employment on her marriage, she did not while away her time in search of other black families who could boast of the same achievement and leisure. In her world privilege carried an obligation to those less fortunate; she became a professional volunteer using her knowledge, expertise, and social and political power for planned change on behalf of African Americans.

Haynes can be described as a "race woman" with a womanist consciousness. The work in which she engaged can best be described, in the vocabulary of her time, as "race work." In contemporary terms, "community work" best identifies her work. For Haynes, this work involved community advocacy coupled with the constant struggle for social justice, race uplift, and gender equity. It included a pride in self, a collective consciousness, and the dynamics of multiple commitments, which according to Higginbotham (1992), resisted white hegemonic discourses. Gilkes (1988, pp. 67–68) used the phrase "lots of small pieces" to describe the "web of affiliations" in which African American women engaged to be effective community advocates. This wide variety of involvement with numerous organizations, whose aims included interracial cooperation, political empowerment, economic advancement, education, cultural enhancement, and community endurance, illustrates the complexity and multiplicity of women's activities. "Lots of small pieces" is a fitting phrase to describe Haynes's "womanist race work."

Preparing Girls for Womanhood through the YWCA

Haynes began her social work career as the first African American national board staff member with the Student Department of the YWCA. Working among college students for more than two years, Haynes traveled extensively throughout the country encouraging, supporting, and modeling expected behavior for African American college women. Her work also included supervisory responsibilities in cities where African American YWCAs had been established.

With a genuine concern for the students' quality of life, Haynes wrote to the national office that "to get a fair and true idea of the girls themselves, the ones in whom we are most deeply interested, it is very necessary to see them in and through their conditions and surroundings to know what they think and what they do." She indicated that "the girls' rooms [on the college campuses], though plainly and poorly furnished, are well kept, are improved by artistic touches here and there, and the girls themselves for the most part are quite tidy in their dress." Haynes further noted with some trepidation that "many work from the early morning hours steadily with just a few minutes between for meals until night and then attend night school. Most of them are able to get work in the schools, but it is necessary for some who support themselves entirely to live out in private families and do the cooking or the laundry work, or the general house work." Haynes felt that in general the students were "cheerful and determined to push ahead, [but] occasionally an almost discouraged girl has made her way to my room seeking advice, information, and more than all a word of encouragement" (Ross, 1909). Haynes had tremendous respect for these young women and saw in them the irrepressible spirit that characterized her own life.

Haynes was realistic and positive in her reports. She also was observant, with a particular eye for the student who showed unusual promise. On visiting Paine College, which Haynes described as "one of the strongest Associations on the field," she found that the young president of the association was "worthy of being kept in mind as a possible Association worker somewhere" (Ross, 1909).

Haynes was proud of her work with the YWCA and noted that after one year as "special worker," the "colored student associations" had increased in number from only 17 in 1909 to 50 by 1910, and that seven associations were subscribers to the *Association Monthly*, the literary organ of the YWCA, whereas only three had subscribed the previous year. She also noted the extent to which the students and the teachers at the various schools had contributed money to the national board in support of the secretary's work and of the conferences sponsored in support of African American YWCAs (Ross, 1910).

Although Haynes acknowledged that the amount contributed was minimal, she felt that "it is a sign of wonderful progress along several lines and especially in self-help" (Ross, 1910). Self-help efforts have a distinguished tradition in the African American community and are recognized as mechanisms for counteracting adverse societal forces and social policies (Hill et al., 1993; Peebles-Wilkins & Francis, 1990). Furthermore, self-help has formed the foundation of social welfare for African Americans. In Haynes's assessment, self-help was a major strength of the African American college YWCA and indicated the students' commitment to participate in determining their life's courses.

When she resigned from the YWCA, Haynes recommended that Cecelia Holloway, a Fisk University graduate, succeed her as "special worker." Her recommendation was accepted, and Haynes worked with Holloway, participating in her training for several months. Such mentoring and training were common among African American women and served to broaden and strengthen the sociopolitical network within which Haynes thrived. Haynes rejoined the YWCA in 1922, when she was named to the newly created Council on Colored Work. In 1924 she became the first African American member of the association's national board, remaining in the post for 10 years.

African American Women's Work

In 1918, when George Edmund Haynes accepted the position of director of Negro economics for the U.S. Department of Labor, Haynes accompanied her husband to Washington, DC, and busied herself with issues of women in industry. In 1919 she became a dollar-a-year worker for the Department's WIS (after World War I, this section became the Women's Bureau). Mary Van Kleeck was the director of WIS; Haynes and Helen Irvin, a Howard University graduate, were appointed to serve as special aides to Van Kleeck (Neverdon-Morton, 1989). *New York City Tribune* reporter Hannah Mitchell found the two women fascinating, but something of an enigma. Mitchell (1919) described in great detail the two women's light skin color, gentle manner, immaculate clothing, physical stature, and diction. Mitchell also spoke of their expertise in the area of women in industry service. But, almost as if to rationalize her praise of the two women, to justify their worthiness, and to account for her own comfort in their presence, the reporter wrote that when Irvin spoke, "she has the charm of not appearing to possess consciousness of race," and "the listener loses race consciousness himself" (p. 7). With a low-key, analytical, and dramatic speaking style (Giddings, 1984), Haynes also may have appeared to be dispassionate (it is more likely, however, that her style was a carefully developed mechanism used to persuade and to put the listener at ease). Furthermore, in describing Haynes's speaking voice as "beautifully modulated" and her diction as "perfect," Mitchell seemed to have felt that these significant attributes were rare among African Americans.

Van Kleeck relied heavily on Haynes and Irvin's expert advice regarding issues of African American women in industry. Haynes believed that many of the problems that African American women faced in industry were the results of inadequate training and preparation, and she was a strong advocate for job training as a prerequisite to economic self-sufficiency. Haynes and Irvin's investigations found conditions very good in two large mail-order houses (presumably Montgomery Ward and Sears and Roebuck) in Chicago. These mail-order houses had certain educational requirements and provided training to new employees. Haynes believed that complaints of absenteeism in some Chicago industries could be accounted for because the young women lived great distances from the factories and did not have access to transportation. Haynes did not blame these young women for their conditions and work habits. Rather, she felt that the women had responded to a national labor crisis in time of war and that "the country should have a sense of duty to them and help them procure the training which they needed" (Mitchell, 1919, p. 7). Haynes also believed that access services such as transportation were essential.

Of economic necessity, African American women had participated in the labor market at a rate much higher than their white counterparts and yet were given limited choices about the types of work in which they engaged (Dill, 1983). Haynes praised "Negro girls" for their willingness "to take up hard and heavy work," or the "dirty work" of industry (Mitchell, 1919, p. 7). She also noted that white girls were unwilling to do these jobs and had refused them in the past. Haynes concluded that "Negro women ... have one advantage over white women as a class. They have the habit of work. ... There are few Negro women in the world who do not do their share, and sometimes more, in the support of their families" (Mitchell, 1919, p. 7). Involvement in the labor market served women in a number of ways. It helped to reduce economic dependence, but it also gave African American women a distinctive set of experiences that provided a different view of their material reality. Furthermore, the world of work provided the women an opportunity to identify with a self-sufficient and powerful group, distinct from their families (Collins, 1989).

Haynes also served as domestic service employment secretary of the U.S. Employment Service in Washington, DC, from January 1920 to May 1922. In 1922 she became the examiner. While in that post, she wrote of the conditions of African American women in labor in an article entitled, "Two Million Negro Women at Work." In that article, Haynes identified (1) domestic and personal service, (2) agriculture and manufacturing, and (3) mechanical industries as the three occupations in which the majority of women were engaged. Haynes found that after the war some women had lost their jobs to returning soldiers and declining labor needs. Companies no longer paid the minimum wage but expanded the duties of workers. Haynes (1922) also noted that with the increasing number of white women available for work, "Negro women were to a very large extent displaced" (p. 64). She also found that "as soon as some of the laundries [in Washington, DC] began to fear that they would be forced to pay the minimum wage they began to ask the employment bureaus about the possibility of obtaining white girls" (p. 65). According to Haynes, these employers were "perfectly satisfied with Negro women" (p. 65) as long as they were not required to pay them a minimum wage.

Haynes's research further revealed that among domestic servants, "the bond between mistress and maid ... is not sufficiently strong for the mistress to learn her maid's surname or her address" (Haynes, 1922, p. 66). In fact, a pattern of exploitation was the norm for domestic workers in both the North and the South, and social distance was the rule. Mistrust and disrespect seemed to form the basis of their relationship, a recapitulation of the mistress-slave relationship. According to Jones (1985), white women justified the low wages they paid their African American servants by arguing that the servants were thieves who took both food and clothing at will. Feeling the weight of disdain and oppression, some African American domestic servants considered "toting" as their right, "a hard earned form of 'pay' for a distasteful job" (Jones, 1985, p. 132). Haynes (1922) noted that neither the domestic servant nor her white mistress "seemed personally interested in the other" and that in "too many cases the feelings of each borders on real dislike for the other." Haynes concluded that "neither has for the other that priceless possession—confidence" (p. 66).

Like many in the African American intelligentsia, Haynes (1922) advocated for "standardization of domestic service" and for "domestic-training schools in connection with public employment agencies" (pp. 66–67). On the other hand, women employed in these areas sought only to escape from what they perceived to be the most degrading of all women's work. The African American factory workers promised never to return to domestic work. Haynes's research showed that with economic shifts, scarcity of jobs, and racial discrimination, these women would easily be displaced, forcing them to return to domestic service. She understood the reality of limited opportunities available to those who lacked marketable skills. More trenchantly, middle-class African American women knew that even when they were well-educated, opportunities for employment commensurate with their training often eluded them because of the hatred and resentment of racism. Haynes emphasized the need for African American women to struggle constantly against restricted job opportunities in search of "economic independence."

In 1923, while pursuing an MA in political science at Columbia University, Haynes wrote an outstanding thesis analyzing domestic working women, entitled "Negroes in Domestic Service in the United States." In this study, she examined numerous issues including demographic data, turnover rates, training and efficiency, and wages. Haynes was holistic in her approach and to that end surveyed the living conditions, health, social life, and organizational affiliations of domestic workers. She found that the church played a significant role in their lives, as did secret orders (for example, the Eastern Star). Younger domestic workers spent leisure time in dance halls and billiard rooms. Haynes (1923) lamented that the meager social options open to younger domestic workers largely were the result of "social stigma attached to domestic service," which barred them from "many of the entertainments of real value and benefit" (p. 442).

The "Lady Politician"

After moving to New York, Haynes worked with her husband while he served as Secretary of the Department of Race Relations of the Federal Council of the Churches of Christ in America, from 1922 to 1946. During this time she also became very involved in the politics of the Harlem community and was elected coleader of the 21st Assembly District in 1935. Haynes was committed to the political process and believed that the time was right for women to seek leadership positions in the political arena (Haynes, n.d.).

As coleader of the 21st district, Haynes worked for two years with a man whom she grew to distrust and with whom she ultimately severed ties. Herbert L. Bruce, a Harlem restauranteur born in Barbados and educated in New York, became the first African American member of the executive committee of Tammany Hall with his election in 1935 as the leader of the 21st district. Haynes served as Bruce's "lady coleader" for two years. Bruce was a well-respected community and business leader in Harlem (Lewinson, 1974; McKay, 1940). During the two years that Haynes worked with Bruce, however, she grew to disrespect him. She believed that he exercised poor judgment in his support of one of New York's elder senators who, as Haynes noted, "in all his years in the United States Senate, never lifted his voice in behalf of the Anti-Lynching Bill, voted to cut off Relief from the poor and [voted] to block the pure Food and Drug Act" (Haynes, 1937). She further criticized Bruce for being a pawn under Al Smith's control, noting that while Smith was New York's governor, he "refused to sign a bill for a Judicial District wherein two Negro magistrates might be elected, saying he could not see two Negro men dressed up in black robes sitting on a judicial bench questioning white women." Haynes (1937) also believed that Bruce's "stubborn intolerance of people whose opinions are different from his, [stood] between him and any great good to the people." Furthermore, she believed that Bruce was mean-spirited and insincere. As an elected official, she felt he had "become too important to treat his electorate courteously, fairly and squarely," ultimately failing to provide genuine service to the people of Harlem. Finally, in 1937, she dissolved her political relationship with Bruce and ran unsuccessfully with Alderman Eustace V. Dench for coleadership of the 21st district.

Haynes (1937) believed that "Negro leadership, which is to serve the people, must be of such sterling character that it could not and would not stoop to any attempt to humiliate or frustrate every effort of any woman, black or white, whose reputation and character are unassailable and whose ability and cooperative spirit have been tried and proven." Haynes obviously felt that Bruce devalued her because of her gender. She proclaimed that as coleader of the 21st district, she had "worked day and night for the people" because of her genuine interest and appreciation of their confidence. Yet she felt that her efforts were taken for granted. She intimated that her former captain, like other male leaders, took credit for the hard work that female coleaders had done. Haynes believed that the time was right "for women ... to step forward as aspirants, bargainers, and if necessary, contenders for the choicest official plums" (Haynes, n.d.). Weary of women staying in their traditional roles as helpmates, Haynes encouraged women to abandon the "hang over training to shove [men] forward instead of ourselves." She further acknowledged that "[women's] petty jealousness of one another are such mill stones about our necks." Always mindful of women's need to mobilize and have a voice in the politics that affect their lives, Haynes (n.d.) said "I have no fears in urging the women of the country, irrespective of race, to awake, register, vote, work and enlarge the fight for equality of opportunity in jobs, in office for women." Haynes clearly had no patience with leaders who were deceitful and who lacked commitment, and she was not reticent about expressing her opinion. In fact, she (1937) stated that her truthful assertions held "malice toward none, and justice for all." Haynes believed that candor and honesty were important qualities, and although she clearly held the honest person in high regard, she also understood that stating certain truths could be unpopular.

Outreach and Organizing with "Lots of Small Pieces"

Haynes was determined to serve wherever need existed and spent some of her vacation time in Alabama tutoring children in her community for several hours each afternoon. As she offered services to poor people, Haynes documented social problems as she saw them. Speaking out on the evils of the system was a hallmark of Haynes's style. On a visit to her home in Alabama, Haynes (Ross, 1910) noted that the

> three greatest immediate evils in the country life of that section of Alabama are the following: very poor school teachers, most incompetent ministers and most unworthy lawmakers and executors, who encouraged crime by permitting men of some means to buy off criminals for a few

dollars, provided the criminals are spoken of as good work hands and are willing to enter a contract and that crimes are committed against other Negroes.

Haynes concluded this reflection of Lowndes County's social problems by citing "the very, very early marriage of so many children" as an evil certain to ensure a life of poverty and want. Acknowledging the desperate social, economic, and political conditions in her community, Haynes made monetary contributions to support African American social welfare. Alabama's Calhoun School benefited from Haynes's benevolence (Jones, 1936). The school's mission—to attack the social conditions diminishing the quality of life for Lowndes County residents—was a goal that Haynes shared. Furthermore, the school represented a grand self-help effort (Lasch-Quinn, 1993), a feature Haynes praised as essential for any successful race work.

Although Haynes engaged in solitary social action, she understood the importance of group efforts. To both surround herself with women who shared her vision of progressive African American womanhood and encourage and influence the lives of younger women, Haynes became a member of the Alpha Kappa Alpha (AKA) sorority in 1923 and a charter member of the Tau Omega graduate chapter in 1925. Through these organizations and others with which she was affiliated, Haynes continued to nurture and strengthen her relationships with other African American women. (This group of college-educated African American women also formed another network through which Haynes could work on behalf of women and girls.) Haynes believed that part of the sorority's purpose was "to build more stately mansions for womanhood" ("Proclamation," 1953) through social welfare programs, race work, and educational opportunities. By 1925 the AKA sorority's national agenda included programs that increased race consciousness and that fostered "aesthetic development of the public" as well as "increased community involvement" (McNealey, 1993, p. 24). In harmony with the national mandate, the New York chapter of the sorority conducted annual literary contests for high school girls in New York and New Jersey. The sorority and its members were prominent enough in the area that literary giants such as Langston Hughes and Countee Cullen, two of the Harlem Renaissance's greatest poets, served as judges for the literary contest at Haynes's request (Haynes, 1926).

Haynes also was a member of the National Association of Colored Women (NACW) and served as chair of the Industry and Housing Department of that organization. Her "web of affiliations" also included the Harlem Branch of the YWCA, the Mary F. Waring Club, the Dorrence Brooks Ladies' Auxiliary No. 528 of the Veterans of Foreign Wars, the New York Fisk University Club, and the Advisory Committee of Harlem Works Progress Administration (WPA) Theatrical Project. She also served as superintendent of the Junior

Department of Abyssinian Baptist Church and as secretary of the board of managers of the Adam Clayton Powell Home for the Aged.

In 1937 New York Governor Herbert H. Lehman appointed Haynes to serve on the Temporary Commission on the Conditions of the Urban Colored Population. The commission was designed to study the economic and social conditions of urban African Americans in the state. Haynes was well-prepared for this charge, having committed much of her career to the study and eradication of social problems affecting African Americans. She was also appointed by Mayor Fiorello La Guardia to serve on the New York City Planning Commission. She was a member of the National Advisory Committee on Women's Participation in the 1939 New York World's Fair. Through her efforts the AKA sorority hosted a luncheon given at the Women's National Advisory Building of the World's Fair, an activity described by sorority members as "one of the most brilliant events of our history" ("Proclamation," 1953).

In addition, Haynes was recognized as a writer of stature. A Los Angeles YWCA girl's group voted to name their club the "Elizabeth Ross Haynes Club" in honor of Haynes's work with the YWCA and her literary contributions. Greater and more public recognition of Haynes's literary prowess came with her acceptance of an invitation to become an honorary member of the International Mark Twain Society. This award was an indication of public recognition of her contributions to literature ("Historical Statement," n.d.). Committed to an accurate historical record of African American people, Haynes wrote two books: *Unsung Heroes* (1921) was written, according to Haynes, to tell of the "victories in spite of the hardships and struggles of Negroes whom the world failed to sing about," and *The Black Boy of Atlanta* (1952) tells the story of Major Richard Robert Wright, a community leader, educator, and banker.

Implications for Social Work Practice

Haynes had a clear understanding that race problems and gender concerns were intertwined, and her work was based on the interconnection between the two. Haynes's work epitomized the elements of feminist organizing as described in contemporary America. Gutierrez and Lewis (1995) indicated that the goal of feminist organizing is to eliminate permanent power hierarchies among all people that can prevent the realization of human potential. They identified six factors that are common to feminist organizing: (1) using a gender lens to analyze the causes and solutions of community problems; (2) attending to the process of practice in an effort to create organizations based on feminist principles; (3) empowering through consciousness-raising; (4) assuming that the personal is political, with organizing therefore taking a grassroots, bottom-up approach; (5) bridging differences among women based on factors like race, class, physical ability, and sexual orientation, with the guiding principle that diversity is strength; and (6) organizing holistically. A discussion of Haynes's work based on these principles follows.

Gender Lens

Haynes recognized that her gender gave her a unique perspective. She was a member of a community of African American women through her sorority, the NACW, and the "colored" branches of the YWCA. Haynes lived and worked near the women and girls she tried to help. She understood their problems, shared their discomfort in race and gender isolation, and rejoiced in their triumphs (Carlton-LaNey, 1996).

Process of Practice

The NACW, one of the many organizations to which Haynes belonged, adhered to the motto "lifting as they climb." This motto suggests that the women's group work affected the conditions of all African American women and simultaneously helped the empowerment process for the race. It also suggests a collective identity and voice in an environment that was nurturing and supportive.

Consciousness-Raising

Through various group activities, Haynes engaged in consciousness-raising. The consummate teacher, she took every available opportunity to expose, educate, and enlighten girls and women to their strengths and potential for personal and system change. These opportunities included holding private, small-group tutorials on her back porch in Alabama, establishing literary contests for high schools in New York and New Jersey, and participating on speaker's bureaus for national organizations. Through these efforts, women were able to see the relationship between personal problems and political issues (Gutierrez & Lewis, 1995).

Grassroots Organizing

Haynes involved herself in service delivery at various points along a continuum. She held elected public office in New York City, served the state and city at the request of the governor and mayor, served on the national board of the YWCA, and served on the board of a local church-affiliated home for elderly people. The creation of services such as the Adam Clayton Powell Home for the Aged and many others were examples of service delivery to meet the needs of African Americans where the white system would not. Providing direct services to girls and women via women's groups like the NACW and the AKA sorority also were significant to Haynes's work as an organizer. One of the most outstanding projects of the sorority was the delivery of alternative health care services to African American sharecroppers in Holms County, Mississippi, during the summers from 1935 to 1942 by the Mississippi Health Project (Gordon, 1991). Haynes's organizing work and that of the myriad organizations with which she was affiliated reflect the issues and problems confronting women and African Americans daily.

Strength through Diversity

During the early 1900s, the Harlem community where Haynes lived was extremely diverse, consisting of African American migrants from the rural South, people from the West Indies, the subculture of extraordinarily talented Harlem Renaissance artists, poor, low-skilled laborers, and wealthy professionals and entrepreneurs. There were individuals who spoke of America with passion and patriotism and those who longed for the land of their ancestry through the Marcus Garvey Pan-African Movement. Within that community, Haynes was a member of an elite group. Her middle-class status set her apart from most other women of her time. Sometimes criticized as "a set of butterflies on dress parade" (DuBois, 1909, p. 88), Haynes and women like her put petty criticisms to rest through their dedication and commitment, through their recognition that diversity is strength, and through their identification with the lifestyles of the people they served (Carlton-LaNey, 1989).

Holistic Organizing

Haynes's career is an example of holistic organizing. Her keen insights and ability to identify needs from the minuscule and personal to the organizational and systemic provided numerous avenues for intervention. Her ability to operate within a holistic framework encouraged her to use the emotional, intellectual, spiritual, and artistic as avenues for creating group identity and solidarity among women and African Americans.

Conclusion

Elizabeth Ross Haynes died in 1953 in New York City at the age of 70. She left a legacy of activism, agitation for change, and effective race work. Her commitment to race work and the economic independence of all women regardless of color set a high standard for others to follow. Haynes's approach to dealing with race and gender oppression was to first prepare herself by gaining the necessary knowledge, skill, and expertise. As she matured personally and professionally, she used her web of affiliations to enhance her political powers, to provide skilled leadership, to model attainable goals for women, to organize communities, and to attack social problems at various levels along the causal chain. The social work profession has yet to recognize the pioneering efforts of Haynes, but it is not too late for social workers to learn from her life's work as a scholar, elected leader, social worker, and womanist.

References

Bogin, R. (1980). Elizabeth Ross Haynes. In B. Sicherman, C.H. Green, I. Kantrov, & H. Walker (Eds.), *Notable American women: The modern period* (pp. 324–325). Cambridge, MA: Belknap Press of Harvard University Press.

Brown, E.B. (1989). Womanist consciousness: Maggie Lena Walker and the Independent Order of Saint Luke. *Signs, 14*, 610–631.

Carlton-LaNey, I. (1989). Old folks' homes for Blacks during the Progressive Era. *Journal of Sociology and Social Welfare, 26,* 43–60.

Carlton-LaNey, I. (1996). George and Birdye Haynes' legacy to community practice. In I. Carlton-LaNey & N. Burwell (Eds.), *African American community practice models historical and contemporary responses* (pp. 27–48). Binghamton, NY: Haworth Press.

Collins, P. (1989). The social construction of black feminist thought. *Signs, 14,* 745–773.

Dill, B. (1983). Race, class, and gender: All-inclusive sisterhood. *Feminist Studies, 9,* 129–150.

DuBois, W.E.B. (1909). *Efforts for social betterment among Negro Americans.* Atlanta: Atlanta University Press.

Giddings, P. (1984). *When and where I enter: The impact of black women on race and sex in America.* New York: Bantam Books.

Gilkes, C.T. (1988). Building in many places: Multiple commitments and ideologies in black women's community work. In A. Bookman & S. Margin (Eds.), *Women and the politics of empowerment* (pp. 53–76). Philadelphia: Temple University Press.

Gordon, L. (1991). Black and white visions of welfare: Women's welfare activism, 1890–1945. *Journal of American History, 78,* 559–590.

Gutierrez, L., & Lewis, E. (1995). A feminist perspective on organizing with women of color. In F.G. Rivera & J.L. Erlich (Eds.), *Community organizing in a diverse society* (pp. 95–112). Boston: Allyn & Bacon.

Haynes, E.R. (1922). Two million Negro women at work. *Southern Workman, 51,* 64–72.

Haynes, E.R. (1923). Negroes in domestic service in the United States. *Journal of Negro History, 8,* 384–442.

Haynes, E.R. (1926, April 20). Letter to Langston Hughes. New Haven, CT: Yale University, James Weldon Johnson Memorial Collection.

Haynes, E.R. (1937, September 11). Open letter to voters. New Haven, CT: Yale University, James Weldon Johnson Memorial Collection.

Haynes, E.R. (n.d.). *Women aspire for political plums.* New Haven, CT: Yale University, James Weldon Johnson Memorial Collection.

Higginbotham, E.B. (1992). African-American women's history and the metalanguage of race. *Signs, 17,* 251–274.

Hill, R.B., Billingsley, A., Engram, E., Malson, M.R., Rubin, R.H., Stack, C.B., Stewart, J.B., & Teele, J.E. (1993). *Research on the African-American family.* Westport, CT: Auburn House.

Hine, D.C. (1996). *Speak truth to power.* New York: Carlson.

Historical Statement of the International Mark Twain Society. (n.d.). New Haven, CT: Yale University, James Weldon Johnson Memorial Collection.

Jones, E.K. (1936, May 7). Letter to Elizabeth Ross Haynes. New Haven, CT: Yale University, James Weldon Johnson Memorial Collection.

Jones, J. (1985). *Labor of love, labor of sorrow.* New York: Vintage Books.

Lasch-Quinn, E. (1993). *Black neighbors race and limits of reform in the American settlement house movement, 1890–1945.* Chapel Hill: University of North Carolina Press.

Lewinson, E.R. (1974). *Black politics in New York City.* New York: Twayne.

McDougald, E.J. (1925). The double task. *Survey Graphics, 53,* 687–691.

McKay, C. (1940). *Harlem: Negro metropolis.* New York: E.P. Dutton.

McNealey, E.G. (1993). Alpha Kappa Alpha sorority. In D. Hine, E. Brown, & R. Terborg-Penn (Eds.), *Black women in America: An historical encyclopedia* (pp. 23–25). Bloomington: Indiana University Press.

Mitchell, H. (1919, March 23). Colored women represent their race in state and nation. *New York City Tribune,* p. 7.

Neverdon-Morton, C. (1989). *Afro-American women of the South and the advancement of the race, 1895–1925.* Knoxville: University of Tennessee Press.

Ogunyemi, C. (1985). Womanism: The dynamics of the contemporary black female novel in English. *Signs, 11,* 63–80.

Palmer, P.M. (1983). White women/black women: The dualism of female identity and experience in the United States. *Feminist Studies, 9,* 151–170.

Peebles-Wilkins, W., & Francis, A. (1990). Two outstanding black women in social welfare history: Mary Church Terrell and Ida B. Wells-Barnett. *Affilia, 5,* 87–100.

Proclamation. (1953, October). New Haven, CT: Yale University, James Weldon Johnson Memorial Collection.

Ross, E. (1909, March 31). *Special worker report to the YWCA*. New York; Archives of the National Board of the YWCA.

Ross, E. (1910, May 25). *Special worker report to the YWCA*. New York: Archives of the National Board of the YWCA.

Smith, B. (1985). Some home truths on the contemporary black feminist movement. *Journal of Black Studies and Research, 16,* 4–13.

Terborg-Penn, R. (1983). Discontented black feminists: Preludes and postscript to the passage of the Nineteenth Amendment. In L. Scharf & J.M. Jensen (Eds.), *Decades of discontent: The woman's movement, 1920–1940* (pp. 261–278). Westport, CT: Greenwood Press.

Walker, A. (1983). *In search of our mothers' gardens: Womanist prose.* New York: Harcourt, Brace.

15

Nursing Science

Womanist Ways of Knowing: Theoretical Considerations
for Research with African American Women (2000)

JoANNE BANKS-WALLACE

Feminist psychologists Mary Belenky, Blythe Clinchy, Nancy Goldberger, and
Jill Tarule caused shock waves in both academia and clinical practice with
the introduction of their book, *Women's Ways of Knowing: The Development
of Self, Voice, and Mind*.[1] In it, they challenged dominant paradigms regarding the nature of truth, reality, knowledge, and one's relationship to the larger
world. As they noted,

> For many women, the real and valued lessons learned did not neces-
> sarily grow out of their academic work but in relationships with friends
> and teachers, life crises, and community involvements. … [E]ducation
> and clinical services, as traditionally defined and practiced, do not ade-
> quately meet the needs of women.[1(p4)]

Their goal was to assist educators in working with women to develop their
own authentic voice and to use women's personal experiences as the foundation for knowledge development. *Women's Ways of Knowing* heralded a major
shift in thinking regarding the significant influence of gender with respect to
how people know and how they respond to this knowledge. The important
contribution of these scholars cannot be overlooked. However, sampling procedures may have greatly compromised the generalizability of these findings.
Current or former students of elite colleges were overrepresented in this study.
The ethnic racial breakdown of participants was not specifically addressed.
However, based on available demographic information regarding these institutions, one could assume that the majority of women recruited from these
places would be European American. In contrast, institutions identified as
either being more ethnically diverse or serving minorities were noted to be
"less advantaged" or "at risk." Furthermore, no information was given about
the women recruited from the family agencies or "invisible colleges." Thus,
one could logically conclude that the sample was sufficiently diverse to allow for

examination of the influence that being a European American or non-European American woman has on knowledge generation and testing. However, interpretations derived from a sample that potentially overrepresents both women of color who are socially or economically disadvantaged and European American women who are socially and economically advantaged are extremely problematic. In addition, the lack of information regarding the specific racial background of the non-European American women makes it impossible to answer questions about variation in ways of knowing within or across racial groups.

There is evidence that race/ethnicity and class significantly influence people's ways of knowing. Turton[2] found that among American Indians living in the Great Lakes region, ways of knowing about health were directly connected to the stories, spiritual practices, and traditions of relationships that have long been a part of the ways of life of their communities. Luttrell[3] concluded that complex gender, class, and racial relations of power influenced differences regarding how Black and White working-class women define and claim knowledge. Study designs and sample sizes that adequately allow researchers to examine inner group diversity among non-European Americans are viewed to be critical prerequisites to the development of culturally competent and relevant scholarship.[4,5]

The purpose of this article is to explicate a womanist epistemologic framework that can undergird the development of intervention research to assist African American women in incorporating health-promoting behaviors into their lives. Many researchers are either unfamiliar with womanist thought, or unsure of how it can be used to inform specific aspects of research design. The importance of research designs that are congruent with theoretical frameworks of African American women[6,7] and other women of color[8-10] has been noted by nursing scholars. Interventions that are consistent with African American women's ways of knowing are more likely to be successful in promoting behavior change amongst this population. Furthermore, research designs grounded in culturally consistent epistemologic frameworks may offer opportunities to integrate healing and scholarly inquiry consciously.[2,6,7,9,11]

The seminal work of Patricia Hill Collins[11] forms the cornerstone of this discussion. An overview of contextual factors influencing the development of an African American woman's perspective is followed by a discussion of the four dimensions of womanist epistemology as articulated by Collins. Implications for research design are addressed throughout the article. Examples are provided to illustrate potential ways of attending to specific dimensions within the research setting. Many of the examples will reflect the author's particular interest in interventions that promote cardiovascular health.

Context, Shared Experiences, and Standpoint Development

The negative impact that living in the United States has on the health and well-being of African American women remains a controversial area of concern.

Scholars have raised questions about the influence of race-, gender-, or class-based oppression on a variety of health issues such as cardiovascular disease,[12] hypertension,[13] obesity,[14] and depression.[15] Byllye Avery,[16] founding president of the National Black Women's Health Project, suggests that daily struggles stemming from being an African American woman may be one of the biggest barriers to self-care among this population. She states:

> I thought, "Oh this is a piece of cake. Obviously these sisters don't have any information. I'll go in there and talk to them about losing weight, talk to them about high blood pressure, talk to them about diabetes—it'll be easy." Little did I know that when I got there, they would be able to tell me everything that went into a 1200-cal-a-day diet. They all had been to Weight Watchers at least five or six times; they all had blood-pressure reading machines in their homes as well as medications they were on. And when we sat down to talk, they said, "We know all that information, but what we also know is that living in the world that we are in, we feel like we are absolutely nothing."[16(p7)]

Avery concluded that a piece of the health puzzle was missing. It was not just about giving information. She argued that providing a space for renewal or "breathing fire and life into ourselves" is crucial to improving the health of African American women.

African American women have many shared experiences and ideas that stem from living in a society that denigrates both women and people of African descent.[17,18] These experiences provide a unique perspective or standpoint for examining self, community, and society. The commonality of experiences is reflected through the prominence of several characteristic themes within an African American woman's standpoint.[11] Core themes include a legacy of struggle against racism, classism, and sexism[19] that is inextricably linked with a parallel struggle for independence, self-reliance, and self-definition.[20,21] These struggles are conceptualized within African American communities as having both spiritual and material components.[22−24] The goal of struggle is to live a meaningful life reflective of the uniqueness of African American culture.

African American women have a range of experiences and responses related to the core themes of struggle against oppression and fight for independence or self-definition. The consciousness of individual women regarding these themes varies widely. Likewise, the ability to articulate one's personal experience and consciousness regarding the presence of these themes varies from woman to woman. However, African American women's ability to aggregate and articulate individual expressions of everyday consciousness as a self-defined, collective standpoint is key to their survival.[11,25] Each woman's theoretical database for decision making is broadened by having access to both her personal experiences and the collective experiences of a population of women living with similar issues. Furthermore, facing the reality of what it is to be an African American woman with all the experiences encompassed therein is integral to maintaining health-promoting behaviors or moving beyond behaviors that are barriers to optimal well-being.[21,26] Stewart states:

> Accepting the truth of one's condition means that both truth and the nascent condition in which one finds oneself can be used as instruments for freeing the mind and spirit. ... Affirming the truth of one's existence creates a freedom of the self that surpasses the superficial constraints created by the realities and mythologies of racial oppression in American society.[24(p37)]

Therefore, interventions that facilitate an increased consciousness and articulation of an African American woman's standpoint may prove an invaluable tool for assisting women in selecting or evaluating the efficacy of health behaviors within the context of their lives.

Womanist Thought

Women scholars of African American descent have developed theoretical frameworks that articulate and interpret an African American woman's standpoint. Analysis of the influence that race, class, and gender have on the lives of women is a central feature of these frameworks. Womanist theory,[27,28] womanism,[7] and Black feminist thought[6,11] have been used interchangeably to designate this body of work. Africana womanism extends the conceptual core to include women of African descent throughout Africa and the African Diaspora, and it prioritizes racism and classism as more critical issues than sexism with respect to the daily lives of women of African descent.[29]

Walker's[28] definition of womanist provides a space to (1) recognize the uniqueness of African American women's experiences, (2) articulate the similarities and differences between these experiences and those of other women of color, and (3) address explicitly the important bond between African American women and men. The ability to see connections between diverse groups and to work toward eliminating all forms of oppression is a defining attribute of womanist thought. Therefore, for the sake of clarity, in this article the term "womanist thought" will be used to denote theoretical frameworks developed by, for, and about African American women.

A defining feature of womanist thought is the interdependence of experience, consciousness, and action.[11] Collins argues that "This standpoint rejects either/or dichotomous thinking that claims that either thought or concrete action is desirable and that merging the two limits the efficacy of both."[11(pp28–29)] The interdependence of thought and action allows for the possibility that changes in thinking will be accompanied by changes in actions and that altered experiences may be a catalyst for a changed consciousness. Collins concludes that womanist thought does not seek to raise consciousness; instead, it seeks to affirm and rearticulate a consciousness that already exists. The goals of womanist thought include stimulating resistance and empowering African American women and others to actualize a humanistic vision of society.

Intersections between Womanist, Afrocentric, and Feminist Theories

Womanist thought encompasses philosophic and cultural elements central to both Afrocentric and feminist theories. This is the result of a shared experience of racial oppression among people of African descent on the one hand and a common history of gender oppression that transcends racial, ethnic, or class groups.[11] An Afrocentric world view exists that is distinct from and in many ways opposed to an Eurocentric world view. This standpoint encompasses both the experience of living as a member of a racially oppressed group as well as group valuation of a longstanding, independent system of beliefs and consciousness among people of African descent.[17,20,23,30] In contrast, a feminist standpoint is an outgrowth of women's self-conscious struggles to among other things: (1) reject patriarchal perceptions of women, (2) place women and women's issues at the center of analysis, and (3) value women's ideas and actions.[31] Feminist standpoints provide a foundation for critiquing male dominance as both a material reality and an ideologic principle.[32,33] Afrocentric and feminist theories overlap with womanist thought in many areas. However, neither Afrocentric nor feminist theories can fully account for the combined effects of being both African American and a woman.

Womanist, Afrocentric, and feminist theories fall within the larger rubric of what Berman and colleagues[34] call a critical paradigm. This term "refers to multiple perspectives that differ on certain dimensions but that share as a goal the generation of knowledge, which contributes to emancipation, empowerment, and change."[34(p3)] From the critical perspective, knowledge is assumed to be value laden and shaped by historical, social, and political concerns stemming from among other things gender, economic, and race conditions. Critical theories posit that "taken for granted" assumptions and values, although usually hidden, create a social structure that oppresses particular groups by limiting their options. Critical scholars embrace the idea of research as a tool that serves dual purposes: knowledge development and promotion of change.

Womanist Epistemology

Womanist epistemology centers the everyday experiences of African American women as a prerequisite to addressing philosophic problems related to the concepts of knowledge and truth.[7,35] Collins[11] delineates four dimensions of womanist epistemology: (1) concrete experience as a criterion of meaning, (2) use of dialogue in assessing knowledge claims, (3) an ethic of caring, and (4) an ethic of personal responsibility. An overview of each dimension follows.

Experience as a Criterion of Meaning

Many African American women view experience as a distinguishing feature that separates knowledge from wisdom. Knowledge in this sense is akin to having particular information, whereas wisdom is understanding how to apply the information appropriately to achieve the desired results in a given situation. Having wisdom based on experience is seen as crucial to individual and collective survival in the midst of an oppressive environment.[11] Collins notes that from an African American woman's standpoint, "individuals who lived through the experiences about which they claim to be experts are more believable and credible than those who have merely read or thought about such experiences."[11(p209)]

The author was a co-principal investigator in a study exploring barriers to women of African descent participating in research.[27,36] During one session, a woman noted the distinction between wisdom and knowledge in the following manner:

> And there's the whole difference that I wanted to speak to when we were talking before, between knowledge—which is what white people went after. It was just knowledge. As opposed to wisdom, but they have very little wisdom, which is the ability to synthesize, to make meaningful discourse between knowledge and whatever you are going to produce.[27]

The importance of experience as a vehicle for developing and testing knowledge is emphasized by womanist,[11] Afrocentric,[22] and feminist scholars. Luttrell[3] found racial and class differences in relationship to the valuing of experiential knowledge. Black women received support from Black communities and institutions for experiential knowledge they had acquired, whereas White communities and institutions did not support experiential knowledge. Therefore, even though White working-class women felt they had experiential knowledge, they did not view it as real intelligence; however, Black women did.

Opportunities to develop or refine particular behaviors and self-monitoring skills are prerequisites to using experience as the basis for generating and critiquing knowledge related to health promotion. Instruction about and practice of specific behaviors and self-monitoring skills can be incorporated into the research design. For example, interventions to promote physical activity can provide opportunities for women to participate in various types of individual and group exercises. This can be accompanied by instruction on using pulse rates, breathing patterns, fatigue level, or other self-monitoring cues to evaluate the appropriateness of a particular activity level. Moreover, this can be supplemented with information on how recording information in diaries or journals can allow women to evaluate change in their experiences over time. Notably, opportunities to experience positive movement toward desired behavior over time[37] and self-monitoring[38] improve the success of behavioral change interventions.

Providing opportunities for women to share their prior experiences may play an important role in establishing the credibility of a given health-promotion intervention. Moreover, investigators must be prepared to discuss their lived experiences as well as their "paper credentials" and theories with potential research participants. Experiences may be shared in several ways. For example, time can be allotted during group interventions for women to share their experiences related to the health issue under investigation. Informal sharing of experiences can take place as part of the "check-in" at the beginning of the group meeting or as part of the debriefing at the end of a session. Interventions that do not take place in a group can also facilitate sharing of experiences. Excellent strategies include incorporating a brief story about the principal investigator's experience with the health issue or intervention strategy into the study information consent form, hosting a group meeting as a recruitment strategy, or designating specific times during the study for participants to come together and share their experiences.

Use of Dialogue in Assessing Knowledge Claims

Dialogue with members of one's community is very important to the development and testing of knowledge claims generated within a womanist framework. It provides a means of reflecting upon or sharing experiential knowledge with others. A primary assumption is that knowledge will be used to build or nurture connections between people.[11] This is accomplished through the selection of specific stories, proverbs, or sayings deemed appropriate for the knowledge to be conveyed.[39] Using dialogue to promote harmony and build connections is also a major focus of Afrocentric[30] and feminist[1] frameworks. Asante argues that "to become human, to realize the promise of becoming human, is the only important task of the person."[30(p185)] He notes that this process takes place only in the midst of others and by striving for individual and collective harmony. Taken together, these perspectives suggest that building community is essential to development of knowledge and that active participation in dialogue by all members is crucial.[23] Womanist and Afrocentric models concerning the use of dialogue are rooted in African oral tradition and African American culture.[39,40]

The choice of words or phrases in a dialogue provides insight into African Americans as a cultural group as well as being a tool for building connections. The language of African Americans is illustrated in casual conversations, sermons, folklore, and song.[39,41] This language conveys both the reality of ongoing struggle against racial oppression and the importance placed on nurturing a unique African American culture.[22,23] Jordan highlights the significance of language in her analysis of Black English:

Black English has been produced by a pre-technocratic, if not anti-technological culture. More, our culture has been constantly threatened by annihilation or, at least, the swallowed blurring of assimilation. Therefore, our language is a system constructed by people constantly needing to insist that we exist, that we are present. Our language devolves from a culture that abhors all abstraction, or anything tending to abhor or delete the fact of the human being who is here and now/the truth of the person who is speaking or listening. Consequently, *there is no passive voice possible in Black English* [italics in original]. … And every sentence assumes the living and active participation of at least two human beings, the speaker and the listener.[20(p129)]

Researchers can gather significant information about the everyday experiences that serve as context for analyzing particular behaviors by paying close attention to the language used by participants.[13] Moreover, research designs that facilitate dialogue, accompanied by reflection on and evaluation of ideas/theories generated through this process, may enhance an individual participant's resources for making decisions about particular health behaviors.[21,27,42] Henderson[43] discusses the important role sharing stories played in the development of a group drug treatment program for women. The stories shared ultimately served as the basis for designing a program that better met the needs of women. Henderson also noted that the process resulted in the enlightenment, empowerment, and emancipation of all participants involved in the group.

Creating vignettes is a more formal way of sharing experiences. As a post-doctoral fellow, the author examined storytelling as a tool for assisting African American women decrease risks related to hypertension. The author and participants created 3- to 5-minute vignettes related to the particular focus of the session. Vignettes allowed women to share information related to a number of issues such as the meaning of being diagnosed as having hypertension, daily management of hypertension, impact of family and other obligations or hypertension management, and concerns about negative impact of hypertension on overall health. The vignettes proved to be an excellent way to link treatment protocols with human experiences. The author does not have hypertension, however, sharing stories about the impact of trying to balance a multitude of obligations and still find time to take care of her own health increased both the sense of community within the group and her credibility as a health provider. Together our stories provided insight into barriers to self-care and resources for optimizing cardiovascular health. The stories also provided a means to think out loud or contemplate the cost and benefits of certain aspects of treatment.[40]

Dialoguing and sharing stories, regardless of the format, provide opportunities for women to share their experience, knowledge, or wisdom. They also promote the development of community among women dealing with a common health issue.[44] Last, dialogue assists investigators in refining health-promotion interventions, taking in account the influence of the context in which women live their lives on their ability to sustain particular behaviors.[10,15]

An Ethic of Caring

The analysis of knowledge from a womanist epistemologic framework also involves an evaluation of the individual making the claim. This evaluation includes the assessment of three interrelated components: (1) personal expressiveness, (2) emotions, and (3) empathy. Together they comprise an ethic of caring.[11]

Personal expressiveness is highly valued in womanist epistemologic frameworks. This emphasis is rooted in African traditions that view each individual as a unique exemplar of the Divine Spirit, which infuses and sustains all creation.[11,24] The affirmation and expression of one's uniqueness are considered essential to the individual and collective well-being of African Americans.[22] Personal expression or style includes but is not limited to language, dress, forms of worship, and ways of interacting with others.

The appropriateness of emotions in dialogues is the second component of the ethic of caring.[11] Knowledge claims are evaluated in terms of both content and depth of feeling associated with them. In other words, it is not just what you say but how you say it.[23] Emotions are considered to be indicative of a speaker's belief in the validity of her or his argument. This is in direct contrast to Eurocentric male models that view emotions as antithetical/inferior to logical or rational thought.[1,31]

The capacity for empathy is the third component of an ethic of caring. A sense of concern or connection between the person making the claim and the individual evaluating the claim is considered an essential part of assessing the claim's validity.[11] Empathy implies a level of concern grounded in the realization that one's own well-being is connected to the well-being of others.[26] It is very different from interactions based on paternalistic or elitist beliefs about one's superiority in relation to another individual or group.[7] The ultimate goal of establishing an empathic relationship is the development or institution of actions that improve the material and social conditions of African American women individually and collectively.

Opportunities for personal expression and nurturing of empathic relationships can be included in an array of research designs. It is important that the researcher as well as the participants engage in activities that promote a sense of community and insight into unique personal attributes.

African American women live in a society where they are often denigrated and/or made invisible.[11,18] Respite from ongoing challenges, accompanied by opportunities to vent frustrations and celebrate the wonderfulness of being an African American woman, may be integral to the success of health-promotion research.[16,42] Effective strategies for replenishing women include providing

15 minutes at the beginning of group sessions for women to share pressing concerns; sharing poetry or short stories; taking breaks to hug one another; singing, chanting, or praying together; and sharing a meal together. The last three strategies have the added benefit of nurturing spiritual development, which has historically played an important role in the meaningful survival of African Americans.[24] Eliciting information about the desire for building community among participants and specific strategies for doing so can be incorporated into recruitment activities.

Activities and incentives that allow each woman to spotlight her uniqueness or contribute to the project also can be incorporated into a variety of research designs. For example, interviews and surveys can be structured in a way that allows women to use their natural language to answer at least some of the questions. If journals are to be used to collect data, the introductory session of a group intervention may include an opportunity for women to decorate their own journal or diary. For individual interventions, the researcher can provide funds so that each woman can select her own journal. Women also can be offered a choice of incentives for participation rather than having only one means of compensation. Finally, attention to aesthetic details with respect to setting, food, and correspondence provide opportunities to celebrate the cultural heritage of participants without expending a lot of money or energy.

Establishing a sense of community between women and investigators is another essential component of developing knowledge within a womanist framework. Ongoing racism, as well as past and current abuses of people in the name of science, have led many African Americans to be leery of participation in research.[45,46] Therefore, demonstrating a commitment to African American communities beyond the immediate research goals is of particular importance. The principal investigator and other research staff should consider attending several cultural or social functions, volunteering to assist in community projects not related to research, and setting aside time to interact periodically with women on an informal basis. These activities will provide an opportunity to build trust and mutual respect.[45] The need to establish trust and respect is not limited to non-African American investigators. Formal educational training often socializes African American scholars away from research frameworks that are more consistent with African American ways of analyzing experiences.[47] Furthermore, African American scientists have participated in research that has been detrimental to other African Americans.[48,49] Thus, African American scholars also must demonstrate their commitment to African American communities and engage in activities that promote the growth of mutual respect and trust.

An Ethic of Personal Responsibility

An ethic of personal responsibility is the final dimension of a womanist epistemology. It stems from the premise that all knowledge claims are grounded in concrete realities rather than in mere abstractions.[11] The views expressed and the actions taken by an individual are assumed to be derivatives of her or his personal core beliefs. Thus, an assessment of an individual's prior history and integrity is an important part of evaluating knowledge claims. Claims made by individuals considered to be morally and ethically connected to their ideas carry more weight than those offered by people not considered as respectable. This stands in contrast to both Eurocentric[31] and Afrocentric[7,25] male models that often privilege role- or class-based authority in assessment of knowledge claims. Belenky and colleagues[1] note that women move beyond relying primarily on role-based authority as a measure of claim validity as they become more secure in their own abilities to think and know. They conclude that an evaluation of the claimant becomes an important part of assessing knowledge claims as women move from simply "receiving knowledge" to "constructing knowledge." Thus, scholars are required to some extent to present insights into themselves as persons in order for women to have sufficient information upon which to assess the validity of a particular knowledge claim.

Establishing credibility ideally will start prior to recruiting for a specific project. Participation in community events, as mentioned earlier, is one technique that can be used. Maintaining professional and personal relationships with several African American women and reading literature produced by African American women also are important. These activities will provide opportunities for investigators to broaden their perspective,[19] understand priorities that might impede research,[35] and develop skills important to working within other cultural frameworks prior to starting a research project.[45] They also may provide an opportunity to network with women who can vouch for the integrity and trustworthiness of the investigator. Researchers should allocate time during recruitment to answer specific questions regarding their connections or commitment to the African American community and how the proposed study fits with their overall goals. This information also could be summarized and included as part of the written information given to potential participants. Developing a plan for dissemination of research findings and sharing it early on with the community could further increase credibility. Finally, working with participants to develop a structure for safely challenging each other and the investigator with regard to the research process is important. In particular, there should be safe spaces for women to dialogue with the investigator regarding racism or other oppressive aspects of the research process. Research designs that include ongoing consultation with other investigators working with African American populations may provide researchers needed support and strategies for minimizing power imbalances.

The ethic of personal responsibility also applies to women participating in a research study. Active participation in development and implementation of interventions increases ownership of solutions provided.[44,45] In turn, this may increase women's willingness to persist through difficulties. Participating in the development or implementation of interventions also may provide women with skills they can use in other aspects of their lives. Moreover, communal ownership of projects or interventions increases the likelihood that they will be continued after the study ends.[50] Women can be invited to participate at several levels depending on the nature of the research. Women meeting eligibility requirements for a study can be employed as research associates and participate in various aspects of the project including recruitment, intervention delivery, data collection, and data analysis. Research participants can help make decisions regarding the manner in which interventions will be delivered or assist in communicating with participants. In one study, the author contracted with a participant working on a degree in graphic arts to design the stationery used to correspond with participants. In this same study participants were invited to serve as co-researchers, raising questions and offering suggestions for improving group dynamics.[27,36] Of course it is important to make sure that participant involvement does not compromise the integrity of the research. However, women should be given every opportunity to develop skills that will assist them in making behavioral changes consistent with the goals of the study or improve their overall quality of life.

Conclusion

"Our basic assumptions about the nature of truth and reality and the origins of knowledge shape the way we see the world and ourselves as participants in it."[1(p3)] In turn, the contexts in which we live our lives and the experiences that we have profoundly influence our construction and validation of knowledge claims.[7,11,21,27] Developing interventions that take into account the various ways of knowing is an important part of promoting health among diverse groups of people.[2,3] Unfortunately, the emphasis of a majority of "culture-based" interventions concerns the use of appropriate language and setting, while the validity of knowledge claims presented within an intervention remains largely unexamined. Development of research designs that attend to African American women's ways of knowing has been the focus of this discussion. However, womanist thought overlaps significantly with feminist and Afrocentric theories. Therefore, suggestions offered could be useful in the design of interventions geared toward other cultural groups as well. The closing quote from a participant in a previous study exemplifies the many possibilities for developing research that is consistent with participants' ways of understanding the world and their place in it:

I think, getting back to your terminology, we need to look at scholarship and teaching and learning as an integrated process (interjection: thank you!). It should involve music, movement, dance: it should appeal to all of the intelligences. We have bought into the fact, if you are not left-brained, if you are not quantitative, you are not intelligent. I think we all know intuitively that's a lie; I think our research should open up new ways to tap into all of our multiple intelligences and to use those to expand our health.[27]

References

1. Belenky M., Clinchy B., Goldberger N., Tarule J. *Women's Ways of Knowing: The Development of Self, Voice, and Mind.* New York: Basic Books; 1986.
2. Turton C. Ways of knowing about health: an Aboriginal perspective. *ANS.* 1997; 19(3): 28–36.
3. Luttrell W. Working-class women's ways of knowing: effects of gender, race, and class. *Sociol Educ.* 1989; 62:33–46.
4. Meleis A. Culturally competent scholarship: substance and rigor. *ANS.* 1996; 19(2): 1–16.
5. Porter C, Villarruel A. Nursing research with African American and Hispanic people: guidelines for action. *Nurs Outlook.* 1993; 41(2): 59–67.
6. Barbee E. A black, feminist approach to nursing research. *West J Nurs Res.* 1994; 16(5): 495–506.
7. Taylor J. Womanism: a methodologic framework for African American women. *ANS.* 1998; 21(1): 53–64.
8. Catolico O. Psychological well-being of Cambodian women in resettlement. *ANS.* 1997; 19(4): 75–84.
9. Henderson D, Sampselle C, Mayes F, Oakley D. Toward culturally sensitive research in a multicultural society. *Health Care Wom Int.* 1992; 13(4): 339–350.
10. Meleis A, Arruda E, Lane S, Bernal P. Veiled, voluminous, and devalued: narrative stories about low-income women from Brazil, Egypt, and Colombia. *ANS.* 1994; 17(2): 1–15.
11. Collins P. *Black Feminist Thought: Knowledge, Consciousness, and the Politics of Empowerment.* Boston: Unwin Hyman; 1990.
12. Kumanyika S, Adams-Campbell L. Obesity, diet, and psychological factors contributing to cardiovascular disease in blacks. In: Saunders E, ed. *Cardiovascular Diseases in Blacks.* Philadelphia: F.A. Davis; 1991.
13. Boutain D. Critical language and discourse study: their transformative relevance for critical nursing inquiry *ANS.* 1999; 21(3): 1–8.
14. Myers B. Hypertension and black female obesity: the role of psychosocial stressors. In: Saunders E, ed. *Cardiovascular Diseases in Blacks.* Philadelphia: F.A. Davis; 1991.
15. Barbee E. African American women and depression: a review and critique of the literature. *Arch Psychiatr Nurs.* 1992; 6(5): 257–265.
16. Avery B. Breathing life into ourselves: the evolution of the National Black Women's Health Project. In: White E, ed. *The Black Women's Health Book: Speaking for Ourselves.* Seattle, WA: Seal Press, 1990.
17. Boutain D. Critical nursing scholarship: exploring critical social theory with African American studies. *ANS.* 1992; 21(4): 37–47.
18. Taylor J. Colonizing images and diagnostic labels: oppressive mechanism for African American winner's health. *ANS.* 1999; 21(3): 32–45.
19. Cannon K. *Black Womanist Ethics.* American Academy of Religion Academy Series #60. Atlanta, GA: Scholars Press; 1988.
20. Jordan J. Nobody mean more to me than you and the future life of Willie Jordan. In: Jordan J, ed. *On Call: Political Essays.* Boston: South End Press; 1985.
21. Scott K. *The Habit of Surviving: Black Women's Strategies for Life.* New Brunswick, NJ: Rutgers University Press; 1991.
22. Cooper-Lewter N, Mitchell H. *Soul Theology: The Heart of American Black Culture.* San Francisco: Harper & Row; 1986.
23. Smitherman G. *Talkin and Testifyin: The Language of Black America.* Boston: Houghton Mifflin; 1986.
24. Stewart C. *Soul Survivors: An African American Spirituality.* Louisville, KY: Westminster John Knox Press; 1997.
25. Lorde A. *Sister Outsider: Essays and Speeches.* Freedom, CA: The Crossing Press; 1984.
26. Cole J. *Conversations: Straight Talk with America's Sister President.* New York: Doubleday; 1993.
27. Banks-Wallace J. Emancipatory potential of storytelling in a group. *Image J Nurs Schol.* 1998; 30(1): 17–21.

28. Walker A. *In Search of Our Mothers' Gardens: Womanist Prose*. San Diego, CA: Harcourt Brace Jovanovich; 1983.
29. Hudson-Weems C. *Africana Womanism: Reclaiming Ourselves*. Troy, Ml: Bedford; 1993.
30. Asante M. *The Afrocentric Idea*. Philadelphia: Temple University Press; 1987.
31. Schaef A. *Women's Reality: An Emerging Female System in a White Male Society*. 3rd ed. New York: HarperSanFrancisco; 1992.
32. The Personal Narratives Group. Origins. In: The Personal Narratives Group, eds. *Interpreting Women's Lives: Feminist Theory and Personal Narratives*. Bloomington, IN: Indiana University Press; 1989.
33. Fonow M, Cook J. eds. *Beyond Methodology: Feminist Scholarship as Lived Research*. Bloomington, IN: Indiana University Press; 1991.
34. Berman H, Ford-Gilboe M, Campbell J. Combining stories and numbers: a methodologic approach for a critical nursing science. *ANS*. 1998; 21(1): 1–15.
35. Brown E. African American women's quilting: a framework for conceptualizing and teaching African American women's history. *Signs J Wom Cult Soc*. 1986; 14(4): 921–929.
36. Banks-Wallace J. Beyond survival: storytelling as an emancipatory tool among women of African descent. *The Womanist*. 1994; (1): 5–8.
37. Bandura A. *Self-efficacy: The Exercise of Control*. New York: W.H. Freeman; 1997.
38. Dishman R, Buckworth J. Increasing physical activity: a quantitative synthesis. *Med Sci Sports Exerc*. 1996; 28(6): 706–719.
39. Goss L, Goss C. *Jump Up and Say: A Collection of Black Storytelling*. New York: Simon & Schuster; 1995.
40. Banks-Wallace J. Storytelling as a tool for providing holistic care to women. *MCN Am J Matern Child Nurs*. 1999; 24(1): 20–24.
41. Tarpley N. On giving testimony, or the process of becoming. In: Tarpley N, ed. *Testimony: Young African Americans on Self-identity and Black Identity*. Boston: Beacon Press; 1995.
42. Boyd J. *Embracing the Fire: Sisters Talk about Sex and Relationships*. New York: Penguin; 1997.
43. Henderson D. Consciousness raising in participatory research: method and methodology for emancipatory nursing inquiry. *ANS*. 1995; 17(3): 58–69.
44. Carter-Nolan P, Adams-Campbell L, Williams J. Recruitment strategies for black women at risk for noninsulin-dependent diabetes mellitus into exercise protocols: a qualitative assessment. *J Natl Med Assoc*. 1996; 88(9): 558–562.
45. Stillman F, Bone L, Rand C, Levine D, Becker D. Heart, body, and soul: a church-based smoking program for urban African Americans. *Prev Med*. 1993; 22(3): 335–349.
46. Thomas S, Quinn. S. The Tuskegee syphilis study 1932–1972: implications for HIV education and AIDS risk education programs in black communities. *Am J Public Health*. 1991; 81(11): 1498–1505.
47. Brown E. Mothers of mind. *Sage* 1989; 6(1): 4–10.
48. Akbar N. *Visions for Black Men*. Tallahassee, FL: Mind Productions & Associates; 1991.
49. Hammonds E. Your silence will not protect you: nurse Eunice Rivers and the Tuskegee syphilis study. In: White E, ed. *The Black Women's Health Book: Speaking for Ourselves*. Rev. ed. Seattle: Seal Press; 1994.
50. Levine D, Becker D, Bone L, et al. A partnership with minority populations: a community model of effectiveness research. *Ethnicity Dis*. 1992; 2(3): 296–305.

16

Sexuality Studies

Kuaering *Queer Theory: My Autocritography*
and a Race-Conscious, Womanist, Transnational Turn (2003)

WENSHU LEE

... My Nameless Everywhere ...

I am a bridge connecting two shores across the Pacific Ocean: Taipei, Taiwan
and San Jose, California, United States. Transnational itinerary, quite obvi-
ously, is my autobiography, and writing myself, I have come to terms with
an elision, a void that has been a nameless, everywhere—*in my youth, in*
my work, in my daily encounters and, most importantly, in my dreams. How
was I awakened to this name and the histories of this namelessness? How
did I manage to erase the memories of romance among my classmates in Bei
Yi Nu, *the best girls' high school in Taipei in the 1970s? How did I bury the*
overtly friendly yet timid interest in me during my graduate school days in
Los Angeles in the 1980s? What persona did I assume in my scholarly writ-
ings on Chinese and Taiwanese women in the U.S. academy in the 1990s?
I have portrayed myself as a liberal straight woman from Taiwan writing
in the United States. I have never been "homophobic" yet I am always
"straight," so I thought.

What has become obvious is that the chi[1] *running through me is deeply*
heteropatriarchal. Do I have a heteropatriarchal mirror which I constantly
have to dust off? But, if there is no mirror, whence comes the dust? For me,
these are big questions, and I am going after them.[2]

This "going after" is tearing me apart, tearing me into pieces. Trying not
to feel like a thief, a language stealer, yet exploring words that reach into the
different sides of me, unseen, unspoken, and untouched, I welcome you into my
bilingual and multi-styled journal—public, private, main text, endnotes,
Mandarin Chinese, United Statesian English, italicized me and nonitalicized
scholar[3]—a written world where there is no common word, no common
sentence ready for me to use.[4]

My formative years offer a glimpse of the national-historical memories in Taiwanese society in the second half of the twentieth century. Quietly embedded in these memories are horrendous acts of discursive amnesia,[5] which I have learned to "see" and "hear" and, ultimately, to "unlearn" its incomprehension. Discursive amnesty,[6] theoretically and in praxis, is the backdrop of my transformed way of seeing. It involves a reorientation of my being. Inwardly, flashbacks and traces of past nu nu guan xi (female–female connections; this expression sometimes will be abbreviated as nu nu *in my journal)[7] dance at the edges of my consciousness. Socially, a cacophony of signs which lay dormant in my nameless everywhere come to speak to me:* jin lan hui (golden orchid association), bu luo jia *(unsettled into her family/home) and* zi shu nu *(self-brushing female) in the 19th century (Chen, 1928/1994; Topley, 1975); school girls' romance in Ling Shuhua's short story, "Once Upon a Time" (1928/1998) in the 1920s;* T *or* tan bao *(tomboy, butch),* puo *(femme),* lazi *(women who love women),* kuer *(queer) and* nu tongzhi *(female comrade or lesbian) in the 1990s in Taiwan (Hong et al., 1997).*

Do you find any of the above Chinese expressions yo yi ci*? Yo yi ci, a Mandarin Chinese phrase, carries three possible interpretations. It is a triple entendre.[8] Translated,* yo yi ci *means: "Do you find any of the above Chinese expressions meaningful?" or "Do you find any of the above Chinese expressions interesting/fun?" or "Do you find yourself romantically interested in any of the above Chinese expressions?" You have just learned* yo yi ci *as a triple entendre. But for me, I am experimenting with myself in two forms of creativity: (a) to feel free to play with words and (b) to learn to understand/interest/love simultaneously. It was through a journey, long but full of surprises and serendipity, that I found the above words from Taiwanese and Chinese* nu nu *worlds* yo yi ci.

Nu Nu Connections and *Nu Nu* Words

In the early 1990s, reading Adrienne Rich's "lesbian existence" and "lesbian continuum" pushed me to pay attention to different forms of woman–woman relationships.[9] Just looking at the list of friends who were invited for dinner at my house on a regular basis, I was dismayed by a horrendous consistency: middle-class professional white males, both gay and straight. No matter how hard I tried to overcome the separation caused by different axes of oppression in theory and in my writing, I could not escape a self-indictment—my life was an affluent, male-centered whiteness. Cherríe Moraga's words drive to the heart of my painful realization: "I felt this [separation] most acutely with Black women—Black dykes—who I felt ignored me, wrote me off because I look white. And yet, the truth was that I didn't know Black women intimately (Barbara says, 'it's about who you can sit down to a meal with, who you can cry with, whose face you can touch'). I had such strong 'colored hunches' about our potential connection, but was basically removed from

the lives of most Black women. The ignorance. The painful, painful igno-
rance" (1981, p. xvii).

When did I or do I know nu nu *intimately? Whom can I sit down to have*
a meal with? Now, I am more conscious of my nu nu guan xi, *and these*
"friends" from different centuries and different races, genders, nationalities,
class and educational backgrounds have gradually assumed different forms of
"primary intensity" in my life. Their biographies accompany me, especially
in waves of vocabulary that have awakened my consciousness, a special
kind of consciousness, which I call "kuaer."[10]

First Awakening: *Jin Lan Hui* and Marriage Resistance

I came across the expression *jin lan hui* when I was doing research on Chinese
feminisms and anti-footbinding discourse at the turn of the 20th century. This
broke the massive silence on Chinese lesbianism for me, a silence that is loudly
naturalized by the Chinese heteropatriarchal normativity (Ng, 1997). Reading
Chen Dongyuan's book on Chinese women's history (1928/1994), I came to
appreciate his progressive criticism of Chinese patriarchy. Rendering Chinese
"female homosexuals" visible, Chen nonetheless advanced a troubling view,
treating female homosexuality as an endemic disease: "Endemic" because it
was unnaturalized and peculiar to an area, and "disease" because it infected
women and damaged their health. Let me explain.

In a 426-page book, Chen spent only two-thirds of a page on "Cantonese
Nu Tong Xing Lian (female same-sex love)" (p. 300), a scant treatment. I was
not surprised by his use of *tong xing lian*,[11] a general concept to refer to homosexuality and homosexuals. This term is old-fashioned and mainly used by
people who accept the framing of homosexuality as unorthodox and deviant,
not seeing alternative reading and naming in their horizons. But the section
where Chen placed his discussion struck me: Chapter Eight and Section Eleven,
entitled "Peculiar Customs in Sundry Places."

Among the other nine customs lumped together with *nu tong xing lian* or
"female homosexuality," the only "peculiar" custom that Chen praised overtly
was the Miao ethnic people's "Dancing to the Moon." The custom, though
"barbaric," was endorsed by Chen because Miao people based the marriage on
free love (vs. arranged marriage) and monogamy (vs. polygamy). This custom,
Chen argued further, emulates the West and is important for the *Han* Chinese
to model themselves after.

Chen condemned *nu tong xing lian*. He quoted extensively from Zhang
Xingtai's *Yue Yo Xiao Zhi (Travel Journal in Canton*, undated):

In Canton, women vow to become sisters under the name of golden
orchid association [*jin lan hui*].[12] Three days after the wedding ceremony,
a woman returns to her natal family for a ritual visit. [Often without prior
consummation], she does not go back to the husband's house until her

association sister gets married. Pressed to the extreme, association sisters would commit suicide together. ... In the recent decade, custom has changed again from sisterhood [*jie mei hua*] to marriage [*lian li zhi*]. When two women live together, one often resembles the husband. This custom was initiated in *Shun De*; it then infected the *Fan Yu* and *Sha Jiao* areas, in which people practiced this custom more severely. It was unavoidable even in the county capital. It's also named *bai xiang zhi* [avowed mutual appreciation]. Engaged as "sisters," women's love for each other is as dense and interwoven as silk, exceeding that between husband and wife, so that they choose to remain unmarried for the life time [translation mine]. (p. 300)

Bolstered by Zhang's travel writing, Chen further asserted that remaining unmarried because of same-sex love violates nature's rule and damages women's health. He remarked that this practice became even more pervasive due to changing economic conditions. It deterred women from marrying and made them *sink* into same-sex love, causing a big problem [for the society] (p. 300).

Chen's judgment of "problem" is couched in terms of his heteropatriarchal value system, treating heterosexuality, monogamy, free love, spouses of small age difference, and getting married when one matures as "natural." Its normative power is made visible when "peculiar" is chosen to mark its undesired other; that is, "peculiar" takes on meaning against the backdrop of Chen's normativity: class-based, *Han*-centric and Western-emulating compulsory heterosexuality. Ethnic minorities (the Manchus, Tibetans, Yaos, Miaos, and Lis) and lower class *Han* people (peasants) were also "peculiar" (read "unnatural"). Finally, not only were Cantonese *nu nu* connections "peculiar/unnatural," but worse yet, they also *shang* (damaged) *shen ti* (body; it is used holistically to mean physical health). Like a disease, *nu nu* connections might deter women from the fulfillment of nature's callings to get married and bear children. They might also cause solitude, isolation, infirmity or suicide. After all, an unmarried and childless life was no life at all.

In Marjorie Topley's historical essay on marriage resistance in Canton,[13] I found two more terms for marriage resisters: *zi shu nu* (self-brushing [the hair] women) and *bu luo jia* (not settling down in the [husband's] family)[14] (1975, p. 67). There was a hairdressing ritual for a bride before marriage. If a single woman chose to take the vow of spinsterhood, she would go through the same hairdressing ritual. But she would be assisted by "an elderly celibate female" rather than "an elderly woman with many sons" (p. 83). Going through the hairdressing ritual by herself, she entered a new stage of life alone, henceforth the term *zi* (self) *shu* (brushing) *nu* (female).

In contrast, some women went through their wedding ceremony but did not consummate their relationship with their husbands. Recall Zhang's travel writing quoted by Chen in my earlier discussion. Three days after the wedding, the bride would be accompanied by the groom to pay a ritual visit to her natal family, called *gui ning. Gui* means returning and *ning* means safe/peaceful. Together, it means the bride returns home to wish her parents a safe and healthy life. The unwilling bride during the resistance era would take advantage of this ritual, refusing to return to the husband's family, henceforth acquiring the name *bu* (not) *luo* (settle down) *jia* (family/home).

In sum, golden orchid association, *jin lan hui,* is a 19th century Chinese vocabulary for *nu nu* connections in Canton. Specificities in *jin lan hui* are further mapped based on (a) whether a woman resisted marriage by not marrying (*zi shu nu*) or by marrying but not returning to the husband's house (*bu luo jia*), and (b) whether their relationship was a celibate sisterhood (*jie mei hua*) or female–female marriage/cohabitation (*bai xiang zhi*).

Economic activities made it possible for unattached women, *zi shu nu* and *bu luo jia,* to be gainfully employed. They became even more economically viable in the mid-nineteenth century when steam-driven machinery (i.e., industrialization) was introduced into the silk factories (p. 72). In addition to financial factors, religion also contributed to the prevalence of marriage resistance. *Bao Juan,* the Precious Volume, printed by a religious sect, *Xien Tien Da Dao*[15] (p. 74), especially influenced many of these unattached women. It preached to women that marriage resistance is not morally wrong; men cannot be trusted; childbirth is a sin; celibacy is the only way to the Happy Land (paradise); and suicide is a virtue if it is committed to preserve purity and chastity.

As the silk industry hit bottom in the great depression of the 1930s, marriage resistance declined. Older unattached women retired early, and younger ones sought employment as domestic servants in Canton as well as Malaya and Singapore. The custom of golden orchid association, which had lasted for one hundred years or so, declined. Established society resumed its silence on this matter in no time.

> *I found myself drawn to these unattached women. What did they look like? What were their dreams, torments and obsessions? Employment and religion, especially the advocacy of celibacy and suicide, were two foundations on which* jin lan hui*'s unorthodox practice stood. These women would have been my great grandmothers' peers. Had I been born into their generation, would or could I have done the same thing?*
>
> *I am an agnostic and a college professor. I am gainfully employed. I have my "modern" beliefs—women should receive education, learn to drive, have the right to divorce, and so on and so forth. The golden orchid sisters seem ghostly. Yet, their existence, in mysterious ways, is beyond me, neither an option nor a challenge, especially for my younger self.*
>
> *I feel thousands of years behind these women. They were never my women, yet I become, little by little, part of these women, leaving my ghostly self behind.*

Second Awakening: *Ai Bao* and 1990s *Nu Nu* Words

In 1993 and 1994, I went back to Taiwan to visit my mother, other family members, and friends. I met three female professor friends at Nu Shu Dien, the Femme Bookstore, across the street from Tai Da (National Taiwan University), where vibrant and often dissenting intellectual movements originated. They talked about the influence of postmodern, poststructuralist and postcolonial theories in the Taiwanese academy. They also mentioned that there's a fierce schism between [heterosexually unconscious] feminists and lesbian feminists. A breakthrough on the front of Taiwanese lesbian organizing/ theorizing, according to them, was the first officially registered lesbian publication in Taiwan, Ai Fu Hao Zi Zai Bao, abbreviated, as Ai Bao—the Love Newspaper/Magazine.[16]

I thoroughly enjoyed our conversations on that hot summer afternoon. Before returning to my mom's house, I picked up all available issues of Ai Bao at the Femme Bookstore. Reading through them, I was struck by many new terms I had never heard of in Chinese. Moreover, what stood out beyond the literal content of their words were Ai Bao's discursive strategies, a marvelous and sophisticated demonstration of the rhetorical art.

Ai Bao and Rhetorical Invention

Rhetoric is a "Greek" term for the study of persuasion in general and the practice of argument in particular. I found this focus useful in appreciating/ understanding the title of the first Taiwanese lesbian magazine, *Ai Bao,* a remarkably complicated text. Here, I would like to focus on rhetoric as the art of invention in words, and on style as an ultimate component of rhetorical invention. Walter Watson (2001) touches on style's oxymoronic essence:

> The style of the speech is thus in its components both familiar and strange, in relation to the case at hand both common and unique, in its forms both recurrent and novel, and in its functioning both known and unknown. This joining of tradition and innovation corresponds to the nature of invention itself. (p. 398)

Relevant to my analysis here are three ways to materialize style: determining word choice, ensuring suitability to the situation, and using vivid/esteemed sayings.

Ai Bao offers an exemplary case study of rhetorical style, specifically in terms of the use of wordplay in the contemporary Taiwanese world. Many different kinds of wordplay exist. Relevant to my rhetorical analyses here are two types of wordplay: homophonic and homonymic. According to Plett (2001), homophonic wordplay (e.g., soul and sole) is one where two words have different spellings and different meanings but identical pronunciation. Homonymic wordplay (e.g., to lie—to prostrate; to lie—to tell an untruth) offers words that have the same phonetic components and the same spelling but different meanings. I will now explicate multiple ways in which *Ai Bao* artfully achieves its rhetorical invention.

First Take. Translated literally, the title of the first Taiwanese lesbian magazine reads "Love, Luck, Good, Self at Ease Newspaper." *Ai* means love, affection and, discursively, it draws people away from hatred. *Fu* means fortune or luck, and it marks the difference from bad luck. *Hao* means good and positive, and it moves people discursively away from things that are bad and disagreeable. "Love," "luck," and "good" are feminine virtues authorized by the traditional Chinese patrilineal-heterosexual hegemony. A good woman is said to bring love, luck, and especially male offspring to the family.

After this parade of feminine virtues, we encounter *Zi* (self) and *Zai* (present). Together, these two characters refer to "self-at-ease, self-content." This contemporary term is derived from the teaching of Confucius, asserting that a man of virtue finds himself at ease (content) wherever he goes. So, "self-at-ease" marks the difference between a man who feels calm and content and desires nothing and a man who feels inadequate and tormented by unfulfilled desires. It is important to note that Confucius, a misogynous philosopher, grouped women and ignoble men into the same category. So self-at-ease is traditionally a gendered elitist virtue. It belongs to the masculine sphere. But unlike the two selfless virtues in traditional worlds—*zhong* (loyalty to the emperor) and *shao*[17] (filial piety to the parents)—*zi zai* focuses more on the delight and joy of the male self.

Even though *Zi Zai* (self-at-ease) and *Ai Fu Hao* (love, luck and good) are both authorized imperial/feudal values, a discursive tension is built into the title because *Zi Zai* is masculine and self-oriented, while *Ai Fu Hao* is feminine and selfless. Together they create a perfectly traditional, innocent and positive title for the new magazine; that is, the title is not only familiar but also good. It is, therefore, persuasive: "Anything that is thought to be good can serve as a basis for a deliberative argument, and so the rhetor needs to know all the kinds of things that are thought to be good" (Watson, 2001, p. 392). Traditional good values are mobilized to break open new rhetorical spaces via subversive turns in meaning; that is, its title allows different readings through wordplay.

Second Take. *Ai Fu* (love luck) is a homophonic wordplay for caress and foreplay. *Hao*, in addition to having the meaning of "good," is a homonymic wordplay for "so, very." *Hao Zi Zai* can be read as "so very great/free!" The title turns "risqué" when we read it as "Caress/foreplay so very great/free!" It liberates a woman from the cage of selfless feminine virtues espoused by the patrilineal and heterosexual status quo. The Confucian "self-at-ease" at first assumes a straight face, only to find itself coupled with "sexual pleasure" replacing a scholarly, canonical image. The title takes hostage two discursive taboos that regulate female identities: (a) a woman is not supposed to mention sexual matters (e.g., caress, foreplay) in public, and (b) a woman is not encouraged

334 • The Womanist Reader

to enjoy sexual pleasure in the private and public spheres, let alone in print. In Taiwanese society, this challenges the core of sexualized and gendered oppression, in Spivak's words, the "effacement of the clitoris" in subordination to a uterine social organization (1988, p. 151).

Third Take. Another combination of homonymic wordplays makes possible a third take on the title. *Ai fu Hao* is a commercial herbal drink manufactured to enhance male energy and, especially, to facilitate heterosexual male potency. *Hao Zi Zai* is the Chinese translation of *Care Free,* a brand name of sanitary napkins imported from the U.S.A. The title turns "indelicate" when it reads, "Chinese traditional potency drinks for men and female sanitary napkins from the U.S."

Chinese patrilineal-heterosexual tradition valorizes male potency. Precious animal parts, for example, deer antlers and penises, have been avidly pursued to aid masculine potency for centuries. One of the imperial herbal doctors' duties was to seek out exotic medicine to aid the Emperor's potency. Taoist treatises were written to help older Chinese men practice sex without losing their "precious fluid," which they believed would help them prolong life.

Women's menstruation, not surprisingly, receives a polar opposite treatment. Menstruation was long held to be "unfortunate." Seeing bloodstains from menstruation brings a man bad luck. Young women, to this day, usually euphemize their monthly flow as "good friend." In a traditional sense, the herbal drink "*Ai Fu Hao*" is discursively acceptable, while sanitary napkins "*Hao Zi Zai*" are hushed into silence. Neither will openly make it into the title of a magazine. A third turn in meanings via wordplay has produced subversive and satirical effects. Male potency and female monthly flow are clandestinely juxtaposed and turned into printable topics.

Fourth and Fifth Take. To make the meanings even more daring, let us consider a fourth and fifth reading of the title: "Caress/foreplay and United Statesian sanitary napkins/feel great/make people self-at-ease" and "Traditional Chinese potency drinks for men feel great/make people self-at-ease." The multiple discursive and bodily possibilities offered by such wordplay maximize a tension between traditional values and an insurgent female sexual agency. By "agency," I mean discursive subjectivity or subject positioning (Spivak, 1988, p. 216). A set of discursive rules allows a specific "I" to speak, and a group of people to grant this "I" a hearing. In the title of this new magazine, I hear a Taiwanese woman marching away from a submissive, silenced non-entity (a role that is always talked to, ordered around, and made ashamed of and invisible) into a speaking, emerging identity (a role that says "I" loud and visible, makes assertions, enjoys sexual pleasure and feels unashamed of menstruation).

"I" have a traditional, good feminine identity coupled with "my" traditional male self-content. But "I" also love caress/foreplay. "I" am no longer the erotic object of male gaze and male fondling. What's more, "I" enjoy potency drinks and menstruation. "I" speak in such a witty yet sophisticated way, attracting a group of people to listen to this irreverent female sexual "I."

When *Ai Fu Hao Zi Zai Bao* is abbreviated for the ease of writing, it is called *Ai Bao*, which means "Love Paper." It is a non-threatening title for those who endorse heteropatriarchy. But subversive readings, as I have shown above, make this title oxymoronically daring for gendered and sexual outcasts in Taiwan: All forms of love between women are possible!

Wordplay as Vision, Morality as Cliché

Different forms of wordplay, in my view, share two discursive acts: creativity and defiance. Wordplay is sign making, a creative association between meanings or between sounds unthought of by unimaginative people. In other words, wordplay breathes the spirit of originality, freshness and spontaneity into the quotidian. In respelling the mundane anew, wordplay also subversively enacts a defiant disassociation from the existing ideologies and moralities that have turned cliché. Going beyond the trite, the banal, and the stale, wordplay invokes experiences unconfined by the present: dream, trance, reverie, vision, the unconscious and the games of the underground (Kennard, 1997).

Performing an aura of creativity, wordplay's simmering defiance renames the Chinese heteropatriarchal morality not so much as a system of negative confinement but as cliché and, by implication, passé—it becomes the overused, excessively applied code that terminates thoughts and should be vanished! Put differently, to urge a different course in *Ai Bao* is less about defying morality/tradition than refusing to be trite, to be banal, and to be stale, a marvelous shift from right/wrong to cliché/creativity. Rhetorically speaking, wordplay, as a creative and defiant move, opens up thinking and offers visions—making the persuasive case that the love between women psychologically and/or sexually is good and, more importantly, original and creative.

Nu Nu Words in the 1990s in Taiwan

Between 1949 and 1987, the Nationalist party ruled Taiwan through Martial Law. Many criminal offenses were tried in military rather than civil courts. Homosexual behavior was regarded as deviant, and, according to Y. Antonia Chao, a professor at Tunghai University in Taiwan,

> ... any offenders of the given social order would be demonized in political terms (usually by being labeled as *fei die* [the Communist spy]), tomboys were frequently charged by the police on the count of treason. (2001, p. 188)

A new rhetorical world emerged in the *nu nu* sphere in Taiwan after July 15, 1987, when the Martial Law of Taiwan was formally ended (Cogswell, 2000). With the loosening of political restraints,[18] especially since the early 1990s, not only did insurgent publications like *Ai Bao* surface, but also new terms from the homosexual underground began to circulate in public.

Tongzhi is an obvious example. Chou Wah-Shan, a Chinese scholar in Hong Kong and one of the pioneers in the gay rights movement and *tongzhi* discourse, explains,

> *Tongzhi* is the most popular contemporary Chinese word for lesbians, bisexuals, and gay people. The word is a Chinese translation from a Soviet communist term "comrade," which refers to the revolutionaries that shared a comradeship. The term was first adopted by Chinese in Republican China, and then taken both by the Communist and Nationalist Party to refer to comrades struggling for the communist/nationalist revolution. *Tong* literally means "same/homo," the same Chinese word for "homo (sexual)," and the word *zhi* means "goal," "spirit," or "orientation." (2001, p. 27)

In other words, *tongzhi* is a homonymic wordplay. It offers three meanings: (a) "revolutionaries" who overthrew the Qing dynasty at the turn of the 20th century, (b) "comrades," a gender-neutral title which functions like "Mr." and "Ms." for men and women in Communist China, and (c) gays, lesbians and bisexuals of Chinese descent in the end of the 20th century and onward.

Tongzhi is the name adopted by gay and lesbian activists/organizers in Taiwan, China and Hong Kong.[19] *Kuer*, a Chinese transliteration of the English word "queer,"[20] a lesser-known term than *tongzhi* in the 1990s, circulates more exclusively in metropolitan areas in Taiwan. Like "queer" in the United States, *kuer* is sensitive to the heterogeneities among sexual minorities. Yet differently nuanced, *kuer* carries another sense in Taiwan. It has an additional meaning of "being cool," a partially transliterated exclamation borrowed from youth cultures in the United States. So being *kuer* is to be playful, fresh, and original in sexuality. It is freer and more porous than *tongzhi*. Discursively, *kuer*, a gender neutral term, is more into pleasure, defiance, heterogeneity, theory and critical discourse; *tongzhi* is also gender neutral, but it is equivalent to lesbians/gays, and more associated with social change projects and activist praxis.[21] Given that the sexual insurgent movement is about one decade young in Taiwan, *tongzhi* and *kuer* have less deep-rooted and politically unresolved issues than those between gay/lesbian activists and queer theorists in the United States. Despite their relatively different sensibilities, *tongzhi* and *kuer* tend to work cooperatively rather than in opposition in Taiwan (Chi, 1997, pp. 15–16).

In addition to gender-neutral terms, there are new expressions in the *nu tongzhi* (female comrades) world and female *kuer* (children who are cool and queer) world. Before *tongzhi* consciousness was named, women who love women romantically were called "*chuan ku zi de*," meaning pants wearer. When the *tongzhi* movement picked up momentum in the 1990s, *nu tongzhi* words like "*T* or *tan bao*," and "*puo*" became more widely known.

Tomboy, abbreviated as "*T*" or transliterated as "*tan bao*," which homophonically also means "juicy dumpling," means a masculine woman who loves other women. Having an English concept as its origin, "*T*" or "*tan bao*" is roughly equivalent to "butch." "*Puo*" has two meanings in a conventional sense: grandmother or wife. It means feminine women who love other women. It also means "the wife" of *T* (Hong et al., 1997, p. 52; Zhang, 2000, pp. 2–26), a role similar to femme in the United States.[22]

Like *T* and *puo*, "*lazi*" is another woman-centered *nu nu* word. However, *lazi* is more fluid and porous, not subscribing to *T* and *puo*'s relatively rigid role-differentiation. According to Wong (1999, p. 256), college educated *lazi* in Taiwan tend to call themselves "*bu fen*" (not differentiating), *bu fen pien T* (not differentiating but leaning toward *T*) and *bu fen pien puo* (not differentiating but leaning toward *puo*).[23]

In addition to its role fluidity, *lazi* is also less *yang pai* or "Westernized" than *kuer*. Even though *lazi* can be easily translated into American English as "lez" (an abbreviation of "lesbian"), *lazi* is more indigenous because it is originated from the main character's name in Qiu Miaojing's novel, *Journal of a Crocodile* (1994). In 1995, Qiu committed suicide in the Montmarte quarter of Paris, France, where she studied as a foreign student from Taiwan. Since then, many *nu tongzhi* and female *kuer* worship her like a cult figure. As indigenous as *nu tongzhi*, *lazi* is more playful and irreverent. Ultimately, *lazi/lez* becomes a popular term in Taiwan, especially on Websites and in chatroom conversations.

From nu tongzhi to lazi, from kuer to T/puo, I feel directly and indirectly the pulse of the United States—lesbian, queer, butch and femme. Yet, Taiwanese nu nu connections emerge with different contours and vibes, vibrating inside me, opening up channels for a new kind of chi[24] running through me. But the voices of womanists—radical women of color—and queers who are not white are yet to reach the shores of Taiwan, its academy and public/private discourse, and vice versa.

I have a deep sense of unease, longing for a different kind of connection. Perhaps, by crossing the ocean and the Internet between Taiwan and the United States, transcending nations and states, more words and spirits will come to speak to me.

Third Awakening: *Kuaer*, a New Name for "Transnational Womanist Quare"

Queer theory[25] and the gay liberation movement have increased the visibility of lesbians, gays, bisexuals and transgenders in the United States. However, black womanists and radical women of color have articulated and challenged a fundamental elision—sexual minorities who are not white, male, and affluent remain relatively invisible in their different localities. Barbara Smith, a long time organizer and cofounder of Kitchen Table: Women of Color Press, confronts this elision and the practical impact it has on grassroots political activity:

> In most cases countercampaigns against the right are led by white gays and lesbians who have little idea how to communicate with and work effectively with members of the Black community. The racism, white solipsism, and elitism that traditionally dominate the mainstream white gay male political agenda spell absolute disaster when what is at stake is changing our own communities' attitudes about issues of sexual orientation and civil rights. (1995/2000, p. 173)

This is not merely a local/national problem. It is inscribed in and produced through "theory":

> I am particularly struck by the fact that for the most part queer theory and queer politics, which are currently so popular, offer neither substantial antiracist analysis nor practice.[26] (1999, p. 18)

Forging coalition politics and building communities among people who exist "as women, as people of color, and as queer," Vera Miao remarks:

> Narratives of rejection and disillusionment by many Asian American lesbians and bisexual women, whose exclusion is caused by the homophobia of racial and ethnic communities and the racism of predominantly white queer populations, are only a few painful interventions in prevailing definitions of "home" and "community." (1998, p. 70)

Addressing the same problem in *Text & Performance Quarterly,* one of the leading journals in Communication Studies, E. Patrick Johnson (2001) recently offered "quare studies," an invention that dreams of the forgotten localities inhabited by shadowy figures—black, poor, male and female—multiply erased in the incubating but hegemonic queer hierarchies. Quare studies, according to Johnson, addresses what is left out[27] in queer theory:

> While queer theory has opened up new possibilities for theorizing gender and sexuality, like a pot of gumbo cooked too quickly, it has failed to live up to its full critical potential by refusing to accommodate *all* the queer ingredients contained inside its theoretical pot. (2001, p. 18)

Johnson, in other words, offers quare theory to redress the omissions of queer theory, featuring the specificities of gays and lesbians of color. His invention emphasizes race and class as interrelated dimensions of sexuality. It pays attention to communities, embodied performativity, and theory in the flesh, taking an interventionist stance in performing critical praxis.

I fully embrace Johnson's move from *queer* to *quare.* Here is a theory that is not merely brilliant but timely and useful. Yet to understand the discursive amnesia in *nu nu* connections in Taiwan and to push theorizing's critical potential, I cannot but move further into *transnational womanist quare studies.* My rearticulation is "womanist" because I insist on noting gendered and racialized experiences in specific localities, honoring the black women and radical women of color who have taught me many important lessons.[28] My rearticulation is "quare" because, like Johnson, I can no longer stomach the naturalized presence of homophobia in heteronormative communities or whiteness in queer communities. Finally, my rearticulation is also "transnational" because I live in an increasingly globalized world that is desperately in need of critical praxis (Hegde, 1998; Shome, 1996, 1999) beyond the reach of International Monetary Fund and World Trade Organization; and I resist the technologies of global domination on the Third World, wittingly or unwittingly exercised by progressive First World *identity academicians,* be they feminists, anti-racists, poststructuralists, Marxists, or queer theorists (Kaplan & Grewal, 1994). In sum, my critical rearticulation[29] speaks to the importance of quare theory and quare coalition politics, making a transnational link between and beyond Taiwanese quare wo/men and radical quare wo/men in the United States.

Resonating with the sensibility of quare theory without fulminating against queer studies, I extend *tongzhi* and *kuer* further into *kuaer, transnational womanist quare/s,* a starting point for subversive strategy as wordplay. *Kuaer* is a transliteration of two Chinese characters *kua* and *er. Er* literally means child/children. Elsewhere I defined it: "… the function of *Er* is like the y added to a person's name in English, for example, Jimmy, Jenny, Tommy. It makes one sound childlike" (Lee, 1999, p. 297). Rather than being childish, *er* connotes vibrant energy, the ability to grow and to learn new things, and is consistent with the move to originality and away from the banal. *Kua* lends itself to multiple meanings. Depending on its tonal differentiations, *Kua* may mean crossing, praised or proud/boastful. Together, *Kuaer* has many shades and colors: *Children who cross horizons. Children who are praised. Children who are proud/boastful. Children who cross worlds and understand quare and womanist politics. Transnational womanist quare children who are proud and praised and whose critical consciousness is multi-racial, multi-sexual, multi-gendered, and multi-class-based. Kuaering* queer theory, my move to a transnational womanist quare theory and politics affords me a more critical assessment of the Chinese *nu nu* world, from *zi shu nu* and *bu luo jia* to *kuer, nu tong zhi,* and *lazi.* One of the main differences between the 19th century and the 1990s *nu nu* worlds lies in whether reform is explicit or not. Topley comments on marriage resistance practice as "nonorthodox but nonreformist" (1975, p. 68). The *nu tongzhi* movement, on the other hand, is consciously reformist, asking for equal rights in marriage, family, employment and personal relationships. The former embraced an ambiguous "celibacy," while the latter champions unambiguous "sexual pleasure."

Both marriage resistance and *nu tongzhi* movement are made possible by women's increased level of education/literacy and the ability to be economically independent. The former phenomenon originated among working classes aided by the silk industry in areas where international trades were prevalent and Western imperialism was dominant; and the latter movement originated with metropolitan elite classes assisted by Western human rights discourse and critical academic discourse, including feminism, postmodern and post-structuralism, lesbian/gay and queer theory (Ho, 2000). What is important to ponder are the opportunities given to the unattached women in the midst of domestic industrialization and foreign imperialism at the turn of the 20th century. What is also important to mark is that, in contemporary Taiwan, the discursive existence and histories of subaltern *nu tongzhi*—those who are from the non-elite classes,[30] factory workers, the modern equivalent of *zi shu nu* and *bu luo jia,* those who are non-Han people, and those who live in rural areas and do not go to college—remain in the shadows.

Kuaering queer theory, our struggles will remain multifaceted and both within and from outside. Standing where we are, we need to organize against what Patricia Hill Collins calls the "matrix of domination" (1990) in our local communities transnationally, heeding how multiple systems of hierarchy in race, class, gender, sexuality, nationality and education work *together* (not in isolation) to create domination, inequality, and opportunities. This call speaks to the bind articulated by Audre Lorde: "Within the lesbian community I am black, and within the black community I am a lesbian" (1999, p. 307). It resonates with Shane Phelan's urging of critical practices:

> We have to stand where we are, acknowledging the links and contradictions between ourselves and other citizens of the world, resisting the temptations to cloak crucial differences with the cloak of universality and to deny generalities for fear of essentialism. Only in this way will we be able to be free from the domination that lives both within and around us. (1993, p. 786)

> *Search your hearts and thoughts and let me ask you, "Does the name* kuaer *make you nervous? Does it stretch your horizons and help you see erasures that once elided you? Does it point to new directions of 'primary intensity' for you? Do you find* kuaer yo yi ci *(meaningful; interesting/ intriguing; romantically engaging)?"*

Postscript

I have labored in two fields of human communication—critical intercultural communication and postcolonial womanist rhetoric. I believe that my research and theorizing is inherently *political* and I work to dismantle hierarchical injustice created by *intersectionality* (i.e., disfavored combinations of race, class, gender, nationality, etc.). I have been voicing the importance of gender, race and transnational/postcolonial power differences in the understanding of human communication. Yet, the lack of dialogue between radical women of color and women who do "high theorizing" in poststructuralism and postcolonialism profoundly disturbs me. I am further troubled by my own deferral in addressing an aspect of intersectionality—sexuality.

A few years ago, in an essay on antifootbinding rhetoric in China, I had to admit, "My femaleness does not address the voices of lesbians living during the footbinding eras" (1998, p. 29). Recently, in a co-authored piece on critical intercultural communication, I asked a question: "We talk about intersectionality and multiple dimensions of oppression. What will a concrete intercultural communication project look like if intersectionality is deeply integrated rather than given lip service? What are the dimensions usually left out? I personally do not see a lot of issues regarding 'sexuality' raised" (Collier et al., 2001, p. 273). Awakened by Audre Lorde's remark, "I simply do not believe that one aspect of myself can possibly profit from the oppression of any other part of my identity" (1999, p. 306), I vow to work in areas that do stretch beyond my earlier consciousness. To go beyond my frequent use of "etc." or the apologia of "future research should," this essay is an "otherwise" project.

Kuaering queer theory, I have made a race-conscious, womanist, and transnational turn at the metatheoretical level. Linking the genealogy from queer to quare and from *kuer* to *kuaer,* I have also made an honest effort to understand and theorize the *nu nu* world in Taiwan at the dawn of a new millennium. But this is not so abstract as it may sound to both those who relish and those who scoff at the merely academic. Beyond "project" and "work," it carries with it a sensual, personal dimension or, better, commitment. I refuse to abandon the poetic in this personal/political struggle. I also strive to perform what Michael Awkward (1999), an African American literary scholar, calls "autocritography"—a self-reflexive academic act that strategically foregrounds multiple genres and provides critical accounts, both institutional and personal, for the production of a scholar and his/her professional concerns (p. 7). Stated differently, my project is a layered reflection on my own marginalities and privileges and how I negotiate them and turn them into scholarly inquiries (Yep, 1998).

Ultimately, I wonder who would invite me and whom I would invite to have dinner? A peacock feather note to these kuaers: *Ziao Yi and Ziao Wei (my* lazi *friends), Audre Lorde, S. and M. (two Mormon feminist friends), Y.S. (my* kuaer *friend from Europe), Moraga and Anzaldúa, Shu Yuan (my* kuaer *friend crossing three continents), Barbara Smith, E. Patrick Johnson, Mab Segrest, and more. I see their voices and they hear my dreams. Awakened to each other's dreams and dreaming each other's awakening, our crossing is, through and through,* kuaer.

Notes

1. It means energy running through the human body.
2. My quest here echoes the journey outlined in Buddy Goodall Jr.'s new ethnography (2000): "I couldn't answer a lot of these questions. But raising them, and finding narrative methods of inquiry to explore them, opened my ethnographic self to a new *rhetorical* frontier of inquiry. I found a way to write about how experiences of the ineffable shape the everyday. I learned what it means to 'read' between the lines of lived experience a variety of alternative interpretive possibilities. I became narratively involved in how individual life quests and communal participation figure into a larger puzzle about human purpose and agency" (p. 188). What concerns me here in this "going after" project lies less in finding answers than experiencing an embodied and evocative process of co-creation with you, my readers and myself. Pursuing shared subjectivities, I experiment with a cacophony of voices as well as genre multiplicity in this essay. See also Kenneth Gergen's works (1999, 2000) for similar advocacy of multiple writing styles and a fundamental rethinking of intellectual/research purposes.
3. The inspiration for my use of personal and scholarly voices in italicized and non-italicized print comes from Michael Awkward's book, *Scenes of Instruction* (1999). As defined and explained in the postscript of this essay, I also perform his genre/method of "autocritography" throughout my writing here.
4. My inspiration comes from Trinh T. Minh-ha (1989, pp. 15–20).
5. Discursive amnesia is defined as "much deeper levels of forgetting, levels far beyond the need of a censor, and levels created both positively through accretions and endorsed recollection (official histories) and negatively through lack of reward (under-funded histories)" (Lee & Wander, 1998, p. 154).
6. I want to make it clear that discursive amnesty is not a wholesale, one-size-fits-all deal. It has to come with a specific ideological shift upheld by a critical community, a community that learns and interrogates forms of "discursive amnesia" and is persuaded by alternative, genealogical histories. The shift such a community urges is not to turn to *dualistic reversal* (e.g., from "whites as superior" to "whites as racists" or "queers as deviant" to "queers as oppressed") but to an anti-unearned-entitlement based program for social change and social justice.
7. I use this term to denote the relationships sensitized by Adrienne Rich's "lesbian existence" in Chinese/Taiwanese contexts. *Nu* means "female/s" and *guan xi* means relationship/s or connections. Together, *nu nu* means female–female and *nu nu guan xi* means the relationships/connections between/among women.
8. One phrase that carries two meanings is called *shuang guan yu* in Mandarin Chinese. Its equivalent in English is double entendre, defined as "a word or expression used in a given context so that it can be understood in two ways esp. when one meaning is indelicate or risqué" (*The Random House Dictionary of the English Language*, 1971, p. 428). "*Yo yi ci,*" here, is an example of triple entendre, which means (1) possessing meaning, (2) interesting/intriguing, and (3) romantically interested.
9. See Rich's essay, "Compulsory Heterosexuality and Lesbian Existence" (1980/1993). I was particularly affected by her appeal:

   > To take the step of questioning heterosexuality as a "preference" or "choice" for women—and to do the intellectual and emotional work that follows—will call for a special quality of courage in heterosexually identified feminists, but I think the rewards will be great: a freeing-up of thinking, the exploring of new paths, the shattering of another great silence, new clarity in personal relationships. (p. 239)

   > Nevertheless, I am aware of objections to her view. For example, Esther Newton (1993) suggests those who work on lesbian cultures and identities not "be gobbled up" by detouring into "generic women's networks or groupings" (p. 538). Personally, I endorse Rich's view. For me, *nu nu guan xi* echoes Rich's definition of lesbian existence, which means "woman-identified experience" and "forms of primary intensity between and among women" (p. 239). But I prefer *nu nu guan xi* or *nu nu* in abbreviation rather than a transliteration of Rich's concept in order to emphasize women–women connections in Taiwanese/Chinese contexts.

10. *Kuaer* is a transliteration, using the pinyin system, of two Mandarin Chinese characters *kua* and *er*. *Kuaer* has the same pronunciation as "quare" coined by E. Patrick Johnson in

his ground breaking essay, " 'Quare' Studies or (Almost) Everything I Know about Queer Studies I Learned from My Grandmother" (2001). As will be explained later in this essay, I appropriate existing words, both Mandarin Chinese and African American, to coin a richly layered term, *kuaer,* to name a coalitional-based positionality—"transnational womanist quare." I urge a transnational study of sexuality with related dimensions of inequality (race, gender, class, and educational background) firmly in mind.

11. *Tong* means the same, *xing* denotes gender/sex/sexuality, and *lian* refers to romantic love.

12. Topley (1975) provides two possible explanations for the meanings of *jin lan hui:* James Liu of Stanford University has suggested to me that it may be derived from the following passage in the *I-Ching:* "When two persons have the same heart its sharpness can cut gold; words from the same heart have a fragrance like the orchid." Winston Hsieh has suggested that the term may be a metaphor referring to structure—i.e., that such associations may "bud" or divide into subgroups as they enlarge, just as orchids bud into several flowers on one stem (p. 76).

13. Topley did her research in the early 1950s and in 1973 in Hong Kong (p. 69). She attempted to offer historical insights into "marriage resistance" among Cantonese women living in a small area for roughly one hundred years, from the early 19th to the early 20th century.

14. I use the Pinyin phonetic system to translate Chinese in this essay. It differs from Topley's translation.

15. This sect was said to derive from the White Lotus Sect. The Qing government in the North suppressed it. This religion entered the marriage resistance areas in the mid-nineteenth century.

16. Translated literally, *Bao* means "newspaper." It is important to note that *Ai Bao* is a quarterly newsletter/magazine not a daily newspaper. For this reason, I use "magazine" rather than "newspaper" throughout the essay.

17. There are three offenses against *xiao* (filial piety). The worst offense is not having male offspring.

18. After 1987, together with the sexual minorities' movement, Taiwan also witnessed unprecedented energy in women's movement, environmental movement and labor movement, challenging "ruling class Confucianism" and opening up political spaces for dissenting viewpoints (Lee et al., 1995, p. 280), marking a transition into a more "democratic" state (Chiang, 1998, p. 380).

19. I do not mean to imply that the use of the term *tongzhi* is uncontested. For an example of such a controversy, see e-mail exchanges triggered by a polemic individual, LuvBangor, after the 1998 *tongzhi* conference in Hong Kong (Lu, 1999, pp. 335–343). LuvBangor indicted that the 1998 conference was part of an "'anti-American style' gay movement" and objected to the use of *tongzhi* in the conference title: "Finally, stop using that fucking word 'Tongzhi,' no one want[s] to be a god damn communist" (LuvBangor, 1999, pp. 336–337).

20. In 1994, Ta-wei Chi, Ling Hong, and Tan-mou Dan coined this term, *kuer,* which is a transliteration of "queer" (Chi, 1997, p. 9 & p. 17). A revised entry on *kuer* in *Little Kuer Encyclopedia* is reprinted in Chi's book (Hong et al., 1997, pp. 55–57).

21. While I agree with Tan's interpretation, "It [*Kuer*] tends generally to denote resistance to mainstream culture and a deliberately pariah stance that aims for subversion. In contrast, *tongzhi* tends to denote more reformist tendency" (2001, p. 134, footnote 13), I disagree with Tan's view that *tongzhi* and *kuer* are both translations of "queer" (see Tan's footnotes 7 and 13). Considering historically different political and social constraints in the United States and Taiwan, I argue in this essay that *tong xing lian* is analogous to "homosexuality," *tongzhi* analogous to "lesbian/gay/bisexual," and *kuer* analogous to "queer."

22. For an excellent essay on lesbian tomboys in Taiwan, see Chao (2001).

23. For a nuanced analysis of *lazi* sensibilities and their heterogeneities, challenging the simple and uncritical dichotomy of *T* and *puo,* see Zhang Juenfeng's field research, *Love's Free Style* (2001).

24. A reader of my earlier draft asked, "You might want to explain what you mean here, Wenshu. What can you imagine? What does it feel like? What kinds of transformations are possible? Tell us! It is so wonderful. You must not tease us. ..." I drew a blank facing this new but ineffable energy (*chi*). Each time I tried to articulate it in a question-and-answer way, I failed. Then it suddenly dawned on me, recalling a passage in a powerful novel written by Alice Walker, "... our affair wasn't like any affair you're likely to read about in *Playboy*. It had this incredible nurturing quality; it was the kind of affectionate

sex that seemed designed to reconnect me to myself, to keep me alive" (1998, p. 132). This new *chi* has helped to "reconnect me to myself, to keep me alive," and an incredibly nurturing relationship, in my view, knows no boundaries marked by homosexuality, bisexuality or heterosexuality.

25. Given the limited space in this essay, I do not provide a systematic treatment of queer theory. For a good starting point to grasp the slippery semantics of queer theory and its genealogy, see William B. Turner (2000).

26. It's hard to find articles challenging racism in the gay and lesbian movement. An example is in Brandt (1999): "One of the biggest frustrations in compiling this book was trying to find a contributor willing to discuss the phenomenon of gay racism ... on the topic of racism in the history of the gay liberation movement, I was faced with a great deal of discomfort and silence" (p. 9).

27. My thinking benefits from the critical scholarship of Philip Wander, a rhetorical critic, who advanced the theoretical terms "third persona" (1984) and "rhetorical contextualization" (1996) to address systematically what's left out and degraded in the discourse authorized by hegemonic ideologies. What Wander argues for is collective struggle critical of its own omissions: "Political struggle too often overlooks the claims of the poor, the immigrants, the minorities, the wives and daughters of the elites, the uneducated, the foreign, the others we are led to ignore, objectify, ridicule, or eliminate" (2001, p. 287).

28. For a systematic introduction of womanism into the communication discipline, see my earlier writing on whiteness and "gendered colorism" (Lee, 1999).

29. For a similar move to connect postcolonial women and minority women of color in literary criticism see Fawzia Afzal-Khan (1996). This coalition refuses to let globalized demagogues profit from socially constructed fissures via the logic of divide and rule.

30. Y. Antonia Chao's work is an exception. Her research focused on "bar-oriented, working-class individuals" and her informants "were working class or had limited access to cultural capital, in contrast with lesbians who have participated in Taiwan's gay rights movement since the early 1990s. These women are exclusively students or graduates of prestigious colleges and universities, and are familiar with North American notions of gay rights and queer theory" (p. 208).

References

Afzal-Khan, F. (1996). Bridging the gap between so-called postcolonial and minority women of color: A comparative methodology for Third World feminist literary criticism. *Womanist Theory and Research, 2*. Retrieved on March 16, 2001, from: http://www.uga.edu/~womanist/Khan2.1.htm.

Awkward, M. (1999). *Scenes of instruction: A memoir*. Durham, NC: Duke University Press.

Brandt, E. (1999). Introduction. In E. Brandt (Ed.), *Dangerous liaisons: Blacks, gays, and the struggle for equality* (pp. 1–11). New York: The New Press.

Chao, Y.A. (2001). Drink, stories, penis, and breasts: Lesbian tomboys in Taiwan from the 1960s to the 1990s. *Journal of Homosexuality, 40*(3/4), 185–209.

Chen, D.Y. (1928/1994). *Zhongguo funu shenghuo shi* [A history of the lives of Chinese women]. Taipei: Chinese Commercial Press.

Chi, T.W. (1997). *Queer archipelago: A reader of the queer discourses in Taiwan*. Taipei: Meta Media Co.

Chiang, M. (1998). Coming out into the global system: Postmodern patriarchies and transnational sexualities in The Wedding Banquet. In D.L. Eng & A.Y. Hom (Eds.), *Q&A: Queer in Asian America* (pp. 374–395). Philadelphia: Temple University Press.

Chou, W.S. (2001). Homosexuality and the cultural politics of *tongzhi* in Chinese societies. *Journal of Homosexuality, 40*(3/4), 27–46.

Cogswell, K. (2000). Lesbian and gay Taiwan: A yardstick of democracy. Retrieved on November 23, 2001, from: http://www.thegully.com/essays/asia/000601gaylestai.html.

Collier, M.J., Hegde, R., Lee, W., Nakayama, T., & Yep, G. (2001). Dialogue on the edges: Ferment in communication and culture. *International & Intercultural Communication Annual, 24*, 219–280.

Collins, P.H. (1990). *Black feminist thought: Knowledge, consciousness and the politics of empowerment*. Boston: Unwin Hyman.

Gergen, K.J. (1999). *An invitation to social construction*. Thousand Oaks, CA: Sage.

Gergen, K.J. (2000). Writing as relationship. Retrieved on October 10, 2001, from: http//:www. swarthmore.edu/SocSci/kgergen1/web/printer-friendly.phtml?id.

Goodall, Jr., B. (2000). *Writing the new ethnography.* Lanham, MD: Alta Mira Press.

Hegde, R. (1998). A view from elsewhere: Locating difference and the politics of representation from a transnational feminist perspective. *Communication Theory, 8*(3), 271–297.

Ho, J. (Ed.). (2000). *Cueng kuer keng jien dao jiao yu keng jien* [From queer space to education space]. Taipei: Rye Field Publishing Company.

Hong, S., Ji, X., & Dan, T. (1997). The encyclopedia of little Kuer (Excerpt). In T. Chi (Ed.), *Queer archipelago: A reader of the queer discourses in Taiwan* (pp. 27–61). Taipei: Meta Media Co.

Johnson, E.P. (2001). "Quare" studies or (almost) everything I know about queer studies I learned from my grandmother. *Text & Performance Quarterly, 21,* 1–25.

Kaplan, C., & Grewal, I. (Eds.). (1994). *Scattered hegemonies: Postmodernity and transnational feminist practices.* Minneapolis, MN: University of Minnesota Press.

Kennard, L.R. (1997). Coleridge, wordplay and dream. *Dreaming, 7.* Retrieved on October 10, 2001, from: http://www.asdreams.org/journal/articles/7-2_kennard.htm.

Lee, W. (1998). Patriotic breeder or colonized converts? A postcolonial feminist approach to antifootbinding discourse in China. In D. Tanno & A. Gonzalez (Eds.), *Communication and identity across cultures* (pp. 11–33). Thousand Oaks, CA: Sage.

Lee, W. (1999). One whiteness veils three uglinesses: From border-crossing to a womanist interrogation of gendered colorism. In T.K. Nakayama & J.N. Martin (Eds.), *Whiteness: The communication of social identity* (pp. 279–298). Thousand Oaks, CA: Sage.

Lee, W., Chung, J., Wang, J., & Hertel, E. (1995). A sociohistorical approach to intercultural communication. *Howard Journal of Communications, 6*(4), 262–291.

Lee, W., & Wander, P. (1998). On discursive amnesia: Reinventing the possibilities for democracy through discursive amnesty. In M. Salvador & P. Sias (Eds.), *The public voice in a democracy at risk: Citizenship for the 21st century* (pp. 151–172). Westport, CT: Praeger.

Ling, S. (1928/1998). Once upon a time. In A. Dooling & K. Torgeson (Eds.), *Writing women in modern China: An anthology of women's literature from the early twentieth century* (pp. 185–195). New York: Columbia University Press.

Lorde, A. (1999). There is no hierarchy of oppressions. In E. Brandt (Ed.), *Dangerous liaisons: Blacks, gays, and the struggle for equality* (pp. 306—7). New York: The New Press.

Lu, J.S. (Ed.). (1999). *1998 Chinese tongzhi conference proceedings.* Hong Kong: Worldson Books.

LuvBangor. (1999). Email: *Tongzhi* conference. In J.S. Lu (Ed.), *1998 Chinese tongzhi conference proceedings* (pp. 336–337). Hong Kong: Worldson Books.

Miao, V. (1998). Coalition politics: (Re)turning the century. In D.L. Eng & A.Y. Hom (Eds.), *Q&A: Queer in Asian America* (pp. 65–78). Philadelphia: Temple University Press.

Moraga, C. (1981). Preface. In C. Moraga & G. Anzaldua (Eds.), *This bridge called my back: Writings by radical women of color* (pp. xiii–xix). New York: Kitchen Table/Women of Color Press.

Moraga, C., & Anzaldua, G. (1981). *This bridge called my back: Writings by radical women of color.* New York: Kitchen Table/Women of Color Press.

Newton, E. (1993). Just one of the boys: Lesbians in Cherry Grove, 1960–1988. In H. Abelove, M.A. Barale and D.M. Halperin (Eds.), *The lesbian and gay studies reader* (pp. 528–41). New York: Routledge.

Ng, V.W. (1997). Looking for lesbians in Chinese history. In M. Duberman (Ed.), *A queer world* (pp. 199–204). New York: New York University Press.

Phelan, S. (1993). (Be)coming out: Lesbian identity and politics. *Signs: Journal of Women in Culture and Society, 18*(4), 765–790.

Plett, H.F. (2001). Paronomasia. In T.O. Sloane (Ed.), *Encyclopedia of rhetoric* (pp. 553–554). New York: Oxford University Press.

Qiu, M. (1994). *Er yu sho ji* [Journal of a crocodile]. Taipei: Shibao Publishing.

Rich, A. (1980/1993). Compulsory heterosexuality and lesbian existence. In H. Abelove, M.A. Barale and D.M. Halperin (Eds.), *The lesbian and gay studies reader* (pp. 227–41). New York: Routledge.

Segrest, M. (1999). Race and the invisible dyke. In E. Brandt (Ed.), *Dangerous liaisons: Blacks, gays, and the struggle for equality* (pp. 45–56) New York: The New Press.

Shome, R. (1996). Postcolonial interventions in the rhetorical canon: An "other" view. *Communication Theory, 6*(1), 40–59.

Shome, R. (1999). Whiteness and the politics of location: Postcolonial reflections. In T.K. Nakayama & J.N. Martin (Eds.), *Whiteness: The communication of social identity* (pp. 107–128). Thousand Oaks, CA: Sage.

Smith, B. (1999). Blacks and gays: Healing the great divide. In E. Brandt (Ed.), *Dangerous liaisons: Blacks, gays, and the struggle for equality* (pp. 15–24). New York: The New Press.

Smith, B. (1995/2000). Doing it from scratch: The challenge of black lesbian organizing. In B. Smith (Ed.), *The truth that never hurts: Writings on race, gender, and freedom* (pp. 167–177). New Brunswick, NJ: Rutgers University Press.

Spivak, G.C. (1988). *In other words: Essays in cultural politics.* New York: Routledge.

Staff. (1993). *Ai Fu Hao Zi Zai Bao* [Love, Luck, Good, Self-at-Ease Newspaper], December, 1–19.

Tan, C.K. (2001). Transcending sexual nationalism and colonialism: Cultural hybridization as process of sexual politics in '90s Taiwan. In J. Hawley (Ed.), *Postcolonial queer: Theoretical intersections* (pp. 123–137). Albany, NY: State University of New York Press.

The Random House Dictionary of the English Language. (1971). J. Stein (Ed.). New York: Random House.

Topley, M. (1975). Marriage resistance in rural Kwangtung. In M. Wolf & R. Witke (Eds.), *Women in Chinese society* (pp. 67–88). Stanford, CA: Stanford University Press.

Trinh, T.M. (1989). *Woman, native, other: Writing postcoloniality and feminism.* Bloomington, IN: Indiana University Press.

Turner, W.B. (2000). *A genealogy of queer theory.* Philadelphia: Temple University Press.

Walker, A. (1998). *By the light of my father's smile.* New York: Random House.

Wander, P. (1984). Third persona: An ideological turn in rhetorical theory. *Central State Speech Journal, 35,* 1–28.

Wander, P. (1996). Marxism, postcolonialism and rhetorical contextualization. *Quarterly Journal of Speech, 82,* 402–426.

Wander, P. (2001). Expediency. In T.O. Sloane (Ed.), *Encyclopedia of rhetoric* (pp. 283–288). New York: Oxford University Press.

Watson, W. (2001). Invention. In T.O. Sloane (Ed.), *Encyclopedia of rhetoric* (pp. 389–404). New York: Oxford University Press.

Wong, Q.N. (1999). Qing ai de XXX [Dear XXX]. In J.S. Lu (Ed.), *1998 Chinese tongzhi conference proceedings* (pp. 254–258). Hong Kong: Worldson Books.

Yep, G.A. (1998). Freire's conscientization, dialogue, and liberation: Personal reflections on classroom discussions of marginality. *Journal of Gay, Lesbian, and Bisexual Identity, 6(3/4),* 159–166.

Zhang, C.T. (2000). *Campus memory, identity and the emerging of lesbian subjectivities in Taiwan.* Taipei: Tangshan Publishing.

Zhang, J.F. (2001). *Ai de zi yo shi* [Love's free style]: *Lesbians like this and that.* Taipei: Shibao Publishing.

17

Architecture/Urban Studies

Critical Spatial Literacy: A Womanist Positionality and the
Spatio-temporal Construction of Black Family Life (2004)

EPIFANIA AKOSUA AMOO-ADARE

Current research on the use of space shows that western design and modern construction technologies challenge household behaviors in many urbanizing societies and confront certain cultural heritages with new models of space and household transactions (Asiama 213; Howell & Tentokali 283; Pellow 1992, 207). In West Africa, the onset of colonization and modernization reconfigured space in such a way that urban centers were favored over rural settlements and men over women within those urban centers. This produced a tendency in populations to migrate from rural areas to urban centers in search of jobs and influenced changes in traditional family household configurations and family roles between men and women. In Ghana, this uneven urban development has had an effect on residential units, lineage groupings, rules of descent, and inheritance (Robertson), thus challenging existing notions of who should be part of one's family and transforming Ghanaian families' traditional household configurations. For example, traditionally in Ghana's Asante region, Asante women and men lived with their *abusua* (matrilineal family) in a communal or compound house. In contrast, nowadays living with one's *abusua* is a diminishing practice in the Asante region and is practically non-existent in urban centers such as Accra where housing is designed using western architectural models such as the nuclear house, which is designed and constructed with a smaller patrilineal conjugal family unit in mind. This contemporary living arrangement has a role in the predisposition of migrant Asante populations' reconfiguration of their households into smaller nuclear family oriented groupings for practical or ideological reasons. It is a phenomenon that begs for investigation into the roles of the urban built environment in the spatio-temporal construction of contemporary Asante families and their social life.

In this paper, I argue for the development of a womanist ethnographic project that constructs a *critical spatial literacy* on how Asante women's socio-spatial environments have changed in Ghana's rapidly urbanizing capital city.

By *critical spatial literacy* I refer to the ability to read codes embedded in the urban built environment in order to understand how they affect social life. To this end, I document and analyze spatial effects, caused by rapid urbanization, on Asante women living in Accra, Ghana, for example, Asante women's household transformation from communal matrikin households to nuclear conjugal households as a consequence of migration to Ghana's capital and the subsequent changes in spatial understandings of what is family and how it manifests in one's household. This includes the kind of spatial understandings these women have about the ideal family configurations required to successfully live in Accra's urban spatial politic. In presenting my work, I describe the significance of a womanist positionality, the spatio-temporal construction of social life, and the importance of a *critical literacy of space* for women of African descent. In addition, I define *critical spatial literacy* and describe how it can be both a domain and the theoretical framework in my study, thus providing the context from which I argue for this *critical spatial literacy*.

A Womanist Positionality

In order to provide a deeper understanding of the rationale for this study, I will briefly describe how my personal experience motivates this research. I make this assertion from the feminist understanding that "(...) feminist researchers begin their investigation of the social world from a grounded position in their own subjective oppression" (Weiler 58), in that, the personal provides an experiential ground from which a theoretical understanding can be made of material structural circumstances. I also make this assertion from a womanist positionality, which recognizes that critical consciousness must incorporate racial, cultural, national, economic, political, and sexual issues into a philosophy that is committed, with love, to the survival and wholeness of an entire people (Ogunyemi 64; Walker xi–xii), within which the structure and ideology of a family has direct social, economic and political significance.

I am an Asante woman who presently lives in an urban diasporic context in Los Angeles, California. I have always lived in urban centers and I have found that my understanding, negotiation, manipulation, and ownership of space (real and imagined) is often predetermined and confined by the prescribed, colonized, gendered, racialized, and class-based social relations of global capitalism. As a woman and as a minority, I am particularly disadvantaged within the politics of space, i.e., I have been privy to a minority and female experience of discrimination by design of a predominantly western man-made built environment (Weisman 2). Ironically, I experience this discrimination despite my access to professional and academic architectural discourse and privilege.[1]

However, through the development of my own *critical spatial literacy,* i.e., an understanding of the dominant ideologies that inform western urban architecture, I have been able to dream of alternative socio-physical space(s). For example, during my preliminary architectural training (from 1987 to 1990)

I found that my personal experience of alternative household configurations, namely my Asante grandmother's communal matrikin house, provided me with concrete examples that contested the Eurocentric and hegemonic spatial conceptions we were being taught, e.g., the belief that nuclear house spatial configurations and women's roles in those *private spaces* was a universal norm. Within my grandmother's Asante courtyard house, located in Kumase,[2] there were very different gender socio-cultural practices and self-perceptions, for example, a woman's ability to share her childrearing responsibilities with her *abusua* rather than bear the urban financial burden of childcare gave her a different conception of what work she could do outside of the family home. And yet in contemporary Ghana, it is those western nuclear household models that prevail in housing development within large urban centers, such as Accra. In 1991, whilst working on a publicly funded building project in Accra (as an assistant site architect) I personally experienced the ludicrous extent to which western models of architecture were uncritically used in housing development. In the design of the project's 76 housing units there was an extensive use of nuclear house designs and imported construction materials, i.e., from the light fittings right down to the concrete used to build the houses. For these reasons, in the Accra community, the houses were perceived as prestigious and valuable properties, despite the impractical fact that in a tropical climate imported English carpets had been laid over expensive imported Italian floor tiles.

The example of my grandmother's house was just one reason for a renegade architectural stance[3] that I developed during my six years of architectural training. In that time, I developed a *critical literacy of space* as an academic survival mechanism and in order to decipher the political ideologies that were hidden in architects, planners, and developers building practices and inscribed in their spatial constructions. I also realized that my singular understandings and/or actions were insignificant in the spatio-political make-up of things. And that perhaps substantial socio-spatial justice would be enabled if more than just the members of the building profession understood, re-invented and owned the vocabulary of the built environment. I began to question how a postmodern spatio-political language could be encouraged and nurtured in the general public, especially those who were the most spatially disadvantaged, thus, my transition into the field of education and my interest in developing an understanding of the use of a *critical literacy of space*.

In addition, as a consequence of my academic pursuits at that time, I developed an analytical understanding of women of African descent's self-perceptions as a consequence of them living in urban London. This was achieved through a small-scale research study that I conducted with 10 women of African descent (with ages ranging from 25 to 55) in 1994. For these women, the city represented entrapment due to gendered racism and yet emancipation from their traditional cultural contexts. Also, the city for them was about a forced anonymity and yet a suitable release from some of the constraining cultural norms of their

African or Caribbean societies. It was through analyzing these women's concerns and experiences that I better understood my own struggles with the urban built environment and my subsequent development of a critical awareness of the politics of space.

I further developed my understanding of urban London and the roles *critical spatial literacy* can play when I worked as a housing administrator for Grand Union Housing Co-operative Ltd. (GUHC) from 1995 to 1997. I worked with the co-op members to manage existing housing and to strategically plan future housing redevelopment projects. In that time, I contributed to our theoretical preparation towards defining strategies for tile re-development and maintenance of their co-operative housing. An important part of this process was the organization of housing training workshops for staff and members in order to critically analyze and understand the multiple dimensions of the urban housing market, including its challenges and possibilities. Knowledge gained in those workshops about housing policy, planning laws, housing finance, tenant participation, and local politics informed how we proactively developed political strategies for garnering local government and private support for our housing interests and needs. In effect, a *critical literacy of space* had been employed to make change in the urban spatial status quo. A *critical literacy of space* enabled our appropriation of dominant spatial ideologies and related discourses in order to understand and contribute to our collective methods for effecting spatial change.

Therefore, as an Asante woman, an architect, and from my autobiographical relationship with the urban built environment, I work from the assumption that the social practice of building is a complex activity that has a significant place in our repertoire of basic human needs and the physical and ideological groupings that we construct in order to survive. Building, both as a noun and a verb, makes people aware at various different levels. First, at the level of having to make pragmatic decisions; secondly, at the level of envisioning architectural spaces in the mind and on paper, and, finally, at the level of committing one's whole being (mind and body) to the creation of a material form that captures an ideal (Tuan 106). Our buildings, neighborhoods and cities are indeed cultural artifacts shaped by our human intention and intervention (Weisman 9). So it follows that even the families that we live in are social representations of the spaces we construct to inhabit, simultaneously the spaces we construct inform and transform those representations of family.

The Spatio-temporal Construction of Social Life

Contemporary critical social theory provides a new theory of spatiality, which is mainly derived from Lefebvre's emphasis on the importance of space for shaping social production. Historically and to date, natural physical space has been appropriated and reconfigured in the social construction of spatiality; thus, spatiality is the material manifestation of social relations in (and through) time (Soja 93). In turn, spatiality situates social life. The built environment clarifies social roles and relations, thus, the built environment provides an essential framework for thinking about the world and the people within it, in that the spatial language used constantly signifies its function (Weisman 2). Spatiality is a product, producer and reproducer of socioeconomic relations (Soja 91). It is the arena within which social practices, power struggles, and identity formations are simultaneously enacted and constituted.

Yet we find that especially in the modern urban context, there is far less awareness of built forms and space than, for example, in a traditional community (Tuan 104). Spatial awareness is crucial especially within capitalist urban contexts where there is an unequal development of space. Keith and Pile argue that the logic of capital produces an uneven development of space. In fact, geographically uneven space is an essential condition of capitalist spatiality, as it is the concretization of capitalist relations of production and division of labor (Soja 118). In a capitalist spatiality, dominant capitalist groups, oftentimes, constrain the economic and political rights of individuals, communities, and nations by restricting and defining their access to space (Hayden). In many instances it is the poor, women, ethnic minorities and children who are subject to restrictive spatial allocation and movement within urban capitalist contexts. This is important to note because there are many poor ethnic minority women without spatial awareness, who are solely or mainly responsible for the economic and sociocultural development of family structures and the ideological maintenance of traditional notions of family in the face of many challenges and changes.

In a postmodern geography, many of us become the social effects of dominant groups' spatial constructs. The planned built environments that we inhabit are embedded with other people's definitions or ideologies of what is housing, leisure space, a business district, etc. The built form creates a predisposition in us to particular spatial functions and practices from which social identities are ascribed (whether or not we choose to contest, subvert, or reject them). Furthermore, as Howell and Tentokali determined from their experience in conducting cross-cultural studies on domestic privacy, western urban spatiality confronts certain cultural heritages with new models of space and household transactions. That is, western design and modern construction technologies challenge household behaviors in many new urbanizing societies and reconstitute what is imagined and constructed as family life. This is certainly the case in modern day West African countries which are challenged with spatial and social structures that are the result of at least three superimposed cultural stratifications: the traditional and pre-industrial phase, the colonial experience and the postcolonial economical-political structure (Boserup; Konadu-Agyemang). Each of these realities varies from country to country, but everywhere the position of women and their families depends on the interplay of these three elements (Boserup).

In traditional West Africa the compound—and the family it encompassed—was usually the minimal unit of political organization. Decisions within the compound had implications for the wider political units in villages and in towns. In effect, the western notion of the house being female and private versus the outside being male and public was non-existent in West Africa. Thus, women could exert direct political influence over males or they themselves play important political roles by virtue of their positions of authority, power or influence in their natal and/or affinal compounds (Sudarkasa 53). For this reason, it was common for women to have important roles within patrilineages as well as matrilineages in West Africa. The onset of colonization, modernization and urbanization reconfigured household space in West African countries along an uneven spatial development that favored urban centers over rural settlements, and within urban centers men over women. Thus they produced a tendency in populations to migrate from rural areas to urban centers in search of jobs and changes in traditional social relations between men and women, within and amongst families. This uneven development was an important factor in some West African women's reduced economic autonomy and public role and their increased dependence on their spouses (Pellow 134), especially when they moved to live in urban city conjugal household configurations.

The uneven development of space in West Africa is clearly expressed in Ghana's capital city (Accra) and its present state of housing and infrastructure underdevelopment that has its roots in British colonialism. The housing problems in Accra are not only a colonial legacy caused by urbanization policies that were insensitive to the local cultural context but also a result of the failure of successive governments to derive appropriate, housing policies and their incorporation of Ghana into a global capitalist economy. Accra is the largest of Ghana's ten urban centers. The population in Accra is 1,657,856 of which 57.1% (i.e., 843,516) are female (Government of Ghana). Presently in the city of Accra, females head 30.5% percent of households, even though there are nearly as many female migrants as male, i.e., 69% and 71%, respectively (Konadu-Agyemang 76). Accra alone accounts for 30% of the urban population of Ghana and 10% of the total population or Ghana. In fact, Accra has the highest rate of urbanization in Ghana and one of the highest in West Africa (Konadu-Agyemang 69). Housing occupancy rates are high in Ghana's capital. In 1990, the UNDP and Ghana government conducted a survey in Accra that found that the average number of persons per room was 2.9, i.e., greater than the UN standard of 2.5, and that 46.3% of the city's households occupied single rooms. This lack of space has grave implications for Ghanaian women living in Accra in part because they spend more time in their houses than the men do (Asiama 213). In addition, lack of space directly impacts how women contribute to the welfare and continuity of existing family structures because they are often solely or mainly responsible for the maintenance and upkeep of families.

Uneven urban development in Accra has had an effect on residential units, lineage groupings, rules of descent, and inheritance (Robertson). These effects are also experienced in other parts of Ghana, for example, the land tenure system in Asante society has undergone change. Land now has an economic value, which was not the case in traditional Asante society. The strong links that existed between land ownership and Asante social and political structures has weakened. Land ownership structures no longer support the continuation of the kingroup, and kinship ties are being weakened. In its place the conjugal family has begun to assert itself against the extended uterine family (i.e., one's matrikin). This means that Asante women's relationship with their kingroup have altered, especially in terms of inheritance and dependence on their spouse versus their matrilineal family (Asiama 225–226). As a result, Asante women living in urban Accra provide the ideal population group and setting for the development of *critical spatial literacy* on how Accra's urban built environment affects household configuration and notions of what family should be. Particularly as they are often migrants, in Accra, with a reduced likelihood of access to land and property than they would have in the Asante region. Research in this location and with this population group contributes to an understanding of a postmodern condition of uneven urban development due to fast encroaching western (capitalist) urban spatiality and its challenging effects on family dwellings and practices.

Women from the Asante clan group also make an ideal sample because they come from matrilineal culture, which has had more obvious and distinct cultural differences than other Ghanaian clan groups. Also, Asante tradition and, to some extent, Asante women's role within it have been carefully and extensively documented over a substantial period of time (e.g., Rattray, McLeod, Allman, Tashjian, Ward, etc.). In addition, I am interested in Asante women for this study because of my adherence to a feminist epistemology that roots investigations of the social world in personal experience. As an Asante woman who has lived in Accra, my personal experience provides a ground from which theoretical understandings can be made of Asante women's structural circumstances in Ghana's capital.

A Womanist Ethnographic Project

Research into African women and their families' spatio-temporal experiences cannot simply be a theoretical and/or empirical endeavor. Instead, it must be a womanist spatial research agenda with a pedagogical praxis that is informed by a critical literacy of gender, race and space to begin with. In other words, it must be an endeavor to develop *critical spatial literacy.* I define this literacy as a praxis that is essentially rooted in a critical understanding of the dynamics of the social construction of postmodern urban space and the spatial construction of social life, its practices, and its identities. So as to guide my research I extracted and layered themes from critical pedagogy, feminist methodology, critical social theory informed by postmodern geography, and postcolonial theory to construct a critical lens with which I develop my theorizations and praxis which in this definition, it reinforces the centrality of critical consciousness in a womanist positionality by deriving its definition from a palimpsest of the essential overlapping themes in the following:

1. Jameson's belief in a new view of political action in space through "an aesthetic of cognitive mapping" (54), which is a concept that comes out of Lynch's work on imageability[4] and the critical social theory understanding of the inherent power struggles in the social construction of the spatial and the spatial construction of the social (Soja 110).
2. A consciousness-raising feminist methodology rooted in a grounded position of one's own female subjective position; a political commitment to changing the position of women; and an emphasis on women's lived experience and the significance of their everyday lives (Weiler 58–59).
3. Fanon's argument that an informed understanding of colonialism as the enforcement arm of western capitalism and its colonizing effects must take place to enable a Third World realization of our own humanity.

I believe that this layered effect is crucial for analyzing and perhaps transforming Black women's urban spatial experiences. I envisage this *critical literacy of space* as a theorizing practice with which to understand the local grounded theories that emerge out of our particular socio-spatial identities, urban spatio-temporal experiences, and spatio-political struggles. In this combination, I utilized this *critical literacy of space* as top-down formative theory to understand the bottom-up results I found in a short study conducted.

In December 2001 and January 2002, I conducted a study (in both English and my mother-tongue Asante Twi). It was a small-scale experimental effort that took qualitative approaches to document Akan women's perspectives (especially Asante)[5] on their socio-spatial household transformations and family life in Accra. In particular I identified six key informants with whom I conducted semistructured interviews. I interviewed Akan women for two reasons: first, because of an initial concern that there would not be a substantial Asante female population in Accra to conduct this study;[6] and, second, to determine whether there may be differences in how Asante women and other Akan women view and articulate their position in Accra.

My Akan informants[7] are all women who have migrated to Accra and have lived there for long periods of time (from 15 to 32 years). In terms of the specific clan group breakdown for each informant within the larger Akan umbrella, three of my informants are Asante, two are Fante, and one is Assin. In general, I found my Asante informants to be the most confident, vocal, articulate, and opinionated of my informants. When I asked whether it was difficult for Asante or Akan females to live in Accra, as it was a Ga[8] town, it was an Asante woman who said that she felt that Asante women do not struggle in Accra because they are more hardworking than the Ga. She believed that Asante females saw no shame in gradually working their way up the socioeconomic ladder, e.g., by selling ice water on the streets, to sweeping in front of stores, to earning enough money to trade, and so on. For these reasons, she went on to jovially state that Asante females had taken ownership of Accra from the Ga.

All my informants lived in nuclear family household configurations as a consequence of moving into urban Accra. This was either by themselves, with their children or with their husband and children. They had all, in contrast, previously lived in extended matrilineal family household configurations in their respective hometowns. Often, this was with their mother, her sisters, her sister's children and their mother's children. None of my informants moved to Accra without some form of prior accommodation and work arrangement. They also strongly advised against anyone moving to Accra without making those arrangements in advance. My informants moved to Accra to initially live with sisters, husbands or friends who provided them with opportunities to come to live in the city. They had since moved into their own places that many of them owned with spouses or alone. My informants described how living in Accra was markedly different from living in their hometowns. They all stated that Accra was a hard place to survive in. As one informant stressed, "Accra's inside is hot!"[9] Her support for this description of Accra was that exorbitant rent payments, high light and water expenses, the cost of food, and the thieves made the city a difficult place to live in. Despite this perception, all my informants also said that even though Accra was not necessarily a better place to live in compared to their hometowns, they would remain in Accra because it provided one with educational and employment opportunities, and the ability to have your *eyes opened*.[10]

In all circumstances, the importance of enduring the struggle in Accra was to gain the finances to build a place of one's own, even if it is a humble chamber and hall arrangement. My informants were also quick to say that the ideal configuration of family, to live in their Accra homes, was small and often nuclear. When asked if they would encourage their *abusua* (matrilineal family) to stay with them in Accra the response was always negative, with some concessions that stemmed from the traditional Akan belief that one cannot progress in life if his or her *abusua* does not also progress with him or her. In deference to this belief, one informant said that she would not allow any of her *abusua* to stay for more than two weeks, after which time they would have to be on their own. Many of the informants also said that they would only allow *abusua* that had some form of education, skill or money to live with them temporarily;

particularly as a way of helping them transition into Accra's hectic lifestyle. Most of the reasons given for discouraging *abusua* to stay were pragmatic and financial, e.g., not having enough money and space for one's own immediate family let alone the extended one. There were also some attitudinal responses that categorized *abusua* who came from their hometown as not sophisticated enough to withstand the norms of city life, thus, liable to annoy their city dwelling relatives and/or embarrass them socially due to ignorance.

This preliminary research suggests that Accra's urban built environment is a text that is transforming Asante female household configurations, thus, socio-cultural practices and notions of what an ideal family should be. In this context, which I term as western urban spatiality, I hypothesize that there is a need for *critical spatial literacy* in order for individuals to understand how the built environment is embedded with codes that both constrain and enable one's ability to participate in the design, construction and/or definition of space. To rest this hypothesis, I will be conducting more specific and rigorous qualitative and quantitative research in a larger field study that should define this complex problem that is experienced by Asante women and their families and is embedded in multiple systems, and to identify and explore the factors associated with the problem by answering the following key research questions: (1) To what extent have Asante women experienced substantial household transformations as a consequence of rapid urbanization in Accra? (2) What are the changes in Asante women's family practices as a consequence of household transformation? (3) What is their spatial self-perception as a consequence of household transformation (i.e., a sense of place)? (4) How has *critical spatial literacy* influenced their understanding and negotiation of Accra's urban space and the spatial changes it has effected?

A Postmodern Pedagogy of Critical Spatial Literacy

Kellner argues that in today's multicultural societies we need to develop a postmodern pedagogy comprised of multiple literacies, such as critical media literacy, print literacy, computer literacy, multimedia literacy, cultural literacy, social literacy, and ecoliteracy. He believes that a postmodern pedagogy is of crucial importance in this period of intense globalization, as it serves to "meet the challenge of new technologies," (103) and in terms of education, it would begin to "foster a variety of literacies to empower students and to make education relevant to the demands of the present and future" (103). I argue that an essential element of this postmodern pedagogy must be a *critical spatial literacy*, which serves to analyze and comprehend the profound spatial effects of a global economy, e.g., uneven urban development, the identity disorienting consequences of rapidly changing landscapes, and the transformation effects on families and their practices.

Critical spatial literacy as a praxis for Asante women and their families in Accra means that it is not enough to take contemporary everyday practices for granted while asserting ownership over the very spaces that transform traditional ways of living. Instead, we need to understand the consequence and implications of the transformative power of Accra's urbanity. In doing so, we must analyze how the continued dismantling of traditional notions of physical and ideological *abusua* affect conceptions of ourselves both inside and out of Asante culture and national heritage. We would also investigate the schizophrenic nature of an Asante female identity that now translates itself through western concepts of the good economics of maintaining nuclear family configurations, while simultaneously adhering to the Akan ethic of always supporting *abusua,* albeit in a temporary fashion. As womanism is about the survival and wholeness of an entire people through love and critical consciousness, investigating and scrutinizing the components of migrant Asante women's—and their families'—spatiality contribute to a global understanding of women's urban spatio-temporal conditions and informs transnational feminist and womanist practices that seek to transform the politics of uneven development of urban space.

Notes

1. I am a Royal Institute of British Architects part II qualified architect.
2. Kumase is the capital of the Asante region.
3. By this I refer to my transition into the field of education in order to redefine my architectural role in the politics of space. It is the boundaries or edge conditions of architecture (and being an architect) that I am interested in shifting, rather than just inhabiting their marginality as I did whilst studying and working in architecture. I enact the reality of this already dreamt spatial imaginary of my diasporic, African, female, architectural permutation mainly within the praxis of critical pedagogy, critical feminist methodology from a womanist positionality, critical social theory as informed by postmodern geography, and postcolonial theory. My present agenda is to facilitate arenas for developing *critical spatial literacy.* In doing this work I will be using both my personal experience of invisible homelessness, being socially housed, and my architectural skills outside the confines of institutionalized architecture for the purpose of doing what I tongue-in-cheek call renegade architecture.
4. Kevin Lynch's work with imageability, in the 1960s and 1970s, was to demonstrate the difficulty citizens had in mapping sprawling, spatially segregated cities. He believed that building professionals were responsible for making the urban city more intelligible for its inhabitants to map. Frederic Jameson draws on Lynch's work to argue for the more political aesthetic of cognitive mapping.
5. In Ghana one of the principal ethnic groups are the Akan within which are the Asante that originate from the Asante Region.
6. It would be possible to make inferences about Asante female experiences if all Akan females are included in the ethnographic field study, mainly because Asantes are part of the larger Akan group, which is linguistically and culturally homogenous. However, significant differences in attitude and self-perception that Asantes have, as a consequence of their historical political dominance in Ghana, would have been lost.
7. Their occupations were as follows: a retired banking professional, a fresh fish seller, a dried fish seller, a cassava seller, a dressmaker who is also a well-known actress in Asante TV productions, and a cosmetics dealer.
8. The Ga are one of the major ethnic groups in Ghana.
9. This phrase is a transliteration of the informant's expletive in Asante-Twi "Accra emu ye hyewl." To say that the inside of a place is hot, often refers to how difficult that place is to be in, i.e., it is as difficult as being on the inside of a boiling pot of hot water or soup.
10. This phrase is a transliteration of the Asante-Twi expression "ani bue" that refers to an increase in cultural awareness with a tint of social sophistication.

References

Asiama, Seth. "Crossing the Barrier of Time: The Asante Woman in Urban Land Development." *Africa*, Vol. 2, 1997. pp. 212–236.

Boserup, Ester. *Woman's Role in Economic Development*. Aberdeen: Aberdeen University, 1970.

Fanon, Frantz. *The Wretched of the Earth*. 2nd Edition. Translated by C. Farrington. London: Penguin Books, 1990 (1961).

Government of Ghana. *2000 Population and Housing Census: Provisional Results*. Accra: Ghana Statistical Service, 2000.

Harvey, David. *The Condition of Postmodernity: An Enquiry into the Origins of Cultural Change*. Cambridge, Massachusetts: Basil Blackwell, 1989.

Hayden, Dolores. *The Power of Place: Urban Landscapes as Public History*. Cambridge, Massachusetts: MIT Press. 1995.

Howell, Sandra; Tentokali, Vana. "Domestic Privacy: Gender, Culture, and Development Issues." In LOW, Setha; CHAMBERS, Erve. *Housing, Culture, and Design: A Comparative Perspective*. University Park: University of Pennsylvania Press, 1989. pp. 281–297.

Jameson, Frederic. *Postmodernism, or the Cultural Logic of Late Capitalism*. London: Verso, 1991.

Keith, Micheal; Pile, Steve. "Introduction: The Politics of Place." In KEITH, Michael; PILE, Steve. *Place and the Politics of Identity*. New York: Routledge, 1993. pp. 1–40.

Kellner, Douglas. "Multiple Literacies and Critical Pedagogy in a Multicultural Society." *Educational Theory*, Vol. 48, 1998. pp. 103–122.

Konadu-Agyemang, Kwadwo. *The Political Economy of Housing and Urban Development in Africa: Ghana's Experience from Colonial Times to 1998*. Westport, Connecticut: Praeger, 2001.

Lefevbre, Henri. *The Production of Space*. Translated by D. Nicholson-Smith. Oxford (United Kingdom): Blackwell, 1991 (1974).

Lynch, Kevin. *Image of the City*. Cambridge and Boston, Massachusetts: Joint Center for Urban Studies, 1964.

Ogunyemi, Chikwenye. "Womanism: The Dynamics of the Contemporary Black Female Novel in English." *Signs: Journal of Women in Culture and Society*, Vol. 11, 1985. pp. 63–80.

Pellow, Deborah. *Women in Accra: Options for Autonomy*. Algonac: Reference Publications, 1977.

———. "Spaces that Teach: Attachment to the African Compound." In ALTMAN, Irwin; LOW, Setha. *Place Attachment*. New York: Plenum Press, 1992. pp. 187–210.

Robertson, Claire. *Sharing the Same Bowl: A Socioeconomic History of Women and Class in Accra, Ghana*. Bloomington: Indiana University, 1984.

Soja, Edward. "The Spatiality of Social Life: Toward a Transformative Retheorisation." In GREGORY, Derek; URRY, John. *Social Relations and Spatial Structures*. Basingstoke: Macmillan, 1985. pp. 90–127.

Sudarkasa, Niara. "Female Employment and Family Organization in West Africa." In STEADY, Filomina. *The Black Woman Cross-Culturally*. 8th Edition. Rochester: Schenkuman Books, 1994. pp. 49–64.

Tuan, Yi-Fu. *Space, and Place: The Perspective of Experience*. Minneapolis: University of Minnesota, 1977.

Walker, Alice. *In Search of Our Mothers' Gardens: Womanist Prose*. San Diego, California: Harcourt Brace, 1983.

Weiler, Kathleen. *Women Teaching for Change: Gender, Class and Power*. South Hadley: Bergin and Hadley, 1988.

Weisman, Leslie. *Discrimination by Design: A Feminist Critique of the Man-made Environment*. Urbana and Chicago: University of Illinois, 1994.

Part 4
Critiquing the Womanist Idea

18

Harmony, Hegemony, or Healing?

The Language of Womanism: Rethinking Difference[1] (1997)

HELEN (charles)

Blanket Terminology and Generalizing Women

The politicization of the western black woman germinates at the moment of recognizable resistance to outside forces which deem her subordinate to others. The potential to understand herself is as justified within the context of a feminist ideology as it is within a non-feminist ideology. This chapter questions the viability of womanism as a doctrine for (black) women activists[2] who have been visibly ignored by the white women's movement. It is an attempt to think further towards an understanding of the notion of difference within the feminist arena and examines the terminology used by women who are conscious of feminism but resistant to taking on the white western labelling that goes with it.

As the focus of this chapter is directed to language, an understanding of feminist nomenclature provides a means to tackle areas of black women's invisibility that have long been ignored. I want to consider placing the black woman activist within mainstream feminist terminology. Using the notions of womanism and difference to illustrate, I argue for an examination of the necessity of a viable language from which the black woman activist can speak and, more importantly, is listened to.

Terminology: why is it needed? In what ways is it used and for what purposes? In terms of progression and development, how does it manifest itself? Terming the activities of the Self—political or otherwise—makes it easier to identify the causes and circumvents the assumption that feminism is essentially white feminism. It takes us to a place where we can question what feminism is *qua* feminism. The possibility within women's activism to overcome racial imbalances opens up greater political autonomy within such a feminism. Before exploring the main themes in detail I will examine briefly some aspects of political activism through an analysis of terminology.

Most would agree that given the worlds that we live in, to hope that a perfect term could exist to encompass all identities (class-wise, gender-wise, colour-wise, race-wise, sexuality-wise, and so on) is a fantasy. A term that does not pay lip-service to, but encompasses black women's activism would recognize the viability and equality of all political women in the main body of the women's movement. The split or the branching away of 'black' and 'other' women from this main body would be a sign that these women are not being recognized for what they are worth by a dominant core. After the split three options are available to a black woman. First, she can join another organization. Second, she can give up the cause altogether and get on with her life, creating her own individual (feminist) framework which is perhaps shared with friends. Third, she can create her own movement, academic or otherwise, to which she attracts others like herself. With this third option, appropriate language is fashioned and treated by her and her followers.

The evolution of the term feminist perhaps initially came about in an attempt to address all the issue-wise aspects of class, colour, race and sexuality. As we move through progressive waves which indicate that the majority view is changing, the etymology of feminism per se also changes. For example, in the early 1980s cultural difference made its debut on the feminist agenda, as some white women in North America collaborated with some black women to address issues of exclusion. Joseph and Lewis write in *Common Differences: Conflicts in Black and White Feminist Perspectives* (1981) that, 'From the early generalizations about "all women", feminists are recognizing the need to understand the specific nature and conditions of women's oppression in differing cultures, societies, and economies' (1981: 67). Significantly, as a consequence of the development of feminism, the term has become not only arguably passé but also one of generalization and exclusion. Feminism now is often linked to the theory that it is not reaching a potential activist populace outside the academe. A manifestation of this was the question which was beginning to be asked at the end of the 1980s. Has feminism gone out of fashion and is it out of date? Maybe, maybe not, but the language of feminism has definitely left newer generations and others who feel like they have seen it, done it, been brought up by it and read all the books, searching for alternative lifestyle politics.

There is no single woman who encompasses all the said issues, and fights for rights to be equated to all of them. Where limitations abide, you will always find the need for acknowledgement. This acknowledgement often arrives via term-creation, adding to already existing terminology. To place the word black, for example, or disabled before the term feminist, does not solve the problem. Instead, it makes it explicit that the term is exclusive of the previously ignored or acknowledged group. This instantly valorizes the situation of non-acknowledgement. The idea of a black, disabled or feminist utopia for instance, is useless as an idea on which to base a reality because its premise is not set up to encompass *all* of the so-called black, disabled or feminist people's realities at once. The view that there are as many definitions of feminism as there are feminists runs counter to what a main definition of feminism ought to be striving for—eliminating the possibility of splits from the main body. While feminism should be the stem from which differences can branch out, instead there is a reluctance to put efforts into maintaining the growth of such a stem. Indeed, it could well be said that it was because of the laxity of a feminism which relied on whiteness, that feminism began to dissipate underground.

Womanism as an (In)Sufficient Strategy for Black Women

The instance of womanism is interesting to examine at this stage, as it seeks to offer a universal means to a black women-based end. When Alice Walker came up with the idea of a special name for black women, her term 'womanist' provided an equivalent to 'feminist'. Composed and placed at the very start of her book, *In Search of Our Mothers' Gardens* (1984a), the definition presents itself as introductory to the book's subheading, *Womanist Prose*. This book begins with the very kernel of its concept: 'Womanist. From *womanish*. ... A black feminist or feminist of color' (Walker, 1984a: xi). The specificity of the black woman's experience becomes a viable basis for feminist interpretation right from the beginning. Although the term 'womanist' has not made head-line news, there was a possibility of it becoming more than just a notion, if only because its germination became possible through Alice Walker. However, this was not to be—at least not in this century [the twentieth century, Edn]—as womanism's seedling struggled from the very beginning when it was placed at diametrically opposed ends with feminism. It has been discussed from some positions in North America. bell hooks argues that womanism is not to be confused as an opposing doctrine to feminism: 'I hear black women academics laying claim to the term "womanist" while rejecting "feminist". I do not think Alice Walker intended this term to deflect from feminist commitment, yet this is often how it is evoked' (hooks, 1989: 181). Here in Britain, the term womanism is barely recognized or used. Nevertheless, the notion was taken up in the late 1980s by West African writer Buchi Emecheta (in Granqvist and Stotesbury, 1989: 19) and on a more local level by the London-based group, Camden Black Sisters (CBS). Valentina Alexander, formally of CBS, viewed activism for black and white women as the 'twin revolutions of Black Womanism and White Feminism'. Under 'Some Statements of Fact', she explains: 'Womanism for the Black Woman/Woman of Colour came about as a direct response to the oppression she experienced, through the exploitation of her gender, race and class' (Alexander, 1989a: 29).

It is not always necessary to look for the origins of terms and concepts but if the etymology exists as womanism did, as a potential twentieth-century phenomenon, then it presents a good opportunity to examine the roots[3] and reasons for invention. The term, 'womanist', whatever its intention, is essentially for black feminists (Walker, 1984a). The black woman activist could not fail to respond to what seems like an answer for the need to re-evaluate an ignored, forgotten, marginalized section of society. The excitement, no doubt, reached many who, like myself, find it difficult not only in terms of what appendage (if any) to attach to themselves but also in terms of what is behind the difficulties of nomenclature: why the need for labels anyhow? If the majority of black women are unhappy about being called feminists then the advent of a new term that has a potential for black women in particular would have inevitable allure on a socio-political platform. But somehow womanism did not make the grade despite Walker's belief that she is, 'offering society a new word when the old word it is using fails to describe behaviour and change that only a new word can help it more fully see' (1984b: 25). The crucial question is not whether womanist as a new word can satisfy a new feminist vision, but whether womanist as a new and viable doctrine can make our ever-changing, traditional white feminism adapt to it. Additionally, it is important to consider at which point womanism as a North American experience departs from the experience of black feminists globally.

I want to now turn to looking closely at four sections of Walker's definition of womanism. In the first section of her definition she states womanism is: 'From the black folk expression of mothers to female 'children', "You acting womanish," ... interchangeable with another black folk expression: "You trying to be grown' " (1984a: xi). Walker shows here that womanish as a term comes from the experience of the language and folk culture which is central to a certain group of people with roots in the southern states of North America. Because black languages differ from place to place, the word womanish from a southern U.S. context is not necessarily linked directly to the same experience of girls and women elsewhere. To adopt language in one culture from another is not unusual, but there must exist some initial identification of whatever the term is or is seen to substitute. Looking closely at Walker's dictionary-style definition of womanism reveals an ambitious attempt to cater for a stylized, individual, all-encompassing woman.

In the second part of Walker's definition, there is evidence of her preference to expand the definition womanism in order to escape the problem of exclusion; which is so much a part of white-dominated women's movements. Here she states that a womanish woman is:

> Also, a woman who loves other women, sexually and/or non-sexually. Appreciates and prefers women's culture, women's emotional flexibility ... and women's strength. Sometimes loves individual men, sexually and/or non-sexually. Committed to survival and wholeness of entire people, male and female. Not separatist, except periodically for health. Traditionally universalist. (Walker, 1984a: xi)

It is punchy and humourous, a very important ingredient for anything new on the market. It is also clear in this definition that Walker, in offering a new concept for black women in particular, does not wish to ignore or not acknowledge 'non-black' women. Interestingly, black as a prefix to woman is not included in this second part of Walker's definition of womanist. While its absence magnifies a feminist need (Walker's?) to accept all women of all skin colours it can also be seen as slightly confusing. If the intention is to make 'womanist' follow a poly-textual mode of definition, then it would be safe to assume the utilization of womanist by white women too; used in preference to, or in conjunction with feminist to illustrate *white women's* development in changing society. However, in acknowledging the viability of black women who are as much women as white women are, the celebration of the possible change from exclusive white feminism to inclusive feminism has potential if we introduce the 'white womanist'. In so doing, the promise of a truly inclusive womanism would be eliminated in favour of a compromisory change, because as black feminists have suggested, in many cases the attitudes of white women researchers towards their Third World women subjects appears to be one of pity and distance (Kazi, 1986: 87–8; Mohanty, 1988).

On the sexuality front, there is an assumption in Walker's second definition that womanist substitutes for lesbian as well as terms like transgendered, bisexual, heterosexual, celibate and so on. Does this term really have the power to account for all these issues, or would it give rise to exhaustive appendages? Having said this, issues such as class and race are strangely unrecorded in this second definition. If Walker presumes their inclusion, it is regretful to misinterpret the reading as equal to their explicit exclusion. Walker's 'universality' in this sense exposes a blanket terminology; a blanketing which attempts to cover up exclusion and is as such questionable in its generalization.

Diana Fuss, having written extensively on the subject of essentialism versus constructionism, attempts to throw up old notions that have been criticized for lacking theoretical substance. In her writings she talks about the work of Luce Irigaray (a scholar who has been labelled 'essentialist' by many in the western academe) who makes an interesting comparison to Walker, here. In *Essentially Speaking* (1989), Fuss talks about Irigaray's 'language of essence' in the search, 'not to create a theory of woman, but to secure a place for the "feminine" within sexual difference' (1989: 72). If the invention of essentialist terminology arrives because of the need to fit in somewhere on a macro level, then linguistically and politically, writers like Irigaray and Walker, as Fuss has said, are opting out of the 'P.C.' rat-race and choosing a path of strategic essentialism. Walker in inventing womanism is, perhaps, not trying to create an essentialist theory of black feminism per se, but seeks to secure a home for the black feminine or essence embodied within racial or skin-colour difference which is strategic.

Walker's use of womanism, in raising the question of an essentialist universality, throws up more than the issue of theorizing. It also offers the chance to tackle the question of politics. The phrase which begins, 'Committed to survival …' spotlights Walker's emphasis on the value of collective commitment as part of this womanist make-up. By referring to this commitment to 'survival and wholeness of entire people' it is difficult to understand the exactitude through which this proposed method ought to be practised. The implications of a politics of 'entire people' and 'wholeness' are at once evaded through a suggestion of global simplicity.[4] Conglomerated into one body, like her view that there can exist a 'woman's culture', it is reminiscent of the notion of an all-encompassing 'single black super-woman'. If 'womanists' were meant to be ubiquitous humanists, committed not merely to international affairs but also to the whole notion and existence of universal affairs, a problem surfaces: if to be womanist means to be black, then the issue of western racism must affect and duly concern the would-be 'womanist', notwithstanding the fact that racism ought not to be a black problem.[5]

Given the triple subordination of the black-identified woman, her experience could be used to gauge the overall development towards attainment for freedom and recognition among all people. As Kwame Nkrumah once said: 'The degree of a country's revolutionary awareness may be measured by the political maturity of its women' (Francis, 1983: 36). Similarly, Staples heroically contends that 'Black women cannot be free *qua* women until all blacks attain their liberation' (Staples, 1985: 348). What is recognized here is a project of universal humanism that black feminism represents. However, this political germination has been prevented. And prevention is no cure as the Combahee River Collective well understand: "If Black women were free, it would mean that everyone else would have to be free, since our freedom would necessitate the destruction of all the systems of oppression' (1983: 278). How is the commitment to universal humanism fostered and developed and in what ways is its development equally beneficial to all black and non-black thinking peoples? Given these problems would it then be safer to accept that womanism can be a viable concept only within the realms and parameters of a Walker-based theory? To foster the womanist thesis may only serve to encourage an essentialist notion based solely on instinct, and in 'nature', rather than in combination with activism or socio-political consciousness:

> I don't choose womanism because it is 'better' than feminism. … I choose it because I prefer the sound, the feel, the fit of it; because I cherish the spirit of the woman (like Sojourner) the word calls to mind and because I share the old ethnic-American *habit* of offering society a new word. (Walker, 1984b; my italics)

If term-proposal is 'habitual' to black people then all the more reason to take a serious look at the terminology.

Walker's third definition of 'womanist' shows further, its apolitical nature. She states: 'Loves music. Loves dance. Loves the moon. Loves the Spirit. Loves love and food and roundness. Loves struggle. Loves the folk. Loves herself. Regardless' (Walker, 1984a: xii). Now, some might say that in being black, one is already political and as Meridy Harris has rightly said, being black is certainly turning the English dictionary definition of woman 'upside down' making it 'an *immediately* satisfying subversion of "the weaker sex" ideology which appears to be contested by far too few to effect any radical change from within white culture' (1991: 4). But suppose I am looking for terminology which will give something more in the way of impact. A terminology that would make not only black women sit up, but will make white women listen. Instead of taking an ambiguous or excluded role, such a terminology would enable black women to be heard. The emphasis of Walker is not on political activism, as many, including bell hooks would like, and because of this, it could be said that Walker does not subscribe to a specific woman-activism. Here is what bell hooks has to say:

> For me, the term 'womanist' is not sufficiently linked to a tradition of radical political commitment to struggle and change. What would a 'womanist' politic look like? If it is a term for black feminism, then why do those who embrace it reject the other? (hooks, 1989: 182)

Coming to Walker's fourth definition, 'Womanist is to feminist as purple to lavender', I would say that it speaks for itself in that Walker places both states of being into a kind of extended family situation, a brave gesture of inclusion. My only difficulty with this is that purple and lavender, being traditional white feminist hues (recall 1970s British sartorial politics), are insinuative of a *plea* for inclusion. This attitude is not very symbolic of the western black woman's *amour propre* and as such, indicates an inevitable death of pride in the family.

For one person to 'offer' society a new term appears somehow uncollective in the decision-making process, though creative. But perhaps because of what appears to be an apolitical gloss on Walker's offer of womanism, this is uncollectively intentional. Her womanist ideology can be seen to describe more the spirit of black women, which also has a place, as opposed to a fiercely political identity. However, having said this, it is quite common for language to evolve naturally alongside political change. Think, for example, of the term 'queer', which has in some circles been appropriated from 'odd' with perjorative connotations, to an umbrella term of (political) pride for those who do not consider themselves heterosexual.

What's the Difference? Ignoring Black Women's Visibility

What can be assumed is the general feeling that black women activists in Britain and in North America do not wish to remain on a perpetual feminist agenda as marginalized contributors to a political, woman-based cause. To be listened to is the *raison d'être*. Moreover, 'Black women *resist* being grafted onto feminism in a tokenistic manner [and] argue that feminism has to be transformed if it is to address them' (Ramdin, 1987: 469; my emphasis). Wanting 'our issues to be on the agendas in a wide range of political organizations [struggling] to raise racism as a central issue within the women's movement' (Amos and Parmar, 1984: 7) was paramount to the black woman activist at a time that seems long ago now. And black women have been re-stating the problem over and over again as they recognize the difference in approach, form, content and attitude within feminism. What that difference is exactly and how it can be attributed to useful and developing practical analysis, is now so important that it must be viewed from as many different angles as possible so as to provide maximum visibility. That this vision produces realization and also sets one up for exposure is inevitable and integral to moving obstinate and lazy ideology. What I have referred to as 'guilt-awareness'[6] among white women activists, goes a long way to localizing very sore points in the activist's consciousness and it is a crucial part of her self-awareness and developing or evolving political clout. But there must be a place at which she surpasses the former condition where practical activism takes over to intercept the potential paralysis that can emanate from guilt-awareness.

The Difference within Difference: Diversity and Binary Oppositions

What follows is a short dialogue in identity politics which necessarily cuts across any discussion about language, terminology and women. A black woman announces a separate identity in adopting womanism as a doctrine viable to her own experience as a black feminist, she could adopt 'black feminism' as an appellation appropriate to her situation as 'black activist', or even place a safe bet and identify with an 'intra-ethnic feminism'.[7] The very existence of all these terms is proof that even in the all-embracing universal world that Walker and her followers espouse, there is (and always will be) difference in black feminist identity. There is difference on two obvious counts. First, within the parameters of blackness, not all black women are the same. They are diverse politically, culturally, sexually; colour, caste and class-wise. Second, within the parameters of whiteness, black women are seen as different and identified as 'other'. The difference here is understood as a binary opposition. So, if a woman is black in, for instance, South Africa she is aware of her blackness as something other than 'coloured-ness'. White South African women are more aware of their whiteness than those in, for example, Britain (Harris, 1991). A woman only knows she is black or white because the woman next to her is non-black or non-white. Walker's view would incorporate elements of the latter notion of binary difference to acknowledge the difference between, for example, women who are 'capable' or have reached the point of understanding and those who are not (yet) 'womanist'. I recall Walker: Tradition *assumes,* because of our experiences during slavery, that black women already *are* capable' (1984b: 25). An example of the binary opposition is for the already capable woman calling herself 'capable' to be placed next to the white woman (against which she must define herself) who is not already 'capable'.

Explanatory of the first point, that not all black women are the same, is the philosophy of bell hooks who tells us that difference can emanate also from a historical praxis: 'Often professional black women with academic degrees are quite conservative politically. Their perspectives differ greatly from our foremothers, who were politically astute, assertive, and radical in their work for social change' (hooks, 1989: 181). Ladner has a similar and perhaps more concise approach: 'In discussing the black woman from a historical perspective, it is important to know that there is no monolithic concept of the black woman, but there are many models of black womanhood' (1985: 271). The diversity among black women can also be seen as integral to the structure of Filomina Chioma Steady's work. She writes,

> From the available literature it is already apparent that the black woman, within a cross-cultural perspective, represents much diversity in terms of nationality, class affiliation, generational differences, and particularly historical experience. The aim of this book is not to present a uniform profile or elicit a monolithic image. (Steady, 1985: 7)

In a pioneering presentation, *The Black Woman Cross-Culturally* (1985), from which the previous extract is taken, the anthology as a whole explores the different experiences of black women cross-culturally. Steady provides food for thought on what she considers to be 'true feminism'.[8] She says:

> True feminism springs from an actual experience of oppression, a lack of the socially prescribed means of ensuring one's well-being, and a true lack of access to resources for survival. True feminism is the reaction which leads to the development of greater resourcefulness for survival and greater self-reliance.

> Above all, true feminism is impossible without intensive involvement in production. All over the African Diaspora, but particularly on the Continent, the black woman's role in this regard is paramount. It can, therefore, be stated with much justification that the black woman is to [a] large extent the original feminist. (Steady, 1985: 36)

True feminism does imply an essentialism and exclusivity here: placing one kind of woman over and above another or others. This can propagate negative divisions and visibility within a woman-based, cross-cultural experience.[9] Conversely, Walker takes another angle on true feminism. For her feminism is true as in applicable to *all* women. She states: 'Feminism (all colors) definitely teaches women they are capable, one reason for its universal appeal' (1984b: 25). If this is the case, it is with some concern to discover that in the early 1980s some women of colour right here in Britain were not aligning themselves to feminism, but were instead opting for a separate black women's movement. This is explained in *The Heart of the Race* (Bryan et al., 1985) and warrants a full citation:

> We began to discuss our common experiences of racial and sexist oppression, and as we forge the links we were unknowingly laying the foundation of the Black Women's Movement which would emerge in the years to follow. (Bryan et al., 1985: 148)

Following on from this is a statement from a member of the Brixton Black Women's Group:

> A lot of people think black women began to challenge what was happening in mixed organisations because we were influenced by what was going on in the white women's movement. But I think we were influenced far more ... by what was happening in the liberation movements on the African continent ... although we had begun to form women's caucuses and women's study groups, what Samora Machel had to say about women's emancipation made a lot more sense to us than what Germaine Greer and other middle-class white feminists were saying. It just didn't make sense for us to be talking about changing life-styles and attitudes, when we were dealing with issues of survival, like housing, education and police brutality. (Bryan et al., 1985: 148)

Does this view make imperative the western (as opposed to universal) need to re-term? What of the non-western black woman activist resident in the west? In an interview Buchi Emecheta states firmly, I will not be called a feminist here, [England] because it is European, it is as simple as that, I just resent that. Otherwise, if you look at everything I do, it is what the feminists do, too; but it is just that it comes from Europe, or European women, and I don't like being defined by them. (Emecheta in Granqvist and Stotesbury, 1989: 19)

The views by black women are numerous. However the distinct differences within black feminist ideology remain distinct and, as such, perpetuate the divisions between different kinds of women, black and non-black.

The general fragmentation of the women's movement into splinter groups that focus on specific oppression (racism, anti-Semitism, homophobia, and so on) on the one hand, and concentrate on theoretical analyses of women's issues on the other, has had a knock-on effect within black women's movements. Here too, recognition and acknowledgement of difference in black women's cultures announce a stalemate: Giving voice to differences of opinion (an aspect that can disrupt or gel), exposes women activists as people who are different from one another. Their difference is, of course, not just because of their genders, their classes, their mobilities, or their nationalities,[10] but also because of the un-sameness of their opinions: 'It is not only that there are differences between different groups of women, but that these differences are often also conflicts of interest' (Bhavnani and Coulson, 1986: 84).

In Britain, the fragmentation of OWAAD[11] and the struggles of pioneering black women's organizations, like the acclaimed Southall Black Sisters and the now defunct Brixton Black Women's Group in London, suggest that enthusiasm for a black woman-based politics has waned to a non-public presence. It would appear that a woman-based politics only exists within smaller groups who practise activism mainly on a local level. Pratibha Parmar looks back in retrospect to the mid-1980s. She writes:

> It seems difficult to fathom where the optimism and stridency which many of us had who were active in the black women's movement has gone, and why. Where are the diverse black feminist perspectives which we felt were in the process of growth? And where, indeed, is the movement itself? In moments of despair, one wonders if those years were merely imagined. (Parmar, 1989: 55)

On the second point of the binary difference between black and white women there are two examples which elucidate the notion of 'otherness'. First, more than two decades ago, Toni Cade questioned the emerging white women's analysis of the black women's experience. She asked whether, as another experience, difference ought to be treated as equivalent:

> How relevant are the truths, the experience, the findings of white women to black women? Are women, after all, simply women? I do not know that our priorities are the same, that our concerns and methods are the same, or even similar enough so that we can afford to deal with this new field of experts [white, female]. (Cade, 1970: 9)

Second, Rosalyn Terborg-Penn has explored the outcome of recognizing difference between black and white women. In her article, 'Discrimination against Afro-American Women in the Woman's Movement, 1830–1920' (1985), she suggests the difference between women in the early women's movement was compounded by the fact of race-consciousness: 'Not all Afro-American women sought to join racially integrated organisations. Some organised separate racial groups in response to common problems and to a common sense of identity' (1985: 302). It must be accepted then, that if all feminists are to be regarded as different though they travel similar paths, the theory of difference ought to connect with the experience of difference within a women-based movement. It could be said that the theory and the experience of difference are separate entities:

> The dialogues that have been attempted have been concentrated more upon viable empirical differences that affect black and white women's lives than upon developing a feminist theoretical approach that would enable a feminist understanding of the basis of these differences. (Carby, 1982: 221)

All too often there is a preoccupation with the assertion of difference within the black (and white) woman activist's text. Once asserted, the recognition of difference leaves no space for a 'come back' to a position where a total reckoning of black and non-black women's work against oppression might begin. It sets the ball rolling toward negating sameness. So, in terms of theory, it can be claimed that acknowledging difference in theory begins with the realization of a political motive. That seed—the one that germinates in the black woman activist—grows, but in its roots there is a (feminist) theory based on recognizing difference which is particular but not necessarily exclusive to black women. This can be seen in early black British feminist theory.

Hazel Carby's then-controversial article, 'White Woman Listen!' (1982), was the beginning of a response to a 'theoretical development of a critique of white feminist theories' (Parmar, 1989: 56). Theories specific to challenging white feminism were present long before and are evident in the many letters and statements produced in nineteenth-century abolitionist literature. Black women fighting to be heard refused the offers by white women abolitionists (Harriet Beecher Stowe, for example) to shadow-write their misfortunes as the slave under-class. Instead black women wrote themselves a place in history. Harriet Jacobs' *Incidents in the Life of a Slave Girl: Written by Herself* (1987) testifies to their determination to be heard.

The Language of Difference: Recognizing the Self

Taking the analysis of difference into the comparative subject area of language develops the theory of difference. It enables us to enhance and draw in interrelated themes without which a substantial and binding case for recognizing diversity could not be found. Language as a medium of communication finds itself as exigent and imperative when a belief is transcended into a movement. It would not be conducive to the development of a theory of difference for views which suggest a hierarchy of difference, such as the following, to be nurtured—'The very language and style of the women's movement of the west is an admission of the women's belief that they are inferior to men' (John, quoted in Steady, 1985: 34). It would be essential that views on relative difference and the possibility of their existence be anticipated along with any other rash conclusions. For it is precisely the publicized views held by people that will dictate the continuance of the ideology that shapes the belief or movement. It is crucial to get the message across, enlighten potential followers and participants, work on manifestos and policies. These are the basic means for fostering whatever belief there is. These aspects need language as a vehicle. In the case of womanism, development of the term in language can only arise if it, as a doctrine, is successful in the transportation of its own meaning and is, therefore, meaningful (and viable) to its prospective supporters.

While difference exists between the black woman and the non-black woman, it also exists between a black woman and her *individual* black woman counterparts. The following linguistic interpretation given by Harland (1987) demonstrates the difficulty in finding a term within feminist language to suit all black and non-black women.

Harland[12] suggests that our ordinary methods of thinking are eventually taken over by the desire to think differently. A change from A to B in our understanding takes place in what Harland calls a 'superstructuralist' way, that is to say, the memory of a particular way of thinking is replaced and becomes more important than the memory of what *used* to be a particular way of thinking. Without entering into the complexities of linguistic analysis, what I want to pinpoint is the need to locate the purveyors of language within political frameworks particular to their set of beliefs. Change, which frames the construction of meaning, can be seen to alter language and thus perception. It is this need or desire felt by Walker and others toward a new politicized meaning which prompts the feeling of a 'habitual offering' of terminology. Words such as womanist show that meaning evolves from the experience of difference. There is nothing inherent or fixed in language. If the meaning of womanism came from the experience of exclusion from feminism then its identity as a term would depend on its difference *from feminism*. This is precisely how bell hooks has treated womanist as distinct from feminist: 'When I hear black women using the term "womanist", it is in opposition to the term feminist; it is viewed as constituting something separate from feminist politics shaped by white women' (hooks, 1989: 181). The existence of difference in whatever form, makes for enquiries into the need for homogeneous terminology which labels representative groups of people in society. Ironically the most obvious reason is for the purposes of differentiation, for example, so that one group can be differentiated from another.

The persistence of reductionist terminology cannot be linked to the pro-woman movement as it changes from suffragette to feminist to potential womanist. These defining terms exist in contemporary obscurity insofar as splits within the movement produce a hazy understanding of what the aims of each phase of the women's movement actually is or was. That labelling gives rise to a form of cohesion, and is used to stabilize and bind together a newly forming group or movement, suggests that the process of naming is integral and imperative to a society that dreams of development. To invent or adopt terminology to suit a proposed development is to trigger a development per se. The remaining question is then, to what extent can the development be sustained?

As a visibilizing process, terming becomes a metalanguage to be used for the voicing of ideas, the standing of ground and the assertion of potentially viable doctrines. In the black feminist or womanist case, it is used as a specifying tool for politicization. It spotlights the seeming desire to call oneself a name which has been chosen by a core of like-minded people. As the black woman's voice is created, be it on a plantation or in a palace, a distinct and recognizable term from which a belief can emanate becomes more important. It stands to reason that if the Self, the Black Self as it is termed, is not given voice within the conglomerating body-term of woman, then the force with which the Self is asserted becomes far more exigent. Consequently, the black woman's Self is shaped by an encounter with the languages of western patriarchal white discourses. The black woman is seen in terms of non-Self. That is, she is untermed, invisible—but not absent.[13]

Being defined in terms of the non-Self never remains a static position. For the condition of being untermed triggers a response among those who are deemed to have no power, a *demand* to be recognized by those in power; a demand that those with power recognize that they have it. It is, therefore, important to foster positive self-recognition in (and outside) the sphere of black feminisms.[14] However, Steady speaks of the black woman's predicament of how to valorize her many 'Selves'. It is neither uncommon nor an arbitrary claim to acknowledge multiple identities:

> Several factors set the black woman apart as having a different order of priorities. She is oppressed not simply because of her sex, but ostensibly because of her race and, for the majority, essentially because of their [*sic*] class. Women belong to different socio-economic groups and do not represent a universal category. (Steady, 1985: 23–4)

From Womanism to Post-Black Feminism

If I reject the notion of womanism the idea of a black feminism still remains. Black feminism remains current to the ideology of many black women in groups, organizations, and individually. Whether this is because womanism has not (yet?) been fully taken up, or whether it is perhaps used simultaneously with 'black feminism', I do not know. What I do know is that despite its relative demise, feminism has met with appreciation for a long time now. Feminism must change with the tide. Whether this is successful or not remains to be seen. Black feminism describes overall black women's activism within a socio-political structuring of black women's thinking. If a black woman wants to call herself 'Black-lesbian-feminist-warrior-poet' as Audre Lorde did, it is because of a desire to voice that which is personally and politically important as well as the almost desperate need to be recognized. In the Combahee River Collective, black women activists expand: 'A political contribution which we feel we [as black women] have already made is the expansion of the feminist principle that the personal is the political' (Combahee River Collective, 1983: 276).

If I embrace womanism and perhaps look to creating further terms to describe essentially black women's activism, the *sine qua non* of new terminology must be approached carefully. It is essential to ascertain the degree of cruciality and what particular *differences* the making of new terms warrant. Some might say that a change in terminology would be prophylactic to the progress of a core idea and struggle. In seeking to clarify the terms under which we struggle and succeed in the west, I have to say that the constant changing of terms can also impede the growth and development of the main aims and ideological development of a movement as well as of a people, never mind the erosion of fundamental racism.

If the focus for too long is on the terminology instead of what I call the inherent 'race-sexism' of feminism, the consequences point to serious circumvention of real change. Localizing the lesion where the black and white women's movements fail to adhere to their own principles of inclusion is to address the problem of adapting to a changing society directly and effectively. Understanding the 'problem' of circumvention can precipitate success. Perhaps the most valuable thing that came out of the birth of womanism was its direct challenge to white feminist racism. It provided an instantaneous critique which some white feminists would find hard to ignore. But what worries me is that the term womanism could be used to further the distance between black and non-black women activists. How easy it would be to assume that the advent of womanism had absolutely nothing to do with anyone but black women, so that within a presumed homogeneous group of women it should stay.

The different and new ways that black women are organizing themselves (more focus on gaining higher education, fighting for better employment, better business opportunities and more improved domestic situations) seems to lead to a much needed expression and acknowledgement of an up-to-date feminism. The possibility of a post-black feminist ideology surfaces to co-join an era of post-modern ethics and theorizing. If feminism exists as 'post', then it could be said that it is still carved out of the present definition. However, there seems to be little point in term-proposal if there is no real demand. To ascertain a term's usefulness, questions must be asked. For example, if a term such as 'post' is agreed, what use, if any, will it have for the development of the movement? Does it make important moves, structurally, towards a specific and positive goal for black feminism? Does it advocate total rejection of prejudice—in a way that Walker's womanism does not clarify? Has the term been agreed collectively? Finally and crucially, does the goal of (black) feminism ultimately embrace a universal unity?

With white feminism's track record, it is not really surprising that younger generations are rejecting what they know older generations have been struggling with for decades. In an article in *The Chronicle of Higher Education* (1994), bell hooks talks about how 'most young black females learn to be suspicious and critical of feminist thinking long before they have any clear understanding of its theory and politics' (1994: A44). She goes on to say that,

> Even though feminist scholars like me have worked to create an inclusive feminist movement, one that acknowledges the importance of race and embraces black perspectives, many of today's black students seem to reject the entire idea of feminism. … Just as some black males hold on to macho

stereotypes about maleness as a way of one-upping white men, whom they characterise as wimpy, some young black females feel that they finally can one-up white girls by insisting that they are already 'real' women, taking care of business, with no need of feminism. (hooks, 1994: A44)

As someone who has 'followed' feminism for two decades, and as a victim of habit I, myself, cannot reject it. But I would favour more the idea of the inclusive feminist movement. I acknowledge the importance of discussing the adoption of more appropriate terminology, but alert the reader to the inevitable and eventual situation of a *fait accompli* in doing so. The preservation of the terminology 'feminism', like the preservation of homogeneous grouping such as 'Asian', 'Black' or 'African-Caribbean' ensures a strategic identity. Within black women's activism it ensures kudos and sets up a legitimate basis for organized action. Feminism is thus constructed not as a strict and impenetrable concept but as one which is pervious to change. If it embraces our differences it can also give rise to our strengths.

My proposal now is for a halt to further umbrella terms until there is more cohesion within especially British black women's networks. Womanist creativity and spirit as an appendage to black feminist activism does provide a much fuller text for feminists to work with. In conclusion, despite Walker having been 'hailed as a developer of the "womanist process" ' (Pinckney, 1987: 18), an upsurge of womanist power and politics, and even spirituality, has yet to come to Britain.

Womanism might be to feminism what purple is to lavender, but it must be remembered that when lavender wanes annually from mid- to late summer, the first task of the western gardener is to lop off its purple flowers so as to benefit the lavender as a plant.

Acknowledgements

Along with Tina Papoulias, I also thank Tiz Cartwright and Heidi Safia Mirza for persuading me to revive this essay.

Notes

1. This paper has been edited from the first time it was published as Occasional Paper no. 21, 1990, University of Kent.
2. The use of the term '(black) woman activists' is deliberate. It is not intended to replace or reject other terms such as 'black feminist'. It is a phrase to describe and convey (black) women's political involvement. The use in this paper of the words 'black' and 'non-black' is also deliberate. It is my preference for clarifying the issue of difference without adding confusion to an already complex debate. 'Black' for me means anyone who wishes to publicly call themselves black for reasons that are political or otherwise. And 'non-black' can mean white, or be appropriated to those who do not feel appropriated as 'black'. This is also a strategy (perhaps not the most effective) of resistance to the continual reading of 'non-white'—as if most of the world operated on a white 'control' basis.
3. I am not using 'roots' in the usual sense as an originating source as I believe that there is no 'origin' as such. Roots, for myself, are the sources that extend *as far back as possible*. But it should be noted that seeds are subsumed as roots come into existence.

4. A dedication in Walker's *The Temple of My Familiar* (1989) displays a projection of the Self which is in juxtaposition with the environment, in a way that is politically suggestive, but evasive all the same. The last sentence under the acknowledgments in *Temple* says, 'I thank the Universe for my participation in Existence' (1989: 405).
5. To illustrate what I mean here, I use the following which is taken from Audre Lorde's presentation on 'The Uses of Anger: Women Responding to Racism' at the National Women's Studies Association Conference, Connecticut, 1981:
   After fifteen years of a women's movement which professes to address the life concerns and possible future of all women, I still hear in campus after campus, 'How can we address the issues of racism? No women of Color attended'. Or, the other side of that statement, 'We have no-one in our department equipped to teach their work'. In other words, racism is a Black woman's problem, a problem of women of Color, and only we can discuss it. (Lorde, 1984: 125)
6. See (charles), H. (1992) 'Whiteness—The Relevance of Politically Colouring the "Non" ', in H. Hinds, A. Phoenix and J. Stacey (eds.) *Working Out: New Directions for Women's Studies*, London: Falmer.
7. Steady explains,
   since sexism exists in the black community as well, sexism is relevant to the black woman, although some aspects of its analysis can best be conducted within a framework of what I term 'intraethnic feminism'—that is, within the black group's experience. (Steady, 1985: 3)
8. This is also taken up by Alexander (1989a).
9. The diversity of Steady's excellent essay-collection defies the unity promised in the title.
10. The pluralization of these issues is in recognition of the multiplicities of cultural make-up in the west today.
11. Organization of Women of Asian and African Descent. For a short historiography see Bryan et al. (1985: 164–81).
12. Because Harland's 'superstructuralist' thesis is taken from specific male-oriented sources it must be understood that his language pertains to something which does not include the feminist theorist. It is to be regarded differently and for illustrative purposes in conjunction with what I am arguing.
13. See Toni Morrison's *Playing in the Dark* (1992). She refers to this issue of the absence of blackness. She argues the narrative of whiteness is shaped by a fear of blackness—which is untermed but ever-present.
14. I pluralize this to illustrate that there are many varied possibilities of black women's activisms, whilst also pinpointing the necessity of a viable political option for black women.

References

Alexander, V. (1989a) 'White Feminism/Black Womanism', *Camden Black Sisters Bulletin*, September, London.
Alexander, V. (1989b) 'Black Woman, Black Womanism: Repainting the Rainbow', *Camden Black Sisters Bulletin*, October, London.
Amos, V. and Parmar, P. (1984) 'Challenging Imperial Feminism', *Feminist Review*, Autumn, 17: 3–19.
Bhavnani, K. and Coulson, M. (1986) 'Transforming Socialist Feminism: The Challenge of Racism', *Feminist Review*, Spring, 22: 81–92.
Bryan, B., Dadzie., S. and Scafe, S. (1985) *The Heart of the Race*, London: Virago Press.
Cade, T. (ed.) (1970) *The Black Woman: An Anthology*, New York: New American Library.
Carby, H. (1982) 'White Woman Listen! Black Feminism and the Boundaries of Sisterhood', in The Centre for Contemporary Studies *The Empire Strikes Back: Race and Realism in 70s Britain*, London: Hutchinson.
Carmen, Gail, Neena and Tamara (1984) 'Becoming Visible: Black Lesbian Discussions', *Feminist Review*, Autumn, 17: 53–72.
Combahee River Collective (1983) 'Combahee River Collective Statement', in B. Smith (ed.) *Home Girls*, New York: Kitchen Table, Women of Color Press.
Feminist Review (1987) *Sexuality*, London: Virago Press.
Francis, A. (1983) *The Black Triangle*, London: Seed Publications.
Fuss, D. (1989) *Essentially Speaking: Feminism, Nature and Difference*, London: Routledge.

Granqvist, R. and Stotesbury, J. (1989) *African Voices: Interviews with Thirteen African Writers,* Sydney: Dangaroo Press.

Harland, R. (1987) *Superstructuralism: The Philosophy of Structuralism and Post Structuralism,* London: Methuen.

Harris, M. (1991) ' "Colour Me Purple": The White "Would-be Womanist" in Search of Community', unpublished paper, Women's Studies MA, University of Kent.

Higginbotham, E.B. (1992) 'African-American Women's History and the Metalanguage of Race', *Signs: Journal of Women in Culture and Society,* vol. 17, no. 2: 251–74.

hooks, b. (1984) *Feminist Theory: From Margin to Center,* Boston: South End Press.

hooks, b. (1986) 'Political Solidarity between Women', *Feminist Review,* Summer, 23: 125–38.

hooks, b. (1989) *Talking Back: Thinking Feminist, Thinking Black,* London: Sheba Feminist Publishers.

hooks, b. (1994) 'Black Students Who Reject Feminism', *The Chronicle of Higher Education,* July 13.

Hull, G.T, Scott, P.B. and Smith, B. (1982) *But Some of Us Are Brave,* New York: The Feminist Press.

Jacobs, H. (1987) *Incidents in the Life of a Slave Girl: Written by Herself,* London: Harvard University Press.

Joseph, G. and Lewis, J. (1981) *Common Differences: Conflicts in Black and White Feminist Perspectives,* New York: Anchor/Doubleday.

Kazi, H. (1986) 'The Beginning of a Debate Long Due: Some Observations on Ethnocentrism and Socialist-Feminist Theory', *Feminist Review,* Spring, 22: 87–91.

Kramarae, C. and Treichler, P.A. (1985) *A Feminist Dictionary,* London: Pandora Press.

Ladner, J.A. (1985) 'Racism and Tradition: Black Womanhood in Historical Perspective', in F.C. Steady (ed.) *The Black Woman Cross-Culturally,* USA: Schenkman Books.

Lorde, A. (1984) *Sister Outsider,* New York: Crossing Press.

Mabey, R. et al. (eds.) (1988) *The Complete Herbal,* London: Guild Publishing.

Mohanty, T.C. (1988) 'Under Western Eyes: Feminist Scholarship and Colonial Discourses', *Feminist Review,* Autumn, 30: 65–88.

Morrison, T. (1992) *Playing in the Dark: Whiteness and the Literary Imagination,* London: Harvard University Press.

Ngcobo, L. (1987) *Let It Be Told,* London: Virago Press.

Parmar, P. (1989) 'Other Kinds of Dreams', *Feminist Review,* Spring, 31: 55–65.

Piercy, M. (1976) *Woman on the Edge of Time,* London: Women's Press.

Pinckney, D. (1987) 'Black Victims, Black Villains', *New York Review,* 29 January: 17–20.

Ramdin, R. (1987) *The Making of the Black Working Class in Britain,* Hampshire: Wildwood House Ltd.

Segal, L. (1987) *Is the Future Female?* London: Virago Press.

Smith, B. (ed.) *Home Girls: A Black Feminist Anthology,* New York: Kitchen Table: Women of Color Press.

Staples, R. (1985) 'Myth of the Black Matriarchy', in F.C. Steady (ed.) *The Black Woman Cross-Culturally,* USA: Schenkman Books.

Steady F.C. (1985) 'The Black Woman Cross-Culturally: An Overview', in F.C. Steady (ed.) *The Black Woman Cross-Culturally,* USA: Schenkman Books.

Terborg-Penn, R. (1985) 'Discrimination against Afro-American Women in the Woman's Movement, 1830–1920', in F.C. Steady (ed.) *The Black Woman Cross-Culturally,* USA: Schenkman Books.

Walker, A. (1984a) *In Search of Our Mothers' Gardens,* London: The Women's Press.

Walker, A. (1984b) *New York Times Magazine,* (interview) January 8: 25.

Walker, A. (1989) *The Temple of My Familiar,* London: The Women's Press.

Weedon, C. (1987) *Feminist Practice and Poststructuralist Theory,* London: Basil Blackwell.

Williams, F. (1996) 'Postmodernism, Feminism and the Question of Difference', in N. Parton (ed.) *Social Theory, Social Change and Social Work,* London: Routledge.

Warrior Marks: Global Womanism's Neo-colonial Discourse in a Multicultural Context (2001)

INDERPAL GREWAL AND CAREN KAPLAN

> Imperialism's image as the establisher of the good society is marked by the espousal of the woman as *object* of protection from her own kind.[1]

—Gayatri Spivak

In the last ten to fifteen years, the fields of colonial and postcolonial discourses have produced a by-now-standard critique of objectification, essentialism, exoticization, and Orientalism as the representational practices of modern Western imperialism. That is, an oppositional power relation between colonizer and colonized has come to be understood as a crucial dynamic at work in the disciplines, institutions, subjects, and practices of modernity. Less understood or less examined in the interdisciplinary cultural studies of colonial and postcolonial discourses are the power relations between the different hybrid subjects produced during centuries of imperialism and modernity. Thus, the center-periphery model, or West/Non-West binary, is inadequate to understand contemporary world conditions under globalization: the relations between gendering practices, class formations, sexual identities, racialized subjects, transnational affiliations, and diasporic nationalisms, etc. Constructing monolithic notions of "Western" and "non-Western" subjects in binary opposition cannot always account for the complex, hybrid, and often contradictory subject positions that mark the era of postmodernity.

We begin with this premise in order to understand the practices, womanist and feminist, that underlie *Warrior Marks* (1993), a film directed by Pratibha Parmar and produced by Alice Walker. Since its first screenings, responses have ranged from celebration to angry denunciation. It has been hailed, on the one hand, as a film that brings to light the misogynistic practice of "female genital mutilation"; and, on the other hand, it has also been condemned as a colonialist narrative that depicts African women as victims of their own culture, a "postcolonial civilizing mission" as Rogaia Mustafa Abusharaf calls it.[2] Sorting through these divergent responses helps us understand the contemporary transnational formations through which sexuality, race, and gender create new subjects. Under globalization, by which we mean the expansionary economic and cultural processes of advanced capitalism, these subjects participate in the construction of an identity politics that draws upon both Euro-American cultural feminism and global feminism to articulate an

379

anti-racist multiculturalism. Such a multiculturalism, as evidenced by the Walker–Parmar film, remains embedded in the practices of Western modernity. The modernity of this multicultural subject lies in the humanist metaphysics and liberal political formations that comprise its liberatory agenda. In *Warrior Marks*, this modernity produces a global womanism—the belief that the intersection of race and gender creates a homogeneous colonized female body as well as the conditions for the liberation of that body. The Walker–Parmar film assumes that a Euro-American multicultural agenda travels freely across national boundaries. Thus, we need to understand multiculturalism in a transnational perspective in order to come to grips with this relatively under-recognized legacy of colonial discourses at work in contemporary Euro-American feminist and womanist practices.

In *Warrior Marks*, a film made presumably with the very best intentions by two committed feminist activists of color, the articulation of a global version of womanism derived from Euro-American cultural feminism results in a neo-colonial representational practice. US cultural feminism constructed an unproblematic narrative of liberation based on a universalized and essentialist identity as "woman."

This form of cultural feminism, as it has been practiced in the US and in Europe from the 1970s to the present, often turns its attention to "global sisterhood" when faced with the dilemma of transnational feminist politics. This form of "global feminism," as Chandra Mohanty and others have pointed out, can result in imperializing and racist forms of "knowing" those constituted as "others."[3] Our task in this chapter is to investigate the complex positionality of the subjects constructed through this representational practice. In order to analyze the contemporary reach of what we call multiculturalism's global sisterhood, we will examine the genealogies of these practices in colonial discourses about women.

As Martin Jay has argued, within Western modernity's "scopic regime" the "visual" plays a primary role in communication and the institutionalization of knowledge.[4] Western ethnographic and documentary film traditions are fully implicated in the empiricist, realist, and positivist ideologies of modernity, ideologies that Walker and Parmar rely upon in their multiculturalist project. While scholars have begun to examine the ways in which multiculturalism has been co-opted and commodified (limiting its oppositional possibilities),[5] we argue that in a transnational framework, US multiculturalists cannot address issues of inequalities and differences if they presume the goal of progressive politics is to construct subjects, feminist or womanist, that are just like themselves.

Multiculturalism's Global Sisterhood: Reading *Warrior Marks*

After several decades of struggle and resistance to ethnocentric and Eurocentric articulations of feminism, multicultural feminism and its variants such as womanism and global womanism have achieved considerable recognition as feminist practices in the United States. Even within the enabling and demystifying paradigms of feminist multiculturalism, a tendency to elide geopolitical considerations and to promote a universalized identity for women of color can also produce points of alliance with colonial discourses. When Euro-American feminist multiculturalism links with colonial discourses that articulate binaries of tradition and progress, for example, or civilized and barbaric, a powerful form of neo-colonialism recurs in activist and progressive representational practices.

The film *Warrior Marks* and its accompanying coffee-table print version, *Warrior Marks: Female Genital Mutilation and the Sexual Blinding of Women*, are recent examples of contemporary Euro-American multicultural feminism in its imperializing vein as global womanism.[6] Proposing "benevolent" rescues and principled interventions, *Warrior Marks* advocates a return to the interlocking traditions of missionary projects, modernizing practices, and global sisterhood. Claiming to demystify a practice from far away lands that appears to have origins deep in a patriarchal past, the *Warrior Marks* texts remystify genital surgeries in Africa, creating conventional subjects of an anthropological gaze already well-known to Western viewers through ethnographic and documentary cinema and their popular and mainstream counterparts.

Ethnography, as Claude Levi-Strauss defined it, represents "societies *other* than the one in which we live."[7] This displacement from the location where "we" live to a gaze upon a place where "others" can be observed forms a foundation for representational practices and discourses under the sign of modernity. The ethnographic impulse, that is, the authority conferred upon the observer by modernity's scopic regime, underlies the birth of cinema itself—the films of Lumière have been referred to as "direct" or "actuality" cinema, terms that can be linked to the rhetorical structure of classic ethnography's reliance upon positivist realism.[8] The rise of modern science and its link to discourses of vision and rationality in the West informs the voyeuristic practices of ethnographic cinema in its documentary mode. Western subjects learn to "see" in a specific set of historically constructed interpretive regimes based upon discourses of unmediated visuality, scientific evidence, objectivity, and the "real."[9]

Ethnographic film as an anthropological practice, David MacDougall has argued, has been defined by its intercultural and interpretive focus, in which foreignness, exoticism, travel, and adventure were necessary elements in constructing knowledge about "others."[10] Visual anthropologists who produce ethnographic films become cultural brokers in what MacDougall calls "the economic exchange of global images."[11] While this tradition has been subverted and critiqued by anthropologists and filmmakers such as MacDougall himself, Jean Rouch, Trinh T. Minh-ha, Laleen Jayamanne, and others, ethnographic cinema, as Fatimah Tobing Rony argues, continues a tradition of "pervasive 'racialization' of indigenous peoples."[12] Such a racialization, according to Rony, denies people of color "historical agency and psychological complexity."[13]

Warrior Marks not only relies on the positivist production of empirical knowledge as documentary testimony but recuperates the racialization and gendered "othering" of non-Western subjects from the ethnographic cinematic tradition. That the cultural producers of this work are two women of color raises important issues about new forms of racialization and power relations between women from First and Third World locations. While we have seen the appropriation and recuperation of positivist visual logics in Third World cultural production (for instance, in nationalist, anti-colonial narratives),[14] what is new here is the construction of a global womanist project framed epistemologically by US multiculturalism.

Given the particular intellectual and political trajectories of both Alice Walker and Pratibha Parmar, respectively, certain questions arise in relation to how *Warrior Marks* continues the tradition of ethnographic visual representation. Walker is best known as an award-winning novelist and anti-racist activist who has refused the label "feminist" in favor of what she terms "womanist."[15] Instrumental in moving US cultural feminism into discussions of racial difference, sexual identities, and resistance to white supremacy, Walker is a primary figure in the US women's movement in general and the movements of women of color in particular. Parmar, who began as an anti-racist feminist activist in Britain, is an increasingly well-known independent filmmaker whose films have ranged from investigations of racialized sexual identity to profiles of well-known women of color writers and activists. Parmar's interest in coalitions with US women of color and Walker's desire to address a topic with "global" dimensions has led to a collaboration that presents the tensions that arise in multicultural feminism's imbrication within racialized diasporas.

The collaboration between Walker and Parmar forms a compelling and complicated coalition between a US-based writer and cultural figure who has struggled to make a space for African-American women's concerns and a British filmmaker whose family's diaspora includes South Asia and East Africa and who has made a commitment to lesbian feminist and anti-racist cultural production. Their process of building an alliance and finding a method of working together is powerfully depicted in the print text of *Warrior Marks*. Consequently, in discussing Walker and Parmar's collaborative work, we need to refer to both the film and the print text. The book *Warrior Marks* records the production of the entire project in both narrative and glossy visuals, giving more context for the project as a whole and adding appendices that document resources. The print text, then, is interesting in and of itself even as it comments self-reflexively on the production of the film. Framed by maps of West Africa, the book utilizes epistolary devices, organizing sections around letters sent between Walker and Parmar throughout the pre- and post-production period. In this text, the narration is evenly divided between Walker, the film's producer and narrator, and Parmar, the director. A third section of the book is devoted to interviews, informational tables, networking information, and other appendices. This section attempts to provide the "voices" of other women, including African and European activists as well as "native" informants. In this sense, the print text differs significantly from the film, providing the kind of production information that is edited out of conventional film products. Nevertheless, both texts adhere to a set of ideological and discursive formations that produce specific subjects; in this case, victimized females in rural Africa and their First World saviors.

Because Walker and Parmar's work has helped to shape both multicultural and anti-racist feminist practices, the emergence of colonial discourse in their collaborative texts raises important questions for many of us who share their political concerns. Thus, the problem is not that Walker and Parmar are not "post-structuralists" or "postcolonial theorists"—Parmar is the author of a significant contribution to feminist postcolonial theory and Walker is a well-respected public intellectual.[16] Our critique does not cast them outside our fields but, rather, seeks to situate our feminist arenas of activism and political struggle within a transnational framework of cultural production that can never be seen to be apart from the politics of representation. As producers of representations, Walker and Parmar can be held accountable for their choices of genre, format, and discursive practices. Since they chose a documentary form for their film, intending to use the techniques of montage, interview, voiceover narration, and travelogue to make a political statement about a set of practices in a distant location, we read the text as feminist cultural critics of the history of modern imperialism. Consequently, we are concerned that such interventions, since they rely on colonial tropes, cannot be effective because they do not provide a socio-cultural and historical context in which activism, as the intersection of gender and agency, can become possible.[17]

The project of *Warrior Marks* is circumscribed at the outset by its rhetorical strategy of global womanism. Given the history of discussions of female genital surgeries in Africa in the anthropological literature and the Western cultural feminist discourses of human rights and domestic violence, the multicultural feminist or womanist approach to the topic cannot escape a colonial legacy. In the history of the multitudinous ways in which the female gender is produced in various cultures, female circumcision has been given an overwhelming and problematic attention in the West.[18] The value-laden terminology justifies and rationalizes interventionist narratives and practices. The surgical removal or alteration of women's genitals is referred to by a range of terms including circumcision, excision, genital mutilation, and clitoridectomy. FGM, the acronym for female genital mutilation, has come to stand for the surgical practice itself in many US feminist/womanist communities. Given that terms are always political and contingent, we are opting to use the phrase "genital surgeries" following Isabelle Gunning's argument that "mutilation" is ethnocentric and judgmental while "circumcision" is misleadingly benign.[19] The problem of terms marks the social relations that structure the sexual-, gender-, and geo-politics of these discourses. That is, each term is attached to a history of colonialism linked to Enlightenment concepts of individuality and bodily integrity, medicalized notions of "cleanliness" and "health," sexualized notions of the primacy of "clitoral orgasm" and cultural organizations of pleasure. Terminologies produce epistemic violence—the silencing and erasure that specialized language enacts in particular situations in reference to particular inequities.[20] Such problems of vocabulary characterize the fraught terrain of cultural commentary in international and cross-cultural contexts.

Alice Walker has been investigating female genital surgeries (although she would insist upon the term FGM—female genital mutilation) for many years. Her novel, *Possessing the Secret of Joy* (1992), revolves around a circumcised protagonist, picking up one of the narrative threads of *The Color Purple* (1982). *Warrior Marks* uses a documentary format to rally opposition to FGM and enhance the international activist movement for its abolition. In the film, Walker interviews women in Europe and Africa to demonstrate the destructive effects of FGM and to draw a connection between violence against women in general and this practice in particular. The film advocates a global sisterhood composed of diverse women of color living in the US and Europe intervening in order to "save" the lives of women and girls in Africa and African immigrant communities in the First World.

In the print text, Walker outlines clearly her personal stake in this project when she discusses her understanding of the metaphorical link between various kinds of "patriarchal wounds." Drawing upon her own experience of violence in a family setting, Walker describes a terrible childhood trauma. Her brother aimed his BB gun straight at her and struck her in the eye. In Walker's recounting of this frightening event, it is clear that her injury was as deeply psychic as it was physical. Her mother and father's distanced response to her pain and fright only compounded her sense of betrayal and danger. Walker makes a direct association between this betrayal and the role that African mothers and grandmothers play in FGM as reproducers of the legitimating ideology and as colluding participants. Her identification with the African victims of FGM is based on her own experience of the vulnerability of young girls in patriarchal families.

This logic of identification is used in the film to link Walker to the African women and children and to link the film spectators to Walker's point of view. Her practice depends upon a notion of interpretation whereby one subject comes to "know" another or others based on a perceived similarity that precludes any self-consciousness of the contingent and power-laden nature of relations between women. In *Writing Diaspora*, Rey Chow argues that several strands of the word "identification" are at stake in the politics of identifying "authentic" natives: "How do we identify the native? How do we identify with

her? How do we construct the native's 'identity'? What processes of identification are involved? We cannot approach this politics without being critical
of a particular relation to *images* that is in question."[21] *Warrior Marks* utilizes visual colonial tropes not only to identify the "natives" but also to enable
Walker herself, as narrator, to identify with this native. Doris Sommer has
argued that a romanticized identification with cultural Others can be "the
ultimate violence" as appropriation and can foreclose the possibility of any
political alliance or solidarity across identities.[22] Thus, Walker legitimates her
view of African genital surgeries by projecting her own tragedy—her brother's
assault and her injured eye—onto the bodies of women whom she perceives to
be in peril from patriarchal violence. "I chose to be part of the subject of *Warrior Marks* and not a distant observer because I wanted to directly align myself
with genitally mutilated women," Walker explains. "Like them, I knew I had a
patriarchal wound."[23] Without taking away from the horror of an attack by a
family member, how can an analogy be made between such different practices
and events? Each has its own complex articulation within a specific patriarchy
and a particular historical context that includes race, nation, gender, class,
and other social factors. Walker's experience of violence can be read through
the lens of a male dominance that is complexly sanctioned within a nuclear
and extended family both shaped and constrained by histories of racism and
class among other social forces at work in the American South. Her identification with the "victims" of female genital surgeries does not inform us about
the nuanced relations between men and women, between women and women
of different classes, ages, nations, ethnicities, and their differential participation in modernity in contemporary Africa. Like so many acts of identification,
it enacts its own epistemic violence and erasures.[24]

As a representational strategy, "identification" requires an elision of material difference in favor of a fantasized similarity. In her section of the print
text, Parmar describes how working on the project caused her to become
increasingly emotionally swept up into Walker's point of view. She reports
that once she arrives in Africa, she wakes up from dreams screaming that she
is in danger of being infibulated. This aura of terror and helpless victimization
pervades the entire film, contradicting some of the footage itself (which shows
local women looking healthy and happy), and punctuating the dry, documentary reportage of health workers, doctors, and activists. Throughout the film,
a dancer is used to demonstrate the filmmakers' emotional projections of terror onto the symbolic body of the African victims. The visual logic brings
viewer and dancer together into a state of fused identification.

Based in part on these kinds of techniques, the film has generated strong
and deeply felt support within particular feminist communities in Europe
and North America. The relatively widespread advance publicity and distribution of the film and print text can be attributed to Walker's popularity as
a novelist and cultural figure as well as to Parmar's growing reputation as

an independent filmmaker. For example, *Warrior Marks* has been picked up for distribution by the influential Women Make Movies group, and flagged for special attention beyond their general catalogue in special flyers on the subject of global feminism tied to the 1995 UN Beijing Women's Conference. We attended the screening of the rough cut of the film at the 1993 San Francisco Gay and Lesbian film festival where a capacity crowd enthusiastically applauded the presentation of a special director's award to Pratibha Parmar. Similarly large crowds greeted with strong emotion the film's opening in several metropolitan locations in the United States. The journalist who covered the Washington, DC, premiere at Howard University for the activist publication *off our backs* described an auditorium-size audience "openly weeping" and "spontaneously cheering," for instance.[25]

The reception of the film in print has been divided between the global womanists (many of whom identified with the film's construction of universalized racial and sexual communities) and those who critiqued the neo-colonial representational practices of the film (many of them Africanists). The film was reviewed positively in most US-based feminist and lesbian-feminist publications, where the global womanist viewpoint was overwhelmingly valorized.[26] The enthusiastic support for the film, reflected in the reviews, may come from an affirmation of the Parmar–Walker project which, at the moment that it constructs the African woman as silent victim or global womanist/feminist, constitutes Western subjectivities. This imperialist subject is affirmed by the film's recuperation of the civilizing project of colonialism within which the figure of the colonized woman as silent victim played a key role.

Although the most prominent mainstream critique of the film appeared as an op-ed piece by Seble Dawit and Salem Mekuria in *The New York Times*,[27] other critiques have built upon earlier responses to Walker's previously published novel on the topic, *Possessing the Secret of Joy*. These reviews argue that Walker's overgeneralizing of African history and culture leads to errors of fact and the reproduction of long-standing stereotypes.[28] Most recently, a special issue of the *Case Western Reserve Law Review* that focused on female circumcision included detailed critiques of Alice Walker's work.[29] For example, while L. Amede Obiora argues that many Western representations of female circumcision ignore the diversity and complexity of this practice, Micere Githae Mugo focuses on Alice Walker's work as an example of a Western "external messiah syndrome" in which activism becomes an invasive practice imbued with unequal power relations.[30]

The Construction of Knowledge through Gendered Representations in Colonial Contexts

The "civilizing" practices of modern European imperialism have generated specifically gendered forms of colonial discourse within which the figure of the "woman" plays a key role in subject constitution. Practices that pertain to women's lives such as *suttee,* seclusion, foot binding, veiling, arranged marriages, and female circumcision have come to symbolize the "barbarism" of non-Western cultures.[31] Singling out such practices as moral anathemas, imperialist discourses condemn entire cultures. Feminist scholarship on colonialism has given us profound insights into the ways in which such isolated tropologies work to mystify histories of social relations, particularly interlocking patriarchal forms and the recastings of various hegemonic formations under colonialisms and nationalisms.[32]

More recently, gendered colonial tropologies are visible in the media as debates over the *hijab* (head covering), in attacks on Muslim fundamentalism, sensationalized accounts of sex tourism, and efforts to legislate against female genital surgeries. These representational practices produce images of Third World women as objects or victims who require First World assistance and direction. Within modernity, First World discourses of the Third World as well as nationalist discourses about its female or subaltern subjects continue such representational practices in a variety of historical contexts. When women are raped during a war, for example, their bodies function symbolically as metaphors for "nation," generating patriotic, patriarchal nationalist responses.[33] Yet, at the same time, local domestic violence and physical abuse do not resonate within geopolitical recuperations of nationalism. For example, the high incidence of rape and domestic violence in the US is not addressed as an international human rights problem in the mainstream press. Our point is not that any of these tropological instances are in and of themselves morally or politically defensible. Rather, their popular representation constructs a binary opposition between West and non-West that disallows an examination of the links between patriarchies in modernity and postmodernity.

For instance, female genital surgeries clearly need to be examined as a problematic social practice within the reconstruction of patriarchies in the context of decolonization. Yet, in Western contexts there is very little discourse on genital surgeries that does not reproduce social relations inherited from European imperialism.[34] Poor women everywhere, especially in the formerly colonized parts of the world, face limited health care and educational opportunities as well as the denial of economic and political agency due to global inequalities, rearticulations of patriarchies in specific regions, and the legacies of colonization. Western discourse on female genital surgeries does not incorporate these complex factors, but continues to direct a "horrified gaze" toward its colonial and post-colonial subjects.

In order to understand what is at stake in such a "horrified gaze," we have to place female genital surgeries in the context of a long representational history in Western cultures. The ascription of such surgeries as a sign of non-Western "barbarism" requires the suppression of the history of this practice in the West, displacing these surgeries onto an ontological "other."[35] This kind of displacement occurs in accounts constructed by colonial bureaucrats, missionaries, health workers, educators, anthropologists, and travelers throughout the nineteenth and twentieth centuries.[36] Such accounts form an important textual archive as well as a discursive practice of empire that disciplines colonized bodies in historically specific ways.[37] This process of "othering" has constructed colonizing subjects as well. Thus the colonial classifications of racial and ethnic types include notions of "whole" and "fragmented" or "mutilated" bodies. The "mutilated" body is at once an object of fascination, desire, and repulsion, differentiating between colonizer "self" and colonized "other."[38] European modernity utilizes horror, romance, and adventure genres to gain power and to construct a Western identity of a fixed and stable self.

The modalities of such knowledge are visible in the binary division between modernity and tradition, the identification processes of humanist subject formation, the construction of subjects and objects through "ethnographic authority," the descriptive and stylistic genres of cultural productions of "difference" as "otherness."[39] In this context, "knowing" can mean the violent imposition of one's values, perspectives, and agendas on those seen as mirrors of the self rather than as complex, historical subjects.[40] These identification practices proliferate in both visual and print traditions in Western modernity.

Reproducing Colonial Discourse: Global Womanism's Narrative and Visual Conventions

Feminist scholarship on colonial discourse has been crucial in pointing out the ways in which imperialist social relations produced the female subaltern as a specifically embodied subject situated in the Third World. Yet, the history of Western feminist ideas and practices includes imperializing and racist formations. Contemporary feminist scholarship on women travelers, for example, has been divided between celebrations of adventurous heroines and condemnations of racist "memsahibs." Such a division in representation can obscure the complicated class and ethnic distinctions that structure Western women's travel and immigration as well as the history of both pro- and anti-imperialist activities on the part of Western feminists. Enmeshed in either the romance of individual achievement over the rigors of travel or a nationalist resistance to European or North American traveling cultures, Western feminist representations of travel remain uneven, under-theorized, and deeply troubling. For instance, the presence of African-American missionaries in Africa in the nineteenth and twentieth centuries requires more research into and discussion of these kinds of complex positionalities that cannot be understood fully within the binary of colonizer/colonized.[41] One of the primary technologies which Walker and Parmar use to convey knowledge is a map of their "travels." It is standard practice in colonial discourse to naturalize the social world through representation. Such maps, used in the broadest metaphorical sense, chart the flows of goods, resources, and peoples in the uneven trajectories of capital. *Warrior Marks,* markedly uninterested in class issues, makes a map of ethnic and racial diaspora that is superimposed upon a map of a unified and universal female body. This complex mapping of modern subjects conflates an "African" diaspora with a Western cultural feminist construction of "woman" to argue for a "return" to the mother country, to the body of the mother, to the source of female identity.[42]

This universalized body—whole, unified, and organic in relation to the circumcised body of the "Other"—forms the standpoint for the feminist practices visible in *Warrior Marks*. Such a standpoint prevents recognition of the ways in which Western patriarchies are inscribed on women's bodies through various technologies and disciplinary practices—breast augmentation, liposuction, rhinoplasty, tubal ligations, *in vitro* fertilization, mastectomies, hysterectomies, cosmetic surgeries, etc.—within the context of a lack of health care and reproductive freedom for metropolitan women, especially poor women and women of color.[43] Geopolitics and cultural asymmetries must be included in our analyses of the formation of specific sexed and gendered subjects in various locations. The histories and relations between such subjects are important topics of analysis in our struggle to deconstruct global feminist discourses. Western feminism's essentialist notions of bodies and sexuality pervade the globalizing discourse of "sisterhood," through imperializing representations. *Warrior Marks* is only one such cultural product in circulation, generating neo-colonialisms in the name of multicultural feminism. One response to *Warrior Marks*, therefore, is to begin a discussion of the ways visual representations, identities, and subjects in modernity collude with the power relations of late capital's colonial ventures.

In the film *Warrior Marks,* the primary tropes of travel that centuries of imperialist economic expansion have engendered are easily identifiable. First and foremost, a designated area—here "Africa"—must be emptied metaphorically and made culturally blank.[44] Thus, the film depicts an overwhelmingly rural Africa peopled only by natives dominated by cultural tradition. *Warrior Marks* acknowledges a few African doctors and activists who work against the practice of genital surgeries but suggests that their actions are ineffectual and can only be strengthened by help from abroad. Both the film and the book present Walker and Parmar on a heroic mission to an Africa that is the site of unspeakable practices against its "women." Indeed, in its portrayal of Africa as a relatively undifferentiated space of "otherness," *Warrior Marks* erases the histories of decolonizations and diverse formations of nation-states including decades of "development," "modernization" programs, and localized strategies of resistance.

Instead, *Warrior Marks* prefers to deploy images that could easily be culled from the magazine pages or documentary footage of *National Geographic*.[45] The world the film conjures for its female heroines to travel through is one in which tradition is drastically differentiated from modernity. This distinction is drawn as a geographical map where some regions remain "dark," unenlightened, and thus more dangerous for women than others. In the print version, this map is rendered literally, complete with insets and scales in a manner reminiscent of such nineteenth-century travel accounts as Mary Kingsley's *Travels in West Africa*.[46] The book is organized into sections that recount the "journeys" of Walker and Parmar. These journeys are further linked to a particular set of Western feminist conventions through the use of epistolary communications: "Dear Pratibha," the book begins.[47] The film also uses the letters between Walker and Parmar as part of its narrative strategy. But before the literary convention of the epistle fully structures our understanding of the film, we see and hear the most typical of colonial discourse tropes—we hear drumming and we see a muscular leg draped in a multipatterned fabric resembling "native garb." We are from the first instant "abroad." More specifically, the drumming signals "Africa" to non-Africans raised on both Hollywood and standard ethnographic films. That is, we, the viewers, must be assumed to be people who are not living in Western Africa—who are not at home there.

Although Walker's early intention was to make a film to educate and raise African consciousness about genital surgeries, she and Parmar soon discover financial and technical constraints—the cost of subtitling a film made in English and the lack of screening or viewing facilities, for example. In the film project, the rhetorical effect of "knowledge" must be produced in the face of a profound lack of information on the part of the filmmakers. African women in diverse locations and of different classes become subsumed under the category "African" as the film's shooting sites in Gambia and Senegal become generalizable to an entire continent and the specific practices of genital surgeries are universalized. Although Parmar and her assistant were able to spend only a week in Gambia researching locations and setting up contacts before Walker arrived and the two-week shoot began, the presentation of information in the text is asserted with great confidence as "fact." Yet, without local guides and with elusive and unreliable contacts, the film crew is literally "lost"; none of the visitors speaks the relevant languages, no one has spent time in these places before, and no one is knowledgeable about this part of Africa. While Parmar spent part of her childhood in Kenya, her adult life in England has not been focused on African topics or studies. By the grace of her research for her novel, *Possessing the Secret of Joy,* Walker becomes the production's "expert" on female genital surgeries. The relatively short pre-production period, the great distances and language barriers, and their difficulties in linking up with prominent activists, such as Awa Thiam, mean that such contacts are more haphazard than they are the product of long-term coalitional activity.

The mistrust of some local figures toward the filmmakers may be justified. For in order to create a global subject—"woman"—as victim of generalized patriarchal oppression, Walker and Parmar have to utilize both anti-feminist and Eurocentric discourses in the form of authoritative texts. The "Selected

Bibliography and Suggested Reading" section that appears at the end of the print version of *Warrior Marks* is interesting in several regards. The key citations fall into categories such as African nationalists (Jomo Kenyatta), Euro-American popular sexologists (Masters and Johnson, Shere Hite, etc.), randomly selected and uncritiqued ethnographies (Marcel Griaule, Jacques Lantier), and African and Euro-American activists on women's health issues who are heavily identified with the fight against FGM. Absent from the bibliography are feminist histories of colonialism and nationalism or decolonization, critiques of ethnographic knowledge in general or the surgeries in particular, and socio-political accounts of the lives of women in Africa. While Walker and Parmar acknowledge that contemporary practices of FGM may be attributed in part to colonialism, such an acknowledgment disallows any infiltration or impact on their own dunking or ideological formation as Western subjects in modernity. The burden of an oppressive practice falls on an ahistorical "tradition" in an exoticized culture.

The appearance of a binary opposition between tradition and modernity is a primary paradigm of colonial discourse. As critics and historians including Edward Said, Talal Asad, Johannes Fabian, Gayatri Spivak, and Ella Shohat have pointed out, this binary division creates a logic for Western intervention because it constructs a view of modernity as a corrective to tradition.[48] Modernity becomes a signifier for a range of attributes including the enlightened West, progress, civilization, democracy, self-determination, and freedom of choice. Tradition becomes the "other" by which non-Western cultures make their own empowerment socially, politically, and culturally. It is only by deconstructing this binary opposition through historicization and contextualization, that tradition and modernity emerge as constructs of a European world view that emphasizes a teleological and rational course over and above other modes of representing change, difference, and similarity. As two aspects of the same paradigm, then, the oppositional relationship between tradition and modernity masks the power of one term to describe and evaluate cultures that are designated as the "other."

Warrior Marks reinscribes this oppositional relationship that is so central to colonial discourse and Western, metropolitan subject formation. Rural Africa comes to signify "tradition," a destructive environment for women. In the film, the camera utilizes standard ethnographic shots to establish cultural difference. The gaze behind the camera penetrates the social space of the local people, moving in and out of doorways, searching for "secrets." The pivotal scene around which all these issues seem to revolve occurs in Walker's interview with an elderly female "circumciser" (who has no identity or name except "Circumciser 1" in both print and film texts). This scene summons many of the tropes of colonial discourse as it is interpellated through global feminism, especially the missionary discourse of eradicating ritual practices by "outing" them, by bringing "light" onto the subject, as it were.

392 • The Womanist Reader

Following Gayatri Spivak's and Rey Chow's examination of the representation of subaltern subjects in colonial discourse, this scene between Walker and the "circumciser" illustrates the way resistance and silence—often coded as "secrets"—challenge Western, liberal political formations.[49] In the interview, the elderly woman is portrayed as sinisterly withholding information from the interviewer, Alice Walker.[50] This "withholding" is presented as being crucial to maintaining tradition. Walker's "telling," on the other hand, is seen as the key to liberating the prisoners of traditional culture. The struggle between Walker and the nameless Gambian "circumciser" is visually and textually presented as a moral victory for Walker's viewpoint. The camera focuses repeatedly on the crude blade the woman holds in her lap, suggesting its deadly and cruel uses. Many reviewers comment on the powerful impact of the struggle between the "circumciser" and Walker's efforts to force her to reveal her "secrets." Indeed, the *San Francisco Chronicle*'s reviewer referred to the elderly woman as "wizened" and "ominous" while applauding Walker's speech, here termed "giving the woman a piece of her mind."[51]

In this and other scenes, the film makes no effort to question ethnographic authority (as the films of Trinh Minh-ha or Laleen Jayamanne have attempted for over a decade) or to make dialogical or epistemological innovations.[52] An uncritical use of ethnographic texts builds upon the nineteenth-century literary tradition that Mary Louise Pratt refers to as "manners and customs description," constructing the "native" as object.[53] Walker and Parmar utilize ethnographic materials as "authoritative" when it suits their end. For example, in the print text at the end of the transcript of Walker's interview with "Circumciser 1," the reader finds a "description" of an infibulation from a 1978 medical thesis from the University of Bordeaux.[54] Parmar cites A.M.I. Vergiat's *Moeurs et Coutumes des Manjas* (1937) as the source of a "ritual" song sung by circumcised girls.[55] Many Third World and anti-imperialist feminist filmmakers and writers have struggled against the reproduction of ethnographic colonial discourses in cinematic and cultural practice, critiquing and resisting its representational strategies. The *Warrior Marks* texts reinforce and reproduce colonial discourse through an unproblematized reliance upon and alliance with "authoritative," Eurocentric studies.

In the standard colonial gesture of constructing a "native" through the operation of difference, the elderly circumciser in *Warrior Marks* is depicted as actively evil and passively deluded by tradition. Walker, the interviewer, on the other hand, throws off the mantle of objective questioner to reveal the enlightened metropolitan subject who "knows" all. In "Can the Subaltern Speak?" Gayatri Spivak calls the position and power of the investigator or interviewer into question in order to examine how the "third-world subject is represented within Western discourse."[56] Rejecting the liberal demand that all subjects constitute themselves through public "speech," Spivak argues that social and political movements cannot break the epistemological stranglehold of imperial culture by resurrecting the "shadows" of subjectivity, the categories that imperialism created. Without deconstruction, the "possibility of collectivity itself is persistently foreclosed through the manipulation of female agency."[57]

Read against the grain, as it were, the print text opens up some questions of knowledge production that could have been pursued in the film itself. For instance, "Pratibha's Journey," Parmar's section of the print text, chronicles, among many things, the contradictions and tensions that emerge in the representational politics of the project. Despite Parmar's increasing identification with Walker's "vision," she expresses concern during pre-production and the shoot about making sufficient contact with local activists. Awa Thiam, for instance, remains relatively elusive for reasons upon which Parmar can only speculate. Parmar worries that if Thiam will not cooperate by leading the filmmakers to the "right" contacts in Senegal and elsewhere or by endorsing the project, their work will be hampered logistically and their credibility will suffer. Thiam, as it happens, is in the midst of a pre-election campaign for the opposition political party in her country and does not seem able to drop everything to meet with Parmar. While Parmar presents this situation as Thiam's obstinate resistance, the text leaves the question open as to whether Thiam is playing the powerful diva/native informant or whether she is just a busy professional who has not been asked far enough ahead of time whether the film schedule would be convenient for her.

In an interview included in the print text, Thiam makes it very clear that she agrees with Walker and Parmar on the symbolic import of female genital surgeries. Since Thiam comes from a local group that practices, as she says, "80 percent female circumcision and sometimes infibulation," she views the situation as urgent and agrees with the filmmakers on the need to organize internationally. However, her analysis of the practice as an indication of women's subordination that is embedded within the power structures of particular societies leads her, after ten years of working in what she calls the "female circle," to "get involved in the sphere of politics," and to "succeed in convincing the decision makers, both male and female, and to try to struggle for the abolition of sexual mutilation."[58]

Thiam's move toward participation in electoral politics highlights the suppression of such socio-political and economic continuums in *Warrior Marks*. In addition to their fuzzy relationship to both state and non-governmental structures, Walker and Parmar's texts erase many facets of transnational economic factors, mystifying the division of labor that makes possible, for instance, the funding of a film instead of a refrigerated truck. In the print version of *Warrior Marks*, the authors recount an extraordinary anecdote that describes a meeting between a group of women who run a collective garden and the filmmakers. Asked their feelings about FGM, these women respond by asking the "rich Americans" for a refrigerated truck they need badly to get their produce to outlying areas. The filmmakers, who do not perceive themselves

as "rich" by their own cultural standards, joke that they could probably only
pay for one tire for such a truck. The request for a truck is not mentioned
again. This will to ignore or misrecognize information that does not seem to
pertain to their own project marks the imperialist tendencies of this project.
The power to set an agenda, to arrive uninvited in a country for a brief period
of time, to tell people how they ought to feel and think about their sexuality
and their bodies, to assume the right to rescue other people's children, and to
use this experience as a yardstick of one's own freedom, is standard operating
procedure in the textual tracks of imperialism's cultural production. These
gestures and moves are an historical legacy—*Warrior Marks* does not take the
opportunity to unlearn or even to question this representational heritage and
thus cannot do more than repeat its signs. As Chandra Mohanty argues in
her critique of Western feminist discourse on female genital surgeries: "Sisterhood cannot be assumed on the basis of gender; it must be forged in concrete
historical and political practice and analysis."[59]

Thus, Walker and Parmar make a film that speaks directly, vividly, and
authoritatively to demand a change in the way people conduct their lives
in particular locations. Their right to make this demand comes through an
unquestioned adherence to Western medical science, and, apparently, through
their superior ethical positioning (their "knowledge" of right and wrong), that
is, they "know better." This positivist ethics is conjoined with an appeal to liberal juridical practices, engendering a powerful set of philosophical, medical,
and legal certainties in the effort to "civilize" in the name of a multicultural
global womanism.

Multiculturalism's Globalizing Discourses

It is clear from the work of many scholars in recent years that what we call
"imperial feminism" emerged during the nineteenth century to create simultaneously new feminist subjects in the West and their objects of rescue in the
"periphery"—"sisters" with drastically different material conditions of life.
The collusion between some Western feminist practices and colonial discourses has been amply documented in over a decade of emergent critical
work. The advent of "postcolonial theory" constructed by diasporas of scholars who settled in Europe or in North America created a new demand for
increased attention to the aftermath of colonialism. Furthermore, the politicization of racial minorities through multiculturalism as a social and cultural
movement in the United States has gained its voice through the articulation
of rights claims against the modern state. These political and cultural movements inform feminist practices in metropolitan locations in a profound and
complex manner.

With this complicated social and cultural field in mind, we might see figures such as Walker and Parmar, with quite different historical trajectories,
coming together for a project such as *Warrior Marks* through their links

with movements that have emerged through anti-colonialist efforts. This means that Walker's concern with the aftermath of slavery in the US and Parmar's participation in anti-racist movements in Britain have contributed to a heightened understanding of present-day gender as constructed through colonized patriarchies around the globe. Multiculturalism, then, has been one way to demand the rights of citizens racialized as well as gendered in particular ways. Yet, when multiculturalism remains fixed upon state remedies, reinforcing national agendas, and placing less emphasis on socio-economic formations, the alliance between "women of color" may become strained.

To a certain extent this dilemma is being addressed by solidarity movements that draw upon a range of ideologies of cosmopolitanism and global unity. Thus, the "global" and "transnational" are all interpellated by feminist subjects who also rely upon a discourse of multiculturalism. Yet differences between subjects of less powerful and more powerful states remain to be addressed. This process conflates the racialized subject of the state with the global feminist or womanist who constructs a universal woman as the paradigmatic female subject of global sisterhood. Thus, Walker and Parmar, in solidarity with this global woman, wish to rescue and include her in the privileges of modernity and its emergent sexual subjectivities and embodied practices. What drops out of this gesture is any recognition that this global woman exists only to reaffirm the metropolitan subject of feminism. The multicultural subject, as it is constituted through such a globalized practice of feminism, may be part of an anti-racist strategy but its only space of negotiation is a modern nation-state.

In order to create a film that satisfies the demands of Western subjectivity and the ethnographic tradition, all the complex negotiations between the multicultural subject and the imperial state fall away so that what remains are the conventional colonial tropes—the very tradition of representation that leads to a racism that the multiculturalism project seeks to resist. To have made a less "popular" film, Walker and Parmar would have had to include many of the tensions and conflicts that emerge in the print text (even if only in passing), such as the links between an analysis of diverse surgical practices as gendered and racialized modes of subject constitution or the difficulty of forging alliances and gaining the cooperation of women activists in the regions of Africa visited by the film crew.

Warrior Marks is just one prominent instance of the difficulties of globalizing a multicultural feminist agenda. It is important to read the texts that come out of the political movements we are committed to not only in a celebratory manner but with an attention to these dilemmas in representational practice and politics. Our aim is not to destroy or take away important icons and cultural practices that support communities of resistance. Rather, we want to generate debate and discussion about our representational practices and politics. In many ways, the dilemma for late twentieth-century multicultural feminists is similar to that faced by late nineteenth-century national feminists—how to work with, around, and against the state. Asking for rights from the nation-state, representing others through identitarian practices, is an inevitable and necessary process for all social movements in modernity. But in acknowledging that inevitability, we should not abandon critique. These are challenges offered by the extremely difficult task of public policy formation and activist work. Our reading of an activist, multiculturalist feminist/womanist film and its accompanying print text is not, therefore, simply one of opposing aesthetic tastes or political correctness. Given that genital surgeries and refugee asylum claims based on FGM are now a matter of governmental debate in the US and Europe,[60] it seems timely and necessary to examine the connections between discourses of human rights, racialized nationalisms, and multiculturalism in feminist and womanist frameworks.

Notes

1. Gayatri Chakravorty Spivak, "Can the Subaltern Speak?" in Cary Nelson and Lawrence Grossberg, eds., *Marxism and the Interpretation of Culture* (Urbana: University of Illinois Press, 1988), 299.
2. Rogaia Mustafa Abusharaf, "The Resurrection of the Savage: *Warrior Marks* Revisited," paper delivered at the seminar on "The Future of Gender" (2 April 1997), at the Pembroke Center for Teaching and Research on Women, 2.
3. Chandra Talpade Mohanty, "Cartographies of Struggle: Third World Women and the Politics of Feminism," and "Under Western Eyes: Feminist Scholarship and Colonial Discourses," in Chandra Talpade Mohanty, Ann Russo, and Lourdes Torres, eds., *Third World Women and the Politics of Feminism* (Bloomington: Indiana University Press, 1991), 1–47, 51–80. See also, Norma Alarcón, "The Theoretical Subject(s) of *This Bridge Called My Back* and Anglo-American Feminism," in Gloria Anzaldúa, ed., *Making Face, Making Soul: Haciendo Caras* (San Francisco: Aunt Lute Books, 1990), 356–369; and Norma Alarcón, "Traddutora, Traditora: A Paradigmatic Figure of Chicana Feminism," in Inderpal Grewal and Caren Kaplan, eds., *Scattered Hegemonies: Postmodernist and Transnational Feminist Practices* (Minneapolis: Minnesota University Press, 1994), 110–133; and Inderpal Grewal and Caren Kaplan, "Introduction: Transnational Feminist Practices and Questions of Postmodernity," in Grewal and Kaplan, *Scattered Hegemonies*, 1–33.
4. Martin Jay, "Scopic Regimes of Modernity," in S. Lash and J. Friedman, eds., *Modernity and Identity* (Oxford: Blackwell, 1994).
5. See Ella Shohat and Robert Stam, *Unthinking Eurocentrism: Multiculturalism and the Media* (New York: Routledge, 1994); Avery F. Gordon and Christopher Newfield, eds., *Mapping Multiculturalism* (Minneapolis: University of Minnesota Press, 1996); David Theo Goldberg, ed., *Multiculturalism: A Critical Reader* (Oxford: Blackwell, 1994).
6. Here we need to differ from approaches such as Faye V. Harrison's toward Alice Walker's representation of women in a global framework. While Harrison argues that Walker's novel, *In the Temple of My Familiar*, is a "world cultural history from a pluralistic Third World feminist perspective" which "deessentializes gender as well as race and class," we view such projects as recuperating new kinds of global gendered subjects. See Faye V. Harrison, "Anthropology, Fiction, and Unequal Relations of Intellectual Production," in Ruth Behar and Deborah A. Gordon, eds., *Women Writing Culture* (Berkeley: University of California Press, 1995), 233–245.
7. Claude Lévi-Strauss, *Structural Anthropology* (New York: Basic Books, 1963), 16–17.
8. Noel Burch, *Life to Those Shadows* (Berkeley: University of California Press, 1990), 16. For discussion of "ethnographic authority" and the history of anthropological cultures of representation see James Clifford and George Marcus, eds., *Writing Culture* (Berkeley: University of California Press, 1986); and James Clifford, *The Predicament of Culture: Twentieth-Century Ethnography, Literature, and Art* (Cambridge, MA: Harvard University Press, 1988).

9. See Denise Albanese, *New Science, New World* (Durham, NC: Duke University Press, 1996); John Berger, *Ways of Seeing* (Harmondsworth: Penguin, 1977); Lisa Cartwright, *Screening the Body: Tracing Medicine's Visual Culture* (Minneapolis: University of Minnesota Press, 1995); and Valerie Hartouni, *Cultural Conceptions: On Reproductive Technologies and the Remaking of Life* (Minneapolis: University of Minnesota Press, 1997).
10. David MacDougall, "Prospects of the Ethnographic Film," in Bill Nichols, ed., *Movies and Methods* (Berkeley: University of California Press, 1976), 136.
11. David MacDougall, "Beyond Observation Cinema," in P. Hockings, ed., *Principles of Visual Anthropology* (Paris: Mouton, 1975), 118, cited in Kathleen Kuehnast, "Visual Imperialism and the Export of Prejudice: An Exploration of Ethnographic Film," in Peter Ian Crawford and David Turton, eds., *Film as Ethnography* (Manchester: Manchester University Press, 1992), 186.
12. Fatimah Tobing Rony, *The Third Eye: Race, Cinema, and Ethnographic Spectacle* (Durham, NC: Duke University Press, 1996), 8.
13. Ibid., 71.
14. See Parama Roy, *Indian Traffic* (Berkeley: University of California Press, 1998); Nalini Natarajan, "Women, Nation, and Narration in *Midnight's Children*," in Grewal and Kaplan, *Scattered Hegemonies*, 76–89; Rey Chow, *Primitive Passions: Visuality, Sexuality, Ethnography, and Contemporary Chinese Cinema* (New York: Columbia University Press, 1995); and Shohat and Stam, *Unthinking Eurocentrism*.
15. Alice Walker, *In Search of Our Mothers' Gardens* (New York: Harcourt, Brace, Jovanovich, 1983).
16. See Valerie Amos and Pratibha Parmar, "Challenging Imperial Feminism," *Feminist Review* 17 (1984), 3–19.
17. For an extended discussion of the importance of "socio-cultural" context for black women cultural producers, see Gloria Gibson-Hudson, "Aspects of Black Feminist Cultural Ideology in Films by Black Women Independent Artists," in Diane Carson, Linda Dittmar, and Janice R. Welsch, eds., *Multiple Voices in Feminist Film Criticism* (Minneapolis: University of Minnesota Press, 1994), 365–379.
18. For a variety of anthropological, legal, historical, and cultural perspectives on female genital surgeries as a question of "tradition" in an era of human rights activism, see Bettina Shell-Duncan and Ylva Hernlund, eds., *Female Circumcision in Africa: Culture, Controversy and Change* (Boulder, CO: Lynne Rienner Publishers, 2000).
19. Isabelle Gunning, "Arrogant Perception, World-Travelling and Multicultural Feminism: The Case of Female Genital Surgeries," *Columbia Human Rights Law Review* 23 (1992), 189. We have been inspired and encouraged by Gunning's interventions in human rights discourse and by her complex, materially grounded theorization of multicultural feminism.
20. For an extremely useful discussion of the history of Western representations of the clitoris see Lisa Jean Moore and Adele E. Clarke, "Clitoral Conventions and Transgressions: Graphic Representations in Anatomy Texts, c. 1900–1991," *Feminist Studies* 21 (2) (Summer 1995), 255–301.
21. Rey Chow, *Writing Diaspora: Tactics of Intervention in Contemporary Cultural Studies* (Bloomington: Indiana University Press, 1993), 28–29.
22. Doris Sommer, "Resistant Texts and Incompetent Readers," *Poetics Today* 15 (4) (Winter 1994), 543, cited in Diana Fuss, *Identification Papers* (New York: Routledge, 1995), 9.
23. Evelyn C. White, "Alice Walker's Compassionate Crusade," *San Francisco Chronicle* (Monday, November 15, 1993), D1.
24. Here we disagree with Diana Fuss and other psychoanalytic feminist theorists who argue for a politicized recognition of the erotic and mobilizing powers of identification as a compensation for lost love-objects. While we acknowledge the rigor of these arguments, examples such as *Warrior Marks* demonstrate the cultural and political limits of such an approach. See Fuss, *Identification Papers*.
25. Amy Hamilton, "Warrior Marks," *off our backs* 23 (11) (December 1993), 2.
26. See Diane Minor, "*Warrior Marks*: Joyous Resistance at Walker Film Debut," *National NOW Times* (January 1994), 7; Mari Keiko Gonzalez, "Culture or Torture?" *Bay Area Reporter* (18 November 1993); White, "Alice Walker's Compassionate Crusade," D1; David A. Kaplan, "Is It Torture or Tradition?" *Newsweek* (December 20, 1993), 124.

27. Seble Dawit and Salem Mekuria, "The West Just Doesn't Get It," *The New York Times* (Tuesday, December 7, 1993), A27. This piece is an exception to the rule. Most *New York Times* op-ed pieces on the topic echo the tone and approach found in A.M. Rosenthal's "Female Genital Torture," *The New York Times* (Friday, November 12, 1993), A33.

28. Critiques of *Possessing the Secret of Joy* include: Margaret Kent Bass, "Alice's Secret," *CLA Journal* (September 1994), 1–10, and Diane C. Menya, "Possessing the Secret of Joy," *Lancet* 341 (February 1993), 423. Critiques of *Warrior Marks* include Leasa Farrar-Frazer, "An Opportunity Missed: A Review of *Warrior Marks*," *Black Film Review* 8 (1) (1994), 41–42; Gay Wilentz, "Healing the Wounds of Time," *Women's Review of Books* 10 (5) (February 1993), 15–16; and Kagendo Murungi, "Get Away from My Genitals: A Commentary on *Warrior Marks*" *Interstices* 2 (1) (Spring 1994), 11–15; and Abusharaf, "The Resurrection of the Savage."

29. *Case Western Reserve Law Review* 47 (2) (Winter 1997). See in particular L. Amede Obiora, "Bridges and Barricades: Rethinking Polemics and Intransigence in the Campaign against Female Circumcision," 275–387; Micere Githae Mugo, "Elitist Anti-Circumcision Discourse as Mutilating and Anti-Feminist," 461–479; and Isabelle R. Gunning, "Uneasy Alliances and Solid Sisterhood: A Response to Professor Obiora's 'Bridges and Barricades,'" 445–459.

30. Mugo, "Elitist Anti-Circumcision Discourse," 462.

31. The second wave, Western feminist salvo against footbinding as "gynocide" was fired by Andrea Dworkin in her well-known text *Woman Hating* (New York: E.P. Dutton, 1974), 95–117. Although Elizabeth Gould Davis also outlines the history of atrocities committed against women, reserving special scorn for those from non-European or non-Christian cultures in *The First Sex* (New York: Penguin Books, 1971), it is Mary Daly who is best known for her analysis of patriarchal violence that includes "Indian" *suttee,* "Chinese" footbinding, and "African" genital mutilation. See *Gyn/Ecology: The Metaethics of Radical Feminism* (Boston: Beacon Press, 1978). This approach lent support to and in many ways instigated the contemporary movement to create International Tribunals on Crimes against Women; see Diane E.H. Russell and Nicole Van de Ven, *Crimes against Women: Proceedings of the International Tribunal* (East Palo Alto, CA: Frog in the Well Press, 1984). Lata Mani has documented both British and South Asian nationalist discourses on *sati* (or *suttee*) in "Contentious Traditions: The Debate on Sati in Colonial India," in KumKum Sangari and Sudesh Vaid, eds., *Recasting Women* (New Delhi: Kali for Women, 1989), 88–126. For a more historically complex approach to footbinding in East Asia, see Alison R. Drucket, "The Influence of Western Women on the Anti-Footbinding Movement, 1840–1911," in Richard W. Guisso and Stanley Johannesen, eds., *Women in China* (Youngstown, NY: Philo Press, 1981).

32. In addition to Gayatri Spivak's groundbreaking work collected in *In Other Worlds* (New York: Methuen, 1987) and *Outside in the Teaching Machine* (New York: Routledge, 1993) as well as in Sarah Harasym, ed., *The Post-colonial Critic* (New York: Routledge, 1990), see also Cynthia Enloe, *Bananas, Beaches, and Bases* (Berkeley: University of California Press, 1989); Trinh T. Minh-ha, *Woman/Native/Other* (Bloomington: Indiana University Press, 1989); Shohat and Scam, *Unthinking Eurocentrism;* Chow, *Writing Diaspora;* Lisa Lowe, *Critical Terrains* (Ithaca, NY: Cornell University Press, 1991); Françoise Lionnet, *Postcolonial Representations* (Ithaca, NY: Cornell University Press, 1995); Nupur Chaudhuri and Margaret Strobel, *Western Women and Imperialism* (Bloomington: Indiana University Press, 1992); Jenny Sharpe, *Allegories of Empire* (Minneapolis: University of Minnesota Press, 1993); Kumari Jayarwardena, *The White Woman's Other Burden* (New York: Routledge, 1995); Antoinette Burton, *Burdens of History* (Chapel Hill: University of North Carolina Press, 1994); Anne McClintock, *Imperial Leather* (New York: Routledge, 1995); and Helen Callaway, *Gender, Culture, and Empire* (Urbana: University of Illinois Press, 1987).

33. See Mary Layoun, "The Female Body and 'Transnational' Reproduction; or, Rape by Any Other Name?" in Grewal and Kaplan, *Scattered Hegemonies,* 63–75; and Sharpe, *Allegories of Empire.* See also Susan Jeffords, "Fantastic Conquests: In U.S. Military History Only Some Rapes Count," *Village Voice* (July 13, 1993), 22–24, 29.

34. Important exceptions include Vicki Kirby, "On the Cutting Edge: Feminism and Clitori-dectomy," *Australian Feminist Studies* 5 (Summer 1987), 35–55; Angela Davis, "Women in Egypt: A Personal View," in *Women, Culture, and Politics* (New York: Vintage, 1990), 116–154; Francoise Lionnet, "Feminisms and Universalisms: 'Universal Rights' and the Legal Debate around the Practice of Female Excision in France," *Inscriptions* 6 (1992), 98–115; and the work of Gunning.

35. See Terry Kapsalis, *Public Privates: Performing Gynecology from Both Ends of the Speculum* (Durham, NC: Duke University Press, 1997); G.J. Barker Benfield, *The Horrors of the Half Known Life: Male Attitudes toward Women and Sexuality in Nineteenth-Century America* (New York: Harper and Row, 1976); Elaine Showalter, *The Female Malady* (New York: Pantheon, 1985), 75–78; John Money, *The Destroying Angel* (Buffalo, NY: Prometheus Books, 1985), 119–120; John Duffy, "Masturbation and Clitoridectomy," *Journal of the American Medical Association* 186 (3) (October 19, 1963), 246–249; J.B. Fleming et al., "Clitoridec-tomy—The Disastrous Downfall of Isaac Baker Brown, F.R.C.S. (1867)," *Journal of Obstetrics and Gynaecology of the British Empire* 67 (6) (October 1960), 1017–1034; and Isaac Baker Brown, *On the Curability of Certain Forms of Insanity, Epilepsy, Catalepsy, and Hysteria in Females* (London: Robert Hardwicke, 1866).

36. Female circumcision or genital surgery in general has been represented in "modern" discussions of anatomy as well as marked as "culturally significant" in ethnographic dis-course. For example, P.C. Remondino's *History of Circumcision from the Earliest Times to the Present* (Philadelphia: F.A. Davis, 1900) combines ethnographic "knowledge," folk legend, and medical "facts." Richard Burton supplied ethnographic data on female infibu-lation and excision in a lost first version of *First Footsteps in East Africa* (1856) that has been recovered by Gordon Waterfield in a 1966 edition. Burton's characterization of this "remarkable method" of maintaining chastity as "barbarous" is continued in the strin-gently "scientific" discourse of an article by Allen Worsley published in the *Journal of Obstetrics and Gynaecology of the British Empire* in 1938 in which the author refers to female circumcision as "evil." The practice is referred to in soft-core pornography in 1939 in Felix Bryk's *Dark Rapture: The Sex-Life of the African Negro* (New York: Walden, 1939) as well as in academia in an article by the celebrated Ashley Montague in *The American Anthropologist* in 1945. "Second wave," Western feminist approaches to the topic follow the parameters and tone established by Fran Hosken in her work since the 1970s (gath-ered in her 1983 *The Hosken Report: Genital and Sexual Mutilation of Females*). See also Henny Lightfoot-Klein, *Prisoners of Ritual: An Odyssey into Female Genital Circumcision in Africa* (New York: Haworth, 1989); Mary Daly, *Gyn/Ecology*, Robin Morgan and Gloria Steinem, "The International Crime of Genital Mutilation," *Ms* 8 (9) (March 1980), 65–69. Third World feminists who have published denunciations of the practice include: Awa Thiam, *Speak Out, Black Sisters: Feminism and Oppression in Black Africa* (London: Pluto Press, 1986); Olayinka Koso-Thomas, *The Circumcision of Women: A Strategy for Eradica-tion* (London: Zed Books, 1987); Asma El Dareer, *Woman, Why Do You Weep?* (London: Zed Books, 1982); Efua Dorkenoo and Scilla Elworthy, *Female Genital Mutilation: Propos-als for Change* (London: Minority Rights Group International, 1992); Nawal el Saadawi, *The Hidden Face of Eve: Women in the Arab World* (London: Zed Books, 1980). Female cir-cumcision has also been featured in nationalist and decolonization discourses. See Jomo Kenyatta, *Facing Mount Kenya: The Tribal Life of the Kikuyu* (New York: Random House, 1975). For a stellar discussion of the politics of female circumcision discourse in the decol-onization struggle in Kenya, see Susan Pedersen, "National Bodies, Unspeakable Acts: The Sexual Politics of Colonial Policy-Making," *Journal of Modern History* 63 (December 1991), 647–680. We identify significant participation in the discourse of sexual surgery in activist writing generated by groups such as the Intersex Society of North America. See, for example, the ISNA's newsletter, *Hermaphrodites with Attitudes,* and their call for an end to "IGM"—Intersexed Genital Mutilation. See also our work-in-progress for a fuller discussion of this complex site of alliance between queer, transgender, and global feminist activism around sexual surgeries.

37. See Ann Laura Stoler's work: "Carnal Knowledge and Imperial Power: Gender, Race, and Morality in Colonial Asia," in Micaela di Leonardo, ed., *Gender at the Crossroads of Knowledge: Feminist Anthropology in the Postmodern Era* (Berkeley: University of Cali-fornia Press, 1991), 51–101; and *Race and the Education of Desire: Foucault's "History of Sexuality" and the Colonial Order of Things* (Durham, NC: Duke University Press, 1995).

38. See Ann Balsamo, *Technologies of the Gendered Body* (Durham, NC: Duke University Press, 1995); Jennifer Terry and Jacqueline Urla, eds., *Deviant Bodies* (Bloomington: Indiana University Press, 1995); Cartwright, *Screening the Body;* Kathy Davis, *Reshaping the Female Body* (New York: Routledge, 1995); David Bell and Gill Valentine, eds., *Mapping Desire: Geographies of Sexualities* (New York: Routledge, 1995); and Mary Jacobus, Evelyn Fox, and Sally Shuttleworth, eds., *Body Politics* (New York: Routledge, 1990).

39. See Edward W. Said, *Orientalism* (New York: Random House, 1978); Clifford and Marcus, *Writing Culture;* and Clifford, *The Predicament of Culture.*

40. See Mary Louise Pratt, *Imperial Eyes: Travel Writing and Transculturation* (London: Routledge, 1992); Shohat and Stam, *Unthinking Eurocentrism;* Inderpal Grewal, *Home and Harem: Nation, Gender, Empire, and the Cultures of Travel* (Durham, NC: Duke University Press, 1996); Caren Kaplan, *Questions of Travel: Postmodern Discourses of Displacement* (Durham, NC: Duke University Press, 1996); and Caren Kaplan, " 'Getting to Know You': Travel, Gender, and the Politics of Representation in *Anna and the King of Siam* and *The King and I,*" in Roman de la Campa, E. Ann Kaplan, and Michael Sprinker, eds., *Late Imperial Culture* (London: Verso, 1995), 33–52.

41. See Sylvia M. Jacobs, ed., *Black Americans and the Missionary Movement in Africa* (Westport, CT: Greenwood Press, 1982). See also Sylvia M. Jacobs, "Give a Thought to Africa: Black Women Missionaries in Southern Africa," in Chaudhuri and Strobel, *Western Women and Imperialism,* 207–228.

42. This point is more fully discussed in our work-in-progress as part of the discourse of global feminism whereby a unified and unfragmented female body becomes equated with an ideal "lesbian body." In this context, female genital surgery eradicates or alters a zone that is configured in historically specific ways by contemporary Western cultural and lesbian feminist discursive practices.

43. See Davis, *Reshaping the Female Body;* Jennifer Craik, *The Face of Fashion: Cultural Studies in Fashion* (London: Routledge, 1994); Hilary Radner, *Shopping Around: Feminine Culture and the Pursuit of Pleasure* (New York: Routledge, 1995); Shari Benstock and Suzanne Ferriss, eds., *On Fashion* (New Brunswick, NJ: Rutgers University Press, 1994); Carol A. Stabile, *Feminism and the Technological Fix* (Manchester: Manchester University Press, 1994); Ann Balsamo, "On the Cutting Edge: Cosmetic Surgery and the Technological Production of the Gendered Body," *Camera Obscura* 28 (1992), 207–238; and Cartwright, *Screening the Body.* Walker does mention cosmetic surgeries and pressures on Western women to conform to patriarchal ideal forms in the written text when she is in the planning stages of the project, but this set of crucial ideas drops out of the film (*Warrior Marks,* 9–10).

44. See Pratt, *Imperial Eyes;* Clifford, *The Predicament of Culture;* Shohat and Stam, *Unthinking Eurocentrism;* and Said, *Orientalism.* See also Christopher Miller, *Blank Darkness: Africanist Discourse in French* (Chicago: University of Chicago Press, 1985).

45. See Lisa Bloom, *Gender on Ice: American Ideologies of Polar Expeditions* (Minneapolis: University of Minnesota Press, 1993); Catherine A. Lutz and Jane L. Collins, *Reading National Geographic* (Chicago: University of Chicago Press, 1993); William M. O'Barr, "Representations of Others," Part 1: Advertisements in the 1929 *National Geographic* Magazine," in *Culture and the Ad: Exploring Otherness in the World of Advertising* (Boulder, CO: Westview Press, 1994), 45–72; Tamar Y. Rothenberg, "Voyeurs of Imperialism: *The National Geographic Magazine* before World War II," in Anne Godlewska and Neil Smith, eds., *Geography and Empire* (Oxford: Basil Blackwell, 1994), 155–172.

46. Mary H. Kingsley, *Travels in West Africa 1897* (Boston: Beacon Press, 1988). Kingsley's influence on contemporary "women's travel" literature can be seen in works such as Caroline Alexander's memoir *One Dry Season: In the Footsteps of Mary Kingsley* (New York: Vintage Books, 1991) and in Alison Blum's critical monograph *Travel, Gender, and Imperialism: Mary Kingsley and West Africa* (New York: Guilford Press, 1994). See also, Katherine Frank, *A Voyager Out: The Life of Mary Kingsley* (New York: Ballantine Books, 1986).

47. For a discussion of epistolary conventions in women's writing, see Linda S. Kauffman, *Special Delivery: Epistolary Modes in Modern Fiction* (Chicago: Chicago University Press, 1992).

48. See Said, *Orientalism;* Spivak, *In Other Worlds* and *Outside in the Teaching Machine;* Shohat and Stam, *Unthinking Eurocentrism;* as well as Johannes Fabian, *Time and the Other: How Anthropology Makes Its Object* (New York: Columbia University Press, 1983); and Talal Asad, *Anthropology and the Colonial Encounter* (London: Ithaca Press, 1973).
49. See Spivak, "Can the Subaltern Speak?" 271–313; and Chow, *Writing Diaspora.*
50. Alice Walker and Pratibha Parmar, *Warrior Marks: Female Genital Mutilation and the Sexual Blinding of Women* (New York: Harcourt Brace, 1993), 301–308.
51. White, "Alice Walker's Compassionate Crusade," D1.
52. For critiques of ethnographic authority in anthropological and cultural discourses see Clifford and Marcus, *Writing Culture;* George E. Marcus and Michael M.J. Fischer, *Anthropology as Cultural Critique: An Experimental Moment in the Human Sciences* (Chicago: University of Chicago Press, 1986); and Clifford, *The Predicament of Culture.* See also, Laleen Jayamanne, "Do You Think I Am a Woman, Ha! Do You?" *Discourse* 11 (2) (Spring-Summer 1989), 49–62; and Trinh T. Minh-ha, *Framer Framed* (New York: Routledge, 1992).
53. Pratt, *Imperial Eyes,* 58–68.
54. See "Alice Walker and Circumciser 1," 301–309 (including the excerpt from Alan David, *Infibulation en République de Djibouti,* 308–309).
55. Walker and Parmar, *Warrior Marks,* 179.
56. Spivak, "Can the Subaltern Speak?" 271.
57. Ibid., 282.
58. Walker and Parmer, *Warrior Marks,* 284.
59. Mohanty, "Under Western Eyes," 58.
60. See Kay Boulware-Miller, "Female Circumcision: Challenges to the Practice as a Human Rights Violation," *Harvard Women's Law Journal* 8 (Spring 1985), 155–177; Isabelle R. Gunning, "Modernizing Customary International Law: The Challenge of Human Rights," *Virginia Journal of International Law* 31 (2) (Winter 1991), 211–247; Georgia Dullea, "Female Circumcision a Topic at U.N. Parley," *The New York Times* (Friday, July 18, 1980), B4; Marlise Simons, "France Jails Woman for Daughter's Circumcision," *The New York Times* (January 11, 1993), A8; Timothy Egan, "An Ancient Ritual and a Mother's Asylum Plea," *The New York Times* (March 4, 1994), A25; Clyde H. Farnsworth, "Canada Gives Somali Mother Refugee Status," *The New York Times* (July 21, 1994), A14; Jill Lawrence, "Women Seek Asylum in West to Avoid Abuses in Homeland," *The San Francisco Chronicle* (March 21, 1994), A3; Sophfronia Scott Gregory, "At Risk of Mutilation," *Time* (March 21, 1994), 45–46. For a vigorous discussion of the pitfalls of cultural defense arguments and the rhetoric of human rights in the context of racism, see Sherene Razack, "What Is To Be Gained by Looking White People in the Eye? Culture, Race, and Gender in Cases of Sexual Violence," *Signs* 19 (4) (Summer 1994), 894–923.

Part 5
Womanist Resources

19

Selections from the First Quarter Century

A Womanist Bibliography (Including Internet Resources)

LAYLI PHILLIPS*

Womanist publications in print and online now number in the thousands. This includes books, book chapters, journal articles, monographs, magazine articles (scholarly and nonscholarly), book reviews, dissertations, theses, news items, multimedia items, arts items, and Web sites, not to mention editorials, interviews, and the occasional conference paper that appears online. The purpose of this selected bibliography is to sample these offerings in a way that is useful to researchers, students, and general interest readers. Three selection criteria have been employed: (1) the publication date must fall within the first 25 years of womanism (1979–2004), (2) the publication must clearly focus on womanism (by containing "womanist" or "womanism" in the title, for instance, or devoting a significant portion of text to either of these), and (3) the selection must contribute to the overall diversity of offerings on womanism in this bibliography. In many cases, these are selections that I would have liked to include in this volume and that, in any case, can be used to supplement the pieces in this collection.

The selections included here are organized mostly by discipline. While I do not wish to reify or reinscribe disciplinary boundaries by using such a scheme, I do want to show the breadth of womanism and the extent to which it has permeated even the most unexpected sectors of academia, linking these together by a common thread. In addition, I want to make it easy for scholars from different disciplines to begin in a familiar place and branch out from there, thus facilitating the dialogue and cross-fertilization among diverse fields of

---

* This bibliography was prepared with the research assistance of numerous people, including Taliba Sikudhani Olugbala, BeAnka Nyela, Melinda Mills, Angel Charmain Dupree Paschall, Kerri Reddick-Morgan, and the twelve students of my Maymester 2003 Womanism seminar that included individuals from Georgia State University, Emory University, and Spelman College.

study that is required for a full grasp of womanism. I have made every attempt to showcase the geographic reach of womanism, although my sampling has been limited to what I can access in English. Readers are encouraged to keep abreast of the rapidly proliferating literature on womanism and, in particular, to notice the emergence of womanist thought in new areas and communities, including communities outside the English-speaking world, outside academia, and in cyberspace.

To give a sense of the historical evolution and proliferation of womanist thought, I arranged this bibliography in a rough chronological order. Disciplines are more or less ordered according to the earliest document using womanist language that I could find. Thus, literature and literary studies, with Alice Walker's "Coming Apart" (1979), is first and architecture/urban studies, with Epifania Akosua Amoo-Adare's "Critical Spatial Literacy: A Womanist Positionality and the Spatio-temporal Construction of Black Family Life" (2004), rounds out the first quarter century of womanism. However, several interdisciplines that have "always already" been interlaced with the womanist project are included at the end, along with categories for critiques of womanism, interviews, journals, and Web sites. Entries are arranged alphabetically within each discipline. Since I have made every attempt to include all of the disciplines in which womanism has made an appearance, and because I fully admit that some articles defy disciplinary classification, I take full responsibility for any inadvertent omissions or misclassifications that others may discover.

Literature and Literary Studies

Adamu, Abdalla Uma. "Parallel Worlds: Reflective Womanism in Balaraba Ramat Yakubu's *Ina Son Sa Haka*," *Jenda: A Journal of Culture and African Women Studies*, 2003, http://www.jendajournal.com/issue4/adamu.html.

Aegerter, Lindsey Pentolfe. "Southern Africa, Womanism, and Postcoloniality: A Dialectical Approach." In *The Postcolonial Condition of African Literature*, ed. Daniel Gover, John Conteh-Morgan, and Jane Bryce, 67–74. Trenton, NJ: Africa World Press, 2000.

Allan, Tuzyline Jita. *Womanist and Feminist Aesthetics: A Comparative Review*. Athens: Ohio University Press, 1995.

Awkward, Michael. "A Black Man's Place in Black Feminist Criticism." In *Negotiating Difference: Race, Gender, and the Politics of Positionality*. Chicago: University of Chicago Press, 1995.

Connor, Kimberly Rae. "Womanist Parables in *Gifts of Power:* The Autobiography of Rebecca Cox Jackson," *a/b: Auto/Biography Studies* 10 (1995): 21–38.

Herndon, Gerise. "Anti-colonialist and Womanist Discourse in the Works of Jamaica Kincaid and Simone Schwarz-Bant." In *Nwanyibu: Womanbeing and African Literature*, ed. Phanuel Akubueza Egejuru and Ketu H. Katrak, 159–71. Trenton, NJ: Africa World Press, 1997.

Hudson-Weems, Clenora. *Africana Womanist Literary Theory*. Trenton, NJ: Africa World Press, 2004.

Jaiswal, Madhavi. *Writing the Ordinary: Indian South African Writing as Womanist Prose*. Ottawa: National Library of Canada, 1996.

Jimoh, A. Yemisi. "Double Consciousness, Modernism, and Womanist Themes in Gwendolyn Brooks's 'The Anniad,'" *MELUS* 23 (1998): 167–86.

Kolawole, Mary E. Modupe. *Womanism and African Gender Consciousness*. Trenton, NJ: Africa World Press, 1997.

Langley, April. "Lucy Terry Prince: The Cultural and Literary Legacy of Africana Womanism," *The Western Journal of Black Studies* 25 (2001): 153–62.

Lee, Valerie. "Testifying Theory: Womanist Intellectual Thought," *Women: A Cultural Review* 6 (1995): 200–206.

Marsh-Lockett, Carol. "Womanism." In *The Oxford Companion to African American Literature*, ed. William L. Andrews, Frances Smith Foster, and Trudier Harris, 784–86. New York: Oxford University Press, 1997.

Montelaro, Janet J. *Producing a Womanist Text: The Maternal as Signifier in Alice Walker's* The Color Purple. Victoria, British Columbia, Canada: English Literary Studies, University of Victoria, 1996.

Mori, Aoi. *Toni Morrison and Womanist Discourse*. New York: Peter Lang, 1999.

Ogunyemi, Chikwenye Okonjo. "Womanism: The Dynamics of the Contemporary Black Female Novel in English," *Signs: Journal of Women in Culture and Society* 11 (1985): 63–80.

———. *Africa Wo/Man Palava: The Nigerian Novel by Women*. Chicago: University of Chicago Press, 1996.

Sherman, Charlotte Watson. *Sisterfire: Black Womanist Fiction and Poetry*. New York: Perennial, 1994.

Stephens, Ronald J., Maureen Keaveny, and Venetria K. Patton. "Come Colour My Rainbow: Themes of Africana Womanism in the Poetic Vision of Audrey Kathryn Bullett," *Journal of Black Studies* 32 (2002): 464–79.

Strong-Leek, Linda. "Emerging Womanism in the Works of Tsitsi Dangarembga, Barbara Mahkalisa, and J. Nozip Maraire." In *African Literature Association Conference Proceedings*, 140–56. Trenton, NJ: Africa World Press, 2001.

Thompson, Betty Taylor. "Common Bonds from Africa to the U.S.: Africana Womanist Literary Analysis," *The Western Journal of Black Studies* 25 (2001): 177–84.

Viswanathan, Meera, and Evangelina Mancikam. "Is Black Woman to White as Female Is to Male? Restoring Alice Walker's Womanist Prose to the Heart of Feminist Literary Criticism," *Indian Journal of American Studies* 28 (1998): 15–20.

Walker, Alice. "Coming Apart." In *Take Back the Night*, ed. Laura Lederer, 84–93. New York: Bantam, 1979.

———. "Gifts of Power: The Writings of Rebecca Jackson." In *In Search of Our Mothers' Gardens: Womanist Prose*, by Alice Walker, 71–82. San Diego: Harcourt Brace Jovanovich, 1983.

———. *In Search of Our Mothers' Gardens: Womanist Prose*. San Diego: Harcourt Brace Jovanovich, 1983.

———. "Womanist." In *In Search of Our Mothers' Gardens: Womanist Prose*, by Alice Walker, xi–xii. San Diego: Harcourt Brace Jovanovich, 1983.

Williams, Sherley Anne. "Some Implications of Womanist Theory," *Callaloo* 9 (1986): 303–308.

Xu, Wenying. "A Womanist Production of Truths: The Use of Myths in Amy Tan," *Paintbrush* 22 (1995): 56–66.

Theology and Religious Studies

Baker-Fletcher, Karen. *A Singing Something: Womanist Reflections on Anna Julia Cooper*. New York: Crossroad, 1994.

———. *Sisters of Dust, Sisters of Spirit: Womanist Wordings on God and Creation*. Minneapolis, MN: Fortress, 1998.

Baker-Fletcher, Karen, and Garth Kasimu Baker-Fletcher. *My Sister, My Brother: Womanist and Xodus God-Talk*. Maryknoll, NY: Orbis, 1997.

Boonprasat-Lewis, Nantawan, and Marie M. Fortune, eds. *Remembering Conquest: Feminist/ Womanist Perspectives on Religion, Colonization, and Sexual Violence*. Binghamton, NY: Haworth Press, 1999.

Brown, Kelly Delaine. "God Is as Christ Does: Toward a Womanist Theology," *Journal of Religious Thought* 46 (1989): 7–16.

Bruce, Beverlee. "The Black Church and Womanist Theology: Implications for Refugee Women." *GEA Publications and Resources*. New York: Global Education Associates, http://www.globaleduc.org/Publications3.shtml.

Burrow Jr., Rufus. "Enter Womanist Theology and Ethics," *Western Journal of Black Studies* 22 (1998): 19–29.

———. "Toward Womanist Theology and Ethics," *Journal of Feminist Studies in Religion* 15 (1999): 77–95.

Cannon, Katie G. *Black Womanist Ethics*. Atlanta: Scholars Press, 1988.

———. *Katie's Canon: Womanism and the Soul of the Black Community*. New York: Continuum, 1995.

———. *A Womanist Theology Primer: Remembering What We Never Knew; The Epistemology of Womanist Theology*. Louisville, KY: Women's Ministries Program Area, National Ministries Division, Presbyterian Church (U.S.A.), 2001.

Cannon, Katie G., Kelly Brown Douglas, Toinette M. James, and Cheryl Townsend Gilkes. "Metalogues and Dialogues: Teaching the Womanist Idea," *Journal of Feminist Studies in Religion* 8 (1992): 125–51.

Carr-Hamilton, Jacquelyn D. "Notes on the Black Womanist Dilemma," *Journal of Religious Thought* 45 (1988): 67–69.

Coleman, Kate. "Black Theology and Black Liberation: A Womanist Perspective," *Black Theology: An International Journal* 1 (1998): 59–69.

Crawford, A. Elaine Brown. *Hope in the Holler: A Womanist Theology*. Louisville, KY: Westminster John Knox, 2002.

Douglas, Kelly Brown. *Sexuality and the Black Church: A Womanist Perspective*. Maryknoll, NY: Orbis, 1999.

Eugene, Toinette M., Ada Maria Isasi-Diaz, Kwok Pui-lan, and Judith Plaskow. "Appropriation and Reciprocity in Womanist/Mujerista/Feminist Work," *Journal of Feminist Studies in Religion* 8 (1992): 91–122.

Gilkes, Cheryl Townsend. *"If It Wasn't for the Women—": Black Women's Experience and Womanist Culture in Church and Community*. Maryknoll, NY: Orbis, 2001.

Grant, Jacquelyn. *White Women's Christ and Black Women's Jesus: Feminist Christology and Womanist Response*. Atlanta: Scholar's Press, 1989.

Hayes, Diana L. *Hagar's Daughters: Womanist Ways of Being in the World*. Mahwah, NJ: Paulist Press, 1995.

Hollies, Linda H. *Bodacious Womanist Wisdom*. Cleveland, OH: Pilgrim Press, 2003.

Hopkins, Dwight N., and Anthony B. Pinn, eds. *Loving the Body: Black Religious Studies and the Erotic*. New York: Palgrave Macmillan, 2004.

Kirk-Duggan, Cheryl A. *Exorcising Evil: A Womanist Perspective on the Spirituals*. Maryknoll, NY: Orbis, 1997.

———. *Refiner's Fire: A Religious Engagement with Violence*. Maryknoll, NY: Orbis, 2001.

Lewis, Marjorie. "Diaspora Dialogue: Womanist Theology in Engagement with Aspects of the Black British and Jamaican Experience," *Black Theology* 2 (2004): 85–109.

Masenya, Madipoane J. "African Womanist Hermeneutics: A Suppressed Voice from South Africa Speaks," *Journal of Feminist Studies in Religion* 11 (1995): 149–55.

Miller-McLemore, Bonnie J., and Brita L. Gill-Austern, eds. *Feminist and Womanist Pastoral Theology*. Maryknoll, NY: Orbis, 2001.

Mitchem, Stephanie Y. *Introducing Womanist Theology*. Maryknoll, NY: Orbis, 2002.

Neuger, Christie Cozad, ed. *The Arts of Ministry: Feminist-Womanist Approaches*. Louisville, KY: Westminster John Knox, 1996.

Paris, Peter J. "From Womanist Thought to Womanist Action," *Journal of Feminist Studies in Religion* 9 (1993): 115–25.

Riggs, Marcia Y. *Awake, Arise, Act: A Womanist Call for Black Liberation*. Cleveland, OH: Pilgrim Press, 1994.

———. *Plenty Good Room: Women versus Male Power in the Black Church*. Cleveland. OH: Pilgrim Press, 2003.

Sanders, Cheryl J. "Afrocentrism and Womanism in the Seminary," *Christianity and Crisis*, April 13, 1992, 123–26.

———. *Living the Intersection: Womanism and Afrocentrism in Theology*. Minneapolis, MN: Fortress, 1995.

Sanders, Cheryl J., Katie G. Cannon, Emilie M. Townes, M. Shawn Copeland, bell hooks, and Cheryl Townsend Gilkes. "Roundtable Discussion: Christian Ethics and Theology in Womanist Perspective," *Journal of Feminist Studies in Religion* 5 (1989): 83–112.

Smith, Pamela A. "Green Lap, Brown Embrace, Blue Body: The Ecospirituality of Alice Walker," *Cross Currents* 48 (1998/1999): 471–87.

Stewart, Dianne. "Womanist Theology in the Caribbean Context: Critiquing Culture, Rethinking Doctrine, and Expanding Boundaries," *Journal of Feminist Studies in Religion* 20 (2004): 61–82.

Townes, Emilie M. *Womanist Justice, Womanist Hope*. Atlanta, GA: Scholars Press, 1993.
———. *In a Blaze of Glory: Womanist Spirituality as Social Witness*. Nashville, TN: Abingdon Press, 1995.
———. *Breaking the Fine Rain of Death: African American Health Issues and a Womanist Ethic of Care*. New York: Continuum, 1998.
Weems, Renita J. *Just a Sister Away: A Womanist Vision of Women's Relationships in the Bible*. San Diego, CA: LuraMedia, 1988.
Westfield, N. Lynne. *Dear Sisters: A Womanist Practice of Hospitality*. Cleveland, OH: Pilgrim Press, 2001.
Williams, Delores S. "Womanist Theology: Black Women's Voices," *Christianity and Crisis*, March 2, 1987, 66–70.
———. *Sisters in the Wilderness: The Challenge of Womanist God-Talk*. Maryknoll, NY: Orbis, 1993.

History

Brown, Elsa Barkley. "Womanist Consciousness: Maggie Lena Walker and the Independent Order of Saint Luke," *Signs: Journal of Women in Culture and Society* 14 (1989): 610–33.
Fulmer, Constance. "A Nineteenth-Century 'Womanist' on Gender Issues: Edith J. Simcox in Her *Autobiography of a Shirtmaker*," *Nineteenth-Century Prose* 26 (1999): 110–26.
Ogunleye, Tolagbe. "Dr. Martin Robison Delaney, 19th-Century Africana Womanist: Reflections on His Avant-Garde Politics Concerning Gender, Colorism, and Nation Building," *Journal of Black Studies* 28 (1998): 628–49.
Steinem, Gloria, and Diana L. Hayes. "Womanism." In *The Reader's Companion to U.S. Women's History*, ed. Barbara Smith, Gloria Steinem, Gwendolyn Mink, Marysa Navarro, and Wilma Mankiller, 639–41. New York: Houghton Mifflin, 1998.

Theater and Film Studies

Carstarphen, Meta G. "Gettin' Real Love: *Waiting to Exhale* and Film Representations of Womanist Identity." In *Mediated Women: Representations in Popular Culture*, ed. Marian Meyers. Cresskill, NJ: Hampton Press, 1999.
Dickerson, Glenda. "The Cult of True Womanhood: Toward a Womanist Attitude in African American Theatre." In *Performing Feminisms: Feminist Critical Theory and Theatre*, ed. Sue-Ellen Case, 109–18. Baltimore, MD: Johns Hopkins University Press, 1990.
Giles, Freda Scott. "Methexis vs. Mimesis: Poetics of Feminist and Womanist Drama." In *Race/Sex: Their Sameness, Difference, and Interplay (Thinking Gender)*, ed. Naomi Zack, 175–82. New York: Routledge, 1997.
Price, Lisa. "Womanism in Film, or Why the Technicolor Dream Is Still in Black and White," 1993, http://www.wrinklybrain.com/WomanisminFilm.pdf.
Reid, Mark A. "Dialogic Modes of Representing Africa(s): Womanist Film," *Black American Literature Forum* 25 (1991): 375–88.
———. *Redefining Black Film*. Berkeley: University of California Press, 1993.
Thackway, Melissa. *Africa Shoots Back: Alternative Perspectives in Sub-Saharan Francophone African Film*. Bloomington: Indiana University Press, 2003.
Tylee, Claire M. "Womanist Propaganda, African American Great War Experience, and Cultural Strategies of Harlem Renaissance Women: Plays by Alice Dunbar-Nelson and Mary P. Burrill," *Women's Studies International Forum* 20 (1997): 153–63.
Willis, Andre. "A Womanist Turn on the Hip-Hop Theme: Leslie Harris's *Just Another Girl on the IRT*." In *Language, Rhythm, and Sound: Black Popular Cultures into the Twenty-first Century*, eds. Joseph K. Adjaye and Adrianne R. Andrews. Pittsburgh: University of Pittsburgh Press, 1997.

Communication and Media Studies

Hamlet, Janice D. "Assessing Womanist Thought: The Rhetoric of Susan L. Taylor," *Communication Quarterly* 48 (2000): 420–36.
Houston, Marsha, and Olga Idriss Davis, eds. *Centering Ourselves: African American Feminist and Womanist Studies of Discourse*. Cresskill, NJ: Hampton Press, 2002.

Smitherman, Geneva. "A Womanist Looks at the Million Man March." In *Million Man March/Day of Absence*, ed. Haki R. Madhubuti and Maulana Karenga, 104–107. Chicago: Third World Press, 1996.

Troutman, Denise. " 'We Be Strong Women': A Womanist Analysis of Black Women's Sociolinguistic Behavior." In *Centering Ourselves: African American Feminist and Womanist Studies of Discourse*, ed. Marsha Houston and Olga Idriss Davis, 99–121. Cresskill, NJ: Hampton Press, 2002.

Walker, Alice. "What That Day Was Like for Me: The Million Man March, October 16, 1995, for My New Brother, Haki." In *Million Man March/Day of Absence*, ed. Haki R. Madhubuti and Maulana Karenga, 42–43. Chicago: Third World Press, 1996.

Psychology

Boisnier, A.D. "Race and Women's Identity Development: Distinguishing between Feminism and Womanism among Black and White Women," *Sex Roles* 49 (2003): 211–18.

Carter, Robert T., and Elizabeth E. Parks. "Womanist Identity and Mental Health," *Journal of Counseling and Development* 74 (1996): 484–89.

Constantine, Madonna G., and Sherry K. Watt. "Cultural Congruity, Womanist Identity Attitudes, and Life Satisfaction among African American College Women Attending Historically Black and Predominantly White Institutions," *Journal of College Student Development* 43 (2002): 184–94.

Letlaka-Rennert, K., P. Luswazi, J.E. Helms, and M.C. Zea. "Does the Womanist Identity Model Predict Aspects of Psychological Functioning in Black South African Women?" *South African Journal of Psychology* 27 (1997): 236–43.

Moradi, Bonnie, Janice D. Yoder, and Lynne L. Berendsen. "An Evaluation of the Psychometric Properties of the Womanist Identity Attitudes Scale," *Sex Roles* 50 (2004): 253–66.

Nabors, Nina A., and Melanie F. Pettee. "Womanist Therapy with African American Women with Disabilities," *Women and Therapy* 26 (2003): 331–41.

Ossana, Shelly M., Janet E. Helms, and Mary M. Leonard. "Do 'Womanist' Identity Attitudes Influence College Women's Self-Esteem and Perceptions of Environmental Bias?" *Journal of Counseling and Development* 70 (1992): 402–408.

Parks, Elizabeth E., Robert T. Carter, and George V. Gushue. "At the Crossroads: Racial and Womanist Identity Development in Black and White Women," *Journal of Counseling and Development* 74 (1996): 624–31.

Poindexter-Cameron, Jan M., and Tracy L. Robinson. "Relationships Among Racial Identity Attitudes, and Womanist Identity Attitudes, and Self-Esteem in African American College Women," *Journal of College Student Development* 38 (1997): 288–95.

Stephens, Dionne Patricia. "Putting Sisters in the Center: Using Womanist Theory and Bronfenbrenner's Ecological Model of Human Development to Examine Young African-American Women's Sexual Education Processes," *Abafazi* 10 (2000): 59–71.

Vaz, Kim Marie. "Womanist Archetypal Psychology: A Model of Counseling for Black Women and Couples Based on Yoruba Mythology." In *The Womanist Reader*, ed. Layli Phillips. New York: Routledge, 2006.

Anthropology

Galván, Ruth Trinidad. "Portraits of *Mujeres Desjuiciadas*: Womanist Pedagogies of the Everyday, the Mundane, and the Ordinary," *Qualitative Studies in Education* 15 (2001): 603–21.

Gourdine, Angeletta K.M. "Postmodern Ethnography and the Womanist Mission: Postcolonial Sensibilities in *Possessing the Secret of Joy*," *African American Review* 30 (1996): 237–44.

Kerns, Virginia. *Black Carib Kinship and Ritual*. 2nd ed. Urbana: University of Illinois Press, 1997.

Rodriguez, Cheryl. "Anthropology and Womanist Theory: Claiming the Discourse on Gender, Race, and Culture," *Womanist Theory and Research* 2 (1996/1997): 3–11.

Thomas, Linda E. "Womanist Theology, Epistemology, and a New Anthropological Paradigm," *Cross Currents* 48 (1998/1999): 488–99.

Education

Beauboeuf-Lafontant, Tamara. "A Womanist Experience of Caring: Understanding the Pedagogy of Exemplary Black Women Teachers," *The Urban Review* 34 (2002): 71–86.

Dlamini, Nombuso. "Literacy, Womanism and Struggle: Reflections on the Practices of an African Woman," *Journal of International Women's Studies* 2 (2001): 78–93.

Garth, Phyllis Ham. "A New Knowledge: Feminism from an Africentric Perspective," *Thresholds in Education* 20 (1994): 8–13.

Henry, Annette. *Taking Back Control toward an Afrocentric Womanist Standpoint on the Education of Black Children.* Ottowa: National Library of Canada, 1993.

Ladson-Billings, Gloria. "Lifting as We Climb: The Womanist Tradition in Multicultural Education." In *Multicultural Education, Transformative Knowledge, and Action: Historical and Contemporary Perspectives,* ed. James A. Banks, 179–200. New York: Teachers College Press.

McCreary, Donald. "Speaking in Tongues: Using Womanist Sermons as Intra-cultural Rhetoric in the Writing Classroom," *Journal of Basic Writing* 20 (2001): 53–70.

———. "Womanist Theology and Its Efficacy for the Writing Classroom," *College Composition and Communication* 52 (2001): 521–52.

Paul, Dierdre Glenn. *Life, Culture and Education on the Academic Plantation: Womanist Thought and Perspective.* New York: Peter Lang.

Sheared, Vanessa. "Giving Voice: An Inclusive Model of Instruction—A Womanist Model," *New Directions for Adult and Continuing Education* 61 (1994): 27–37.

Smith, Dianne. "Womanism and Me: An (Un)Caged Black Bird Sings for Freedom," *The High School Journal* 79 (1996): 176–82.

Social Work

Carlton-LaNey, Iris. "Elizabeth Ross Haynes: An African American Reformer of Womanist Consciousness, 1908–1940," *Social Work* 42 (1997): 573–83.

Littlefield, Melissa. "A Womanist Perspective for Social Work with African American Women," *Social Thought: Journal of Religion in the Social Services* 22 (2003): 3–18.

Peebles-Wilkins, Wilma. "Historical Perspectives on Social Welfare in the Black Community (1886–1939)," http://people.bu.edu/wpeebles/.

Nursing Science

Banks-Wallace, JoAnne. "Womanist Ways of Knowing: Theoretical Considerations for Research with African American Women," *Advances in Nursing Science* 22 (2000): 33–45.

Taylor, Janette Y. "Womanism: A Methodologic Framework for African American Women," *Advances in Nursing Science* 21 (1998): 53–64.

Public Health

Heath, Corliss D. "A Womanist Approach to Understanding and Assessing the Relationship Between Spirituality and Mental Health," *Mental Health, Religion, and Culture,* n.d., http://www.taylorandfrancis.metapress.com/.

Architecture/Urban Studies

Amoo-Adare, Epifania Akosua. "Critical Spatial Literacy: A Womanist Positionality and the Spatio-temporal Construction of Black Family Life." In *La Familia en Africa y la Diaspora Africana: Estudio Multidisciplinar/Family in Africa and the African Diaspora: A Multidisciplinary Approach,* ed. Olga Barrios and Frances Smith Foster, 63–73. Salamanca, Spain: Ediciones Almar, 2004.

Africana Studies

Aldridge, Delores P. "Womanist Issues in Black Studies: Towards Integrating Africana Womanism into African Studies." In *Out of the Revolution: The Development of Africana Studies,* ed. Delores P. Aldridge and Carlene Young, 157–66. Lanham, MD: Lexington Books, 2002.

Beckmann, Felicia. "The Portrayal of Africana Males in Achebe, Marshall, Morrison, and Wideman," *Journal of Black Studies* 32 (2002): 405–21.

Dove, Nah. "African Womanism: An Afrocentric Theory," *Journal of Black Studies* 28 (1998): 515–39.

———. "Defining African Womanist Theory." In *The Afrocentric Paradigm*, ed. Ama Mazama, 165–84. Trenton, NJ: Africa World Press, 2003.

Hudson-Weems, Clenora. "Cultural and Agenda Conflicts in Academia: Critical Issues for Africana Women's Studies," *Western Journal of Black Studies* 13 (1989): 185–89.

———. "Africana Womanism." In *Africana Womanism: Reclaiming Ourselves*, by Clenora Hudson-Weems, 17–32. Troy, MI: Bedford, 1993.

———. *Africana Womanism: Reclaiming Ourselves*. Troy, MI: Bedford, 1993.

———. "Africana Womanism and the Critical Need for Africana Theory and Thought," *Western Journal of Black Studies* 21 (1997): 79–84.

———. "Africana Womanism." In *Sisterhood, Feminisms and Power: From Africa to the Diaspora*, ed. Obioma Nnaemeka, 149–62. Trenton, NJ: Africa World Press, 1998.

———. "Africana Womanism: The Flip Side of a Coin," *The Western Journal of Black Studies* 25 (2001): 137–45.

———. "Africana Womanism: An Overview." In *Out of the Revolution: The Development of Africana Studies*, ed. Delores P. Aldridge and Carlene Young, 145–56. Lanham, MD: Lexington Books, 2002.

Jennings, Regina. "Africana Womanism in the Black Panther Party: A Personal Story," *The Western Journal of Black Studies* 25 (2001): 146–52.

Ntiri, Daphne. "The WAAD Conference and Beyond: A Look at Africana Womanism." In *Sisterhood, Feminisms and Power: From Africa to the Diaspora*, ed. Obioma Nnaemeka, 461–63. Trenton, NJ: Africa World Press, 1998.

———. "Reassessing Africana Womanism: Continuity and Change," *The Western Journal of Black Studies* 25 (2001): 163–76.

Reed, Pamela Yaa Asantewaa. "Africana Womanism and Africana Feminism: A Philosophical, Literary, and Cosmological Dialectic on Family," *The Western Journal of Black Studies* 25 (2001): 168–76.

Splawn, Jane. "Cross-Atlantic Womanism(s): An African American Woman's Reflections on the Women in Africa and the African Diaspora Conference, 1992." In *Sisterhood, Feminisms and Power: From Africa to the Diaspora*, ed. Obioma Nnaemeka, 445–47. Trenton, NJ: Africa World Press, 1998.

Ethnic Studies

Jaimes-Guerrero, M.A. "Red Warrior Women: Exemplars of Indigenism in 'Native Womanism,'" *Asian Women* 9 (1999): 1–25.

———. "Native Womanism: Exemplars of Indigenism in Sacred Traditions of Kinship." In *Indigenous Religions: A Companion*, ed. Graham Harvey. London: Cassell, 2000.

———. "'Patriarchal Colonialism' and Indigenism: Implications for Native Feminist Spirituality and Native Womanism," *Hypatia: A Journal of Feminist Philosophy* 18 (2003): 58–69.

Women's and Gender Studies

Collins, Patricia Hill. "What's in a Name? Womanism, Black Feminism, and Beyond," *The Black Scholar* 26 (1996): 9–17.

———. *Fighting Words: Black Women and the Search for Justice*. Minneapolis: University of Minnesota Press, 1998.

Delveaux, Martin. "Transcending Ecofeminism: Alice Walker, Spiritual Ecowomanism, and Environmental Ethics," 2001, http://www.ecofem.org/journal.

Heilmann, Anne. *Feminist Forerunners: Womanism and Feminism in the Early 20th Century*. Kitchener, Ontario, Canada: Pandora Press, 2003.

Lemons, Gary L. "To Be Black, Male, and 'Feminist': Making Womanist Space for Black Men," *International Journal of Sociology and Social Policy* 17 (1997): 35–61.

———. "'When and Where [We] Enter': In Search of a Feminist Forefather—Reclaiming the Womanist Legacy of W.E.B. DuBois." In *Traps: African American Men on Gender and Sexuality*, ed. Rudolph P. Byrd and Beverly Guy-Sheftall, 71–89. Bloomington: Indiana University Press, 2001.

———. "Womanism in the Name of the 'Father': W.E.B. DuBois and the Problematics of Race, Patriarchy, and Art," *Phylon* 49 (2001): 185–203.

McCaskill, Barbara, and Layli Phillips. "We Are All 'Good Woman!': A Womanist Critique of the Current Feminist Conflict." In *"Bad Girls"/"Good Girls": Women, Sex, and Power in the Nineties,* ed. Nan Bauer Maglin and Donna Perry, 106–22. Newark, NJ: Rutgers University Press.

Neal, Mark Anthony. "My Black Male Feminist Heroes," February 26, 2003, http://www.popmatters.com/features/030226-blackfeminists.shtml.

Pattel-Gray, Anne. "The Hard Truth: White Secrets, Black Realities," *Australian Feminist Studies* 14 (1999): 259–66.

Phillips, Layli, and Barbara McCaskill. "Who's Schooling Who? Black Women and the Bringing of the Everyday into Academe, or Why We Started *The Womanist*," *Signs: Journal of Women in Culture and Society* 20 (1995): 1007–18.

Sexuality Studies

Fraile-Marcos, Ana Maria. " 'As Purple to Lavender': Alice Walker's Womanist Representations of Lesbianism." In *Literature and Homosexuality,* ed. Michael J. Meyer, 111–34. Amsterdam: Editions Rodopi B.V., 2000.

Lee, Wenshu. "*Kuaering* Queer Theory: My Autocritography and a Race-Conscious, Womanist, Transnational Turn," *Journal of Homosexuality* 45 (2003): 147–70.

Critiques of Womanism

(charles), Helen. "The Language of Womanism: Re-thinking Difference." In *British Black Feminism: A Reader,* ed. Heidi Safia Mirza, 278–97. London: Routledge, 1997.

Grewal, Inderpal, and Caren Kaplan. "*Warrior Marks*: Global Womanism's Neo-colonial Discourse in a Multicultural Context." In *Keyframes: Popular Cinema and Cultural Studies,* ed. Matthew Tinkcom and Amy Villarejo, New York: Routledge, 52–71.

Haraway, Donna. "Reading Buchi Emecheta: Contests for Women's Experience in Women's Studies," *Inscriptions: The Center for Cultural Studies Journal* 3/4 (1988), http://humwww.ucsc.edu/CultStudies/PUBS/Inscriptions/vol_3-4/DonnaHaraway.html.

hooks, bell. "Black Women and Feminism." In *Talking Back: Thinking Feminist, Thinking Black,* 177–82. Boston: South End Press, 1989.

Mwale, Pascal Newbourne. "Where Is the Foundation of African Gender? The Case of Malawi," *Nordic Journal of African Studies* 11 (2002): 114–37.

Walker, Alice. "Audre's Voice." In *Anything We Love Can Be Saved,* by Alice Walker, 79–82. New York: Random House, 1997.

Interviews

Arndt, Susan. "African Gender Trouble and African Womanism: An Interview with Chikwenye Ogunyemi and Wanjira Muthoni," *Signs: Journal of Women in Culture and Society* 25 (2000): 709–26.

Bradley, David. "Novelist Alice Walker: Telling the Black Woman's Story," *New York Times Magazine,* January 8, 1984, 22–39.

Journals

McCaskill, Barbara, and Layli Phillips, eds. *Womanist Theory and Research,* 1996/97, 1998, 2000.

Phillips, Layli, and Barbara McCaskill, eds. *The Womanist: A Newsletter for Afrocentric Feminist Researchers,* 1994, 1995.

Web Sites

Barnes, Sherri L. "Black American Feminisms: A Multidisciplinary Bibliography," http://www.library.ucsb.edu/subjects/blackfeminism/introduction.html.

Misra, Joya. "Black Feminist/Womanist Works: A Beginning List," http://research.umbc.edu/~korenman/wmst/womanistbib.html.

Name Index

Subject Index

A

abolitionism, 39, 105, 372

abusua, 347, 355–357

Abyssinian Baptist Church, 307

academics

and Black culture, 92–93

and everyday experience, 86–89, 94

Accra, 347, 352–353, 354–356

activism

Civil Rights, xxix

gay/lesbian, 198, 336

human rights, 109

woman-, 47, 367

activist, black, 368

Adam Clayton Powell Home for the Aged, 307, 308

adult education, 272–278

aesthetics, 159, 160

affirmation, self-, 222–223

Afose, 222

Africa, depiction of in *Warrior Marks*, 389

Africana Womanism: Reclaiming Ourselves (Hudson-Weems), xx, xlii, xliii, 44–53

Africana Womanist Literary Theory (Hudson-Weems), xliii

"African Feminism: A Worldwide Perspective" (Steady), 45, 49

African Methodist Episcopal church, 12, 15

Africa Wo/Man Palava: The Nigerian Novel by Women (Ogunyemi), xlii

Africentrism, feminist epistemology, 274–278

Afrocentrism, 66

aggression, 236

Ai Bao, 332–337

Ai Fu, 333

Ai Fu Hao, 333–334

Ai Fu Hao Zi Zai Bao, 332–337

Akan, 354–356

All the Women Are White, All the Blacks Are Men, but Some of Us Are Brave: Black Women's Studies, 85

aloneness, 243

Alpha Kappa Alpha (AKA), 306–307, 308

American Indians, 314

American Woman Suffrage Association, 46

amnesia, discursive, 328, 342n5

ancestry, reverence for, 223–224, *see also* foreparents

androcentrism, 69–70

dangers of, 75

in sermons, 136

animadora, 248, 266n3

anti-feminism, 101–102, 104

anti-footbinding, 329, 341

Anti-Lynching Bill, 304

antioppressionist, xxiv

arbitration, xxvii–xxviii

architecture, womanist positionality, 348–350

M